THE ARMENIANS

To my parents
Stephan and Sona Panossian

RAZMIK PANOSSIAN

The Armenians

From Kings and Priests to Merchants and Commissars

Columbia University Press New York

Columbia University Press
Publishers since 1893
New York

Library of Congress Cataloging-in-Publication Data
A complete CIP record is available from the Library of Congress
ISBN 978–0–231–13926–7 (cloth: alk. paper)
ISBN 978–0–231–51133–9 (e-book)

♾ Columbia University Press books are printed on permanent and durable acid-free paper.
c 10 9 8 7 6 5 4 3 2

'*The life of a nation is a sea, and those who look at it from the shore cannot know its depths.*'—Armenian proverb

'*The man who finds his homeland sweet is still a tender beginner; he to whom every soil is as his native one is already strong; but he is perfect to whom the entire world is as a foreign land. The tender soul has fixed his love on one spot in the world; the strong man has extended his love to all places; the perfect man has extinguished his.*'—Hugo of St Victor (monk from Saxony, 12th century)

The proverb is from Mary Matossian, *The Impact of Soviet Policies in Armenia.* Hugo of St Victor is cited in Edward Said, 'Reflections on Exile', *Granta*, no. 13.

CONTENTS

MAPS

PREFACE AND ACKNOWLEDGEMENTS

My grandfather Hagop Panossian, who was generally known by the Turkish honorific title *Onbashi* (corporal), spoke six languages without having any formal education beyond primary school. He had two mother tongues: Armenian and the local village dialect of Kessab (Kesap), a 'language' incomprehensible to outsiders that is a mixture of old and new Armenian at its root with much Turkish and Arabic vocabulary, peppered with Persian, Greek and even the odd French and English words. He knew Turkish, since he grew up in what was then the Ottoman empire. He spoke Arabic, because his village—a six hundred year old Armenian settlement in the diaspora—became part of Syria. English was picked up in the United States, where he migrated to as a labourer in the early 1910s, and he learnt French when he joined the French Legion during the First World War to fight against Ottoman armies. After the War he resettled in his native village, being the only survivor in his immediate family of the Armenian Genocide.

In contrast, as I was growing up in Lebanon in the 1970s I was supposed to learn one language properly: Armenian. Of course the 'natural' process of picking up languages continued for many individuals based on the circumstances of diasporan life, but there was a clear policy and an exerted effort at the communal level to emphasise Armenian as the language to master. Within one generation it had become the key cultural marker of national identity. Turkish was frowned upon as the language of the enemy. The village dialect was considered too parochial to teach the young. To be fair, the Armenian community school I attended recognised the importance of learning other languages. French, Arabic and later English were taught—in that order and often badly—as second or 'foreign' languages. They were mere tools or skills, whereas Armenian was the 'essence' of identity.

I do not wish to generalise this process of linguistic nationalisation to all Armenians. However, it was—and is—an important component of the construction of Armenian identity, particularly in the Middle Eastern communities and of course in Armenia. There are needless to say quite a few multilingual Armenians around the world, along with a large number of Armenians in the diaspora who do not speak the 'national language'. But the emphasis on language as a 'natural' component of being Armenian is generally accepted, although the reality of hundreds of thousands of non-Armenian speaking Armenians in North America and Europe is leading to the re-evaluation of the link between language and national identity, at least in the diaspora.

One important clarification must at once be made about the concept of 'construction' of identity. I do not at all imply that Armenian identity itself is a modern or artificial creation. Armenians have existed for nearly 3,000 years as a distinct linguistic and ethno-religious community. And similar processes of collective identity (re)formulation, as described above, have taken place before—for example, in the fourth and fifth centuries with Armenians' conversion to Christianity and the invention of a unique alphabet. Even in adverse conditions, when they were living under the suzerainty of foreign powers, most Armenians maintained their separate cultural identity. This ancient identity was transformed into a modern national identity between the eighteenth and twentieth centuries. It is in this context that I use the words construction, creation, evolution and formulation of identity, more or less interchangeably. National identity, like all other collective identities, is a socially constructed reality.

To use the metaphor of the family story above, this book analyses the 'how' and the 'why' of the historical transformation from the grandfather who spoke six languages to the grandson who was being taught one national language. The personal story demonstrates the change from one generation to the next; the collective history demonstrates the change from one century to the next. This book is concerned with the latter, with the evolution of Armenian national identity.

Research for the project was carried out both in Armenia and in the diaspora. I spent a total of eight months in Armenia on four separate occasions (1996, 1997, 1999 and 2002) when I conducted formal and informal interviews, consulted archival sources (the State

Central Archives of History and Contemporary History), and attended various press conferences, protests, public meetings, demonstrations, election rallies and the two Armenia-diaspora conferences. I also examined the press, Armenian language textbooks and *samizdat* literature. Much anthropological research was also done in the form of informal and extensive discussions with scores of individuals from various strata of society. As a diaspora Armenian I have also collected much anecdotal and formal information over the years from, and about, various communities, most notably in Canada, Britain, France, Lebanon and Syria. I have used some of this material throughout the book, but most extensively in the last two chapters on the twentieth century.

The overall approach of the book is that of interpretative political history and comparative analysis (between Armenia and the diaspora). It is written by a political 'scientist' who believes in the crucial importance of history and culture in the study of modern politics and identities. No doubt 'purist' historians, political scientists and anthropologists who have strict loyalties to their disciplines will find faults with my casual treatment of disciplinary boundaries, or the eclectic theoretical approach. However, in interpreting and explaining national identity it is essential to use various tools of analysis. A combination of political studies, history, anthropology and cultural studies provides the most fruitful results in terms of a deeper understanding of Armenian national identity and the modern politics of nationalism. The book therefore examines culture and structure, ideas and institutions, symbols and organisations, myths and state policies.

Nationalists too will criticise the book as yet another 'Western' attack on Armenian identity; the very use of the word 'construction' in relation to national identity or the modernity of the nation is anathema to such people. However, it is important to situate the Armenian example in—and analyse it through—the overall theoretical body of literature on nations and nationalism, but not in a mechanistic manner that would undermine the unique characteristics of the Armenian case. Such an approach helps us to understand the evolution of Armenian identity better (rather than taking it as a 'given'), and to assess critically the usefulness of various aspects of the theoretical literature—particularly its more Eurocentric and extreme modernist assertions.

On more technical matters, transliteration from Armenian to English is problematic because of phonetic differences between eastern and western Armenian dialects. For the sake of simplification I have used the *Armenian Review* key based on the eastern pronunciation for all names and titles. For some of the well known names or words in western Armenian I have maintained the more widely accepted version but have given the eastern transliteration in round parenthesis the first time the word is used—e.g. Catholicos Karekin I (Garegin). All translations of sources into English are mine.

In general I have used the Armenian name for indigenous cities, places and individuals—e.g. Mountainous Gharabagh and not Nagorno-Karabakh. I have also used place names current to the time in which they are mentioned—e.g. Constantinople until the early twentieth century, but Istanbul thereafter.

In the footnotes reference is given to the interviewees I cite by their name—e.g. 'Author's interview with Karlen Dallakian' (unless it is 'off the record'). The list of interviewees used, with relevant details (short biographies, dates, length etc.), is found at the end of the Bibliography.

On a personal note, academically objective as I have sought to be, I am sure my experiences as a diasporan Armenian who has lived in London, but was born in Beirut and raised in Canada, in a family engaged with community affairs, have influenced my approach, research and analysis. The inspiration for this book comes from a specific social milieu: on the boundaries of many cultures, aware of the ideology of nationalism while being at home in Western society and liberal politics, amidst the parochialism of an ethnic kitchen and the cosmopolitanism of world-class universities, between the knowledge of the remarkable lives of grandparents (and parents) and the full embrace of the methodology of serious academic research.

Such closeness to the Armenian community is, I believe, a mixed blessing. Having a foot in the Armenian world enables me to understand Armenian identity and nationalism in a more profound manner than an 'outsider'. This 'membership' in the community has certainly opened many doors and given voice to many opinions which are usually not volunteered to *odars*—i.e. non-Armenians. But I am also aware that some people will assume that I am being partisan because of my ethnic background and socialisation in a specific sector of the Armenian community. I hope, as the reader progresses, it will become apparent that I have provided above all a critical and objective analysis while not betraying the trust of the Armenian community.

Acknowledgements

This book is a slightly shorter version of my PhD dissertation written at the London School of Economics and Political Science. My studies at the LSE were made possible by the generous assistance of the following scholarship programmes: the Overseas Research Students Awards Scheme (ORS), various scholarships from the London School of Economics, including the Alfred Zauberman Award, School Graduate Studentships and other bursaries. The Central Research Fund of the University of London provided the funds for one of my research trips to Armenia. My thanks to all.

Various organisations within, or affiliated with, the Armenian community were generous in their assistance as well. I am very grateful to the scholarships programme of the London Trust of the Armenian General Benevolent Union (AGBU), particularly to their Nevarte and Hasmik Krikorian Fund; an additional grant from the AGBU London Trust enabled me to work on the book manuscript throughout the summer of 2001. Assistance for three years from the Gulbenkian Foundation in Lisbon is also much appreciated.

The maps printed in this volume were created by Robert Hewsen and borrowed from Richard Hovannisian's two-volume *The Armenian People from Ancient to Modern Times* (New York: St Martin's Press, 1997). I thank them for kindly granting me permission to reproduce the maps.

When I began my PhD I was intent on writing a dissertation on Armenian nationalism after 1988. I ended up writing a thesis on Armenian national identity before 1988! This was largely due to my thesis supervisor, Professor Dominic Lieven, who insisted rightly that one could not understand nationalism without 'a bit' of history. His guidance both threw me into, and then enabled me to navigate through, the stormy seas of Armenian history. Our numerous discussions and his detailed comments on my work also enabled me to situate Armenia within the wider parameters of the Russian and Soviet empires. I am grateful for all his support.

I also appreciate the suggestions given by Professors Ronald Suny and Anthony Smith who were my thesis examiners. They made perceptive remarks on how to improve the manuscript for publication. A heartfelt thank you goes to Dr Ara Sanjian for giving me detailed and extremely useful comments, as well as for providing sources such as newspaper clippings and Lebanese-Armenian publications. His encyclopaedic knowledge of Armenian issues is gratefully acknowledged.

I received much academic and personal assistance from a number of close friends. Some read and commented on various sections of the manuscript, others provided valuable information, ideas and intense forums for discussion. They include: Pamela Young, Susan Pattie, Hratch Tchilingirian, Sebouh Aslanian, Arild Ruud, Ayla Göl, Gloria Totoricaguena, Khachig Tölölyan, Lucia Garcia, Ara Sarafian, Zhand Shakibi, Gwen Sasse, Jim Hughes, Ani King-Underwood and George Shirinian. I must also express my deep appreciation to the two reviewers who provided detailed suggestions and useful ways to improve the manuscript.

In Armenia I was generously helped by distant relatives, particularly Shahen and Hnazant. They took me in, as one of their own, and not only made my stay in Armenia so much easier, but also provided a wealth of information. Being an appendix to their family was at times a challenge, but it was always educational. Through them and their network of friends and relatives I came to understand what Armenia was really like, often over meals and family gatherings. Garnik too was most helpful, accompanying me on some of my trips outside Yerevan. Finally, I appreciate the help and advice received from Armineh and Vova.

Needless to say, thanks go to all of my interviewees, informants and everyone else who provided me with vital information. Without them the research for this book would not have been possible and I would not have understood the realities of Armenia and Armenian identity. The 'informal' list is too long to allow for names to be mentioned individually; it is perhaps best that some of them remain anonymous, lest I betray their trust by disclosing information that was told to me in confidence, during that peculiar 'Soviet ritual' centred around the vodka bottle!

Most important, my profound thanks and appreciation go to my family: my parents, my sister Arpi and her family, my brothers Raffi and Asbed. All, in their own particular ways, made this project possible. I am grateful for their constant support and encouragement. I must particularly express my gratitude to Asbed, who diligently scanned the Armenian press and sent me many of the important articles, magazines and books that ended up in the manuscript.

This book is dedicated to my parents. It is from my father, Stephan, that I have learnt to respect national identity and carry the responsibility (and burden!) of being Armenian. But it is from my mother Sona that I have learned to love humanity and to transcend the narrow confines of the nation and nationalism. I hope this work reflects the synthesis of those (often contradictory!) values.

London and Oxford RAZMIK PANOSSIAN

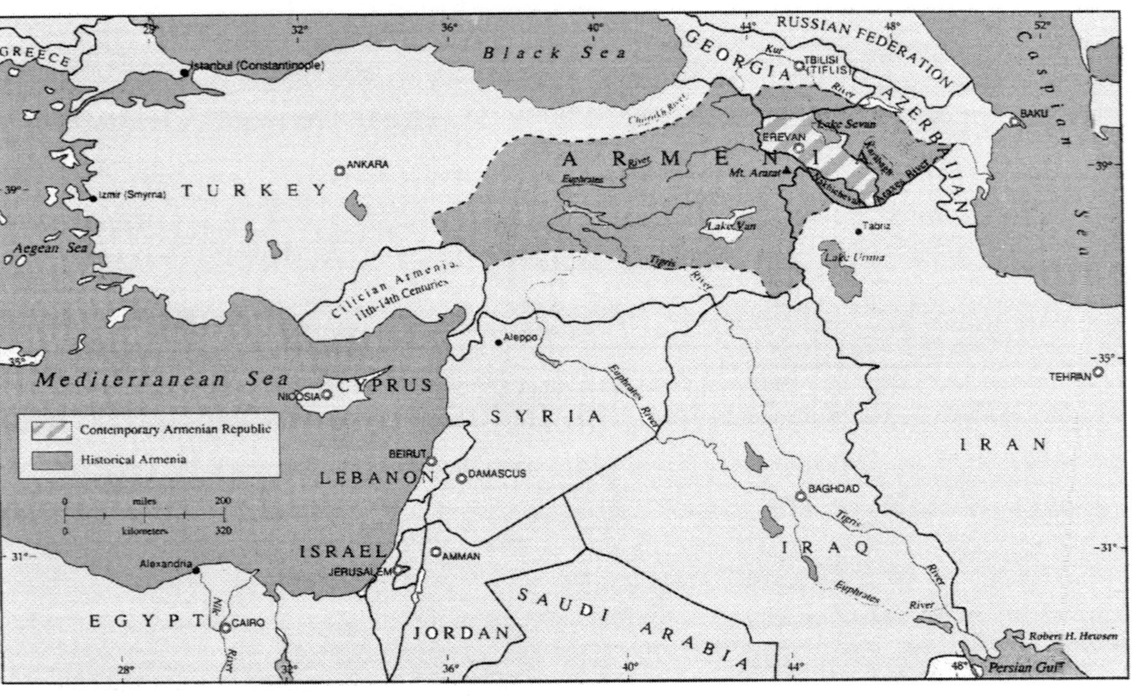

Historic and present-day Armenia.

1

INTRODUCTION

Writing about Armenia and the Armenians entails writing about dispersion, diaspora, a multitude of intellectual centres and about developments in the homeland. It entails examining history and conducting research on current politics. Therefore, this book is both geographically wide and historically 'deep' in its scope. To analyse Armenian national identity one must examine ethnic roots and the effects of modernity, networks of dispersed communities and conditions in Armenia, nationalist intellectuals and imperial policies, revolutionary endeavours and the church, genocide and survival, diasporan organisations and Soviet policies. The Armenian case study is complex, but it also provides scholars a unique opportunity to examine theories of nations and nationalism against the backdrop of a collective which contains within it almost all of the factors analysed by the theoretical literature. 'In reality every nation is a unique socio-historical construct,' says Adrian Hastings, adding that each 'case [must be] examined in its own historical evolution.'[1] This book aims to do that for the Armenians. It is an interpretative analysis of how Armenian identity was shaped and reshaped over the centuries, and how nationalism arose and was manifested. The emphasis is on the modern period—developments from the seventeenth century onward.

The endeavour of writing such a study proved to be more complicated than I had originally anticipated. The first hurdles that needed to be overcome were theoretical issues. The literature on nations and nationalism is divided along various cleavages, and it soon became clear that any rigid framework or a single theory would

[1] A. Hastings, *The Construction of Nationhood*, p. 25.

not suffice. The complex historical phenomena of national identity and nationalism do not fit into a 'neat' typology, nor can they be explained through one theoretical approach, no matter how inclusive. There are always exceptions, and one of the most notable is the Armenian case. It made much more sense to adopt a flexible framework of analysis that draws on various schools of thought and paradigms. The theoretical framework of this book is, therefore, eclectic and flexible. It does not dismiss any theory of nationalism, rather, it incorporates useful elements from various approaches. The basic argument is that nations are modern entities, but they do have (or believe that they have) deep historical roots which affect their evolution profoundly. Moreover, it argues that to understand national identity, subjectivity—i.e. the subjective sense of belonging to the same nation despite real differences—has to be situated at the core of any definition of the nation. The argument does not dismiss other, more 'tangible' factors such as states, institutions, intellectuals and organisations. These are all important, but without the subjective sense one cannot speak of 'belonging' to a nation.

The theoretical framework also questions the wisdom of making the state the central institution in the formation of national identity. A more general focus on the role of organisations is more advisable given that Armenian national identity and nationalism evolved and were maintained without an Armenian state. Related to this is the issue of the homogenisation of identity as a precondition to nation-formation. This too is questioned given the reality that culturally very diverse individuals can claim to be part of the same nation.

As always, the theory and the case study influence one another considerably in such projects. Applying theories to a case mechanically results in omissions and skewed conclusions. My analysis of the evolution of Armenian identity and nationalism is thoroughly informed—implicitly or explicitly—by theories of nationalism, but my theoretical framework and definitions are also heavily influenced by the Armenian case study. I hope that through this interaction I have been able to strike a balance between being a prisoner of theory and a prisoner of the details of history. This approach thus examines the relationship between subjectivity and objective cultural markers, between the state and community institutions, and between the modernity of nations and their ancient roots.

The second set of complications relates to the Armenian case study. As I was writing about the construction and evolution of identity, it became increasingly obvious that the various sources of Armenian identity formulation were quite different from one another. It could not have been otherwise with such a dispersed ethnic group and with a homeland divided between three empires for many centuries. Not only were the Armenian people and their intellectuals geographically apart, but their notions of nationhood, of what an Armenian should be, and many of the cultural markers they were employing were also different, particularly in the modern period. A national 'awakening' was taking place, connected to the ideals of modernity, but at various points affected by an assortment of environments—from India to Venice, from Moscow to Constantinople, from Russian Armenia to Ottoman Armenia. As an ethnic community Armenians of course had certain commonalities (e.g. a unique national church), but deep divisions were infused into the emerging sense of modern national identity. A good part of the book discusses these vicissitudes based on multiple sources of, and influences on, national identity. But in my examination, it also became apparent that Armenians were developing a sense of identity as part of *one* nation despite the objective differences and the historical as well as sociological divisions.

The different threads of identity, along with the uniting force of subjectivity, are woven with one another in the book, but in a manner that does not imply any kind of essentialist outcome. I do not argue that this evolution of identity was part of a greater 'plan' or an inevitable teleological process. There were discontinuities, breaks and dissolutions. Many people did lose their identity as Armenians, being assimilated into other societies and cultures. These 'silences' are also profoundly important. What I examine is one part of the 'story', the element that continued as a distinct group and eventually acquired modern national identity.

The multilocal interpretation of Armenian identity, highlighting not only the binding ties but also the differences, is new in the study of Armenian history and nationalism. Armenians and Armenia experts do acknowledge the obvious differences in the eastern and western dialects of the language, and scholars discuss the variations in literature. Some writers examine the history of eastern Armenia/ns, others of western Armenia/ns. But to date such social, cultural and political differences are not tied to national identity. Consequently, the notion that there is a profound divide in Armenian collective identity is not systematically analysed. More generally, the multilocal perspective to the study of national identity is also uncommon in the wider theoretical literature on nationalism. The emphasis is usually on the homogenisation process in the formulation and dissemination of national identity.[2]

The historical evolution of Armenian national identity continued into the twentieth century, but as before it continued along more than one track. There was a narrowing of 'identity points' from various centres to two overall tracks. One was the Sovietised republic of Armenia, the other the post-Genocide diaspora. Once again identity construction continued in a multilocal manner, through two parallel processes. The old east/west divide remained, but it now manifested in the form of the homeland/diaspora duality. Because of the Iron Curtain, the two parts of the nation remained divided. In both spheres, in Soviet Armenia and in the diaspora, there was a process of nation-building and identity construction. But in both cases this was conducted outside the parameters of a 'normal' nation state. The state that Armenians had was one of the constituent republics of the USSR, at best a semi-independent part of the Soviet 'family', whereas the diaspora, by definition, did not have a state; however, diasporan organisations did in many ways carry out the nationalising role of a state.

In sum, the overall questions this book addresses are: how was Armenian national identity constructed? How and why did it evolve in a multilocal manner? Why is it still possible to speak of one unified Armenian nation despite profound differences? How did Armenian nationalism emerge historically and what were its demands? And, more specifically, how was multilocal national identity reinforced in the twentieth century under Soviet and diasporan conditions?

The book is structured in a loose chronological order. After a few comments on theoretical issues in the remainder of the Introduction, Chapter 2 begins the historical narrative. It examines three thousand years of Armenian history up to the seventeenth century.

[2] A very few scholars—such as Partha Chatterjee in *The Nation and its Fragments*—highlight the fragmentary nature of national identity.

The 'building blocks' of Armenian ethnic identity are highlighted, as are the historical roots of subsequent divisions. Chapter 3 covers the seventeenth to nineteenth centuries, analysing the factors that led to the evolution of modern Armenian identity as a nation. Chapter 4 presents the argument of multilocality; it examines language, literary culture and political ideology in the nineteenth century 'awakening'. Chapter 5 outlines the organisational dimension of national consciousness, bringing the narrative up to the early twentieth century. Chapters 6 and 7 are on the Soviet period, analysing Soviet and diasporan processes of identity formulation and strengthening. The book ends in 1987, on the eve of the outburst of the nationalist movement in the Armenian SSR over Mountainous Gharabagh. At various points the narrative is 'interrupted' by Theoretical Interludes that address specific theoretical points in the context of the case study.

THEORETICAL CONSIDERATIONS AND DEFINITIONS

No single theory of nationalism can explain the historically and socially complex dynamics of national identity formation and its political manifestation in the form nationalism. Certain theories or approaches to nationalism are more useful to understand modern developments, while others are more appropriate for analysis of ancient socio-cultural and political evolutions. This is particularly true if the nation being analysed has deep historical roots. In some cases a single nation embodies both sets of dynamics—as is the case with the Armenians, Jews and Greeks. It is therefore essential to approach a specific case study—particularly one that has millennia-old roots—with a certain amount of theoretical flexibility.

The main theories of nationalism are not mutually exclusive. For example, the sharp distinction between the 'modernists' and the 'primordialists' is mostly unwarranted. There can be fruitful discussion among them. Each camp does not necessarily negate the validity of the other's position *in toto*. Each school emphasises a different set of factors as the more important. But both approaches have valid points which must be taken into account. After all, most nations have both modernist and primordialist/perennialist elements to them. The same is true of the civic/ethnic and the subjective/

objective 'debates'. To understand the formation of national identity and nationalism in a specific case it is, therefore, important to examine and to combine various theories of nationalism from 'opposing camps'. This approach is more than just a 'middle position'. It is the acceptance of theoretical diversity as the basis of analysis.

A brief overview: going beyond dichotomies

Anthony Smith provides a useful categorisation of the literature on nations and nationalism in one of his more recent books. He situates each of the major thinkers in five paradigms: primordial, perennial, ethno-symbolic, modernist and post-modernist.[3] In another recent book, Umut Özkırımlı provides a similar survey of the main schools: primordialism, modernism and ethno-symbolism.[4] Thankfully, both writers go beyond the usual (and now stale) ethnic/civic or eastern/western (occasionally implying bad/good) dichotomies. The critical overview of the various theories that the two scholars provide is more or less similar. However, their conclusions—the theoretical 'what is to be done'—are diametrically opposed. Smith talks of the possibility of 'accommodation', 'agreement' or 'theoretical convergence' between the various approaches. His compromise is based on the sociological acceptance that, 'some nations and their particular nationalisms have existed well before the advent of modernity.... At the same time, the modernists are surely right to insist on the modernity of many nations, as well as of "nationalism-in-general."'[5] Özkırımlı opts for 'a binary classification consisting of "essentialist" and "constructivist" approaches'.[6] He conflates the ethno-symbolic and primordial schools in the 'essentialist' category, and situates the modernists in the 'constructivist' category. He favours the constructivist and modernist approach.

Smith's call for a 'theoretical convergence' between the various approaches is laudable, but his middle ground position is still based on situating nations along the modern/pre-modern dichotomy. It does not bridge the dichotomy itself but maintains it, albeit not as

[3] A. Smith, *Nationalism and Modernism*, part II; for a succinct summary see pp. 222–5.

[4] U. Özkırımlı, *Theories of Nationalism*, chapters 3–5.

[5] A. Smith, *Nationalism and Modernism*, p. 226.

[6] U. Özkırımlı, *Theories of Nationalism*, p. 215.

sharply. At best it conceptualises it as a continuum. Two fundamental issues at the heart of the dichotomy continue to divide scholars. The first is the relationship between modernity and nationhood—i.e. how are the two connected. The second is the extent to which nations are rooted in the past—i.e. issues of historical continuity, symbolic links etc. These two sets of inquiry are usually conflated rather than separated. Both issues are related to the debate over the 'age' of nations—that is, to the definitional problem plaguing the discipline of nationalism studies. Modernists and post-modernists, in general, are preoccupied with the first relationship (the nation and modernity); primordialists, perennialists, and ethno-symbolists with the second (the nation and the past). In both cases a theoretical convergence is possible on the 'practical' level of a concrete case study, and within the given set of questions. But there is not much convergence between the two sets of questions being asked.

For example, a modernist like Ernest Gellner could say, tongue in cheek, 'the world was created round about the end of the eighteenth century, and nothing before that makes the slightest difference to the issues we face [i.e. the origin of nations],' and, 'Some nations have [navels] and some don't and in any case it's inessential.'[7] The core of the modernists' argument is not that nations do not have historical roots, but that these roots do not matter in our understanding of the present. Hence, links with the past do not need to be studied to understand the present. Conversely, a perennialist like John Armstrong, or an ethno-symbolist like Anthony Smith, would generally agree that nations as they exist today are modern entities, but these scholars are more interested in the roots of modern identity; the questions they ask relate to the relationship between the modern and the pre-modern and not so much to the relationship between modernity and nationhood.[8] The theoretical

[7] E. Gellner, 'Do Nations Have Navels?', pp. 366 and 367 respectively, emphasis added. In a subsequently expanded version of his argument, published posthumously, Gellner was much more accommodating toward the past and did not dismiss it as totally irrelevant. He admitted that both the 'continuity' and the 'invention' arguments have valid points (E. Gellner, *Nationalism*, pp. 93–4).

[8] For Anthony Smith, the shape of the modern world cannot be fully understood without the pre-modern sense of ethnic identity. As he puts it, 'Without the initial networks of ethnic ties underpinning the competition of states, modern capitalism, bureaucracy, and communications could not have conjured into being the world of nations that we know' (A. Smith, 'Formation of National Identity', p. 153; cf. A. Smith,

divergence of these two schools is mostly the result of their differences in focus. In short, modernists in general study the relationship between the nation and modernity: which came first, what were the cause and effect factors, and how nations were 'created' through the process of modernisation (or vice versa). Non-modernists[9] want to know how nations are rooted in the past, what are the connections between past entities and the nation, and how modernity has shaped and reshaped pre-modern identities into a modern national identity. In some respects the argument between the two approaches is one of 'the glass is half full/the glass is half empty.'[10]

Within this perspective it becomes clear that one approach does not have to be chosen at the expense of the other. Both have valid points. And both must be used to examine any nation that has ethnic roots going to the medieval period—and practically all nations claim such ancestry. Therefore, nations must be analysed using the questions that are asked by both schools of thought: how did the forces of modernity affect collective identity, and what is the relationship between national identity and past ethnic identities. There is no point in trying to give a definitive and generally applicable answer to the core divisive question: do roots matter or not? My research on the Armenians shows that they do and that one there-

---

Myths and Memories, p. 11; and A. Smith, 'Ethnic Identity', p. 49). At the root of Smith's ethno-symbolic approach lies the concept of *la longue durée* (borrowed from John Armstrong)—that nations are a historical phenomenon and to understand them one must examine their evolution over a long period of time (J. Armstrong, *Nations Before Nationalism*). In the continuity between the past and the modern, ethno-symbolists particularly emphasise cultural markers and focus on myths of origin and descent, symbols of territory, language and, in J. Armstrong's word, '*mythomoteurs*'.

[9] I disagree with the 'essentialist'/'constructivist' terminology (Özkırımlı) or other categorisations such as 'modernist'/'primordialist'. Essentialism implies unavoidability (be it natural or cultural), which almost all non-modernist scholars reject. Non-modernist writers are also constructivists insofar as they examine the reformulation or reconstruction of identity along national lines, and almost all reject the primordial argument of nationalists. I prefer the term 'non-modernist' even though it has a negative connotation because it is the negation of another term. I simply use it as a neutral category that groups together all the scholars who do not subscribe to the modernist school.

[10] For example, contrast the statement of J. Breuilly—'It is the discontinuities with modern national identity that I find most striking' ('Approaches to Nationalism', p. 151)—with that of J. Armstrong who emphasises the '*persistence* rather than genesis of particular patterns' (*Nations Before Nationalism*, p. 4).

fore has to look at the non-modernist approach for fruitful insights in this case. But this is half the analysis. Modernists raise many valid points as well, especially regarding the eighteenth and nineteenth centuries. These too have to be taken into account and analysed. In some other cases, such as settler nations (the United States, Canada, Australia), it might be that roots do not matter as much since the imperative of modernisation was a more powerful social force. Or in the case of France where a specific type of 'civic nationalism' was clearly associated with the 1789 break from the past. In these instances the emphasis of the analysis would be different, but still the past—that reservoir of 'national' myths, symbols and traditions—cannot be dismissed as irrelevant.

The approach in this book does not derive from the 'categorisation' of nations as modern or pre-modern. It rejects the dichotomy which Smith, Özkırımlı and others are preoccupied with or take for granted. There is no point in putting nations on such a continuum (usually for the sake of sociological classification). Rather, their evolution must be analysed through the factors highlighted by the theoretical literature—both modernist and non-modernist. Nations as we know and experience them are modern constructs with their legitimacy based on popular sovereignty, but they do have pre-modern roots that affect and define contemporary identity and politics in different ways and degrees. Nationalists certainly believe that the deeper the roots, the more legitimacy or prestige a nation would have, and hence project the nation backwards into history. But, as I will argue later, the fact that roots matter does not, no matter how deep they are, make nations pre-modern entities. There is something qualitatively different between modern and premodern collective identities.

In addition to the modernist/non-modernist divide, the theoretical literature on nations and nationalism can be divided a number of other ways. One traditional categorisation has been the ethnic/civic distinction, and its derivative of 'Eastern' and 'Western' nationalism. This approach is now widely criticised, and it is accepted that nations have both ethnic and civic components (albeit to varying degrees).[11] The objective/subjective divide is another cleavage in

[11] For an article that criticises the ethnic/civic divide see T. Nieguth, 'Beyond Dichotomy', pp. 155–73.

the literature—i.e. should nations be defined primarily on the basis of objective or subjective characteristics? I will discuss this issue in my definition of the nation below. One other way of examining nationalism is through the division between cultural and political nationalism.[12] Modernists are generally more concerned with the political and economic aspects of nationalism, whereas non-modernists examine the cultural component more. Once again, I do not agree that a sharp distinction between the cultural and political components of nationalism is all that fruitful. Politics is part of a wider cultural web of meanings, and culture can certainly be politicised (as was the case with the Armenians in the nineteenth century). Rather than dividing nationalism between these two components, the relationship between the two must be examined. As one scholar puts it, 'All nationalisms are cultural nationalisms of one kind or another. There is no purely political conception of the nation, liberal or otherwise.'[13]

Questionable assumptions: homogenisation and the role of the state

It is often stated, or at the very least implicitly assumed, in nationalism literature that the formulation of national identity entails a rigorous process of homogenisation—particularly of culture. Ernest Gellner makes this point most explicitly in *Nations and Nationalism*. This assumption is predicated upon the argument that nationalisation entails the centralisation of the various sources of identity into a single overall process controlled either by a state or by an intellectual elite (and often emanating from a capital city). I do not dispute that this is indeed the case in many instances. Peter Alter is correct when he writes that 'The aim of nation-building is to integrate and harmonize socially, regionally or even politically and institutionally divided sections of a people.'[14] However, I do question the a priori assumption that this is always the case, that such homogenisation has

[12] See, for example, J. Hutchinson, *Modern Nationalism*, particularly chapter 2. Hutchinson does not dismiss the importance of politics. His argument is against modernists who interpret 'nationalism as just a political movement' (p. 40).

[13] K. Nielsen, 'Cultural Nationalism', p. 127.

[14] P. Alter, *Nationalism*, p. 21.

to succeed in order for the nation to emerge. The Armenian example shows otherwise. Because of various diasporan sources of identity, a homeland divided between empires, and deep cultural differences, Armenian national identity emerged in more than one centre and was therefore diverse in its cultural composition. The emergence of national identity can be multilocal, multifaceted, and heterogeneous. It could emerge as a result of unconnected endeavours by various intellectuals in many parts of the world and at different times. The fact that Armenians constituted—and still constitute—a heterogeneous nation demonstrates that the homogenisation argument, often at the heart of theories of nationalism, is rather problematic.

From this perspective the role of the (centralising) state is somewhat diminished. The evolution of national identity is not dependent on states because it can also emerge through community structures. But such structures are often themselves fragmented or unconnected. The Armenian case shows that eighteenth century Armenian merchants in India, or a religious brotherhood in Venice, played a similar role in the financing and directing endeavours of national identity creation as did states in Europe. But merchants are dispersed and small religious orders do not have the long and strong arm of a state to enforce exclusively their vision of the nation. The eventual result was a non-homogenised but nevertheless unified nation without the intervention of a state. In short, non-state actors outside the homeland can also be crucial in the reformulation of identity and in the creation of the nation. This questions another central argument in theories of nationalism: the assumption that states are crucial in the formation of nations.[15] As this book shows, national identity can be constructed without a state.[16]

[15] Benjamin Braude, on the basis of the example of the Armenians and Jews, makes a wider point about modern historiography's overemphasis on the state and its neglect of stateless people and diasporas (B. Braude, 'Nexus of Diaspora', pp. 9–10). He too highlights the 'polycentricity' of the Armenian diaspora (p. 16) and discusses the process of 'extraterritorial nation-building' among diasporas (p. 37). Shifting some of the focus away from the state expands historical analysis by including non-state actors—an increasingly prevalent trend in Western scholarship. However, in Soviet-inspired historiography the state remains the central legitimating force of history and therefore the lack of a state is used to delegitimate the history of a people. Such arguments are used by Azerbaijani and Armenian historians to negate each other's historical claims over Gharabagh.

[16] Another facet of the state-centric argument is the explanation of diasporan nationalism as a reaction to the nationalism of the dominant group which controls the state.

The points raised above barely touch upon some of the 'core' issues in the vast literature on the subject of nationalism and nation formation. But there is no need here to examine the details of the theoretical literature. I have done this elsewhere,[17] and both Anthony Smith and Umut Özkırımlı provide excellent critical overviews of the literature in their books mentioned above.[18]

The Armenian view

The scholarly, theoretical and critical examination of the topic of nationalism is quite an underdeveloped field in Armenian language literature, although there is an abundance of nationalist publications. The post-Soviet treatment of the subject in Armenia is almost always subject to nationalist political considerations, just as earlier theoretical work in the Armenian SSR was subject to the predictable Soviet denunciations of nationalism (making certain diaspora intellectuals the sole 'bearers' of the idea of nationalism). From this

---

According to Ernest Gellner, such nationalism is the response of the diasporan minority to the nationalist assertions of the majority in a modernising and hence nationalising state. The diasporan group, in order to protect itself, can either assimilate or develop its own nationalism—including claims to its own territory (E. Gellner, *Nations and Nationalism*, pp. 106ff.). But Gellner's analysis does not explain the Armenian case. He is partially correct regarding the lack of political power of a diasporan minority in such situations, and its attempts to acquire it through nationalism. However, Gellner is wrong when treating diasporan nationalism as a reaction to the nationalism of the dominant group. Armenian diasporan nationalism was informed by conditions in the historic homeland—and hence was tied to territory—but it preceded, possibly by as much as a century, the nationalism of the dominant groups in control of that homeland (i.e. Turkish and Persian nationalism). The emergence of Armenian nationalism in the diaspora, particularly before the mid-nineteenth century, was tied much more to European ideas than to Ottoman and Persian ideas and modernisation. The diaspora communities in which nationalism initially emerged were not even in these two empires. Of course, it was a reaction to the conditions of the Armenians in these empires, but those conditions had nothing to do with the modernisation of the empires, and the accompanying nationalism, before the latter part of the nineteenth century. The circumstances were different vis-à-vis the Russian empire. Early Armenian nationalists were inspired by Russia and were not seeking liberation from it, but through it.

[17] R. Panossian, *The Evolution of Multilocal National Identity*, chapter 1.

[18] Prominent scholars associated with the modernist school include Elie Kedourie, Ernest Gellner, Benedict Anderson, Eric Hobsbawm, Paul Brass and John Breuilly. The non-modernists include Steven Grosby, Pierre van den Berghe, Walker Connor, John Armstrong, Anthony Smith and Adrian Hastings.

currently burgeoning domain, I will select only four works, which deal with the issue from three time periods.

The guiding thread in the conventional 'Armenian approach' is to present nationhood as ancient and as natural as possible, in contrast to modernist approaches. The first work is by the prominent diasporan intellectual Levon Shant. Writing in the early 1920s, his main aim was to counter the Socialists' dismissal of national identity as false consciousness. Shant emphasises blood ties, territory, national character and the role of history as the four points which together lead to the formation of a unique nation and guarantee its survival and progress. Civilisational characteristics such as religion, language and cultural production tie the members of the nation together as a specific group.[19] Shant's main concern is to make the national an essential category of identity given the diasporan and socialist conditions in which Armenians were forced to live: 'The individual cut off from his nation is the same as a word outside a sentence; it has no role; and it has and does not have meaning. In order to receive a role and a certain meaning, to be able to express its real meaning and inner nuance, it must be woven into a sentence. Under normal circumstances the most appropriate context of an individual's life is the nation.'[20]

Half a century later this 'organic' approach is taken further by another intellectual writing in the same nationalist tradition. According to Edik Hovhannisian (a Soviet Armenian who had fled to the diaspora and joined the Dashnak party) the 'philosophy of national politics' is losing its importance in world affairs.[21] This is wrong because it negates a crucial element of human identity. Hovhannisian sees the nation not only as a natural and perennial entity, but also a collective imbued with certain esoteric qualities:

> National will is not decided by a majority; it is not the sum of the will of all. Not only the living, but also the dead speak in the national will. The past speaks, as well as the puzzling [i.e. unknown] future. Not only human generations are part of the nation, but also the khachkars [i.e. Armenian stone-crosses], churches, miniature paintings, ancient manuscripts, books, songs etc.... And if these voices are being heard by only one group, one

[19] L. Shant, *Azgutiune*, pp. 11 and 19.
[20] Ibid., p. 54.
[21] E. Hovhannisian, *Azgayin*, p. 12.

party, or even one person, that is where the will of the nation is being expressed, and not the majority who cannot see or hear.[22]

This romantic view of the nation is still prevalent among most Armenian intellectuals. I cite Hovhannisian because he tries to give this notion a philosophical and quasi-scholarly basis.[23]

A recent publication by a scholar in post-Soviet Armenia explicitly engages in the debate against the modernist approach of Eric Hobsbawm and Ernest Gellner. Hamlet Gevorgian (of the Institute for Philosophy and Law of the Armenian Academy of Sciences) bases his argument on the classical perennial approach. Armenian national identity is ancient and those who insist that nations are modern creations simply have it wrong. Gevorgian asks: 'What "re-creation" of historical memory is it possible to talk about in the case of a people who has continuously maintained and visited for sixteen centuries the memorial of the inventor of its alphabet, and whose main cathedral at Holy Ejmiatzin has been operating continuously for seventeen centuries....'[24] Armenia, the author points out, is one of those very few countries that existed in the period of classical civilisation and managed to combine its ancient culture with Christianity in a unique synthesis. He cites examples from medieval Armenian legal codes that distinguish between the 'us' and the 'them', and points out how the church played a crucial role in the intra-national organisation of communal life in the absence of statehood.[25] For Gevorgian the very existence of Armenia and Armenians disproves the modernist approach to the study of nations and nationalism.

Finally, these arguments are radicalised further by Lendrush Khurshudian in a 1999 book entitled *Hayots Azgayin Gaghaparakhosutiun* [Armenians' National Ideology]. Khurshudian's enemies are a-national [*apazgayin*] thinking and cosmopolitanism. His agenda is much more proactive than scholarly criticism. He appropriates elements

22 Ibid., pp. 166–7.

23 The literary version of this idea is provided by the famous diasporan writer Andranik Tzarukian. For him 'A nation can have many layers, different psychological elements in its make up and character; it can even have specific divisions emanating from ancient racial [tribal] origins. But a nation has only one ideal, like the human body has one heart' (A. Tzarukian, *Amerikian*, p. 196).

24 H. Gevorgian, *Azg*, p. 23.

25 Ibid., pp. 30–2.

from Western scholarship, namely Anthony Smith's *National Identity*, quoting it selectively or out of context to suit his programme. Smith's description of nationalism is interpreted as justification, and his emphasis on its resilience is taken as proof of its natural pervasiveness. As such, a sociological study by a Western scholar is transformed in a few pages by Khurshudian into a normative statement advocating the nation and nationalism.[26] But Khurshudian goes much further than Smith. He combines the biological drive for self-preservation in nature with the imperative of preserving the nation. Using the terms 'nation', 'race' and 'ethnos' interchangeably, he argues that a nation is doomed to disappear unless it develops and pursues a clear national ideology. Nationalism, embodying this ideology, is for him a 'weapon for self-defence' because it 'is the mode of expression of the nation's instinct for self-preservation'.[27] The nation, he maintains, 'is a live organism, a historio-ethnic category. For the preservation of each nation the following national factors are necessary: *language, culture, historical memory, thinking, self-consciousness, personal nature, psychology, spiritual composition, character, feeling, love of nation, love of fatherland and pride, spirit, family, religion, taste, habitat, ethnic folklore and habits etc.*'[28]

Khurshudian's 'analysis' has a very clear political aim: to nationalise Armenians so that they can struggle against internal and external enemies. The external enemy is the Turk (pan-Turkism) who in this view is intent on destroying the Armenians. The internal enemy is a-nationalist or cosmopolitan Armenians, more specifically the country's president and ruling party until 1998 (Levon Ter Petrosian and the Armenian Pan-national Movement—people with weak instincts of national self-preservation, or none, according to Khurshudian).[29] The nation must be saved from such people through the inculcation of national ideology taught at schools, and nationalist cultural expression. The ultimate goal is a free and united Armenia, including the historic Armenian territories in Turkey.

[26] L. Khurshudian, *Hayots azgayin*, pp. 26–9.

[27] Ibid., p. 24, cf. pp. 7–8. He also mentions that 'national ideology is in the blood of the nation' (p. 163), and yet a-national 'defeatism' can negatively affect the genes of the nation (p. 240).

[28] Ibid., p. 15 (emphasis in original).

[29] Ibid., pp. 219 and 240.

Written in the same tone as a Soviet text—which would both utilise Marxism-Leninism for historical analysis and praise its virtues as the Truth—Khurshudian's book merely replaces the category of class with that of the nation.[30] The nation embodies the true essence of humanity and must be defended from enemies everywhere. Importantly, the views expressed in *Armenians' National Ideology* do not represent the fringe or most radical elements of Armenian nationalism, but opinions shared by the mainstream of intellectuals in Armenia.[31] Lendrush Khurshudian is considered a prominent scholar in the republic; he is the Director of the Armenian History Department at Yerevan State University, the President of the Historians' Association of Armenia and a member of the Armenian Academy of Sciences. His work is demonstrative of the current academic approaches and level of analysis on nations and nationalism in Armenia. Critical (Western) thought on the subject, if it is engaged with at all, is either dismissed as irrelevant and antinational,[32] or selectively and mendaciously appropriated to justify the nationalist agenda in Armenia.

[30] Another interesting piece written from this perspective is H. Hakobian, 'Hairenikn ibrev patmakan kategoria'. The author first asserts that the notion of fatherland or homeland (*hairenik*) must be accepted as a 'category of history' (p. 143). He then argues that Armenians were one of the first people to develop the concept of a fatherland, the roots of the idea probably stretching back to 'the new stone age', and having one of the earliest states in humanity—15th to 14th century BC (p. 150). All this is tied to modern political concerns: having a nation state is the 'natural right' of all nations. This right must be accepted 'without reservation [and] without a referendum for all those nations who have been exiled from their national-historical territories, that is from their fatherland, because of genocide and deportation' (p. 150). Finally, international law must take into account the right to territorial integrity of the ethnic group ('ethnic territory'), and not just the integrity of the existing state (p. 160).

[31] For a brief analysis of radical nationalism in contemporary Armenia see R. Panossian, 'The Past as Nation', pp. 130–6.

[32] Western scholars of Armenian origin who do not subscribe to the nationalist line emanating from Armenia are often dismissed as 'traitors' by most intellectuals and historians in Armenia, and nationalists in the diaspora. 'Modernist' views on the construction of national identity are not only considered wrong, but 'treacherous'. Any suggestion that Armenian *nationality* is a modern social construct is seen as 'anti-Armenian' because it undermines, in the view of the nationalists, claims to Armenian territory—even if an author steadfastly maintains that Armenian identity itself is indeed very old. There is not much of a debate between the modernist/constructivist and the perennialist/primordialist schools in the Armenian context. Rather there is an acrimonious denunciation of academics who are (or are perceived to be) modern-

Setting aside the nationalism of scholars in Armenia, primordial and perennial approaches to the study of nations and nationalism are quite appealing to anyone who studies the Armenian case. In fact Western scholars in this category, far from being either Armenian or nationalist, often mention the Armenians as an example

---

ists. For example, Ronald Suny was publicly labelled a 'traitor' by one speaker at an opposition rally organised by the Armenian Democratic Party and the National Self-Determination Union in Yerevan on 14 November 1997. The speaker referred to Suny as the 'so-called historian' and the 'so-called Armenian'. (For Suny's basic argument see his *Looking toward Ararat*, Chapters 1 and 3.) A more sustained and sophisticated critique of Suny and Western Armenianology comes from Armen Aivazian. Although he raises some valid criticisms based on historical facts that Suny does not take into account, his book is infused with snide and derogatory comments about Suny and other prominent Western scholars of Armenia(ns), whom he accuses of 'hypocritical-Armeneology', intent on destroying Armenian identity with their 'pro-Turkish' approaches and collaboration with 'Azerbaijani hypocrisy' (A. Aivazian, *Hayastani patumtian lusabanume*, pp. 10, 35, 40, cf. Preface and Part I). Even most of the young and upcoming generation of historians in Armenia, and some in the diaspora, see the writing of history as a *tool* to be used for nationalist purposes. Writing in 1998 (and not 1898 or 1948!) Aivazian puts it explicitly: 'Armenian history is the inviolable strategic resource pool [*razmavarakan andzernmkheli pashar*] of Armenia.... Therefore, the scientific study of Armenian history... is not only a pure academic endeavour, but also a necessary and productive means to benefit the newly formed Armenian state' (pp. 8–9). Aivazian tries to do precisely this in his own work (for his recent attempt, reading nationalism in the work of Catholicos Ghazar Jahketsi who reigned 1737–51, see A. Aivazian, 'Ghazar Jahketsu'). Significantly, most of the historiographical establishment in Armenia rallied around Aivazian in denouncing Western approaches to Armenian studies, largely because of their modernist/constructivist approach. The Department of Armenian History of Yerevan State University even took the extraordinary step (harking back to Soviet times!) of issuing a Declaration on 19 December 2001 condemning historical research (in the diaspora) which it believes undermines the Armenian nation and statehood. Armen Aivazian's book was reviewed widely (and almost always favourably) in the republic's press. For example, one review in the respected *Patma-banasirakan handes* went as far as saying that 'the American authors mentioned in Aivazian's book [i.e. practically all the 'big names' in Armenian studies] not only are pro-Turkish in their thinking, *but directly take its false formulations*, explicitly defend them and *act as the lawyers* [of this approach]' (M. Zulalian, [Review], p. 351; see also A. Sargsian, 'Patmutian chisht chanaparhe'; V. Devrikian, 'Hayots patmutiune'). For a lone critical review of Aivazian in Armenia see K. Iuzbashian, 'Amerikian hayagitutiune'; for a superb and systematic critique of Aivazian's book and the entire nationalist discourse in Armenia's academia see S. Aslanian, 'Treason of the Intellectuals'; cf. A. Sanjian [Review]. Serious diaspora-based scholars of Armenia(ns) have condemned Aivazian's book, and the US-based Society for Armenian Studies itself issued a Statement on 24 July 2002 condemning the Declaration of Yerevan State University!

which proves their argument regarding the ancientness of nations (e.g. Steven Grosby and John Armstrong).[33] However, these approaches—both in Armenia and in Western academia—do not take into account the fundamental changes that took place in Armenian identity in the nineteenth century. Nationhood cannot be projected backwards into antiquity because the very definition of a nation is based on thoroughly modern concepts.

Defining the nation

How to define a nation—which includes the question of dating nationhood—is the most divisive issue in the theoretical literature on the subject. Consequently, it is essential to provide at least a 'working definition' in order to have some of the conceptual clarity necessary in the examination of historical developments. However, there has to be a certain amount of flexibility built into such a definition. A wide variety of factors must be taken into account, and yet the definition must be precise enough to be useful as an analytical tool. I would like to present a two-pronged argument in this respect: the subjective nature of national identity, and the modernity of nations. This definition and characterisation of nation will be useful in the analysis of the Armenian case, and others.

Before tackling the difficult concept of nation, I will quickly define related terms that are used throughout this book. The terms 'national identity' and 'national consciousness' are used interchangeably to denote a sense of belonging to a nation. If someone says 'I am Armenian' or 'I am English', or whatever other nation, the person is asserting his or her national identity based on his or her consciousness as belonging to a collective which is known (to him or her and to many others) as a nation. 'Nationhood' is a descriptive terms for a group of people most of whom identify themselves as

[33] Steven Grosby's argument is particularly interesting in this respect. In addition to the Jewish case he cites the Armenians as an ancient nation with the distinguishing markers of religion, a common enough language (i.e. cultural homogeneity), clear territory, a sense of ancestry and even a political assembly. These led to a collective self-consciousness that could be considered as national according to him (S. Grosby, 'Borders', pp. 19–25; cf. S. Grosby, 'Territoriality' and 'Religion and Nationality'). Grosby is not arguing that nations have always existed as part of nature, but that some nations do go very far back, and that national identity is tied to very basic human characteristics such as kinship, language and religion.

members of a specific nation and have the general attributes of that nation. Hence, to develop nationhood a majority of a people must have a sense of national consciousness and identity. The 'nation-state' is mostly a juridical-political concept—and a misnomer. As Walker Connor has shown, very few countries in this world are 'true' nation-states with a complete overlap between national identity and the boundaries of the state.[34] Contemporary Armenia, in its homogeneity, is one of the few exceptions that comes close; over 95 per cent of its population is ethnically Armenian. The establishment of a nation-state is often the *desire* of various nationalist movements, but nationalist movements are not necessarily confined to this goal.

'Nationalism' is *predominantly*, but not exclusively, a political concept. It is an active endeavour to either create national identity, or to maintain, advance, augment and strengthen it. It seeks to establish or to redefine a political order based on the principle of belonging to a nation. Although a political ideology, nationalism usually incorporates cultural elements and historical symbols in its worldview.[35] It can be organised into a movement or it can be expressed in a diffused and informal manner. Nationalism is often associated with the desire to establish a state for the nation (i.e. independence), but that is not always the case. Nevertheless, nationalism includes demands for at least a certain degree of self-rule (be it political, cultural or economic). Militancy, rebellion and secession are certainly associated with nationalism and are its most visible manifestations. But nationalism is also expressed peacefully through reform, and can be confined to calls for cultural autonomy or respect for national rights. In short, nationalism is the ideology of acting politically, in either an explicit or an implicit manner, on behalf of the nation. However, it should be pointed out that although nationalism as a policy device can be used instrumentally by a particular elite, nationalism in itself

[34] W. Connor, *Ethnonationalism*, p. 96.

[35] The 'core' doctrine of this worldview—in its 'classical' version—is outlined by Anthony Smith (*Theories of Nationalism*, p. 21). The doctrine stipulates: (1) humanity is naturally divided into nations; (2) each nation is unique; (3) the nation, in its collectivity, is the source of all political power; (4) everyone must belong to a nation because freedom and self-realisation are experienced through the nation; (5) nations can be fulfilled in their own autonomous states; (6) loyalty to the nation overrides other loyalties; (7) strong and free nations are essential if the world order is to be free and harmonious.

is not just a tool. It is broader than the political process in the strict sense of parties, elites and state activities. Nationalism has an element of being 'felt'—and not only used—by the elite, intellectuals and masses. For all of them the nation, as a politico-cultural entity, is the central point of reference. Nationalism is a wide concept indeed, as applicable to contemporary Quebec as to eighteenth-century Armenian printers in India.

But what is a nation? As mentioned, it is not possible to give a precise definition to the term 'nation'. The phenomenon itself is fluid and subject to many variations. I agree with Seton-Watson that 'no "scientific definition" of a nation can be devised'.[36] For example, how can an exact definition apply to nations with as diverse historical evolutions and experiences, not to mention cultural contents, as the Americans and the Armenians? There are two main components to the definitional problem. The first relates to the variables based on which the term can be defined. The second is the temporal question of how far back nations can be traced or projected. I start with the first issue and highlight the importance of subjectivity.

The importance of subjectivity. Scholars of nationalism generally do not dismiss subjectivity as a factor, pointing out that a nation contains both objective and subjective elements. The main argument is one of emphasis. More than a dichotomy these factors are part of a continuum. Some scholars emphasise the subjective factors, while others highlight the objective characteristics. The subjective approach is usually traced to Ernest Renan and his famous phrase of 1882: 'A nation is a soul, a spiritual principle.... A nation's existence is, if you will pardon the metaphor, a daily plebiscite, just as an individual's existence is a perpetual affirmation of life.'[37] At the other end of the spectrum one finds Stalin's oft-cited definition from 1913: 'A nation is a historically constituted, stable community of people, formed on the basis of a common language, territory, economic life, and psychological make-up manifested in a common culture.'[38] Stalin's definition does allow for a subjective component

[36] H. Seton-Watson, *Nations and States*, p. 5; cf. V. Tishkov, *Ethnicity*, p. 21.
[37] E. Renan, 'What is a Nation?' pp. 52–3.
[38] J. Stalin, 'The Nation', p. 20.

(psychological make-up), but it is a predominantly objective definition. More recently, scholars whose definitions are closer to the subjective pole of the continuum include Hugh Seton-Watson and Walker Connor. The latter says: 'The essence of the nation is not tangible. It is psychological, a matter of attitude rather than of fact.' Furthermore, it is 'the self-view of one's group, rather than the tangible characteristics, that is of essence in determining the existence or non-existence of a nation.'[39] Anthony Smith is the closest scholar to the objective pole. According to him, a nation is 'a named human population sharing an historic territory, common myths and historical memories, a mass, public culture, a common economy and common legal rights and duties for all members.'[40] Other scholars of nations and nationalism fall between these two poles, combining both subjective and objective elements.[41]

While accepting that a nation is a combination of objective and subjective factors, I place more emphasis on the subjective component in my own definition of nations. It is for this reason that I do not project nationhood backwards onto pre-modern Armenians. My argument consists of two points. First, national identity is about belonging, and any sense of belonging is above all else a subjective projection of identity. Objective factors do come into play, but as mechanisms to reinforce or define that sense. Of course there are limits to the extent of subjectivity. A group of people might feel that it constitutes a nation, but without some sort of 'objective' distinguishing markers it will be very difficult for the group to maintain such a claim (hence the importance of historians and cultural workers in the imagination of *difference*). Moreover, there is an external component. Not only must the group claim to be a nation, but others have to grant it recognition as such. The international dimension is important as a yardstick of measurement and emulation. Hence, a nation has to be recognised and 'subjectively' defined *as* a nation by its members and others. This of course does not 'neatly' apply to some cases and a good many conflicts are waged because of it; peo-

[39] W. Connor, *Ethnonationalism*, pp. 42 and 43, cf. pp. 112–13, 202; see also H. Seton-Watson, *Nations and States*, p. 5.

[40] A. Smith, *National Identity*, p. 14, cf. p. 69; A. Smith, *Theories of Nationalism*, p. 186.

[41] For some examples see E. Gellner, *Nations and Nationalism*, p. 7; S. Grosby, 'Borders', pp. 26–7; E. Tiryakian and N. Nevitte, 'Nationalism and Modernity', pp. 58, 65–6.

ple struggle to assert their national identity or rights against those who dismiss the group's 'nationness' (for example, the case of the Kurds). The lines defining both objective and, especially, subjective divisions are fuzzy. In some cases, therefore, the first task of a nationalist movement is to 'prove' that its constituency does indeed constitute a nation. In sum, a nation is a nation when it says it is, on the basis of some differences from its neighbours, and when it is accepted by others as such. National identity is primarily a 'felt' category of self-definition, but it is tied to certain objective characteristics. Importantly, as I argue below, *what* is being felt is profoundly connected to modernity.

The second reason why I emphasise the subjective dimension emanates from the specific case of the Armenians, notably in the modern period. The subjective element allows intellectuals and members of a group to gloss over objective differences within the community. As the following chapters argue, Armenian nationalists—and subsequently the masses—defined themselves as members of one nation despite a number profound differences within the pre-existing ethno-religious community. What united such activities, and situated what had become a disjoined people under the rubric of the Armenian nation, was the subjective sense of belonging to *one* nation despite those differences. A predominantly objective definition of nationhood would not be able to account for such cases where deep divisions are subordinated to the overall sense of national identity. Armenians felt—and still do feel—as part of one nation even if they hardly have anything in common with many other Armenians. A workable definition of nations, and by extension nationalism, has to be able to take this into account. It is subjectivity that allows for all members of a collective to gloss over divisive realities and to feel part of one and the same nation.

However, the Armenian case also shows the importance of theoretical flexibility in this respect. While I agree with John Edwards when he says, 'Any analysis of nationalism which concentrates upon objective characteristics misses the essential point,'[42] I would maintain that proper analysis requires the ability to shift theoretical emphasis from one period to another. After all, the basis of identity, as

[42] J. Edwards, *Language, Society and Identity*, p. 15.

well as the ideological legitimisation of power relations, changes from one period to the next. Historical dynamism requires theoretical versatility. The objective dimension must be woven into the analysis because it has more explanatory value than the subjective argument when discussing ancient identities. It can account for the cultural, ethnic and geographic boundaries within which the nation eventually emerges. As will be clear in the next chapter, focusing on the objective dimension is particularly relevant in the analysis of pre-modern identities as it highlights the cultural 'content' and the specific characteristics of an ethnic group. Pillars of the distinguishing features of Armenian identity—the building blocks—were laid in ancient times: religion, language, territorial basis, myths and symbols. These objective historical characteristics of 'Armenianness' enabled the group to survive into the modern period when the subjective dimension was introduced on the road to nationhood, transforming the collective from an ethnic group into a nation.

National identity is created, consciously or not, through various factors such as mass education and culture; it is generally situated on—or inspired by—a specific territory (with relatively clear boundaries); and it usually takes place within the parameters of a specific legal code, or at the very least, specific community organisations.[43] In this creation process the past plays a crucial role. It provides the images, the examples, the cultural markers and the community institutions through which identity is reformulated and shaped into a modern sense of nationality. Roots do matter; and roots set the boundaries, providing the objective elements of national identity. How the 'greater community'—i.e. the general boundaries around a more or less distinct group of people—is defined almost always has historical antecedents in the form of pre-existing ethno-religious communities. Most commonly these antecedents evolve around language (classic-*cum*-vernacular), a separate religion and/or church institutions, other communal structures, a shared sense of history and/or ancestry and, of course, a connection—be it real or imagined—with a specific territory.

The emphasis on subjectivity goes to the core of the argument in this book because of its importance in the modern period (i.e. the

[43] Partly based on A. Smith, *National Identity*, p. 69.

seventeenth century onwards). In the past four centuries or so the disparate efforts of nationalists produced one overarching national identity as differences that had emerged after the Armenian classical period, in diasporan and imperial conditions, were 'unified'. My subsequent 'multilocality' argument emerges from this realisation and suggests that diverse collectives can become one nation because they subjectively believe themselves to be part of one entity. In sum, by using the word 'subjective' I am not at all suggesting that structures and objective characteristics do not matter as crucial building blocks in history. But it is the subjective element that unites—and not necessarily in a homogeneous manner—people as *one* nation. This is the crux of my approach.

The importance of modernity. The second dimension of the two-pronged definition of nation has to do with the question of 'dating'—or, as one scholar poignantly asks, 'When is a nation?'[44] Conflicting answers are at the core of the modernist/non-modernist divide. 'The key issue at the heart of our schism,' writes Adrian Hastings, 'lies in the date of commencement.'[45] Are nations modern or not? How far back can they be projected? My argument is that *nations are modern political constructs but with pre-modern socio-cultural roots which give them specific characteristics.* These roots do not have to be confined to one ethnic group or *ethnie*—i.e. I do not accept that there has to be *one* ethnic core or one *predominant* core (although often there is).[46] By roots I do not mean a clearly distinguished *ethnie* in the sense employed by Anthony Smith, but simply cultural

[44] W. Connor, 'When is a Nation?'

[45] A. Hastings, p. 9; cf. J. Breuilly, *Nationalism and the State*, pp. 2–5.

[46] For example, the ethnic core centred in Paris enforced its notion of 'Frenchness' on to the rest of the country (more or less successfully) in the centuries-long nation-building process of France. A counter-example would be Canada (or similar settler countries). If it is accepted that Canadians constitute one nation, then it would have to be accepted that it has, officially, three ethnic 'cores': English, French and the indigenous first nations, which currently co-exist with one another. To these one could add the many ethnic identities of the immigrant minorities, which are subsumed under the overall identity of 'Canadianness'. A similar argument can be made with 'Britishness' and the various ethnic and regional identities that are inherent in it, often in tension with 'Englishness'. In the Armenian case there has been one ethnic core but not a singular cultural core which could (in the modern period) enforce its notion of Armenianness onto the rest of the ethnic group.

and symbolic links to past ethnic identities.[47] Furthermore, roots should not be confused with dominant characteristics. The dominant characteristic of a nation is its modernity, not its perennial or primordial connections—even if these give it a deep sense of history in some cases. Something modern can, and often does, have ancient roots; this does not make it any less modern.

As mentioned, the main reason I argue that nations are modern constructs is connected to the subjective argument presented above. National identity is contingent upon a subjective sense of belonging which is predominantly based on notions of citizenship and popular sovereignty—i.e. *modern, secular* and *political* ideas of belonging to a collective. I do not mean this in a mechanistic manner, that a nation does not exist until there is full enfranchisement, but I do accept that 'national consciousness [and nationalism] is a mass not an elite phenomenon.'[48] In a fully 'developed' nation, almost all individuals would conceive of themselves as members and citizens of that *nation qua nation* (despite objective differences). This, figuratively, is a post-1776/1789 idea. At the heart of this notion of belonging lies the belief that *everyone* matters as a political entity or subject (even if he or she does not have the right to vote). Everyone is considered to be, and must feel as, part of the greater *political* community—at least in rhetoric. It is assumed that there is a common secular and political bond between all sectors of society, between the leaders and the masses, between the city and the countryside, between one region and the next. This is a modern phenomenon—especially the idea that 'commoners' do matter and that their lives and their views should be taken into account as part of the collec-

[47] My argument differs from Anthony Smith's approach. For him, 'Modern nations may have pre-modern precursors and can form around recurrent ethnic antecedents.' Thus nations usually have an 'ethnic basis' in the form of 'ethnic communities', which he calls *ethnies* (A. Smith, *Myths and Memories*, p. 11); these are the 'nuclei of subsequent "nation states"' (A. Smith, 'Ethnic Identity', p. 49). Smith is preoccupied with 'precursors' and 'antecedents' which constitute clearly defined pre-modern cultural units. My argument is much more flexible because it concentrates on roots that are diffused and decentralised—i.e. my approach is broader and more applicable to cases where an ethnic 'core' is missing but there exist obvious connections to various pre-modern entities and identities. Smith's argument is applicable to the Armenians but excludes other cases that cannot be traced to a clear-cut ethnic core or *ethnie*. My argument includes the Armenians while being wide enough to include most other cases.

[48] W. Connor, 'When is a Nation?' p. 92.

tive-*cum*-nation. The French revolution was the most powerful expression of this idea, the one 'moment' in which it crystallised.[49] In short, when serfs and slaves began to matter as political subjects, as potential citizens, as part of the same cultural background as the rulers, nations began to emerge.[50]

Intrinsically connected to this political idea is the cultural component of the argument: the idea that the 'commoners'—i.e. the people—and the ruling elite must necessarily be of the same cultural background and collective identity. This too is a profoundly modern idea, going to the heart of political legitimacy. For the elite to be considered legitimate in its rule, it must share the same cultural heritage or assumed ancestry of the people. Modern political ideology stipulates that rulers must derive their legitimacy from the population who are 'alike'—at least in popular belief if not in reality. Legitimate sovereignty no longer lies in divine rights embodied by kings, aristocrats and religious leaders but in the people. Put differently, there is a lack of *political* legitimacy if ruler and ruled are not from the same *cultural* background.[51] This lack of legitimacy undermines popular sovereignty, one of the 'sacred' principles of modern politics.

I do not mean to suggest that there were, for example, no Armenians or Russians or English before the nineteenth century. But most Armenians, Russians and (*au contraire* to Adrian Hastings and Liah Greenfeld) English had a *pre*-national ethno-religious sense of belonging—i.e. their collective identity was not national identity.

[49] Jean-Jacques Rousseau (1712–72), for example, expressed the idea—very directly and powerfully—that the nation is not confined to the (aristocratic) elite but incorporates within it the entire population of the 'fatherland' bound together by similar customs, morals, laws and so forth.

[50] In this respect, nation and democracy—in its widest sense—are interlinked. For a brief overview on the issue of citizenship and nationalism see M. Guibernau, *Nationalisms*, pp. 51–5.

[51] Benedict Anderson highlights that in the past the prestige of rulers (e.g. royal families) rested on their *difference* from the masses they ruled, not on similarities (B. Anderson, 'Western Nationalism', p. 36). Benjamin Braude makes a related point, but in connection to territory: in pre-modern times ideas of attachment to a homeland were quite different from territorial exclusivity at the core of the modern national-state, he argues (B. Braude, 'The Nexus of Diaspora', pp. 32–3). He then adds, 'The apolitical quality of pre-modern national [*sic*] existence is crucial' (p. 34). I am making a general point here, and not implying that Armenian rulers and their subjects were not of the same cultural background in the classical period (notwithstanding Cilicia).

Certainly their intellectual elite might have conceived of themselves and even their fellow 'countrymen' as part of the Armenian, Russian or English nation, but the vast majority of the population certainly did not see itself in national terms, nor did the elite really care to know the terms in which the majority of the population did perceive itself. It is possible to argue that certain elements that led to nationhood (especially in the cultural realm) were in incubation for centuries. But the *idea* of the nation, as we understand it today, is inexorably connected to modernity. Nations did not exist in antiquity. One could not, in the pre-modern period, feel part of an entity that only came into being with modernity, with its notions of popular sovereignty and the importance of the masses.

To sum up, a nation is the combination of objective (ethno-cultural) factors rooted in the past and a particular sense of subjective (political) belonging emanating from modernity. The modern component outweighs the historical element because it sets the parameters within which we can speak of a nation, but it cannot explain the shape and content of nations. Simply put, even if all the objective factors are there, it is not possible to speak of a nation in a non-national (that is, in a pre- or post-national) age. As John Breuilly points out, Shakespeare might have used the term 'nation' to refer to a distinct group of people, but it meant something else.[52] As an *analytical category* the concept of a nation should be confined to the modern period. Earlier entities can just as easily be referred to as proto-nations, pre-nations, ethnic groups or *ethnies*.[53] The three

[52] J. Breuilly, *Nationalism*, p. 4. It is the same in the case of the Armenian language. The word *azg* currently means 'nation', but it was in use a millennium or so earlier to denote family or kinship. In fact, the modern word for 'family name' (or surname)—*azganun*—is a derivative of the term *azg*. If literally translated in its modern use, *azganun* would mean 'name of nation'. Other meanings of the word *azg* in the past included 'people', '*ethnos*' and '*natio*' in its Latin sense (cf. K. Tololyan, 'Textual Nation', pp. 86–7.

[53] I will discuss the concept of *ethnie* in the next chapter. Suffice to mention here that the term 'ethnicity' is much more suitable in reference to pre-modern identity. Ethnicity and nation are often conflated, but this is erroneous. A brief definition of ethnicity will hopefully clarify the confusion. Ethnic identity is an older and broader phenomenon than national identity. It is not 'imagined' as a *political* community, but as a familial community. Ancestry and kinship are crucial to ethnic identity in ways that they are not to national identity. As Donald Horowitz states, 'Ethnic identity is established at birth for most group members....Ethnicity is based on a myth of collective ancestry, which usually carries with it traits believed to be innate' (D. Horowitz, *Ethnic*

dimensions of the above argument come together in my definition of nation: *it is a modern entity, based on a subjective sense of political belonging, but rooted in objective—and often pre-modern—factors such as myths, symbols and cultural markers.*[54]

The characteristics of nations. Before concluding this section on the definition of nation, it is necessary to outline some of the central characteristics of nations. What concrete properties or features do nations have? First, nations must have histories—be they 'real' or 'constructed', 'deep' or 'shallow'. Some nations take their history very seriously, others less so: for example, history is 'everything' for Armenians and Georgians, but that is not the case for Americans or Canadians. History is the 'pool' out of which ancient myths and collective memory emerge. 'Nations without a past are contradictions in terms,' says Eric Hobsbawm, adding, 'What makes a nation is the past.'[55] Such 'faith in history'[56] is what sustains identity among the Armenians.

Second, even though nations are based on a political sense of belonging, they are also cultural categories. As much as history, nations do need a distinct culture that nationalists seek to protect and advance.[57] Culture sets the boundaries of the nation in its totality

Groups, p. 52; cf. J. Fishman, 'Social Theory and Ethnography', pp. 84–5). Ethnicity expresses the human need of belonging at a more personal level. Generally, ethnic politics do not seek to address the 'wide' issues of autonomy, independence, statehood etc.—i.e. issues related to a political sense of belonging. Some nations are more 'ethnic' than others (e.g. Armenians and Japanese in contrast to Americans and French) because, in their case, there existed a clearly defined core ethnic community, perhaps a proto-nation, which was transformed to a modern nation. For some of the literature on ethnicity that examines its links with nationality and politics see F. Barth, 'Introduction'; T. Eriksen, *Ethnicity and Nationalism*; P. Brass, *Ethnicity and Nationalism*; A. Smith, *Ethnic Origins of Nations*.

54 This eclectic definition of nation bridges the gap between the modernist and non-modernist schools, as well as between the 'objective' and 'subjective' perspectives; it borrows relevant points from various approaches.

55 E. Hobsbawm, 'Opiate Ethnicity', p. 8. He colourfully adds: 'Historians are to nationalism what poppy-growers in Pakistan are to heroin-addicts: we supply the essential raw material for the market.' Of course some nations or would-be nations imagine futures more than pasts; the Soviet 'nation' is one failed example; but the American nation can be considered a successful example.

56 S. Pattie, *Faith in History*, pp. 232ff.

57 Almost all scholars discuss the relationship between culture and nation. See, among others, A. Smith, *Ethnic Origins of Nations* (chapter 8) and *National Identity* (chapter 4); E. Gellner, *Nations and Nationalism* (chapter 4); J. Hutchinson, *Modern Nationalism*

and therefore has to have a 'mass' component to it. High cultures are not enough, as Ernest Gellner has shown, they have to become mass cultures. 'National culture' has to incorporate everyone within it. In some cases cultural markers are based on very stark differences; in others there could be quite a bit of overlap in the culture of two nations. But there have to be clearly accepted differences.

Third, nations must have some sort of political structure that tie its members together. These can be states (as is the case with the 'established' nations), or they can be community structures (as is the case with diaspora nations).[58] States are not essential to the existence of a nation and, in fact, nations can precede or follow state creation. Nations can exist without a state at all, as long as they have other mechanisms that tie the community together as a political unit. Nationalism too can precede or follow the nation—although in most cases nationalism, through the work of intellectuals, precedes the formation of mass national identity. Nationalism, as a clearly articulated ideology, 'follows' nations only in particular circumstances, such as the unique experience of Soviet-style nation formation.

Fourth, the nation has a territorial component to it. It believes that a certain territory *exclusively* belongs to it. This is often expressed as an ancestral right. Hence it follows that the nation should enjoy a right to self-determination (independence or autonomy). On this view, a nation must have a home*land* in which it can exercise some form of home-rule. It does not always live on its territory (as in the case of nations in diaspora), but the notion of a homeland—either concretely or in the abstract—is always infused with national identity.[59]

Fifth, nations and nationalisms are not tied to one specific political ideology. They can accommodate right-wing or left-wing politics, they can have deep historical roots or be an immigrant society,

---

(chapter 2); B. Anderson, *Imagined Communities* (chapter 2); E. Tiryakian and N. Nevitte, 'Nationalism and Modernity', p. 65.

[58] The relationship between state and nation is discussed much in literature (e.g. J. Breuilly, E. Gellner, L. Greenfeld). But community organisations, except the church, are not generally analysed as political instruments. One important exception is J. Armstrong's detailed study, *Nations Before Nationalism*, in which he examines group identities within wider structures such as empires and civilisations.

[59] For further elaboration on the nation-territory link see A. Smith, *Theories of Nationalism*, p. 186; J. Armstrong, *Nations Before Nationalism*, Chapter 2.

they can emerge out of the 'romantic' or 'liberal' traditions (or both, as in the Armenian case), and they can be democratic or repressive (i.e. claim popular sovereignty without democracy). These categorisations demonstrate the possible variations in the phenomenon called nation and the terms derived from it; but they are not part of its definition *per se*. A nation that has a totalitarian state is as much a nation as one that has a liberal state.

And finally, nations are dynamic constructs and not just 'given' entities that exist in an unchanging manner. All scholars agree at least on this point. National identity is constantly in flux because it is an ongoing development. Ronald Suny calls it an 'open ended process, never fully complete'.[60] Homi Bhabha mentions the '*instability* of cultural signification' of the nation.[61] And Anthony Smith writes, 'Creating nations is a recurrent activity, which has to be renewed periodically. It is one that involves ceaseless re-interpretations, rediscoveries and reconstructions; each generation must refashion national institutions.'[62] What is most interesting about this dynamic is the fact that the very basis of nationhood can change, but without undermining a group's sense of national identity. From one generation to the next, within the *same* nation, the basis of belonging might change. For example, for a 1935 Armenian in Lebanon, being Armenian would have been based on 'objective' characteristics such as language and community structures. For a 1995 Armenian in the United States, a purely subjective sense of 'feeling' part of the nation might suffice. It is important to keep such heterogeneity in mind.

Five themes emerge from the theoretical discussion above. These themes form the guiding threads in my subsequent analysis of the evolution of Armenian national identity and nationalism. First, the modernist/non-modernist dichotomy in the literature on nations and nationalism must not be adhered to in analysing a case study. All useful elements of the literature should be used because nations have both modern and pre-modern components that must be

[60] R. Suny, *Looking Toward Ararat*, p. 11.
[61] H. Bhabha, 'DissemiNation', p. 303.
[62] A. Smith, *Ethnic Origins of Nations*, p. 206.

examined. Second, it must not be assumed that nationalism is necessarily a homogenising force (although it might present itself as such). Differences must be analysed as well, and heterogeneity in national identity must be explored. The multilocal nature of Armenian identity is a testament to such diversity. Third, national identity can be constructed without a central point 'directing' it. Hence the centrality of the state must be questioned and the role of non-state actors examined—e.g., the role of diaspora institutions and agents. Much of Armenian nationalism in the modern period was diasporan in its origin and nature. Fourth, the subjective component of national identity must be emphasised, especially given the second point above. If there are fundamental differences between various components of the same nation, then what unites them is a subjective sense of belonging. And fifth, nations on the whole are modern constructs because their basis of identity is qualitatively different from the pre-modern period. This might seem a contradiction of the first point, but is in fact addressing a different issue. The first point calls for analytical sophistication in the need to recognise all components of nations by rejecting the dichotomy in the literature, and the tendency to classify nations as modern or pre-modern. What I am arguing here is that the predominant characteristic of national identity, and its basis of legitimacy, are modern. However, it is not sufficient to examine just this, and it is certainly problematic to base one's analysis entirely on the modern characteristics of nations.

I now turn to the analysis of the evolution of Armenian national identity based on the above preliminary theoretical comments. Throughout the book, I will touch upon certain other theoretical points in specific historical contexts.

2

THE INITIAL BUILDING BLOCKS

FROM THE 'BEGINNING OF TIME' TO THE 17TH CENTURY

In an interview I conducted with a Member of the Armenian National Assembly in 1997, the genealogy of the Armenian nation came up as 'essential' background to explain the basis of the 'Armenian Cause' today. Mr Khachik Safarian explained:

> Humanity has not developed a hundred times and in a thousand places. This is against the laws of evolution of nature. This point of origin is the Near East—especially for all the religions which believe that humanity originated from one couple (in this locale). So, humanity has originated in one spot, in the Near East, and then, independently of one another, [the various tribes] have multiplied. Those who were capable of adapting to their milieu, to the local conditions, stayed; and those who could not, the riffraff, wandered throughout the earth, and adapted to different conditions and environments, developing different languages, customs etc.... The environment also caused changes in anatomy. Those who stayed in the original location developed into sedentary life....and, therefore, they considerably advanced because they started thinking about creating things. Those who moved on, could still live with hunting and gathering, and therefore lagged behind in their development....We [the Armenians] stayed here. We did not go anywhere, nor did we come from anyplace. [It has been] determined in scientific studies, with thousands of facts, that the fatherland of Indo-Europeans is found in the Armenian mountain ranges or nearby territories. And the closest language today to the original Indo-European language is Armenian....[1]

Such 'explanations' of Armenian ethnogenesis and history are quite prevalent in Armenia, even at the elite level. They bring together

[1] Author's interview with Khachik Safarian.

myth, religion, history and scientific research, as Armenian historians did centuries earlier, to prove that the Armenian nation has been on its land since the 'beginning of time', and that the actual territory is much larger than the current republic. At the extreme it is suggested that Armenians were the originators of all the Indo-European races, if not of humanity, and hence the embodiment of the purest lineage. Of course the arguments of the professional historians are much more sophisticated and measured than those of my interviewee, but they all come down to the same basic theme: Armenians are at the very least the natives of their land.

This chapter provides the historical background on which such assertions are based. It covers, briefly, ancient history and discusses some of the political, social, cultural and intellectual forces that have shaped Armenian national identity. My aim is not to write Armenian history *per se*, but to highlight key developments and trends that have symbolic links to the modern period and are therefore relevant to understanding Armenian nationalism. What follows is an interpretative rather than a descriptive account. I argue that a distinct Armenian collective identity—already in the making for many centuries—was cemented further with the adoption of Christianity and a unique alphabet in the fourth and fifth centuries AD. Nevertheless, this does not mean that nationhood itself can be projected back to the pre-modern era.

MYTHS, KINGS, CHRISTIANITY AND THE *ETHNIE*: FROM NOAH TO MOVSES KHORENATSI

Being autochthonous to the land is one of the most important themes in nationalist discourse. In this respect Armenians do indeed go very far back. The date accepted by mainstream historians for the existence of a distinct Armenian collective is the sixth century BC although, according to James Russell, it is 'indisputable that there were Armenians in Armenia by the late second millennium BC, speaking their own [Indo-European] language.'[2] They had emerged from the mix of indigenous Hurro-Urartean tribes and Indo-European people who had migrated to the region from Europe in the second millennium BC. Some revisionist (more nationalist) histori-

[2] J. Russell, 'Formation of the Armenian Nation', p. 26.

ans counter this argument. They insist that the Armenian proto-nation and language existed as early as from the sixth to the fourth millennia BC in Armenia (Anatolia), and that this was the birthplace of Indo-Europeans. Hence the Armenian language, and therefore the people, are the true natives of the land.[3]

However, it is clear that by the ninth century BC a tribal confederation had formed the first politically unified kingdom on the territory of what subsequently became Armenia. The dynastic state of Urartu (870–590 BC) centred around Lake Van and was a rival to the Assyrians.[4] Eventually the Armenian component within this confederation became dominant and assimilated the other tribes within itself. After the collapse of the Urartian kingdom the first recorded reference to 'Armenia' and 'Armenian' (written as 'Armina' and 'Arminiya') appears in 520–518 BC on the Behistun rock (presently Bisotun in north-western Iran) erected by Darius I of Persia commemorating his victories over conquered peoples. By this time the Armenians—especially at the elite level—had emerged as one people, perhaps a proto-*ethnie*, from the coalitions and assimilation of various tribes.

The historic territory on which the Armenian people lived stretched between the Kur river to the east, the Pontic mountain range to the north, the Euphrates river to the west and the Taurus Mountains to the south. This vast land was composed of mountain ranges, valleys and rivers. Such geographical features had political consequences: the physical composition of the territory mitigated

[3] For these debates between the 'classical' and 'revisionist' approaches see S. Astourian, 'In Search of their Forefathers', pp. 43–52; J. Russell, 'The Formation of the Armenian Nation', pp. 24–6. The revisionists base their approach on the work of Soviet linguists Thomas Gamkrelidze and Vyacheslav Ivanov. For a recent study that looks at the tribal foundations of the Armenians and hence stretches Armenian roots to prehistory see M. Ohanian, 'Hai zhoghovrdi'. What was the revisionist thesis in the Soviet period is now the widely accepted orthodoxy in Armenia. The preoccupation with trying to prove that Armenians are autochthonous to the land continues unabated—if anything, it has intensified largely due to the Gharabagh conflict and 'debates' with Azerbaijanis over the national ownership rights to territory.

[4] The partially preserved ruins of one of the important fortresses of this kingdom, Erebuni, built in 782 BC, are in present-day Yerevan, giving the capital city of Armenia 2,800 year old historical roots—a fact not lost on the current leaders of the country. In October 1998 the 2,780th anniversary of the founding of Yerevan was officially celebrated with much fanfare and publicity. The practice of celebrating the founding of the city dates back to the last two decades of Soviet rule in Armenia.

against the emergence of a strong central political power throughout much of Armenian history. Consequently, various regions and enclaves, at different times, could maintain a degree of autonomy from the centralising tendencies of both domestic and external (imperial) sources of political power. As one historian sums up this widely accepted view, it was 'a blessing in disguise' since 'Armenia's lack of political unity meant the survival of its culture even while its kings were deposed and its capital cities destroyed,' unlike highly centralised Assyria 'whose entire culture vanished with the collapse of its capital city.'[5]

Whichever theory of ethnogenesis one accepts, it is clear that the first dynasty to rule over Armenia (notwithstanding Urartu) as a distinct administrative unit was that of the Yervandunis (a.k.a. Orontids, c. 585–200 BC). They were initially appointed as governors by the Medes (early sixth century BC) and Persians (Achaemenids 550–331 BC) and, subsequent to Alexander the Great's defeat of the Persian empire in 331 BC, ruled Armenia independently until they were (internally) overthrown more than a century later. The Hellenistic empire of Alexander and his Seleucid successors was unable to assert full control over the Yervandunis who refused to pay tribute to the Persian empire's inheritors.

It is not known whether the Yervandunis were ethnically Armenian. They probably had marriage links to the rulers of Persia and other leading noble houses in Armenia. They were formally appointed *satraps* (governors) by the Achaemenid kings to whom they paid tribute in the form of taxes, horses etc., and fought alongside the imperial armies against foreign enemies. As long as these obligations were met without turmoil the Achaemenids left their subject peoples alone and did not interfere with local customs and religions. It seems that the satraps of the Yervanduni family ruled Armenia more or less independently.

During this period Armenian identity was being solidified as various regions and peoples who lived on the Armenian plateau were integrated into the imperial administrative structure. This was made easier with the construction of the Achaemenid royal road. Interregional trade also developed and new cities were built. Consequently, a more unified and homogeneous culture emerged. Although heavily influenced by Persian language, customs and Zoroastrian

[5] G. Bournoutian, *History of the Armenian People*, vol. I, p. 6.

religion, an Armenian identity, rooted in local cultural markers and customs, was clearly being formed. The existence of a separate Armenian entity is affirmed by the Greek historian Xenophon when he, along with the retreating Greek army from Persia, passed through Armenia in 401–400 BC. In the *Anabasis* he recorded his observations about the language, politics and social habits of a distinct people known as Armenians.

The Hellenistic invasion of Persia partially influenced Armenia as well, but Persian and local Armenian culture remained the strongest element within society and the elites. The latter retained local customs rather than assimilating into the all-imperial aristocratic culture. For example, Aramaic remained the language of administration, although Greek did make inroads at the leadership level. In sum, the Yervanduni dynasty of almost four centuries was the period during which the Armenian *ethnie* (or proto-nation) consolidated, based on a specific administrative region, a separate language and identity. However, in terms of social structure, dress, religious practices etc., the region was heavily influenced by Persia.[6]

Around 200 BC a coup by the Armenian noble family of Artashes (Artaxias) toppled the Yervanduni dynasty. This move was encouraged and supported by the Seleucids under Antiochus III (223–187 BC) who, in his attempts to revive the Hellenistic empire, wished to eliminate Yervanduni independence and make Armenia a vassal state. In this way, ironically, the foundations of the first truly Armenian kingdom were laid. The Artashesian dynasty lasted from 188/9 BC to AD 10. Artashes's rule began as governor of Armenia, with allegiance to Antiochus for approximately a decade. But the latter was defeated by the Romans in 190 BC, as the Roman empire established a firm base in Asia Minor. Simultaneously Parthians invaded from the east and took control of Persia. In these monumental changes

[6] N. Garsoïan, 'Emergence of Armenia', p. 42, cf. pp. 38–48. For Xenophon's account see G. Bournoutian, *A History of the Armenian People*, vol. I, pp. 29–30. It should be noted that by the third century BC three Armenias had emerged. In addition to Greater Armenia (east of the Euphrates, to Lake Sevan in the north-east, to Lake Urmia in the south-east), there was Lesser Armenia (north-west of the Euphrates) and Dsopk or Sophene (in the south-west of Greater Armenia). Lesser Armenia fell under Hellenistic influence, Greater Armenia maintained its autonomy, and Dsopk, along the royal road, oscillated between independence and Yervanduni rule. Such divisions remained throughout Armenian history, as each region developed separate characteristics and some were assimilated into other cultures (particularly Lesser Armenia).

to the geopolitics of the region Artashes (188/9–*c.* 160 BC) allied himself with the Romans. Consequently, in AD 188 or 189 he was recognised by Rome as the king of a sovereign Armenia. Parthians too recognised the independence of Artashesian rule over Armenia. Under this dynasty a new capital city was built on the Arax river (Artashat/Artaxata), a new administrative and tax system was established, and boundaries were clearly demarcated. These had retracted in the west, but were expanded in the south and in the east, stretching all the way to the Caspian Sea.

The independence of Artashesian Armenia was conditional on the balance of power between the two new major empires in the region: the Romans in the west, and the Parthians in the south-east. Thus, when the former temporarily withdrew from Asia Minor, Armenia was subjugated to the wishes of the latter and had to pay tribute to Parthian kings. The order would occasionally reverse in the future, but the basic dynamic would remain. However, for a short period (*c.* 85–69 BC), when both major powers were preoccupied with their internal problems, the Armenian king Tigran II ('The Great', 95–55 BC) seized the opportunity and expanded his kingdom into an empire stretching from the Caspian Sea to the Mediterranean, including Damascus. This short-lived empire retracted back to the Armenian plateau when both Romans and Parthians once again asserted their influence in the region. After Tigran the Artashesian dynasty continued its balancing act between the two empires, despite the occasional attacks. The dynasty died out by AD 10 after a period of internal turmoil over succession. Subsequently Armenia fell to Roman rule.

In the Artashesian period the elite, in all probability, spoke Greek and Persian while Aramaic remained the language of administration. But Armenian was the spoken language of the common people (according to Strabo) and distinct customs were maintained. Iranian and Greek influences were undeniable in religion, administration, architecture and commerce—especially since Armenia's role further developed as a trade route between the east and the west. But these various traditions were combined in the region. They formed the basis of a more sophisticated and unique Armenian civilisation. It seems that there was already a strong sense of local identity that resisted the dynamics of complete assimilation into the much more powerful neighbouring empires. On the basis of various primary sources Nina Garsoïan points out that by the first half of the second century BC the general population of Greater Armenia spoke the same language. While the various districts of Greater Armenia were being unified, Garsoïan concludes that the 'Armenization of the entire area was progressing apace.'[7] However, it should be pointed out that none of the surviving written records on this period are in Armenian. The earliest historical sources in Armenian are from the fifth century AD, after the script was invented.

Approximately half a century after the collapse of the Artashesian dynasty Armenia was ruled by the Arshakunis, the Armenian branch of the Parthian Arsacids. This dynasty ended in AD 428, but it is not clear when it began because of confusing chronologies and differing founding 'acts'. The various dates given are AD 12, 66 and 180. The dynasty was established and survived as an acceptable solution to both Roman and the Parthian demands on Armenia. It was based on the Compromise of Rhandeia (in western Armenia) negotiated in AD 63. According to this agreement, which was generally adhered to during the next two-and-a-half centuries, but with some notable exceptions, a branch of the Parthian Arshakuni dynasty reigned in Armenia, but received its crown from Rome. Hence, King Trdat I went to Rome and in a magnificent ceremony in AD 66 received his crown from Nero. Armenia was therefore a 'dependent kingdom with some internal autonomy'.[8] Significantly, it was not, as a rule, annexed by the Romans and ruled as a province.

In this period Armenia had closer relations with Parthia not only in terms of dynastic rule, but also culturally and socially. There was some antagonism towards—and even rebellion against—the Romans, especially when the latter interfered too much in Armenia's internal affairs. However, this was reversed in the third century when the Parthian dynasty of Persia was overthrown by the Sasanians in 224. The established balance of power between the Roman and Persian empires was broken. In the ensuing wars Armenia was once again caught in the middle and oscillated between the Romans and the new rulers of Iran. But this time the Armenian Arshakunis were

[7] N. Garsoïan, 'Emergence of Armenia', p. 50, cf. pp. 48–62; Lang, *Armenia*, p. 126.
[8] N. Garsoïan, 'Arsakuni Dynasty', p. 63, p. 67.

against the Sasanian rulers who attacked Armenia, undermined the established dynasty, annexed the country, and enforced their version of Zoroastrianism as the official religion of the empire. Such opposition reinforced Armenian identity in relation to Persian rule and culture.

By the end of the third century the former equilibrium between Rome and Persia was reestablished and once again Arshakunis reigned in Armenia. But this dynasty had itself become Armenian (and presumably Armenian-speaking) along with the other Parthian ruling families of the region. Descendants of Persian Parthians were now the creators of 'a truly Armenian Arshakuni dynasty'.[9] They reflected 'a highly individual and identifiable Armenian entity with its own life and institutions', which had clearly consolidated in the Arshakuni period, and was recorded by contemporary historians.[10]

This centuries-long process seems to have taken place in the reverse order of modern nation-formation. Instead of the elite 'creating' the mass basis of the nation, the foreign-originated ruling class had itself become slowly 'nationalised' over centuries. By the end of the third century AD Parthian-Armenian opposition to Rome, followed by Roman-Armenian opposition to Sasanian Persia, had led to the development of a separate identity among the Armenian noble families that was much closer to the people they ruled than to any of the other royal families they were historically related to. This identity was based on a culture that partly borrowed from Rome and from Persia, but was rooted in Armenia. The Armenian language was also influenced by Persian loan words, but continued to be used widely.

Despite its unique identity the social structure of Arshakuni Armenia was heavily influenced by Iran, and closely resembled the feudal system of the European Middle Ages. The king was the first among equals, directly ruling the core of the country. The nobles (*nakharars*) below him headed their own clans and had inalienable titles and lands inherited through the law of primogeniture. The whole system was based on an elaborate hierarchy of offices and duties. The army was composed of a feudal force of knights, princes

[9] G. Bournoutian, *History of the Armenian People*, vol. I, p. 60.
[10] N. Garsoïan, 'Arsakuni Dynasty', p. 75.

and commoners (serving as infantry when needed), headed by a commander from the Mamikonian family. The Bagratunis held the office of the coronant (i.e. they were responsible for the coronation of the king); Gnunis were in charge of taxation, and so forth.

The most important characteristic of this *nakharar* system was its decentralised nature. The noble families ruled their domains autonomously, resisting both foreign domination and their own kings' attempts to centralise power. They had their own territorial, economic and political power bases which paralleled the role of a (mini-) state. Such a social structure was 'capable of surviving even in moments of political eclipse' and could thwart the 'chances of total annexation'.[11] But it also meant that there were many regional differences within the Armenian people. However, all indications are that an overriding cultural-linguistic common core had emerged which unified the various regions, noble houses and clans in their attempt to resist assimilation into the neighbouring imperial domains. Structure and culture both reinforced the distinct Armenian identity, which was a unique synthesis of local, Persian and Hellenistic/Roman elements.

Intertwined with this identity were some of the major characteristics that had emerged by AD 300. These would be dominant traits throughout subsequent Armenian history. The first is the position of Armenia between two (and sometimes three) major powers, the cleavage usually being one of east/west rivalry between empires, with Armenia in the middle as a buffer zone. This meant that Armenians had to play a delicate game of balancing major powers in order to maintain independence—the great balancing game had begun. However, more often than not this could not be done successfully, owing to internal divisions and the whims of the imperial powers. Subsequently, Armenia throughout most of its history was either directly subjugated to empires or at the very least had to pay tribute to them, but always as a distinct administrative-political unit.

Second, such regional rivalries, as well as the decentralised feudal system both in the Artashesian and particularly in the Arshakuni periods, meant that political unity was difficult to maintain within Armenia. Different elements of the elite allied themselves with dif-

[11] Ibid., pp. 77–8, 79.

ferent external powers (which, of course, could play one element against the other). Thus, some leading figures—sometimes within the same family—would support rival empires undermining any chance of political unity (e.g. Tigran the Great's two sons 'betrayed' their father: one joined the Parthians, the other joined the Romans). This lack of political unity became, and still is, a very important theme in Armenian thinking. The sigh 'if we can only unite!' is heard often, examples of disunity are cited from history, and then used to explain the current political situation at the national and the community level.

Of course, such lack of unity could also be indicative of a weak sense of political allegiance to the 'nation' implying that personal, local or clan interests took precedence over collective 'national' interests. This is not to say that common cultural markers did not exist, or that there was no sense of unity as the same people. But the modern conception that allegiance to the nation above all other collective identities should be maintained does not seem to have been present at this point.

The third characteristic is one of rebellion against too much intrusion by external powers. When suzerainty became unacceptable owing to high taxes or, later on, to forceful attempts at religious and cultural assimilation, Armenians reacted by rebelling and asserting their autonomy. It is unlikely that in the first millennium BC there were conscious attempts by Armenians to resist assimilation because they had a strong 'national identity'—this came later, although the roots were laid in this period. But what is important is that subsequently, in modern times (seventeenth century onwards), ancient history was interpreted as such. Nationality was projected backwards so that Yervandunis and early Artashesians were seen as protectors of Armenian identity and culture (whereas their drive for autonomy—which was only occasional in any case—was probably due to more mundane factors such as amount of tribute paid, honour and the extent of the family domain).

Finally, the fourth characteristic is that of Armenia being a battlefield for major empires and therefore constantly suffering due to forces beyond its control. This mentality of always being a victim has affected the Armenian popular psyche. Again, history is invoked, starting with the beginning of the Armenians. It is noteworthy that the present conflict with Azerbaijan is sometimes put in this perspective with such comments as: 'We have not had this much military success since Tigran the Great; it's about time we go on the offensive...!' In a long history of defeats and persecution, Tigran the Great's brief empire of 2,000 years ago is still a source of pride for Armenian nationalists.[12]

The conversion to Christianity

The formal adoption of Christianity as the state religion of Armenia in 314–15[13] has probably been the most important event in terms of maintaining a separate identity. In fact it was Christianity that cemented the distinctiveness of Armenian identity in the classical period. In the early fourth century the Sasanid Persians increased pressure on the Armenians to accept the official Zoroastrian religion of the empire. In their centralising attempts the Sasanids did not tolerate religious freedoms and differences based on local or Hellenistic traditions. However, by this point Armenians had developed a strong enough identity to resist such assimilating tendencies which were threatening their religious-cultural traditions and the political control of their territory. In this context King Trdat III ('the Great'), who was educated in Rome, converted to Christianity—as did many of the other Armenian noble families.[14] Almost at

12 After the collapse of Soviet rule in Armenia October Avenue in Yerevan was renamed after Tigran the Great. He is the only king to have his image imprinted on an Armenian banknote.

13 The traditional date given by Armenians for the conversion is 301, but the more probable date now accepted by a growing number of historians is after Emperor Constantine's Edict of Milan in 313 when Christianity was legalised in the Roman empire (see A. Redgate, *Armenians*, pp. 115–16).

14 The myth surrounding Trdat's acceptance of Christianity is, of course, based on divine intervention. According to the fifth century Armenian historian Agathangelos, the King was turned into a wild boar because of his sins, which included the violent persecution of Christians. He was healed by his former assistant Gregory. The latter had been incarcerated years earlier on the order of the King for being a Christian. But he miraculously survived the deadly pit of Khor Virap where he was thrown until Trdat's sister had a divine vision to release him to cure the King. Subsequently, Trdat 'The Great' and St Gregory 'The Illuminator', the founder of the Armenian Church, set about Christianising Armenia.

a stroke Armenians defiantly turned their backs on Persia and its attempts to culturally and politically absorb Armenia.[15]

Once Christianity had become a state religion an intense—and at times violent—proselytising campaign began to enforce the new religion on the entire population. In this way the Zoroastrian fervour of Persia was countered. Armenians therefore destroyed their own Hellenic and pagan or Zoroastrian temples and replaced them with Christian sites.[16] But it is noteworthy that the church did not become subservient to the kings of Armenia and evolved into a relatively autonomous institution. It fitted into the feudal system in its structure (initially even the position of the Patriarch/Catholicos was hereditary), and its top clergy came from the noble families. Hence it provided a powerful new cultural and institutional framework that transformed and strengthened Armenianness into a unique ethno-religious identity. As Nina Garsoïan puts it, 'From the start, the church helped to create a separate Armenian identity and provided a focus for the allegiance of the entire population that was independent of the political framework and consequently from the fate of the realm.'[17]

In a period when religion was a central element of identity, such a conscious decision to convert en masse to a new faith so different from that of their neighbours already indicates a sense of distinctiveness that Armenians sought to maintain. Later, when the Roman empire embraced Christianity itself, Armenians held on to tenets of the faith which were different from the other major churches. They rejected the decision of the Council of Chalcedon (451) on the nature of Christ[18] and subsequently seceded from the Byzantian branch of Orthodoxy. The Armenian Apostolic Church[19] formally became

[15] N. Garsoïan, 'Arsakuni Dynasty', pp. 81–4; D. Lang, *Armenia*, pp. 155–60.

[16] Underneath the altar of Ejmiatzin, the central Armenian church, one can see the remains of a pagan temple. Interestingly, Ejmiatzin means '[where] the only-begotten [Son] descended'; it was, according to myth, the location to which Christ directed Gregory in a vision to build a church.

[17] N. Garsoïan, 'Arsakuni Dynasty', p. 84.

[18] The Armenian church is closer to the Monophysite doctrine of the nature of Christ. Its theology accepts the two natures of Christ—divine and human—but in one person (see G. Guaïta, *Between Heaven and Earth*, pp. 95–7; D. Lang, *Armenia*, pp. 169–71).

[19] It is believed that Christianity was first brought to Armenia much earlier by the apostles Thaddeus and Bartholomew. Hence the church is formally referred to as 'apostolic'. This also suggests that there was a long tradition of Christian activity in underground congregations before it became official state religion.

autocephalous—i.e. independent of external authority—in 554 by severing its links with the patriarchate of Constantinople. 'During the Middle Ages, before the invention of the modern political party system,' writes Lang, 'these religious distinctions had enormous importance and often determined political and military alignments.'[20] Quite simply, Armenians wanted to retain a separate identity both against the east and the west, and their unique brand of Christianity was the means to do so. Their emphasis was not on converting people outside their ethnic group, but on maintaining cultural boundaries that would assure their uniqueness.

Being the first nation to officially accept Christianity as the state religion also gave Armenians—and especially later nationalists—a powerful claim to be a 'chosen people'.[21] The textual basis of this notion was already set in the fifth century by the Armenian historian Agathangelos who wrote about Armenians' conversion to Christianity. According to him, Armenia was 'where God's grace has been manifested'.[22] Such claims were further augmented by Bagraduni presumptions that they were related to the Jews—i.e. the original chosen people. The notion of being the first Christian people who originally received the word of God directly from the apostles has remained with the Armenians throughout the centuries; it became a core element of their national identity. As such, Christianity became a rigid distinguishing marker, a cultural and symbolic boundary. Once a person crossed this boundary by converting to another faith—especially to Islam—he or she was no longer considered to be Armenian. This has remained the case, even if the idea of being a chosen people is no longer widely believed by contemporary Armenians.

The alphabet and the Golden Century

Christianity, it seemed, was not going to be enough to maintain Armenian cultural distinctiveness. Another instrument was needed to reflect the difference in language and to maintain 'national' unity, especially after Armenia was re-partitioned between the Byzantine

[20] D. Lang, *Armenians*, p. 50; cf. D. Lang, *Armenia*, p. 169.

[21] For a discussion on the theory of chosen people and its importance in the survival of ethnic groups see A. Smith, 'Chosen Peoples'. For an extensive analysis of chosen peoples see the Special Issue of *Nations and Nationalism*, 5/3, July 1999.

[22] As cited by R. Thomson in his 'Introduction' to Ełishe, *History of Vardan*, p. 2.

and Persian empires in 387. It is likely, as George Bournoutian suggests, that the King of Armenia (Vramshapuh) and its religious leader (Catholicos Sahak) were conscious of this need for cultural unity for the survival of their people. They therefore commissioned a learned clergyman-scholar, Mesrop Mashtots, to create an alphabet for the Armenian language.[23] He accomplished this between 400 and 405 and soon afterwards, along with his students, opened schools throughout Armenia to teach the new script.

For Mashtots and the church leaders, teaching the new Armenian alphabet (and therefore religious texts) was inextricably tied to their Christian missionary zeal. They wanted to convert the entire Armenian population, especially the mass of the people who had not yet heard the Christian message, to the new faith. But through this religious conversion church leaders were also producing a uniform literary tradition—and vice versa. In a crucial respect they were 'creating' Armenians. It is important to note the centralised and planned manner in which this was done at *this* juncture of Armenian history. At a stroke, again, a unique textual basis was established with the invention (rather than evolution) of a new script. It seems that the work of eighteenth-century nationalist intellectuals was being done in the fifth.

With the new religion on the one hand and the new alphabet on the other the fifth century became the 'golden' period of Armenian learning and language. The Bible was of course immediately translated/transcribed into Armenian, as were other religious works, Greek scientific texts and philosophical treatises (including Aristotle). A rich tradition of manuscript writing began. Mashtots's entrusted pupil, Koriun, wrote the first original composition in Armenian (mid-fifth century): a biography of his master. Soon thereafter Armenians started to write their own history in their own language.[24]

The alphabet gave Armenians a unique textual-literary basis for their language and linguistic identity. Greek, Latin, Aramaic or Syriac scripts were no longer needed for written communication. This further isolated Armenians from external cultural influences as it made their written language even more inaccessible to people

[23] G. Bournoutian, *History of the Armenian People*, vol. I, pp. 69–71; cf. A. Redgate, *Armenians*, pp. 140–1.

[24] For further detail see R. Thomson, 'Armenian Literary Culture', pp. 201–7.

outside the community, while it standardised written communication among Armenians themselves, particularly at the elite and religious levels. The 'divinely inspired' script[25] eventually acquired the aura of a 'secret code'—specific only to those who spoke Armenian. Language, script and religion all complemented each other in emphasising the distinctness of the Armenians vis-à-vis others, while further binding them together through common cultural markers.[26]

The paradigm of rebellion: the Battle of Avarayr

Such distinctiveness was not in the interest of the Sasanid kings of Persia. Nor were relations between the different ruling families so harmonious. There were intense and violent conflicts between them, between the *nakharars* and the Arshakuni kings, and between the kings and the church leadership. These were usually over power and opposing political allegiances with the Persians or the Byzantines who had partitioned Armenia under their respective spheres of control. Consequently, the last Arshakuni king was removed from the throne by the Persians in 428 at the request of the Armenian magnates who preferred to manage their own affairs directly under

[25] According to myth (propagated by some of the early teachers themselves) the alphabet was revealed to Mashtots in a divine vision. This made the actual script the product of Godly intervention and therefore more acceptable to the newly converted Christians. Consequently, it is interesting to note, the sacred basis of the Armenian alphabet has made it more important than the language itself in many instances. In the eighteenth and nineteenth centuries it was not uncommon for Armenians who did not speak Armenian to write other languages which they did speak, particularly Turkish in the Ottoman empire, in the Armenian script. Books were published in this format (mostly religious texts) and there were even Bibles (printed by Catholic and Protestant missionaries for Armenians) that were in Turkish but in the Armenian alphabet. The actual script is often revered more than the language itself. This remains true to this day, with the symbolic value of the alphabet. Its image, along with Mount Ararat and other such symbols, adorns many homes both in Armenia and in the diaspora—even in households where Armenian is not necessarily spoken. Since its inception the alphabet has not changed, except with the addition of two new letters nine centuries later.

[26] The celebration of the alphabet and the literary work of the fifth century is sanctioned by the Armenian church as an official holiday (in October) called Surb Tarkmanchats (Holy Translators). It is noted both by the church and the laity in Armenia and in the diaspora as a celebration of Armenian literature and books. It was also celebrated by cultural-literary organisations in Soviet Armenia.

Sasanid control. For the next two centuries Persian Armenia was ruled by *marzpans* (governors) who were appointed by the Sasanid rulers. However, unlike Byzantine Armenia, 'national' institutions—namely the *nakharar* socio-political system and the autonomous church—survived because they were not substantially altered. They in fact became the principal agents of repeated revolts against the Persians.

Conversely, in Byzantine Armenia Emperor Justinian I (527–65) rearranged the administrative structure of the region. Four provinces were created, which made Armenia no different from other administrative units. Autonomy, privileges and recognition as Armenian ruled territories were eliminated. Further changes in the legal code were detrimental to the *nakharar* system as well. According to Byzantine law, which rejected the notion of primogeniture, inheritance was to be divided between all the children, including daughters. Consequently, rather than remaining intact and being inherited by the eldest son, the great territorial estates—which were the power basis of Armenian noble families—quickly fragmented. Powerless Armenian elites were quickly absorbed into the Byzantine hierarchy and eventually assimilated.[27]

However, in Persian Armenia Sasanid rulers had not given up their desire to enforce Zoroastrianism on the Armenians, continuing to view Christians as agents of Byzantium. These attempts intensified with the accession in 439 of the new king, Yazdgird II, who sent Zoroastrian priests to Armenia to impose the state religion. Even with such direct imperial intervention to re-convert Armenians, the Persians could not eradicate Christianity in Armenia. The Armenian elite, including the church organisation, could still rely on their independent power bases to resist the Persians. After years of low intensity conflict the decisive battle came in 451 when Armenians openly rebelled against the Persians. Led by the commander Vardan Mamikonian and supported by the church, as well as many other *nakharars* (but by no means all),[28] Armenians faced the much superior Persian army in the plain of Avarayr (presently in Iran). In the

[27] For further detail see N. Garsoïan, '*Marzpanate*', pp. 103–7.

[28] These were led by the *marzpan* of Armenia, Vasak Siuni, who did not want to have antagonistic relations with the Persians. He did not join the battle and is remembered to this day as the quintessential national 'traitor'.

ensuing battle the Armenian forces were crushed—or 'martyred' as church historians put it. However, resistance and minor incidents of rebellion continued, especially by the Mamikonian family. Within a few years the Persians adopted a more lenient approach toward the Armenians. In 484 the head of the Mamikonian family was again appointed commander of Armenia and, more significantly, the treaty of Nvarsak was signed which granted Armenians a large degree of autonomy and freedom of religion.

Among all the other instances of rebellion and war against external forces, the Battle of Avarayr (Avarair) became the paradigm of resistance in Armenian history, complementing the founding myth of Haik and Bel (discussed below). It sharpened the divide between the Christian Armenians and the 'evil' and 'impious' Persians. It was a specific event—a prism—through which the differences between the two peoples could clearly be seen.[29] Although Avarayr was a military defeat, it was (and is) celebrated as a 'moral victory' because Christianity remained the religion of the country, and was (is) used as a rallying cry against the 'Other'. The battle is part of the church calendar since Vardan and his followers were elevated to sainthood. However, its commemoration has become much wider than a religious celebration. In addition to inserting martyrdom at the heart of Armenian history, Avarayr is also interpreted—specially in the last few decades—as *national* resistance against oppression, fought in defence of church, nation, truth and justice. By falling in battle in 451, Vardan entered *modern* Armenian consciousness as a national hero to be celebrated and emulated.[30]

[29] The prominent Armenian historian Nicholas Adonts sees two opposing trends in Armenian history that are characterised by the Avarayr Battle: the tension between rebellion, as exemplified by the Mamikonian family, and prudence or conservatism, as exemplified by the Siuni family (L. Abrahamian, 'Armenia i diaspora', p. 62).

[30] In the *Soviet Armenian Encyclopaedia* the Mamikonians are mentioned as the household 'around whom gathered the patriotic [*hairenaser*] forces and continued the liberation struggle against Sasanid Persia' (vol. 7, p. 193). The Battle of Avarayr is referred to as a 'popular-liberation war' (vol. 7, p. 314) and 'a heroic page in the Armenian people's liberation struggle for national self-determination' (vol. 11, p. 316). In the diaspora the religious dimension of the struggle is not shunned as much as in Soviet publications, but it is infused with national liberation. For one example see the 11 Feb. 1999 editorial published in the popular Los Angeles based *Nor Gyank* (New Life) weekly; the writer equates Avarayr with the national struggles in contemporary Armenia, Gharabagh and even in the diaspora, while Azerbaijan and Turkey are

Movses Khorenatsi and the writing of history

Armenians started to write their own history in the fifth century. In fact many of the 'national' themes in Vardan's epic struggle are found in two sources from the fifth to sixth centuries. The more important of these is Eghishe's *History of Vardan and the Armenian War.* Although he stresses the nobility of fighting for Christianity and Truth, Eghishe also highlights the need to protect ancestral customs; personal salvation is important, but it is not the only motivating factor because national survival is also essential.[31]

Significant as Eghishe's text has been in subsequent nationalist discourse, the title of 'the father of Armenian historiography' (*patmahair*) belongs to Movses Khorenatsi (Moses of Khoren). Khorenatsi complemented his Greek, Assyrian and Hebrew written sources with traditional oral chronicles, as well as with fictitious inventions. Among the classic historians he stands out since his *History of the Armenians* 'had the greatest influence on later generations'[32]—both on other historians and nationalist intellectuals.

---

equated with the attacking Persians of old (pp. 1, 36). Another Armenian magazine, *Khosnak* (Speaker) (8:1–2, January–February 1999), published in Beirut, had a series of articles (based on local events and speeches) devoted to the meaning of the Battle of Avarayr. The following three passages, among many others, are indicative of the contemporary meaning attached to the 451 battle. From a speech to schoolchildren: 'We gave 1036 sacrifices [i.e. victims], we lost but you see that we still live; the evidence is in you, in us, in our fatherland and in our holy church' (p. 54). From an event organised by Catholic Armenians: 451 'was the first amazing [*hrashali*, also meaning 'miraculous'] national liberation struggle in the history of the Armenian people....Perhaps for the first time in the history of nations all strata of a people united under the direction of the political and religious leaders of the country, [with the motto] "for Christ, for the fatherland"' (p. 8). And from a speech explicitly making the modern connection: 'What has changed from Avarayr to Artsakh [i.e. Gharabagh]?... Hazkert [the Persian Shah], convinced that it is not possible to convert [to Zoroastrianism] this people, withdrew and granted [to the Armenians] self-rule....Today we indispensably need Vardans..' (p. 13).

[31] Ełishe (Eghishe), *History of Vardan*, pp. 105–30, 153–73. The other historian of this period is Ghazar Parpetsi who gives a similar account of the war. See R. Thomson, 'Armenian Literary Culture', pp. 212–14, and his Introduction in Ełishe, *History of Vardan*, for commentary; Ghazar's text is also found as an appendix in Ełishe's *History of Vardan*.

[32] R. Thomson, 'Armenian Literary Culture', pp. 215–16, cf. pp. 208–15 for a concise exposition of the other significant early historians. Some of these were: Agathangelos (fifth century), who wrote about King Trdat's conversion to Christianity, and Pavstos Buzand (around 500), who described the social life and the political intrigue in

Despite many debates and arguments about the factual basis of his history,[33] Khorenatsi's work is instrumental in giving Armenians a sense of belonging that stretches back over two millennia or more. He was the first to write the entire history of the Armenians—from the beginning to his purported present time—in a systematic manner. He claims to have been a disciple of Mesrop Mashtots, writing in the second half of the fifth century. However, Robert Thomson presents what seems to be convincing arguments that Khorenatsi belongs to the middle of the eighth century.[34] This is not generally accepted by Armenians, particularly historians in Armenia, who take Khorenatsi's word at face value and place him in the 410 to 490 period.[35]

It is not terribly important for my argument when Khorenatsi lived, or how much of his *History* deviates from truth. What is important is that he gave Armenians a long and continuous sense of history that was integrated in world civilisation and in the Biblical narrative.[36] And he did this *consciously.* In the introduction to the last part of his book, entitled 'The Conclusion [of the History] of Our Fatherland', he writes: 'We shall deal with this history in simple

---

fourth century Armenia, and the country's division between empires. Along with Eghishe and Ghazar, these men provided invaluable texts, which were later used by nationalist intellectuals. According to Thomson, the trio of Khorenatsi, Agathangelos and Eghishe enshrined the received accounts of Armenian history and therefore have a particular place in Armenian tradition ('Introduction' in Ełishe, *History of Vardan*).

33 Thomson, in his 'Introduction' to Khorenatsi, *History of the Armenians*, concludes that 'Moses is an audacious, and mendacious, faker' (p. 58). He 'was a mystifier of the first order. He quotes sources at second hand as if he had read the original; he invents archives to lend the credence of the written word to oral tradition or to his own inventions; he rewrites Armenian history in a completely fictitious manner....' (p. 56). Thomson is vehemently criticised by most historians in Armenia who revere Khorenatsi (for a scathing denounciation see A. Aivazian, *Hayastani patmutian lusabanume*, pp. 122ff; for a more reasonable critique see L. Ter-Petrosian, 'Review').

34 In 'Introduction' to Khorenatsi, *History of the Armenians*, particularly pp. 7–8, 58–60.

35 See the Introduction of the Armenian version of Khorenatsi, *Hayots patmutiun*, pp. 8–9; P. Hovhannisian, 'Movses Khorenatsu', pp. 238–9. For one argument dating Khorenatsi to the fifth century see A. Matevosian, 'Movses Khorenatsin', pp. 226ff. Incidently, Marx Street in Yerevan was renamed Khorenatsi Street after independence, symbolising the move from dialectical history to national history.

36 In the genealogy provided by Khorenatsi, Haik, the father of the Armenians (and consequently later Armenian kings) is presented as a descendant from Noah (Khorenatsi, *History of the Armenians*, pp. 74–5). Khorenatsi's link between the Armenians and Noah was based on the account of the first Christian author, Eusebius of Caesaria (not Armenian). Khorenatsi introduced Haik into the lineage.

terms so that no one may seem attracted to it because of its rhetoric, but rather that desiring truth in our account, people may read carefully and avidly the history of our fatherland.'[37] Thomson concludes his critical Introduction to *History* by pointing out that 'Moses' interest in historical explanations is his particular contribution to [the] process of tradition forming.' This created the basis of subsequent '"received" tradition [which] was of major significance in the emergence of Armenian nationalism in the nineteenth century and is still a vital force in today's debates on national identity.'[38] Khorenatsi, in short, was the first 'nationalist' Armenian historian. He was, in turn, used by later intellectuals—who cite him as a definitive source—first to prove and then to further national consciousness.

Importantly, Khorenatsi was also the author of the Armenian myth of origin, the Haik and Bel story. In terms of popular perceptions this story is just as important in modern nationalist thinking as 'objective' history. The myth asserts that Armenians are direct descendants of Noah, through his son Japheth. Haik,[39] the father of Armenians, comes from this lineage. Being a righteous man, he rebelled against Bel, the evil leader of Babylon. Haik then moved from Babylon back to the land of the Ark where he settled along with his family and followers. But Bel pursued Haik and his clan to subjugate them. In the subsequent battle good won over evil and Bel was slain. The roots of the Armenian nation were thus established around Mount Ararat with Haik and his family.[40]

This story, taught to all primary students in Armenian schools around the world, has a number of powerful symbolic components. First, it makes Armenia the cradle of all civilisation since Noah's Ark landed on the 'Armenian' mountain of Ararat. Second, it connects Armenians to the biblical narrative of human development. Third, it infuses a very important element of righteous rebellion against tyranny and oppression (of Babylon). Fourth, it situates freedom, independence and justice at the centre of the nation's origins. And finally, it makes Mount Ararat the national symbol of all Armenians, and the territory around it the Armenian homeland from time

[37] Khorenatsi, *History of the Armenians*, pp. 254–5.

[38] In 'Introduction' to Khorenatsi, *History of the Armenians*, p. 61.

[39] Note that *hai* is the word for 'Armenian' in Armenian; *hayastan* means Armenia.

[40] For the story see Khorenatsi, *History of the Armenians*, pp. 85–8.

immemorial. With such powerful symbolic resonance, the Haik and Bel story is often cited by nationalists as the paradigm of Armenian identity.[41]

Theoretical interlude: the concept of ethnie

It seems that ancient Armenians possessed many of the characteristics of modern nations, including features missing in subsequent (eighteenth century onward) Armenian nationalism—i.e. a state that harboured a centralised culture, and a drive to create a homogeneous collective identity in the face of political disunity. In fact, as mentioned earlier, some scholars in the perennial tradition of analysis do use the Armenians as an example of an ancient nation.[42] Given such ancient historiographical and literary traditions, a unique religion and language, a bounded territory, a collective sense of belonging to the same group that distinguished them from their neighbours, and an elite consciously rejecting assimilation, can it not be argued that Armenians already constituted a *nation* by the fifth and sixth centuries?

The answer to this question has to be 'no'. Nations, as explained in the previous chapter, are modern creations because of their political connotations relating to popular sovereignty and legitimacy. Such sentiments were absent in fifth century Armenia (as they were absent everywhere else in the world). Moreover, Armenian identity did not remain constant. Just as collective identity can be constructed in a unifying manner, it can also be fragmented. This is what had happened to the Armenians by the seventeenth century. And yet there clearly remained a collective known as Armenians (which was eventually transformed into modern nationality).

The most appropriate term for such pre-national ethnic identities is *ethnie*, a word favoured by Anthony Smith. The use of the term and its analysis are his major contributions to the field of

41 The date on some of the nationalist *samizdat* literature published after 1987 in Soviet Armenia did not count the years from the date of the birth of Christ, but from Haik's victory over Bel. Such magazines had the 'real Armenian' dates of 4480, 4481 and so forth (instead of 1988, 1989...). The publishers took the Haik and Bel story as the real founding act of the nation (in 2492 BC) from which Armenians should date their calendar. Some nationalist publications continued this practice into the post-Soviet period. A few fringe journals in the diaspora (e.g. *Spiurk* [Diaspora] of Lebanon) also use the 'real Armenian' date (R. Panossian, 'The Past as Nation', p. 130).

42 S. Grosby, 'Borders, Territory and Nationality'; J. Armstrong, *Nations Before Nationalism*.

nationalism studies. An *ethnie* is a 'named human population with shared ancestry myths, histories and cultures, having an association with a specific territory and a sense of solidarity.'[43] More specifically, there are six characteristics associated with *ethnie*: a collective name (*hai*, in the case of the Armenians); a widespread myth of common descent (the story of Haik); a fund of shared historical memories (Noah, the ancient kings, saints); a distinctive shared culture (language, alphabet and religion); association with a specific territory (Ararat and the other mountains on the Armenian Plateau, the capital cities and religious centres); and a sense of solidarity (with the church, the *nakharars*, kings and other Armenians). Clearly Smith's analysis of *ethnie* is based on objective features.

In many instances *ethnies* are 'proto-nations'. According to Smith they are the roots out of which modern nationality grows. *Ethnies* do not have the mass-based and political dimension of nationality; an *ethnie* differs from a nation insofar as it lacks notions of citizenship, of political rights for all, and of political control based on cultural similarities—all ideas associated with modernity.[44] It also lacks the subjectively 'felt' category of nationhood. Once formed, *ethnies* are 'exceptionally durable' because of their symbolic character. But, Smith adds, 'the *ethnie* is anything but primordial' (despite the claims of nationalists), and it is in flux, subject to dissolution or absorption. He warns, however, that the mutability of ethnic boundaries must not be overstated.[45]

Structural-institutional factors are important in the formation, maintenance, and strengthening of an *ethnie.* Two such elements stand out in fifth century Armenia: the *nakharar* system of rule (predicated on family/blood ties among the elites) and the separate church organisation. The first played an important role in integrating, at least culturally, the elite and the masses both vertically (within each family domain) and horizontally (interaction among the *nakharars*). This was similar to the role played by 'nationalising' states in the modern period, but on very different criteria. As to the second,

[43] A. Smith, *Ethnic Origins of Nations*, pp. 32, 22–30; cf. A. Smith, *National Identity*, pp. 21–2.

[44] A. Smith, *Ethnic Origins of Nations*, p. 31. Smith also adds the modern attribute of economic unity in his distinction between ethnie and nation.

[45] A. Smith, *Ethnic Origins of Nations*, p. 16, and A. Smith, *National Identity*, pp. 23–4.

Smith does emphasise the religious component of an *ethnie*: 'It may safely be argued that lack of religious and cultural individuality over the longer term is more important for ethnic survival potential than even conquest or eviction from the homeland.' It is particularly important for the church to be organisationally separate from—or at least not be too dependent on—the indigenous state (as was the case with the Armenians). If the latter collapses, the former could carry on being the symbolic and institutional reservoir of the *ethnie*.[46] *Ethnies* are not contingent upon the control of one's own state or the political process. *Ethnies* could survive, and even flourish, outside political control.

These fundamental structural attributes were infused with the symbolic elements, together reinforcing the Armenian *ethnie*. When the structural factors disappeared, as in Byzantine Armenia after the Justinian reforms, the Armenian *ethnie*—after initial resistance—substantially weakened and was eventually assimilated as a distinct group. Myth-symbol complexes are interconnected with (and I deliberately do not use the term 'based on') socio-political structures. As the Armenian case demonstrates, both culture and structure, in conjunction with one another, were crucial for ethnic survival.

Smith's argument in analysing the roots of nations through the concept of *ethnie* is taken a few steps further back by Adrian Hastings in his book *The Construction of Nationhood*. According to him, nationhood can be found as early as a millennium ago in the 'prototype' of the English. His thesis is predicated upon the importance of religion (viz. Christianity) and the development of written language: 'I will argue that ethnicities naturally turn into nations... at the point when their specific vernacular moves from an oral to written usage to the extent that it is being regularly employed for the production of a literature, and particularly for the translation of the Bible.'[47] And in the case of the Armenians: 'The key to their

46 A. Smith, *Ethnic Origins of Nations*, p. 100 for the quote, p. 103, cf. pp. 110–11, 114–16, 120–1, 124. For Smith's use of the Armenian example (as a diaspora *ethnie*) see pp. 115–16.

47 A. Hastings, *Construction of Nationhood*, p. 12, cf. pp. 24–5, 29. In this context the Bible is quite important as a prime lens 'through which the nation is imagined by biblically literate people' (p. 12). This is very true for Khorenatsi, Eghishe and the Armenian historians in the classical period—some of whom even mentioned links (probably presumed) between the Armenian nobility and the Jews (e.g. Khorenatsi, *History of the Armenians*, p. 112; cf. R. Thomson, 'Armenian Literary', p. 214).

national survival seems to [b]e the way that Christian conversion produced both a vernacular literature and the idea of a nation out of which grew a real nation able to endure across the political vicissitudes of the centuries.'[48] For Hastings mass literacy is not as important as the 'bond between the written language, perhaps used only by the few, [and] the oral language forms used by everyone' (which was achieved by the clergy through religious service etc.). Such a bond 'can ensure that a linguistically based nationalism quickly gains support even in largely non-literate communities.'[49] On this view Armenian nationhood—or at the very least, its literary-religious form—can be traced as far back as the fifth to sixth centuries. If Hastings' argument is taken to its logical conclusion, then the Armenian nation predates the 'prototype' of the English by a good half a millennium, as Hastings himself implies.[50] A tantalising proposition indeed (especially for nationalists), but one that cannot be taken too far.

There are two problems with such an approach. First, in relation to the pre-alphabet literary languages (Greek, Aramaic, Syriac), Armenian was the vernacular language. But to what extent was fifth century literary (liturgical) Armenian itself understood by the majority of the population? Even if Hastings' point is accepted, that the bond between the literary language and the oral language is more important than mass literacy, it cannot be taken for granted that those using oral Armenian necessarily comprehended the language of the literary texts. This is an impossible question to answer. But it is a crucial point if mass identification with, and participation in, high culture are intrinsic elements of nationhood. Second, if national self-identification is to include more than the religious and linguistic dimensions (which goes to the core of my argument and my definition of nation), then it cannot be said that an Armenian 'nation' existed in the Middle Ages. After all, survival as an ethno-religious

[48] A. Hastings, *Construction of Nationhood*, p. 198.

[49] Ibid., p. 31, see pp. 191–3 for the social role of the clergy in affirming nationhood by diffusing literature in the vernacular.

[50] Ibid., p. 187. One Armenian academic, writing more than twenty years before Hastings, supports this proposition: 'The basic components of the Armenian personality had fused together by the... seventh century.' Thus, 'The forging of the Armenian nation preceded the more recent European period of nationhood by many centuries' (R. Dekmejian, 'Armenians', pp. 27 and 30 respectively).

Arshakuni Armenia, 1st–5th centuries AD.

group does not necessarily mean the existence of nationhood. However, Hastings is right in highlighting the very long and deep religious and linguistic roots some nations have. He does not employ Smith's terminology of *ethnie*, but he does show how modern nations evolved through very deep linguistic roots.

The Armenian *ethnie* was powerful and united enough in some of its crucial components to withstand the tribulations and invasions of the next thousand years. Its core had cemented around the church and the Armenian brand of Christianity. Even though many Armenians did indeed assimilate, particularly into the more powerful Christian civilisations to the west, and some converted to Islam during the Arab invasions, nevertheless a critical mass remained, both in its homeland and in diasporan communities. It was this critical mass, the surviving Armenian *ethnie*, which was nationalised in the modern period, but in a multilocal and heterogeneous manner. Armenians did not have statehood, or even a powerful political centre, for many centuries, but a sense of ethno-cultural and religious belonging sustained the people as a distinct group into the age of nationalism. I will now turn to the centuries between the Armenian classical period and the dawn of modernity.

THE NEXT THOUSAND YEARS...

In the ten or so centuries between the seventh and the seventeenth, Armenian identity evolved in various directions. At certain times and in some places it was weakened, at other times and places it was reinforced. New developments in terms of the 'building blocks' of national identity were rare,[51] although there were bursts of significant intellectual activity. However, the most important factor in this period did not so much relate to the 'content' of identity, but was the very fact of the actual *survival* of the Armenian *ethnie*. In the remainder of this chapter I will focus on some key events that had important socio-political consequences or affected Armenian collective identity in one way or another during this period.

[51] I realise that this is a generalisation and students in other disciplines such as architecture and art will profoundly disagree. Indeed, Armenians have left a very rich (church) architectural legacy from this period. There is much literature on this subject. See, for example, D. Lang, *Armenia*, pp. 212–32; A. Novello, 'Armenian Architecture'; G. Jeni, 'Architectural Typologies'.

Arab rule

For over two centuries after the fall of the Arshakuni dynasty in 428, the eastern parts of Greater Armenia were ruled as a semi-autonomous region by the Sasanids. Despite many problems and rebellions, Armenian civilisation and identity were 'nurtured' and 'solidified'.[52] In 661, after being a theatre of war between the Byzantine empire and Arabs for twenty years, Armenia was subdued by the conquest of the latter. Arab rule was initially tolerant of (and at times even benevolent to) the Armenians. However, in the eighth century it became unbearable owing to its heavy taxation policies. Consequently the Armenian nobles, despite their inter-clan disunity, rebelled in 705, 748, 774 and 850. They were usually urged on by the church leadership. Each time the rebellion was crushed and each time an entire generation of *nakharars* perished.

Consequently, the *nakharar* system was substantially weakened and many of the noble families, having lost control of their lands, perished (including the powerful Mamikonians, the usual leaders of the rebellions). The vacuum was partially filled by Arab/Muslim migration to the country, which began to alter the demographic composition of society. This was especially the case in the southern parts of Armenia where in some cities Arabs and other Muslims became the majority. There was a handful of Armenian noble households which did benefit from Arab domination, the most important of which was the Bagratunis, who had come to terms with Arab rule fairly early on.[53]

[52] N. Garsoïan, '*Marzpana*te', pp. 114–15.

[53] Based on N. Garsoïan, 'Arab Invasions' and 'Independent Kingdoms', and on A. Redgate, *Armenians*, Chapter 8. It should be mentioned that the rebellions against the Arabs inspired one of the more popular oral epics of heroism in the form of the legendary figure David of Sasun (a Bagratuni). This tale eventually became part of Armenian literature with clear national(ist) overtones against tyranny and foreign occupation. It is widely taught to school children in both Armenia and the diaspora. It was first published in 1874 (by Father Garegin Srvandztiantsin in Constantinople). One of the most popular versions was composed by Hovhannes Tumanian (1869–1923); it appears in many textbooks and children's books (for one example see *Mankakan ashkharh entertsaran* [Children's World Reader], compiled for fourth graders by the prominent diasporan intellectual Levon Shant, and published in Beirut by Hamazgayin Press, 1968). In 1938 Armenians celebrated the one thousandth anniversary of the epic. And in November 1998 an exhibition was organised in the Armenian National Library dedicated to the 125th anniversary of the tale's first publication.

The Bagratuni dynasty

In 884 the Arab Caliph al-Mutamid sent Ashot, the head of the Bagratuni clan, a crown in acknowledgement of the latter's *de facto* status as the most powerful prince of Armenia. Al-Mutamid wished to maintain Ashot's loyalty to the Caliphate, and the granting of the crown was a means to that end. Although Ashot never achieved full sovereignty, he nevertheless acquired the title of King in a coronation ceremony officiated by the Catholicos. As such, a new Armenian dynasty had begun, albeit as a tributary to the Caliphate—at least initially.[54] Not to be outdone by the Arabs, the Byzantine Emperor, Basil I, shortly thereafter also sent a crown to Ashot. Despite their elevated status the Bagratunis could not unite the entire country under their domain (especially the rival Artsruni house), except in brief moments. Nor could they generally stop Arab and Byzantine intrusion into, and campaigns against, Armenia. The apex of Bagratuni rule was reached in the second half of the tenth century. Soon afterwards, again because of internal divisions and external pressures, the dynasty collapsed in 1045 when Ani, the capital city of the Bagratunis, was surrendered to the attacking Byzantine forces. In 1064 Kars, another Bagratuni kingdom but of less importance, was annexed as well. With the end of Bagratuni rule came the end of Armenian kingdoms and statehood in historic Armenia.

Byzantine control of Armenia, although short-lived, had a 'deleterious effect on the country'.[55] It decreased the Armenian population of Greater Armenia because many lords and princes left the country (some voluntarily, others under pressure) and moved west, closer to the empire's centre, taking with them their peasants and followers. As part of Byzantine policy they were given lands in Cappadocia in exchange for their annexed estates in Armenia. Thus they were integrated into the imperial socio-political hierarchy, accepting the official (Chalcedonian) church dogma, and henceforth being cut off from the Armenian church. Consequently most of them assimilated. This meant that Armenia proper was drained of its military defence and political leadership; only the 'national' clergy remained.[56]

[54] The Armenian Bagratunis had close family relations with the Iberian (Georgian) Bagratunis, and the two closely collaborated on certain occasions.

[55] N. Garsoïan, 'Byzantine Annexation', pp. 195, 195–7; cf. R. Bedrosian, 'Armenia', p. 243.

[56] The Armenian church was undoubtedly a powerful institution in its own right. It

However, despite the political misfortunes, the Armenian literary tradition continued, and even flourished, both within and beyond the Bagratuni domains. Usually affiliated with the church, historians, poets (the famous religious poet Grigor Narekatsi is from the tenth century), translators, miniature painters and manuscript scribes continued to produce a rich repertoire of Armenian culture well into the thirteenth century.[57] That is to say, the cultural basis of collective identity was continuing to be enriched and reinforced even when there was no Armenian state *per se*.

In this respect, special mention must be given to the Bagratuni capital, the city of Ani, not least for its important place in current Armenian thinking. By medieval standards Ani was truly a magnificent metropolis, of 100,000 people at its peak—a city of '1001 churches', of trade, commerce and wealth, as well as of impenetrable fortifications at the height of its power. It was already in existence as a town centuries before it became the capital of the Bagratunis in 961. Even after the end of the dynasty it remained an important centre of the arts and learning. Sacked by the Mongols in 1236 it declined to the status of a village, especially after it was destroyed in an earthquake in 1319. By the seventeenth century it was completely abandoned, and remains so to this day. But Ani, in its splendour, never left Armenian popular imagination. Today the ruins of the city, like Ararat, can been seen from Armenia, but are located in Turkey, across the Akhurian river (i.e. the border of the two countries). This symbolic 'insult' to the national pride of Armenians is augmented by the ancient city's Armenian past being denied by Turkey in its official historiography. Not only is Ani one of the most visible and 'tangible' symbols of past Armenian greatness (hence a source of pride), it is a 'forbidden' territory (hence simultaneously a source of frustration).

The Turkic invasions

Less than twenty years after the Byzantine takeover of Armenia, the Seljuk Turks sacked and occupied Ani in 1064 and Kars in 1065. In

had already asserted its hegemony over the Caucasian Albanian (the precursors of Gharabagh Armenians) church, subordinating it to the Armenian Catholicos both in its dogma and jurisdiction (N. Garsoïan, 'Independent Kingdoms', p. 173).

57 For details see R. Thomson, 'Armenian Literary Culture', pp. 226–38; R. Bedrosian, 'Armenia', p. 264.

1071 the Byzantine Emperor himself was defeated by the Seljuks and captured in battle at Manzikert, just north of Lake Van. Seemingly oblivious to the Turkic threat from the east, Byzantium had weakened Armenia in the preceding decades, facilitating the Turkic invasion of its own empire. In fact, Byzantine rule had antagonised some Armenian princes so much that the latter sided with the Seljuks. But with Turkic rule came what Armenians call the 'dark centuries' of Turkish domination in Greater Armenia. This period augmented the Armenian sense of victimhood, as subjects of forces beyond their control. According to Christopher Walker, 'In the centuries that followed, the history of Armenia is of almost uninterrupted woe and disaster.'[58] The Mongol invasion of 1236 was an even greater disaster. But the most violent and disruptive attacks were those of Tamerlane in the 1380s and 1390s. With each wave of invading tribesmen the country was devastated further and depopulated. Trade ceased and cities and farmland were destroyed. The indigenous *nakharar* system was obliterated as the last vestiges of the Armenian noble families were removed from positions of political leadership (except in some mountainous enclaves).[59] However, certain crucial elements did remain that assured the continuation of the Armenian *ethnie*.

First, a new set of eminent Armenian families such as the Zakarids emerged, although they were mostly affiliated with the Georgian kingdom, which achieved its apex of power and glory in the twelfth and thirteenth centuries. Also a new class of extremely wealthy Armenian merchant families appeared with vast trade networks stretching from Central Asia to the Italian city states. Some of these prominent families were favoured, sporadically, by the Seljuks, the Mongols and even Tamerlane, enjoying the support and protection of the conquerors. Others were systematically destroyed. Nonetheless, a secular elite, despite being battered and weakened by multiple invasions, did survive in various locations in one form or another.

Secondly and most importantly, the clergy and church institutions continued to operate. They were in fact assisted on occasion

[58] C. Walker, *Armenia*, p. 31.

[59] Some difficult-to-access Armenian mountainous principalities (usually of no great military significance to the invading armies of the time) were never—or very rarely—captured. They remained (semi-)autonomous. Among them were: Siunik, Artsakh (present-day Gharabagh), Sasun and Mush.

by the Seljuks and the Mongols, but more frequently they were persecuted. In addition to the harassment by Muslim rulers, the Armenian church continually resisted the relentless pressure from both the Byzantine and Latin churches to accept their authority. On more than one occasion leaders who did agree to subjugate the Armenian church to the Pope or to the Greek Patriarch were killed by other Armenian princes. Of course, many leading figures did convert to the other religions, including Islam. In that way their careers were advanced but they were, as mentioned earlier, quickly assimilated. However, on the whole Armenians stubbornly clung to the autocephalous nature of the institutional church and the bulk of the population remained faithful.

Owing to these two factors, there remained a strong material basis to maintain and even to produce a distinctly Armenian culture in medieval Armenia. History was still written, the arts and higher learning (in monasteries) carried on, legal and medical knowledge advanced, and new manuscripts were produced—albeit not as vigorously as before, owing to the political turmoil. Seljuk and Mongol rule, as destructive as it was, did not obliterate Armenian identity, and in fact gave it other avenues to flourish and transform. Nor should it be assumed that Armenians were intrinsically opposed to, or remained immune to, Turkic/Islamic cultural influences.

The 'clash of civilisations' on the territory of Armenia produced a cultural dynamism that influenced both the conquered and the conquerors—notwithstanding Tamerlane. There were inter-ethnic cultural borrowings and intermarriages at the elite level. If anything, the turbulent years of the invasions show how ethnic identity is malleable, subject to both cultural and structural pressures from without.

Peter Cowe demonstrates how Armenian literature, law, medicine and even religion were influenced by various other cultures, notably Greek (Byzantine), Arabic, Turkish, Persian and Latin (European). However, cultural malleability does not mean assimilation as long as core characteristics are preserved. Cowe does point out that borrowings from the west were in general limited to 'form and methodology rather than content'[60]—particularly in the religious

60 P. Cowe, 'Medieval Armenian', p. 312. His article provides a detailed examination of Armenian arts, culture and learning in this period.

field. Armenians maintained their identity because they did adapt without assimilating en masse. An autocephalous church (institutionally and theologically), an elite that could still support cultural production, and the distinct language (and script) were the keys to their survival even in the most adverse conditions.

The 'Diasporan Kingdom' of Cilicia

Before concluding this chapter with Ottoman rule over Armenia an important historical 'detour' must be mentioned: the Armenian 'diasporan kingdom' of Cilicia, or Lesser Armenia (not to be confused with the Lesser Armenia of Hellenistic times). After the downfall of the Bagratuni dynasty a number of Armenian noble families migrated out of Greater Armenia. Some went north to Georgia, many moved to the heartland of the Byzantine empire, while others migrated to the south-west, establishing themselves on the territories between the Taurus Mountains and the Mediterranean Sea. One of the most notable of these families, the Rubenians (who emphasised their links with the Bagratunis), eventually established the Cilician Armenian kingdom in 1199 when prince Levon was crowned King. Once again, confirmation of his status came from abroad. And again, an Armenian king was sent not one, but two crowns (owing to imperial rivalries). One came from the German (i.e. Holy Roman) Emperor, and the other from the Byzantine Emperor. After 1230 the Rubenian kingdom was co-ruled with another (initially rival) Armenian noble family, the Hetumids.

Cilician history is intertwined with the advances of various powers into Asia Minor and the Middle East, each with its own religious ideology. There were the crusades of the European powers; the Turkic and Mongol invasions; the Mamluk advances of Egypt-Syria; and the ever present Byzantine threat. Politically, Cilicia's existence was predicated upon its successful balancing act between all of these forces, which it managed to continue for certain periods. Economically, when there was peace the kingdom flourished as a major land and sea trade route. Culturally, it played an important role in the further development of Armenian identity, which I will focus on.

Cilicia was quite heterogenous demographically. Its population was composed of Greeks, Jews, Muslims, various Europeans and Armenians. The latter never formed an absolute majority, although they were the ruling class. Such a population, along with trade and political links with various peoples meant that Cilician Armenia was heavily influenced by other cultures. Leading Armenian families had marriage links with Europeans, crusader city-states, Byzantium etc.[61] Consequently, the French and Italian languages, as well as western social and governmental habits, made significant inroads. New Latin-based words were added to Armenian, and two new letters to the alphabet ('f' and 'o') so that the sounds of the western languages could be better accommodated.

But in terms of language the most important development was that vernacular Armenian began to be used in written texts. This trend had begun before the founding of Cilicia. As early as the twelfth century a medical writer acknowledged the need to use 'common' Armenian: 'I wrote this in the free, colloquial language so as to be accessible to all readers.'[62] However, it was in the Cilician kingdom that the written use of colloquial Armenian became much more widespread. It was utilised in documents at the official state level. Some religious compositions were also written in simpler style in order to be accessible to a wider readership not familiar with the rigid forms of classical Armenian. The same was the case for legal texts.[63]

Cilicia has been a bridge in the development of Armenian identity on two fronts. First, although Armenia was always influenced by other cultures, in Cilicia these influences came directly from the European west for the first time. Armenians were thus linked to the

[61] For a study of the links between Cilicia and the Crusades see J. Ghazarian, *The Armenian Kingdom in Cilicia.*

[62] Mkhitar Heratsi as quoted in P. Cowe, 'Medieval Armenian', p. 297.

[63] P. Cowe, 'Medieval Armenian', pp. 287, 300. It should be noted that the first systematic Armenian legal code was written by Mkhitar Gosh (d. 1213) in this period too. The code was used in Cilicia, and then spread to the Armenian colonies abroad; it was used to regulate their community life. Parts of the code survived as late as the middle of the nineteenth century in India. Although Armenians were subject to the legal system of host countries, Gosh's code was another element which tied various communities with a common legal bond. I do not want to emphasise this factor too much because it is not clear the extent to which it played a role in the development of a common identity. It was a rather loose bond.

non-Byzantine western civilisations. Second, Cilicia acted as a bridge between classical and modern Armenian. Its vernacular reflected this transitionary period and in many ways it was closer to the modern language (the western dialect) rather than the classical written language. Importantly, Cilician Armenians provided a textual basis for this vernacular (in the forms of manuscripts)—centuries earlier than the age of mass nationalism in Europe. Of course, being before the emergence of print capitalism, such literature was not widespread. It does, however, show that there was a conscious will among the elite to reach out to a wider audience than the narrow literary class.

In the long run, the Cilician kingdom could not be sustained because of political turmoil. Internal infighting, differences between leading families in terms of alliances, instances of regicide, external attacks and so forth led to the crown being passed to the French Lusignans of Cyprus in 1342. The kingdom formally came to an end in 1375 when the Mamluks of Egypt occupied Cilicia. Its last king, Levon V, died in Paris in 1393 after unsuccessful attempts to solicit aid from European monarchs to retake his kingdom.[64] Cilicia was the last Armenian entity that had the vestiges of statehood (between 1375 and the establishment of the 1918 republic no Armenian state existed).

In the following century the territory of the kingdom, along with the rest of Armenia, was firmly under Ottoman control. In the meantime, the Armenian elite—the merchants and the nobles—were once again on the move, establishing themselves in various European countries. This was the second major push of leading families out of Armenian regions since the middle of the eleventh century. Conversely, it was the beginning of an organised diaspora far away from the homeland.

After Cilicia fell themes of exile, loss of country and of leadership became significant subjects in Armenian literature and art (in songs, poetry, folklore etc.). The trend was already in evidence as early as the thirteenth century when Stepanos Orbelian, through his writings, sought to 'apply psychological pressure on the conscience of

[64] Incidentally, the Cilician title of 'King of Armenia' formally survived up to 1946; it was among the titles inherited by the princes of Savoy in Italy who continued to use it until the nineteenth century (A. Bournoutian, 'Cilician Armenia', p. 290).

nobles to return and reestablish an Armenian state [in Armenian plateau].' Once it became obvious that that was not going to materialise, others lamented 'the émigré's alienation, lack of rights, and vulnerability'. As a fifteenth century bishop wrote, 'The exile in a foreign land is indeed extremely wretched.'[65] Clearly, themes of exile and dispersion were woven into Armenian culture much before the final act of expulsion through the genocide of 1915.

The last point that needs to be made about the Cilician kingdom is how it entered Armenian national memory not as an established diasporan community, but as part of the historic homeland. A new territory was imbued with the meaning of homeland because part of the elite established structural roots there. Major Armenian settlements—cities and villages—remained in this region until 1921.[66] Hence, the 'sea to sea' Armenia envisioned by nationalists takes Cilicia into account as the basis of territorial claims on the coast of the Mediterranean Sea.

Subjects of empires, again: maintaining identity as a religious community

By the beginning of the sixteenth century the political turmoil in Armenia proper and in Cilicia were no longer contingent on the remaining Armenians themselves, but on imperial politics. Two new empires had established their control in the region: the Turkish Ottomans (Sunni Muslims) and the Persian Safavids (Shi'i Muslims). As in the past, Armenian territories were divided between them.[67]

[65] P. Cowe, 'Medieval Armenian', pp. 314–15.

[66] In fact, one such community near the Mediterranean coast still survives to this day by a fluke of history. The village of Kessab (Kesap), and its surrounding hamlets, fell on the Syrian side of the border instead of the Turkish side after the annexation of the Sanjak of Alexandretta (Hatay) by Turkey in 1939. It is therefore still populated by a few thousand Armenians, with their own dialect and folklore. There is also a surviving Armenian hamlet comprising a handful of families a few miles away, at Musa Dagh in Turkey. This is Vakifli, which is considered the only remaining Armenian village in Turkey; it has a population of some 125 people.

[67] The Safavids came to power in Persia in 1501, replacing the descendants of the Mongols and the Turkmens (among them the Akkoyunlu). Half a century earlier the Ottomans had already consolidated their complete control over Asia Minor, bringing under their control other Turkic confederations (among them the Karakoyunlu). Their capture of Constantinople in 1453 was the crowning glory of their successes

This did not bring peace to Armenia, as the two empires fought many wars against each other (especially in the sixteenth century) over the frontier that ran through Armenia. Once again the country was a battlefield, a subjugated buffer zone between empires. During these wars hundreds of thousands of Armenians either were forcibly moved out of the region, or had to flee the scorched-earth policies of each of the armies. The greater part of the region remained in the Ottoman sphere, although the borders continuously shifted. For example, the town (and fort) of Yerevan changed hands at least fourteen times between the Ottoman and Persian empires between the fifteenth and seventeenth centuries.

But this was a socio-politically different Armenia. It was no longer just a divided state, but a divided territory that had become a demographically mixed provincial borderland with a ruined economy. It no longer had an indigenous secular leadership to speak of (except in the highlands of Gharabagh), and Armenia itself ceased to be a political, economic, intellectual or cultural centre of any significance. Owing to the many wars, repression and Islamic laws of inheritance, the traditional leadership of *nakharars* and noble families disappeared (with very few exceptions in mountainous areas). As their estates were reduced in size or disappeared altogether, the leading families themselves lost their power and disappeared. In accordance with Islamic laws some gave their lands to the local church (headed by a related bishop) as an inalienable religious grant to avoid sequestration of their estates. As such, the property would at least remain unified and under Armenian control. But the upshot was the same: the Armenian nobility no longer had an economic and political basis of power, and thus it withered away.

This leadership vacuum was filled with two other strata. On the one hand the church leaders began to assume the role of the secular elite, thinking of themselves (and being seen by their followers) as both national leaders and religious heads. On the other hand a new class of merchants and traders emerged called *khojas* and *chelebis* (who later became the *amiras*). But, unlike the church and the disappeared *nakharars*, this dominant class was not tied to the land of Armenia for its power or wealth. Their dominance was conditional

---

hitherto. For further details see Barraclough and Parker, *Times Atlas*, pp. 126, 132, 136, 166; D. Kouymjian, 'Armenia'; and G. Bournoutian, 'Eastern Armenia'.

upon forces beyond their control, such as wars, the whims of the local rulers, foreign laws and royal edicts. In short, they were subject to sudden changes in fortune. But with their mobile capital, they could travel and establish themselves elsewhere, as many of them did, abandoning the Armenian heartland and settling in other parts of the Ottoman and Persian empires, as well as in various other countries.

Obviously, political instability and the lack of a consistent culture-sponsoring elite affected the cultural production of this period in Armenia itself. The confident strides taken by Armenian historiography, law, literature etc. of the previous centuries were reduced to faltering steps. For example, manuscript production dramatically declined, as did the construction of new churches. Very few significant history texts were written. However, literature was produced, almost exclusively in a religious context, in the form of lamentations about the tragedies that had befallen Armenia. There were also significant cultural expressions at the more popular level: poems and songs of exile which longed for security and prosperity. Monasteries continued to run theology schools where wider subjects of philosophy and science were also taught. In fact, some churches and monasteries grew in wealth and land through the endowments of the dwindling noble families.[68]

Amidst the devastation of the Armenian heartland the region ceased to be a cultural centre in terms of innovations and identity construction. Rather, as the next chapter will show, diasporan communities became such centres of learning and identity (re)formulation. In many regions of the historic homeland the Armenian language itself either was lost at the mass level, or had become a localised dialect. Dress and everyday norms did not differ too much from the local Muslims and other local people. However, Armenians did not assimilate and die out as a collective. Greatly reduced in numbers and wealth, Armenians survived as a distinct group on the Armenian plateau because of their separate religious beliefs and habits, sense of history and community structures (viz. the church). Eventually these remaining Armenians—almost exclusively peasants—became the 'raw material' of subsequent nationalism.

[68] D. Kouymjian, 'Armenia', pp. 41–8.

One major but slow change must be noted during these centuries that had important consequences later. As a result of the decline in formal literary media of expression, the classical written language was further 'corrupted' by the vernacular. This process that had begun in the Cilician kingdom was accelerated during these centuries in Armenian texts. Popular language—the Armenian vernacular (*ashkharabar*)—came to be used more and more as a language of (popular) cultural expression. Importantly, the many travelling bards and minstrels were composing poetry and songs in the vernacular. Insofar as such compositions were written down, the vernacular began to acquire some acceptance as a legitimate medium of literary expression. Simultaneously, as a mutually comprehensible popular language (much more so than the formal literary style) it was a linguistic link between regions and generations.

The dire conditions in Armenia did not mean that all Armenian subjects were pauperised and the 'nation' leaderless. The capitals of the Persian and Ottoman empires also became the 'community capitals' of the Armenians. The religious centre, however, remained in Ejmiatzin, which was an important focal point for the church, at least symbolically.[69] In the Persian empire New Julfa, attached to the Safavid capital of Isfahan, became the new centre of Armenians. It emerged both as the core of Armenian affairs in the Persian empire, and an international hub of commerce. As will be discussed in the next chapter, such centres played a major role in the subsequent national revival of Armenians.

In the Ottoman empire the Armenian community formed one of its (self-governing) *millets*. According to the *millet* system, imposed by the rulers of the empire, a community was distinguished by its religion, no matter where its members lived in the empire. Hence identity was based on religion and was formally divorced from territory, as well as ethnicity and language. But since the Armenian church was an autocephalous national institution with 'exclusive'

[69] It would be more correct to say that Ejmiatzin resumed its importance in 1441 as the seat of the Catholicos was reestablished there by a decision of Armenian bishops. Institutionally and financially Ejmiatzin could not at this point compete with some of the more powerful patriarchates, but symbolically it was the centre of the Armenian church. There were also other religious seats that were referred to as Catholicosates, notably in Van and Sis; the latter is the ancestor of the present Catholicosate of Cilicia in Lebanon.

membership, ethnicity and religion completely overlapped.[70] (By mid-nineteenth century Armenian Catholics and Protestants were part of those religious communities, and not the Armenian *millet*, as far as Ottoman administration was concerned.)[71] As the religious heads of the community, the church hierarchy—namely, the patriarch of Constantinople—assumed *the* leadership position of the community in both religious and secular matters. The authority and powers of the church leadership were accepted (and legitimated) by the Sultan, while its jurisdiction increased or decreased in proportion to the expansion or contraction of the Ottoman empire.[72] The *millet* system institutionally complemented socio-political developments in the Armenian heartland: the decline of the secular leadership of noble houses and the survival of religious foundations fitted well with the administrative arrangement of the empire. Thus the ethno-religious identity of the Armenians was further reinforced at the expense of the secular. In the absence of their own political, secular or state institutions, Armenian culture and identity were maintained by an increasingly powerful church.

In addition, since the *millet* system created a clear administrative and theological divide between the Armenians and the other communities—be they Christians or Muslims—Armenians were fur-

[70] Kemal Karpat makes the wider point that 'the *millet* system emphasized the universality of the faith and superseded ethnic and linguistic differences without destroying them' (K. Karpat, '*Millets* and Nationality', p. 143).

[71] The Catholics were recognised as a separate *millet* in 1831, and the Protestants in 1847. But at the turn of the nineteenth century there were only three major non-Muslim *millets*: the Greek (the largest and including other orthodox subjects such as the Serbs, Bulgarians *et al.*), the Armenian and the Jewish. For a brief overview of the Armenian *millet* see H. Barsoumian, 'Eastern Question', pp. 182ff.

[72] For the powers of the Patriarch of Constantinople see V. Artinian, *Armenian Constitutional System*, pp. 15–8. The Catholicos of Ejmiatzin formally remained the supreme ecclesiastical head of the church, but the Patriarch of Constantinople was more powerful in administrative matters, had a wider jurisdiction, and probably controlled more wealth. He was also the community's official link with the Sultan. For the details of the evolution of the Armenian Patriarchate in Constantinople see K. Bardakjian, 'Rise of the Armenian Patriarchate'. Bardakjian concludes: 'The transformation of the seat of Constantinople from a vicariate into a universal patriarchate was due not to an explicit, or conscious Ottoman policy, but to an evolutionary historical process' (p. 97; cf. B. Braude, 'Foundation Myths', p. 81). However, the 'founding myth' of the Armenian *millet* is that Mehmet the Conqueror granted the Armenian patriarchate authority and jurisdiction in 1461. This founding act is still commemorated by the Armenian community in Istanbul.

ther isolated from the cultural and religious influences of the more powerful and numerous communities. Hence their identity was protected against assimilation or en masse proselytisation (except in the case of the Janissaries). Some Armenians did convert to Islam because of personal economic considerations, and there were occasional drives to forcefully convert certain communities. But these were not systematic, consistent and empire-wide attempts. Ottoman rule, ironically, gave Armenians a structure through which their collective identity as a (religious) *ethnie* could be maintained, albeit 'frozen'—at least until the 'age of nationalism'—within the parameters of a more or less culturally isolated *millet.* The *millet* system, in short, considerably helped to assure the survival of Armenians as a distinct group.

To conclude, the three hundred years between the early fifteenth and late seventeenth centuries were simultaneously a period of the destruction of the Armenian heartland, and of the transformation of traditional structures. No new significant identity or cultural markers emerged in these 'dark centuries', but certain structural changes took place that were vital for future developments in terms of national identity construction and the politics of nationalism. First, the old feudal ruling classes tied to specific land completely disappeared. In their place a new class of merchants and traders began to emerge which was city-based. As the next chapter will show, they eventually became the main cultural patrons, supporters of the church and the funders of intellectual endeavours. Second, the centres (religious, cultural, economic, political) of the community began to shift from Armenia proper to the diasporan communities in the imperial capitals (and other major cities outside the two empires). These then became the bases of the national intellectuals. Third, the church leadership was recognised as the sole 'official' head of the community (especially in the Ottoman empire). Hence Armenians did not remain leaderless when the traditional political elite disappeared, or when secular leadership was in flux or persecuted. At crucial moments there was at least a religious elite that could act on behalf of the community and provide a rallying point. Centuries later this leadership came to be challenged by secular intellectuals, but at the very least they had managed to remain as heads of a distinct collective while ensuring its survival. Finally, related to the previous point, during this period of fundamental structural shifts ethnic identity remained secure because it was infused with the officially sanctioned religious identity. The latter was accepted as a collective demarcation line between communities within the Muslim empires (most clearly in the *millet* administrative system) and separated Armenians from the 'others'. Again a distinct identity remained—albeit a religious one—and therefore was open to reinterpretation in secular terms in the nineteenth century. In 1375 the last Armenian state fell, but the collective survived because of these factors. Moreover, these changes contained elements that in the next two centuries greatly facilitated the formation of a modern Armenian nation.

The roots of the Armenian people do indeed go very far back. During three thousand or so years the 'building blocks' of Armenian identity were set, shaped and reshaped. The thumbnail-sketch provided here does not do justice to the many arguments and debates in this field. However, my intent has not been to provide a detailed historical account, but to highlight the structural, cultural, symbolic and historiographical sources of the Armenian *ethnie*, and eventually the Armenian nation. The most notable period in solidifying the distinctness of the already existing Armenian ethnic group was the two hundred or so years after the adoption of Christianity early in the fourth century. This period included the creation of the Armenian alphabet, the subsequent 'Golden Century' of literary output and a major rebellion (at Avarayr in 451 AD) in defence of the new faith and the unique culture. In the following millennium, despite tumultuous transformations and invasions, socio-economic crises and demographic changes, the core element of the Armenian *ethnie* survived. This was largely due to the powerful ethno-religious foundations established in this period. Language and culture were reshaped (some would argue 'diluted'), but Armenian identity remained in Armenia and in the newly established diasporan communities, which included the diasporan kingdom of Cilicia.

Throughout this chapter I have consciously avoided the term 'nation' when refering to the Armenian collective in ancient times; '*ethnie*' or 'ethnic group' are much more appropriate terms given the modernity of national identity. Neither Armenians nor any other group were a nation, as defined by our modern conceptions of nationality. But by the seventeenth century all the main components were in place for the construction of nationhood once that became the dominant paradigm of collective identity and international politics. Ancient roots and the survival of the Armenians under adverse conditions were a major source of national pride for subsequent generations, as was the mentality of '*We* were here first, on our lands'. The long and deep Armenian history was—and is—used and abused by nationalists for political purposes. Intellectuals quoted, and continue to quote, Movses Khorenatsi, for example, to assert Armenian rights. It is impossible to fully comprehend modern Armenian nationalism without being aware of the basic parameters of ancient Armenian history.

I now turn to the next period in the history of the Armenians, the modern era, and examine the rise of the early national(ist) intellectual movements and the attempts to liberate Armenia. In this process the Armenian *ethnie* began to be transformed into a nation.

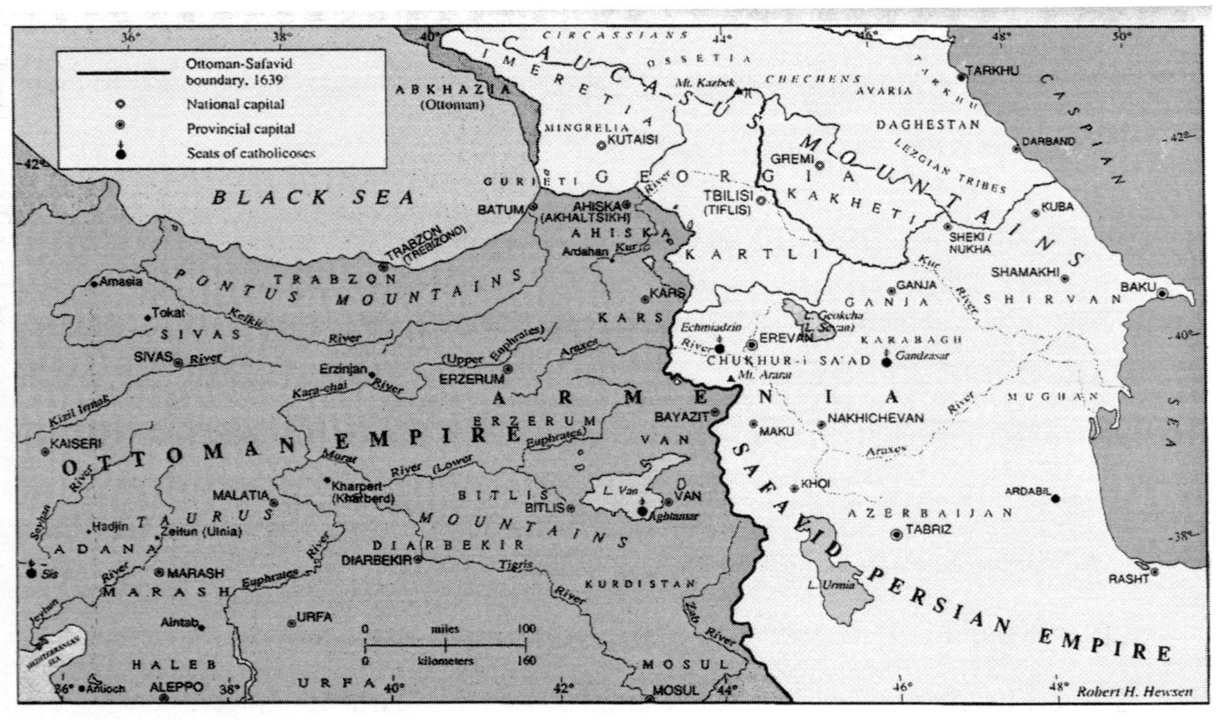

Ottoman–Persian treaty, 1639.

3

MERCHANTS, DIASPORA COMMUNITIES AND LIBERATION ATTEMPTS

THE 17TH TO THE 19TH CENTURY

Between the seventeenth and the nineteenth centuries much intellectual work was done which prepared the groundwork leading to the 'national awakening' of the Armenians in the second half of the 1800s, and to clearly articulated nationalism from the 1880s onward. In these two centuries collective consciousness began to evolve in a national direction. The actual 'awakening' and the politics of nationalism are the subjects of subsequent chapters. Here I focus on the preceding factors and examine the ideas, and the socio-structural bases, that led to the Armenian renaissance.

The history of these centuries comprises a complicated web of networks and dynamics. It is no longer the history of a people in one specific homeland, but also of communities that were scattered globally, with the various threads of their 'stories' being intertwined—at least in hindsight—both geographically and temporally. Because of such dispersion the intellectual process of modern Armenian national identity formation became a *multilocal* experience. That is to say, it took place in a decentralised manner in various communities, many of them far away from Armenia proper (the multilocal argument is discussed in more detail in the next chapter). To highlight the issues related to this process, I follow a more thematic approach in this chapter (at the risk of some repetition), rather than a strictly chronological narrative. As this multilocal process of identity formation is traced, the argument criss-crosses over three centuries, two continents and a number of empires and states. Despite the wide scope, some important historical events have to be left out, or glanced over. It would otherwise be impossible to cover this complex period in one chapter.

Three components are elaborated in my analysis: (1) the establishment of major diasporan centres, particularly merchant communities; (2) the Mkhitarist Catholic Brotherhood based in Venice and their intellectual work; and (3) initial attempts at liberation from Muslim rule in western Armenia, and Russian rule in eastern Armenia. I discuss the diaspora element at length because of its significance in the intellectual endeavours in the reformulation of Armenian identity.

PREPARING THE GROUNDWORK, I: MERCHANT COMMUNITIES AND DIASPORA CENTRES

As the heart of Armenia was being ravished and depopulated in imperial wars, a new Armenian socio-economic force was emerging in the fourteenth to sixteenth centuries: that of the merchant diaspora. The establishment or reinforcement of this diaspora is immensely important in terms of the evolution of national identity. Both the physical and intellectual location of identity formulation shifted from the historic homeland to the diasporan communities in these centuries. The diaspora remained the intellectual 'centre' of the nation until the second half of the nineteenth century when a significant intellectual movement emerged in Armenia itself, complementing the efforts of the diaspora. In this way, despite the unfavourable conditions of the homeland, the evolution of national identity not only continued, but flourished in various locations outside Armenia proper.[1]

Vartan Gregorian summarises the extent of the early network of the Armenian merchants, based on some primary sources:

> During the sixteenth century there were Armenians in India and Goa. In the court of the Mughal emperors, Armenians occupied high administrative posts and served as interpreters. As early as the fifteenth century and the beginning of the sixteenth, there were Armenian merchants in Malabar and Cochin. There are reports of Armenian merchants in Central Asia

[1] John Armstrong, using the example of the Armenians and the Jews, also argues that 'archetypal diasporas' have historically been locations where ethnic identity is maintained, centred around a distinct religion and other cultural markers (J. Armstrong, *Nations before Nationalism*, pp. 206–13; cf. A. Smith, *Ethnic Origins*, pp. 64ff., 86ff., and 114ff.).

at the turn of the sixteenth century. By the end of the sixteenth and beginning of the seventeenth century, English merchants were purchasing some of their major wares (silk, spices, rugs etc.) from the Armenian merchants of Constantinople, who had brought them from India and Persia via the overland route. There were Armenian merchant communities in Georgia, the Crimea, Kiev and Volga regions, Russia, Poland, Bulgaria and Rumania.... There was a caravanserai in Moscow in the late sixteenth century and many active merchants trading for Czar Ivan IV.... [I]n 1596 there was an Armenian shop... in Venice.[2]

Later in the essay Gregorian also mentions the Netherlands, Sweden, Java and the Philippines, Kabul etc., as other centres where Armenian merchants were active. Merchant communities reached their apex in the seventeenth century and continued to be important throughout the eighteenth. Subsequently other, more permanent, diasporan centres (e.g. Constantinople and Tiflis) emerged, with their own banker/capitalist elites at the forefront of the nation. They, along with the clergy, remained the leading elements of Armenians until the second half of the nineteenth century when they began to be challenged by the newly emerging (more secular) intellectual-cum-political elite.

It is not possible to deal with all of the merchant/diaspora communities and hence I focus on a few of the more significant ones.[3] It is also necessary in this section to back track as early as the sixteenth century to cover the background of some of these communities. First, I give a brief historical background on a colony-by-colony basis and then discuss the significance of these diasporan centres in relation to national identity on a thematic basis. The most important colony before the nineteenth century was that of New Julfa (in the Persian empire), which was the hub of the vast Armenian trade network in the seventeenth century. It was an international centre of commerce and the initial financial catalyst of the subsequent national revival of Armenians.

[2] V. Gregorian, 'Minorities of Isfahan', p. 662, cf. p. 668. See also, K. Papazian, *Merchants from Ararat*, pp. 17–28; D. Kouymjian, 'Armenia', p. 23; M. Seth, *Armenians in India*, p. 613.

[3] For a an extensive historical survey of Armenian diasporan communities see A. Abrahamian's two-volume study (*Hamarot urvagitz*) published in Yerevan in the 1960s. For a more accessible source see H. Atikian, *Hamarot Patmutiun*. Unfortunately there is not a comparable source in English. There are, however, studies of specific communities or regions which I will use below.

New Julfa

The original city of Julfa on the Arax river in Nakhijevan (historic Armenia, present day Azerbaijan) had already emerged as an important centre of the overland east-west trade route by the second half of the sixteenth century. Its network stretched from Central Asia to the Italian city states, while its merchants acted as representatives and brokers for European trading houses.[4] During the intervals in the Ottoman-Persian wars the city had become quite wealthy. When Shah Abbas I (1588–1629) relaunched his campaigns against the Ottomans in 1603 he arrived in Julfa where he was greeted with open arms, honoured and hosted by the merchant families. He was impressed by the wealth amassed, and by the contacts and trade networks of the Armenians. This 'prompted Shah Abbas I to transplant the Armenians of Julfa en masse from their homeland to Isfahan' (his capital city), for he saw that they could 'perform well as the economic entrepreneurs of the Safavid dynasty.'[5] And so, in 1604, as he was retreating from the campaign, the Shah forcefully moved the entire town of Julfa (10–12,000 people), along with the entire population of the Ararat valley (close to 300,000), to Persia. Half of the people uprooted died en route, but special care was taken for the Julfa merchants, who were resettled near Isfahan in a new town named New Julfa.[6] As such, one of the most important Armenian

[4] For a good overview on Julfa see E. Herzig, 'Rise of the Julfa Merchants'.

[5] V. Gregorian, 'Minorities of Isfahan', pp. 662–3.

[6] In the second half of the sixteenth century some Armenians had already moved to Isfahan in order to escape the devastation in Armenia. For details of Shah Abbas' deportation see, E. Herzig, 'Deportation of the Armenians'; Leo, vol. III(a), pp. 223–63. The following lamentation written at the beginning of the seventeenth century by clergyman Stepannos Vardapet (as cited in V. Gregorian, 'Minorities of Isfahan', p. 665) captures the sorrow and the suffering felt by the Armenians at being deported from their homeland:

> *Poor, Armenian people, innocent and without advice*
> *Dispersed, hungry, thirsty and naked*
> *On your way to captivity in Khurasan [Persia]*
> *You endured hundreds and thousands of ills*
> *But you did not set foot out of your sweet country.*
> *Now you are abandoning your fathers' and mothers' graves*
> *And surrendering your houses and churches to others…*

The full Armenian version ends thus (in Leo, vol. III(a), p. 247):

> I wish I was blinded, my neck broken,
> And had not seen you like this, poor Armenia.

diaspora communities was formally born, while old Julfa, along with the rest of Armenia conquered by Abbas, was completely destroyed by the Persian forces.[7]

The Shah granted Persian residency to the Armenians of New Julfa, freedom to travel and gave them internal autonomy to govern their community. They were allowed to practice their religion freely, elect a mayor, and build churches and other communal structures, as well as have their own courts in civil matters. Initially the Armenians also received economic assistance. By 1630 New Julfa had become quite prosperous, with an estimated population of 30,000 Armenians (plus 50,000 in the surrounding villages). By the second half of the seventeenth century some of the Armenian traders of New Julfa were among the richest merchants in the world, living opulent lives, as they handled a substantial component of Persia's foreign trade, including that with India, Russia and Europe.[8]

> I would have preferred to be dead,
> Rather than be alive to see you thus.

Edmund Herzig ('Deportation of the Armenians') also cites a number of descriptive passages from similar sources.

[7] By moving the Armenians to his capital, Shah Abbas achieved a number of strategic and economic goals. First, he laid waste territories which Ottomans would eventually reconquer. Second, he removed from their control an important revenue generating centre. Third, he rerouted the trade network to go via the Persian empire, which meant that he could control the lucrative silk trade. Abbas gave Armenians the monopoly to be silk merchants. Finally, the Shah ensured that economic wealth was in the hands of a minority that could compete with the Europeans and yet could easily be controlled without being a political threat (V. Gregorian, 'Minorities of Isfahan', p. 663). For two excellent and detailed studies of New Julfa see E. Herzig, *Armenian Merchants*, and I. Baghdiantz McCabe, *Shah's Silk*.

[8] V. Gregorian, 'Minorities of Isfahan', pp. 665–8. According to him, there were three factors that worked in the Armenians' favour, enabling them to amass such huge fortunes: (a) they enjoyed the protection of the Safavids and hence capital could stay within the community to be reinvested; (b) they were granted the monopoly over the silk trade of the Persian empire (silk production being a state monopoly and Armenians its sole merchants) and; (c) the merchants were situated at the crossroads of both overland and maritime trade which enabled them to successfully compete with all the major trading companies of Europe (cf. pp. 669–70 for some of the figures attesting to the size of the transactions of these merchants). In a wider scope, Philip Curtin enumerates other factors including mutual self-support and trust (usually organised and expressed through the church), skill in 'diplomacy and cross-cultural brokerage', and usually becoming subjects of local governments while not having a powerful homeland that could be threatening (P. Curtin, *Cross-cultural Trade*, pp. 198–204). The last point also meant that they could be persecuted without the threat of retaliation from their own state.

Shah Abbas's calculations had paid off. The wealth of the Armenians was based in Persia where they paid taxes and supported the state. However, the privileges of the community were not formalised within state structures and, without any political power, its well-being was left to the whims of the Shahs. From 1666 onward the Shahs turned against the Armenians and taxed them heavily while making deals directly with European merchants in order to diminish their wealth and economic importance. Pressure was put on them to convert to Islam.[9] As Gregorian puts it, 'New Julfa was no longer treated as the economic arm of the Safavid ruler, but rather as an open target and limitless source of money.'[10] The community did survive this onslaught, but it ceased being a leading trade hub. The Safavid dynasty ended in 1722 owing to the Afghan invasions, but New Julfa never regained its importance as a world trade centre. On the one hand the merchants did not enjoy the patronage of the new rulers as in the time of Shah Abbas. On the other global trade dynamics had changed; Europeans began to outflank Asian traders, and political upheavals in Europe by the end of the eighteenth century (the French Revolution and the subsequent wars) greatly reduced inter-continental overland trade. However, the New Julfa community had already spawned a number of other prominent merchant communities, many of them in India and the Far East.

India

Although Armenians had arrived in India before 1500, the first notable Armenian there was a merchant called Hakob, originally from Aleppo. He settled in Agra upon the invitation of the Mogul emperor Akbar in 1560, serving in the Mogul court. Soon a small Armenian community was established in Agra, where it built a

[9] Shah Abbas's benevolent attitude towards the Armenians was countered by a law he enacted which stipulated that any Christian who converted to Islam would automatically inherit the entire wealth of his family and of his relatives. A few individuals did convert for such reasons, but on the whole the community staunchly held on to its religion (and therefore identity) and refused to assimilate. During Abbas's time there were no forced conversions, but later Shahs, in combination with this law, tried to forcefully Islamise Armenians to the point of death. Some did change their faith, others fled, while others managed to avoid being converted (V. Gregorian, 'Minorities of Isfahan', pp. 656, 671).

[10] V. Gregorian, 'Minorities of Isfahan', p. 671.

church in 1562.[11] Most of the Armenians who came to India (from Persia) from the seventeenth century onward were from New Julfa. With their mobile capital they settled in Madras, Delhi, Calcutta, Surat and Bombay, among other towns, building churches and establishing a stable community life. Armenians stayed close to the Moguls and often acted as intermediaries and interpreters between the local Muslim rulers and European representatives. In the process they prospered as merchants. Once again Armenians were playing the role of the quintessential middleman and becoming very wealthy in the process. The merchants based in India replaced New Julfa as a leading hub of world trade by the second half of the eighteenth century.[12]

The English first came across the 'well established' and prosperous Armenians in Surat in the seventeenth century and used them by 'cultivating their friendship'. In this manner they gained access to the Mogul court and negotiated concessions in favour of English merchants.[13] By the early 1800s Armenians were, however, outdone by the European—particularly the British—maritime trade routes.[14] Never numerous, the various communities across the sub-continent withered away as they lost their trading niche and therefore their potential to generate wealth. Some moved further east (Singapore, Hong Kong, Manila etc.) or north (Russia), while others were

[11] M. Seth, *Armenians in India*, pp. 1–2; K. Papazian, *Merchants from Ararat*, p. 30, cf. pp. 29–40 for an overview. Seth's book is a fascinating and detailed account of the history of Armenian communities and individuals on the Indian subcontinent.

[12] One interesting story is that of an Armenian jewel merchant from Surat, Khojah Johannes Rafael, who sold a 195-carat diamond to the Russian Prince Orloff in Amsterdam in 1775 for 90,000 pounds. Orloff presented Catherine II with the stone which she had set in the Imperial Russian sceptre (K. Papazian, *Merchants from Ararat*, p. 35).

[13] M. Seth, *Armenians in India*, pp. 227–9; cf. pp. 281ff.

[14] The English and the Armenians of India (represented by one of the most wealthy merchants, Khojah Panos) signed a trade agreement in 1688 that gave the Armenians equal rights as the English in dealing with English companies, living in their settlements and shipping on their vessels. This treaty, although initially advantageous for both sides, was the 'death knell' or the 'Death Warrant' of the Armenian trade communities in India according to Mesrovb Seth (*Armenians in India*, pp. 231–2). Armenians moved to the settlements of the English Company and were eventually absorbed in the overall British trade pattern and community. They therefore dissolved as a separate and distinct trading community. The entire treaty is reproduced in Seth's *Armenians in India*, chapter 18; see also chapter 24 for Armenians' relations with the East India Company.

absorbed in the English/European settler communities. A small Armenian community survives to this day in Calcutta, while individuals as well as church buildings can still be found in Madras and Dhaka. As it will be discussed later, despite its size and relatively short-lived prominence, the Armenian community of India played a crucial role in the development of Armenian nationalism.

Europe

As an extension of the trade network based in New Julfa and India, Armenian communities were also established in western Europe: Amsterdam, Genoa, Venice, Leghorn, Vienna etc. At various times some of these commercial colonies developed into organised communities with churches, trade guilds, hostels and cultural centres.[15] However, by the middle of the nineteenth century none of these merchant-based communities had survived as major Armenian centres. As extensions of the New Julfa and Indian colonies, they withered away when the latter declined.

The dynamics of the Armenian communities were different in eastern Europe. They were more established, with longer histories and a more varied social composition. The roots of these centres are to be found in Crimea, where a large number of Armenians had emigrated. Armenians had settled in Crimea as early as the eleventh century, but in the thirteenth and fourteenth centuries immigration became large scale as more and more people fled the devastation of Armenia. By the 1400s there was an 'impressive' Armenian presence in Crimea, and according to Genoese sources—Genoa then controlled the region—there were 46,000 Armenians in Kaffa (now Feodosiia) alone.[16] Armenians were once again involved in commerce,

[15] For example, Armenians in Venice had their own community constitution (as of 1579), a church and a hospice for merchants. In the seventeenth century they were granted citizenship rights as well. In Amsterdam the city administration had given permission to the Armenians to build a church in 1713; it closed in 1874 due to the lack of a congregation (K. Papazian, *Merchants from Ararat*, pp. 21–2, 54).

[16] K. Maksoudian, 'Armenian Communities', pp. 54–5. Some have suggested that as many as 300,000 Armenians had migrated to Crimea (G. Bournoutian, *History of the Armenian People*, Vol. II, p. 73). This might be an inflated number, but the Crimean peninsula was sometimes called '*Armenia maritima*' and the Azov sea '*Lacus armeniacus*' in the fifteenth century (K. Maksoudian, 'Armenian Communities', p. 55). Although Armenians in Crimea kept their identity and loyalty to their church, they neverthe-

but many were also farmers and artisans. The community survived the Ottoman capture of the region in 1475, although it declined in importance and numbers due to persecution as a conquered people. In 1778, after Russian influence in the region was established, Armenians were encouraged to move from Crimea deeper into the Russian empire. The entire remaining community of 12,000 emigrated to the Rostov-on-Don region and established a new community called Nor (New) Nakhijevan which still survives.[17]

Crimea was the springboard for Armenian settlements in the rest of eastern Europe, the most important of these being in Lwow, Poland (now in Ukraine and called Lviv). Again, Armenians had settled in Poland centuries earlier (the Armenian cathedral there dates from 1363). The community enjoyed internal autonomy and reached its peak in the 1630s with the influx from Crimea. Merchants occupied a prominent place here as well, but Armenians were also tradesmen and peasants. The Armenian community in Poland declined in the eighteenth century owing to imperial wars, the loss of its communal autonomy and migration to other cities. Most importantly, in 1689, under pressure from the Catholic church, the Armenian Bishop of Poland accepted the supremacy of the Pope and cut his church off from Ejmiatzin. Unable to maintain its distinct form of Christianity, the Armenian congregation was eventually absorbed in the Catholic church. Without the religious difference much of the basis of ethnic distinctiveness was lost, which led to accelerated assimilation.[18]

Constantinople

The Constantinople Armenian community had the most complex social composition in the diaspora. Armenians in the Ottoman imperial capital were much more than a trade colony. They were members of an established community, the leadership of which was seen

less began to speak Tatar (and later Kipchak Turkish) as an everyday language, but wrote it with the Armenian script (P. Curtin, *Cross-cultural Trade*, p. 186).

[17] K. Maksoudian, 'Armenian Communities', pp. 58–60.

[18] Based on K. Maksoudian, 'Armenian Communities', pp. 62–9, cf. pp. 69–78 for details on Armenian communities in Bulgaria, Romania and Hungary. For details on the formation of the Polish and Ukrainian colonies see J. Galstian, 'Haikakan gaghtavaireri arajatsume'.

as the leadership of the entire Armenian *millet* in the Ottoman empire. By the nineteenth century Constantinople was not only the administrative, religious, political, economic and cultural centre of Ottoman Armenians, but also the most significant Armenian centre in the world—much more so than towns in historic Armenia and other diasporan communities.[19] Its importance increased just as the wealth and prominence of the trade colonies diminished. It became the undisputed capital of Armenian finance, community power and culture outside the Russian empire. Towards the end of the nineteenth century Armenians in Tiflis/Tbilisi could compete with Constantinople as a primary intellectual centre as well, with their own capital might and intra-community political influence.

Armenians had resided in Constantinople even before it was captured by the Ottomans. But under Ottoman rule Armenians continuously migrated to the city. Many came on their own initiative because of the pull of the imperial centre for career advancement (some Armenians did achieve prominent positions in the Ottoman administration), trade, commerce, industry, employment as artisans etc. Others came in waves as captives from military campaigns. Many Armenians were forcibly moved from their traditional lands (and other territories conquered by the Ottomans) to the capital and surrounding areas (as in Persia under Shah Abbas). Eventually Constantinople became the city with the largest number of Armenian inhabitants (200,000–300,000 by the nineteenth century).[20]

[19] It should be noted that Armenians in Constantinople did not conceive of themselves as a true 'diaspora'. Being in the capital of the empire that ruled most of Armenia, and the centre of the community, did not make them feel like a diasporan colony—although in reality Constantinople was as far from Armenian lands as Crimea. They were, after all, in the same state that ruled the homeland. This sentiment persists to this day. As the editor of an Istanbul based Armenian newspaper, Robert Haddejian of *Marmara*, put it in an interview, 'Istanbul is not a settlement of immigrants (*kaghut* [colony]) like Beirut. It is something unique, between the fatherland… and the Diaspora.… We are a community (*hamaynk*)' (T. Voskeritchian, 'Armenians of Istanbul', p. 38). Interestingly, however, Armenians in Isfahan, the Persian capital, were much more readily referred to (by themselves and others) as a colony. The *millet* system of administration, the self-perception as an old and integrated community in the capital and the elite's close connections with the Ottoman state were the main causes of this feeling of being at 'home' in a city which was, in reality, very much part of the diaspora. Issues of diaspora identity will be explored further in subsequent chapters.

[20] D. Kouymjian, 'Armenia', p. 26; V. Artinian, 'Armenian Constitutional System', p. 6; H. Barsoumian, 'Eastern Question', p. 188; for details of migration patterns see

Although the Constantinople community was multi-classed, with fairly large artisan/service and labour sectors, it was nevertheless dominated (by the late eighteenth century) by a particular class of *amiras* (the successors of *khojas* or *chelepis*). *Amira*s were not simply merchants, but also bankers, money lenders and industrialists who worked in conjunction with—or for—the Ottoman state, particularly in its taxation system. They were 'capitalists par excellence' whose capital and function as bankers was 'essential for the functioning of Ottoman financial structure'.[21] Moreover, they were at the forefront of the empire's industrialisation process, often being the agents of innovation, bringing the latest European technology to Ottoman industry. Some families had acquired their prestige and wealth by being employed by the Ottoman state. They had specific tasks in the service of the government that were passed down from one generation to the next: Balians were architects, Dadians ran the government arsenal factory (as well as their own industries), Duzians were in charge of the imperial mint, and Bezjians looked after trade.[22] The *amiras* were not very large in number (approximately 165 individuals and their families),[23] but they were favoured subjects of the Ottoman government and enjoyed tremendous prestige.

This prestige and their wealth was translated into power in the Armenian community. The *amiras* were the intermediaries between the Sublime Porte and the community. They were its undisputed and 'all-powerful' leaders in the first half of the nineteenth century; they controlled the patriarchate and could in practice appoint or dismiss the Armenian patriarch 'at will'.[24] This was indeed significant, given that the patriarch of Constantinople was the recognised head of the Armenians throughout the empire, and in many ways church institutions functioned as the community's government. The patriarch himself was legally vested with absolute power over the

---

D. Kouymjian, 'Armenia', pp. 13–5, 25–6, 40; see also K. Maksoudian, 'Armenian Communities', p. 56, for Armenian migration from Crimea to Constantinople (in 1475).

[21] H. Barsoumian, 'Economic Role', p. 314.

[22] V. Artinian, *Armenian Constitutional System*, pp. 20–4; K. Papazian, *Merchants from Ararat*, pp. 1–9; H. Barsoumian, 'Economic Role', pp. 312–13.

[23] H. Barsoumian, 'Dual Role', p. 172.

[24] Ibid., p. 177; H. Barsoumian, 'Eastern Question', pp. 184–5, 189.

lives of the members of his *millet*. Not only did the patriarchate administer churches, but also schools, charity organisations and even a small prison. Whoever controlled it controlled the entire community (as much as this was possible in the outlying areas of the empire). The *amiras* were also the major financiers of Armenian social, educational and religious institutions (mostly concentrated in Constantinople and Smyrna) through their large donations. This earned them even more power and prestige in the eyes of the community.

Despite the decline of the Ottoman empire, its internal turmoil and massacres of Armenians in the latter part of the nineteenth century, Constantinople remained the main Armenian centre in the empire and western Europe until the catastrophic destruction of the Ottoman Armenians in 1915.

Tiflis

In many respects Tiflis (Tbilisi) was the Constantinople of the east for the Armenians—minus the *millet* system. Armenian presence in the city dates back to the foundation of the city as Georgia's capital in the third century. By the eighth century there was an Armenian church in the city and during the medieval period there were close relations between the princely families of Armenia and their Georgian counterparts. At the end of the eighteenth century many Armenians either were forcibly moved to Georgia by King Herakl II, or fled north to the relative safety of Georgia from the Ottoman-Persian wars. The pattern continued in the early nineteenth century owing to the Russian-Persian wars.

Similar to their role in other major cities where they did not have political control, Armenians became Tiflis' leading merchants, artisans and professionals (e.g. doctors). Their prominence was already obvious by the seventeenth century. Many Armenians served in the Georgian court, but they did not acquire direct political power. Nevertheless, Armenians were in control of considerable economic resources and trade networks. By the nineteenth century Tiflis had become one of the most important Armenian economic centres. Moreover, after the 1840s the city administration was mostly controlled by the Armenian bourgeoisie, as were 62 per cent of its commercial and industrial enterprises. As elsewhere, economic well-being also translated into cultural production and Tiflis became one of the most important Armenian cultural centres.[25] As will be discussed in the next chapter, the city played a crucial role in the reformulation of Armenian identity and nationalism in the second half of the nineteenth century.

Diaspora/merchant communities and national identity

All of these diasporan centres played significant roles that led to the 'awakening' of national consciousness among the Armenians in the nineteenth century. When the Armenian homeland had fallen into the 'dark centuries'—as the preceding period is popularly known—of destitution and war, these communities either became centres of culture and learning themselves, or they financed individuals and organisations elsewhere. In this way, not only was ethnic identity kept alive, but it evolved and was modernised with new innovations, forming the basis of subsequent *national* identity. In short, it was in the diaspora that the Armenian *ethnie* began to be politicised into nationalism—both consciously and inadvertently. There are two elements in this process which need to be examined here: (1) the relationship between the merchants and cultural-intellectual production, and (2) Armenian printing as a crucial element in this link.

Diaspora merchants as the financiers of culture, learning and identity

Wherever Armenians settled they tried to establish some sort of a community life by at the very least opening an Armenian church. This was seen as both a 'safeguard' to maintain communal identity, and a nucleus for community activity and mutual support. Merchants were particularly active in this respect because they had the capital to finance the building and maintenance of such structures. For example, two merchants (Hakob and Panos) financed the building of the Armenian cathedral in Lwow in 1363,[26] while subsequent wealthy patrons paid for its upkeep. In addition to religious institutions, in many colonies schools were built and cultural activity was supported. Thanks to merchant sponsorship New Julfa became an important cultural centre producing, for example, its own particular style of distinctly Armenian miniature paintings, but influenced by

[25] Based on A. Petrosian, *Hayern ashkharhum*, pp. 94–7.
[26] K. Maksoudian, 'Armenian Communities', p. 63.

Persian and European motifs. In the 1630s an advanced school supported by the rich of the city was also established there. The school produced some of the most important Armenian intellectuals of the period.[27] Elsewhere, 'Crimea became a major center of Armenian art' where manuscripts were being produced in the monastic complex of Surb Khach (Holy Cross).[28] The first play in the Armenian language in modern times was staged in Lwow in 1668 by the Armenian school there.[29] A century and a half later, Seth pointed out:

> Whilst the Armenian merchants of his day were piling up huge fortunes at Calcutta and elsewhere in India and the East, Manatsakan Sumbat Vardon, a merchant of Saidabad, saw the urgent need of national education in India and with a praiseworthy zeal, he founded after strenuous efforts, the 'Armenian Philanthropic Academy' in Calcutta. The Academy, which opened its doors on the 2nd of April 1821, still continues its useful work in educating poor boys...

The first school in Calcutta was opened in 1798 because 'the Armenian colonists in India... have neither been backward in the matter of education nor indifferent to the advancement of their national literature.'[30] In Constantinople the *amiras* contributed large sums for the construction of churches, hospitals and schools for the entire community, and funded cultural societies and publications.[31]

However, it should also be noted that wealthy Armenians did not only support their own communities, but also other diasporan centres, as well as institutions in Armenia proper. Hence, many merchants donated money to Ejmiatzin. In fact the printing press of the Catholicosate was established in 1771 by funds from Armenian notables in India. Two Madras Armenians (Samuel Mooradian and Raphael Gharamiantz) bequeathed substantial sums to the Mkhitarist order of Venice and Vienna to open colleges in the early nine-

[27] V. Gregorian, 'Minorities of Isfahan', pp. 667–8.

[28] K. Maksoudian, 'Armenian Communities', pp. 57–8; cf. D. Kouymjian, 'Armenia', pp. 47–8, 25–6. Some monastic centres continued to function in Armenia as well, as did the St James monastery in Jerusalem.

[29] The subject was the religious-national theme of the martyrdom of St Hripsime in Armenia. According to Leo, the play had a 'religious-didactic' character and was part of the 'Catholic propaganda' to convince the Armenians of the city to join the Roman church (Leo, vol. III(a), p. 408; K. Maksoudian, 'Armenian Communities', p. 66).

[30] M. Seth, *Armenians in India*, p. 356 for the first quote, p. 481 for the second.

[31] H. Barsoumian, 'Dual Role', pp. 177–8. See also V. Oshagan, 'Modern Armenian Literature', pp. 140–1.

teenth century.[32] Similarly the Lazarians (Lazarev), initially from New Julfa, set up a college in Moscow (where they had settled) in 1815.[33]

Despite the geographic distance between these various communities there was contact between them, and between them and Armenia. The two main agents were the merchants themselves and celibate/learned priests (*vardapets*)—the 'intellectuals' of the church who went from community to community transferring knowledge while gathering and disseminating information. Often they also collected funds for specific churches or projects.[34] To give one example, there was an intellectual 'give-and-take' between Armenia and the colonies in Poland/Ukraine, which meant that 'certain traditional literary genres flourished', contributing a great deal to the intellectual revival of Armenians.[35] Not only trade wares were exchanged between these Armenian centres, but also ideas, knowledge and information.

A final point needs to be made here. By virtue of their role as agents between different countries and cultures, Armenian merchants were also interlocutors of ideas between the East and the West as a whole. This was often reflected in their role as interpreters, as transferers of technology, bearers of European ideas in their own societies and agents of modernisation in host societies. According to Boghos Levon Zekiyan, 'Both the attitudes of eth[n]icity and of cosmopolitan openness have been a distinguishing feature of the behaviour of many Armenian merchants as a commercial group.'[36]

It is possible to give a multitude of other specific examples of the cultural role of merchants. The point, however, is obvious. In the process of establishing community life in the diaspora which acted

[32] M. Seth, *Armenians in India*, pp. 593–5.

[33] Wealthy Armenians also engaged in charitable endeavours to help the poor. Certain families in India, for example, bequeathed their wealth to religious, educational and charitable organisations with the explicit purpose of helping the poor. For some examples see M. Seth, *Armenians in India*, pp. 106, 354, 484–7, 501ff, 523ff, 551–2; K. Papazian, *Merchants from Ararat*, pp. 35, 39, 40, 51. Some even left money for Muslim sanctuaries in Mecca, and the Holy See of Rome (B. Zekiyan, *Armenian Way to Modernity*, p. 44).

[34] *Vardapets* and bishops whose main task was this were called *nvirak*s (literally meaning 'the committed', but usually translated as nuncio or legate).

[35] K. Maksoudian, 'Armenian Communities', p. 66.

[36] B. Zekiyan, *Armenian Way to Modernity*, p. 44.

as a basis of social support for themselves, Armenian merchants—consciously or subconsciously—became agents of identity maintenance. Partly out of a sense of duty, partly on the basis of belief and partly out of social and commercial necessity they funded churches, schools, publications and various intellectual endeavours that maintained their ethno-religious distinctness.[37] Therefore, diasporan communities, despite their heterogeneity, became key locations of national identity when cultural and intellectual production in the homeland was reduced to a trickle. New Julfa, India, Amsterdam, Constantinople etc. became 'Armenian' centres. It could be argued that such diasporan communities played the same role as the state did in Europe in encouraging or sponsoring the evolution of national identity. Zekiyan too appreciates this point: 'Sensitivity to culture has been…a real, if not always dominant feature of Armenian capitalism. The thick network of schools, institutions, charitable societies and other social works, functioning without any financial support from any State, would have been unthinkable without that sensitivity.'[38] But these activities were not organisationally centralised, systematised or coordinated into an overall 'plan'. Each community, and often each individual, did its or his 'own thing' for the benefit of the 'nation'. There was, however, unity in the process insofar as various people in various locations were engaging in similar activities.

Armenian printing. The most profound impact that diasporan communities had in terms of national identity and the emergence of nationalism was through the printing press. In this case the merchants' support of culture was not just limited to maintaining identity, but also led to the dissemination of new and radical ideas. This is not to say that initially there was a conscious attempt to use the printing press for national(ist) purposes. Most early publications were of a religious nature. However, various publications (religious

[37] According to Zekiyan, merchants contributed so much to culture because in terms of their mentality they were situated 'somewhere between modernity and non-modernity'—i.e. they were not yet totally free from the primacy of 'ethical values'. They did not think of wealth only in economic terms, but also in terms of social responsibility and moral duty; Christian ethics were reconciled with the intense pursuit of economic aims and profit (B. Zekiyan, *Armenian Way to Modernity*, pp. 43–4).

[38] B. Zekiyan, *Armenian Way to Modernity*, p. 46; cf. V. Oshagan, 'Modern Armenian Literature', p. 142.

or secular) made an impact on the national imagination beyond the confines of the specific community in which they were printed. Printing as a whole was both a powerful tool for identity maintenance, (re)construction and advancement, and an indication that there was already a strong sense of cultural pride which had found a new avenue of expression.

The first Armenian book was published between 1511 and 1513 (half a century after Gutenberg set up his press) in Venice, where many Armenian merchants were based, particularly from Julfa. It was a book of talismans called *Urbatagirk* (Friday Book).[39] The first Armenian printing press was established in 1565 (by Abgar Dpir of Tokat), also in Venice, where a Psalter was initially published, before the press moved to Constantinople in 1567. In 1636 Armenian printing began in New Julfa. In fact Armenians pioneered the introduction of print technology to the Ottoman and Persian empires.[40] The Bible was printed in (classical) Armenian in Amsterdam between 1666 and 1668.[41] In the same city the first Armenian map was printed in 1695 and, significantly, Movses Khorenatsi's *History of the Armenians* (which was soon translated into and published in Latin in 1736).[42] In 1685 the first Armenian vernacular book—called *Elucidation of the Psalms of David*—was published in

[39] It was published by Hakob Meghapart, who printed five other titles. This made Armenian the tenth language in which books were printed (D. Kouymjian, 'Armenia', p. 45).

[40] Some other centres of early Armenian publications include: Lulu (1616), Milan (1621), Paris (1633), Leghorn (1643), Amsterdam (1658), Leipzig (1680), Padua (1690), London (1736), Ejmiatzin (1771), St Petersburg (1781), Nor Nakhijevan (1786), Astrakhan (1796), Calcutta (1796) etc. See C. Mouradian, *L'Arménie*, p. 40; cf. P. Cowe, 'Medieval Armenian Literary', pp. 321–4; B. Zekiyan, *Armenian Way to Modernity*, pp. 32–6. For a comprehensive overview of early Armenian printing see R. Kévorkian and J.-P. Mahé, *Le livre arménien*; Teodik, *Tip u tar*; Leo, vol. III(a), pp. 427–73, vol. III(b), pp. 523–58, and most of vol. V. The latter has produced a considerable amount of work on the subject of Armenian printing which appears in some of his other publications. For a more concise and modern account see R. Ishkhanian, *Hai girke*. There is much literature on this subject in Armenian, some in French, but it remains an understudied topic in English.

[41] The Rev. Voskan Yerevantsi was assigned the task of printing the Armenian Bible under the sponsorship of Ejmiatzin. However, the expenses were paid by three New Julfa merchants in Leghorn (Leo, vol. III(a), p. 437).

[42] B. Zekiyan, *Armenian Way to Modernity*, pp. 48–9. Another history text was also published by a contemporary historian, Arakel Tavrizhetsi (Arakel of Tabriz), in 1669. Such publication were part of the wider European humanist movement and the revival of interest in the Greek and Roman antiquity.

Venice at the request of a prominent New Julfa merchant.[43] All these were important building blocks in the maintenance and advancement of Armenian identity because they gave a new (printed) basis to its culture. However, it was in India that Armenian printing took a new and decisive turn towards secular and explicitly nationalistic books and journals.

Armenian publishing in India began with the establishment of a press in Madras by a merchant called Shahamir Shahamirian (born in New Julfa) and his two sons Hakob and Yeghiazar. Between 1772 and 1783 they published eight titles, relatively poorly written and presented, but rich in ideas of national liberation. The first four titles are the most significant in this respect. Initially they published a book called *Aibbenaran* (Alphabet). It was an Armenian language text to teach the mother tongue to the younger generation. The second book had the aim of familiarising Armenians of India with their homeland. It was a geography book called *Ashkharhagrutiun Hayastani* (Geography of Armenia).[44]

The third book printed by the Shahamirians (in 1772) is their most significant publication. It was authored by Movses Baghramian, an intellectual-activist originally from the Gharabagh region.[45] The book was called *Nor Tetrak vor ge kochi Hordorak* (New Book which is called Exhortation). The exhortation was to 'awaken the Armenian youth and the young from their drowsiness and lazy sleep'[46] so that they would liberate Armenia from the yoke and slavery of foreigners (i.e. Muslims), and the prevailing lawlessness of the homeland. For the first time the idea of Armenia's national liberation was made the subject of a printed book—published, of all places, in far

[43] K. Sarafian, *History of Education*, p. 147. It is possible that a mathematics book published in Marseilles in vernacular Armenian predates the *Elucidation* by a few years.

[44] H. Irazek, *Patmutiun hndkahai tpagrutian*, pp. 53–4, cf. pp. 47–79.

[45] Baghramian had collaborated with Joseph Emin (more about him below), and accompanied Emin on some of his travels in the 1760s.

[46] As quoted in H. Irazek, *Patmutiun hndkahai tpagrutian*, p. 54; for the details of the content of the book see pp. 55–9. Seth provides a translation of the title page: 'New pamphlet, called *Exhortation*, composed for the awakening of the Armenian youth from the weak and idle drowsiness of the sleep of slothfulness, and with an ardent and tender desire printed at the expense and through the exertions of Jacob [Hakob] Shameer by his tutor Moses Bagram, for the benefit of the tender Armenian youth, in the year of the incarnation of the World 1772 and in the year 1221 of the Armenian era. In India, at the city of Madras, at the press of the said Jacob Shameer' (M. Seth, *Armenians in India*, p. 596, cf. pp. 596–8).

away Madras. 'The aim [was] clear,' says Marc Nichanian, 'today we would call it purely nationalistic.'[47] The press also published an equally remarkable book (probably in the late 1780s, but dated 1773): a compilation of laws, a proposed constitution, a plan of the army and even a suggested budget for liberated Armenia! This was indeed building castles in the air, but it does show the extent to which the Shahamirians were thinking about the liberation of their homeland and the establishment of an Armenian state. The book was called *Vorogait parats* (Snare [or Entrapment] of Glory). It was based on principles of self rule, a republican government of free citizens and liberation through the rule of law. It is obvious from its pages that contemporary European enlightenment ideas and social contract theories (viz. Locke, Montesquieu *et al.*) had found their way to Madras and were being put to use—on printed paper—in the 'liberation' of Armenia.[48] These books were the first publications that dealt explicitly with the national(ist) themes of liberation. They did not have a religious 'world view' insofar as they did not blame, as in the past, the 'sins' of the Armenians for their own subjugation and misery, but foreign domination and its despotic rule.

[47] M. Nichanian, 'Enlightenment and Historical Thought', p. 116. This was 'long-distance nationalism' *par excellence*, to use Benedict Anderson's phrase (B. Anderson, *Spectre of Comparisons*, Chapter 3).

[48] For details see H. Irazek, *Patmutiun hndkahai tpagrutian*, pp. 61–79. The discrepancy between the actual listed publication date and the real date was brought to my attention by Sebouh Aslanian, based on his research on the subject. Interestingly, in the Preface to *Snare of Glory* there is even a reference to George Washington, according to Zekiyan (*Armenian Way to Modernity*, p. 64). In Soviet Armenian publications the Madras press is characterised in terms of a 'national liberation movement', which 'exploded like a bomb'. But there was much opposition to such radical ideas in the Armenian establishment, particularly in religious circles. Catholicos Simeon Yerevantsi opposed the publication of the *Exhortation*, ordered all copies of the book to be burnt, and even excommunicated Baghramian (A. Abrahamian, *Hamarot urvagitz*, vol. I, p. 474; cf. pp. 471–4; see also Leo, vol. III(b), pp. 526ff; V. Ghougassian, 'Quest for Enlightenment', p. 253). It is also interesting to note that in July 1999 the chairman of the Armenian Constitutional Court (Gagik Harutiunian) mentions the Shahamirians' Constitution and their *Snare of Glory* as a point of reference while discussing the principle of the supremacy of the law in *today's* Armenia. It is, he says, 'essentially our first Constitution', which is 'almost in conformance with today's requirements for the protection of individual rights and freedoms…' (Interview with Gagik Arutyunyan [*sic*] in *Respublika Armeniya*, 8 July 1999, p. 2, as posted on *Groong Armenian News Network*, 29 July 1999).

Another important event in the history of Armenian printing was the publication of the first periodical, again in Madras. Between 1794 and 1796 the Rev. Harutiun Shmavonian published a journal called *Azdarar* (Monitor). The idea had come to him from the English who had embarked on a similar endeavour in India a few year earlier. *Azdarar* not only gave local news, but it also covered events in Armenia, and even had a 'correspondent' in Russia.[49] Its 'serious' pieces were written in *grabar* (classical Armenian), but the overall language of the journal (announcements etc.) was mixed with the vernacular dialect of the Armenians in India, which was based on the Julfa dialect. *Azdarar* was the precedent of Armenian journalism. Within a decade other periodicals were established in Venice (by the Mkhitarist fathers) and Constantinople. Some of these were published in modern vernacular Armenian and sought to 'bring culture nearer to the popular masses, to build standards of mass education.'[50] The first Armenian daily began publication in Smyrna in 1840.

Theoretical interlude: print capitalism

One of the pillars of Benedict Anderson's thesis on the rise of nationalism is print capitalism: the convergence between cultural production and the profit motive. Print capitalists sought to maximise their markets and in the process a mass cultural basis was created—an 'imagined community'—where everyone felt connected to other members of the same community. Anderson's argument is quite powerful and his phrase 'imagined community' is often used almost synonymously with the word 'nation'.

Armenian commercial printers in the nineteenth century did indeed pursue profit through publishing. But it should also be emphasised that not all Armenian printing—especially in the early period—was motivated thus. It was not necessarily print 'capitalism'

[49] It was published monthly for eighteen consecutive issues. See H. Irazek, *Patmutiun hndkahai tpagrutian*, pp. 444–50; V. Ghougassian, 'Quest for Enlightenment', p. 260; M. Seth, *Armenians in India*, pp. 597ff, cf. pp. 601–3 for other publications in India. According to Seth, journals published in India, with two exceptions, did not have great literary merit because they were founded and run by businessmen and not literary figures. According to one count, 200 books (mostly secular in nature, including translations) were published in Madras and Calcutta, and ten journals, by sixteen Armenian presses (V. Ghougassian, 'Quest for Enlightenment', p. 243).

[50] B. Zekiyan, *Armenian Way to Modernity*, p. 65.

in Benedict Anderson's sense.[51] Rather it was an enterprise in which capitalists engaged for 'national' and charitable purposes and sometimes as a 'Christian sacrifice' for the greater good. This was particularly true in the case of the Indian publishers, who explicitly stated that they had engaged in a money-losing enterprise for the sake of the nation. To quote them, they wanted 'to benefit the nation', 'to brighten and illuminate our nation...for the spiritual benefit of Armenians' etc.[52] This trend continued with some of the presses right up to the nineteenth and twentieth centuries. There was a conscious attempt to use the press for national purposes. For these men the printing press was the means for a greater good, rather than a profit instrument that had the unintended consequence of creating a collective national identity, as Anderson's argument suggests.[53]

However, this is only one side of the equation. Citing the example of Abgar Dpir of Tokat (operating in Venice and then Constantinople in the 1560s), Boghos Levon Zekiyan points out that many Armenian printers in Europe were 'busy in worldly affairs' as merchants or tradesmen. For them printing had 'the essential features of an economic enterprise'. It was an individual initiative (and not the monopoly of monastic institutions) that aimed to provide a product for the merchants—to 'satisfy [their] needs'—because they were 'at the same time deeply religious and even superstitious people...'[54] Hence calendars, almanacs, horoscopes, exchange rates etc. were the subjects of the early Armenian books that were printed for profit. By the nineteenth century there was a thriving commercial press, especially in Constantinople and Smyrna, which was run on 'busi-

[51] B. Anderson, *Imagined Communities*, p. 38.

[52] H. Irazek, *Patmutiun hndkahai tpagrutian*, pp. 44–5, xii–xiii. Some merchants assisted the presses, in addition to churches, in memory of their deceased ancestors.

[53] H. F. B. Lynch, the early twentieth century English traveller in Armenia, appreciated this link between publishing and the Armenians. He wrote in his 1901 book: 'Armenians prize [the printing press] with the same childish affection and reverence as the Persian highlanders value a rifle or sporting gun.' (H. F. B. Lynch, *Armenia*, vol. I, p. 240). For the Armenians, unarmed and without their own state or army, the printing press was perhaps the best self-defence against cultural obliteration.

[54] B. Zekiyan, *Armenian Way to Modernity*, pp. 35–6. In the second half of the seventeenth century the publication of books dealing with commercial activities flourished. In 1699, for example, a book printed in Amsterdam dealt with the regulations, weights, measures, tariffs, prices etc. of various countries in which Armenians traded. Around the same time there was also a 'business school' for apprentice merchants in New Julfa (P. Curtin, *Cross-cultural Trade*, pp. 192–3).

ness' principles, publishing popular novels, translations, journals and similar marketable items.

The fact that both of these trends existed in the case of the Armenians suggests that a cause and effect relationship cannot be established between capitalist profit making, printing and national consciousness—particularly at the initial stages of the printing industry. Furthermore, as will be discussed below, much of the printing with national themes was done by the Mkhitarist monastic institution for the sake of knowledge and the nation and not for profit. The motives of profit (capitalist enterprise) and strengthening national identify occasionally ran parallel, at other times one or the other took precedence.

Has Anderson put the cart before the horse? In the case of the Armenians it seems so. He is of course correct in highlighting the close connection between publishing and the emergence or dissemination of national identity, and many aspects of his rich argument are applicable to the Armenians. But before the printing press was invented there was already an explicit understanding among the Armenians that they constituted a specific ethno-religious community with a common bond. Print capitalism, and more generally the printing press itself, was an instrument that transformed (rather than created) this identity into nationality—something that was often done self-consciously by the men who operated the presses; they fully appreciated the power of the press as a tool for raising national consciousness.[55] The press became a mechanism of further national unification once a reading public emerged in the nineteenth century.

Of course before the nineteenth century the circulation of books and journals was limited. For example, the Shahamirians of Madras printed only some 100 copies of their 'nationalist' books. One can therefore assume that the immediate impact of these publications was also limited.[56] Lack of a large audience, backlash by conservative

[55] As Zekiyan affirms, the printers 'were aware enough of what was new in the social, economical and even political order in which they were acting', but, he quickly adds, such 'awareness [would] still have to go a long way before reaching the masses' (B. Zekiyan, *Armenian Way to Modernity*, p. 38).

[56] In other words, they did not 'explode like a bomb' as Soviet Armenian commentators would have liked to believe (as mentioned in note 48). Another (non-Soviet) commentator emphasises the point that such early attempts as the 'Madras program' did not develop into a sustained ideological or theoretical mode of thinking in their own time (G. Libaridian, *Ideology of Armenian Liberation*, p. 11).

elements opposed to secular-political interpretations of Armenian reality, and a dearth of resources led to the closure of many of the early presses, especially in India and Europe after the decline of the merchant communities. However, not only had a precedent been set, but the books were actually circulated in important circles—they were often sent to prominent Armenians (in Armenia and in the diaspora) and to foreign dignitaries.[57] Such publications began the accumulation of knowledge on national themes and as such had an impact on the future generation of intellectuals. Hence there was an intellectual precedent to look back to when the time came for the popularisation of the ideas of liberation in the nineteenth century through the mass printing of novels, journals, newspapers etc. In fact part of this was the writing of the history of earlier publications and the celebration of their existence.[58] In other words, the impact of early Armenian publications was felt strongly a century later, giving nationalists a pedigree of ideas of liberation and materials which could be put to use in their nationalist discourse. Their work was presented as continuation of earlier beacons of freedom.

Commerce, religion and ethnicity came together in the case of the Armenian diaspora between the seventeenth and nineteenth centuries. As a result Armenian identity was not only maintained, but strengthened, as Armenia itself was in a state of decline. This 'capital-culture marriage'[59] had a number of characteristics that had important ramifications for Armenian national identity and subsequent developments.

[57] For example, Shahamir Shahamirian not only corresponded with the prominent Armenians such as the princes of Gharabagh and church leaders, he was also in contact with the King of Georgia, Heraclius II, having sent him a copy of his *Vorogait Parats*, urging the King to use it in his rule of Georgia (and hopefully Armenia). The Shahamirians even translated their *Hordorak* into Russian in 1786 in St Petersburg and purportedly printed 2,000 copies! (V. Ghougassian, 'The Quest for Enlightenment', pp. 253, 258–9; Tz. Aghayan, *Hai zhoghovrdi azatagrakan*, p. 34).

[58] For example, both G. Galemkiarian (*Patmutiun hai lragrutian*, 1893) and Teodik (*Tip u tar*, 1912) fall in this category. Even H. Irazek (*Patmutiun hndkahai tpagrutian*), written in the 1930s but published in 1986, is a celebration of the Armenian-Indian press in terms of the antecedents of national liberation. In its Preface, Catholicos Karekin (Garegin) II (of Cilicia) writes: 'A handful of Armenians was able to live Armenia in India…, or put differently, to live life for Armenia in India….' (p. xvi).

[59] The term is borrowed from B. Zekiyan, *Armenian Way to Modernity*, p. 46.

First, however wealthy certain Armenians had become in the diaspora, they nevertheless lacked real political power in their host states and were at the mercy of non-Armenian rulers. For example, as one scholar points out, the *amiras* of Constantinople 'had a complex and vital *function* in the financial and economic administration of the Ottoman Empire, but lacked any real *power* in that sphere.'[60] They were in a precarious position. Because of their different ethnicity/religion they could not translate their economic power into political power outside the Armenian community and therefore could very easily fall out of favour with the political masters of the Ottoman empire and be persecuted, losing their wealth and status. As a consequence their influence was limited on state policy and rarely would they oppose the Sultan (or the Shah etc.) if the latter was persecuting Armenians (in the provinces or elsewhere).[61]

Second, partly because of this fear of losing their wealth and well-being if disfavoured, most—but by no means all—Armenian merchants tended to be conservative in their politics. They resisted innovation in the political sphere, for fear of 'rocking the boat', while supporting cultural development. They were, therefore, conservative in both senses of the word: on the one hand supporting the status quo and on the other conserving their identity and culture and being open to innovation in that sphere. However, as we shall see, by the end of the nineteenth century this contradiction could no longer be sustained.

The third point is that the merchant diaspora, by virtue of its trade niche and location, was subject to global economic trends and political realignments or wars. It was also reliant on the favourable policies of the host states. All of this meant that their prosperity, and even existence, depended on forces beyond their control. In favourable conditions merchants could become extremely prosperous. But when the situation became unfavourable they could decline rapidly

[60] H. Barsoumian, 'Dual Role', p. 180. The *amiras* were dependent on the good will of the pashas who sponsored them, and their fate was tied to the pasha's political position. Some were directly dependent on the Sultan and his whims. One contemporary historian put it as such: the bankers 'can reduce any Turkish governor to the condition of a private individual' in terms of finances, but they 'have no power of their own, they have not distinct influence... they are wholly deprived of all political importance' (David Urquhart, as cited in H. Barsoumian, 'Dual Role', p. 176; cf. H. Barsoumian, 'Economic Role', pp. 314–15).

[61] H. Barsoumian, 'Dual Role', pp. 179, 181.

and disappear as a community, either through assimilation (if deep roots had been established in the host society) or expulsion (if such roots were weak). This happened to almost all of the significant diasporan centres in India and Europe (except Constantinople and the special case of the Mkhitarians who were not merchants).

Fourth, despite their eventual decline, the merchants (along with the church) were instrumental in maintaining a link between the various diasporan communities, no matter how far flung, and between the diaspora as a whole and the homeland. The catalyst for these links was trade, but the product was cultural exchange and subjective connections with one another. Songs of exile had become popular forms of cultural expression in these centuries.[62]

Fifth, another by-product of merchant activity was the urbanisation of the Armenian elite, and later of the middle classes. Because of the merchants Constantinople, Venice, Tiflis etc. became the centres of the national elite. This meant that modern Armenian culture developed as a mostly urban phenomenon in cities outside Armenia proper.[63] It was the culture of a 'mobilised diaspora', to use the phrase of John Armstrong,[64] residing in major (imperial) cities.

Consequently, and as the sixth factor, modern Armenian (political) thinking and identity were heavily influenced by a variety of host cultures namely the French, Italian, German and Russian and to a lesser degree the English (in India). In fact Armenian intellectuals had a 'xenophilia' towards the West.[65] Hence Armenians became agents of western ideas, technology and language in their own traditional communities of the homeland, and the wider society of Muslims. This westernisation was not uniform in its content. That is to say, different ideas were picked up from different host countries, which were then synthesised with the Armenian experience, sometimes in a contradictory manner.

And seventh, as emphasised earlier, merchants were the financiers of culture, church, printing and intellectuals. Ironically it was the

[62] For example, Leo, vol. III(a), p. 383, quotes the most famous of these songs, still sung today, called *Krunk* (Crane, as in the migratory bird found in Armenia): '...Crane, don't you have any news from our world?' This quintessentially Armenian song is all about longing for home and loved ones, while being stranded in foreign lands.

[63] V. Oshagan, 'Modern Armenian Literature', p. 142.

[64] J. Armstrong, 'Mobilized and Proletarian Diasporas'; cf. J. Armstrong, *Nations Before Nationalism*, p. 209.

[65] V. Oshagan, 'Modern Armenian Literature', p. 142.

amiras who financed the education of bright students who went to Europe on scholarships in the 1840s. These students became the fiercest critics of the conservatives since they came back full of revolutionary ideas and set to work to transform Armenian traditional structures, and to radicalise the masses—much to the detriment of the *amiras*![66]

Before moving on to the next section one final point needs to be made. I have concentrated on the merchants' role in the maintenance and advancement of Armenian identity. However, it should not be assumed that all merchants or all diasporan communities made such a contribution. Many simply did not care, while others who cherished the culture did not want anything to do with the political aspect of liberating Armenia.[67] As Gerard Libaridian rightly points out, 'The merchant class displayed no more than a passing involvement in these schemes for liberation.'[68] Numerous Armenians (merchant or otherwise) did assimilate, converted to Catholicism or Islam, either willingly or forcefully. It is impossible to say how much of the community was 'lost' through such means. In no way do I want to imply that there has been a universal desire to maintain a distinct identity (or to contribute to the emancipation of Armenia). Obviously what I concentrate on is the element that survived, and consciously so, becoming the basis of the Armenian nation

[66] Some of the above points will be elaborated further in the section on the national awakening below.

[67] The most telling example of this is recounted by Joseph Emin (see below). Writing in the 1790s, he recounts an experience he had had earlier in Moscow with the wealthy Lazar(ev) merchant family who typified 'the stinginess of Armenians' when it came to supporting the cause of national liberation:

> If the Armenian merchants had half the attachment to liberty that they have to money and to superstitions [that Armenia could not be free],... they would have been made free long ago.... They actually do not know what liberty is; could they once but taste the sweetness of it, and drive old women's stories out of their good hearts, they would certainly be a great nation. It has been Emin's [i.e. the author referring to himself] darling ambition only to tear off that obscure curtain from before their eyes, which motive forced [*sic*] him to go through such a multitude of toils (J. Emin, *Life and Adventures*, pp. 197, 198).

It is interesting to observe that two centuries later a similar dynamic continues in the Armenian diaspora with some latter day 'merchants' who are very willing to fund a church or a school, but would not contribute a penny to anything that might be politically controversial.

[68] G. Libaridian, *Ideology of Armenian Liberation*, p. 9.

as we know it today. The element that did disappear, the silences, would be the topic of another book in itself.

PREPARING THE GROUNDWORK, II: THE MKHITARIST BROTHERHOOD

The most influential intellectuals who directly contributed to the creation of modern Armenian national identity were, remarkably, the *Catholic* monks organised in the Mkhitarist monastic order based in Venice (and later partly in Vienna). It is not surprising to find clergy at the forefront of national consciousness. What is surprising in this case is that, first, the clergy were Catholic despite the fact that Armenian identity was based on the Apostolic 'national' church and second, the Mkhitarists' ethno-religious work paved the way for the secular ideology of nationalism, which consequently did not have the strong anti-clerical component usually associated with it.

The founder of the order, Mkhitar, was born in Sebastia/Sivas (Armenia) in 1676. At an early age he decided to become a monk, but found no intellectual satisfaction in the inadequate teachings of the Armenian church around him, or in Ejmiatzin. He travelled around Asia Minor, coming into contact with Catholic missionaries in Syria in 1695. He eventually moved to Constantinople to start a monastic order. He was already a *vardapet* in the Armenian church, but did not get enough support and encouragement to establish a monastic order within it. In 1701 he did formally establish such an order, but within the Catholic church, having converted to that faith.[69] He and his ten or so followers were soon chased out of the capital by the Armenian patriarch and his conservative supporters. Mkhitar established a monastery at Modon in Morea (Greece), then under the jurisdiction of Venice. But he had to abandon that site in 1715 owing to the Ottoman re-invasion of the territory. In 1717 he and his followers were finally granted the island of San Lazzaro in

[69] Papal recognition was granted to the order in 1712. The information in this section is based on Leo, vol. III(b), pp. 482ff. Just about every item of literature on Armenian modern history, identity, historiography or printing mentions the Mkhitarists. For a brief overview of Mkhitar and the Mkhitarists in English see K. Bardakjian, *Mekhitarist Contributions*.

Venice by the Senate, where they established their order permanently—it exists to this day. Mkhitar died on San Lazzaro in 1749. The order, named after him, is called Mkhitarist or Mkhitarian.

Mkhitar became a Catholic partly because of Rome's active proselytisation campaign in the Ottoman empire and partly because of his desire for learning, which he could not obtain in the morbid and conservative atmosphere of the Armenian church. But he rejected the excessive Latinisation practices advocated by other Catholic converts and preachers. Until the end of his life Mkhitar, and subsequently his followers, remained both 'good Catholics' and 'good Armenians'. In the Preface of his book on St Matthew's Gospel Mkhitar writes: 'I do not sacrifice neither my nation for my confession nor my confession for my nation.'[70] There was no contradiction in this as far as the Mkhitarists were concerned. Their order was exclusively for Armenians, but their teachings were for the Catholic church. Hence Mkhitarists were active in both fields. They sent priests to Armenia to convert the inhabitants to Catholicism, they engaged in fierce (and acrimonious) debates against the Apostolic church, and they published volume upon volume of religious texts. This was one side of their work. I will concentrate on the other—national—side of their activities, for which they are revered and remembered because of their impact.

It would not be an exaggeration to say that on the terrain of intellectual work the Mkhitarists played the most crucial role in the 'national awakening' of the Armenians. Quite simply, they retrieved and researched Armenian history, literature, geography and language, and presented it to their contemporary world through their publications. Aware of and in conjunction with the intellectual currents of European thought they were very consciously and systematically carrying out an enlightenment project on behalf of the nation. Its motivating force and style were European (and more particularly Catholic ideology), but its content was Armenian.[71] The conse-

[70] As cited by B. Zekiyan, *Armenian Way to Modernity*, p. 55. V. Oshagan ('Modern Armenian Literature', p. 144) adds: 'Mekhitar achieved his triple goal of preparing Catholic priests of deep religious devotion, accomplished scholars and highly motivated patriots.' For the details of early Catholic activities and propaganda in Armenia see Leo, vol. III(a), pp. 316–48.

[71] Mkhitarists of course interpreted the wider European Enlightenment project in a selective manner, which was in congruence with their religious/Catholic world view.

quence was the modern intellectual foundation of national identity and consciousness.

In this respect the first phase of their work entailed gathering scattered manuscripts from all over Armenia. As Leo puts it,

> Members [of the order] were wandering around various parts of Armenia to save souls, but more than souls, they were saving from destruction the fruits of ancient Armenian thinking, past literature in manuscript form, scattered in monasteries, churches, and private homes. Like bees, the Mkhitarian fathers were gathering these precious items of national culture, and with care taking them to Italy... and preserving them.[72]

But the Mkhitarian monks not only preserved these documents in their libraries, they also studied them, published some of them, and translated a few others into European languages. In all cases they were used as the primary basis of further research on Armenia and Armenians.

There were two main avenues through which this work was done in the order. The first was in the field of linguistics which Mkhitar himself pioneered. In 1727 he published a grammar book for vernacular Armenian (called *Grammar in Armeno-Turkish*) and in 1730 a more substantial and authoritative grammar of classical Armenian—the first such book. The crowning moment of his efforts was the publication in 1749 (three weeks after his death) of Volume I of the first comprehensive dictionary of the Armenian language. Mkhitar had worked on this for over twenty years and eventually put together a 'definitive' dictionary after much research on the true or original meanings of the words (Volume II was published in 1769). Through his dictionary of classical Armenian, he established the foundations of the Armenian language as a modern and standardised literary medium, expunging from it foreign words and regional variations. This work was continued by his disciples who completed and perfected the project in the next fifty years, giving the modern Armenian vernacular (of the west) a standardised basis rooted in classical Armenian. Mkhitarists also published other linguistic texts (and textbooks), both in classical Armenian

---

They objected to the secularisation inherent in the Enlightenment, and the more radical ideas that questioned the authority and legitimacy of the church.

[72] Leo, vol. III(b), p. 502.

and, very importantly, in the vernacular, firmly establishing the latter as a literary language.[73] In short, Mkhitarists were instrumental in the formation of the linguistic basis of modern Armenian identity.[74]

The second field in which Mkhitarists played an extremely significant role was in historiography. The towering figure in this endeavour was Father Mikayel Chamchian (1738–1823). In addition to many studies on religious themes and the publication of an Armenian grammar textbook in 1779, Chamchian wrote a three volume *History of the Armenians* (published 1784–6). This became the definitive Armenian history text in this formative period of mass national identity. Not since Movses Khorenatsi (fifth/eighth century) was there such a comprehensive and systematic treatment of Armenian history in its entirety. Chamchian's book remained the most authoritative source on the subject until the end of the nineteenth century. It was significant on two grounds. First, it was extremely well researched, using all the available sources (manuscripts) of the time, both in Armenian and in European languages. This was the 'scientific' side of the work. Second, on its 'theological' side, Chamchian's work was heavily influenced by Catholic themes as they applied to the Armenians. Once again Armenians were situated at

[73] For example, Father Arsen Aydenian (1824–1902) published in 1866 a seminal work called *Critical Grammar of Ashkharhabar* [i.e. vernacular] *Modern Armenian Language.* This, according to V. Oshagan ('Modern Armenian Literature', p. 157), 'is considered an epoch-making achievement in the study of the Armenian language, its dialects, and its periods. His work has contributed perhaps more than any other [Mkhitarist] work to the establishment of the *ashkharhabar* as the literary language of modern times.'

[74] Mkhitar's linguistic work was in the context of the wider European movement of similar research and publication, starting in the middle of the sixteenth century with Latin, and then Greek, French etc. dictionaries. The publication of the Armenian dictionary preceded that of the English and the German. In the 1745 Preface to the dictionary Mkhitar explains the need for the dictionary in terms of the importance for 'people to use their language in a uniform way when they speak and write. Otherwise, everything blends together and decomposes as we can witness it in our vulgar language [i.e. the vernacular]. Because it is so irregular and without guide, the vulgar language is torn and scattered into as many pieces as there are regions, or even cities and villages. This language is sometimes so decomposed that people seem to speak another language and not Armenian. They speak a barbarian dialect...' (as quoted by M. Nichanian, 'Enlightenment and Historical Thought', p. 120). Mkhitar wanted a uniform classical Armenian to be the foundation of language. For further details see Leo, vol. III(b), pp. 506–9; K. Sarafian, *History of Education*, pp. 146–7.

the centre of Christian civilisation and at the very centre of humanity. The argument went as follows: According to the Bible the Garden of Eden was in Armenia, therefore Adam must have spoken Armenian, and since Adam spoke to God, Jehovah too must have spoken Armenian! Noah (who died in Armenia after the ark landed on Mount Ararat) and his offspring spoke in Armenian too. This Armenian language, spoken by Adam and Noah in Armenia, still exists; it 'did not mix, it did not disappear, and it did not change, and it is the same [language] that currently exists in Armenia'.[75] This made the Armenians the chosen people, the inhabitants of the sacred land of Eden, and speakers of the sacred language, which was also the original language of humanity (all others being derivatives of it). Chamchian was thus 'robbing the myths of the Jewish nation' and bestowing the honour of being the 'real' chosen people on the Armenians.[76]

Despite these religious excesses, which many intellectuals either disregarded or toned down, Chamchian's work was a crucial contribution to national identity formation. Both its research and its conception emphasised that Armenians had a continuous existence and a history to be proud of. Perhaps God did not speak Armenian, but Armenians were the first 'nation' to embrace His word, to fight and die for His Truth and for their nation, to have victorious kings and martyred saints...In short, historiography was 'picked up'—with the

[75] M. Chamchiants, *Patmutiun hayots*, vol. I, pp. 153–4, 143, 57.

[76] Leo, vol. III(b), pp. 517, 519, cf. pp. 513–21. This 'naïve' religious side of Chamchian is usually not dwelt upon by later historians who emphasise the research/secular side of his work. But Leo, having to write/publish in the Soviet context of Armenia in the 1920s, highlights these religious components so that he could dismiss them. Leo's approach is quite telling. He critiques the religious elements, and the excessive nationalistic tones, only to praise in the very next paragraph the contribution Chamchian, or Mkhitar, made to Armenian national identity formation. For example, he sarcastically criticises Chamchian for asserting that Armenians are a 'chosen people' and therefore 'fetishising' the idea of nation (p. 518), and yet heralding the publication of his *History* as the beginning of patriotism (or 'love of nation', *azgasirutiun*) which had a 'huge impact on our intellectual advancement' (p. 519). In 1985 the Yerevan State University republished Chamchian's *History* on the occasion of the 200th anniversary of the original publication. Despite its 'serious shortcoming' as an 'idealistic historical outlook' which approaches history from the perspective of the 'exploiting classes', Chamchian's work, according to the editorial committee, was considered of 'undeniable value for those studying Armenian history' (pp. vii–viii of the Introduction in volume I). For a critical assessment of Chamchian (and his relationship to Khorenatsi) see M. Nichanian, 'Enlightenment and Historical Thought', pp. 101ff.

'assistance' of various other intermediate historians—where Movses Khorenatsi had left off a millennium or so earlier, updated and modernised.[77] In fact, according to one scholar, 'Chamchian's *History* is a *national* one. He wanted to write the history of a nation (*azg*), the history of the greatness and decline of a nation.'[78] And he did. Importantly, Chamchian affirmed the belief that Armenians are the natives of their land, the original people who lived there and spoke the original language of humanity. The roots of this theme, of being autochthonous to the land, which is constantly emphasised by current nationalists, lie in Chamchian's *History*.

Chamchian's work was complemented by numerous other Mkhitarist scholars who wrote on different aspects of history, literature and linguistics and translated into Armenian the classics, and current European philosophical, theological and even scientific texts. Among the next generation of scholars Father Ghevond Alishan stands out (1820–1901). He wrote masterly studies of the geography and nature of Armenia (without ever setting foot in the country). From 1843 onward the Mkhitarist order also published influential journals/periodicals on Armenian subjects in the vernacular.

In addition to their multitude of research projects and publications the Mkhitarists opened and administered their own schools outside the monastery (although this was not their primary aim). Some were preparatory schools in Europe or the Ottoman empire. The most famous is the Murad-Raphaelian college in Venice. Funded by Armenian merchants from India, its roots date to the 1830s; it remained operational until very recently. A number of students who studied there became prominent intellectuals of the late nineteenth and early twentieth centuries.[79]

Leo believes that the period between the 1720s and 1840s should be called 'Mkhitar's century' because his monastic order became the leading centre of learning and intellectual development in the Armenian world.[80] In this period the Mkhitarist monk-intellectuals were

[77] For example, whereas Khorenatsi had provided genealogies to situate the story of the battle of Haik and Bel (the 'founding myth' of the nation) in Armenian history, Chamchian gave an exact date: 2492 BC. Similarly it is Chamchian who calculated the traditionally accepted date of AD 301 for Armenia's acceptance of Christianity.

[78] M. Nichanian, 'Enlightenment and Historical Thought', p. 90.

[79] By the First World War, Mkhitarians had opened 28 schools, according to V. Oshagan, 'Modern Armenian Literature', p. 158; cf. K. Sarafian, *History of Education*, pp. 150–4.

[80] Leo, vol. III(b), p. 495.

researching Armenian history, language and culture, writing about their findings, and most importantly *disseminating* their knowledge and information through their very own printing presses (and later schools).[81] For the first time a much wider group of people (intellectuals beyond the narrow confines of manuscript libraries) was exposed to national ideas. As one historian puts it, this 'encouraged the development of a consciousness of national ideals and a general desire for a re-awakening.'[82]

The whole Mkhitarian endeavour was obviously not a profit-making enterprise, but work for the sake of enlightening the nation and advancing religious education—although it seemed the latter had taken a back seat by the beginning of the nineteenth century. It should be noted that a good part of the funding of the Mkhitarist order, particularly its publication projects and schools, came from wealthy Armenian merchants (especially from India).

Mkhitarists did not create or invent the Armenian nation, but retrieved it—and in the process helped to reshape it for the modern period. By reprinting the generally inaccessible works of the early medieval Armenian historians, and writing their own histories based on them, these Catholic monks produced works which 'did nothing less than *lay the foundation for the emergence of secular Armenian nationalism*.' Subsequent writers 'constantly circled back to the themes that had their origin in the classical Armenian texts', which the Mkhitarist had made available and contributed to.[83]

What is particularly interesting here is the fact that a Catholic religious order is responsible for the rise of *secular* nationalism. One line of argument to explain this curious contradiction is that the Mkhitarists were apolitical patriots, unaware of the political consequences of their work. In the age of secular nationalism they had no

[81] The Mkhitarists had two presses: in Venice and in Trieste (the latter had relocated to Vienna by 1811). The second press belonged to a group of dissenters who had split from the main order in the mid-1770s, moved to Trieste in 1775, and then to Vienna in 1811. Both groups pursued similar goals and the division between them was over administrative matters. By the second half of the nineteenth century an informal intellectual division of labour had taken place: the group in Vienna specialised in linguistic scholarship, while Venice was more devoted to history and literature. The two Mkhitarist congregations formally united in 2000, with Venice as the headquarters.

[82] K. Sarafian, *History of Education*, pp. 145–6; Sarafian adds, Mkhitarian publications were seen as the 'intellectual food' for many growing up in the nineteenth century (p. 149).

[83] R. Suny, *Looking toward Ararat*, p. 6 (emphasis added), cf. pp. 56–7.

control over the ideological use of their printed texts. There is some truth in this, especially as far as the eighteenth century is concerned. But a second line of argument provides a deeper analysis. It is important to note that the Mkhitarists themselves, because they were Catholics, consciously separated national identity (the basis of nationalism) from religion. They wanted to be Armenian without being part of the 'national' Apostolic church. Leo picks up this point when he writes:

> Mkhitar was the first to declare with a loud voice and openly that by religion he was a devoted Catholic, and by nationality a devoted Armenian, and that it is possible to be a good Catholic and a good Armenian, and that nationality is not dependent on religion, and that he can love both the Roman church and the Armenian nation. This principle puts Mkhitar in the category of great men not understood by their times.[84]

The publications, schools and teachings of the Mkhitarists thus contributed to this division between church/religion and nation.

Importantly, this separation was not based on an inherent antagonism toward the church. Partly because the impetus of the divide came from a religious source, and partly because the Armenian church was such a unique focal point of ethnic identity, subsequent Armenian secular nationalism did not go through a sustained anti-church/religion backlash of any significance. Hence on the one hand nationalism could emerge as a secular idea, while on the other the church could remain as a pillar of identity—partly thanks to Mkhitar. After all, according to Zekiyan (himself a product of the Mkhitarist establishment), the founder of the order, while a devout Catholic, was also devoted to the 'ideal of national unity'.[85]

[84] Leo, vol. III(b), p. 496.

[85] B. Zekiyan, *Armenian Way to Modernity*, p. 55. Projecting backwards, he adds, Mkhitar was the 'heir of that national ideology that we find already clearly formulated by the father of Armenian historiography, Movses Khorenatsi' (p. 55). A propos, Zekiyan interprets Mkhitarists' contribution to the secularisation of Armenian identity in terms of their full immersion in the humanist tradition (p. 52). Vahé Oshagan gives a similar interpretation. He points out that Mkhitarists were concerned with two themes: 'One was the national ethos—the unending struggle for national liberation, the heroic and glorious past of Armenia, the beauty of the motherland, the mythic figure of Haik the ancestor, and the virtues of Haikanush, his wife. The other was the general aesthetic issues of classicism...' (V. Oshagan, 'Modern Armenian Literature', p. 153).

Much like his contemporary merchants Mkhitar was a bridge between the East (his people and his homeland) and the West (his religion and final home). His followers continued this tradition and became key agents in the dissemination of many European ideas and approaches (particularly in cultural, historical, linguistic and of course religious matters) into Armenian thinking, especially in Ottoman Armenia. Mkhitarists, however, were not only trading in intellectual products, but also creating them. They were instrumental in retrieving Armenia's 'golden age'[86] and putting it in the service of nationalism. In fact by the early nineteenth century Mkhitarists were even publishing books that consciously promoted the idea of the love of nation. In a 1815 tome called *Azgaser, char asatsial* (A Discourse Called Love of Nation), they wrote:

> Love has order; man must first love his parents [and] close relations, then distant relations. And as he owes it first of all and utmost to love his parents, from that it comes to him the duty to love foremost his nation or fatherland, because his grandparents are his nation.[87]

The book then goes on to argue that this is a natural and normal condition and provides proof for the assertion by citing examples from other nations. It is crucial to note that the word 'nation' is used in this volume in the modern (European) sense of the word, denoting a distinct cultural community and not just a familial or religious community.

PREPARING THE GROUNDWORK, III: EARLY ATTEMPTS AT LIBERATION AND RUSSIAN RULE

The last two major factors that prepared the groundwork for the Armenian 'national awakening' in the nineteenth century were the precedent of previous attempts at liberation by Armenians and the expansion of the Russian empire into eastern Armenia. The first was an important factor on the ideological level, the second on the structural-social level. Both prepared the terrain for the politics of nationalism in the late nineteenth century. In the next few pages it

[86] For a discussion of the importance of the 'golden age' in nationalist discourse see A. Smith, 'Golden Age'. As he puts it, 'The greater, the more glorious that antiquity appears, the easier it becomes to mobilize people around a common culture' (p. 39).

[87] *Azgaser*, p. 11. This rare book was brought to my attention by Sebouh Aslanian.

is therefore necessary to shift the focus from intellectual developments in diasporan centres to political-military activity in Armenia.

The precedent of rebellion

The idea of liberating Armenia from Muslim rule was not merely a diasporan intellectual endeavour. The impetus for liberation also came from 'the ground'. Rebellion, or plans for rebellion, failed to achieve their goal, but they did enter Armenian consciousness as important precedents of national liberation attempts—as examples to be emulated by the nineteenth century revolutionary movement. It should be noted that these early endeavours took place *before* the 'age of nationalism' had reached Armenia itself, but they nevertheless had an explicit agenda of liberation. All of the attempts were based in eastern (i.e. Persian) Armenia and relied upon the (usually naively) expected support of foreign powers. Hence wider geopolitical dynamics of the region—particularly between the Persian, Russian and Ottoman empires—were an important dimension of Armenian calculations. In the eighteenth century these three empires clashed over Armenia and Georgia a number of times, vying for control of the South Caucasus.

Initial attempts. The first plan (after the classical period) to free Armenia was initiated by the Catholicos of Ejmiatzin (then under Persian rule), Stepanos Salmastetsi, who invited certain bishops and lay notables to a secret meeting in 1547 to discuss the possibility. It was decided that a delegation headed by the Catholicos should go to Rome to request the Pope's assistance. Stepanos reached Rome in 1550, met the Pope, then went to Vienna to meet the Emperor Charles V, then to Lwow to have an audience with the Polish King Sigismund II. All along the delegation relied on Armenian communities in Europe for assistance and support. Nothing tangible came out of the mission. European powers were not terribly interested in getting involved in such a far flung area. One thing did become clear, that any potential western involvement was preconditioned on the Armenian church accepting the supremacy of the Pope and unity with the Catholic church.[88]

[88] Supposedly Stepanos had accepted union with the Catholic Church so that Rome would take action on behalf of Armenia. But such unity was never accepted by the

Another secret meeting was held by the next Catholicos, Mikayel of Sebastia, in 1562. This time Abgar Dpir of Tokat, a layman, was sent to Europe for the same reason of soliciting support for Armenian emancipation from Muslim rule. Again, nothing came out of the attempt, except for the fact that Abgar, as mentioned earlier, set up the first Armenian printing press in Venice. Catholicos Azaria Jughayetsi initiated another such mission in 1585, as did Catholicos Hakob IV Jughayetsi in 1677/8. All of these attempts were initiated by the church leadership and supported by lay leaders (in the 1677/8 secret meeting there were six clerics and six lay leaders). All were aimed at convincing Europe to intervene on behalf of the Armenians for the sake of protecting Christians in a Muslim environment.[89] As we shall see, this reliance on foreign powers was ingrained in subsequent Armenian political thinking.

Israel Ori. The secret council of 1678 was the impetus for the remarkable diplomatic activities of one individual, Israel Ori, who was not a clergyman. If the church—specifically Ejmiatzin—was one locus of the liberation 'movement', the other was the lay leadership of the mountainous parts of eastern Armenia, namely in Gharabagh and Zangezur. These impregnable regions were ruled by a number of Armenian principalities led by local chieftains called *meliks.* Even under Mongol, Turkic and Persian rule *meliks* and their families ruled their mountain domains as autonomous regions. They were the last remnants of the Armenian aristocracy, isolated pockets of nobility that still had a role as secular leaders in their domains. Israel Ori, son of a *melik*, was from one of these families in Zangezur.

Born in 1659, Ori spent most of his life seeking the support of European powers to militarily liberate eastern Armenia from Persian domination and to create an independent state. He started off

---

majority of the Armenian church leaders, and no changes were made to church doctrine, structure or liturgy (D. Kouymjian, 'Armenia', p. 31).

89 D. Kouymjian, 'Armenia', pp. 31–2; G. Bournoutian, 'Eastern Armenia', pp. 85–6; L. Nalbandian, *Armenian Revolutionary Movement*, p. 21 (cf. pp. 18–24 for a concise account of 'movements for independence' between the fifteenth and nineteenth centuries). G. Libaridian (*Ideology of Armenian Liberation*, pp. 16ff.) labels these attempts by church leaders as 'clerical diplomacy'. According to him, they were based on a residue of 'medieval, crusader mentality' and on a moral view of history and politics which would ensure 'a dominant position' for the church (pp. 19–20).

his attempts as a member of the 1678 delegation of Catholicos Hakob IV. When the Catholicos died on the way to Europe and the delegation disbanded Ori continued his journey as a one-man mission. He arrived in Venice, then went to France and joined the army of Louis XIV for a few years. He was promoted to the rank of major, fought the English, was captured and then released. He then went to Prussia and became a merchant. He married and then entered the service of Prince Johann Wilhelm of the Palatinate. He offered Wilhelm the crown of an independent Armenia if the prince would accept his plan to liberate Armenia. In 1699 Ori returned to Armenia with letters of support from Wilhelm. Some of the *meliks* lent their support to Ori, who then returned to Prussia. Wilhelm suggested that Ori see Emperor Leopold in Vienna for further support. Leopold was favourable to Ori, but pointed out that it was essential for Russia to agree to the plan if Armenia's liberation were to succeed. Ori then proceeded to Russia and in 1701 met Peter the Great, outlining his plan to the Tsar. Peter sent a delegation to Ejmiatzin regarding a proposed Russian expedition against the Ottoman and Persian empires. But at that point Russia was busy with the Swedish war. Ori went back to Europe, only to return to Russia in 1704 to enter the service of Peter. In 1708 he was sent to Persia as a special envoy of the Tsar to assess the situation and to solicit local Armenian aid for Russian conquest. Ori died in Astrakhan in 1711 on his way back to St Petersburg. His mission had failed and ended with his death.[90] But he entered Armenian history as the indefatigable individual who wandered around the world with a vision and plan to liberate Armenia. Again, in his travels Ori could rely on Armenian communities scattered throughout Europe for assistance.

Davit Bek. In the 1720s Armenian rebellion went beyond the planning stages and developed into a well-organised and sustained military movement. The main protagonist was Davit Bek, a general in the service of the Georgian king. In 1722 he led a force to Persian Armenia at the request of the *melik*s to support their fight against unruly Turkic and Persian lords who were harassing their domains. But soon the dynamics of the region changed when the Ottoman

[90] For further detail see G. Bournoutian, 'Eastern Armenia', pp. 86–7; G. Libaridian, *Ideology of Armenian Liberation*, pp. 34–6.

empire, alarmed by Russian advances towards the South Caucasus, and capitalising on the internal turmoil of Persia, breached its 1639 agreement[91] with the latter by attacking Armenia and Georgia. Davit Bek, having succeeded in defeating the local Muslim tribesmen, continued to unite the squabbling and usually divided *meliks* who now turned against the Ottoman armies. The Armenian forces waged a guerrilla war on the invaders upon whom they managed to inflict heavy losses. Davit Bek and his followers could not prevent Ottoman occupation of Yerevan and large parts of eastern Armenia, but they did manage to successfully defend the autonomous mountain principalities of the *meliks*, now in alliance with the Persians, while anticipating the arrival of the Russian army to assist them.

This was the last major political-military activity of the *meliks* as independent actors on the Armenian scene. With the end of the rebellion *meliks* ceased to be important regional forces. Many migrated to Georgia and were fused with the latter's aristocracy or joined the Russian military service. The arrival of Russian administration a century later further eroded their autonomy as local rulers. Thus the last remnants of the Armenian aristocracy withered away as a socio-political and military factor.

Davit Bek's rebellion was in the context of the Russian advance in the South Caucasus and the weakening of Persian central authority. It sought to capitalise on these two developments to liberate eastern Armenia (along the general parameters of Israel Ori's vision). But Peter the Great was more interested in gaining a foothold on the shores of the Caspian than in engaging in a war with the Ottoman empire for the sake of the Armenians and the Georgians. Hence the promised—or at least expected—Russian help did not arrive. In fact Russia and the Ottoman state signed an agreement in 1724 dividing the South Caucasus between them, which left Armenia and part of Georgia under Ottoman jurisdiction. Nevertheless, the

[91] After decades of war over Armenia and Georgia the Ottomans and the Persians had signed an agreement in 1639 that delineated the boundary between the two empires. This agreement divided Armenia between the eastern (Persian) and western (Ottoman) sectors. Subsequent boundary changes between Iran and Russia (1828 and earlier) did not affect the Ottoman boundary too much (until the 1870s). This division was similar to the imperial divisions of Armenia centuries earlier (with the Romans, Byzantines, Persians etc.). The main division within the Armenian nation in terms of language (dialect) and culture (which will be discussed below) emanates to some extent from the eastern-western split formalised in 1639.

mountainous territories held by Davit Bek and the *meliks* (Gharabagh and Zangezur) were never fully subjugated. This Russo-Ottoman arrangement did not last too long since after Peter's death in 1725 Russia, faced with the huge costs of maintaining the new frontier, lost interest in the region and eventually withdrew. The Persians on the other hand reinstated their authority under Nadir Shah, and in 1736 the Ottomans were pushed back to the 1639 borders. Davit Bek had died sometime between 1726 and 1728, but the *meliks* were again granted autonomy by the new Shah, and their domains were left in peace.[92]

The rebellion of the 1720s did not change much for the Armenians. But, like Vardan Mamikonian of the Battle of Avarayr in 451 AD, Davit Bek and his associates (particularly Mkhitar Sparapet) entered Armenian consciousness as heroic leaders who successfully fought the Ottoman armies. Even during the rebellion Davit Bek's reputation had spread far and wide. Hundreds of Armenians in Crimea and in Poland had volunteered to join his forces of liberation. In the nineteenth century Davit Bek and his struggle became the subject of patriotic stories and novels (most famously by the novelist Raffi), as well as of an opera written by Armen Tigranian in the 1940s in Soviet Armenia. Davit Bek's example is still considered relevant today in the struggle for Gharabagh. Moreover, some contemporary historians argue that his war was much more than a self-defensive struggle, but a fine example of national liberation. One nationalist academic from Armenia writes:

> The Armenian liberation attempt of the 1720s, although it had many elements of self-defence,... had been planned decades before and therefore affords a unique case of rebellion whose original aim was—as stressed at the clandestine meeting of the Vaspurakan Armenians in September 1722 where there was a broad representation of the population— '*the liberation of all of blood-drenched Armenia.*'[93]

[92] For further detail see G. Bournoutian, 'Eastern Armenia', pp. 88–9; K. Maksoudian, 'Armenian Communities', pp. 60, 68; G. Libaridian, *Ideology of Armenian Liberation*, pp. 36–41.

[93] A. Aivazian, *Armenian Rebellion*, pp. 48–9 (emphasis in the original). The roots of this interpretation go to the Soviet period. Soviet publications presented Davit Bek's struggle as a national liberation movement, but with a class component added, and the Russian role overemphasised (see, for example, *Haikakan sovetakan hanragitaran* [Soviet Armenian Encyclopaedia], vol. III, pp. 302–3). The *Davit Bek* opera was part

Joseph Emin. The last significant individual in this period who tried to rally both Armenians and Europeans to liberate Armenia was Joseph Emin (1726–1809). Emin's life is just as remarkable as that of Israel Ori. In general his vision was similar to Ori's, as were his mistakes and assumptions.[94] Emin too wanted to establish an independent kingdom of Armenia in alliance with Georgia and under Russian protection. However, one important difference between them was that Emin was not a native of Armenia, but came from Calcutta, where his family had settled (he was born in Iran). But like Ori he travelled and acted in—or on behalf of—Armenia. As a diasporan he not only envisioned a free Armenia but tried to actualise it. Moreover, Emin wrote an autobiography (in English and published in London in 1792) in which he outlined his activities and his beliefs. As he puts it, writing about himself in the third person, 'His ambition has always been to see his countrymen free, which he hopes to be the wish of every honest man.'[95]

Emin's travels took him to England where he befriended Lord Northumberland and other aristocrats. He convinced them to support his attempts to liberate Armenia and throughout his endeavours some of his 'English friends' did assist him. But first he learned the 'art of war' in the British and Prussian armies (fighting against the French). After ten years in England (London) he left for (Ottoman) Armenia for the first time, but within a year returned. In 1761 he left London again and went to Russia to solicit assistance for his plans from the court there. He then travelled to the Caucasus and tried to get the Georgian king Erekle II to join his plans to create a common front against Turks and other Muslims who had reduced Armenians and other Christians to 'slavery'.[96] Emin spent eight years

---

of the regular repertoire of the Armenian SSR opera company, and a film with the same title was made in 1944 by Hamo Beknazarian, the 'father' of Soviet Armenian cinematography.

[94] It is clear from his autobiography that Emin knew of Ori's attempts two generations earlier. In a speech to the Russians he (unjustly) attributes Ori's failure to the latter's lack of courage to take command of armed forces which, supposedly, Peter the Great had so magnanimously been willing to put under Ori's command (J. Emin, *Life and Adventures*, pp. 189–90).

[95] J. Emin, *Life and Adventures*, p. 270. The next paragraph is based on Emin's book.

[96] J. Emin, *Life and Adventures*, pp. 133–61, 174–5, 190–2, 206ff., 158.

in the Caucasus region, in Ottoman and Persian Armenia, getting involved in various schemes and adventures, relying on not much more than his powers of persuasion, his inflated reputation based on conduct and oft-mentioned contacts with European courts. As he travelled he tried to preach liberation to Armenians[97]—to conscientise them (to use a modern term)—but he did not succeed in gaining much support.[98] Most significantly, Catholicos Simeon was 'absolutely opposed to rebellion'[99] and had no interest whatsoever in Emin's schemes, except to thwart them. At best success was limited and only confined to promises. Emin then returned to India, in 1773 visiting Madras where he became close to the Shahamirians who had just published their first books on Armenian liberation.[100] In 1775 Emin was in New Julfa, where he stayed for six years, dabbling in trade and trying to rekindle his schemes to free Armenia. Finally, after some more travels, he settled in Calcutta in 1785, spending the remaining years of his long life in India. Having failed in his grand attempts to free Armenia from Muslim rule Emin nevertheless wrote his biography so that through it he could continue the educational process of national liberation. He concluded his text by paraphrasing the Shahamirians' publications two decades earlier:

> Who knows but [this book] may throw some light into their [young Armenians'] minds, if they communicate the substance of it to others, or translate it into their own language? In time to come it may be of service to them, and rouse them from their slumber, till they open their eyes by degrees, and understand the true meaning of liberty; of which all Asia, from the creation of the world to this moment, have been, and are blindly ignorant...[101]

A number of important factors must be mentioned in relation to these attempts to liberate Armenia. First, they all had one thing in common: an intrinsic reliance on external—European—powers to come to the assistance of the Armenians. Some three centuries ear-

[97] Ibid., pp. 141–4.

[98] Benjanmin Braude puts if forcefully: 'Emin's memoirs were... wildly irrelevent to the consciousness of the Armenians of his homeland' (B. Braude, 'Nexus of Diaspora', p. 32).

[99] L. Nalbandian, *Armenian Revolutionary Movement*, p. 24.

[100] J. Emin, *Life and Adventures*, pp. 235, 444–7.

[101] Ibid., p. 484. The book was first translated into Armenian in 1958 in Lebanon.

lier the last king of Cilician Armenia had died in Paris, soliciting French aid to restore his kingdom. And now his mantle was being picked up by the Catholicoi and individuals like Ori and Emin. But more importantly the approach of these latter liberators laid the foundations of *all* subsequent attempts to emancipate Armenians. This was to be done *through* European (and/or Russian) intervention in one way or another. This mentality of reliance on outside powers exists to this day. Another issue related to this factor is the 'internationalisation' of Armenian issues. Although the 'Armenian Question' formally became part of the European political agenda in the last quarter of the nineteenth century, there were precedents for its inclusion due to the efforts of these early pioneers—at least as far as Armenians were concerned.

The second factor is the appearance of Russia as a new major actor in the region. Partly because of Russia's (intermittent) political promises and partly because of religious affinity with the Russian Orthodox church, Armenians began to pin their hopes on their northerly 'saviour'. As pointed out, Israel Ori, Davit Bek and Joseph Emin all had high hopes for Russian intervention on Armenians' behalf. In this sense Ori and Emin were the transitional figures who began their 'diplomatic careers' in Europe, but soon concluded that Armenia's path to liberation went through the Russian capital. This approach, which was another important precedent from this period, came to be ingrained in the mentality of future Armenians.

The third factor is specifically related to Joseph Emin and Israel Ori. They are yet again transitional figures, but this time between pre-modern church diplomacy (based on moral arguments, i.e. the crusader mentality of saving poor Christians in a sea of unbelievers) on the one hand and on the other modern secular considerations of geopolitical calculations and state interests. This is most obvious in Emin's autobiography. While he exalts his own as well as the Armenians' Christian virtues in the abstract (honesty, truth etc.), he vehemently criticises Armenian clerics for being vain, conservative, selfish, cunning and dishonourable. He blames them for the failure of his liberation attempts and for plotting against him to keep the people in darkness.[102] Both Ori and Emin had to wrestle with the tension

[102] For examples of Emin's steadfast belief in Christianity see J. Emin, *Life and Adventures*, pp. 237–41, 362, 445–7; but he also goes as far as equating church fathers with 'dogs' (p. 157) for preaching to their flock that they ought to be subservient to

between their religious beliefs, which distinguished them as 'enlightened' Christian Armenians from the 'impostor Mohammedans' and conservative church structures and leaders that opposed their liberation efforts (partly because Muslim rule ensured the clerics' prominent positions in society). This tension, and their European experience, led them to the separation of religious/church considerations from secular (geo)political calculations. They developed an understanding of Armenian conditions in terms of political interests rather than moral imperatives. Furthermore, they reinterpreted the causes of the oppression of the Armenians; they did not view it as a result of the people's sin, but understood it as the result of foreign oppression and misrule. It would take another century after Emin's activities for this separation between moral or religious understanding, and political or secular interpretation of Armenians' reality, to fully mature. The clear division that eventually emerged in the last third of the nineteenth century, between religion-church and political activity-organisation, clearly had its seeds in Emin's and Ori's vision and programmes (as well as, in a much more pronounced manner, in the publications of Emin's contemporary Shahamirian press in India). In some ways they did, from the ground up, what Mkhitarist fathers were doing intellectually in their works: beginning the trend of separating the church from the nation.

In Emin there is also a clear anti-merchant dimension. He objected to anyone who did not support, or was against, the liberation of Armenia. He does not clearly articulate it in class terms, as later revolutionaries did, but his attacks on merchants parallel his attacks on clerics.[103]

The final point to be made is once again a word of caution. It is wrong to interpret these attempts at and plans for 'national liberation' from an overly essentialist perspective. First, with the important exception of Emin's efforts, the earlier plans or rebellions did not have a clear nationalist agenda in the sense of seeking to liberate the entire nation on the basis of modern ideas of national sover-

---

Muslims. He does however speak highly of priests who supported him (pp. 234–6). For Israel Ori's transformation into a 'diplomat' see G. Libaridian, *Ideology of Armenian Liberation*, pp. 34–6. Neither a merchant by profession nor a cleric, Ori, as Libaridian puts it, 'became the first full time propagandist-diplomat devoted to Armenian liberation' (p. 36). Joseph Emin was the second.

[103] J. Emin, *Life and Adventures*, pp. 197–8, 426–8.

eignty. Yes, they are very important insofar as they manifested the idea of liberating Armenians from oppression and, in this way, were the precedents that later nationalists imbued with much meaning. But these attempts were either individual initiatives or isolated and specific instances of rebellion; even Davit Bek's united effort was a relatively short lived regional phenomenon. Second, as Gerard Libaridian points out, future Armenian historians interpreted these attempts as a series of historic struggles, all part of a greater movement toward national liberation. But in fact they were not 'a continuous chain of events'. Rather the individuals were 'like characters in one act plays that succeed each other but [were] not related. It is the historian's conceptualization, not any units of ploy, that brings them together.'[104] Nevertheless, men like the Catholicoi, Israel Ori, Davit Bek and Joseph Emin kept the idea of Armenian liberation alive until the nineteenth century—i.e. *before* the 'age of nationalism'—when such ideas acquired broad political significance. As these events and plans were *subsequently* brought together in a teleological manner by the thread of nationalist ideology,[105] a sense of crucial importance in relation to national identity formation was attached to them. They were placed into a pattern, as men ahead of their times, or as sparks which would eventually 'awaken' the 'dormant' nation. This later interpretation was far more significant than the immediate impact of these events or individuals in their own times. In short, their attempts might not have been part of a nationalist endeavour during their lifetimes (although Joseph Emin comes very close in his own thinking), but they certainly contained seeds of nationalism which allowed them to be inserted into the subsequent 'great plot' of nationalist history and ideology.

The Russian conquest of eastern Armenia

Russia's expansion into the South Caucasus is well documented and therefore there is no need to repeat the details once again.

[104] G. Libaridian, *Ideology of Armenian Liberation*, pp. 8, cf. pp. 1, 11, 36. Both Ori and Emin were, after all, individuals with grand schemes who thought that they could single-handedly change, or at least influence, the course of events relating to Armenia.

[105] In the case of Soviet inspired historiography, the teleology was in the form of dialectical materialism. It is interesting that both the ideology of nationalists and socialists converged in their interpretation of the evolution of national liberation—that all the events were somehow part of the larger dynamic of historical progress towards a specific 'end'.

Suffice to point out that it was a gradual process which lasted approximately a century, at the end of which, in 1828 the Arax river was recognised as the border between the Russian (expanding) and Persian (retracting) empires.[106] Russia made three major attempts to occupy eastern Armenia. The first was during the time of Peter the Great (coinciding with the activities of Israel Ori and then Davit Bek). The second was during the reign of Catherine the Great (about the same time as Joseph Emin's efforts). Success finally came with the signing of the treaty of Turkmanchai in 1828, after another series of wars with the Persians in the preceding twenty-five years.[107] Thus, in bits and pieces, the region between the Caucasus mountains, the Arax River, the Caspian Sea and the eastern border of the Ottoman empire came under Russian control.

The Ottoman-Russian border was expanded in favour of Russia when the Armenian regions of Kars and Ardahan were incorporated into the Russian empire after the 1877–8 Russo-Turkish war. The settlement was finalised with the 1878 treaty of Berlin. Almost always Russian advances into Armenia were welcomed by the local Armenians who on many occasions (especially in Gharabagh before 1828) lent considerable military assistance to the Tsar's army. Armenians, at least initially, viewed the great 'Christian' empire of the north as their 'liberators' from Muslim rule.[108]

[106] To this day the Arax remains the border between Iran and the former Soviet republics of Armenia and Azerbaijan.

[107] Armenians had settled in Russian controlled territories centuries before Armenia's incorporation into the empire. Even before the fall of Astrakhan to Muscovy, Armenians were involved with the Volga trade (P. Curtin, *Cross-cultural Trade*, p. 189). As mentioned earlier, there was a large Armenian community in Crimea which then moved to Nor Nakhijevan (Rostov-on-Don) in the 1770s. Merchants from New Julfa and eastern (Persian) Armenia had settled in Moscow from the seventeenth century onwards. In 1815 an Armenian school of higher learning was opened in Moscow (specialising in the teaching of oriental languages), bearing the name of its benefactors, the Lazarian (Lazarev) family. Hence there was an Armenian presence in the Russian empire long before the Russian presence in Armenia. For a brief overview of Russian-Armenian relations before 1828 see, R. Hewsen, 'Russian-Armenian Relations'; V. Gregorian, 'Impact of Russia', pp. 169–78. See also Zh. Ananian, *Hai vacharakanutiune*, for an interesting argument regarding the role of Armenian merchants in the economic development of the Russian empire in the eighteenth century. Most of these merchants were eventually assimilated into Russian culture.

[108] For details in English see G. Bournoutian, 'Eastern Armenia', pp. 98–105; R. Suny, *Looking toward Ararat*, pp. 32–7; C. Walker, *Armenia*, pp. 39–49, 64–6. For a detailed

More important than the actual details of the Russian advance are the consequences of Russian rule. Russian policy was not consistent and oscillated between repressive measures to Russify the population and a more tolerant attitude of giving the Armenians (and other minorities) some autonomy over cultural, educational and religious institutions. State policies depended on the attitude of the Tsar and/or the local governor appointed by the Tsar.[109] But there were certain overall trends that can be highlighted.

The most significant of these consequences is the mass population transfers between the empires. The trend had already begun before 1828 when many Armenians left their traditional lands in Persian Armenia and moved to Russian domains, either in Georgia or further north. Whenever a Russian military campaign retreated from conquered territories thousands of Armenians, fearing Persian persecution, also left—particularly the leading sectors of the population and their followers. Those who settled in Tiflis joined the substantial Armenian sector of the city. But many of these notables joined the Georgian nobility, while others were integrated into Russian society. These families in general tended to assimilate into the dominant elite culture. This trend of moving out of their lands and assimilating depopulated parts of eastern Armenia was, however, drastically reversed after 1828.

The treaty of Turkmanchai stipulated mass population transfers: Armenians were to move to the Russian held domains, and Muslims were to leave them. Consequently, after 1828, 30,000 people from various parts of (northern) Iran crossed the Arax river into now

---

archival source see, G. Bournoutian, *Russia and the Armenians*. There are, of course, a multitude of Armenian language sources on the subject as well. Obviously, those published in Soviet Armenia lionised the role of Russia's advance in the South Caucasus (cf. Tz. Aghayan, *Rusastani dere*; and for a more sophisticated analysis, Leo, Vol. IV). Diasporan—specially Dashnak sponsored—publications were more critical of Russian control, although their criticisms were measured compared with their denunciation of Turkish/Ottoman rule of western Armenia (cf. G. Lazian, *Hayastan*).

[109] The clearest change of policy toward the minorities was in 1881, with the inauguration of Alexander III after the assassination of Alexander II; the latter had been much more tolerant towards minorities. Alexander III ushered in a period of rising Russian nationalism and chauvinism and attempts of forced Russification. Despite the overt anti-Armenian attitudes of some of the officials, Russian authorities did not go as far as the Ottoman regime. They did not instigate or carry out massacres against the Armenians—at least, not during the nineteenth century.

Russian Armenia (a 'homecoming' of sorts, 225 years after Shah Abbas' forced migration of Armenians in the opposite direction). Similarly, after the 1828–9 Russo-Turkish war and the treaty of Adrianople, thousands of Armenians moved to Russia from the Ottoman empire. Whereas before 1828 there were 87,000 Muslims and 20,000 Armenians in the Yerevan khanate/province, after the mass migrations Armenians constituted the majority population: 65,000, as opposed to 50,000 Muslims. This trend continued as more population transfers took place after the Crimean war (1853–6) and the 1877–8 war. Hence Armenians became the dominant majority in Yerevan Province (although not in the town of Yerevan until the early twentieth century).[110] There were also significant numbers of Armenians in surrounding provinces/regions of Nakhijevan, Gharabagh, Ganja, Akhalkalak and in the city of Tiflis (where close to half the population was Armenian by the end of the nineteenth century).

The second consequence of Russian rule was the territorial division of eastern Armenia. Although a distinct administrative unit called the 'Armenian Province' existed only between 1828 and 1840, there remained a compact territory (Yerevan Province) where Armenians constituted the majority. This did not include other (adjacent) Armenian populated areas and most notably left out the Gharabagh region (the ramifications of which are felt to this day). But it was, nevertheless, the embryonic core of the future Armenian state.

Third, despite the Russian state administrative centralisation and integration, Armenians were given a degree of autonomy in cultural and religious matters and therefore could easily maintain their distinct communal identity. This was formalised in the *Polozhenie* of 1836 which regulated the powers and mechanisms of communal organisations (viz. the church) without too much interference from

[110] Figures based on R. Suny, 'Eastern Armenians', pp. 112, 121, 126–7, 133; G. Bournoutian, 'Eastern Armenia', pp. 100–1, 105; for a more detailed study see G. Bournoutian, 'Ethnic Composition'. By the mid-nineteenth century there were approximately 565,000 Armenians in the South Caucasus. This number had risen to 1.24 million at the turn of the century, and almost 1.8 million by 1917. In 1900 there were 506,000 Armenians in Yerevan Province. The main reason for the drastic jump was the additional conquest of Armenian territories (which did not become part of Yerevan Province, but many Armenians did move to it) in 1878 and migration from the Ottoman empire. The annexation of Kars and Ardahan (1878) increased the Armenian population of the Russian empire by approximately 100,000.

the state. This 'nominal degree of self-government'[111] recognised the autonomy of the Armenian church and gave Armenians freedom of worship in their own brand of Christianity. The church was also given control over religious/community education, freed from taxation, and allowed ownership of land for income. However, it was made very clear that ultimate authority lay with the Tsar and the state. Armenian regions were *not* organised into an autonomous province under Russian suzerainty as Armenians had initially hoped. They were administered like any other Russian province without any special status. But the '*Polozhenie* established a working relationship and cooperation' between the Armenian church and the Russian state and hence regulated relations between the community and the imperial administration, generally in a cordial manner, for approximately half a century.[112] This state-church/community relationship resembled in many ways the sultan-*millet* relationship in the Ottoman empire, but without formally bestowing on the church head the leadership position of the entire community. Armenians were recognised as a distinct community and the institutional mechanisms, and cultural markers necessary to maintain this distinctiveness, were respected—at least until the 1880s.

After initial hardships immediately following the incorporation of the new territories into Russia, Armenia's and Armenians' socioeconomic conditions improved considerably. Consequently, as a fourth point, a significant middle class emerged which was comprised of traders, financiers, industrialists and a technical intelligentsia. The wealthy among this class acquired a status and function within the community similar to that of the Constantinople *amira*s (but without being so entrenched or formalised in their titles). Some of these families, many with Russified names, were: Arzumanov, Avetisian, Tumaniants, Kevorkov, Egiazarov, Ter-Asaturov *et al.* In the absence of an Armenian aristocratic class the middle class assumed the role of community leadership. The Armenian leading class was, therefore, urban based, but its members lived in urban centres *outside*—but near—the Armenian provinces, predominantly in Tiflis and Baku. Some did move further north and settled in Russian cities where they were quickly absorbed into the dominant culture. But

[111] L. Nalbandian, *Armenian Revolutionary Movement*, p. 24.
[112] R. Suny, 'Eastern Armenians', p. 115.

Tiflis, and later but to a lesser degree Baku, became centres of Armenian intellectual life and culture. In short, Armenians of the Russian empire went through the process of urbanisation and modernisation, but outside Armenia proper—i.e. the modernisation experience was once again diaspora based, albeit relatively close to the homeland. As in the Ottoman empire, Armenians forged ahead in urban centres while Yerevan Province remained a backwater rural area.[113]

The fifth consequence followed from the last point. It was the emergence of a lay Armenian intelligentsia that eventually generated a new sense of modern collective identity: that of nationality, or the idea of belonging to a *nation*. Again, in a way similar to developments in Constantinople, the sons of the upper and middle classes went abroad to study and were influenced by European ideas which

[113] Ronald Suny points out that 'This class of propertied Armenians... emerged as the most influential social group in Transcaucasian towns, as a new capitalist-industrial environment began to take shape in Caucasia' (R. Suny, 'Eastern Armenians', p. 114, cf. pp. 121, 125; cf. Suny, *Looking toward Ararat*, pp. 40–2). For a more comprehensive account see V. Gregorian, 'Impact of Russia', pp. 186–94. In a section entitled 'The Growth of the Armenian Bourgeoisie' he gives detailed figures of the urbanisation process. By 1897 among the 1,173,096 Armenians in the South Caucasus the class breakdown (%) was as follows (p. 189):

0.8 Landholding nobility and clergy,
70.0 Peasantry (9.1 per cent well-to-do, the remainder middle income or poor),
7.3 Bourgeoisie (industrial and commercial),
16.2 Workers,
5.7 Artisans, retail merchants, home industries.

In terms of ethnic/territorial breakdown, at the turn of the century, only 40.9 per cent of Armenians lived in territories of what is now Armenia (as opposed to 99.7 per cent of Georgians, and 64.6 per cent of Azerbaijanis—i.e. Turco-Tatar—living in their respective territories). In 1900 Tiflis, Yerevan, Alexandropol (Leninakan, now Gyumri) and some other major towns had Armenian mayors and municipal councils dominated by Armenians. Baku had a Russian mayor, but in its city council Armenians had 21 seats, Muslims 27, Russians none (p. 189). For figures of economic development see pp. 190–4. In the urban centres, class and ethnicity/religion overlapped and reinforced social distinctions. In Baku, for example, the hierarchy was roughly thus: Russians (and European) at the top, then Armenians (and other Christians), and at the very bottom Tatar (and other Muslims). As to Tiflis, with a total population of 71,000 in 1865, 31,000 were Armenians, 15,000 Georgians and 12,000 Russians. By 1897 the numbers were: 55,500, 38,000 and 36,000 respectively. Armenians remained the largest ethnic group until 1917 (R. Suny, 'Eastern Armenians', pp. 125–6).

they brought back with them to the South Caucasus. But in this case the influence was from Russian radical thought and German philosophy (rather than French and Italian). Simultaneously, Russian administration put eastern Armenia under the jurisdiction of one state and one set of laws governing the conduct of individuals and community institutions in a uniform manner. As the 'divided and diverse' Armenian people were brought together 'under the same laws, taxes, and political authority,'[114] the community acquired a uniformity that enhanced both its sense of unity and an identity separate from their neighbours as a result of the *Polozhenie*. Hence, on the one hand an intelligentsia emerged that was in tune with radical thought (populism, socialism, nationalism etc.), and on the other a 'people' emerged whose ethno-religious identity was augmented by unifying administrative structures, a school system and semi-autonomous community organisations.

Finally, Russian conquest of eastern Armenia once again put a geopolitical fault line within Armenian territories. In the first quarter of the century the dynamics were between Russia and Persia (supported by the French in the context of the Napoleonic wars). In the last quarter of the nineteenth century European 'grand politics' aimed to contain Russia, and consequently the Ottoman-Russian conflicts drew in the British who sought to limit Russia's power and expansion by assisting the Ottoman empire when needed. As it will be discussed in the next chapter, Armenia and Armenians were once again caught in the middle of these manoeuvres and suffered in the geopolitical 'games'. Millennia-old dynamics were again at play: as if, loosely put, Russia had been substituted for Parthia, and the Turks and the British for the Romans.

All of these factors—the groundwork prepared by the merchant diaspora and the Mkhitarists, the early liberation attempts, the Ottoman *millet* system and Russian rule—were different moments in the multilocal process of the formation of modern Armenian national identity. They all came together or, more correctly, were brought together by intellectuals in the middle of the nineteenth century, and this led to the 'awakening' of Armenian national consciousness.

[114] R. Suny, 'Eastern Armenians', p. 120.

But, as this chapter has shown, much of the necessary preparatory work done in this direction took place in the preceding two centuries. Some Armenians (from Mkhitarist Catholic monks to world-travelling merchants and 'adventurers') were quick to pick up the cause of 'nation-building' or 'national liberation' because they had a strong sense of community, history and ethno-religious difference on the one hand, and knowledge of European intellectual currents, literature and technology on the other. It was the combination of these two dynamics, taking place in various communities from India to Amsterdam, that led to the intellectual movement known in Armenian as *zartonk* ('awakening' or 'renaissance'). This 'awakening' was translated into social changes and concrete political action in the last quarter of the century. It is crucial to highlight that the construction of modern Armenian identity and nationalism began *without* the intervention of an Armenian state. Hence linking, *a priori*, the state with nationalism is not warranted. Merchants, monks and revolutionaries, working through community structures and institutions, were playing the same role as the state did in western European nationalisms.

Russian Expansion into South Caucasus, 1774–1878.

4

A MULTILOCAL AWAKENING

THE CONSOLIDATION AND RADICALISATION OF COLLECTIVE IDENTITY IN THE 19TH CENTURY

In the Armenian collective memory and in much of the historiographical literature the overall process of the formation of modern nationality in the middle part of the nineteenth century is referred to as the 'awakening' or the 'renaissance' (*zartonk*) of the nation. Different elements of this process are emphasised, but it is almost uniformly accepted that the 'dormant' Armenian nation 'awoke' after centuries of Turkish and Persian misrule. This traditional approach, typical in the approach of nationalist intellectuals, does not however explain the complex process through which Armenian identity was *transformed* in the nineteenth century. The fact of the matter is that this process of identity transformation was not so much the 'awakening' of a pre-existing nation as the construction of the modern Armenian nation. I should immediately emphasise that this argument does not imply that what emerged was the artificial or illegitimate creation of intellectuals. Rather, modern Armenian nationality was based on a pre-existing and a very deep ethno-religious identity, which in itself was intertwined with unique local identities and cultural markers (such as dialects). In other words, the Armenian nation, like all other nations, was an 'imagined community', but it was based on real and concrete pillars rooted in the Armenian past and the intellectual work of earlier generations. That is why, once it emerged, Armenian nationalism became a potent mobilising force with powerful historical resonance.

Western academic literature has recently began using the word 'revival' to refer to the nineteenth century *zartonk*. However, in this chapter I will continue to employ the words 'awakening' and 'renaissance' since they are the widely accepted terms denoting a specific process in Armenian history, even though 'metamorphosis' would be a more appropriate expression and image. I will examine the three main elements of the renaissance in the second half of the nineteenth century. The focus will be on key elements which were linked to the formation of modern national identity and nationalism, and how the awakening process itself was *multilocal*. The three elements I examine in greater detail are language, literature and political ideology. I concentrate on these three factors because as both loci and agents of change they were instrumental in the reformulation of Armenian identity along national (and later radical) lines. I will discuss the related religious/church dimension and its relationship to national identity in the next chapter.

I begin this chapter with my core argument regarding the multilocal process of the fundamental transformation of Armenian collective identity along national(ist) lines. I emphasise the differences between the main points of Armenian cultural production and nationalism. As a result of this multiple process national identity was divided into two overall linguistic and cultural patterns and into three general ideological positions. It is through this overall dynamic that I analyse the three core elements of language, literature and political ideology. This was a turbulent period in Armenian history—when the collective gelled as a modern nation, when the politics of nationalism and radicalism emerged, when a new wave of anti-Armenian massacres was unleashed and when the 'Armenian Cause' was internationalised.

THE MULTILOCAL ARGUMENT

'The modern Armenian renaissance', writes Ronald Suny, was 'not a spontaneous release of deep-seated Armenian spirit but the product of hard political and intellectual work by Armenian scholars, teachers and political activists.'[1] This was indeed the case. Moreover, unlike many of the earlier activities of merchants and other individuals, the nineteenth century efforts of national awakening were systematic, often coordinated and largely successful. Intellectuals and

[1] R. Suny, 'Eastern Armenians', p. 116.

activists managed to create a modern national identity (even though they failed in their ultimate political objective of national liberation because Armenian aspirations were met by genocidal policies that eliminated Armenians from their homeland). In the previous chapter the various centres and diverse efforts of Armenian cultural production, as well as political thinking and activity, were discussed. In the second half of the nineteenth century this multilocal dynamic remained, but it was either directly or indirectly incorporated into three overall patterns. Through this triple process, and based on the earlier pillars of identity, modern Armenian nationality was constructed. Hence the emergent sense of collective belonging itself reflected this multiplicity (and multilocality).

These dynamics—though placed under the single rubric of the renaissance—entailed three sources of imagining the same nation, that is, three general sets of parallel awakenings: a *western* point, an *eastern* point and a *central* point. Geographically these came from different directions, but were intertwined in their common goal of forming one nation. The political projects differed too, although the main aim was to reform or liberate Turkish Armenia(ns). The western component of the awakening, based in Constantinople (as well as some west European cities), evolved around the liberal reform project influenced by French and Italian thought, constitutionalism and 'Western' nationalism. The eastern component, based in Tiflis (and other cities of the Russian empire), was influenced by Russian and German thought, radicalism and 'Eastern' nationalism. The central point was based on the indigenous conditions in the Ottoman Armenian provinces. None of the points was affiliated with an Armenian state or anything resembling a state structure. By the end of the nineteenth century these trends co-existed in Armenian national identity and in the nationalist and revolutionary programmes of the Armenian intelligentsia. But there was tension between the three approaches, both in identity and in politics, even though they were part of the national movement of the same people. The attributes of this tension are still existent in Armenian national life.

Dividing identity and nationalism into 'eastern' and 'western' is, of course, a generalisation. And the categories of the division are not new.[2] I use the east/west/central divide to denote a geograph-

[2] John Plamenatz, for instance, makes the distinction in his 'Two Types of Nationalism'. Whereas his categorisation is useful, his analysis is flawed, not least because it interprets

ical division that encapsulated three separate spheres of ideological influence; I am not passing a value judgement as to one being better, more or less nationalistic than the other. What I am arguing is that these trends existed in the same national movement, striving to create one collective identity. The outcome was indeed the creation of *one* overarching identity as members of the Armenian *nation*, but this identity had profoundly different elements, which in fact subdivided the nation into two parts in terms of language and literature, and into three spheres in terms of political ideology. The division was due to the dispersion of the Armenian intelligentsia in various locales, situated on different sides of imperial, cultural and ideological boundaries. Therefore, the 'western', the 'eastern' and the 'central' points overlapped and conflicted—and at times synthesised—on the terrain of Armenia, in various diasporan communities and in the very notion of Armenianness. In this process Armenian identity was reformulated and nationalised.

The radicalisation of identity and politics (associated with the eastern point) could also be interpreted as a consequence of the failure of the liberal programme.[3] After all, the liberal project of the western point preceded the radicalisation process by two to three decades. I am discounting neither this nor the close relationship between the three points. My argument is that the sources—be they theoretical, ideological or sociological—of the three trends had separate origins which influenced intellectuals and subsequently the masses. This multiplicity became an intrinsic characteristic of Armenian national identity and its politics, instituting (or reinforcing) a deep divide within the collective consciousness of the nation.

Historians of Armenia, while aware of this east/west division (especially in language and literature[4]), do not analyse its ramifications for national identity formation. What I argue is that examination of this east/west/central split is essential to understand modern

---

the eastern variant of nationalism as something inferior to the western variant. The east/west division is also expressed more fruitfully in the dichotomy of civic/ethnic, territorial/blood-based (*ius soli*/*ius sanguinis*) nationalism.

[3] This is Gerard Libaridian's approach in his *Ideology of Armenian Liberation*; cf. G. Libaridian, 'Nation and Fatherland'.

[4] For example, Kevork Bardakjian, in his book on modern Armenian literature, alludes to it as the 'larger cultural context' in which literature was produced. (K. Bardakjian, *Reference Guide*, pp. 105–6). He focuses on the literary manifestation of this divide.

Armenian national identity and nationalism. As I trace this divide I will argue in subsequent chapters that it continued to affect Armenian identity, becoming the root of the post-Genocide homeland/diaspora division. This analytical perspective takes me into uncharted territory in terms of interpretation. Although there are many studies of the Armenian awakening and its politics, none analyses how this multilocal process affected the construction of an Armenian national identity that was *heterogeneous* in its essence.

What emerges is a triangular relationship with two of the three ideological sources of 'imagining' the nation based in diasporan communities: the western point, embodied by Constantinople, but also including Venice, Vienna, Paris etc.; and the eastern point of Tiflis, including Moscow, St Petersburg, Dorpat (now Tartu, Estonia) etc. The third point of the triangle was the actual homeland, the local realities, thinking, and developments in Armenia itself—i.e. the six *vilayets* of Ottoman Armenia: Van, Bitlis, Erzerum, Diarbekir, Sivas and Kharput. The emphasis of socio-political reform was on these provinces, although from the 1880s onward some of the focus shifted onto Russian Armenia as a result of increased Tsarist repression. However, the situation in Turkish Armenia remained at the core of the national movement.

In sum, the Armenian awakening was a multilocal experience—both in its roots (as discussed hitherto) and in its nineteenth century evolution and politicisation (as analysed next). But it was also a totalising experience insofar as it transformed, or at least affected, all the crucial elements of identity: language, literature, political ideology and religion. I will now explore the first two of these domains while highlighting the east/west division only; for language and literature the main intellectual input came from the eastern and western points and not from the central point of Ottoman Armenia. Political ideology will be analysed in greater detail on the basis of all three points since it was in this domain that the central (Armenia) point made its most significant contribution to identity and to nationalism.

LANGUAGE

The need for a standardised and commonly understandable language had become clear to Armenian intellectuals as early as the eighteenth century (e.g. Mkhitar and his dictionary). By the first half of the nineteenth century this view was cemented further: language had to be transformed into a medium of unification instead of being a source of division.[5] The question was which language, classical Armenian or the modern vernacular? After much debate and struggle, by the second half of the century the vernacular was victorious as the hegemonic language.[6] However, owing to the lack of close cultural and institutional bonds between the two sectors of Armenia divided between two empires, two vernaculars

[5] One telling example of the linguistic mixture before the standardisation of the vernacular is a letter written to the Dutch States-General by Armenian merchants in Aleppo in 1568. The address is in Italian but written in Armenian letters, the introduction is in classical Armenian and the body of the text is in the eastern Armenian dialect! (K. Papazian, *Merchants from Ararat*, pp. 53–4). Around the same time Armenians of Crimea and Poland were conducting business in Kipchak Turkish, but written in the Armenian alphabet. Later, when Ottoman Turkish became the lingua franca of the empire, many Armenians wrote it in the Armenian alphabet. As mentioned, the first Armenian periodical, *Azdarar*, published in India in the 1790s, used a mixture of classical Armenian and the Indian-Armenian dialect. These examples are an indication of the multiplicity of vernacular linguistic expression among the dispersed Armenians (classical Armenian remained the language of the Church and the written medium of high culture until the nineteenth century). The common element among these various modes of expression was that they were all written in the 'sacred' Armenian alphabet. This linguistic mixture persisted into the nineteenth century. In the 1860s the satirist Harutiun Sevajian wrote that in a 'typical' upper class family, in 'the home of a rich Armenian of Constantinople the Agha speaks Turkish, his wife speaks either Armenian or Turkish, his elder son speaks either English or Italian, his daughter French, his younger son Greek' (as quoted in V. Oshagan, 'Self-Image of Western Armenians', pp. 203–4).

[6] The most important point in the relationship between language and nationalism is the emergence of the vernacular as a literary language that binds together all members of the (potential or proto-) nation into one cultural unit. A number of scholars of nations and nationalism, writing from various perspectives, make this a central element of their theory (cf. B. Anderson, *Imagined Communities*, pp. 44–6; A. Hastings, *Construction of Nationhood*, p. 12); K. Deutsch, *Nationalism and Social Communication*, p. 96). More broadly, the connections between language and identity, as well as nationalism and the vernacular language, are a much discussed subject in the literature on nationalism (cf. J. Edwards, *Language*; J. Fishman, 'Social Theory and Ethnography'; R. Taras, 'Nations and Language-Building'). The idea that language and national identity are inseparable goes as far back as Herder (1744–1803) and Fichte (1762–1814). However, it is generally accepted that language is not *necessarily* tied to ethnic identity or nationalism in every case, even though linguistic distinction (as one element of culture) is often used as a marker of the uniqueness of the nation (cf. J. Armstrong, *Nations Before Nationalism*, pp. 242, 282; A. Smith, *National Identity*, pp. 88–91).

emerged: the western one based on the dialect of Constantinople, and the eastern one based on the dialect of Yerevan. The classical (literary) language, known only by the small group of *belles lettres* intellectuals and the clergy (for liturgy), was not suitable for linguistic unity as it was incomprehensible to the majority of the population. It was also deemed by many modernising intellectuals to be inadequate for contemporary communication.

It is interesting to draw a parallel here between the fifth and the nineteenth centuries. In both instances language was used as a unifying mechanism. In the first case the alphabet was invented to bond Armenians together through a written and standardised language. In the second, common language was modernised and once again standardised as a medium of *written* expression. While some Armenians spoke a form of vernacular Armenian—mostly the (semi-)educated in towns—the rest of the population (in the provinces) spoke either Turkish or various Armenian-based but often mutually incomprehensible dialects, some of which were heavily influenced by Turkish and other languages.[7]

In the west

The western Armenian vernacular evolved out of the intellectual milieu of Constantinople and the work of the Mkhitarist monks in Venice and Vienna. The proponents of the classical language and the vernacular debated the issue for twenty years. By the 1880s it was clear that the vernacular had become the undisputed spoken

[7] Vahé Oshagan suggests that in the first half of the nineteenth century Turkish words made up 85 per cent of the 'Armenian' spoken by the common people in some regions of Armenia. By one estimate this number was 60 per cent in 1860 (V. Oshagan, 'Cultural and Literary Awakening', p. 59). Some old regional dialects survive to the present and are used as a 'home language', especially by the elderly in the diaspora. In some pockets dialects are still used as an everyday medium of expression. The most notable case is that of the Gharabagh dialect. Some regions in Armenia have also retained their local dialects (e.g. in Meghri). In the diaspora the dialect of the village of Kessab (in Syria) survives and, similar to it, that of Musa Ler (originally in Turkey, but since the 1930s relocated in Anjar, Lebanon). These dialects are incomprehensible to other Armenians, a sort of 'secret code' of communication among people from a very particular region. In the dialect of Kessab, for example, one can very clearly notice the mixture of Armenian, Turkish, Arabic and even a few Greek, French and English words. The grammatical root, however, is (classical) Armenian (cf. H. Cholakian, *Kesapi barbare*).

and literary language of western Armenians. The first journal in the vernacular was published in 1840 in Smyrna (Izmir),[8] but its crowning moment was the publication of a new influential daily called *Hairenik* (Fatherland) in Constantinople in 1891. By this point poetry, literature, academic and even patriarchate publications were all appearing in the vernacular.[9] It should be emphasised that these texts catered to the readership of western Armenians concentrated in Constantinople, Smyrna and the rest of the Ottoman empire, as well as Armenian communities in western Europe. Some of the ideas contained in these publications—especially in progressive periodicals—were disseminated in eastern Armenia, but on the whole the publications themselves (novels, journals etc.) were not widely circulated among Russian Armenians. Geographical barriers, border controls, the difference in dialects and differing socio-cultural experiences as subject matter mitigated against such diffusion across the political and identity frontiers between the two Armenian regions. Hence the evolution of the dialects continued more or less independently of each other's influence.

In the east

Eastern Armenia developed its own literature and written language, paralleling the similar process in the west. This too was a conscious effort to forge a standard written language based on the spoken. Except that in this case the research and intellectual work was mostly done in the Lazarian/Lazarev (in Moscow) and the Nersisian (in Tiflis) colleges, as well as the Gevorgian seminary in Ejmiatzin. Various regional dialects were studied and 'purified' of foreign words to

[8] It was called *Arshaluis Araratian* (Dawn of Ararat) (V. Oshagan, 'Modern Armenian Literature', pp. 155–6). However, A. Ter Minassian ('Sociétés de culture', p. 13) maintains that the first Armenian periodical in the Ottoman empire—called *Shtemaran pitani giteliats* (Storehouse of Useful Knowledge)—was published by American missionaries in 1839 in Smyrna. She highlights the importance of the missionaries as agents for the dissemination of the vernacular. They not only translated the Bible into the 'common language', but in many cases also used the vernacular as the language of instruction in their schools.

[9] Some of the prominent Constantinople intellectuals who advocated and wrote in the vernacular were Karapet Utudjian, Nahapet Rusinian, Nikoghos Zorayan, Grigor Otian and Nikoghos Balian; many of them were European-educated.

form a common language based on the Yerevan (Ararat valley) dialect. Again there was a debate between those advocating the vernacular and those clinging to the classical language—the first representing reform (and secularism) and the second conservatism (and the church). In 1846 Stepanos Nazariants wrote a book in defence of the vernacular and in 1855 Rafayel Patkanian (a.k.a. Kamar-Katipa) published (patriotic) poetry in the 'common language'. This, according to Vahé Oshagan, ensured the victory of the eastern vernacular in Russian Armenia. Subsequently there was a revival of all sorts of literature, songs, travel books and other written texts.[10] By the 1870s the vernacular was the hegemonic language of eastern Armenians.

In an 1871 article entitled 'Modern Armenian Language' published in a new Armenian progressive journal called *Arevelian Mamul* (Eastern Press) (in Smyrna), the author argues that one of the factors of Armenians' backwardness is 'the varying mix of our current written language. This is the place to say: [we have] as many dialects as Armenians, [and] as many grammars as literates.' The article then goes on to advocate some sort of unity between the various dialects, which should be the responsibility of a committee of experts. A few issues later in an article called 'When are we Going to Construct our Language?' the author once again suggests that we 'must give unity to the written vernacular', which is essential 'for all acts of progress'.[11] It is obvious that there was a conscious and systematic effort to create a united and modern vernacular language for the Armenians. The modernising intellectuals failed to do this at the pan-Armenian level, but they did succeed in doing so within each of their spheres. Hence Ottoman Armenians (including the provinces) fell under the linguistic influence of Constantinople, while Russian Armenians used the eastern vernacular. Consequently the two main vernaculars in modern Armenian, the eastern and western, although

[10] V. Oshagan, 'Modern Armenian Literature', p. 150; V. Oshagan, 'Cultural and Literary Awakening', p. 61; S. Shmavonian, 'Mikayel Nalbandian', pp. 43–4.

[11] The first article is from *Arevelian Mamul*, 1:3, March 1871, pp. 103–9 (p. 103 for the quote). The second is from 1:12, December 1871, pp. 579–82 (p. 579 for the quotes). See V. Oshagan, 'Self-Image of Western Armenians', for a brief summary of the contemporary press' constant complaints about the lack of Armenian speakers and readers (pp. 203ff.).

mutually comprehensible, developed different spelling rules, pronunciation of some letters, declensions and conjugations. Thus on one level language unifies Armenians on a pan-national plane, but simultaneously the two vernaculars divide them into eastern and western spheres.[12] This is the most noticeable difference between eastern and western Armenians to this day.

LITERARY CULTURE

Modern Armenian literary production took off after the 1840s. Texts were first published in the classical language, but within decades a larger mass readership had emerged in the vernacular idiom. Hence hundreds of books (novels, history, poetry, translations etc.), newspapers and journals were printed.[13] Oshagan highlights the multiple influences on Armenian literature and culture in this period:

> Modern Armenian culture is an essentially urban phenomenon and has flowered in large cities at the periphery of the Armenian world, at the points of contact with foreign cultures—with English culture in Madras and Calcutta; with French culture in Smyrna, Constantinople and Paris; with Italian culture in Venice; with German culture in Dorpat... and Vienna; with Russian culture in St Petersburg, Moscow and Tiflis. This fact gives modern Armenian culture a somewhat cosmopolitan character, provoking inner tensions that other cultures, developing within their own and stable national structures, do not experience.[14]

It is impossible to trace all of these influences in a few paragraphs, or to elaborate on the 'inner tensions' in a satisfactory manner. Suffice to say that the literature reflected the arguments between the con-

[12] Presently classical (*grabar*) Armenian survives as a public language only in the formal liturgy of the church—as a 'ritual' language (the sermon is in vernacular Armenian and, in some churches in North America, in English). For all intents and purposes *grabar* has become a 'dead' language for the overwhelming majority of the Armenian population. However, it might be more appropriate to call it an 'ancient' language since, similar to Latin, it is still learnt by church officials and a few historians, linguists and classicists.

[13] The periodical press alone, published in various communities across the globe, numbered some 300 journals and papers in the nineteenth century (V. Oshagan, 'Modern Armenian Literature', p. 169). Some only lasted for a few issues, others carried on for years, while a few survive to the present.

[14] V. Oshagan, 'Modern Armenian Literature', p. 142.

servatives and the liberals or radicals, between the clerics or clerical minded and the secularists, between the city and the countryside, between the upper classes and those representing the interests of the poor, the anxieties within the middle class and so forth. However, the tension I would highlight is the east/west division in literary culture. Whereas in both the east and the west many writers focused on national issues and themes of liberation, there was an overall difference of style and content that affected identity.

In the west

Once again the Mkhitarist brotherhood was at the forefront of cultural and academic production. The Order broke new ground in 1843 by publishing in Venice (and continuing to this day) the first scholarly journal in modern Armenian: *Bazmavep* (Polyhistory).[15] The Vienna Mkhitarists followed suit by beginning the literary-scholarly journal *Yevropa* (Europe) in 1847 (to 1863) and *Handes amsorya* (Monthly Journal) (1887 to the present). In 1847 the patriarchate in Constantinople also founded its own journal called *Hayastan* (Armenia). In the pages of these and other more popular magazines published later, the first generation of western intellectuals, mostly Constantinople-based but educated in Europe—many of them graduates of the Mkhitarist schools began their writing careers.[16] And just as importantly, through such periodicals, as well as publishing presses catering to the more popular tastes of the general reading public, European literature, good and bad, was disseminated (in translation) within the Armenian community.

[15] Although *Bazmavep* was the fourth periodical published by the Mkhitarists since 1799, it nevertheless became their most significant publication. It played on the one hand an instrumental role 'in the formation of Modern Armenian [language]' by refining it and adopting it to contemporary needs. On the other hand it was a crucial medium in introducing (selectively) western European ideas and innovations into the Armenian context: the 'introduction of Western civilization as a model for the advancement of the Armenians was one of the major aims of *Bazmavep*'s publishers' (K. Bardakjian, *Mekhitarist Contributions*, p. 20 [first quote], p. 19 [second quote]).

[16] These men included Nahabet Rusinian and Khachatur Misakian (linguists), Hovhannes Hisarian (editor and ethnographer) and Grigor Otian (jurist, writer and the force behind the drafting of the Armenian and Ottoman Constitutions). Rusinian is the author of the famous patriotic poem-song *Cilicia*. It continues in the tradition of songs of exile, longing for the homeland—in this case, Cilician Armenia.

Between 1825 and 1850 130 volumes of European literature (both classical and modern) were translated and published in Armenian by the Mkhitarists. The practice was picked up in the second half of the century by the commercial presses of Constantinople and Smyrna which printed hundreds of French, English, Italian etc. novels in Armenian translations (Alexandre Dumas, Jules Verne, Victor Hugo, Sir Walter Scott and others). In this way print capitalism (especially the Dedeyan Press) reinforced and widened a process of westernisation that had been started earlier by Mkhitarist and other intellectuals.[17] Through such works of literature, and translations of non-fiction essays, European ideological currents and literary genres entered western Armenian culture.[18]

The dominating trend in western Armenian literature after the 1880s was the realist school. In addition to national liberation the main themes it dealt with were class exploitation, alienation, social ills, the hypocrisy of the upper classes, relations between the sexes and so forth. The intellectual-activist Arpiar Arpiarian (1852–1908) ushered in this trend. In 1884 he founded the journal *Arevelk* (Orient or East), which gathered around it the realist writers of Constantinople. He also published a powerful novella (in 1901 called *Karmir Zhamuts* [The Red Offering]) on class conflict and the need for national reconciliation and self-defence.[19] Some realist writers only

[17] The theoretical underpinnings that link print capitalism to the homogenisation of culture and language, as well as the dissemination of national ideas, comes from B. Anderson, *Imagined Communities*.

[18] V. Oshagan, 'Modern Armenian Literature', pp. 156–8. According to Oshagan, a respected literary critic and author himself, such foreign influences 'inhibited' the growth of 'authentically national genres' and it 'consolidated the hold of French cultural values on the Western Armenians' (pp. 156–7). For example, Molière's influence can clearly be seen on the 'master' of Armenian satire, Hakob Paronian (1841–92), who caricatured the vanity of the Armenian upper classes. Similarly, Tzerents (1822–88) wrote three historical novels which were inspired by Sir Walter Scott in their style, but situated within the Armenian historical context, calling for the liberation of Armenia. In the above mentioned journal, *Arevelian Mamul*, Walter Scott's novel *Ivanhoe* is serialised. In its preface the editor of the journal deplores the dearth of Armenian national literature. We wish we had national literature, he asserts, and then rhetorically asks: but who is to support our suffering writers? (1:1, January 1871, p. 36).

[19] The next generation of writer-activists in the realist school included Grigor Zohrap (Krikor Zohrab) (1861–1915), Tigran Kamsarakan (1866–1940), Ruben Zardarian (1874–1915) and Yervand Otian (1869–1926) who—it is worth noting—satirically ridiculed eastern Armenian revolutionaries trying to politicise the peasants of western Armenia. Poets were part of this movement as well: Vahan Tekeyan (1878–1945), Levon Shant (1869–1951), Siamanto (1878–1915), Misak Metzarents (1886–1908)

dealt with social and existential issues (e.g. the early Levon Shant), while many others intertwined their social realism with national(ist)—or even racialist—themes (e.g. Daniel Varuzhan).

The fact that realism had become the dominant literary current in the last quarter of the nineteenth century does not mean that other currents were excluded, especially before the 1870s. The romantic style was also present but it did not remain as prevalent. Romanticism was best exemplified by the poetry of the Mkhitarist Father Ghevond Alishan (1820–1901), whose love of nature and of the fatherland reflected the post-1848 French romantics.[20]

Another important genre was 'provincial literature'—i.e. literature written by authors in the Armenian provinces of the Ottoman empire. These writers offset the snobbery of the Constantinople elite and were much more reflective of the conditions, needs and aspirations of Armenian peasants and the lower classes in the interior of the empire. They put them at the centre of attention instead of the 'decadence' of urban life in the capital. The towering figure in this genre was Father Mkrtich Khrimian (1820–1907), who later became Patriarch of Constantinople and then Catholicos of All Armenians. His book *Hravirak Ayraratian* (Invitation to Ararat) (1850) 'was fashioned after the classical model of Virgil's *Pastoral Poems*...[and was] an exhortation to love the land and to liberate it from oppression[. It] had a tremendous impact on the minds of the enlightened people.'[21] Through Khrimian and similar intellectuals from the interior the Armenians of the provinces were knocking on the doors of the Constantinople elite to draw its attention to the appalling conditions of the Armenian peasantry. But as a literary genre provincial literature did not have the same impact on identity as realism—

---

and Daniel Varuzhan (1884–1915). The last significant generation of Constantinople writers included Zapel Yesayan (1878–1943), Hakob Oshakan (1883–1948) and Kostan Zarian (1885–1969). For a basic overview see V. Oshagan, 'Modern Armenian Literature', pp. 169–74; for a comprehensive study see K. Bardakjian, *Reference Guide*, pp. 99–200; H. Chanashian, *Hai grakanutian*, pp. 115–266. Of these intellectuals who survived 1915, all had emigrated from Turkey by the 1920s and settled in various diasporan communities.

20 For details see H. Chanashian, *Hai grakanutian*, pp. 47–71, 95–104. Other western Armenian romantic poets included Petros Durian (1852–72) and Mkrtich Peshiktashlian (1828–68).

21 V. Oshagan, 'Modern Armenian Literature', pp. 152–3, cf. p. 171. Other authors in this genre included Melkon Kiurchian (1859–1915), Tlkatintsi (1860–1915) and the realist Ruben Zardarian (1874–1915).

although, as will be discussed below, Khrimian himself had a powerful influence on political thinking and nationalism.

Finally, in 1856 a permanent Armenian theatre was established in Constantinople by Mkrtich Peshiktashlian (Mkhitarist educated) who staged plays (in the vernacular) with national themes, based on Armenian historic figures. One of these plays, *Arshak II*, put together by Tigran Chukhachian and Tovmas Terzian in 1868, became the first Armenian classical opera. It was about King Arshak who in the fourth century battled for 'national unification' and independence against Persia and Byzantium.[22]

In sum, by the end of the nineteenth century western Armenian literature was dominated by the realist school of writing, though other trends also existed. This European-inspired style was woven with Armenian content. Consequently wider social/existential concerns were intertwined with national(ist) themes. Although western Armenian literature in the late nineteenth and early twentieth centuries highlighted the exploitation of Armenians and the need for national liberation, it did not in general glorify the nation as an organic whole the way the romantics did. Rather, it explored human values and universalistic themes in the context of Armenian—usually *Constantinople*—society.[23] The nationalist project of liberation became more prevalent in this literature after the massacres of 1896, but on the whole it remained one of its important elements, not its core. Nor was realist literature as socially radical, or as intense and consuming as the passion of the romantics.[24] Western Armenian literature was as concerned with the human condition of the individ-

[22] It is noteworthy that in 1998–9 there was a fundraising drive in the United States to stage the *Arshak II* opera at the San Francisco Opera Company. One million dollars was raised. In the Armenian community press the opera was described thus: 'At the core of the story is the will of the Armenian people to defend their Christianity, protect their right to religious freedom, and maintain national independence and unity' (*California Courier On-Line*, 21 January 1999, as posted on *Groong Armenian News Network*, 19 January 1999).

[23] For example H. Chanashian, commenting on the work of Grigor Zohrap (one of the more prominent writer-intellectual-politicians of this period) says: 'In general, he portrays human existence, a life full of dreams, with sexual misadventures, in its naked misery, with difficulties and disappointments' (H. Chanashian, *Hai grakanutian*, p. 144).

[24] Even in the poetry of Daniel Varuzhan, existential concerns are woven into racial and nationalist themes without being subordinated to the imperatives of nationalism; cf. H. Chanashian, *Hai grakanutian*, pp. 229–31; K. Bardakjian, *Reference Guide*, pp. 157–8.

ual as it was with the nation. In short, it was not the literature of radical nationalism, but of liberalism, embodying the liberal view of the individual and of the nation while reflecting the middle class attitudes of Constantinople Armenians. Nevertheless, it was national literature insofar as it accepted the nation as the 'natural' or 'given' basis of collective identity.

In the east

In contrast to the western point, the dominant current in eastern Armenian literature was romanticism, while the realist school remained much less prevalent. Whereas in the west young Armenians went to Paris and Venice for their higher education, in the east they went to Dorpat University and St Petersburg. The role of Dorpat (Tartu) in Estonia is particularly important in this context. From the 1830s onward Russian Armenians went there to study the humanities and fell under the spell of the work of the romantic poets Goethe and Schiller, as well as German thought. Later generations were also influenced by the revolutionary fervour inspired by 1848 Paris. 'They were fired up with nationalist fervour, with the ideals of the Enlightenment, and the revolutionary spirit of the times. They wrote passionate poetry about the woes and hopes of Armenia, set it to music, and sang it.'[25] The total number of Armenians who went to these universities was never large, but their impact on eastern Armenian literature and culture was tremendous.[26] This romantic literature, with patriotic and populist strains, remained the main literary current until the end of the nineteenth century.

Among many writers in this genre two emerge as the towering giants of eastern Armenian literature.[27] These two men were instrumental in creating the literary basis of the nationalist literature (in

[25] V. Oshagan, 'Modern Armenian Literature', pp. 150, 163; cf. H. Chanashian, *Hai grakanutian*, pp. 72–94.

[26] By 1892 fifty-two Armenians had studied at Dorpat. But many of these became the most influential intellectuals within Russian Armenia, such as the educator Stepanos Nazariants (W. Balekjian, 'University of Dorpat', p. 336 [n. 9]).

[27] Of course there were other significant authors, namely Rafayel Patkanian (Kamar-Katipa) and Mikayel Nalbandian. For such men literature was only one of their vocations and their impact—as activists—was more notable in other fields such as journalism.

the vernacular) of the awakening. The first was Khachatur Abovian (*c.* 1809–48) who was an educator, an advocate of modernisation and a poet. However, he is best remembered as the author of the powerful novel *Verk Hayastani* (Wounds of Armenia), which set the trend in both style and content for subsequent literature. Written in 1841, but published posthumously in 1858, it was the first novel in the eastern Armenian (Yerevan based) dialect. The story describes the misery of Armenia under Persian and Turkish rule before 1828 and the need for self defence. It also highlights the *continuation* of such misery under Russian domination. Through his novel Abovian not only attacked foreign control of Armenia he also criticised the conservatism of the clergy and the backwardness of the region. His romantic novel, historical in theme, was written in the context of Abovian's constant efforts to modernise Armenia, especially through education. Not only did this book provide the basis of eastern Armenian (and nationalist) literature, it ushered in the new modern age of Armenian literature in general. Its intensely emotional and tragic story, which contained the 'prototype of the freedom fighter' in the novels of subsequent authors, was meant 'to appeal to the people, [to] move their feelings, and [to] direct their will.'[28] And it did—and it still does—just that.

Abovian was born near Yerevan and received his early education at the seminary of Ejmiatzin. He then went to study at the Nersisian

[28] The quotes are from V. Oshagan, 'Modern Armenian Literature', p. 161. Another commentator calls Aghasi, the hero of *Wounds of Armenia*, 'the first rebel in modern Armenian literature [who] fights and dies for the liberation of his country' (K. Bardakjian, *Reference Guide*, p. 137; cf. L. Nalbandian, *Armenian Revolutionary Movement*, pp. 38–40). Although Abovian's *Wounds of Armenia* is the first significant modern Armenian novel, the Indian Armenian community must (once again) be given credit for publishing the very first work of fiction in modern Armenian literature. It was a 'partly historical and partly psychological' novel written by Mesrob Taghiatiants and published in 1846 in Calcutta. The book did not gain a wide readership outside India (V. Oshagan, 'Modern Armenian Literature', p. 147). Taghiatiants was a Russian Armenian who had ended up in Calcutta where he founded the Araratian Society and published a magazine called *Azgaser Araratian* (Patriot of Ararat) between 1848 and 1852 (this was a follow-up on an earlier publication he had embarked on; Taghiatiants published in both classical and modern Armenian). As Mesrovb Seth puts it, 'To his efforts the revival of Armenian literature and nationalism in India is mainly due; for, through the medium of his journal, the *Patriot of Ararat*, he revived the dying embers of patriotism amongst the Armenians in this country' (M. Seth, *Armenians in India*, p. 521, cf. pp. 515–22). This was the last notable contribution of the Indian Armenian community to national(ist) culture and identity.

Academy in Tiflis, being one of its first graduates. Subsequently, with the help of Professor Johann J. F. W. Parrot (1791–1841)—with whom, as a guide, he climbed Mount Ararat in September-October 1829—he went to the University of Dorpat, where he studied the humanities and philosophy for five years (1830–5).[29] It was there that he fell under the influence of German Romanticism. He returned to Tiflis, and then Yerevan, with the knowledge and determination to enlighten the Armenians, to modernise them, and to 'awaken' them as a nation. He tried to do this through the means of education and his writings. But he encountered resistance and much opposition from the conservative clergy, who controlled education, and the Tsarist bureaucracy, who were suspicious of his innovative ideas. In a state of depression (it is assumed), Abovian disappeared in 1848, ten years before his *Wounds of Armenia* was published.

The second writer who must be noted is Hakob Melik-Hakobian, better known as Raffi (1832–88). A prolific novelist, Raffi wrote in the same vein as Abovian, but in a more refined and sophisticated style. His historical novels took episodes from Armenia's past and presented them in a rebellious and revolutionary manner. Unlike Abovian's, Raffi's heroes, instead of meeting tragic deaths, succeeded in their liberating projects. However, like Abovian, Raffi used history and literature to enlighten people and to imbue them with the love of the nation. Hence his novels—especially *Davit Bek* (based on the life of the leader of the 1720s rebellion) and *Kaitzer* (Sparks)—are full of nationalist sermons advocating the struggle for liberation against oppressive rule, corruption and evil. The subject of one of his best novels, *Samvel*, is the struggle of a patriotic young man for his nation and religion against Persia, and against his very own traitor parents who have rejected Christianity and joined the enemy.

Raffi was born in northern Iran and educated in Tiflis. Unable to complete his formal higher education (owing to the financial constraints of his family), he nevertheless acquired knowledge of European literature through Mkhitarist translations and Russian publications. He became a teacher in an Armenian school in Tabriz (Iran), travelled throughout eastern and western Armenia, and finally settled in Tiflis where he devoted all of his time to writing. Through his widely read romantic works Raffi became the 'ideological

[29] For Abovian's relation with Dorpat University see W. Balekjian, 'University of Dorpat'.

father of the Armenian revolutionary movements', successfully applying 'the ideas of enlightenment and political awakening' to the Armenians.[30]

As in the west, Armenians in the east developed their own theatre and opera, based in Tiflis. Gabriel Sundukian (1825–1912), a student of Abovian but a realist in his style, is considered the father of eastern Armenian theatre. His plays 'derided the corruption in the Armenian middle class, the superstitions of the lower classes and their exploitation by the bureaucracy of Tiflis.'[31] In 1912 the immensely popular opera *Anush* was staged in Alexandropol (eastern Armenia, now Gyumri in Armenia) for the first time. This Armenian version of *Romeo and Juliet* (but set in village life) was based on a long poem by Hovhannes Tumanian and put to music by Armen Tigranian.

As in language, Armenian literature in the second half of the nineteenth century was divided into western and eastern variants. Each used its own vernacular language and each was influenced by different trends of European thought. However, this conclusion is based on general traits, and the east/west division, along with the spheres of European influence, was not absolute. The realist and the romantic schools influenced each other and both had certain common characteristics in their focus on national as well as social issues, enlightenment and liberation. Nonetheless, there are two interconnected points that need to be made here: eastern and western literature had different types and levels of impact on the construction of Armenian national identity.

Eastern romantic literature played much more of a prominent role in nationalising the Armenian renaissance. It explicitly sought to create a collective national identity. Both its style and its content were meant to educate and mobilise people around the idea of the Armenian nation and its struggle for liberation. Hence the impact it

[30] V. Oshagan, 'Modern Armenian Literature', pp. 164, 166–7; cf. L. Nalbandian, *Armenian Revolutionary Movement*, pp. 63–6; H. Chanashian, *Hai grakanutian*, pp. 86–94. The next generation of eastern Armenian writers (not all of them romantics) included Avetis Aharonian (1866–1948), Hovhannes Hovhannesian (1864–1929), Hovhannes Tumanian (1869–1923), Avetik Isahakian (1875–1957), Vahan Terian (1885–1920). They all included patriotic themes in their work, but after 1915 had a different set of problems to contend with.

[31] V. Oshagan, 'Modern Armenian Literature', p. 165.

had was predominantly nationalist. To this day Abovian, Raffi and the romantic writer-intellectuals are seen as the quintessential authors belonging to the genre of 'national liberation' literature. Pre-1915 western Armenian writers on the other hand had less of an impact in terms of the national(ist) content of their literature (although they took the nation for granted as the basis of Armenian identity). Nevertheless, they were influential in other realms. The works of these writers helped shape Armenian identity through their social critique, their inner meaning and their aesthetic beauty—for which they are still applauded. In short, eastern and western literature had different types of influence in the process of shaping modern Armenian identity. This is the first point.

The second point—the level of impact—is best expressed in terms of a sociological question: To what extent did these bodies of literature influence the masses? It is difficult to come to a definite conclusion about this in the absence of available research on the subject. But it does seem that eastern authors and intellectuals were much more successful in bridging the gap between them and the general population as their literature found a deeper resonance at the mass level. They managed to establish 'organic' links with the people largely because of their ideological commitment to the masses. Their work captured the imagination of the 'common' Armenian who could relate his or her experiences to the characters and stories found in Abovian's, Raffi's and others' texts—and as such could reformulate his or her identity along national(ist) lines. Romantic novels also reached western Armenians, including readers in Constantinople and Smyrna, but their impact was less powerful, largely on account of their eastern vernacular language.[32]

Western realist literature was not as successful in terms of its level of influence on the Armenians of the Ottoman empire as was eastern romantic literature on the Armenians of the Russian empire and beyond. Realist literature was more or less confined to a small intellectual class based in Constantinople, Smyrna and other cities in the western sphere of Armenian cultural production. They did

[32] In the *Arevelian Mamul* (1:1, January 1871) article quoted above some eastern Armenian writers are mentioned (Abovian, Nalbandian, Patkanian etc.). While they are applauded for their commitment to liberating ideas and to the creation of a new 'national school' of literature, the language they use—the eastern Armenian vernacular—is referred to as 'spurious and strange [*anhetet yev khort*]' (p. 36).

not have much of a following among, or influence on, the general Armenian population (until well into the twentieth century). The 'high culture' they created could not link itself with the masses as it did not on the whole 'speak' to the everyday realities of the homeland—i.e. to the Armenians of the provinces. The concerns of cosmopolitan urbanites seemed too foreign and too complicated for the majority of the Armenian population. Vahé Oshagan highlights the weak link between writers and the people of western (Ottoman) Armenia:

> The end result of all the frantic activity to put together a cultural infrastructure and sustain a literary life, the effort to awaken and educate a humiliated, ignorant, and docile nation in order to catch up with the rest of the world was meagre. Generally, writers had no clear notion of their identity as such and there was no tradition of national literature yet.[33]

In sum, both western realist and eastern romantic literature influenced Armenian national identity, but in different ways, in different places and in differing degrees. Together they constituted the basis of modern Armenian literature, but in their differences (as in language) they also manifested and shaped the east-west divide in Armenian culture. Each body of literature shaped the identity of Armenians in its sphere of influence, although eastern romanticism was more influential at the mass level.

POLITICAL IDEOLOGY

If language and literature provided the cultural context of the Armenian awakening in terms of national identity, political ideology provided the clearly articulated expression in terms of Armenian nationalism. Hence the cultural renaissance entered the stage of the politics of nationalism. Once again the sources of this ideology were multilocal, but the two overall trends roughly corresponded to the east-west divide. However, in this case the third point of the triangle mentioned above—the Armenian homeland—also played a crucial role. By the first decade of the twentieth century the eastern radical trend, combined with indigenous elements within (Turkish)

[33] V. Oshagan, 'Cultural and Literary Awakening', p. 69. Gerard Libaridian makes a similar point but in the context of ideology rather than literature (G. Libaridian, 'Nation and Fatherland', pp. 87–9).

Armenia, came to dominate Armenian political thinking, at least in terms of setting the agenda of national politics.

The Armenian awakening did not have a clear cut political ideology with one set of coherent principles. There were various elements to it as many concepts were intertwined to form a heterogeneous set of ideas.[34] This multiplicity of ideas was reflected in the activities and deeds of various individuals and organisations. I will concentrate on three overall ideological positions or locations that affected identity: the liberal constitutionalism of the west (viz. in Constantinople); the radical leftism—be it socialist or populist—of the east and; the rebellious or revolutionary ideas and activities emanating from Armenia itself. All of these trends, it must be emphasised, were infused *into* Armenian nationalism. That is to say, in general they were not alternatives to nationalism but constituted different core elements within the *same* national movement.[35]

In the west

Until the arrival of revolutionary ideas from Russian Armenia in the 1890s, the dominant ideology among western Armenians evolved around the reforms of the Ottoman empire and the Armenian *millet* therein. This emphasis on reforms—in thinking and in structures—was nothing less than a liberal (and fundamental) transformation taking place within the political centre of the community in Constantinople as a result of which the powers of the conservative 'aristocratic' elements—the *amira* class and their supporters—were curtailed. The main agents of change were students and young intellectuals who had studied in Europe, mostly in Paris. Ironically some

[34] There are various studies of the political ideology of this period. For general studies see L. Nalbandian, *Armenian Revolutionary Movement*; G. Libaridian, *Ideology of Armenian Liberation* and 'Nation and Fatherland'; S. Atamian, *Armenian Community*; R. Suny, *Looking toward Ararat*; A. Ter Minassian, *Nationalism and Socialism*; H. Tasnapetian, *Hai heghapokhakan sharjume.*

[35] This is a simplification of the complex relations between nationalism and socialism/populism within the Armenian revolutionary movement. From the 1880s to the 1910s there were fierce debates between socialist and nationalist Armenians. Nationalism, however, emerged as the dominant paradigm while 'socialism remained a rhetorical cover behind which the national struggle was fought' (R. Suny, *Looking toward Ararat*, p. 93, see pp. 63–93 for an overview; cf. Ter Minassian, *Nationalism and Socialism*). This point will be discussed in further detail in the next chapter.

of these men were themselves from *amira* families or had gone abroad with scholarships provided by the *amiras*. However, they returned full of 'revolutionary' ideas such as the equality of individuals, representative government, constitutional rule, intellectual enlightenment, secularisation of politics etc., and were eager to put some of these progressive ideas into practice within the Armenian *millet*.[36] These individuals were not large in number,[37] but they—and their followers—had a substantial impact on the political thinking of the community. I will concentrate on the most significant political achievement of this liberal approach: the intra-community reform process, which led to the adoption of the 'Armenian National Constitution'.

As mentioned in the previous chapter, the Armenian *millet* was ruled by the *amira* class who dominated the community and controlled its official leadership: the patriarchate of Constantinople. The ideologically conservative *amiras* were uninterested in both inter- and intra-*millet* reforms. Their standing was in 'perfect accord with Ottoman policy' and they did not hesitate 'to use their financial generosity [i.e. charitable donations to the community] to preserve and further their influence and control over the millet.'[38] However, in the second half of the nineteenth century the *amiras* did lose their undisputed control. The forces of change were represented by the 'constitutionalists' (known as the 'enlightened'). These young western-educated men were supported by the middle and working classes organised in the *esnafs* (tradesmen/artisans guilds). Together

[36] For example, in an article called 'Freedom' in the progressive journal edited by Matteos Mamurian, *Arevelian Mamul* (1:8, August 1871, pp. 478–84), a liberal conception of freedom is expounded: 'Freedom begins with the individual, and man is born with the [right of] ownership' (p. 480). Of all the different types of freedom listed in this article—personal, household, economic, religious, political (which it says is the 'shield' of other rights)—national rights are not mentioned.

[37] Initially, in the 1840s, no more than thirty were sent abroad, but the practice continued in the next few decades. Many of these men became the most influential thinkers and leaders in Constantinople. They included Grigor Otian (1834–87), writer, jurist, driving force behind the Armenian Constitution of 1863 and the Ottoman Constitution of 1878; the brothers Mkrtich (1818–90) and Grigor (1825–68) Aghaton, editors, educators and civil servants; Matteos Mamurian (1830–1901), writer and publisher; Dr Nahapet Rusinian (1819–76), writer, linguist and philosopher; Dr Serovbe Vichenian (1815–97), writer and educator (cf. V. Oshagan, 'Modern Armenian Literature', pp. 151–5).

[38] H. Barsoumian, 'Dual Role', pp. 179, 178.

they managed to dislodge the *amira*'s absolute domination of the community.[39] This had wide ramifications. As Hagop Barsoumian points out, 'The conflict between these two antagonistic groups [*amiras* and the constitutionalists] was not only political, it was also cultural, economic and social.'[40] Each side represented a different world view, set of principles and agenda.

In the context of the overall *Tanzimat* reforms of the Ottoman empire,[41] the progressive elements eventually succeeded in passing a constitution for the *internal* administration of the Armenian *millet* which was ratified by the Sultan in 1863.[42] This document is a fasci-

39 *Esnafs* were long established guilds that contributed funds toward the expenses of the *millet* as well, but without much of a say in its running until the 1840s. For details see V. Artinian, *Armenian Constitutional System*, pp. 24–9; H. Barsoumian, 'Eastern Question', pp. 190, 195–6.

40 H. Barsoumian, 'Dual Role', p. 180.

41 The reform process in the empire began in 1839 and continued on and off for the rest of the century. The highlight was the adoption at the end of 1876 of a Constitution, which was abrogated a year later by Sultan Abdul Hamid II. The reforms were partly due to the internal stagnation of the empire and partly induced by Western powers. They did not accomplish much in terms of ameliorating in practice the living conditions of the Armenian (and other minority) subjects—especially in the provinces. However, on the conceptual level the reforms did introduce the radical liberal idea that all subjects of the Sultan, Muslim and non-Muslim, were equal. This was a fundamental break with the Ottoman/Muslim conception that non-Muslims were inferior in status (cf. H. Barsoumian, 'Eastern Question', pp. 180–2, 198–200). Kemal Karpat suggests that by incorporating a notion of equality and citizenship the reforms actually undermined the *millets*' autonomy vis-à-vis the Ottoman state (K. Karpat, '*Millets* and Nationality', pp. 163–6). It should also be noted that the non-Muslim *millets* were often the 'agents or channels of Westernization in the Ottoman Empire'—i.e. as the sources of reform at the pan-empire level (R. Davidson, '*Millets* as Agents of Change', p. 319). For example, Davidson points out that 'Some of the Western influence that contributed to that momentous document [i.e. the Ottoman Constitution of 1876] flowed through the filter of the Armenian *millet* constitution' (p. 330), with Grigor Otian playing a particularly important role (p. 327).

42 It was formally known as the National Constitution of the Armenians (for details of the content of the constitution see V. Artinian, *Armenian Constitutional System*, pp. 93–101; for a critical analysis from a more radical perspective see S. Atamian, *Armenian Community*, pp. 30–41; for a good overview see H. Barsoumian, 'Eastern Question', pp. 195–9; the entire document is reprinted in English in H. Lynch, *Armenia*, Vol. II, pp. 445–67; for comments and assessments on the Constitution's relevance to contemporary Armenian communities in the diaspora see the round table discussion, 'Azgayin sahmanadrutian aizhmeakanutiune'). It should, however, be clear that the Constitution (more correctly a 'code of regulations') was purely a rearrangement of formal power relations *within* the Armenian community and in no way affected rela-

nating example of a constitution of a nation without a state. It was not tied to any specific territory, but was based on community institutions and structures. The Constitution created a series of elected bodies to run the affairs of the community, which were very much dominated by the laity and the middle classes. It considerably curtailed the formal powers of the *amiras* (who did remain powerful individuals), and of the Patriarch, in the (secular) leadership of the *millet*. In short, the patriarchate and other community organisations such as schools, hospitals and charitable institutions were now controlled by a much broader sector of the community according to a codified legal-institutional framework.[43]

However, this was not just a question of who was to control the levers of power in the *millet*. It was indicative of the emergence of a new political stratum which sought to lead the Armenian *nation* based on a different set of principles. Liberalism and nationalism came to replace 'the notion of social order represented by the [*millet*] system of religious communities.'[44] The Constitution was the symbol and the structure of a new way of organising the Armenians into a community that resembled a modern nation. It did not grant separate citizenship to them (all residents of the Ottoman empire were subjects of the Sultan),[45] nor did it give them a clear-cut terri-

---

tions between the *millet* and the general Muslim community or the Ottoman state—i.e. Armenians did not get any new rights or safeguards against maltreatment. The passing of the Constitution was not a smooth affair. Between 1840 and 1863 it engendered bitter antagonisms between the *amiras* and other conservatives on the one side, and the 'young Armenians/enlighteners' and the *esnafs* on the other, with the Patriarch in the middle. The disputes were over the control of the institutions governing the *millet* (details are recounted in V. Artinian, *Armenian Constitutional System*, pp. 52ff.).

43 Lay participation in—and even control of—the administration of the church had been an Armenian tradition since its foundation. The Constitution formalised this arrangement in a way that generally favoured the middle classes. The patriarch retained substantial powers, but he could not remain on the throne without the support of the elected bodies. Of the 140 deputies in the Armenian National Assembly only twenty were reserved for clerics; the rest of the seats were allocated to (elected) lay members (A. Ter Minassian, 'Sociétés de culture', p. 11).

44 H. Barsoumian, 'Eastern Question', p. 183. More generally, on how the *millet* system led to nationalism see K. Karpat, '*Millets* and Nationality', pp. 147ff.

45 Article IX of the preface to the Constitution explicitly states: the National Administration's (i.e. the Assembly's) first obligation is 'towards the Imperial Government, that is to preserve the nation in perfectly loyal subjection and to secure to the nation

torial basis, but it did provide Armenians with a more representative leadership, an elected 'National General Assembly' and a secularised system of internal governance. In short, the Constitution, in a very visible manner, manifested the victory of the new set of political principles through which Armenian identity was being reconstructed based on notions of modernity, liberalism and nationality. These were the recurrent themes in the political writings, publications and activities of the 'enlighteners'.

Accordingly Armenian intellectuals and the (city-based) middle classes were no longer 'imagining' themselves and their people exclusively as an ethno-religious community, but as a modernising nation. At this point national independence was not part of their political framework, but liberal reforms were. They wanted Armenians to be treated as equal citizens of the Ottoman empire while enjoying communal autonomy. There were two sides to this: the internal dimension of an Armenian constitution-based society, and the external dimension of a law-and-order-based Ottoman state which would provide protection to the Armenian *community* and to the Armenian *citizens* from arbitrary taxes, coercion, Kurdish raids and other abuses of power. The issue of autonomy also was raised (based on the example of Lebanon) as early as 1878, and remained part of the Armenian political debate; it became a central demand of the Armenian political parties in the mid-1890s. Nevertheless, the liberal Armenians of Constantinople envisioned nationhood *within* the Ottoman domains, as a self-governing (and dispersed) nation within a reforming empire. In the Ottoman context these were rad-

---

in general and to individuals in particular the preservation of their rights and privileges on the part of the Government.' The second is to the nation 'in a paternal way'. And the third is to Ejmiatzin—i.e. to the Catholicos of All Armenians. The first point under the section 'Fundamental Principles' states: 'Each individual has obligations towards the nation. The nation, in its turn, has obligation towards each individual. Again, each individual and the nation have their respective rights over one another' (H. Lynch, *Armenia*, vol. II, pp. 448–9). It is interesting to note in these articles how the constitution tries to balance between Armenians as subjects of the Ottoman empire and as members of an autonomous community within it. The whole document is also an embodiment of liberal contract theory with its emphasis on 'written regulations, defining the functions, duties, jurisdictions and methods of election of the patriarch' and of the administration of other community structures (H. Barsoumian, 'Eastern Question', pp. 197–8). *Amiras* were against such codification because it limited their unofficial powers.

ical ideas, but they were in no way revolutionary in their means or aspirations.

This 'western' notion of nationhood did not remain the dominant mode of thinking, owing on the one hand to the failure of the Ottoman reforms and on the other to the challenge from the radical nationalists of the east and of Armenia itself, as we shall see next. However, it did leave a profound mark on Armenian identity. The idea of citizenship, of individual rights and civic duties, of constitutionalism and reform-based politics, all entered Armenian political consciousness through the western point of identity formation. Finally, and very importantly, the liberal nationalism of Constantinople perceived the nation in a way that was not necessarily or exclusively based on a compact territory or statehood, although it was obviously related to the Armenian provinces and communal autonomy. There was a diasporan sense of identity built into the very meaning of Armenian nationhood. This was reflected in the 1863 Constitution, which was drawn up in—and mostly for—Constantinople and kept power in the hands of the Armenian elite in the capital. Of the 140 seats in the newly formed National Assembly, eighty were reserved for deputies from Constantinople, while representatives from the Ottoman provinces (where more than eighty per cent of the Armenian population lived) were only allocated forty seats.[46]

In the east

As on the western side, nationalism in eastern Armenia emerged through young intellectuals who were knowledgeable about—and in contact with—European political ideas and movements, having attended mostly Russian and German universities (Dorpat, Heidelberg, Moscow etc.).[47] The first generation of writers, publishers, educators, poets and activists who advocated reform and modernisation were *liberals* eager to transform Armenians into a modern nation. For example, Grigor Artzruni, 'armed with European knowledge,... was the inoculator of progressive ideas in the barren reality of Armenia, preaching the enlightened ideas of renewal'; he was like

[46] A. Ter Minassian, 'Sociétés de culture', pp. 11–12.

[47] These men included Mikayel Nalbandian (1829–66), Stepanos Nazariants (1812–79), Gabriel (1802–89), Rafayel and Patkanian (1830–92), Grigor Artzruni (1845–92).

a 'cultivator who sowed the seeds of progress'.[48] Stepanos Nazariants situated language at the centre of national identity and tied the well-being of the latter to the attainment of statehood, the highest form of social organisation and freedom.[49] Meanwhile Mikayel Nalbandian advocated a new conception of the Armenian nation which was based on the common people and a secular sense of belonging. The principle of nationality was to replace the principle of a religious community.[50]

The principle of nationality was taken a step further by the next generation of activists, as revolutionary ideas were infused into Armenian political identity. By the 1880s young intellectuals and students—themselves testimony to the success of the earlier educators—were no longer content to confine their activities to schools, publications and other cultural forms of expression. No longer satisfied with just

[48] The quotes are from an article commemorating the 25th anniversary of Artzruni's death: '25-amiak taghman Grigor Artzrunu' in *Mshak*, 28 Dec. 1917, no. 273, p. 1. He had established the progressive newspaper *Mshak* in 1872 in Tiflis; it ceased publication in 1920.

[49] R. Mirumian, 'Azg-petutiun'.

[50] R. Suny, 'Eastern Armenians', p. 119. Mikayel Nalbandian also introduced the first ethnographic novel in Armenian literature. He 'believed that the function of the Armenian writer was to enlighten the Armenian people through proper education in literary ashkharhabar [i.e. the vernacular]' (V. Oshagan, 'Modern Armenian Literature', p. 162). He was one of the most important eastern nationalist intellectuals—an activist, educator, writer and poet. One of his patriotic poems (written in celebration of the Italian struggle for independence) has become the current national anthem of Armenia—which is the same as that of the independent republic of 1918. The last verse of this poem-song is as follows:

Death is the same everywhere.
Man will only die once,
But blessed is he who
sacrifices [his life] for the liberty of his nation.

It should be noted that some changes were made to the original version to 'update it' for the 1990s—minor verbal changes but with great symbolic value. Hence, the opening lines which were (in the 1860s):

Our Fatherland, miserable and without leadership,
Trampled by its enemies...

have become in the official 1991 version:

Our Fatherland, free and independent,
Which has lived from century to century...

For an exposition of the thought of Nalbandian and his activities see S. Shmavonian, 'Mikayel Nalbandian'.

'imagining' the nation they wanted to engage in political action to liberate it. With them Armenian nationalism came of age.

Although they lived and organised in the Russian empire, mostly in Tiflis, these revolutionaries almost exclusively turned their attention to the emancipation of Ottoman Armenia, at least until 1903. Some of these Russian Armenians operated in other European cities outside the empire. They were heavily influenced by radical Russian political thought and some were even active in local revolutionary organisations in Moscow and St Petersburg. The ideas of Mikhail Bakunin, Alexander Herzen and Visarion Belinsky most strongly influenced the young Armenians of the Russian empire. The Russian populists' idealisation of the 'people' was internalised by the Armenian radical intelligentsia. But, very importantly, this social activism was infused with romantic nationalism. Hence, the notion of 'going to the people' propagated by the populists—viz. People's Will—was reinterpreted by the Armenians as 'going to the homeland' (*'depi yerkir'*). Going to '*yerkir*' meant going to Turkish Armenia to defend and free its oppressed Armenian population, with the use of arms if needed.[51] Later when socialism also made inroads into Armenian thinking (from the late 1880s onwards) it too was merged with nationalism. As Ronald Suny puts it, 'For most Armenian revolutionaries, nationality was the touchstone of their worldview'; they emphasised 'the unity of the Armenian nation, of the solidarity of goals of all Armenians, and the danger of class division among this small people.'[52] Intra-community class antagonisms did exist, especially when radical elements began to organise in Constantinople and other large cities, but they remained subordinate to the national struggle.

By the 1890s romantic nationalism had emerged as the main current of political thought and action. The national had clearly become the dominant mode of (political) identity, subordinating and absorbing other identities and ideologies. The deep sense of already existing ethno-religious identity, the efforts of the earlier generation

[51] One scholar characterises 'the Armenian movement as national populism' (A. Ter Minassian, *Nationalism and Socialism*, p. 21).

[52] R. Suny, *Looking toward Ararat*, p. 71; cf. R. Suny, 'Eastern Armenians', p. 131. For a good discussion of the Armenian intelligentsia of this period, and the relationship between populism, socialism and nationalism see R. Suny, *Looking toward Ararat*, Chapters 4 and 5; A. Ter Minassian, *Nationalism and Socialism*.

of intellectuals and novelists to nationalise it according to modernist principles, and now the national liberation movement of the radicals contributed to the establishment of a powerful sense of all-encompassing Armenianness that was based on a secular political sense of belonging.[53]

The melange of romantic nationalism and social radicalism can be seen in the early publications of the newly established Federation of Armenian Revolutionaries (more about this in the next chapter). In its first propaganda leaflet, printed in the second half of 1890, the revolutionaries wrote:

> Today Europe is seeing in front of it an entire people, an entire nation, which has begun to defend its human rights.... In such a historically critical junction the first issue, which should concern every patriot, is the unity and federation of all revolutionary forces.... The Federation of Armenian Revolutionaries is appealing to all Armenians and inviting them to stand under one flag.... Having as its aim the political and economic emancipation of Turkish Armenia, the Federation has entered that struggle which has been started by the people itself against the Turkish government, vowing to fight until the last drop of its blood for the freedom of the fatherland.... Hence, brothers, let us unite for the sake of the holy effort against the common enemy. And you, the youth,... unite with the people.... And you, the wealthy, open your purses to provide weapons to the people to defend itself.... And you, Armenian women, infuse spirit into the holy endeavour. And you, Armenian clergy, bless the soldiers of freedom.... It is not the time to wait.... Let us unite Armenians, and bravely advance the holy endeavour of liberating the fatherland.[54]

A few months later, in its 1891 Proclamation, the Federation added: 'Turkish Armenia, enslaved for centuries, is now demanding its freedom.... The Armenian is no longer imploring—he now demands, with gun in hand.'[55] In 1892 the organisation published its prog-

[53] I do not wish to suggest that the revolutionary approach was the only mode of thought. But it did become the politically dominant ideology by the turn of the century. Liberalism also existed and was best represented by the newspaper *Mshak*. However, almost all Armenian activists were nationalist insofar as they struggled for national rights. The very few Armenian 'internationalist' activists emphasising the primacy of class conflict over national issues operated within Russian Marxist organisations.

[54] As quoted in M. Varandian, *H. H. Dashnaktsutian patmutiun*, pp. 74–5; and in G. Lazian, *Hayastan yev hai date*, pp. 66–7; cf. *H.H.D. 100*, pp. 10–11.

[55] S. Atamian, *Armenian Community*, p. 104; cf. A. Sevian, 'Founding', pp. 128ff.; L. Nalbandian, *Armenian Revolutionary Movement*, pp. 156–7.

ramme, which included among other points the 'creation of a popular-democratic government based on free election'; the 'equality of all nationalities and religions before the law'; 'freedom of speech, press and assembly'; land redistribution; compulsory education; and 'communal principles as a means to greater production and distribution.'[56] These were to be achieved by propaganda as well as revolutionary and terrorist activities against the Ottoman state.

These statements reflect the predominant mode of thinking among the Armenian revolutionaries. It evolved around a united, nationwide struggle to defend the Armenian population of the Armenian provinces in the Ottoman empire. It incorporated liberal political ideas and socialist principles into a nationalist project directed against the Ottoman state and menacing Kurdish tribes. Activists in Tiflis and in other Armenian intellectual centres believed that national liberation, through a general rebellion was imminent. Varandian himself labels this as the 'romantic period of the Armenian movement'.[57]

Three qualifying points need to be made here. First, Armenian liberation did not necessarily mean independence from the Ottoman empire. Even the most fervent revolutionaries did not think this was feasible at any time in the foreseeable future. They called for fundamental reform, autonomy and self defence. Their means (armed struggle and rebellion) and their ideals (populist-nationalist and socialist) were revolutionary in this context. They wanted to liberate the Armenian *people*; independence and statehood were of secondary considerations. Second, it should be noted that at this point Armenians (with some minor exceptions) did not mobilise against Russian autocracy, and they did not oppose Russian rule of eastern Armenia in any significant manner. Despite increasing persecution by Tsarist authorities of the Armenians, the latter took for granted that Russian administration was better than Turkish domination.

The third point is a significant element of Armenian national identity. As at the western point of identity formation, Armenian nationalism in the east was not confined to territoriality—i.e. having to live exclusively on their own historic lands. True, the main geographic focus of the nationalists was on historic Armenia where

[56] As quoted in R. Hovannisian, *Armenia*, p. 17.
[57] M. Varandian, *H. H. Dashnaktsutian patmutiun*, p. 77.

Armenians had originated and where most of them lived. No doubt these Armenians had to be liberated on their own land. However, the nation was not necessarily confined to the Armenian lands in the Ottoman or Russian empires or, even more specifically, to the six *vilayets* of Turkish Armenia on which the nationalists concentrated.[58] Rather, the most important dimension of Armenian national identity and nationalism at this point was based on communal rights and autonomy largely manifested through community institutions (as formalised by the 1836 *Polozhenie*) rather than state structures. Armenians were after all dispersed throughout the two empires and various other countries, with significant elements living outside Armenia proper (in Tiflis, Baku, Moscow and so forth). What is more, on a more practical level they rarely constituted a majority, even in the Armenian provinces of the Ottoman empire.[59] Hence

[58] For example, nationalist parties defended Armenians wherever they were threatened, but in all the programmes and proclamations of these organisations the notion that Armenians should only live on their own land was absent.

[59] Population figures for the Armenians, particularly for the Ottoman empire, are a controversial topic. Simply put, historians close to the Turkish view (e.g. Justin McCarthy, Kemal Karpat, Heath Lowry, Stanford Shaw, Bernard Lewis) downsize the number, while scholars sympathetic to the Armenians (e.g. Richard Hovannisian, Vahakn Dadrian, Christopher Walker, Gérard Chaliand and Yves Ternon) try to maintain as high a number as possible. There is no consensus because there is a wide discrepancy in the figures given in the primary sources of the period. It is, however, clear that Armenians constituted a minority in all of the six *vilayets*. Only in some specific areas (e.g. the cities of Van and Zeytun) were they the majority, in some *vilayets* they were a plurality, while in others (e.g. Diarbekir) they may have been outnumbered six to one by Muslims (Kurds and Turks). Their share of the population varied from 18 per cent to 42 per cent in each of the *vilayets*. Overall in 1844 there were 2.4 million Armenians in all of the Ottoman empire. This figure was approximately two million in 1912 (or about 13 per cent of the Ottoman population of 15 million in Anatolia and Constantinople). The decline was due to massacres, emigration and the incorporation of the Kars and Artahan regions in Russia after the 1878 Russo-Turkish war. Of the two million, half lived in the six Armenian provinces (approximately 200,000 in Bitlis, Van, Erzerum and Sivas each and 100,000 in Diarbekir and Kharput each). Another 640,000 lived in the remainder of Anatolia, 161,000 in Constantinople and about 40,000 in other parts of the empire (in Europe and in the Middle East). This leaves about 150,000 people who cannot be placed in a specific region. The 1912 figures are based on the Armenian patriarchate census returns, which seem the most reliable, and are corroborated by other sources (L. Marashlian, *Politics and Demography*, pp. 49, 51, 58; R. Kévorkian and P. Paboudjian, *Arméniens*, pp. 53–60; H. Barsoumian, 'Eastern Question', pp. 191–2). Levon Marashlian's book outlines the demographic debate and debunks the arguments for the lower figures, particularly that of Justin McCarthy. H. F. B. Lynch, writing at the turn of the twentieth century, gives a total 1890s figure

eastern and western Armenian nationalism did not base national identity on independent statehood and territoriality.[60] Of course there was a very clear notion of the Armenian homeland and historic territories. But Armenian nationalism could not be reduced to territorial demands. Nor could nationalists make demographic/electoral arguments a basis of their demands for rights and autonomy. In this view the nation did not *have* to live on its own territory to be defined as such, or to have collective rights; Armenians living on their own land must be protected, *and so must Armenians living elsewhere.*

The other side of this ethno-cultural and communal-based nationalism was the exclusion of other peoples who did not share the same ethnicity, culture, religion or language (be it actual or symbolic) as the Armenians, but resided in the historic Armenian homeland. By definition they could not be part of the Armenian nation even though they lived on historic Armenian territories. In sum, Armenian nationalism was diffused to include all Armenians no matter where they had settled, but very specifically excluded all those who lived on traditional Armenian lands but were not part of the ethnocultural space of Armenians. National identity was very much blood-based. The old and rigid ethnic and religious boundaries were very much maintained as the boundaries of the emerging nation. Territorial demands for an exclusive homeland and independence were secondary to this.

In conclusion, at the eastern point of the evolution of Armenian national identity socio-economic issues and individual rights, radi-

---

of 2.4 to possibly 3.0 million Armenians worldwide, with 1.5 million in the Ottoman empire (H. Lynch, *Armenia*, vol. II, pp. 412–14, 427–8).

In the Russian empire, it was more or less the same scenario. Armenians constituted approximately half the population of the city of Tiflis and were the majority (56 per cent) in the province of Yerevan. Everywhere else—including the city of Yerevan (until the turn of the twentieth century)—they were clearly a minority. Only in the mountainous Gharabagh district did Armenians remain an overwhelming majority. On the whole the Armenian population in the Russian provinces south of the Caucasus in 1886 was approximately 20 per cent, or 940,000 people out of a total South Caucasian population of 4.7 million; 45 per cent were Tatar/Muslim and 25–30 per cent were Georgians (V. Gregorian, 'Impact of Russia', p. 190; cf. H. Lynch, *Armenia*, Vol. I, pp. 249, 447–51).

[60] Sarkis Shmavonian makes a similar point with regards to the 'non-territorial' cultural nationalism of Mikayel Nalbandian and his focus on the people rather than territory (S. Shmavonian, 'Mikayel Nalbandian', pp. 35, 44, 52–3).

cal politics and communal liberation were all woven into the nationalist movement. Hence Russian and European revolutionary ideas were 'nationalised' and combined with the Armenian national identity. The Populists' idealisation of 'the people' became the idealisation of the *Armenian* people (particularly the ones residing in the Ottoman empire). Social radicalism and the already established cultural markers of Armenianness—the vernacular language and literature, the schools, the distinct religion, the land, the sense of history etc.—were intertwined, forming a nationalist movement which both led (and redefined) the nation and was sustained by it.

In Ottoman Armenia

But what exactly was going on in Armenia, particularly in Ottoman Armenia?[61] Important as the roles of nationalist intellectuals are, 'ground conditions' are just as crucial elements in a national movement and its ideology. In addition, even though Constantinople was the centre of Armenian intellectual work and political activity, Armenian towns and individuals in the interior provinces played an important role in identity formation and nationalism.[62] There is no need to recount the details of the living conditions of the Armenian peasantry. They were heavily taxed and at the mercy of official and/or unofficial local rulers including Kurdish and other nomadic

[61] I focus on Ottoman, and not Russian, Armenia because of its significance in terms of indigenous political developments and ideology. Russian Armenia proper—i.e. outside Tiflis (and later Baku as well as Shushi to a lesser extent)—was not an important intellectual, political or cultural centre, nor was it an independent actor on its own.

[62] Constantinople Armenians were aware of the plight of their ethnic brethren in the provinces. The modern equivalent of economic refugees or migrant workers emigrated to the capital (or to other major cities such as Smyrna) from the interior of the empire in search of work and a meagre existence. They usually lived in appalling slum conditions and worked at backbreaking jobs. They were called *pandukhts* (émigrés). In 1860 there were 15,000 of them in Constantinople; by the 1870s their numbers had risen to 45,000. With their strong sense of attachment to their families and villages in Armenia, and as living testimony to the conditions in Armenia, the *pandukhts* 'awakened in the hearts and minds of the bourgeois and cosmopolitan Armenians in the capital an awareness, and even a concern, for the *gavar* (province, in the sense of homeland) that for a long time had been neglected, if not actually ignored' (H. Barsoumian, 'Eastern Question', p. 191). The *Mshak* newspaper of Tiflis covered the plight of these refugees as well, adding, 'Due to the unbearable conditions in Turkish Armenia, the number of Armenians spreading to the corners of the world is increasing day by day' (27 Sept. 1894, no. 111).

tribes who appropriated almost all the surplus of the farmers. Many individuals (especially young women) and sometimes entire villages were forced to convert to Islam by the sword. With no political rights or recourse to self defence the peasantry (approximately 75–80 per cent of the Armenian population) was being drained of its livelihood. Conditions were a bit better in local urban centres, but still Armenians were very much second class subjects, and always vulnerable to arbitrary rule and violence (pogroms, massacres, raids). There were some better-off traders, artisans and land owners, but the entire Christian population was deprived of political rights.[63]

If these conditions were believed to be part of the 'natural order of things' (or 'heaven sent' punishments) until the middle of the nineteenth century, they were no longer being accepted as such owing to the rise of national and political consciousness particularly in the towns of Armenia. Hence resistance to arbitrary rule, to Kurdish raids and to ruthless officials increased from the 1860s onward. The first challenge to Ottoman rule was in the form of a major rebellion in the semi-autonomous Armenian district of Zeytun in 1862. Accusing the Armenians of non-payment of taxes, the Ottoman government sent a regular army of 12,000 soldiers to subdue the town. Zeytun Armenians managed to defeat the army, but were put under siege. The standoff ended with the intervention of Emperor Napoleon III. The Armenians of the region were spared death, but their local autonomy ended. In the same year Armenians of Van also staged a rebellion. In 1863 in Erzerum Armenians rebelled against the Kurds. In the following decades skirmishes continued until the 1890s when major rebellions took place in Sasun (1893–94), once again in Zeytun (1895–96) and in Van (1896). By the 1890s a clear revolutionary leadership had emerged spearheading these military endeavours (which will be discussed in the next chapter). What is important to note here is the effect of these rebellions, especially the earlier ones, on Armenian thinking. They became part of folklore, providing examples of popular resistance. They were

[63] For Western travellers' accounts of Armenian life see C. Walker, *Visions of Ararat*, particularly Chapter 8; H. Lynch, *Armenia*, vol. II. For a brief description see H. Barsoumian, 'Eastern Question', pp. 191–5. Libaridian discusses the role of the Sultan in making conditions worse: 'Abdul-Hamid II systematically transformed the evils that preyed on powerless subjects in a corrupt society into regular tools of repression' (G. Libaridian, *Ideology of Armenian Liberation*, p. 178).

seen in the same light as ancient rebellions against oppressive rulers, and they had electrifying effects on intellectuals and activists who realised that their endeavours to liberate the people had some resonance. In this respect the first Zeytun rebellion was particularly important. As one historian puts it,

> The Zeitun [*sic*] rebellion... had deep and far-reaching repercussions among all the Armenians, both in the Ottoman Empire and in tsarist Russia.... [I]t inspired pride and self-confidence because of the heroic struggle of the Zeituntsis, and... it awakened nationalist feelings and desires.... [T]he Zeitun rebellion was the fledging beginning of Armenian nationalism [from the ground up].[64]

In conjunction with the intellectual work of nationalist writers, and the organisational skills of activists, local Armenians—in their deeds—contributed to the rise and radicalisation of national identity.

Increasing radicalisation, rebellion and nationalism among the Armenians was met with massacres by the Ottoman state. But the massacres themselves further radicalised Armenians as they realised that the Sultan was promising reforms, but in fact delivering further death and destruction. Minor local massacres and pogroms against the Armenians had become part of the 'normal' socio-political landscape in the Armenian provinces. But the intensity and the systematic nature of these mass killings increased in the 1890s. The 1895–6 massacres took the lives of at least 90–100,000 Armenians in a number of provinces and cities: Erzinjan, Erzerum, Urfa, Bitlis, Diarbekir, Sasun, Kharput etc. Armenians of Sasun and of Van resisted the Turkish onslaught, but this was the exception rather than the norm. By the time the mass violence ebbed in 1896 2,500 towns and villages had been plundered, 456 villages forced to convert to

[64] H. Barsoumian, 'Eastern Question', pp. 200–1. For additional details see L. Nalbandian, *Armenian Revolutionary Movement*, pp. 69–74, 78–9, 102–3, 120–2; C. Walker, *Armenia*, pp. 100–2, 161–2. There is of course a patriotic song about the Zeytun rebellion which emphasises the fighting spirit of the Zeytun people and their rejection of Turkish subjugation (*Heghapokhakan yergaran*, pp. 104–5). See also the poems called *Zeytuni yerger* (Songs of Zeytun) by the Constantinople-based poet Mkrtich Peshiktashlian (1828–68) in M. Peshiktashlian, *Yerker*, pp. 54–61. It should be made clear that however important these rebellions became in the formation and radicalisation of national identity, they were not widespread phenomena. They were important as examples and precedents, but never did they threaten Ottoman rule in any serious manner. Even in 1915 Armenians on the whole did not resist the government.

Islam, 649 churches and monasteries desecrated and 328 churches converted to mosques. More than half a million victims were left destitute, with their properties looted or burnt.[65]

The massacres, Armenian radicalism and threats of European intervention on behalf of the Armenians (to implement the Sublime Porte's promised reforms) were intrinsically tied together. The European connection will be discussed in the next chapter. The relationship between the massacres and Armenian agitation—i.e. the cause-effect dynamic—was in all probability a dialectical relationship in which the Ottoman side massively overreacted, trying to eradicate Armenian demands by eradicating Armenian civilians. This is not my main concern here. What needs to be elucidated in connection with my argument are the effects of the massacres on Armenian identity.

There were two contradictory outcomes. On the one hand the massacres reinforced the mentality of Armenians being perpetual victims at the mercy of the 'evil Turks'. In this perspective obedience was the key to survival and resistance was futile—it only made conditions worse.[66] But more importantly there was a causal relationship between the massacres and the radicalisation of the Armenians in the provinces. Hence the second effect of the mass violence was to push Armenian thinking increasingly towards radical nationalism. As they were subjugated to violence *because* they were Armenian, many hitherto unpoliticised Armenians came to the conclusion

[65] The figures are from Johannes Lepsius and based on German sources as cited in R. Hovannisian, 'Armenian Question', p. 224, cf. pp. 219–26. For details on the 1895–6 massacres see C. Walker, *Armenia*, pp. 156–64; for an in-depth analysis of the massacres as a 'proto-genocidal policy' see V. Dadrian, *History of the Armenian Genocide*, Chapter 8; for a contemporary (anti-Turkish) account see J. Hopkins, *Sword of Islam*, pp. 294–378; for a pro-Turkish view, which puts the blame on the Armenians for being rebellious and provocative see J. Salt, *Imperialism*, pp. 60–106.

[66] Another important element of this sense of victimhood was the reinforcement of the notion of exile in Armenian thinking. As many men left their villages and towns because of economic hardship or political persecution and longing for the homeland—and longing by family members left behind for those who have departed—once again became important themes in national culture. Two powerful examples can be found in the popular poetry of the Akn region (in Kharberd province). The first is entitled *Kine ir gharipin* (The Wife to her Emigrant [Husband])', and the second *Gharipin mahe* (The Death of the Emigrant) (reproduced in M. Barsamian, *Histoire du village qui meurt*, pp. 12, 24). In more formal literature Mkrtich Peshiktashlian, writing in the romantic tradition, has penned a poem called *Mah Pandkhtin* (The Death of the Emigrant) (M. Peshiktashlian, *Yerker*, p. 64). All of these poems underscore the tragedy of both the émigré and his family in the provinces.

that their salvation rested on armed struggle for national rights, including autonomy for the Armenian provinces. This contrast of views is clearly articulated in an article entitled 'An Armenian Soldier' in *Arevelian Mamul* (1871). It is presented in the form of a dialogue between a father and his son who wants to become a soldier. The father tries to dissuade the son because it is pointless to fight, and one should accept the prevalent conditions and make do. The son retorts: 'What value is [our] religion, historic glory,... national feelings, the call for freedom' if one does not have a place 'in armies which determine the fate of nations.' He then concludes: 'Currently, rights are found at the edge of the sword, at the mouth of the cannon...'[67]

The victim-radicalisation link was also explicitly made in the programmes of revolutionary organisations. For example, in the above cited 1890 manifesto of the Federation of Armenian Revolutionaries the third paragraph begins: 'For centuries the Armenian people have been repressed under the yoke of Turkish tyrants. For centuries they have sown but not picked the fruit [of their labour]...'[68] Even the organisation's anthem draws on this link between victimhood and the need of revolutionary action. The last verse is:

Eh, black days, turn into protest,
Blood and sweat become parturient,

[67] *Arevelian Mamul*, 1:11, November 1871, pp. 531–8, p. 536 for the quotes. The negative self-image of Armenians was a common theme in the period press of Constantinople and Smyrna. In describing what they were combating in a self-critical manner, the press ironically 'gradually [created] the image of a nation of ignorant, illiterate, selfish and servile people good only at imitating others' (V. Oshagan, 'Self-Image', p. 205, cf. pp. 204–8). This was contrasted with the revolutionary spirit of self-defence and change. Gerard Libaridian argues that Armenians had developed three sets of self-images under Ottoman rule: (1) as rebels specifically associated with Zeytun, but eventually absorbed by radical Armenian political ideology; (2) as prosperous and loyal middle/upper class communities of merchants, bankers etc. in Constantinople and other coastal cities and; (3) as the poor, defenceless and oppressed victim in the provinces who is 'looted, killed, and raped by the Kurd; exploited by the landlord, tax collector, administrator, and the Armenian moneylender' (G. Libaridian, 'Changing Armenian Self-Image', pp. 157, 155–8). All three images corresponded to different aspects of Armenian political ideology and identity as discussed throughout this chapter: the revolutionary (of the east), the liberal constitutionalist (of the west), and the reality at the root of the indigenous nationalism (of the central—Armenian provincial—point).

[68] *H.H.D. 100*, pp. 10–11; for the lyrics of the anthem quoted see *Heghpokhakan yergaran*, p. 5.

Suffering and deprivation, speak,
Open the way for the [Armenian Revolutionary] Federation.

Both themes of martyrdom and radicalisation along nationalist lines can also be seen in an Armenian history textbook (for middle level students) published twenty years later in Constantinople in 1910—i.e. after the reinstatement of the Ottoman Constitution due to the 1908 Young Turk revolution. On the penultimate page of the last lesson there is a paragraph entitled 'The Martyred Nation'. It points out that in the past twenty-one years (1888–1909, the last two-thirds of the reign of Sultan Abdul Hamid II, known as the 'Red Sultan') all Armenians were affected by his repressive government; some were massacred, others exiled and imprisoned, yet others could only save themselves through bribery etc. This paragraph is followed by another on the role of the 'Armenian *Fedayee*' (i.e. the Armenian freedom fighter). It states: 'As much as the Russian and Turkish governments increased the pressure on the Armenians hoping to destroy them, the work of the revolution was proportionally increased and was popularised.' The lesson, and the main body of the textbook, ends with slogans, the first three of which encapsulate both notions of victimhood and radical nationalism: 'Respect to the Armenian *fedayee* [*fitayi*]! Blessed [are] Armenian martyrs! Embrace the lands filled with Armenian blood!'[69]

Christopher Walker argues that Ottoman misrule and the example of a better-off Russian Armenia, 'rather than arid intellectual theories from western Europe, led Armenians to reject the [Ottoman] imperial system and develop national sentiment. Armenian nationalism was not a transplanted poisonous weed, but a natural organic growth from the circumstances of Ottoman Armenians.'[70] Walker understates the significance of the 'arid intellectual theories' from Europe, which were important as the general framework through which Armenian intellectuals interpreted the plight of their people. But he does have a point insofar as he emphasises the link between nationalism and local conditions.

Conditions in Armenia also led to important intellectual responses by local thinkers and activists. Such indigenous efforts to mobilise Armenians around the notion of national liberation fed into the

[69] D. Khachkonts, *Hayots patmutiun*, pp. 270–1.
[70] C. Walker, *Armenia*, p. 172.

efforts of the Constantinople, Tiflis and Europe-based intellectuals. Two figures towered in this respect. The first was Father Khrimian (1820–1907) and the second was Mkrtich Portukalian (1848–1921).

Mkrtich Portukalian was a ceaseless educator, writer and activist. Although he was born in Constantinople, he is considered an intellectual of the provinces since he travelled extensively in Armenia setting up schools and other educational organisations (e.g. branches of the Araratian Society) in various regions. He wrote for newspapers and/or edited them and in general mobilised people around progressive (liberal) ideas. Among other places he settled in Van, but also visited Tiflis in the Russian empire, where he established contact with Grigor Artzruni, the editor of *Mshak*. First arrested (but soon released) in 1869 by the Ottoman authorities, he was finally expelled from the empire in 1885 (which was welcomed by conservative Armenians who had done much to hamper his efforts to modernise education). He subsequently settled in Marseilles where he founded the journal *Armenia*, becoming the 'spiritual father' of the first Armenian political party, the Armenakans of Van (to be discussed in the next chapter). Portukalian 'was a pivotal figure in the transition from a middle class liberalism... to the armed defence of the interests of the peasantry', to whom—and to the lower classes—he was sympathetic.[71] As one of his contemporaries put it, 'Without pronouncing the word revolution...[, Portukalian] prepared a revolutionary generation.'[72]

In fact, Portukalian did advocate armed self-defence against Turkish oppression, and was a supporter of revolution—at least intermittently. But he shunned the opportunity to become a revolutionary leader himself and at times questioned the very wisdom of such means in such a backward area as the Armenian provinces. At other times he advocated guerrilla warfare. Although he was indecisive on the means, oscillating between reform and revolution, he was nevertheless consistent on the need for national liberation. He elevated 'the task of liberation of the homeland to the level of religion',[73] and appreciated the need for cultural and psychological changes among the people. Education was particularly important in this respect.

[71] G. Libaridian, *Ideology of Armenian Liberation*, p. 221, cf. pp. 221–34.
[72] Arpiar Arpiarian, as quoted in L. Nalbandian, *Armenian Revolutionary Movement*, p. 94.
[73] G. Libaridian, *Ideology of Armenian Liberation*, p. 232, cf. pp. 222–34 for details.

Portukalian's main contribution to Armenian nationalism was his activism, particularly his publication of the first Armenian newspaper, which was primarily dedicated to the liberation of the suffering people.

The cornerstone of Portukalian's worldview was the nation, which he believed gave a people their legitimacy in the world—although he was inconsistent on the best means of its survival and advancement. He was instrumental in disseminating this self-perception among the Armenian population. National liberation for him meant the transformation of the Armenians into a modern, European style, confident nation, equal in status with the Turks and other neighbouring peoples, willing to fight in order to protect its rights and ready to take its destiny into its own hands. He systematically campaigned against the notion of victimhood ingrained in Armenian mentality. He wanted Armenians to defend their honour and their economic interests. Portukalian severely criticised the use of popular Armenian proverbs and maxims that perpetuated the image of victim; maxims such as 'It will all end up the same anyway, woe to the one who thinks deeply' and 'Where there is an Armenian, there is suffering.'[74] It is important to remember that these ideas came from an intellectual who had settled in Armenia, who had based his views on the realities and conditions in the provinces, who had an important indigenous following (especially in Van), and who continued to present the interests of the downtrodden Armenians of the interior provinces while in exile in France.

The single most important nineteenth century figure to have entered Armenian consciousness as the bearer of the radical message of national liberation is the clergyman Mkrtich Khrimian, affectionately called Khrimian *Hairik* (meaning 'little father'). Khrimian was born in Van in 1820 to a well-to-do family of merchants who apparently had some links with Crimea, as the family name suggests. In 1842 Mkrtich moved to Constantinople where he became a teacher. He was subsequently sent back to the Armenian provinces by the patriarchate to investigate and report back on the conditions of the Armenians living in the interior of the empire. This began Khrimian's life-long commitment to the betterment of the conditions of the Armenians of the provinces, and of Armenian

[74] Ibid., pp. 225, 231.

rights in general. He was from the 'hinterland', he travelled extensively throughout Armenia (including, in the 1860s, Russian Armenia and Tiflis), he lived in various provinces, and acquired an intimate knowledge of the problems and aspirations of common Armenians. The avenue Khrimian chose for his activism was the church. At the age of 34, in 1854, after his wife and daughter died, he became an archimandrite (celibate priest or *vardapet*). After holding important church positions in the provinces he was elected the Patriarch of Constantinople between 1869 and 1873, a position he used to advance the interests and conditions of the poor and oppressed provincial Armenians. Khrimian died in 1907, as the Catholicos of All Armenians in Ejmiatzin (located in the Russian empire), having been elected to that position in 1892.

Khrimian's activism extended from education to writing and publishing, from verbal support for revolutionary activism to diplomacy. For example, in 1855 he began publishing the periodical *Artzvi Vaspurkan* (Eagle of Van), the first journal published in western Armenia, although initially it was set up and printed in Constantinople. Through this journal a written forum was provided to the voice of Armenians in the provinces. The publication was also instrumental in the awakening of the Armenian masses in the interior as it printed articles and stories on Armenian history, cultural figures (Mesrop Mashtots, Movses Khorenatsi etc.), heroic fighters, kings and princes. While posted in Mush in the 1860s, Khrimian helped to establish in 1863 a similar publication called *Artzvik Tarono* (Eagle of Taron), which was closed down by the Ottoman authorities in 1865 because of its 'radical' content. Khrimian headed the Armenian delegation to the Berlin Congress of June 1878 after travelling to Italy, France and Britain, where he tried to garner support for European-guaranteed reforms of the Armenian provinces in the Ottoman empire.[75] It was upon his empty-handed return from the

[75] Details are from A. Petrosian, *Haikakan harts*, pp. 171–2, 64; cf. L. Nalbandian, *Armenian Revolutionary Movement*, pp. 53–4. For a wonderful eyewitness description of Khrimian, and his consecration as Catholicos of All Armenians in October 1893, see H. Lynch, *Armenia*, vol. I, pp. 231–56. In a poignant passage Lynch writes of Khrimian: 'He is a figure who steps straight out from the Old Testament with all the fire and all the poetry.... What is more rare among this people is the spirituality and refinement which is written in every line of his handsome face. But the whole character of the man would seem to have been moulded upon a Biblical model rather

Berlin Congress that Khrimian gave a series of speeches which secured him a place in the radicalisation of Armenian thinking, and the clear and forceful articulation of demands based on nationalist principles. It is therefore important to briefly outline the issues relating to this congress, and the internationalisation of the Armenian cause by contemporary powers.

The Berlin Congress was convened in order to settle the Russo-Turkish war of 1877–8 which was fought on two fronts: in the Balkans and in Armenia.[76] All the major European powers were present at the congress. Britain, though not a direct participant in the conflict, was particularly keen to limit Russian advances and influence gained at the expense of the Ottomans. Specifically, Prime Minister Benjamin Disraeli sought to reverse some of the concessions Russians had secured in the earlier treaty of San Stefano (March 1878). The 'Armenian Question'—i.e. the implementation of reforms in the Armenian provinces of the Ottoman empire and respect of the rights of the population—was, as part of the larger 'Eastern Ques-

---

than upon that of the Christian hierarchy. He is the tried statesman to whom the people look for guidance in the abeyance of the kingly office. *With him religion and patriotism are almost interchangeable terms*...' (vol. I, pp. 236–7, emphasis added). A few pages later, in reference to Khrimian's *Eagle of Van*, Lynch adds: 'His avowed object and real aim was the elevation of the Armenians and their preparation for the new era which he foresaw. That era he conceived as one of *national* activity...' (vol. I, p. 240, emphasis added, cf. vol. II, p. 86).

[76] On the eastern (Armenian) front Russian troops had pushed all the way to Erzerum, and on the western front they were close to capturing Constantinople when the Ottomans agreed to an armistice. According to the final peace agreement (of Berlin), Russians withdrew from Erzerum, surrendering the town to the Ottomans, but they kept Kars and Batum. Hence the Russian empire's southern border expanded westward to include certain parts of Ottoman Armenia. Armenians in these territories greeted Russian advances with much enthusiasm and saw it as liberation from the Ottoman yoke, especially after witnessing the burning and looting of Armenian villages by Kurdish and Ottoman irregular bands in the wake of Russian withdrawal from some areas. A similar pro-Russian view was held by the Armenians of the Russian empire and was highlighted further by the fact that certain important officers in the Tsar's army were of Armenian descent (M. T. Loris-Melikov, A. A. Gusakov and I. I. Lazarev). Western Armenians in Constantinople were much more guarded in their views regarding the Russians. In general they condemned Russian advances. In fact the Patriarch of Constantinople issued a pastoral letter urging Armenians to support and pray for an Ottoman victory. This was partly due to astute politics, but it also reflected the deep suspicions held by the Constantinople Armenian elite toward the Russians (R. Hovannisian, 'Armenian Question', pp. 207–8).

tion', an integral part of these negotiations. The treaty of San Stefano stipulated that Russian withdrawal from occupied Ottoman territories was conditional on reforms carried out by the Sublime Porte in order to protect the Armenian population. Article 16 read:

> As the evacuation of the Russian troops of the territory which they occupy in Armenia, and which is to be restored to Turkey, might give rise to conflicts and complications detrimental to the maintenance of good relations between the two countries, the Sublime Porte engages to carry into effect, without further delay, the improvements and reforms demanded by local requirements in the provinces inhabited by Armenians, and to guarantee their security from Kurds and Circassians.[77]

Although there was no mention of autonomy or self-rule, Russia was to be the guarantor of Armenian security.[78]

Khrimian's delegation at the Berlin Congress (which was to supersede San Stefano) pressed ahead with the Armenian demands. It sought to obtain concrete actions from European powers that would lead to the implementation of tangible reforms in the Armenian provinces by the Sublime Porte. Part of the demand included some form of autonomy for the Armenian provinces. The Armenians wanted European powers to guarantee these reforms, to supervise them, and if need be, to intervene in the Ottoman empire on behalf of the Armenian population. In short, European governments—which in reality meant Russia, since its troops were already stationed in Armenia—were to make sure that the Porte would ameliorate conditions in the provinces, to apply the Ottoman Constitution to the Armenian subjects, and to defend Armenian security and autonomy. The Armenian delegation, and western Armenians on the whole, did not demand independence, or the break-up of the Ottoman empire, or the incorporation of western Armenian territories into the Russian empire. Their demands were limited to reform, civil rights and partial autonomy. The example of the Maronites of Mount Lebanon was their point of reference.

However, all the Armenian delegation received were toothless promises and a watered down version of the San Stefano agreement.

[77] As cited in R. Hovannisian, 'Armenian Question', pp. 208–9.

[78] There was an earlier precedent for this. The treaty of Kuchuk Kainarji of July 1774 gave the Russians the right to intervene in the Ottoman empire on behalf of Orthodox Christians (H. Barsoumian, 'Eastern Question', p. 176).

Largely owing to British pressure, Russia was no longer made guarantor of Armenian reforms and the withdrawal of its troops was no longer conditional on security guarantees for the Armenians. Article 61 of the Berlin treaty read:

> The Sublime Porte undertakes to carry out, without further delay, the improvements and reforms demanded by local requirements in the provinces inhabited by Armenians, and to guarantee their security against the Circassians and Kurds. It will periodically make known the steps taken to this effect to the powers, who will superintend their application.[79]

By making the Armenian Question the responsibility of all the European powers rather than entrusting Russia with it, and without any real stipulation of how and when the reforms were to be carried out, the Berlin treaty relegated the issue to discussion fora, diplomatic protests and ineffectual pronouncements or pledges. As the Duke of Argyll subsequently put it, 'What was everybody's business was nobody's business.'[80] The Berlin Congress divided up the territories of the Balkans, giving independence to some of the Christian subjects of the Ottoman empire.[81] However, Armenians—who were asking for reform, good governance and at the most limited self-rule—came away empty-handed, while witnessing the liberation of other Christian peoples (Serbs, Bulgarians etc.). Armenians were extremely disappointed and their hopes were dashed.

It was in this context that Khrimian analysed his delegation's failure, concluding that force was necessary in order to be listened to, even by the 'Christian powers' of Europe. He realised that no European power was going to help Armenians based on their suffering, historic rights or moral argument. 'The Armenians have just real-

[79] As cited in R. Hovannisian, 'Armenian Question', p. 210.

[80] Ibid.

[81] According to Jeremy Salt, after the San Stefano and Berlin treaties the Sultan believed that his empire was being subjugated to 'piecemeal partition' or 'dismemberment', especially because of British policies (J. Salt, *Imperialism*, pp. 48, 52). At this point the British were on the one hand trying to weaken the Ottoman empire and bring it under their influence and on the other trying to prop it up to keep Russian advances and power in check. The British were not going to allow the development of the Armenian Question in any direction which would have increased the influence of Russia. For a good overview of the San Stefano and Berlin congresses, and the Armenian Question in the geopolitical context of the period, see R. Hovannisian, 'Armenian Question', pp. 206–12; C. Walker, *Armenia*, pp. 108–17; A. Nasibian, *Britain and the Armenian Question*, chapter 1.

ised that they have been deceived,' he wrote in a protest note the day the Berlin treaty was signed (13 July 1878), and 'that their rights have not been recognised, because they have been pacific...'[82] However, Khrimian's message acquired a powerful resonance once he returned to Constantinople. In a series of forceful speeches, which Gerard Libaridian terms 'The Sermon of the Sword', Khrimian spoke metaphorically of the 'dish of liberty' from which Serbs and Bulgarians served themselves using 'iron ladles' (weapons and force). Armenians went to get their fill, but they only had 'paper ladles' (petitions and promises), which dissolved and were useless to serve liberty.[83] They therefore remained hungry. The moral of the story was clear: in order to obtain freedom, arms had to be used.[84]

Khrimian's 'iron ladle' message became—and still is—the most widely used metaphor for rallying Armenians in support of radical policies. It reoriented Armenian nationalism toward a new and revolutionary direction, and pervaded the very essence of Armenianness, imbuing collective identity with an unprecedented sense of national purpose. Not only had the message come from such a respected church leader, but it was also based on the realities of the Armenian homeland and its abandonment by the international community. It was a call to arms emanating not from theoretical arguments regarding world revolution, but from the hard realities of

82 As cited in C. Walker, *Armenia*, p. 117; and in R. Hovannisian, 'Armenian Question', p. 210.

83 For a good analysis of Khrimian's thought see G. Libaridian, *Ideology of Armenian Liberation*, pp. 160ff.

84 As a man of the cloth, Khrimian never openly advocated violence and revolution. He remained cryptic in his pronouncements and did not accept that his message was responsible for Armenian revolutionary activity. More than a decade after his sermon he said that he remained 'convinced that no nation can make its voice heard without force.... [But that it was not] possible to have the Armenian people rise up and free itself from oppression with a couple of... guns. [Nor was it] possible to bring the Ottoman empire to its knees or with a couple of demonstrations have the bastard European diplomacy side with the Armenian people' (cited in G. Libaridian, *Ideology of Armenian Liberation*, pp. 165–6). However, as his own words suggest, it seems that he objected more to the inefficient means of the revolutionaries rather than the principle of using force. It should also be noted that Khrimian did publicly object to the Patriarch of Constantinople, Nerses Varjapetian, who in 1878 'swore fidelity to the sultan and emphasized that efforts to surmount Armenian misfortunes would be made within the framework of the beloved Ottoman homeland.... [At this point] the Armenians still shunned any hint of separatism.' (R. Hovannisian, 'Armenian Question', p. 212; cf. G. Libaridian, *Ideology of Armenian Liberation*, pp. 146–7).

Armenian life and politics. Through its simplicity and in its use of familiar images to express new and radical ideas it undermined the sense of victimhood, voiced the profound frustration felt by Armenians, called for action (without explicitly defining how), and focused attention on conditions in Armenia itself rather than on abstract constitutional issues or social theories. As such, 'Khrimian characterized the shift in Armenian political thought from an abstract nationalism to concrete populism,'[85] and in the process he himself entered national consciousness as a hero who fought for liberation.

Moreover, Khrimian's basic framework of analysis and outlook was the Armenian nation rather than the ethno-religious community. He talked of *national* rights and freedoms and he clearly *tied these to the Armenians of the provinces and their territory* in the Ottoman empire. Khrimian linked salvation to earthly conditions, to the importance of leading a moral life and to the collective responsibility for the betterment of the nation. In his sermons and writings he focused on the ideas of 'progress, education, freedom, self-consciousness and human dignity'.[86] As a church leader Khrimian interpreted religion not as an ideology to accept present conditions as God-given, but as a moral basis that should lead to progress and collective liberation in earthly life.[87] He symbolised the concluding 'act' of the transition—began by Israel Ori, Joseph Emin and the Shahamirian publishers in Madras a century or more earlier—from a religious interpretation of Armenian suffering to a political understanding.

Both Portukalian and Khrimian were crucial figures in the transformation of Armenian political identity. The most obvious change was the move towards the radicalisation of political thinking based on nationalist principles. Both sanctioned the use of arms, although they stopped short of advocating outright revolution (Portukalian did at times call for a revolutionary movement, but he did not take part in such activities, nor was he consistent in his views). Furthermore, Portukalian and Khrimian were instrumental in situating Armenia—the actual Armenian provinces of the Ottoman interior—on the map of nationalist thinking. They perceived the home-

[85] G. Libaridian, *Ideology of Armenian Liberation*, p. 190.

[86] Ibid., p. 164.

[87] In this respect Khrimian was quite close to the Catholic liberation theologians who emerged in the wake of the Second Vatican Council after 1965.

land not only as the subject of liberation, but also as its agent and contributor. Through their and their followers' efforts, the homeland and its people entered the multilocal nationalist project as the 'ground point', supplementing the eastern and western points. Armenian nationalism, therefore, was not limited to European-inspired liberal or radical trends; rather it developed an indigenous basis which asserted itself forcefully on the plane of national identity formation and its politics. There were two elements to the provinces' contribution to this dynamic.

The first was the predication that what should matter in Armenian politics could not be based only on the interests of the metropolitan centres (e.g. Constantinople and Tiflis), and on how *those centres* defined national interests and identity, but also on the conditions and demands of the provinces. Gerard Libaridian spends a good portion of his study analysing the various aspects of this tension, the centre-periphery antagonism vis-à-vis Constantinople, as well as its class dimension.[88] However, for the purposes of my argument, what is more important to note is the second element of the dynamic: the territorial link the provinces brought to Armenian nationalism, especially to the liberal nationalism of the western point.

The Armenian homeland situated in the interior of the Ottoman empire was an abstract entity for most Constantinople-based intellectuals. Even for the eastern radicals, who had more of an intimate knowledge of the *yerkir* (homeland), Armenia was the land for which (or on behalf of which) they were struggling. Such diaspora-

[88] See G. Libaridian, *Ideology of Armenian Liberation*, pp. 119–20, 181–99, particularly pp. 186–7; he cites some long primary passages that give an indication of the gulf between the conditions of the provinces and the nonchalant attitude of the elite in Constantinople. He also draws attention to the relationship between economic issues and nationalism—i.e. the importance some intellectuals attached to national liberation as the only avenue for economic success (p. 171). For a summary of some of his main arguments see, G. Libaridian, 'Nation and Fatherland', pp. 79–90. It is important to note that Khrimian was forced to resign as the Patriarch of Constantinople because his 'support of provincial Armenians made him an enemy of many influential Armenians in Istanbul. His enemies charged that [among other accusations] Khrimian spent too much money on pantukhts [migrant workers from the interior], neglected the prestige of the Church, diminished the power of Istanbul in favour of the provinces, and supported the cause of the poor and oppressed at the expense of others.… Finally, he spoke so much of the conditions and problems of the provinces, remarked an opponent, that he "endangered the nation"' (G. Libaridian, 'Nation and Fatherland', pp. 82–3).

based nationalism concentrated on the Armenian people rather than the territory. But, as mentioned, through men like Portukalian and Khrimian Armenia itself became a *source* of identity and political activism in its own right. At its roots this nationalism was very much tied to the Armenian lands. 'The peasants' link to the land of Armenia was neither culturally inspired nor politically negotiable. Rather it represented the most basic relationship between man and nature.'[89] Once peasants and other provincial residents began to mobilise for self-defence and around national issues, as they defined them, they brought the territorial component to national identity and liberation with them. As such the liberal and culture-based nationalism of the west, and the radical romantic social issues-based nationalism of the east, were complemented by the home*land*-based nationalism of Armenia. As Libaridian explains, whereas Constantinople Armenians were thinking in terms of 'love of nation' (*azgasirutiun*) in a 'culture-laden' manner, while discussing the politics of a *millet* constitution that was not very representative of the provinces, Armenians living on their own lands were expounding their views in terms of 'love of fatherland' (*hayrenasirutiun*). For them culture and politics were intertwined with their land 'invested with historical and spiritual significance'.[90] Therefore, territoriality entered Armenian nationalism largely through the efforts of Mkrtich Portukalian, Khrimian Hairik and their followers in Armenia, balancing out the 'diasporan' element of the eastern and western points.

The political ideology behind Armenian nationalism was the product of various influences based on the western, eastern and central points of its source. All these influences had an impact on Armenian thinking and identity in different ways: the liberal constitutionalism of the west, the romantic social movements of the east, the indigenous land-based patriotism of Ottoman Armenia. In all three cases collective identity was recast in terms of *nationality* rather than an ethno-religious community. This does not mean that *all* Armenians (especially in the provinces) reinterpreted themselves in terms of national identity within one or two generations. Regional, religious and family identities persisted. But as the framework of collective

[89] G. Libaridian, 'Nation and Fatherland', p. 85.
[90] Ibid., p. 86.

loyalty and especially as the basis of the ideology of socio-political activism national consciousness had clearly become the dominant paradigm.

It is not possible to denote exactly how prevalent national(ist) ideas were among the general Armenian population, but there are indicators which suggest that both national identity and nationalism had developed a broad base by the last decades of the nineteenth century. Popular participation in rebellions, the establishment and circulation of Armenian-language newspapers,[91] the testimonials of intellectuals and activists,[92] the proliferation of cultural-educational societies,[93] the founding of political parties and of course the opening of new schools testify to the nationalisation of Armenian thinking and identity on a broader mass level than the narrow circles of metropolitan intellectuals.

One way of gauging the impact of nationalist thinkers and activists is through the increase of Armenian educational establishments and numbers of students. By 1902 there were 82,695 students (of all levels—60,315 boys, 22,380 girls) in 818 Armenian 'national schools' throughout the Ottoman empire. Of these, 56 schools (1887 figure) were located in Constantinople (the figure was 37 in 1840), and 61 were for the Armenian communities in Egypt, Cyprus and Bulgaria. The rest were in or near the Armenian provinces. The curriculum and textbooks of these schools were set by the Armenian National Assembly and its Educational Council based in Constantinople and administered on the whole by the 'enlightened intellectuals'. In addition there were scores of benevolent society schools (46 in 1882, 56 in 1909, and 85 in 1910, with 2,820, 5,100 and 6,810 pupils respectively), as well as American and European missionary schools for the

[91] In Ottoman Armenia alone 197 periodicals were published between 1825 and 1900 (V. Oshagan, 'Self-Image', p. 202; cf. G. Galemkiarian, *Patmutiun hai lragrutian*).

[92] Many individuals active in the Armenian revolutionary movement of 1880s onwards left behind memoirs, books, notes and letters. As some of the literature used in the next chapter indicates, these activists were operating under the assumption that large segments of the Armenian masses (especially in the towns) had acquired a sense of national identity by the end of the century.

[93] There were close to 690 Armenian cultural organisations in the Ottoman empire (350 of them in Constantinople) in the second half of the nineteenth century. In addition to literary/cultural, patriotic and educational groups, these included charity organisations as well as professional unions (A. Ter Minassian, 'Sociétés de culture', pp. 7–8).

Armenians and notable private schools. Practically all of these educational establishments had at the very least accepted the modern paradigm of Armenian nationhood. Despite wide regional discrepancies the average percentage of the population outside of the capital who had had some access to education (by 1913) was in the range of 13 per cent.[94]

In Russian Armenia Armenian students attended either parochial (i.e. church administered) schools or Russian (state) schools. There were also private schools with modern curricula. The overall figures for the state schools in the South Caucasus were as follows: in 1878 there were 583 elementary schools with 2,037 Armenian pupils in attendance and 24 secondary schools with 1,257 Armenian students. By 1900 the numbers had increased thus: 1,693 elementary and 51 secondary schools with 23,218 and 5,250 Armenian students in attendance respectively—that is more than a tenfold increase in number of elementary students and a fourfold increase for secondary students. As to parochial schools, in 1885 the Armenian church controlled some 330 schools in the Transcaucasus and

[94] Figures based on A. Ter Minassian, 'Sociétés de culture', pp. 18, 21–5; V. Oshagan, 'Modern Armenian Literature', p. 151; K. Sarafian, *History of Education*, pp. 202–3; R. Kévorkian and P. Paboudjian, *Arméniens*, p. 79, cf. pp. 76–9. According to the calculations of one recent study, there was nearly a sevenfold increase in student numbers (from 23,026 to 153,404) between 1872 and 1913 as the number of Armenian community schools in the Ottoman provinces went up from 446 to 1,746 (P. Young, *Knowledge*, p. 97). For a specific examination of the role of the Sanasarian Academy (a hotbed of nationalist activity in Erzerum) in the radicalisation of education see P. Young, 'Making a People into a Nation'. For a general overview of the history of Armenian education see K. Sarafian, *History of Education*, chapters 14 and 15 for the Ottoman empire, 17 and 18 for the Russian empire. For a contemporary (1890s) description of some of the Armenian schools and education see H. Lynch, *Armenia*, vol. I, pp. 129, 218–24, for the Russian empire, and vol. II, pp. 94–101, 213–17, for the Ottoman empire. Oshagan quotes a number of articles from the 1850s to 1890s that are critical of the contemporary educational system for its lack of innovation and its limited extent; one columnist in 1877 wrote: 'Our schools [in Constantinople] are in a lamentable state; only four or five of the fifty-three are worthy of the name' (V. Oshagan, 'Self-Image', p. 204, cf. p. 206). This negative side must also be mentioned. As much as the situation had improved and modernised, it was still not enough as far as nationalist intellectuals were concerned. For example, Mkrtich Portukalian, among others, was critical of higher education as administered by the liberal establishment, which regarded it as 'the panacea for the Armenian problem. Portukalian himself observed that Europeanization rather than dedication to liberation was the ultimate effect of higher education on Armenians' of the Ottoman empire (G. Libaridian, 'Changing Armenian Self-Image', p. 161).

in south Russia (including 83 for girls). However, it is important to note that although these were church-administered institutions, education in them no longer consisted of 'moribund' religious instruction, but had been 'revitalized', 'modernized' and 'secularized' by the Russian and European trained Armenian intellectuals.[95] Even the Ejmiatzin Seminary and the Nersisian Academy of Tiflis (both opened by Catholicos Nerses Ashtaraktsi in 1813 and 1823/4 respectively) had become from 1843 onward important centres of secular education not to mention nationalist thought.[96]

Despite the evolution of a three-pronged nationalism, there was an overarching sense of Armenian national identity which glossed over real differences and ontological contradictions before these could develop into serious or irreconcilable positions. The emergence of a pan-Armenian identity was largely due to two interrelated factors. The first was the very fact that *political ideology prevailed as a unifying force irrespective of linguistic and cultural differences.* Armenian nationalist thinkers and activists envisioned one nation, despite its geographic dispersion and regional variations. Hence they grouped Turkish-speaking peasants of Anatolia, the Russian-speaking bourgeoisie of Tiflis, the middle classes of Constantinople and so forth under the rubric of the Armenian nation on the basis of their historic ethno-religious commonality, even if there was no contact, or a tangible bond initially, between these diverse groups. This testifies to the power of the subjective imagining of a nation by intellectuals, *coupled with* existing objective historical factors which act as the basis of that imagination.

The second factor was *the victory of the eastern form of radical nationalism at the pan-Armenian level* by the turn of the twentieth century. This triumph, which will be most obvious in the next chapter, was due to a number of components. First, the eastern and central points

[95] V. Gregorian, 'Impact of Russia', pp. 195–6.

[96] R. Suny, 'Eastern Armenians', pp. 117–18. Note that by 1914 there were 34,845 pupils in Armenian parochial schools in the South Caucasus, but 42,594 Armenian students in Russian state schools. Moreover, the ratio was 'worse' at the secondary level: 1,528 attended Armenian diocesan schools, but 8,713 Russian secondary schools (V. Gregorian, 'Impact of Russia', p. 198). Russian schools were preferred because of their higher quality (much like the situation in Soviet Armenia in the 1970s!), but this did not necessarily mean the 'denationalisation' of Armenians; many of the radical intellectuals were themselves 'products' of the Russian schools.

of nationalism were combined in their approach to national liberation and in their activities. The inclusive nature of romantic nationalism and its ideological flexibility enabled a synthesis of thought between the territorial-based and people/culture-based nationalisms of the period. This was a powerful combination which put the 'ground conditions' in Armenia at the centre of the nationalist movement at the expense of western liberalism. Second, again because of its flexible nature eastern nationalism also incorporated some elements of the western liberal tradition. As such populism and later socialism, territoriality, individual rights and representative democracy all coexisted in the programmes of Armenian nationalists. Third, the western point itself had failed to extend its ideological influence much beyond Constantinople and Smyrna. Liberal nationalists were unable or unwilling to seriously address the concerns of the mass Armenian population in the provinces and hence could not develop a support base beyond the narrow confines of the metropolitan centres in the Ottoman empire. Nor could they effectively counter the cosmopolitan attitudes of many middle and upper class Armenians who believed they had more in common with European cultures than with Armenian peasants. Fourth, on the other side of the ideological spectrum radical socialists and internationalists (mainly in the Russian empire) faced the same problem of generating popular support. They remained confined to a few like-minded intellectuals unable to address national issues dear to the Armenians. Fifth, conversely, although the prevailing eastern nationalists were not on the whole overly burdened with ideological matters or nuances, and therefore could subordinate them to the national imperative, they nevertheless were associated with international ideological currents that seemed progressive, dynamic and revolutionary. Finally, as discussed in the next chapter, it was the organisational dimension and activism of eastern Armenian political ideology that sustained and expanded its brand of nationalism. More than any other organisation the Armenian Revolutionary Federation was able to consistently synthesise the various elements of Armenian nationalism in its programme, while developing close links with the masses and maintaining a presence in the eastern, central and western points of the Armenian world. Its eastern-based nationalism had become the dominant mode of thinking among political activists, while the western liberal trend continued as a weaker bourgeois counter-current to the radicalism of the revolutionaries. National identity remained blood-based.

Theoretical interlude: intellectuals and phases

Two interlinked theoretical points should be made here. The first relates to the role of intellectuals in the rise of national consciousness. Intellectuals are the most important agents in the advancement of nationalism. Their role and endeavours are extensively discussed in the literature of nationalism; each scholar examines such activities from whatever framework he or she has adopted. Intellectuals are the inventors of tradition, the instrumental elites who use nationalism for advancement, and the purveyors of mass culture and education. They are, in short, the people who 'make' nations and nationalism:

> It is the intellectuals—poets, musicians, painters, sculptors, novelists, historians and archaeologists, playwrights, philologists, anthropologists and folklorists—who have proposed and elaborated the concepts and language of the nation and nationalism and have, through their musings and research, given voice to wider aspirations that they have conveyed in appropriate images, myths and symbols. The ideology and cultural core doctrines of nationalism may also be ascribed to social philosophers, orators and historians [and, in the Armenian case, some priests]…, each elaborating elements fitted to the situation of the particular community for which he spoke.[97]

This quote from Anthony Smith demonstrates the extent to which intellectuals are involved in the creation and reformulation of national identity. But, naturally, intellectuals act within specific time periods and conditions. They reflect and react to existing social, political, cultural and ideological trends. They respond to other nations and to the socio-political conditions of their people and in the process set the trend in the construction and evolution of their own nation. The Armenian case (as discussed so far and as elaborated in the next chapter) is a perfect example of this process.

The trends within which intellectuals operate vary from one situation to another. Based on his study of 'small' European nations,

[97] A. Smith, *National Identity*, p. 93; cf. A. Smith, *State and Nation*, Chapter 5; A. Smith, 'Nationalism and the Historians'.

Miroslav Hroch provides a useful categorisation of the phases of nationalism and nation-creation. He argues that a national movement can be divided into three structural phases. During Phase A (as he calls it) 'the energies of the activists [are] above all devoted to scholarly enquiry into and dissemination of an awareness of the linguistic, cultural, social and sometimes historical attributes' of the potential nation. They do not have any overt political demands. In Phase B the task is 'to win over' as many converts as possible to the goal of creating the nation—i.e. to '"awaken" national consciousness'. Phase C is the period when 'the major part of the population [comes] to set special store by their national identity, [and] a mass movement [is] formed.'[98] In Phase A research is carried out, books written and published, and the people are envisioned as a nation; the groundwork for the subsequent formation of national identity is laid (e.g. what the Mkhitarists did). In Phase B cultural, linguistic and social demands are put forth on behalf of the emerging nation (e.g. what the Constantinople intellectuals did). In some cases political demands are put forth as well. In Phase C political demands are formulated and put forth much more forcefully (e.g. what the revolutionary parties did). The 'final' shape of the nation is moulded in this phase as well.[99]

Hroch's schema is a good way of categorising and examining the rise of national identity and its politics. It is not meant to be a rigid formula, but a flexible way of making sense of various trends. The three phases do overlap, the length of each varying from nation to nation, and intertwined with other factors lead to different outcomes.[100] The various phases of Armenian nationalism can be analysed through this approach, but in this case Hroch's periodisation must be questioned. He is right that in general Phase A is followed by B and then C. But it is also possible that all three phases can operate simultaneously within the life of one nation-to-be. While

[98] M. Hroch, 'From National Movement', pp. 6–7; cf. M. Hroch, 'National Self-Determination', p. 67.

[99] M. Hroch, 'Real and Constructed', pp. 97–102; M. Hroch, 'From National Movement', p. 9.

[100] Four types of national movements historically emerged in Europe; national agitation took place in the context of (i) political upheaval, (ii) constitutional revolution, (iii) armed insurrection and (iv) constitutional reform (M. Hroch, 'From National Movement', pp. 7–8).

Joseph Emin, ahead of his times by a century, was riding through Armenia to liberate it, intellectuals in Constantinople had barely begun to envision the Armenian collective in terms of a nation. And while revolutionaries in Tiflis were demanding political rights, Armenian peasants were far from constituting a 'mass movement'. In short, Hroch's schema can be employed fruitfully to examine the Armenian case, but with the caveat that the chronological order of the phases must not be maintained too rigidly.

There is one other point in Hroch's approach that should be questioned: the assertion that small nation nationalism necessarily reacts to the political conditions of the dominating state—i.e. the shape and content of the national movement is dependent upon the political system of the state in which its people live (i.e. whether it is an old regime, new regime, constitutional or repressive). This is true, but only partially. A nationalist movement, especially one that is heavily based on diasporan communities, can be affected by a much wider range of influences—ideological and structural—than the conditions of the dominating state in which the people of the nation-to-be live. As Hroch himself asserts, any explanation of the rise, success or failure of nationalist movements must 'be multi-causal, and move between different levels of generalization'.[101]

Modern Armenian identity and nationalism emerged in the nineteenth century, but did not develop in a unified, centralised or consistent manner. There was a complicated web of internal and external influences which affected collective identity: European and local education, imperial rivalries, massacres, class differences, linguistic formations, various ideological trends, charismatic individuals etc. I have discussed many of these issues in this chapter, but given its length and complexity it is worth summarising the main arguments. There were two overall trends at the heart of Armenian collective identity formation: first, the link between the awakening in the nineteenth century and the formation of modern national identity and nationalism; second, the heterogeneous and multilocal process through which this was done. Two key 'objective factors' highlighted the east/west division—language (dialects) and literature—

[101] M. Hroch, 'From National Movement', p. 8.

and one 'subjective factor': the political ideology of nationalism. All of these factors encapsulated essential differences in terms of identity formation. For example, the distinction between 'love of nation' and 'love of fatherland', not to mention romantic and liberal literature and nationalism, reflected the plurality in the ways in which the Armenian nation envisioned itself.

However, these differences, profound as they were, did not lead to the formation of more than one nation. This was because the ideology of Armenian nationalism, and more specifically the triumph of its eastern point (helped by the popularity of eastern romantic literature), united under its banner the various local, linguistic, religious and imperial identities, but without resolving the inherent tensions (often expressed in class, regional and urban-rural terms). Consequently one modern nation emerged, stretching from Tiflis to Yerevan to Van to Constantinople and to western Europe, which was governed by a more or less coherent set of 'eastern' nationalist principles. The prevailing—but by no means exclusive—means to achieve the end of national liberation was to be revolutionary activity.

Five conclusions can be reached based on my arguments in this chapter. The first is the obvious point that much of the intellectual work done in the process of forming Armenian national identity was carried out in diasporan communities *outside* the homeland *per se*. It is important to note this for two reasons: that activities leading to nationalism do not have to be confined to the territories of the homeland; and that in the specific case of the Armenians the diaspora played an absolutely crucial role in the cultural and political redefinition of Armenian collective identity.

Second, the ethno-religious Armenian community (or *ethnie*), which was already a clearly defined unique collective in the fourth century AD with roots stretching well into the first millennium BC, was now redefined and perceived as a modern nation both by itself (on the whole) and by other nations. It had developed a secularised conception of belonging akin to the concept of 'citizenship', but without the territorial basis or the state structures. The emergence of Armenian national identity and nationalism was not tied to an Armenian state; it was rather linked to communal organisations and autonomy. The nation had its own vernacular(s), national(ising) literature(s), political leadership(s) and pan-national organisations. The problem was that it did not form a majority on its own land, but was divided between two empires (not taking Persia into account) and dispersed with its main intellectual centres in neighbouring regions or imperial capitals. Nonetheless, it was a nation awaiting 'liberation'. All the previous efforts and endeavours to enlighten and to educate, from the Mkhitarists of Venice to the Armenian printers in India, had paid off.

Third, it should however be emphasised that no *new* ethnic identity was created. Rather, an old one was reinterpreted, reinvigorated, modernised and eventually politicised. In this process the political and intellectual authority within the community was relocated to a new group of people whose legitimacy was based on a different set of principles congruent with modernity (political rights, representation, secularisation, liberty, rationality etc.). Armenian nationalism was not a question of gelling different peoples together with the intention of creating a new collective identity—i.e. the issue was not to answer the query 'Who are we?' Rather it was a question of redefining the pre-existing sense of identity—i.e. taking the 'who' for granted, but giving it a new definition: we are no longer a *millet* or an ethnic group or a religious community, but a nation.[102] In this process new ethnic boundaries were not created, but existing ones redefined and strengthened. 'Who is the nation' was not debated by intellectuals, but 'What is the nation', 'Why should it be free' and 'How' were debated. It was accepted that Armenians 'always' existed in history, delineated by their religion which was then formalised by the *millet* system and the *Polozhenie.* It was the same with the Armenian 'homeland'. It was not specifically defined by intellectuals, although the Ottoman *vilayet* demarcations were generally accepted as the Armenian provinces, plus Russian Armenia. The complications of uncertain borders were not addressed; Armenians believed that their homeland constituted the historic territories of

[102] For example, despite profound cultural differences between eastern and western Armenians, no Armenian on either side maintained that the others were not Armenian, even if they did not speak the language. What is more, even assimilated Armenians in the Russian aristocracy were referred to as Armenians for generations. Armenians who had converted to Catholicism or had become Protestant were considered part of the nation as well (sometimes barely, in popular view!), but an Armenian who converted to Islam was 'lost', no longer part of the nation. This religion-based definition, as will be discussed in the next chapter, remained a central core of national identity.

their ancient kingdoms and principalities, despite current unfavourable population ratios.

The fourth conclusion is that the process of national identity formation does not have to be a homogeneous and centralised endeavour—although it does need to have a totalising 'pan' component in its worldview in order to transcend existing differences, at least at the ideological level. Beneath the surface of pan-Armenian identity there were real differences in the very content of nationality and nationalism. Whereas ancient heroes and myths and the alphabet and religion were shared (either in reality or symbolically), current activities, elites, the vernacular, literature, culture, ideology and geographical location embodied fundamental differences. Consequently the Armenian road to modern nationality was heterogeneous and even fragmented. But the end result of this multilocal process was the same because there was a subjective sense of unity among the nationalist intellectuals and activists. However, this was based on one or more *existent* historical factors which provided the initial linkage to begin with (in this case, the national church).

This leads to my fifth and last conclusion: that the subjective dimension in national identity formation is absolutely crucial. Without such subjective unity, at least at the ideological level, collective identity could gel around two or more 'cores', giving rise to more than one nation, or to a civil conflict over what constituted the core values, characteristics and identity of the nation. This is a hypothetical point, but the fact that there have emerged in the world two or more nations with similar cultural backgrounds and religions attest to this possibility (Canada and the United States, Malaysia and Indonesia, the states of the Arab world and so forth). Hence, without the subjective element in the thinking of nineteenth century nationalists, which envisioned *all* Armenians as part of *one* nation (and this was largely due to the victory of the eastern point on the pan-Armenian level), there *could* have been two Armenian nations today. I am not suggesting that the only—or even the predominant—factor in the emergence of a specific nationality is always the subjective dimension, but that it is a crucial component, especially when there are so many 'objective' differences between the various components of the potential nation.

So who were the Armenians at the end of the nineteenth century? They were a modern nation, defined as such by themselves and others, based on common ethno-religious ties, with their own national church, mutually comprehensible vernacular language, unique alphabet, common set of historical symbols and myths, shared pool(s) of literature and other cultural markers, community institutions (schools etc.), a newly emerged but fragmented secular political leadership and, very importantly, a secular collective consciousness as one nation. In short, they had developed a common identity as a nation that bridged—but did not unite or standardise—the deep divisions within the collective consciousness of the nation. The Armenian Revolutionary Federation, quite conscious of its important role in this process of the reconstitution of the Armenian nation from diverse components, put it this way in a 1931 editorial celebrating the Party's fortieth anniversary:

> One of the greatest historical services of the A.R. Federation was the unprecedented impetus it gave to Armenian spiritual and physical national consolidation [*azgahavakum*]. By demolishing provincial, segmental and denominational prejudices, as well as divisions due to the artificial walls imposed by external political borders, the Federation, for the first time in the contemporary history of the Armenian people, cemented a *new* Armenian collective through the force of many sacrifices and efforts; it was inspired by the ideal of pan-national unity [and] with its miraculous breath created a whole new generation of dynamic and self-sacrificing Armenians, who not only did not accept the cursed borders which divided the Armenians, but also with their personal example, their imposing life and with their spilled blood knew how to tie with one another the scattered fragments of our people through inseparable ideological and moral ties.
>
> To be able to understand the great value of this huge revolutionary task, it should be taken into consideration how deeply the Armenian people was subject to religious, segmental and provincial divisions, and how much effort is required to repress [and] to stifle the passionate sentiments and prejudices emanating from such divisions.[103]

No doubt, in its celebratory tone, the ARF was lionising its role as it claimed, *ex post facto*, the overall success of national consolidation under its leadership. But its acknowledgement of the diversity and opposition it needed to overcome is quite telling. After all, Armenians lacked a common state, a unified homeland, autonomy and pan-

[103] 'H. H. D. Karasnamiake', p. 5. The same thesis is repeated in various other Dashnak publications. See also S. Atamian, *Armenian Community*, p. 270.

national political ideals and parties pursuing the nationalist cause. These parties emerged in the mid-1880s and by 1900 they had assumed the leadership of the nation. To this organisational dimension of nationalism we now turn.

5

REVOLUTIONARY PARTIES AND GENOCIDE, INDEPENDENCE AND SOVIETISATION

THE LATE 19TH AND EARLY 20TH CENTURIES

National identity, consciousness, nationalism and liberation remain ineffectual and abstract concepts without the organisational work done by specific associations, political parties and groups of activists. This chapter focuses on these bodies and examines their activities. Two other crucial developments must also be examined since they had a profound impact on Armenian collective identity: the Genocide of Ottoman Armenians, and the independence of Russian Armenia. The time period covered is from the 1880s, when the first political organisations were formed, to 1921, when the republic was Sovietised. In these forty or so years the eastern point of Armenian nationalism consolidated its domination of Armenian politics organisationally, while mass identity was further nationalised and radicalised. Nevertheless, deep cultural fissures remained, along with political disconnections in terms of pan-national linkages.

However, before dealing with the detail of the organisational dimension, two particular features must be analysed in the character of Armenian nationalism and identity. The first point is Armenians' reliance on foreign powers to assist them in their liberation attempts. The second is the relationship between nationalism and the church. I have alluded to these two issues throughout the previous chapters, but they now need to be discussed in greater detail because they both profoundly affected organisational activity. The chapter starts with the first point, then the religious dimension is analysed; followed by a discussion of political parties and their activities. The

Genocide and its relationship to identity will then be examined, before ending the chapter with the independent republic and its Sovietisation.

NATIONALISM THROUGH OTHERS: RELIANCE ON EXTERNAL FORCES

It is quite common for a small people to seek external support in its struggle against a powerful state. In this case, however, this expectation that European (imperial) forces ought to—*and therefore will*—liberate Armenia(ns) from the Ottoman yoke had become an ingrained element in Armenian collective consciousness. Such reliance was much more than a political calculation; it was woven into national identity, becoming an inherent element of Armenians' liberation struggle in the nineteenth century. Armenians, therefore, based their politics on the lofty (and mostly empty) promises of various external powers, which led to the worst kind of dependence: on words not founded on deeds.

Such expectations were common to both the liberals of the west and the radicals of the east. They all understood that the 'Armenian Question' entailed European great power rivalries. They knew that Britain, Russia, Germany, Austria-Hungary and France were the key players and that the Ottoman empire was the subject of their struggles. But they failed to appreciate that Armenians were *only* pawns in this 'game', that the issue of reform in the Armenian *vilayets* was merely used as a means of putting pressure on the Sublime Porte. They failed to see that no power was going to go as far as intervening on behalf of the minority Armenians situated in the heartland of the Ottoman empire just to ameliorate their situation. Reforms were discussed in European capitals, official protests sent, and decrees signed, but in reality conditions worsened. Armenians, however, kept trying to elicit European sympathy and attention.

Two examples illustrate this dependence inherent to Armenian thinking. Khrimian Hairik's protest note on the Berlin treaty of 1878 was cited in the previous chapter as indicative of the radicalisation of Armenian nationalism. Khrimian after all had realised that Armenians would not be able to obtain liberty without the use of force. But in the very same note Khrimian concludes: 'The Armenian delegation is going to return to the east, taking this lesson with it.

It declares nevertheless that the Armenian people will never cease from crying out until *Europe gives its legitimate demands satisfaction.*'[1] Such thinking was also ingrained in the mentality of the later generation of revolutionaries. For example, the preamble to the section on tactics in the report of the Second General (i.e. World) Congress (1898) of the Armenian Revolutionary Federation says:

> ...the Congress unanimously accepted the principle that without European intervention it would be impossible to bring to a successful conclusion the struggle to free our people and that, therefore, before choosing the methods and times of operations, efforts must be funnelled into the task of bringing about such intervention through all means.[2]

The experiences of the preceding twenty years—no intervention, but more massacres—and contemporary geopolitical realities had not made much of an impact on Armenian thinking. The reliance on outside forces continued right through the twentieth century.

There were two reasons behind such expectations of intervention. The first is the obvious point that Armenians were aware of their political surroundings. They saw the example of the Balkans—i.e. Russian (and other European) assistance to the Serbs, Bulgarians and the Montenegrins struggling against Ottoman rule. They saw the Russian victory over the Ottomans in 1878 and the 'liberation' of the Armenian regions of Kars and Artahan. Furthermore, various powers had declared that they would put pressure on the Sublime Porte to reform the Armenian provinces. Armenians naively took all of these as signs of imminent European intervention, which if not forthcoming immediately needed to be induced—at least according to some revolutionaries. In this respect policies and actions were based on untenable assumptions.[3]

[1] Cited in C. Walker, *Armenia*, p. 117, emphasis added.

[2] S. Vratzian, 'Second World Congress', p. 243, cf. p. 246. Louise Nalbandian confirms that assistance from European powers was 'a vital factor in [the revolutionaries'] program' (L. Nalbandian, *Armenian Revolutionary Movement*, p. 184).

[3] H. Barsoumian, 'Eastern Question', pp. 177–80; J. Salt, *Imperialism*, pp. 11, 53, 63, 142. Two in depth studies deal with the geopolitical issues in this period and their effect on the Armenians: M. Somakian, *Empires in Conflict* (his basic argument is that Russian policies and actions do not warrant the conclusion that it supported the Armenians while the Ottomans persecuted them: both empires pursued their interests against the Armenians, and Russians had become as anti-Armenian as the Turks by the First World War); A. Nassibian, *Britain and the Armenian Question* (she is mostly concerned

The second reason behind Armenians' expectations from Europe went deeper than current politics. It was based on 'a Messianic hope' placed in western Christian powers. Armenians did not realise that there was no longer a 'Christian Europe in politics'. They 'could not liberate themselves from their Medieval Messianism vis-à-vis Europe, and hoped against hope, that the "Christian" Europe would save them, and would, at least, not allow them to perish.'[4] This belief was part of Armenian identity rooted in ancient contacts with European empires. It became particularly important in the religion-based politics of Christianity. And, as mentioned in the previous chapter, it was at the core of the early liberation attempts by Armenians (including in varying degrees those of Israel Ori and Joseph Emin). At the end of the nineteenth century the belief still existed that Europe would eventually come to the assistance of suffering Christians. This is clearly seen in the following passage from a joint 1897 manifesto from the Armenian revolutionaries to European embassies in Constantinople:

> Despite bleeding to the end, we did not lose hope. We were satisfied that the bleeding of the martyrised Armenians was reaching the ears of the Europeans and were hoping that a helping hand will be extended to us.... But the torrential blood of the Armenians did not shake the European powers... Unfortunately we had bitter deception.... [Armenian] mountains and valleys have been dyed with the blood of the martyrs.... But all these were not enough to awaken the conscience of sleeping Europe and remind them of Christian mercy.[5]

Nationalists did not always put the argument in these terms, but also framed the issue in terms of democracy, human rights, socialism etc.[6] Nonetheless, the underlying assumptions were the same—that

---

with Britain's attitude toward the Armenians, focusing on the first quarter of the twentieth century).

[4] B. Zekiyan, *Armenian Way to Modernity*, pp. 82, 88–9.

[5] Cited in M. Somakian, *Empires in Conflict*, p. 22. This statement was issued after a series of sensational 'revolutionary activities' in Constantinople—demonstrations and terrorist activities—in the mid-1890s aimed at inducing European intervention. Many Armenians genuinely believed that Europe (especially Britain) was at this point ready to intervene to overthrow the Sultan (cf. S. Atamian, *Armenian Community*, p. 143).

[6] There was a two-pronged approach in this view. One was the dependence on European imperial powers, as mentioned. The other was reliance on the support of European socialist-revolutionary forces. The 'human rights' argument was articulated most forcefully in such forums. In a tract addressed to the Socialist Congress of 1896 in

Armenians deserved to be helped, and that their liberation was dependent on Europe.

The most tangible manifestation of such dependence at the heart of Armenian nationalism was the Russophilia of most eastern intellectuals, and of many Armenians living in the provinces. This was an extension of the old Christian view that the Orthodox Russians were the natural allies and defenders of the Armenians. In an article published in December 1917 A. Chopanian argued that Russia was Armenians' 'primary protector'. If victorious in the war it would, along with the allies, reward Armenia with self-rule.[7] Four years later, in 1921 and after the Sovietisation of Armenia, independent Armenia's ambassador to the United States, Armen Garo (Garegin Pastermajian), still maintained:

> Without Russia's active assistance, we will not have the opportunity to even half-way realize our national ideal: to have our own homeland, independent or even semi-independent, where our people will have the chance to live and work, away from the Turkish sword. From this perspective our 'red brothers' in Yerevan are standing on more realistic ground.[8]

This pro-Russian attitude, as part of the more general reliance on Western powers (Britain and France), remained ingrained in Armenian nationalism and its world view. The debates were over which foreign power Armenians must rely on.[9]

London the ARF, based on such premises, tried to mobilise support from progressive European forces: *'Nous ne poursuivons pas la chimère de la résurrection de l'antique Arménie politique, mais nous voulons les mêmes libertés et les mêmes droits pour toutes les populations de notre pays dans une Fédération libre et égalitaire. Nous espérons qu'un régime politique meilleur seul peut éliminer ces antagonismes inhérents de culture, de races et de religions, que le gouvernement actuel tend à perpétuer pour conserver son existence'* (ARF, *Au Congrès*, p. 3).

[7] 'Vana Luise [Light of Van]', *Mshak*, 30 Dec. 1917, no. 275, pp. 1–2.

[8] The quote is reproduced in *Armenian International Magazine*, June 1999, p. 13. It originally appeared in Simon Vratsian's *Andsink Nvirialk* (Dedicated Individuals) (Beirut: Hamazkayin, 1969). There was a counter-argument to this Russophile position. It was forcefully expressed in a pamphlet written by Ruben Darbinian (also of the ARF) in April 1920, months before Armenia's Sovietisation. It provides a systematic critique of Russian rule over Armenia. Russia, Darbinian states, is our 'friend' as long as we were its slaves; but it became our enemy, 'perhaps our most dangerous enemy', when we sought freedom and self-rule (R. Darbinian, *Rusakan vtange*, p. 78). This view acquired some prevalence in the diaspora after Armenia's Sovietisation, but by no means did it replace the reliance on outside forces. Significantly, this pamphlet was republished in Yerevan in 1991.

[9] Armenian history textbooks published in the Russian empire were important instru-

However, far from liberation, such reliance on external forces had disastrous consequences. Without falling into the trap of blaming the victims for their suffering, it should be pointed out that the Sultan viewed such Armenian demands and agitation with great suspicion. He was paranoid about European intervention, having lost the Balkan territories, and quite aware that the Armenians of the provinces could easily be used as an excuse by Britain and Russia to undermine his empire. His answer was further repression and massacres.[10]

Richard Hovannisian writes that because of the 1896 massacres, 'Armenians were learning the price for looking to the West and daring to challenge the theocracy of Sultan Abdul-Hamid. And once again the European powers stood by passively, limiting themselves to joint and identic [sic] notes of protest to the Sublime Porte.'[11] But Armenians were not learning 'the price', and they continued to look to the West for support and protection. As Louise Nalbandian puts it,

> The idealistic revolutionists were persistently naive in their evaluation of European politics and diplomacy: they never gave up hope for some kind of assistance, military or otherwise; and after nearly 20 years they continued to hope that Article LXI of the Treaty of Berlin would be enforced—a treaty long forgotten in international politics.[12]

---

ments in inculcating a pro-Russian and anti-Turkish attitude in Armenian students (see, for example, R. Khan-Azat and G. Vardanian, *Hayastani patmusiun*, pp. 143–57). Textbooks in the Ottoman empire tried to do the reverse, but in general had a more complex attitude towards Russia—especially after the 1908 Young Turk revolution. On the one hand they admired the freedoms granted to the Armenians and their social development, on the other they criticised the increased repression after 1881—i.e. Alexander III onward (see, for example, D. Khachkonts, *Hayots patmutiun*, pp. 252–4, 269). In the Ottoman case, at least until 1908, it was not so easy to propagate a Turcophilia comparable to that of the Russophile attitudes of the eastern Armenians, owing to the realities of massacres, repression and the second-class status of the Armenians.

[10] Jeremy Salt takes this argument further and suggests that Armenian radicals deliberately provoked Ottoman authorities to massacre the Armenians in order to invite European intervention (J. Salt, *Imperialism*, p. 157). This was vehemently denied by the Armenian revolutionaries. The Second General Congress of the ARF (1898) explicitly addressed this issue: 'It is erroneous to believe that our operation in the Old Country [i.e. the Armenian provinces] have been the cause of the massacres.' At most, revolutionary activity was a pretext for the massacres (S. Vratzian, 'Second World Congress', p. 245; cf. K. Mikayelian, *Heghapokhakani mtkere*, p. 26).

[11] R. Hovannisian, 'Armenian Question', p. 223.

[12] L. Nalbandian, *Armenian Revolutionary Movement*, p. 184.

Revolutionaries declared that Europe was betraying the Armenians who must, therefore, begin to rely on themselves. For example, the Hnchak party anthem even includes the lines:

> *The deaf European only rumbled in council[s],*
> *The Armenian was shocked, the bell turned red.*[13]

But Armenians on the whole, including the radical nationalists, could not let go of their reliance on foreign powers, despite their occasional pronouncements. As part of their national identity it was ingrained in their mentality that as a small victim nation they needed external support to survive and to be free—and they mobilised and organised within this frame of mind.

THE 'RELIGIOUS' DIMENSION IN SECULAR NATIONALISM

The relationship between the Armenian church and nationalism is a complex issue. In this section I focus on the ideological component of this relationship. I argue that there was no clear-cut contrast between religious identity and the secular(ising) ideology of nationalism. The two were compatible and in fact reinforced one another. This is not to say that Armenian nationalism can be characterised as 'religious nationalism', rather that it cannot be counterposed to religion in a clear-cut dichotomy. After all, religion had been the most basic unifying factor for more than a millennium, and the church had remained the only major pan-Armenian institution.[14]

[13] As reproduced in A. Kitur, *Patmutiun*, vol. I, p. 7.

[14] The Armenian church was organisationally divided along the east/west/central lines as well; but there were no theological differences between the various spheres. The spiritual head of all Armenians was the Catholicos of Ejmiatzin, but in terms of administrative jurisdiction the Patriarch of Constantinople was the head of Ottoman Armenians. He did, however, have to share some of his jurisdiction with the Cilician Catholicosates of Sis and of Aghtamar (at Van), and with the patriarchate of Jerusalem; nevertheless, the Constantinople patriarch undoubtedly held the most influential (and most wealthy) seat. On the one hand the church was a uniform source of identity for all Armenians, but on the other it too was subject to—and perpetuated—the physical and intellectual divides between the various parts of the nation. Currently the patriarchates of Constantinople and Jerusalem, as well as the Catholicosate of All Armenians in Ejmiatzin (Armenia), remain in their original locations. The Catholicosate of Sis has moved to Antilias (Lebanon). And the Aghtamar see is no more because of the Genocide.

Part of the nineteenth century awakening process was the secularisation of Armenian society and the reconstruction of identity based on national, rather than religious principles.[15] This entailed a certain element of anti-religious feeling, which was particularly prevalent with some of the earlier nationalist intellectuals—especially in the east. Raffi, for example, mused:

> O fathers! O forefathers! I drink this glass, but not as a toast to your remains. Had you built fortresses, instead of monasteries with which our country is full; had you guns and ammunitions, instead of squandering fortunes on Holy urns; had you burned gun-powder, instead of perfumery incense at the Holy altars, our country would have been more fortunate than she is today.... From these very monasteries the doom of our country was sealed.[16]

Others, such as Mikayel Nalbandian in the Russian empire, went further than Raffi and specifically asked Armenians to rally around the concept of nation rather than religion.[17] In the Ottoman empire, around the same time, the poet Mkrtich Peshiktashlian of Constantinople established a society called *Hamazgiats* (pan-national) which was inspired by the secularised idea of the nation and explicitly rejected the religious definition of Armenianness as embodied by the *millet* system.[18]

[15] For the process of the secularisation of the Armenian school system in the Russian empire see V. Gregorian, 'Impact of Russia', pp. 195ff; S. Shmavonian, 'Mikayel Nalbandian', pp. 36ff. Khachig Tölölyan analyses a key poem in which this transition was made from the desire 'for the restoration of a religion-dominated prenationalist past [as represented] in the first three stanzas, [to] the installation of a more secular and protonationalist future [as represented] in the last two' (K. Tololyan, 'Textual Nation', p. 84). The poem, called 'Lord, Sustain the Armenian People' or simply 'Lord, Sustain', was first published in 1820 in Calcutta. Subsequently, after its republication in 1847 (with its authorship widely attributed to Mesrop Taghiatiantz in India), it was circulated among the Armenian elites and picked up and published by Russian Armenians (viz. by Mikayel Nalbandian) in the mid-nineteenth century. It henceforth became a 'cultural icon' as a national song (K. Tololyan, 'Textual Nation', pp. 80–1).

[16] Cited in S. Atamian, *Armenian Community*, p. 79. Other such thinkers included Khachatur Abovian and Grigor Artzruni. Similar views were expressed by some western intellectuals. Grigor Otian of Constantinople, for example, wrote: 'Each hood of a [priest] hides a devil!' (R. Suny, *Looking toward Ararat*, p. 10).

[17] S. Shmavonian, 'Mikayel Nalbandian', pp. 49–52.

[18] B. Zekiyan, 'Armenian Way to Enlightenment', pp. 76–7.

But a closer examination of Armenian anti-religious sentiment suggests that it was more of a response to the conservatism of the clergy than a deep seated opposition to the church. It was, no doubt, anti-clerical, but not necessarily anti-religious in the full sense. Nationalists could not deny that the church had given the Armenians a unique identity which enabled them to survive as a distrinct group throughout the centuries. Both of these thoughts are apparent in the writings of Kristapor Mikayelian (one of the founders of the Armenian Revolutionary Federation). In 1903 he stated, 'The Armenian of the Caucasus is needlessly following the cleric, that historic invalid, who is clinging onto the tired and bloody body of the people, while sitting in Ejmiatzin, in patriarchates, in state schools... so that it can implement the orders of [Russian] prosecutors, governors and police.' However, the same Mikayelian had written in 1885, 'from our glorious past we have been left two holy things—the national church and the national schools. These two holy things, having preserved our language, have preserved us as a nation....'[19] Maturity as a revolutionary can perhaps explain Mikayelian's apparent change of views, but his 1885 belief did remain an inherent element of Armenian nationalism.

The use of religious imagery in nationalist discourse is the most obvious dimension of this relationship. 'The blood shed by our 100,000 *martyrs* gives us the right to demand liberty,' declared the revolutionaries who occupied the Imperial Ottoman Bank in 1896.[20] The paradigm of the battle of Avarayr led by Vardan Mamikonian

[19] The first quote is from K. Mikayelian, *Heghapokhakani mtkere*, p. 93. It was written in the aftermath of the appropriation of church property by the Russian state in 1903. The second is from R. Suny, 'Eastern Armenians', p. 131. It was written in the aftermath of the closing of the Armenian schools in 1885 by the Tsarist authorities (more about this later). This mentality continues to the present day; in an interview given to the Snark news agency in Yerevan in August 1999, Armen Rustamian, one of the ARF leaders in Armenia, stated: 'The Armenian Church always promoted the unity of the nation and played an important role in the self-preservation of the nation. I hope that it will remain faithful to its roots and will continue performing its Apostolic mission more vigorously. The need for that is more than topical today' (as posted on *Groong Armenian News Network*, 10 Aug. 1999). Note how the roots of the church and its 'apostolic mission' are equated not with religion, but with the preservation of the nation.

[20] Cited in M. Somakian, *Empires in Conflict*, p. 19, emphasis added. The martyrs refer to the massacred Armenians that year. The occupation of the Bank will be discussed below.

in 451 for the sake of Christianity was constantly evoked, as was the fifth-to-sixth century historian Eghishe's famous phrase regarding this battle: 'Death consciously accepted is immortality.' Such terms and images were appropriated from their religious contexts and used for nationalist purposes. Whereas Eghishe's point of reference was Christian truth and life after death, revolutionaries reinterpreted his message to mean that dying consciously for the national cause would lead to their eternal remembrance by the nation. Their 'holy endeavour' seemed like a natural extension of the age-old Armenian struggle to maintain their identity and to liberate themselves from foreign rule.[21] The religion-nationalism mélange was very clear, for example, in many of the revolutionary songs of the period. In one song, entitled *To the Memory of Petros Seremchian* (a fallen hero), the following lines appear:

> *I was called dear fedayee [fitayi*—i.e. freedom fighter*]*
> *I became a soldier of ideology/....*
> *I was crucified; dear fedayee,*
> *May your principle remain holy,*
> *With the drops of my blood,*
> *May the Armenian soldier strengthen/....*
> *I carried the cross of life [to the mountains of Sasun]/....*
> *My Macedonian brother*
> *Was crowned with my cross/....*
> *When the wind on the gallows*
> *swings me back and forth,*
> *Remember Petros Seremchian*
> *Roaring revenge to the enemy.*
> *I am being buried with comfort,*
> *You are my hope, comrades,*
> *Continue our holy endeavour,*
> *Majestic heroes of the [Armenian Revolutionary] Federation.*[22]

[21] Khachig Tölölyan makes a similar point in discussing the cultural narrative of Armenian terrorism in the 1970s and 1980s. He shows how the fifth century hero Vardan Mamikonian was linked to the nineteenth century revolutionaries, and then to the latter day terrorists. In the following passage he is writing about the terrorists of the 1980s, but what he says is absolutely true for the 1890s as well: 'The terrorist can see himself not as a marginal outcast from his society but as a paradigmatic figure of its deepest values—as a martyr... and witness—living and dying in the central martyrological tradition of the culture, while remaining resolutely secular, disdaining the promise and reward of any paradise' (K. Tololyan, 'Martyrdom as Legitimacy', pp. 102, 91–2; cf. K. Tololyan, 'Cultural Narrative', pp. 223, 231).

[22] *Heghapokhakan yergaran*, pp. 18–19.

A second dimension of the religion-nationalism link came from the Armenian church itself, since many of its elements easily lent themselves to the cause of national liberation. For centuries the church had struggled for the Armenians. As early as the fifth century it had fused 'secular heroism and religious martyrdom'.[23] As discussed earlier, it never was a purely religious institution—a fact that was formalised by the *millet* structure and the 1836 *Polozhenie.* Hence, when nationalism emerged in the nineteenth century, this new ideology could fuse with religion *within* the church itself, as long as it was not inherently anti-religious. While there were conservative clergy who fought against the reconceptualisation of Armenians as a nation rather than a religious community, others were more than willing to interpret the Armenian condition from a national(ist) perspective. For example, Bishop Garegin Srvantstiants declared in 1861 that 'patriotism [is] "the real root of all good" and defined "good" as the welfare of the community.' He then added, 'Our fatherland is where our history, our heroes and our saints are. It is the people there that make our fatherland real with their sufferings.'[24] Khrimian Hairik (by then Catholicos) went further by explicitly endorsing the revolutionary movement. In a 1896 letter to the Armenians of Van he wrote,

> The appearance of political parties among you is an example of the rebirth of the historical houses of our nobility, while the Dashnaktsoutune Party [i.e. ARF] is the new Armenian knighthood. Its pioneers have shown themselves to be true knights in Vaspourakan [i.e. the region around Van] and elsewhere. Rise, rise, Armenians, join this new Armenian knighthood, take heart...[25]

The church was therefore itself radicalised (only to a certain degree, needless to say) and as such 'secularised' in its vision of the Armenian nation. As Boghos Levon Zekiyan puts it, Armenians could

[23] K. Tololyan, 'Martyrdom as Legitimacy', p. 102.

[24] Cited in G. Libaridian, *Ideology of Armenian Liberation*, pp. 184–5 and 188, cf. pp. 153–6, 181–5. Bishop (later Patriarch) Maghakia Ormanian had a similar conception of a united Armenian identity which was broader than the religious definition. In fact Ormanian went further and in his *The Church of Armenia* situated the clergy at the centre of the Armenian 'movement towards civilisation, progress and liberty' (M. Ormanian, *Church of Armenia*, p. 94).

[25] Cited in H. Dasnabedian, 'ARF Record', p. 121.

'secularize without rejecting religious faith'.[26] The nationalist elements within the church made the institution itself, and religion generally, more acceptable to the revolutionaries.[27]

Certainly the overall Armenian vision changed from primarily a religious view of the world to a more secular one. In this sense it was a victory for nationalism, but ironically not at the expense of the church. The latter remained a core element of national identity and its politics even though the religious world outlook was no

[26] B. Zekiyan, *Armenian Way to Modernity*, p. 85. A modern expression of this thinking is found in the writings or statements of contemporary heads of the Armenian church. For example, Bishop Aram Keshishian (now Catholicos Aram I of Cilicia) writes in his 1978 book *The Witness of the Armenian Church in a Diaspora Situation*: 'The political involvement of the Armenian Church has been and still is, with a renewed impetus indeed, so deep and extensive that it is often quite difficult, if not impossible, in any given stand or function of the Church to distinguish between faith and politics, theology and ideology. The Church is a political factor par excellence in the Armenian Diaspora' (p. 42). Catholicos Karekin I (first of Cilicia and then of Ejmiatzin) reconciled the church and the nation as such:

> The national element in the church is a natural phenomenon. Christ's Incarnation represents God's direct intervention in history. The church has manifested God's presence in the world throughout the centuries. Christ said: *'My Kingdom is not of this world'* (St John 18:36), but we know also that it is not out of this world. It is in us: *'Behold, the kingdom of God is in the midst of you'* (St Luke 17:21), in which nations—taken in the broadest sense of the term—have a permanent place which the church must recognize, just as Christ recognized the national expressions of his own people (Karekin I, *In Search of Spiritual Life*, p. 259).

This article was written first in 1964, but republished with the approval of the Catholicos in 1991 and 1995. Finally, just before his election as the new Catholicos of Ejmiatzin in October 1999, Archbishop Garegin Nersesian (now Catholicos Karekin [Garegin] II) stated in an interview: 'The catholicos should be a man of God and of the nation, willing and able to serve both God and nation.' He added a few moments later, 'You know, for us church-nation-Christianity are united in one' ('Interview with Archbishop Karekin Nercessian [*sic*]', *Azg/Mirror On-Line*, 14 Oct. 1999, as posted on *Groong Armenian News Network*, 15 Oct. 1999).

[27] I have only looked at two dimensions of the church's transformation: the internal ideological impetus and its relationship with the revolutionaries. There are many more internal and external factors, related to the awakening, that led the church to modernise itself. These cannot be elaborated here, but one factor that must be mentioned is the competition the church had from the Protestant missionaries from the west (and their promise of education), and from the Catholic church (including the Mkhitarian brotherhood), both of which were active among the Christian population of the Ottoman empire (see B. Zekiyan, *Armenian Way to Modernity*, pp. 70–9; R. Davison, '*Millets* as Agents of Change', p. 329; H. Barsoumian, 'Eastern Question', pp. 185–8). The church-nationalism symbiosis was cemented in the face of such competition. Compared to this challenge the onset from the nationalists seemed less serious and in line with the mission of the church.

longer the main prism through which Armenians saw themselves and their surroundings. The religious idea that Armenians were a 'chosen people' was fused with the secular idea of being a repressed people. Some priests became national liberation fighters, and secular fighters received the blessings of priests. All were part of the nation which might not have been 'chosen' but was certainly unique and worth fighting for.

POLITICAL AND REVOLUTIONARY ORGANISATIONS

The 'crowning moment' for the new politics of nationalism was the 1885–95 decade when Armenian revolutionary parties were formed and began their struggle for national liberation. They had evolved within the context of the Armenian renaissance and were its organisational expressions. The parties put into practice the principles inherent in the awakening. They were on the whole nationalist organisations, although some would have objected to the label because of their socialist-internationalist principles. In a characteristically colourful (and orientalist) passage, H. F. B. Lynch alludes to this general process in his 1901 book (even though he does not seem much impressed by the political capabilities of the Armenians!):

> But the spirit of truth is too often akin to the spirit of revolution, and there are bonds from without as well as from within. When the scales fell from the eyes of this downtrodden people, the naked ugliness of their lot as helots was revealed. Their native energies were transferred from the domain of money-making to that of social improvement and political emancipation. The craft of their minds, abnormally quickened by the long habit of oblique methods, exchanged the sphere of commerce for that of politics. Armenians have been a subject race for over nine centuries, are honeycombed with the little vices inherent in such a status, and are quite unused and as yet unfit to govern themselves.[28]

Early attempts at organisation

Before the establishment of actual political parties individuals concerned with the emancipation of Armenians grouped around Masonic

[28] H. Lynch, *Armenia*, vol. II, p. 86. For a good overview of the emergence of revolutionary organisations among the Russian Armenians see R. Suny, 'Populism'; R. Suny, *Looking toward Ararat*, Chapter 4. For an overview of the same or similar organisations in the Ottoman empire see A. Ter Minassian, 'Role of the Armenian Community'.

lodges or other similar societies.[29] In 1869 the short-lived *Barenpatak Enkerutiun* (Good Intention [i.e. philanthropic] Society) was formed in Alexandropol (Gyumri) in Russian Armenia. It was the first somewhat organised group dedicated to the liberation of Armenians in the Russian empire. In 1872 an 'ephemeral association' with no 'formal organization' emerged in Van, which 'petitioned the Russians for protection against [Ottoman] governmental outrages.' They threatened both the Ottoman state and the Armenian establishment suggesting that unless something was done to defend their interests they would adopt Russian Orthodoxy.[30] Not much came from this loose association called *Miutiun i Prkutiun* (Union for Salvation) or its threats, but it was significant insofar as it used religion and reliance on the Russian empire as a 'means' for attaining emancipation.

More important, *Pashtpan Haireniats* (Defence of the Fatherland) was founded in Erzerum in Ottoman Armenia in 1881. It advocated self-defence to counter anti-Armenian violence and adopted the slogan 'Liberty or Death!' (which became a rallying cry for subsequent revolutionaries). The organisation was suppressed by the Ottoman authorities within a year, but only after it had achieved some resonance among the local population. It was the first Armenian organisation with a mass membership. Its approximately 5,000 members came mostly from the lower middle classes, peasants and students.[31]

None of these groupings had a clear ideology or programme beyond the idea of self-defence and vague notions of the liberation and salvation of the oppressed Armenians. They were not advocating open revolution or independence of the Armenian provinces. Limited to specific regions, they sought to put into practice the ideas of such men as Mkrtich Portukalian and Khrimian Hairik without really knowing how.

The Armenakans and their continuations

The 'honour' of being the first formal Armenian political party goes to the Armenakan society. It was established in Van in the autumn

[29] The *Ser* [Love] Masonic Lodge was founded in 1866 in Constantinople by prominent Armenian intellectuals, although there seems to have been an earlier (1850s) *Ser* society in Cilicia. The Constantinople branch was officially approved by the Grand Orient Lodge of France (L. Nalbandian, *Armenian Revolutionary Movement*, p. 75; G. Libaridian, *Ideology of Armenian Liberation*, p. 204).

[30] G. Libaridian, *Ideology of Armenian Liberation*, p. 206.

[31] Ibid., pp. 209–10.

of 1885 as a direct consequence of the influence of Mkrtich Portukalian's radical views. Portukalian's students formed the organisation months after their teacher had been exiled to France. The name Armenakan came from the newspaper *Armenia*, which he had established in Paris in August 1885.

The Armenakans were essentially a local party, although they did have some branches in Persia, in the South Caucasus and even in the United States. They were 'revolutionary' insofar as they advocated Armenian self-rule and self-defence through violent means if and when other avenues failed. But they believed that much preparatory work needed to be done through the political and cultural education of the masses, propaganda, teaching of military discipline etc. Armenians had to be prepared (i.e. made conscious of the need) to liberate and govern themselves when external circumstances favoured their cause. In other words, Armenian identity had to be nationalised and radicalised further. On this view an 'immediate revolution was not desirable'.[32] Armenakans did not accept socialism, nor did they want to expand their struggle beyond the Armenian community.

It should be noted that this first Armenian political party was founded in the 'central point' of Armenia. The Armenakan movement was more of a response to local conditions in line with Portukalian's thought, rather than being based on ideological premises. The party was more revolutionary in its rhetoric than in its activities. On the whole it did not promote terror, although some of its members did engage in a few political assassinations of Turkish/Kurdish officials and took part in the 1896 defence of Van. However, by then Armenakans were already upstaged by the other two more radical political-revolutionary parties.

The Armenakan tradition continued in Armenian political life through the liberal streak inherent in the party. By the 1900s the actual organisation had ceased to have any significant presence as its more radical and nationalist elements had already been assimilated into other parties (in the 1890s). But the liberal oriented members formally joined the newly established bourgeois-liberal *Sahmanadrakan Ramkavar Kusaktsutiun* (Constitutional Democratic Party) at its founding in 1908 in Alexandria in Egypt. The organisation

[32] L. Nalbandian, *Armenian Revolutionary Movement*, pp. 99, 94ff., 171.

became popular among the upper and middle classes, especially in Constantinople; it also allied itself with the Patriarchate. Having lost its raison d'être of betterment through constitutional reform and cooperation with the Turkish authorities, the Constitutional Party was reorganised in Istanbul in 1921, renaming itself *Ramkavar Azatakan Kusaktsutiun* (Democratic Liberal Party). It is usually referred to by the acronym ADL (Armenian Democratic Liberal).

The Ramkavar party came to embody the liberalism of the western point of Armenian identity. It eschewed radicalism and violence, providing an alternative programme that emphasised political and individual rights, market economics, private property etc. It remained committed to the freedom and unity of Armenia, but this aim was to be achieved through peaceful means and negotiations, and with reliance on Russia/the Soviet Union. Despite their liberal orientation Ramkavars proudly highlight their descent from the Armenakans as the first Armenian political organisation. The ADL became the second most important diasporan political party; it is still active.

The Hnchakian Party

The Hnchakian Revolutionary Party embodied most clearly the radicalism of the eastern point of Armenian nationalism. It was founded in 1887 by seven Russian Armenian students in Geneva. The party was explicitly socialist in its ideology. In fact its name—*Hnchak*—meant 'bell' in Armenian, reflecting Alexander Herzen's *Kolokol*. The organisation changed its name to Hnchakian Social Democrat Party in 1905 and in 1909 to Social Democrat Hnchakian Party (SDHP), the name it still maintains. The force behind the formation of the party was Avetis Nazarbekian and his fiancée Maro Vardanian. They, along with their founding colleagues, had grown impatient with Portukalian's wavering and reserved attitude towards revolution and consequently launched their own party. They were not influenced only by Portukalian, but also by the romanticism of the Russian Narodniks, as well as by more 'scientific' Marxist theory. Unlike Portukalian, Hnchaks were—at least initially—much more consistent in their views and their desire for immediate radical change. As Libaridian puts it, 'It was the Hnchakian program, with its clear and comprehensive treatment of the Armenian question, that ushered in the revolutionary phase of the Armenian liberation movement, beginning in 1887.'[33]

Hnchaks unwaveringly insisted on the immediate independence of Ottoman Armenia through revolutionary means and the subsequent creation of a socialist state. In addition to propaganda and education, agitation, mass protests, assassinations, terror and other violent means were used. Party members were active in the Sasun, Zeytun and Van rebellions and defensive operations (1893–96). They did believe that European intervention was necessary for the attainment of Armenian independence, although, as socialists, they were wary of the imperialism of Western powers. Hnchaks emphasised both the class and national elements in their struggle. On the one hand they sought, as 'internationalists', to establish alliances with non-Armenian (including Muslim) oppressed classes in their battle against Ottoman oppression (although this policy had no success). On the other their point of reference was the liberation of Armenia and Armenians. In Richard Hovannisian's words, 'Hnchakists [*sic*] saw no serious contradiction between patriotism and socialism or between nationalism and internationalism.'[34] In the long run they wanted to see a free and independent Armenia in a socialist world order. Organisationally the party was centralised in its decision making and command structure (based in Geneva), but it had soon developed more than one hundred cells active in Armenia, Constantinople and the South Caucasus as well as in various Armenian communities in the United States and Europe. Most of its members were young people, students and intellectuals, with a few workers and fewer peasants. When it mobilised for specific actions (e.g. demonstrations) its wider constituency came from the lower-middle and working classes.

Hnchaks were most active and well organised in the 1890–6 period. However, in the absence of immediate results (on both the socialist and nationalist fronts), dissent grew within the party and it splintered into various groups from 1896 onwards. The anti-Nazarbekian Reformed Hnchaks wanted to eliminate socialism from the party programme since they saw it as an impediment to the more

[33] G. Libaridian, *Ideology of Armenian Liberation*, p. 248; cf. H. Dasnabedian, 'Hunchakian [*sic*] Party'. A sympathetic account of the party and its heroes is provided in the two-volume history of the organisation by A. Kitur, *Patmutiun*.

[34] R. Hovannisian, 'Armenian Question', p. 214.

important cause of the liberation of Armenia. Further divisions, dissensions and even fratricide completely weakened the party. By the 1910s it was a minor if not insignificant revolutionary and political organisation. The reformed Hnchaks merged with the Ramkavars in 1908 and in 1921, whereas the core of the party remained loyal to socialism. In 1924 the Eighth Congress of the party accepted Soviet Armenia as 'the realization of the goal we have pursued for thirty-eight years', and it decided to support the Soviet republic 'without reservation'.[35] Henceforth Hnchaks became Soviet Armenia's staunchest ideological allies in the diaspora (after the Armenian Communists). The party became less and less significant after the 1950s; it was confined to a few neighbourhoods in Beirut, showed some activism in Aleppo, Damascus and Cairo, and maintained a handful of cells in the western diaspora.

With the exception of a few years in the 1890s the Hnchak party failed to capture the imagination of the Armenian people. No doubt the splits and internal quarrelling weakened the organisation, creating a vacuum which was quickly filled by the ARF. However, the core Hnchak party's influence remained limited because it refused to subordinate socialism to nationalism. Socialist ideology did not 'speak' to the identity of the Armenian masses—comprising mostly peasants and some (petty) bourgeois elements—to the extent that nationalism did. The prominence of an Armenian political party that in its ideology gave socialism an equal position with nationalism was therefore short-lived, having passed its peak by the turn of the twentieth century. Ultimately the Hnchak Party symbolised the failure of ideologies oriented towards more internationalist and social issues to have a profound impact on Armenian collective identity.

The Armenian Revolutionary Federation

The Federation of Armenian Revolutionaries was founded in the summer of 1890 in Tiflis. It was renamed a year later as the Armenian Revolutionary Federation (ARF)—*Hai Heghapokhakan Dashnaktsutiun*.[36] By the second half of the 1890s it had already emerged as the

[35] H. Dasnabedian, 'Hunchakian [*sic*] Party', p. 35.

[36] The party is usually referred to as *Dashnaktsutiun* (Federation), and its members are known as Dashnaks or Dashnaktsakans.

most significant revolutionary-political party, with a wide network of cells and activities in Ottoman and Russian Armenia, as well as in various diasporan communities within and beyond these empires (including western Europe and the United States). After the early 1920s the ARF came to be the predominant Armenian political organisation in the diaspora, in opposition to the Soviet regime in the Armenian SSR. As its name suggests, it began as a federation of various small radical Armenian groups and individuals mostly based in the Russian empire (viz. in the South Caucasus). It was established primarily by students and enjoyed the support of certain progressive 'bourgeois' individuals. Initially the Hnchaks were part of the organisation, but they withdrew their participation in 1891, unhappy with their treatment and unsatisfied with the ARF's vague commitment to socialism. For two years the new party maintained a precarious existence, beset by splits, an unclear agenda and disappointment that the revolutionary spark was not immediately igniting the masses. In the summer of 1892 the party developed a clearer agenda—in the form of the party Programme—during its first General Congress (held in Tiflis). Soon thereafter the ARF began organising revolutionary activities in earnest, becoming a force to contend with.

The main objective of the Dashnaks was the liberation of Ottoman (western) Armenia. They too were committed to socialism, but not as staunchly or rigidly as the Hnchaks. Their 1890 manifesto (partially quoted in the previous chapter) managed to square the circle of 'uniting' socialism with middle class nationalism by referring to it as 'economic and political freedom'.[37] The ARF did use class language and analysis in the introduction of its 1892 Programme, denouncing the bourgeoisie, the conservative clergy and the 'nobility' for their collaboration with the Ottoman government in exploiting the working classes. In fact in 1907 the party joined

[37] L. Nalbandian, *Armenian Revolutionary Movement*, p. 154. Of all the Armenian organisations, the ARF has the most literature on it. This is partly because of its importance and partly because of the historiographical work of its own intellectuals. Mikayel Varandian's history remains a classic source, as are the memoirs of many of the first and second generation Dashnaks (e.g. Rouben [Ruben], *Mémoires*; A. Garo, *Bank Ottoman* etc.). For two noteworthy ARF publications in Armenian see the three volume *Hushamatian* and H. Tasnapetian, *Niuter.* For general overviews in English see L. Nalbandian, *Armenian Revolutionary Movement*, chapter 7; V. Lima, 'Evolving Goals and Strategies'.

the Second Socialist International and to this day it remains committed to socialism—at least nominally.[38] However, unlike the Hnchaks, Dashnaks were not overly concerned with theoretical nuances and rejected the rigidity and determinism of Marxism. They also did not place socialism on a par with national liberation. The struggle for the nation took precedence over the class struggle. 'From its inception, the Dashnaktsutiun subordinated the social question to the national,' writes Ronald Suny, 'Dashnaks did not see themselves as the representatives of any single group or class, but as the revolutionary vanguard of the entire nation.'[39] They saw socialism, adds Anahide Ter Minassian, as 'a means of defence against national oppression more than an inevitable stage in economic development.'[40] In other words, for the ARF socialism was a means to achieve a nationalist goal and not an end in itself.

The 1892 Dashnak Programme is indicative of its ideological eclecticism. It was a mélange of nationalist goals, socialist values, populist ideas (especially communalism) and liberal demands. It stated that the ARF's aim was to bring about 'the political and economic

[38] M. Hassassian, *ARF*, pp. 8–9. For the latest party programme (1998) addressing the issue of socialism see Hai Heghapokhakan Dashnaktsutiun, *Tzragir*, pp. 11–13. Before the adoption of the new party programme in 1998 there was some debate over certain issues in the Party's central organ, *Droshak*. One commentator from Armenia urged the Party to eliminate socialism from its programme; instead he advocated a nationally specific form of social justice within the parameters of pursuing the Armenian Cause as the supreme goal (Ashot Petrosian, 'H.H.D.', p. 9). The Party's theoretical statement on the relationship between socialism and the ARF remains the classic work of A. Jamalian, *H. H. Dashnaktsutiune*. First published in the early 1930s, it maintains that contrasting the internationalism of socialism with national interests is 'nonsense.... [b]ecause *for socialists, there is no incompatibility between national and international interests, nor can there be any*' (p. 116). In a more current article E. Hovhannisian ('Enkervarutiune') argues that Dashnaks are socialists but not Marxists; he rejects the dogmatic element of Marxism while emphasising the pluralistic dimension of the socialism of the ARF. Interestingly, the party's website in Armenia 'translated' *Hai Heghapokhakan Dashnaktsutiun* (Armenian Revolutionary Federation) as 'The Armenian Socialist Party' (http://www.arf.am, as checked in August 1999). In August 2002, when last checked, the correct translation was given and below it was added in parentheses, 'Armenian Socialist Party'.

[39] R. Suny, 'Eastern Armenians', p. 132; cf. R. Hovannisian, 'Armenian Question', pp. 216–17; M. Varandian, *H. H. Dashnaktsutian Patmutiun*, pp. 58ff. The latter interprets the socialism of ARF's founders as an ideology based on their 'worship of the people' and their wish to 'liberate the working and suffering masses from all types of repression—political, economic, religious...' (p. 58).

[40] A. Ter Minassian, *Nationalism and Socialism*, p. 47.

freedom of Turkish Armenia by means of rebellion'. More specifically the party demanded

> (1) democratic government of free Armenia [based on] free elections...;
> (2) the strictest provisions for the security of life and labour;
> (3) equality of all nationalities and creeds before the law;
> (4) freedom of speech, press and assembly;
> (5) land be given to [the landless] and the tiller guaranteed the opportunity to benefit from the land;
> (6) [taxation based on] ability to pay and according to communal principles, which for centuries have been deeply rooted in our people;
> (7) elimination of all forced and unpaid labor....;
> (8) elimination of the military exemption tax and establish conscription....;
> (9) assistance to... the intellectual progress of the people, making education compulsory;
> (10) assistance to the industrial progress of the people by giving them modern methods of production based on the principle of communal enterprise....;
> (11) assistance in strengthening the communal principles of the peasants and artisans...which have appeared on the soil of Armenia as a result of local and historic influences. Broadening the area of such communal establishments... [eventually] to the whole country.[41]

It should be noted that, in contrast to the Hnchaks, there was *no* mention of *independence* for Armenia. Dashnak demands were essentially for fundamental reforms and freedom in Armenia, but within the Ottoman framework. The means to achieve this end were to be revolutionary and violent since these were, it was believed, the only avenues left to demand changes from the Ottoman authorities.

Through this and subsequent programmes, as well as activities based on them, the ARF struck a balance in its approach which had a wider appeal than other radical organisations. The party could, therefore, establish roots not only in the eastern point of Armenian nationalism (where it was born) but also in the western point, as

[41] L. Nalbandian, *Armenian Revolutionary Movement*, pp. 167–8.

well as in the central point of Armenia itself. Dashnaks also had wider room to manoeuvre. With socialists they would highlight their socialist credentials; with nationalists, their national liberation ideology; with the middle classes, their liberal demands. But above all, they presented themselves as the defenders of the entire Armenian nation.

Like the Hnchak party, the ARF too was willing to collaborate with non-Armenian progressive elements, be they Turkish or Kurdish, although, again, this was not pursued in earnest at the local level, particularly until the Young Turk revolution of 1908. And, as with all the revolutionaries, the linchpin in the Dashnak approach was European assistance and intervention in the Ottoman empire to ensure the freedom of the Armenians.

Dashnaks and Hnchaks were similar in many ways in their radicalism and commitment to liberate Armenia.[42] But whereas the Hnchak party practically withered away, the ARF succeeded because it always placed the national imperative at the forefront of its struggle, subordinating socialism to it. Furthermore, it mixed in its ideology, programme and activities various elements from the eastern, western and central points of Armenian nationalism. Ultimately the ARF was successful because it could bring together the various elements of Armenian identity. It was very much an 'eastern' romantic and radical organisation at its inception, but it 'spoke' to the peasants of Armenia and related to their realities, and to the middle classes of Constantinople. Being more inclusive in their ideology Dashnaks could develop a much wider constituency than Hnchaks and Ramkavars. Their approach was neither too local and parochial in its concerns, nor too internationalist and theoretically abstract.

More concretely, Dashnaks were also well organised, but with a relatively decentralised structure (unlike the Hnchaks). They produced much propaganda (journals, papers, pamphlets etc.); they had charismatic and capable leaders who travelled, mobilised, fought, and died in the line of duty in Armenia and elsewhere;[43] and they

[42] In fact Louise Nalbandian minimises the substantive differences in the programmes of the two parties and states that they could not collaborate because of petty jealousies and personal feuds between Dashnak and Hnchak leaders, which made theoretical differences insurmountable (L. Nalbandian, *Armenian Revolutionary Movement*, pp. 172, 184).

[43] 'Hero worship' is an important element of Dashnak culture. The three most impor-

engaged in daring acts of bravery—the assassination of officials or informers, the arming and defence of Armenian villages and towns, taking punitive measures against Kurdish tribes and oppressive individuals, and performing various terrorist acts.

Armenian Marxists/Social Democrats

If class and ethnicity were mixed to reinforce one another in the politics of the Dashnaks and Hnchaks, there were a few Armenian radicals who altogether rejected the nationalist element of the equation as liberating and focused exclusively on the class struggle. These internationalists insisted on the cooperation between workers of all ethnicities. They were part of the wider Russian and Georgian based Social Democratic movement that began to make inroads in the major industrialising cities of the South Caucasus (mainly Baku and Tiflis) in the last few years of the nineteenth century. A few Armenian intellectuals tried to mobilise their brethren along these lines by establishing in the summer of 1902 the Union of Armenian Social Democrats. But the Union dissolved into the Tiflis Social Democratic organisation within six months.

Social Democracy reached its peak in 1903 among the Armenians, but it very much remained an insignificant movement until 1917. The 'scientific' Marxism of the Social Democrats was at least in theory an ideological rival to the nationalist revolutionaries (i.e. the Dashnaks). However, in reality it never became a serious threat and did not at all assume any kind of centrality in the Armenian national movement. Hence Social Democracy did not affect Armenian national identity or nationalism, at least until the ascendency of the Bolsheviks in Russia and the subsequent Sovietisation of Armenia in December 1920.

---

tant men lionised in the party's mythology are its founding fathers, the 'trinity' of Kristapor Mikayelian (1859–1905), Simon Zavarian (1866–1913) and Stepan Zorian (a.k.a. Rostom, 1867–1919). In addition, there is a whole array of revered *fedayees*, whose images and biographies are constantly reproduced in party publications. Revolutionary songs (either about individuals or events) are also a rich source of historical repertoire. For two examples of this popular culture see *H.H.D. 100* and the magazine *Kaitzer* (Special Issue on Kristapor Mikayelian, verging on the 'cult of personality' literature). Each of the founders has also merited commemorative books on his own. One example is the impressive collection of letters and other documents on Stepan Zorian, edited by H. Tasnapetian, *Rostom*.

Social Democrats did not appeal to too many Armenians for two main reasons. First, they were seen to be members of a predominantly Georgian movement. Almost all members of the party were Georgian and its 'internationalism' was becoming the *de facto* ideology of *Georgian* national liberation.[44] Second, and more importantly, the Social Democrats, as Marxists, were not concerned with the liberation of Ottoman Armenia, but with the workers' struggle against Russian autocracy and the Romanov dynasty. The primary goal was to emancipate the workers of the Caucasus regardless of their nationality. As Suny puts it, 'Armenian Marxists, equipped now with an internationalist analysis based on class struggle, turned their back on the Arax and their face to the workers of Transcaucasia.'[45] But the recently mobilised Armenians were much more concerned with the conditions of the Ottoman Armenians and national unity than with cross-ethnic solidarity. They were, therefore, drawn to the Armenian nationalist parties whose programmes, incidentally, also promised to deliver social justice. In fact organisations such as the Dashnaks 'discouraged Armenian workers from participating in strikes and directed all efforts toward the struggle in Turkey'[46]—at least until 1903 when Russian repressive measures directly targeted Armenian national interests (as will be discussed later).

Some of the Armenian Social Democratic leaders of note were Arshak Zurabian, Bogdan Knuniants and Stepan Shahumian. The latter became one of the most celebrated leaders of the communist movement in the Caucasus, sometimes referred to as the 'Caucasian Lenin'. As one of the leaders (chairman) of the 1918 Baku commune he was executed—along with the other 25 commissars—by the anti-Bolshevik Socialist Revolutionaries on 20 September 1918, after fleeing (as a prisoner) the Turkish/Muslim occupation of Baku. Soviet authorities lionised Shahumian as a great fallen hero of the 1917 revolution.[47]

[44] R. Suny, *Looking toward Ararat*, p. 90; cf. R. Suny, *Making of the Georgian Nation*, pp. 156–64.

[45] R. Suny, *Looking toward Ararat*, p. 91.

[46] R. Suny, 'Eastern Armenians', p. 133.

[47] R. Suny, *Baku Commune*, pp. 337–43. There is much Soviet Armenian literature on Shahumian—his collected writings, detailed biographies etc. For one example see the short biography by V. Avetisian, *Stepan Shahumian*. As in Russia proper, Bolsheviks in the Caucasus had to collaborate with 'bourgeois specialists' in 1917–18 to hold on to

The Armenian revolutionaries of all persuasions encountered many problems: the fear and conservatism of the populace who had internalised their second-class status; the wrath of the clergy who were appalled by the radicals' anti-clerical pronouncements; the opposition of the upper classes who objected to socialism etc. Many in the Armenian establishment (*amiras*, church leaders, landowners) were against the revolutionaries because fundamental change in the Ottoman system was not in their economic interests; and the loss of the Sultan's 'favour' towards the 'loyal *millet*' was detrimental to their status. The parties—especially the ones informed by socialist analysis—were aware of this and they therefore tried to establish direct links with the masses. They realised the importance of educating and conscientising the Armenian peasants and lower classes through education, propaganda and the examples of their deeds.[48]

Revolutionary organisations did not have mass membership,[49] but they did have a powerful impact on Armenian politics and identity in a number of ways. First, they shifted political representation from the conservative elements within society (the wealthy bourgeoisie and the clergy) to a new and dynamic group of young intellectuals, students, *fedayees*, party workers/members and affiliates, who claimed to represent the interests of the lower (middle) classes and the peasantry, bringing them into the heart of national affairs.

Second, these parties adopted popular movement politics as the new strategy of liberation. Hence they 'created a new reality not so much by fighting against the Church and capital as by developing a new arena of activity.'[50] In their strikes, mobilisation efforts, rebellions, assassinations and military endeavours the parties (re)opened a

---

power, without being ideologically too rigid. Hence Shahumian in Baku worked with Dashnaks in defending the city. In fact it was a Dashnak commander who assisted Shahumian and the other commissars to flee Baku during the chaos of 14–16 September 1918 when the city fell to Azerbaijani and Turkish forces. It seems that when push came to shove Armenian national solidarity prevailed over bitter ideological antagonisms.

48 For example, one of the major discussion topics of the ARF Second General Congress in 1898 was the issue of preparing the masses for revolution; see S. Vratzian, 'Second World Congress'. The same theme was also central in the Hnchakian programme.

49 I have not come across reliable figures, as the parties themselves kept membership numbers secret. Both the ARF and the Hnchak party considered themselves an elite 'vanguard'. Their active membership was probably no more than a few thousand.

50 G. Libaridian, *Ideology of Armenian Liberation*, p. 250.

whole new dimension of political and military activity within the Ottoman and Russian empires.

Third, in this radicalisation process socialism was brought into Armenian politics—either on a par with nationalism, in service to it as an instrument or in replacement of it. Between the late 1880s and the early 1920s socialism and nationalism were linked 'inextricably'.[51] Moreover, this link between the nation and socialist ideology continued throughout the twentieth century. As is discussed in subsequent chapters, it was formalised and regulated during Soviet rule over Armenia, but it continued to be used in the service of national(ist) goals.

The fourth point is the undisputed victory of the eastern radical point of Armenian nationalism at a pan-national level. Revolutionary parties born from eastern Armenians came to dominate national politics in the east, in the west and in Armenia itself. More specifically, the Hnchak and Dashnak parties became the predominant political organisations setting the national agenda.

Fifth, the parties, and especially the ARF, succeeded in further articulating and reinforcing a new hegemonic vision of what it meant to be Armenian. Revolutionary intellectuals and their followers delineated the image of the Armenians as a modern, essentially secular nation that was demanding individual and collective rights based on European principles of freedom. As such the parties became the new brokers of identity, which they defined in terms of both nationality and (subsequently) class. In reality their vision was not based on a synthesis of the various sources of Armenian identity, but reflected the aggregation of diverse elements under the umbrella of 'Armenianness'—i.e. it *inferred* an organic unity around certain 'core' cultural and political characteristics such as language and national liberation. In this process of amalgamating the nation further, the *subjective will* of the parties was of paramount importance.

Finally, the parties were the key instruments in the shift of Armenian self-image from defenceless victim to rebellious fighter—a notion that had historic precedents and a literary tradition. They sought to redefine what it meant to be Armenian in a radical direction.[52] Their means of doing this was propaganda, heroic activities and

[51] A. Ter Minassian, 'Role of the Armenian Community', pp. 110–11.

[52] G. Libaridian, 'Changing Armenian Self Image', p. 168, cf. pp. 164–9.

self-sacrifice. Many of the revolutionaries, along with their deeds, entered popular culture (particularly through songs), helping it to radicalise further. They were seen by their followers and sympathisers as the embodiments of the fictional heroes in the novels of Raffi and other writers of the earlier generation. We now turn to some of their activities.

REVOLUTIONARY ACTIVITIES

The Armenian revolutionaries mobilised people through both pre-existing national institutions[53] and their own organisations. I will focus on the latter since they had more of a tangible impact. The most obvious medium for the parties to spread their word was the printed page: the media and other party literature. For example, the ARF published close to 150 titles, many of them periodicals, between 1890 and 1925 in the Ottoman empire/Turkey alone.[54] The Hnchaks were active publishers too, albeit not as prolific as the Dashnaks. But paper propaganda could only go so far; hence revolutionaries also embarked on activities which they classified as 'propaganda of the deed'. These can be divided into three overlapping categories: activities primarily aimed at European attention, intra-community deeds, and self-defence.

Protests and terrorism

Mass protests were the preferred method of the Hnchaks. Through such demonstrations they sought to achieve two ends: to draw European attention to the Armenian cause and to spark revolutionary fervour among the Armenian masses. In June 1890 they were behind such a protest in Erzerum which turned violent. More importantly they staged a much better organised demonstration a month later in Constantinople. The Kum Kapu protest (named after the Armenian quarter of the city where it began) was the first time

[53] For example, both Simon Zavarian and Stepan Zorian, leaders of the ARF, were active in the administration of Armenian national schools in the Ottoman empire in the early 1910s—a platform they used to propagate progressive ideas. The first was active in Mush and Sasun, the second in Erzerum, as general directors of the schools (*H.H.D. 100*, p. 14; Ghazar-Chareg, *Hushamatian*, p. 238).

[54] A. Ter Minassian, 'Role of the Armenian Community', p. 124, cf. pp. 121–34.

The Western (Ottoman) Armenian provinces, 1878–1914.

Christian subjects of the Sultan were openly demonstrating against him in the capital. Moreover, it was a protest against the Constantinople Armenian liberal leadership. It began in the patriarchate when Hnchaks interrupted mass, read out a manifesto (which also denounced the head of the church and the Armenian National Assembly for neglecting the provinces), forced the Patriarch to join the protesters, and marched to the Palace to demand the improvement of conditions in Armenia and the implementation of article 61 of the Treaty of Berlin. The procession did not reach the palace as it was terminated by the police, causing the death of a few people.

Hnchaks continued their protests in the following years. In September 1895 they once again organised a mass rally, having notified foreign embassies of their intent. Two thousand people took part in what was planned to be a peaceful march from the Armenian quarters of the city to the Bab Ali (the Sublime Porte). They once again demanded civil liberties, reform in the Armenian provinces and a European governor for these provinces, the right of the Armenians to join the police force and to bear arms, and the denunciation of the 1894 Sasun massacres. Again the police intercepted the protest and arrested its leaders. But this time the outcome was much bloodier. For three days Constantinople witnessed an anti-Armenian pogrom in which hundreds were killed by Muslim theological students with the assistance or acquiescence of the police.

Dashnaks did not agree with the method of mass protests and concentrated their efforts on guerrilla activities in the provinces and terrorist attacks in the cities. The most daring—and therefore celebrated—example of their attempts to 'shock the Europeans into action'[55] was their takeover of Banque Ottomane, the central bank of the empire, which was administered by the French. Twenty-six ARF commandos stormed the building, held its staff and wealth hostage, and threatened to blow it up if their demands were not met within forty-eight hours. These included the appointment of European commissioners to preside over the Armenian provinces, police forces that included Armenians, judicial, tax and land reforms, and the usual civil liberties of freedom of press, assembly, speech etc. Instead of reforms the surviving commandos only received safe passage out of the empire (to France)—negotiated by the Russian

[55] R. Hovannisian, 'Armenian Question', p. 224.

dragoman Maximov—and promises of future European support. In the two days after the incident 6,000 Armenians were killed in yet another pogrom in Constantinople.[56]

The ARF also decided to assassinate Sultan Abdul Hamid II. An attempt was made in July 1905, but the Sultan survived the massive bomb explosion by a fluke. Months earlier, in March, during the preparation of the bomb in Bulgaria, Kristapor Mikayelian, the foremost leader of the ARF, had died from an accidental detonation.[57]

Far from sparking mass rebellion and European assistance—the two main intended goals of the Armenian revolutionaries—such activities did not produce any tangible results except further repression and massacres. Armenian radicals mistakenly believed that the Sultan's position was so precarious that any major crisis, especially in the capital, would entice European intervention, leading to the restructuring of the Ottoman empire. Their agitation was aimed at ensuring such an outcome, but they were unaware of the gap between the words of European statesmen and their national interests. They also did not appreciate the complexities of international relations which necessitated the survival of the Ottoman empire (and the Sultan). As to their own people, much as Armenians were struck by the heroism of the revolutionaries, repression, fear, conservatism and a lack of widespread organisation prevented them from joining the radicals en masse.

Intra-community activities

The revolutionary parties were quite active within the Armenian communities in both the cities and provinces of the Ottoman and Russian empires. In addition to holding meetings, disseminating propaganda, and organising other educational activities, they manufactured arms and mobilised guerrilla forces and terrorist groups as needed. They assassinated (both in Ottoman and Russian domains) local government officials, brutal police chiefs, Kurdish chieftains

[56] For further details on these events see L. Nalbandian, *Armenian Revolutionary Movement*, pp. 118–20, 122–6, 176–8; R. Hovannisian, 'Armenian Question', pp. 218–25; C. Walker, *Armenia*, pp. 132–3, 152–6, 164–8. For an eyewitness account of one of the participants in the Banque Ottomane raid see A. Garo, *Bank Ottoman*, chapters 11–14.

[57] M. Varandian, *H. H. Dashnaktsutian Patmutiun*, pp. 363–9.

and others who were particularly oppressive or cruel towards the Armenians. They also murdered Armenian informers and other collaborators with the imperial regimes. However, the revolutionaries also tried to project a friendly image: kind to and supportive of the peasantry and poor Armenians. As such they acquired an aura of brave defenders of the people, as freedom fighters or *fedayees* who were to be respected and feared.

The revolutionaries funded their activities and their organisations through dues and local 'donations'. Some of these came from voluntary support, but more often than that, rich Armenians were forced to make a 'contribution' or else face the terrorist arm of the organisation. Through such extortion, funds were raised for party activities and community self-defence (which basically entailed the purchase and manufacture of arms in the South Caucasus or Iran and their transport to Ottoman Armenia).[58]

Interestingly, despite such practices, the revolutionaries introduced a moral dimension into Armenian politics. Their integrity, commitment to justice and honesty, disinclination for personal material gain and their total commitment to the nation endeared them to many people—particularly to the lower classes. Of course the parties themselves emphasised their upright commitment to the national cause in contrast to the corruption and sly self-interest of the

58 There is a revealing account of such an incident by an eyewitness of the 1905 Baku battles. After Dashnak forces had defended the Armenian community from Muslim (Tatar) attack, the ARF commander, Nikol Duman (Niko), gathered all the rich Armenians of the city and said in a speech:

> 'You have summoned me from the Turkish border to come to your aid. This I have done. But I want you to know that there are in Turkey hundreds of thousands of Armenians who are always in need of our help, even more so than you.... [O]ur party is doing all it can to parry [the Hamidian] massacres. Armenians in Turkey are threatened with extermination, but have no means to defend themselves. They are poor.... You, here, are rich, and you must help us. You, too, must contribute to the defence of our people.'

He then demanded a list of all the rich Armenians with the contributions they were to make. Unhappy with the sums they had volunteered, Duman increased each of the contributions, adding, 'Those who refuse to pay will be killed.' Sure enough, when one of the rich Armenians fled from Baku to St Petersburg in order to avoid payment, he was tracked down and murdered by a Dashnak in the St Petersburg Armenian church yard; for maximum effect, the killer, after the deed, announced to the exiting congregation why he had carried out his task (M. Mathossentz, *Black Raven*, pp. 20–1).

upper classes. Such 'symbolic capital' served the parties well into the twentieth century.

For example, writing in the 1950s Sarkis Atamian uses such arguments in his sympathetic account of the ARF:

> The Dashnaktzoutyoun [*sic*] and its deeds and fighters of the time, are defined as a group, indeed as the only group, with such traits of heroism, gallantry, valor, self-sacrifice, loyalty to duty and nation, patriotism, and martyrdom. By identification with those values, Dashnaks or Dashnak sympathizers are able to obtain directly or vicariously a sense of courage and victory—a sense of having cheated the Turk to some extent of an inevitable fate.... Dashnaktzoutyoun and its adherents who constantly commemorate, in many social and political functions through the year, the heroism and valor of those men who attained a moral victory in the resistence or helped many Armenians to escape a certain death. These commemorative exercises continue to release or neutralize residual hostility.[59]

Of course the other, non-Dashnak side of the Armenian community mirrored similar arguments about their own glorious past and patriotic deeds. The point is that intra-community relations and politics heavily relied on the revolutionary past in order to justify the activities and existence of various organisations even when, decades later, they had absolutely nothing to do with revolution.

Self-defence in east and west

The third category of revolutionary activity was in the realm of self-defence. Hnchaks were instrumental in the instigation of the 1894 Sasun rebellion against the repressive measures and excessive taxation of the local Kurdish chieftains and the Ottoman government. The Armenians eventually surrendered, believing the word of honour of the Turkish commander. A massacre of thousands of local Armenians followed. In October 1895, weeks after the bloody

[59] S. Atamian, *Armenian Community*, pp. 264–5. He continues his biased analysis to argue that the anti-Dashnak Armenians (i.e. the non-ARF side of the community, particularly the Ramkavars) do not have the benefit of such a heroic past and therefore base their identity on an anti-Dashnak and pro-Soviet Armenia *Weltanschauung* that emanates from 'autistic thinking' (pp. 273–305, 316–17). The main motif of Atamian's 1955 book, it should be noted, is to vindicate the Dashnak party from accusations of 'terrorism' and being 'Turkophile' and 'unpatriotic'—particularly in reference to the scathing attacks in an anti-ARF book published earlier in the United States (in 1934) by K. S. Papazian (K. Papazian, *Patriotism Perverted*).

repression of their protest march in Constantinople, Hnchaks again guided the Armenians to rebel, this time in Zeytun, in the face of imminent massacres as reprisals. The rebellion ended with European mediation in February 1896. Again massacres ensued—triggered by the rebellion as well as by the Constantinople protests—which took the lives of 100,000 to 200,000 Armenians. In defence of their town Armenians of Van, led by Armenakans and assisted by Hnchaks, rose up in rebellion in June 1896. This was the most—and last—significant endeavour of the Armenakans. After 1896 much of the onus of national self-defence fell on the Hnchaks (who soon lost their momentum) and the Dashnaks (whose significance increased).[60]

Another example of large scale guerrilla activity was the punitive attack at Khanasor (July 1897). ARF forces of 250 men (including two *fedayee* priests) destroyed a particularly menacing Kurdish tribe, part of the Hamidiye forces, to avenge the tribe's participation in massacres. This, along with the Banque Ottomane attack, was the turning point in the ascendancy of the ARF as a revolutionary party.[61]

The events which really galvanised the ARF and turned it into the major Armenian political and military force were the confiscation of Armenian church properties in 1903 and the Armeno-Tatar wars of 1905, both in the Russian empire. Russian authorities had

[60] L. Nalbandian, *Armenian Revolutionary Movement*, pp. 102–3, 120–2, 126–7. My thanks to Aram Arkun for bringing to my attention the role of the Constantinople protest as a trigger for the Zeitun massacres.

[61] For details on Khanasor see M. Varandian, *H. H. Dashnaktsutian Patmutiun*, pp. 149–56. Such military activities in the Ottoman empire, particularly in the Armenian provinces, received much assistance—both in terms of personnel and material—from Russian Armenians, despite the harsh clampdown by the Tsarist administration. The first attempt by Armenian armed bands to penetrate the Ottoman domains from Russia took place in 1890. An expedition was organised on the private initiative of a student, Sargis Kukunian. In September 125 revolutionaries left Kars to begin the liberation of Ottoman Armenians. The expedition failed even before reaching the frontier, as its members were arrested by Russian forces. They were put on trial and received harsh sentences. A most interesting element of the group was its banner: among other things it had five stars (symbolising five of the Armenian provinces) surrounding the number 61—i.e. article 61 of the treaty of Berlin. It also had the drawing of a skull and the words 'Revenge! Revenge!' (L. Nalbandian, *Armenian Revolutionary Movement*, p. 158). Revolutionaries also used Iranian territory as a rear support base for their activities in the Ottoman empire. Moreover, the ARF and the Hnchak party were quite active in the revolutionary movement within Iran as well (1900–10s). They supported the indigenous progressive (constitutionalist) forces (for a detailed study see C. Chaqueri, *Armenians of Iran*).

already tried to close down the Armenian national schools in 1885,[62] but backed down in 1886 after encountering much resistance. However, the Russification efforts begun in 1885 intensified even more after Nicholas II's accession to the throne in 1894. Repressive measures against the Armenians (and other ethnic minorities) increased considerably—particularly during Prince Golitsyn's tenure as governor-general of the Caucasus (1896–1905). Golitsyn crudely implemented a policy of forced Russification. The most severe blow came in June 1903 when a decree was issued in violation of the 1836 *Polozhenie* dictating that all properties of the Armenian church (including the schools) were to be managed by the Russian state. Armenians resisted the order en masse and Khrimian Hairik, now Catholicos of Ejmiatzin, refused to hand over the church deeds.[63]

The standoff between the Armenians and the Tsarist authorities continued until 1905. In February clashes broke out in Baku between the Armenians and the Muslims (usually referred to as Tatars). The latter were encouraged to attack Armenians by the governor of Baku, Prince Nakashidze (later assassinated by the ARF). Close to 900 Armenians were killed, and some 600 Muslims.[64] But the Armenian population on the whole was defended by small Dashnak units. Subsequently clashes also broke out in Gharabagh and Nakhijevan. When Baku was once again engulfed in ethnic and class violence in September, Armenians and the ARF were much better prepared to defend their quarters. By October the situation had calmed down in the region. In August 1905 the Russian Council of Ministers had already repealed the 1903 act confiscating Armenian church properties.[65]

[62] 500 schools, with 900 teachers and 20,000 students, were closed down for one year in the Caucasus (R. Suny, *Looking toward Ararat*, p. 45).

[63] For further details see V. Gregorian, 'Impact of Russia', pp. 197–8; R. Suny, 'Eastern Armenians', pp. 129–37.

[64] C. Walker, *Armenia*, p. 74; cf. pp. 69–78.

[65] R. Suny, 'Eastern Armenians', pp. 134–5. These regional dynamics took place within important developments in the international context. The Russo-Japanese war, the February 1905 uprising in St Petersburg and the subsequent promise of reforms by the Tsar were all part of the bigger picture of upheaval in the empire at this point. More specific to the Armenians,

> Russian attitudes towards the Armenians had changed greatly since the Congress of Berlin. The Russian government had entered a period of *rapprochement* with the sultan, and was too alarmed at the revolutionary and nationalist tendencies of its own Armenians… to want to stimulate them among Armenians elsewhere. It was well

Between 1903 and 1905 Russian Armenians were radicalised considerably owing to the repressive policies of the Tsar. As Christopher Walker puts it, 'Overnight [in June 1903], the entire Armenian nation in the Russian empire became converted to the cause of the revolutionaries.'[66] This is perhaps an exaggeration, but the effects of the closing of the schools in Russia paralleled the effects of the massacres in the Ottoman empire; they both had a considerable impact in the radicalisation process of the masses. Dashnaks were the main beneficiaries of this process since they spearheaded both the anti-Tsar and the anti-Tatar struggles. Their respect and reputation as defenders of both the Armenian people and national rights increased, especially among the church leaders and the middle classes. The ARF was, after all, defending the church institution.

The 1903–5 events had four consequences on the ARF. First, it reoriented its focus towards Russian Armenia. At its Third General Congress in 1904 (in Sofia) it decided to take up the defence of Caucasian Armenians. Taking this logic further, at its 1907 Fourth Congress (in Vienna) the ARF split its programme into an eastern and western component, pursuing a dual policy of liberating both Ottoman and Russian Armenia. Henceforth the party programme directly reflected the east/west divide among the Armenians—at least in the realm of politics. Second, the party itself was further radicalised in a socialist direction. In the 1907 Congress it officially accepted a socialist programme, joining the Socialist International.[67] Third, after 1903 a clear anti-autocracy and anti-Russian stream developed within the ARF. Although this never became predominant, it always existed within the party, reflecting the erosion of Russophilia among the Armenians.[68] Finally, given the weakness of the Hnchaks due to organisational and ideological splits, the ARF filled

---

aware that the ultimate aim of many Russian Armenians—'the intellectuals and the clergy'—was independence and not assimilation (J. Salt, *Imperialism*, pp. 90–1).

Russians no longer wanted to keep the Armenian question alive as a pressure mechanism against the Ottomans. This policy, however, changed once more 'in favour' of the Armenians in late 1912 owing to geo-strategic calculations on the eve of the First World War (see M. Somakian, *Empires in Conflict*, pp. 46–9).

66 C. Walker, *Armenia*, p. 70.

67 A. Ter Minassian, 'Role of the Armenian Community', pp. 119–20.

68 A very clear expression of this anti-Russian attitude is found in the already mentioned pamphlet by Ruben Darbinian entitled *Rusakan Vtange* (The Danger of Russia), written in 1920, at a moment of extreme threat from the Bolsheviks.

the void, consolidating its position as the primary defender of national rights.

After 1905 the Armenian middle classes did not on the whole strongly oppose the Tsar. The revolutionaries were persecuted, but they remained active and continued to function in a semi-legal manner. Once again they focused more on the Ottoman empire but no longer neglected the Caucasian Armenians. The radicals, especially the Dashnaks, remained popular among the lower classes. During the First World War Armenians in Russia supported the Russian war effort. In addition to the conscripts (150,000) in the imperial army, volunteer units were set up to fight alongside the regular troops. They expected the liberation of Ottoman Armenia with the victory of Russia. By 1917 Armenians too had realised that the Tsar was unable or unwilling to fulfil their aspirations, and greeted the February revolution with joy.

Alliance with the Young Turks

Although not directly related to identity construction, the issue of Armenian alliance with the Young Turks must be addressed. This was an important dimension of Armenian political activity before the First World War and the Genocide. It shows that some Armenian and Turkish nationalists were willing to collaborate with one another as long as they perceived that they had a common goal. However, at the end the two nationalisms could not coexist within the same state and the result was the almost total destruction of the Armenian community in the Ottoman empire. The Armenian and Turkish nationalist goals were incompatible. One side wished to create a unified Ottoman society—after 1911 interpreted as a Turkish society—while the other side advocated local autonomy and communal rights.[69] Both were fighting over the same land and mutually exclusive collective rights.

Dashnaks and some Reformed Hnchaks participated in the first Congress of Ottoman Liberals held in Paris in 1902. Relations continued with the Young Turks who reformed and redirected the Committee of Union and Progress (CUP) in 1907. When the latter

[69] Feroz Ahmad has come to a similar conclusion, using the word 'antithetical'. But he exaggerates the Armenian demands to include total independence, which was not often the case (F. Ahmad, 'Unionist Relations', p. 419).

marched on Constantinople and took power from the Sultan in July 1908, Armenians hailed the 'revolution' and the restoration of the abrogated constitution. The mood was one of cooperation, unity and common destiny between the Turks and the minorities despite ethnic and religious differences. However, this was not to last.

The first major shock came with the Adana (in Cilicia) massacres of 20,000 Armenians in 1909. The CUP blamed the reactionaries sympathetic to the Sultan. The ARF continued to cooperate with the Young Turks, believing that constitutional reform, which would grant autonomy to the Armenian provinces, was still possible. In fact the party—much to the objection of many members who broke ranks—supported the Ottomans against the combined Greek, Bulgarian, Serbian and Montenegrin forces in the Balkan wars of 1912.[70] It became impossible for Dashnaks and other Armenians to cooperate with the Committee after the triumvirate of Enver Bey, Talaat Pasha and Jemal Pasha (the ministers of War, the Interior and Marine respectively) consolidated their power in 1913. These men were nationalists who were intent on Turkifying the Ottoman empire. In fact relations between the ARF and the CUP were formally broken off in May 1912.[71] However, contacts between the Young Turks and the Armenians continued. Between 1912 and 1914 the former used such opportunities to clearly warn the Armenian revolutionaries to steer away from their reliance on foreign powers to guarantee the reforms in the Armenian provinces. The CUP promised that it would implement the necessary changes, but the Armenians were convinced that without external guarantees Turkish promises would come to naught.[72]

As long as the Young Turks were concerned about rights, reforms and autonomy in the Armenian provinces, as it seemed that they were until 1910 or so, cooperation was possible. However, by

[70] General Andranik, on the other hand, a former ARF *fedayee* in Armenia with a legendary reputation, played a key role in the Bulgarian army. He was instrumental in the defeat of the superior Ottoman forces in October 1912 (V. Dadrian, *Warrant for Genocide*, pp. 108–10).

[71] At the Sixth General Congress of the ARF (August-September 1911), it was already decided to break relations with the CUP unless the latter began to reverse its oppression of national rights and to act on its earlier promises of reform (H. Dasnabedian, *Histoire*, p. 100).

[72] For further details see R. Hovannisian, 'Armenian Question', pp. 229–35; M. Varandian, *H. H. Dashnaktsutian Patmutiun*, pp. 421–43. For a detailed study of ARF-CUP relations see G. Minassian, 'Relations'.

1911 Young Turk ideology had shifted from the concept of 'Ottomanisation' as understood by the Armenians and other minorities—which at least theoretically entailed the equality of all subject people—to 'Turkification' of all the subjects and the inherent superiority of the Muslims. In short, Ottomanism had come to mean very different things for the Young Turks and for the Armenians. The Young Turk approach was coupled with a centralised and dictatorial administration, and policies based on force. Consequently the Armenians realised that even their minimal demands could not be met by the Porte. In the meantime Armenians were encouraged by the facts that (a) Russia had once again taken up the Armenian cause and for the first time in fifteen years was making demands on behalf of the Armenians, and (b) Balkan Christian nations were continuing to succeed in their liberation struggles against the Ottomans.[73] The CUP was thus convinced that the Armenians had become, or would become, 'instruments of Russian policy'. Meanwhile European powers (the Triple Entente) were once again putting pressure on the Ottoman empire to implement reforms in the Armenian provinces. An agreement was reached in February 1914; it was formally signed by representatives of the Ottoman and Russian empires. The Reform Act, accepted by the Ottomans under pressure from European powers, and Russian involvement in its implementation, seemed to the Turks 'like a prelude to a Russian protectorate over eastern Anatolia, with eventual Armenian independence.'[74] By the spring of 1914 a Dutchman and a Norwegian

[73] Even liberal and conservative Constantinople intellectuals, in addition to the Armenians of the provinces, were increasingly banking on the Russian empire to liberate the Armenians. As Manoug Somakian explains,

> The inability or unwillingness of the Ottoman government to enforce security and order in its Asiatic domains had compelled Armenian leaders in Turkey to seek Russian protection. Krikor Zohrab, a former deputy of the Ottoman Parliament, and Mardigian, the representative of the Armenian Patriarchate, conferring with N. G. Giers, the Russian ambassador at Constantinople, stated that the Armenian people saw no other way for salvation but to appeal to Russia. They further stressed that the Armenians had 'completely lost faith' in Turkish reforms, even if they were to be under European auspices (M. Somakian, *Empires in Conflict*, p. 49).

For further details of the ideological shift in the Young Turk approach see C. Walker, *Armenia*, pp. 181–93; M. Somakian, *Empires in Conflict*, pp. 39–40. My thanks to Erik Zurcher for comments on Ottomanism that enabled me to fine-tune this parapgraph.

[74] Both quotes are from F. Ahmad, 'Unionist Relations', p. 424. In his analysis of the ARF-CUP collaboration Ahmad also introduces—rightly—the class dimension.

were selected as the foreign inspectors-general to supervise the far reaching reforms and reorganisation of the Ottoman Armenian provinces. But war broke out and the mission of the two men did not get off the ground.

The revolutionaries of the late nineteenth and early twentieth centuries had one eye on the Armenian masses, and one eye on the European powers. They dirtied their hands mostly in the Ottoman and to a lesser degree the Russian empires. Their hearts were rooted in Armenia but their minds wandered across Europe and Russia. In short, Armenian nationalism reflected a complex web of ideologies and activities, but always remained focused on the liberation of the Armenian nation and its territories. Hence the activities of the revolutionaries conscientised and galvanised the Armenians. Objectively most major acts were failures—i.e. they did not achieve their intended goals (except individual assassinations, Khanasor, some of the self-defence battles in the South Caucasus and the school and church standoffs in the Russian empire). But failure did not matter in terms of the evolution of national identity and the strengthening of the nationalist cause. In the collective consciousness of the Armenians such acts were instances of heroic rebellion, moral victory and great national achievement (except the alliance with the CUP).[75] These activities affected identity by making revolutionary politics and nationalism a 'normal' part of Armenian life. Revolu-

---

Both organisations had progressive ideologies and were against the traditional elements and upper classes of their societies—e.g. the religious hierarchy and the *amiras* (cf. p. 403, 419). However, Ahmad does not appreciate the fact that the nationalism of the ARF, and that of the CUP, was deeper than class loyalty. Neither party would have jeopardised the security of ethnic kin (e.g. the *amiras* in the Armenian case) and national institutions (e.g. religious establishments) in the name of cooperation with one another.

[75] For example, if someone who is ignorant of Armenian history examines the revolutionary songs from this period, he or she would never guess that Armenians were ultimately crushed by the Ottoman empire during the First World War. Rather that the Sultan and his empire were brought down to their knees by Armenian freedom fighters! Some of the lines in one popular Dashnak song (*Ariunot Drosh* [Bloodied Flag]) go as follows:

Hope filled the hearts of the Armenians
Fear surrounded the Ottoman emperor/...
Arms at hand, stood up
dear fedayees like lions/...
Intense fear reigned in the Ottoman army (*Heghapokhakan yergaran*, p. 16).

tionary acts became the politics of the nation. They are commemorated as great moments in the history of the Armenian nation. Many of these acts are celebrated on a regular basis to this day by Armenian political and cultural organisations.

Each party has its own pool of activities to remember, using their commemoration as occasions to propagate its message. The ARF, for instance, celebrates its founding, the Khanasor battle, the Banque Ottomane takeover, the proclamation of the 1918 republic and the 1921 rebellion (see below for the latter two) as well as other events. In the diaspora these dates are occasions to have community dances, concerts, lectures, dinners and other such events. After the 1990s with the establishment of ARF, ADL and SDHP branches in Armenia, similar events are being held in the republic.

For example, Dashnaks in Yerevan organised a Banque Ottomane centennial commemorative event on 14 August 1996. The gathering was held in a semi-clandestine manner since the ARF was officially banned in Armenia at that point. In two hours of speeches, songs and other displays of 'revolutionary culture' certain interesting themes emerged. The most striking feature was the ease with which speakers and images moved from the past to the present and to the future. The glory of the nineteenth century revolutionaries was tied to the assassins who in the 1920s killed Turkish officials responsible for the Genocide, to the 1980s terrorists who struck Turkish embassies, to the ARF members who died in the post-1988 Gharabagh struggle, and finally to the party members and leaders who were jailed in independent Armenia in the 1990s. The latter were explicitly paralleled to the jailed commandos of the Banque Ottomane operation. Of course the future was not neglected: Mount Ararat, Kars and Artahan (all in Turkey) were waiting to be liberated.... All these were part of the same chain of revolutionary activity spearheaded by the ARF. Other themes included: (1) The ARF revolutionary is a Christian soldier (although in contrast to similar events in the diaspora, there was no priest or any other religious participation at the Armenia gathering); (2) the moral superiority of the ARF fighters; (3) the indifference of foreign powers to the plight of the Armenians and; (4) Dashnaks will always struggle against injustice, be it in Armenia or elsewhere, and are willing to gloriously die for the Armenian cause. This is one example of many similar events the ARF organises for its members and sympathisers both in Armenia and in the diaspora. It uses such occasions to present a revolutionary image that is a mélange of the past, the present and the future, of activities in the Ottoman empire, Turkey and Azerbaijan, and of history, politics and culture—all enmeshed in the ideology of Armenian nationalism.[76]

Of course until 1988 Soviet Armenian authorities and historians vehemently countered the Dashnak view of history. ARF revolutionary activities were dismissed as an 'adventurism' that caused much more pain to the Armenians than gain. More specifically, Dashnaks were blamed for causing the Ottoman wrath which was manifested in anti-Armenian massacres. The progressive and 'saviour' role of the Russians was, needless to say, emphasised, and reliance on Turks—and later the West—was criticised as detrimental to the Armenians.[77]

THE GENOCIDE

The 1915–16 Genocide of the Armenians in the Ottoman empire is the cornerstone of modern Armenian identity, particularly in the diaspora. It is a defining moment, which on the one hand acts as a fundamental break with the past and the historic homeland, while on the other it serves as a prism through which national identity is seen, politics interpreted, and culture redefined.[78] The Armenian Genocide is the subject of much literature, but the topic itself remains understudied—especially its effects on identity. Because of the denial of genocide by the Turkish state and its supporters, most of the academic and semi-academic work on the issue is devoted to the factual proof of the event, its different aspects, and the refutation of its negation. Some interpretive work is done on how the Geno-

[76] Based on field notes taken by the author.

[77] The classic statement of this view is provided by the prominent Soviet Armenian historian H. Simonian, *Spiurkahayutiune* (see particularly pp. 499ff.). His massive book, published in 1968, is a systematic but highly ideologised criticism of the ARF. The work was a culmination of the Soviet view and set the tone for subsequent treatments of the subject.

[78] The schism created by the Genocide is clearly represented in the architecture of some of the commemorative monuments (e.g. the Tzitzernakaberd memorial in Yerevan, the Genocide Monument in Montreal). Another motif is that of a *khachkar* (the classical carved-in-stone cross) emphasising the martyrdom of the victims (e.g. Sydney, London, Paris). In some memorials the themes of protest and resistance are built-in (e.g. Athens, Aix-en-Provence). For some of the images see *Armenian International Magazine*, April 1999, pp. 48–50.

cide affected identity (especially in literary works), but it is impossible to say that there is a body of academic literature on the subject of genocide and Armenian identity. However, even if this link is academically underanalysed, the Genocide remains the key to understanding Armenian identity in the twentieth century. Although I barely scratch the surface of the Genocide topic in the next few pages, I highlight some of the issues and questions that are related to my analysis.[79]

There are two overall arguments regarding the Genocide. The first is the 'debate' over the very fact that the massacres constituted a genocide—i.e. were they the intentional destruction of the Armenians, planned and executed by the CUP administration and the Ottoman state. This is an extremely politicised issue and the word 'debate' is a misnomer. All Armenian scholars and mainstream historiography accept that the Young Turks' elimination of the Armenians was a genocide. Almost all Turkish historians, and some Western historians close to Turkey, deny that it was a genocide. They question the intent to destroy the Armenians, the number of deaths, the

[79] For a brief overview on the Genocide see C. Walker, 'World War I'; V. Dadrian, 'Determinants'; R. Suny, *Looking toward Ararat*, pp. 94–115. The most authoritative studies on the subject are written by Vahakn Dadrian. For two comprehensive studies see V. Dadrian, *History of the Armenian Genocide*, and V. Dadrian, *Warrant for Genocide*. Some of his significant essays are collected in the Special Issue of *Journal of Political and Military Sociology*, 22:1, Summer 1994. See also his seminal essay on the legal aspects of the extermination of the Armenians, V. Dadrian, 'Genocide as a Problem'. Three significant volumes on the different aspects of the Genocide and its denial are edited by Richard Hovannisian, *The Armenian Genocide in Perspective, The Armenian Genocide* and *Remembrance and Denial*. For two eyewitness accounts, among many, see A. Hartunian, *Neither to Laugh nor to Weep* and H. Riggs, *Days of Tragedy*. For a compilation of primary documents see A. Sarafian, *United States*. For an excellent comparative study looking at the Armenian and Jewish cases see R. Melson, *Revolution and Genocide*; see also L. Chorbajian and G. Shirinian, *Studies*, for a wider comparative perspective. For studies which focus on Genocide and memory, identity and literature see L. Shirinian's 'Impact' and *Armenian-North American Literature*; R. Peroomian, 'Armenian Literary'. I have listed only some of the more significant English language sources. There is of course considerable literature in Armenian on the topic. In the diaspora Armenians wrote about the Genocide on a regular basis (especially in the form of commemorative books, special issue newspapers and magazines). In Soviet Armenia the Genocide was a taboo subject until the late 1950s, but there was much written about it after 1965. One of the earlier publications, focusing on the Russian response to the Armenian 'tragedy' of massacres and genocide, is A. Mnatsakanian, *Hai zhoghovrdi voghbergutiune*; for an influential work condemning the Young Turks see, J. Kirakosian, *Yeritturkere*. For a recent overview of Armenian-language historiography on the Genocide (mostly an exegesis) see M. Karapetian, *Hayots*.

loyalty of the Armenians and the role of the Ottoman state. At best they accept that hundreds of thousands of Armenians died, but say this was due to wartime conditions, problems with their relocation, disease and the excesses of unruly elements (e.g. Kurdish irregulars). At worst they reverse the argument, blaming the Armenians for massacring Turks, terrorism and rebellion, which some argue constituted an anti-Turkish genocide.[80]

The second argument is over the questions of when and why the Genocide was planned? Was it the pinnacle of a long term Ottoman trend to get rid of the Armenians and therefore the Armenian question—that is, the end of a decades-long process which the Young Turks intensified and successfully actualised? Or was it a hastily planned and haphazardly executed decision based on First World War contingencies? In the first view, the Hamidian massacres of the

[80] For some of this revisionist and even apologist literature see T. Ataöv, '*Armenian Question*' (a criticism of Dadrian); K. Gürün, *Armenian File* (focusing on the terrorism of the Armenians); S. Sonyel, *Ottoman Armenians* (the fifth column thesis); A. Süslü *et al., Armenians* (rebellion and relocation arguments); M. Öke, *Armenian Question* (revolutionaries, geopolitics and relocation arguments); Ş. Orel and S. Yuca, *Talât Pasha* (false documents); H. Türközü, *Armenian Atrocity* (Turks as victims of the Armenians); J. McCarthy, 'Anatolian Armenians' (the 'numbers game' and war conditions); H. Lowry, *Story Behind* (unreliable sources); S. Shaw and E. Shaw, *History* (population figures, rebellion, fifth column and lack of intent; all these arguments are condensed on pp. 314–17). J. McCarthy, in a particularly mendacious book (*Death and Exile*), turns history on its head by arguing that the Muslims were the victims of Armenian aggression: 'The Armenian revolution' (p. 185) led to 'intercommunal war' (p. 187); all the Ottomans wanted to do was to peacefully and comfortably move the Armenians for their own safety (pp. 193ff, cf. pp. 185–218)! For commentary on such denialism see C. Foss, 'Armenian History'; R. Smith *et al.*, 'Professional Ethic'; V. Dadrian, 'Ottoman Archives'; V. Dadrian, *Key Elements*; M. Nichanian, 'Truth of the Facts'; R. Hovannisian, 'Denial of the Armenian Genocide'; and D. Papazian, 'Misplaced Credulity'. A very small number of Turkish historians accept the Genocide as fact. One such scholar, Taner Akçam (based in Germany and United States), examines its role in Turkish national identity. Many Armenians believe that his bold move and his criticisms of the Turkish denial constitute a first step towards Genocide recognition by more Turkish scholars and ultimately the Turkish state. For an excerpt from Akçam work translated into Armenian see T. Akçam, 'Turk azgayin'; for his massive study in German see T. Akçam, *Armenien* (his work is just beginning to be published in English; see for example his *From Empire to Republic: Turkish Nationalism and the Armenian Genocide*, London: Zed Press, 2004). For a good review of his arguments see Ara Sanjian, 'Taner Akçam's'. In the early 2000s a handful of Turkish and Armenian scholars, along with some Western colleagues, participated in a series of workshops (organised by Ronald Suny and Fatma Müge Göçek) collectively examining the Genocide. The workshops were held at the Universities of Chicago, Michigan (Ann Arbor) and the Minnesota (Minneapolis).

1890s (and earlier) and the 1909 Adana massacres are analysed as part of the same process which eventually led to genocide. In the second view, 1915 is interpreted quite differently, as part of the CUP nationalist programme, the geopolitics of the First World War (especially the Russian front) and therefore specific to the Young Turk regime.[81]

I will not engage in any of these issues since they could be the subject of another book or two. Rather I highlight, very briefly, two points related to the causes of the Genocide, and then focus on its effects on Armenian identity. But first some of the basic facts. The Genocide killed in 1915 one to one-and-a-half million Armenians, roughly one-third to one-half of the entire Armenian population. The actual number of Armenians living in the Ottoman empire is, as mentioned, debated. According to Armenian primary sources there were close to 2.1 million Armenians in the Ottoman empire on the eve of the First World War (a similar number lived in the Russian empire).[82] What is not debated is the fact that by 1923, when the modern Turkish republic was declared, there were hardly any Armenians left in the territories of what used to be the Armenian provinces of the Ottoman empire. Approximately 70,000 Armenians remained in Turkey, almost all in Constantinople/Istanbul. In a space of seven years the rest of the Armenian population

[81] The clearest expression of this debate is found in the exchange between Vahakn Dadrian, who argues the first thesis, and Ronald Suny, who maintains the second thesis. The exchange is published in *Armenian Forum*, 1:2, Summer 1998 (R. Suny, 'Empire and Nation', and 'Reply', especially p. 135; V. Dadrian, 'Armenian Genocide'. The first argument is taken to an extreme by A. Aivazian (*Armenian Rebellion*, particularly p. 46) who traces Turkish genocidal policies to the 1720s.

[82] For a brief overview of the numbers see R. Hovannisian, 'Armenian Question', pp. 233–5; L. Marashlian, *Politics and Demography*. Justin McCarthy (of the denialist camp), basing his research on Ottoman governmental sources, gives the following figures for the 1915–22 population changes: of the 1.3 million Armenians in Anatolia (i.e. the Asian territory of modern Turkey): 81,000 Armenians fled from Anatolia, 70,000 Armenians remained in Turkey, 880,000 Anatolian Armenians survived the war, 600,000 Armenians (40 per cent of the population) died. Of the survivors 400,000 went to the Russian empire/Armenia as refugees, the rest resettled elsewhere (J. McCarthy, *Muslims and Minorities*, p. 130, cf. pp. 121–30, 47–88 for details).

In contrast, Raymond Kevorkian, on the basis of the Armenian Patriarchate's census of 1912–13, gives the following calculations: 172,000 escaped to Russia, Bulgaria etc.; 115,000 remained in Constantinople and Smyrna; 120,000 converted to Islam, but then reconverted to Christianity; 75,000 survived in hiding; 1,430,000 were either massacred or forcibly converted to Islam (R. Kévorkian, 'L'Extermination').

living on their ancestral lands had disappeared. Most were killed, some were forcefully converted to Islam, while a few survived the death marches that were at the core of the genocidal process.[83] As such the central point (the provinces) of Armenian identity was eliminated and the western point (Constantinople) was no longer a vibrant political and cultural centre of Armenianness. Whatever survived did so in the form of diasporacised refugees concentrated in the Middle East, with some in France, Greece and elsewhere.

The most common explanation as to why the Genocide took place centres around the 'fifth column' argument: that the Armenians were, or potentially could have been, supporters of external powers (viz. Russia). Therefore, their threat had to be eliminated as part of the Ottoman war effort. It was strategically expedient to get rid of the Armenian population so that the Balkan dynamic would not be repeated in the heart of Anatolia. This is the favoured position of pro-Turkish analysts, but by no means confined to them. There is after all *some* truth in this. The Young Turks did fear that the Armenians would be used by the Russians and European powers against the Ottoman state.[84]

[83] 'Most', 'some' and 'a few' are not exact terms, but it is impossible to give reliable numbers. There were approximately 100,000 Armenian survivors in Syria after the First World War (mostly in refugee camps at or near Deir ez-Zor). Perhaps a few thousand Armenians did remain in their remote villages, escaping the deportations and death. Some of these people had formally converted to Islam, but kept their Armenian faith as a 'home religion'. It is remarkable that even eighty years later, there are certain families and villages which privately and/or secretly maintain elements of Armenian identity, or claim Armenian ancestry. Their numbers are believed to be insignificant, although the Armenian Patriarchate of Istanbul claims that it could be as high as 250,000 (*Turkish Probe*, Issue 361, as posted on *Groong Armenian News Network*, 14 Dec. 1999, p. 5). For obvious reasons there are no formal studies of these people. Recently, however, a young student has written a Master's thesis on the subject in Paris (see O. Akkus, 'Arméniens').

[84] It is noteworthy that the 'fifth column' argument, and therefore the imperative to get rid of the Armenians, was purportedly articulated as early as 1878 at the very dawn of Armenian political activity by Kamil Pasha, who became the Ottoman Grand Vizier in 1885. He said:

> If in European Turkey we kept warm the snakes [i.e. gave in to the Balkan nationalisms], in Asian Turkey we must not repeat the same stupidity. Common sense dictates that we destroy and eliminate from our soil all those elements which can endanger us and serve as weapons and means in the hands of European powers to intervene [in the Ottoman empire].... The rights of the state demand that we remove even the slightest suspect appearances and elements, and secure our future;

However, this view does not take into account that the Armenian communities in each of the two empires generally supported—both immediately before the First World War (1912–14) and during the initial stages of the war—the state in which they lived. Ottoman Armenians were urged by their leadership to support the Ottoman war effort, and they did. This was the declared and practised policy of the Armenian authorities and important parties, including the ARF.[85] Even after the First World War erupted the Dashnak party, not to mention the non-revolutionary liberals, did not go beyond demands for autonomy, reform and protection from Kurdish tribes. The ARF and the Ottoman Armenian leadership did not want to see the Russian army occupying the western Armenian provinces, even though there was undeniably some popular excitement for the advancing Russian forces within the Armenian population of the provinces.[86] Moreover, on the other side of the

---

> and therefore we must eliminate without a trace the Armenian nation from the surface of our soil. We have the means to realise this plan, such as the Kurds, the Circassians, governors, judges, tax collectors, the police, and all those who have declared a holy war against that nation which does not have weapons and protection; while we, in complete contrast, have arms and an army, and the world's largest [and] richest state [i.e. Britain] as our ally.... If the Armenian nation is eliminated and Christian Europe does not find a single Christian in Asia Minor, then they will leave us alone and we can concentrate on our internal affairs and state reforms... (Cited in A. Yeapuchian, 'Haikakan hartsin tzagume', pp. 3–4; and partially in A. Mnatsakanian, *Hai zhoghovrdi voghberguthune*, p. 7).

The original quote comes from an 1879 article in the Tiflis-based Armenian monthly, *Pordz* (Vol. 7–8, pp. 204–5). It is not clear where the author of the article, Tzerents, has obtained the quotation from. I am grateful to Vahakn Dadrian for pointing out the 1879 source of this citation to me in a personal communication.

[85] The ARF policy was adopted at its Seventh General Congress (August 1913), and reaffirmed, after intense debates, in its Eighth General Congress in July 1914 (H. Dasnabedian, *Histoire*, p. 107; cf. R. Melson, *Revolution and Genocide*, pp. 155–9). In fact the ARF responded to the 1914 Young Turk request to use the Armenians of the South Caucasus against the Russian empire by formally stating that Armenians in each of the empires must remain loyal to their government, executing their duties and serving in the respective armies as loyal subjects (A. Ter Minassian, 'Role of the Armenian Community', p. 120). Some Armenians, including former Dashnaks, did oppose this approach and wanted to form an alliance against the Ottoman empire. Hnchaks, for example, were much more oppositional in their views of the Ottomans. But these were minority voices and usually based outside the Ottoman empire.

[86] Ronald Suny, for example, writes: 'The Russian advances [early in the First World War] and the evident Armenian enthusiasm for the tsar's armies were the final incen-

front Russian Armenians publicly stated their desire to support the Tsar's armies against the Ottoman empire in order to 'liberate' Turkish Armenia and mobilised to this effect. As one historian puts it, at 'this stage Ottoman Armenian and Russian Armenian leaders were apparently working independently, each upholding the interests of their respective governments. The declaration of war had drawn a distinct line between them.'[87] The 'fifth column' argument regarding the Armenian Genocide is at most a partial explanation—and then primarily in terms of the *perceptions* of the Young Turks and the aspirations of the Russians. Given the actual reality on the ground, important reservations must be maintained regarding this thesis.

Another, deeper argument—to which I alluded above—can go further in explaining the causes of the Genocide. By 1915 there were two incompatible nationalisms competing for the same land. They were exclusive of one another. One concentrated on the Turkification of the Ottoman empire (especially in Anatolia, but also with pan-Turkic expansionist aspirations), the other demanded Armenian autonomy and communal rights and most certainly protection from Turkification. Both looked at the Balkan wars of 1912–13 as an example: one with the horror of defeat, the other with the inspiration of victory.

At a special CUP congress in October 1911 the following resolution was passed:

> The character of the Empire must be Mohammedan, and respect must be secured for Mohammedan institutions and traditions. Other nationalities must be denied the right of organisation, for decentralisation and autonomy are treason to the Turkish Empire. The nationalities are a negligible quantity. They can keep their religion but not their language. The propagation of the Turkish language is a sovereign means of confirming the other elements.[88]

---

tives for the Young Turk government in Istanbul to begin massive deportations and massacres of its own Armenian subjects' (R. Suny, 'Eastern Armenians', p. 136).

[87] M. Somakian, *Empires in Conflict*, p. 74.

[88] Cited in ibid., p. 40. A similar point was made by Talaat Pasha in a speech in August 1910 at another CUP meeting (V. Dadrian, *Warrant for Genocide*, p. 96, cf. pp. 96–101). According to Dadrian, the decision to Turkify the empire at the expense of the minorities was taken at this point. A discussion of Turkish nationalism is beyond the scope of this work; but it is worth noting the argument that Turkish nationalism was in many ways a reaction to the nationalism of the empire's minorities, including the

By 1911 the initial Young Turk ideology of Ottomanism, which was projected to be an inclusive approach to the empire's nationalities problem, was completely transformed. With the exception of some negligible groups neither the important minorities of the empire, nor the Turks themselves, accepted Ottomanism. For the minorities Ottomanism was a different form of Turkishness, especially since the symbols used to promote this supposedly 'supranational' identity were exclusively Turkish. For the Turks it was a dilution of the true Turkish and Muslim character of the empire. In fact, Şükrü Hanioğlu demonstrates that Young Turks had a strong nationalist sentiment even before their 1908 revolution, but they used Ottomanism for 'tactical' reasons and 'political opportunism' to obtain minorities' support in their revolution. Once firmly in power they no longer felt the need to sideline their 'Turkist ideology' and turned to Turkish nationalism with great zeal.[89] It subsequently became clear to the Armenians that their place in the empire was indeed precarious. Hence the ARF decided at its Eighth General Congress (July 1914) to adopt 'an inflexible position of opposition vis-à-vis the Ittihadists [CUP], to struggle against their injuriously chauvinistic and illegitimate politics.'[90]

At the end there was no contest between these two forces. The more powerful, state sponsored and virulently violent nationalism of the Young Turks, based on the precedents of anti-Armenian massacres, won.[91] Armenians did not have a chance. This was not a

Armenians. Roderic Davison concludes that 'nationalism, a modern Western invention, was communicated to the Turks themselves. In part they received it directly from Europe. But in part they received it from the non-Muslims of the Ottoman Empire, both by contagion and by revulsion' (R. Davison, '*Millets* as Agents of Change', p. 333). A similar and detailed, argument is made by Evan Siegel in relation to turn-of-the century Azerbaijani progressive or nationalist intellectuals and publications. Siegel shows the Armenophilia of such men insofar as they exhorted their own kin (at least until 1908) to follow the Armenian example of encouraging education, westernisation, philanthropy and nationalism (E. Siegel, 'Armenophilia').

[89] Ş. Hanioğlu, 'Turkish Nationalism', pp. 86, 88, 94. Hanioğlu also demonstrates the pedigree of anti-Christian nationalism in Young Turk thinking, based on fears of minority separatism (p. 91).

[90] Cited in H. Dasnabedian, *Histoire*, p. 107. The original French text is: '*vis-à-vis de l'Ittihad [CUP], un position d'opposant inflexible, de lutter contre sa politique chauviniste nuisible et illégitime.*'

[91] Although Bernard Lewis dismisses the use of the word 'genocide' in his later writings, and overestimates the threat of the Armenians to the Ottomans, he does nevertheless

struggle between two relatively equal nationalisms in terms of military force and other resources. It cannot even be characterised as a war. With no political power of any significance within the Ottoman state (despite their economic importance), very limited means for self-defence and no adequate community structures that could resist the might of the state, Armenians were easily rounded up and sent to their deaths. Whereas before 1908 the Sultan used massacres to maintain his rule, and to 'teach' the minorities 'a lesson', the motives of the Young Turks were quite different: they perpetrated genocide—eliminating an entire people from their lands—to create a new Turkish society in which there was no room for the Armenians and other non-Muslim minorities who could not be assimilated.[92] In this overall nationalistic process Armenian 'rebellion', the fifth column argument, war conditions and other such explanations were pretexts to get rid of the Armenians, not the causes of the Genocide.

Armenian national identity went through a profound transformation due to the Genocide. I will examine different elements of the post-Genocide identity in the next two chapters. Here I will briefly highlight six points as the precursors to subsequent analysis. These six factors defined to a large degree what it meant to be Armenian in the twentieth century.

First and foremost, the Genocide was the great 'equalizer' of identity.[93] *Everyone* became a victim. Being Armenian meant being a survivor of the Genocide and therefore a member of a community of sufferers. This mentality of victimhood, which was an important part of Armenian identity for centuries and which the revolutionary parties had tried so hard to overcome from the late nineteenth

---

interpret the elimination of the Armenians from a similar perspective: 'A desperate struggle between [Turks and Armenians over Anatolia] began—a struggle between two nations for the possession of a single homeland, that ended with the terrible slaughter of 1915' (B. Lewis, *Emergence of Modern Turkey*, p. 356).

[92] R. Hovannisian, 'Armenian Question', (p. 226) and R. Melson, *Revolution and Genocide* (pp. 152–70) make a similar argument. Melson situates Turkish nationalism in the context of military defeats and revolutionary fervour, and debunks the 'provocation' thesis. Vahakn Dadrian minimises the differences between the Hamidian massacres and the Young Turk genocide; he argues that the latter could take place because of the prevailing 'culture of massacre' (V. Dadrian, *History of the Armenian Genocide*, pp. 157ff.).

[93] G. Libaridian, 'Changing Armenian Self-Image', p. 158.

century onwards, was once again ingrained as the central element of Armenian collective consciousness—at least until the 1970s, when a new wave of Armenian radicalism arose. Post-Genocide literature reflected the mentality of victimhood and trauma.[94] The notion was perpetuated from year to year at Genocide commemorations and publications.[95]

Armenians commemorate the Genocide every 24 April. On that evening in 1915 close to 600 Armenian intellectuals and political leaders were arrested in Constantinople and eventually killed. This decapitated the nation and it was the opening act of the Genocide. The first formal commemoration was in 1919, and since then Armenians world-wide have remembered the victims every year. In Armenia the population visits the Genocide memorial (Tzitzernakaberd in Yerevan), while in the diaspora commemorative events are held in community centres and churches and at local Genocide monu-

[94] One of the most moving is a poem by Siamanto, a Genocide victim himself, called *The Dance* (G. Papasian, *Sojourn at Ararat*, pp. 37–8, cf. other poems on pp. 35–52; see also C. Forché, *Against Forgetting*, pp. 56–62). Both Rubina Peroomian and Lorne Shirinian discuss the issue of literature and genocide, including literary manifestations of dealing with the post-Genocide diaspora condition (R. Peroomian, 'Armenian Literary Responses' and 'Problematic Aspects'; L. Shirinian, *Armenian-North American Literature*). The latter, focusing on North American Armenian literature written in the English language (i.e. diasporan literature *par excellence*), concludes: 'In these texts, pain, loss, dispersion, bewilderment, and frustration, for example, have particular connotations to Armenians arising from recent historical events. Genocide and the larger category to which it belongs, destruction, create a framework within which the specific collective symbol is created.... The collective symbol shapes the structure of its various representations and their networks to the point that they become the dominant theme in the narrative' (L. Shirinian, *Armenian-North American Literature*, pp. 258–9).

[95] Gerard Libaridian ties the notion of victimhood to modern politics. In the Introduction to a book on the early phase of the Gharabagh conflict (1991) he writes:

> The Genocide, its exploitation, and its denial by Turkey have paralyzed the collective psyche of the Armenian people. A nation of victims—at first, of violence, and subsequently of its denial—is incapable of sustaining a rational discourse. A nation cannot imagine a future if the only thing it can imagine the future bringing is further victimization. The denial of the future justifies the denial of the present and mandates an obsessive treatment of an overburdened past. Under the circumstances, the function of history is merely to chronicle and legitimize this fear (G. Libaridian, *Armenia at the Crossroads*, p. 2).

He quotes the same passage in his recent book, commenting on post independence Armenian politics in which he played an active role as a senior presidential adviser (G. Libaridian, *Challenge of Statehood*, p. 4). Libaridian's point is that the Armenian National Movement (the post-1988 nationalists) tried to break out of this mentality.

ments. Four themes are intertwined in such commemorations: (1) the obvious point that 'we are a victim nation' and all of our dead of 1915 are 'martyrs'; (2) tied to this, the notion of suffering a great injustice which still continues because (3) 'we have been expelled from our historic homeland'. This leads to a longing for the 'lost lands' which is awaiting the return of its 'true inhabitants'. Finally, (4) the more radical use the opportunity to demand justice, revenge and retribution, often using the Armenian word *pahanjatirutiun* (to demand and protect what is your own).[96]

The last theme had its precedent in the 1920s. It is based on the desire to redress the sense of victimhood through acts of revenge. In the early 1920s the ARF devised a secret programme to punish the main perpetrators of the Genocide and the 1918 Baku massacres. In what was known as 'Operation Nemesis' Dashnak volunteers tracked down and assassinated some of the key CUP members and a few other officials. Most famously Soghomon Tehlirian killed the former Young Turk Interior Minister, a key architect of the Genocide, Talaat Pasha in Berlin in March 1921. Tehlirian was subsequently acquitted by a German court.[97] Importantly, despite the overwhelming sense of victimhood, the acts of these assassins wove an element of revenge and retribution into post-Genocide Armenian mentality, especially among the Dashnak side of the diaspora.

Even though the Genocide was the complete defeat of western Armenia, there were nevertheless instances of resistance and rebellion. Coupled with the 1920s punitive assassinations these moments of armed action entered Armenian consciousness as yet other examples of heroic defence of the fatherland. The Armenians of Van defended their city against Ottoman forces in April-May 1915. But after a few weeks they had to abandon the city in a new Turkish

[96] Based on the author's personal observations of Genocide commemoration events in London, Toronto and Montreal in the past ten years, as well as a plethora of Armenian newspaper, magazine, and other media sources.

[97] In total six men were assassinated by Dashnaks between 1920 and 1922, while the seventh, Enver Pasha, was gunned down in a battle near Samarkand by Bolshevik forces (it is widely believed that it was, rather ironically, a unit of Armenian Bolsheviks who shot him). The Nemesis operation was headed by Armen Garo and Shahan Natali. The first was one of the young militants who had taken over Banque Ottomane in 1896 and who was the ambassador of the 1918–20 Armenian republic to the United States. For details on Operation Nemesis see J. Derogy, *Resistance and Revenge*.

offensive. The surviving Armenians of Van retreated along with the Russian armies. Without the latter's continuing support resistance would have been futile. The most significant action celebrated by Armenians is the battle of Musa Ler (or Musa Dagh in south eastern Turkey near the Mediterranean coast) where a small group of villages chose to resist rather than obey the deportation order. For nearly two months (July-August 1915) they held the far superior Ottoman army at bay. Close to 4,000 Armenians were eventually rescued by passing French ships. After moving around many times the survivors were relocated to northern Lebanon (in Anjar) in the 1930s. This was a small victory given the scale of destruction elsewhere, and by no means typical of Armenian behaviour during the Genocide. Musa Ler, and to a lesser degree Van, occupy significant places in national identity because they symbolise the Armenians' will to resist.[98]

The second point about the Genocide and identity continues from the notion of victimhood. It is the transformation of the diaspora into a community of genocide victims. Diaspora, by definition, was always associated with exile and hardship, but after 1915 these notions were magnified and reinforced. It was no longer a diaspora of merchants, labourers, fortune seekers, intellectuals and political exiles. Rather it was of refugees, starving survivors and a deeply scarred people. Moreover, the diaspora and the homeland no longer co-existed as two parts of the same nation with their strong reinforcing links. Since the homeland side was completely decimated—physically lost—the diaspora no longer had the option to return. This exacerbated the sense of loss and of victimhood.

The western and central points of Armenian identity survived in diasporan form, but in a much weakened condition. This meant that western Armenianness acquired additional layers of identity; not only as victims of genocide, but also as victims condemned to live in dispersion. The diaspora condition was seen as a perpetuation of the Genocide: the loss of the homeland followed by the loss of identity through the dangers of cultural assimilation in foreign lands. Armenians powerfully call the assimilation process 'the white massacre'.

[98] The story of Musa Ler is immortalised in a powerful novel by Franz Werfel called *The Forty Days of Musa Dagh*. It was first published in 1933 in German and subsequently translated into many languages.

Decades after 1915 genocide remained—and for many still remains—the core attribute of modern Armenian identity, woven with diasporan identity.[99]

The third point about identity has to do with territory. The Armenian provinces were of course at the centre of the political programme of the nationalists before 1915. But the existence of the land itself was taken for granted—i.e. nationalists were not claiming 'lost lands'. After the Genocide the Armenian cause was very much territorialised; that is, it was focused on getting back the homeland. Nationalist demands were reoriented towards a specific territory. Communal rights, autonomy, independence etc. no longer made sense when the land itself was violently stolen. Post-Genocide Armenian identity (especially in the diaspora) therefore came to be associated with a 'lost homeland' and the need to regain it.

Fourth, the Muslim and the Turk were historically the 'Other' for Armenian identity. After the Genocide this Other also came to embody evil. Due to the Turkish denial of the Genocide the wounds of 1915 remained open, and the notion of the 'evil Turk' was perpetuated in popular Armenian culture. Turkishness was considered immoral, unclean and violent. Anti-Turkishness was therefore accepted as a 'natural' and inherently good attitude. Only after three generations is this attitude beginning to change, particularly in the western diaspora.

The issue of identity politics and the Genocide, particularly in the diaspora, is the fifth point. Much of the work of the Armenian lobby in Washington, in Paris and in other capitals around the world centres on the recognition of the Genocide by different governments as a means to put pressure on Turkey. For example, every April the Armenian lobby in the United States tries to get a Genocide resolution passed in Congress. Part of the Armenian effort has to do with

[99] The sense of being in exile has occasionally been reinforced in certain parts of the diaspora because of the successive waves of emigration (roughly once every generation) from many Middle Eastern countries to Europe and North America. This movement, usually due to civil war or political crisis and hardship in the initial host country, has intensified notions of longing for a lost place, of being forced to get uprooted again, of becoming refugees again. Even though these experiences are not comparable to the Genocide in terms of their causes, violence and magnitude, they do nevertheless act as reminders of the hardships of exile, of not having 'a home' in the broad sense.

the terminology used to refer to the events of 1915. Armenians insist on the use of the word *genocide* by the world community rather than the less forceful term massacres (which does not necessarily imply intent to eliminate a people or have international legal ramifications).[100] The politics of genocide recognition has come to affect Armenian political identity in the diaspora, especially after the 1970s. One of the terrorist organisations active in the 1980s was even called 'the Justice Commandos of the Armenian Genocide'—i.e. commandos for the recognition of the Genocide.

The sixth and final point to be made is a partial qualification of the preceding arguments. It also highlights the continuing division between the eastern and western points of Armenian identity construction in the twentieth century. Although the Genocide was a pan-Armenian wound, it physically affected only the western Armenians. Eastern Armenians, in the Russian empire, did not experience it first hand, nor did they lose their land, although hundreds of thousands of refugees from the Ottoman empire did escape to Russian (subsequently independent and then Soviet) Armenia. Moreover, the Soviet Union put a freeze on the Armenian Genocide issue until 1965, when it was officially commemorated for the first time in Yerevan. Thus the Genocide did not become the central element of Armenian identity in the eastern point until a couple of generations later.

However, it did permeate eastern Armenian identity. The Genocide entered Soviet Armenian consciousness as a *learnt* injustice rather than as an experienced reality. The idea of being victims of the Turks did exist and was further nurtured by Soviet-inspired historiography. After 1965 eastern Armenians too had the 1915 Genocide at the core of their identity, albeit not as prevalently as their western diasporised brethren.

I will elaborate on many of these issues in subsequent chapters. What is important to note at this point is the centrality of 1915 to subsequent Armenian identity. It is impossible to understand twen-

[100] For example, when Bernard Lewis, a historian of the Ottoman empire and Turkey, referred to the Armenian Genocide as the 'Armenian version of the story' in a *Le Monde* interview in November 1993, the Armenian community in France mobilised to sue him successfully in a civil action (Y. Ternon, 'Freedom and Responsibility'; *Les Nouvelles d'Arménie*, no. 14, November 1994, pp. 8–13).

tieth-century Armenian consciousness—particularly until 1988—without situating the Genocide at its very centre. The elimination of Armenians from their historic lands in the Ottoman empire was the ultimate 'Catastrophe'.[101] Despite the devastation and the loss of western Armenia the Young Turks did not succeed in eliminating the Armenian nation. In fact many of the survivors developed a stronger sense of national consciousness. Again, having been on the verge of annihilation Armenians developed a powerful will to survive. Once the sense of victimhood eased its debilitating hold on the Armenian psyche, martyrdom—mixed with rage and a national cause—drove subsequent generations to pursue national(ist) goals. The Genocide itself (including its denial) became the defining moment—the founding 'moment'—of contemporary Armenian identity. Post-1915 Armenians, particularly in the diaspora, saw themselves as 'the first Christian nation' and 'the first victims of genocide in the twentieth century'.

THE INDEPENDENT REPUBLIC AND SOVIETISATION

The Bolshevik revolution and the withdrawal of the Russian army from the South Caucasus created an imperial power vacuum in the region, including Russian Armenia. Ottoman forces tried to fill this vacuum by advancing on Armenia and hoping to reach Baku. But the Ottoman empire itself was on the losing side in the First World War and eventually had to cease hostilities short of achieving its aim of occupying eastern Armenia and controlling Azerbaijan. In the subsequent two-year hiatus of imperial power struggles between the Russians and the Ottomans in the South Caucasus, three independent republics emerged in the region between 1918 and 1920: Georgia, Azerbaijan and Armenia. The creation of a however short-lived independent country had important effects on Armenian national identity. But first some of the facts.

By early 1918 the Russian army had mostly withdrawn from the Ottoman front. Article 4 of the Brest-Litovsk Treaty (signed on 3 March 1918) formalised this arrangement, once again transferring the Armenian-populated regions of Kars and Artahan (as well as

101 Certain scholars such as Marc Nichanian make a point of referring to the Genocide as the 'Catastrophe' (M. Nichanian, 'Style of Violence').

Batum) to Turkey. Armenian units fighting alongside the Russian army were to be demobilised, and the pre-1878 border between the two empires was to be the new frontier. Armenians and the other peoples south of the Caucasus were left alone to fend for themselves. On 12 March 1918 Erzerum fell to the Turkish forces, Van followed on 7 April and Kars on 25 April. In this way the battle for Ottoman Armenia came to an end. There remained, however, the struggle for Russian Armenia.[102]

In the absence of Russian administration, the political vacuum in the South Caucasus was briefly filled by the Transcaucasian Federative Republic. The regional (non-Bolshevik) Seim (sitting in Tiflis), comprising Georgian, Azerbaijani and Armenian delegates, formally declared its independence on 22 April 1918—much to the chagrin of the Armenians who opposed any kind of formal separation from Russia. But in the end they too had to agree to it in order to have some sort of formal structure that could oppose the Turkish advances. However, the Federation did not have the strength to deal with the Turkish onslaught, nor did it have the internal unity necessary to continue its existence. It fell apart in less than five weeks as Turkish forces crossed the borders agreed at Brest-Litovsk and advanced toward Yerevan, Baku and the southern parts of Georgia. It had become obvious that the Federation was unworkable owing to the fundamentally differing interests of the Georgians, the Azerbaijanis (Tatars) and the Armenians. The Georgians wished to ally with the Germans, the Azerbaijanis with the Ottoman Turks and the Armenians—in the absence of Russia—with the Allied forces led by Britain and France and supported by the United States. Hence the leadership of each of the three peoples decided to follow a separate path.

Georgian delegates (mostly Mensheviks) in the Seim proclaimed the independence of their country on 26 May, dissolving the Federation. The following day the Muslim National Council decided to do the same for Azerbaijan (although Baku was still ruled by the Bolsheviks[103]), formally announcing independence on 28 May. With no other choice the Armenian National Council—led by Dash-

[102] R. Hovannisian, 'Armenia's Road', p. 292, cf. pp. 286–301 for further details.

[103] Baku was 'liberated' by the Ottoman Turkish forces on the night of 14–15 September 1918, as the small British contingent there fled on ships. Subsequently, approximately 20,000 Armenians were massacred (C. Walker, *Armenia*, p. 261). For further details on developments leading to the fall of Baku see B. Gökay, 'Battle of Baku'.

naks—had to declare the independence of Armenia as well (in Tiflis!). Thus on 28 May 1918 the 'inglorious birth' of an independent Armenia took place, 'a mangled bit of land that, for a lack of a better term, [was] called a republic'.[104] It did not even comprise all the territories on the Russian side of the 1828 Ottoman-Russian frontier (let alone of the 1878 border)—lands west of Yerevan, the city of Alexandropol (Leninakan/Gyumri) and the north-south railroad (Alexandropol-Julfa), remained under Turkish occupation.

'Inglorious' as its political birth was, the republic did survive thanks to military successes in some fierce battles between 21 and 28 May. After months of retreats in the face of Ottoman advances led by the Young Turk military men, Armenians fought back: 'To the astonishment of friend and foe alike, the unexpected came to pass. The Armenians stopped running, for there was nowhere to flee.... As the ordeal of battle entered its final phase, the temper of defenders and populace alike transformed. Resolution supplanted panic.... Armenians were now ready "to die with weapons in hand".'[105] In the battles of Bash-Aparan, Gharakilise and particularly Sardarapat the outnumbered and outgunned Armenian soldiers, irregulars, peasants and other ordinary folk finally managed to stop the Turkish advances, securing the independence of the republic and preventing Ottoman troops from reaching Baku at that time.

The first Prime Minister of Armenia, Hovhannes Kajaznuni, referred to the country in his inaugural address as 'chaos without bounds'. Of a population of nearly one million, one quarter to one half were refugees from the Ottoman empire; 200,000 died from famine, disease and exposure in the winter of 1918–19.[106] The economy was practically destroyed due to the wars, agricultural production had declined by close to 70 per cent. People could barely survive on humanitarian aid from the West. However, after the first winter the republic slowly began to establish the foundations of a feasible country. Politically there were the rudiments of a function-

[104] R. Hovannisian, 'Armenia's Road', p. 301. For a comprehensive study of the months leading to Armenia's independence see R. Hovannisian, *Armenia*, particularly chapters 8–10.

[105] R. Hovannisian, *Armenia*, p. 192, cf. pp. 191–4.

[106] Kajaznuni's citation is from R. Hovannisian, 'Republic of Armenia', p. 306; cf. pp. 307, 311, 313 for the population figures; R. Hovannisian, *Republic*, vol. I, pp. 126ff. (in the first source, the refugee population is cited as 500,000, in the second as 250,000).

ing parliamentary democracy (with the ARF always in firm control of the key ministries). Economically the infrastructure was being rebuilt and production slowly increased. Militarily peace was established on its western (Turkish) front and the border even expanded to include Kars, after the defeat of the Ottoman empire in the First World War and the Mudros Armistice (30 October 1918); Nakhijevan came to be governed briefly by Armenians as well, while Armenian units drove out or killed thousands of Muslims (particularly in the region of Zangezur, southern Armenia), consolidating their control over the country. Internationally Armenia's representatives were active in the European peace conferences and in various capitals. Socially, however, conditions remained bleak, but the initial threats of mass starvation subsided.[107]

Despite its modest successes Armenia was not to survive as an independent country. By late 1920 Communist Russia was eager to assert its influence on all three South Caucasian republics. The Soviet representative to Armenia, Boris Legran, was insisting that Armenia accept Soviet rule (Azerbaijan was Sovietised on 27–8 April 1920). Meanwhile Turkish forces—now reorganised under Mustafa Kemal (Ataturk)—once again were on the attack to subdue Armenia and to expand the frontiers of Turkey eastwards; on 6 November Alexandropol had fallen again to the Turkish 15th army corps (commanded by General Kiazim Karabekir) and Yerevan was under threat. Moreover, Kemalists and the Moscow government were engaged in friendly negotiations while the Soviets supported (in arms and gold) Kemal's 'national liberation' struggle against Western encroachment in Turkey (viz. in opposition to the Sèvres Treaty of 10 August 1920). Finally Western powers, which had promised much to Armenia, were nowhere to be seen. Given these circumstances Armenia was caught, in the words of Simon Vratsian, the last Prime Minister of the independent republic, between the 'Bolshevik hammer and the Turkish anvil'.[108]

[107] By mid-1919 the Armenian republic had expanded from its initial 4,500 square miles to 17,000 square miles, taking up practically the entire area of what was Russian Armenia (R. Hovannisian, 'Republic', p. 319). For an extremely detailed history of the independent republic see Richard Hovannisian's four-volume magnum opus, *The Republic of Armenia.* Independent Armenia lasted a little over 900 days; Hovannisian's massive volumes add up to more than 2,200 pages!

[108] This is from the title of his short book (S. Vratsian, *Hayastane*), in which he is more

On 2 December 1920 the Dashnak-led government resigned and Armenia was declared an 'independent socialist republic'. On 4 December the Communist Military Revolutionary Committee of Armenia (*heghkom* [Revkom]) assumed power and on 6 December Red Army units entered Yerevan. Henceforth, in its policies and structures Armenia was further integrated into the Russian Soviet Federated Socialist Republic (RSFSR), particularly in the second half of 1921. On 12 March 1922 it became part of the Federative Union of Soviet Socialist Republics of Transcaucasia. This in turn became a single federated republic on 13 December 1922. Two weeks later the Transcaucasian Federal Socialist Republic entered the USSR as one of its seven constituent republics when the latter was established on 30 December 1922.[109] After a short break of two-and-a-half years Armenia was once again under the firm control of much larger imperial powers.

A number of international treaties pertained to the Armenians in the 1918–23 period.[110] There is no need to elaborate on these, save

---

concerned with the Bolshevik hammer than the Turkish anvil. Vratsian (1882–1969) also wrote a number of other books based on his experiences, including a history of the republic. For an English-language text summarising his views, but written in the early 1940s with the aim of re-inserting the Armenian question onto the political and military agenda of the West, see S. Vratzian [*sic*], *Armenia*. For brief overviews of the circumstances of the republic's Sovietisation see R. Hovannisian, 'Republic', pp. 339–46; R. Suny, *Looking toward Ararat*, pp. 124–31; for detailed accounts, see R. Hovannisian, *Republic*, Vol. IV; C. Walker, *Armenia*, pp. 256–330. Ayla Göl provides a comprehensive study of Turkish foreign policy towards Armenia and the South Caucasus in this period, linking Turkish foreign policies with its drive for modernisation (A. Göl, *Place of Foreign Policy*).

109 R. Pipes, *Formation of the Soviet Union*, pp. 229–33, 252–4, and more generally, Chapter 5.

110 Some of the more important treaties affecting the Armenians were the following: the *Batum Treaty* (4 June 1918) between the Ottoman empire and the Armenian republic assured the existence of the republic and its recognition by the Ottoman government. Under the terms of the *Mudros Armistice* (30 October 1918), the Ottoman empire capitulated, and it stipulated that Ottoman forces were to withdraw to pre-war borders; this meant that Armenia's frontiers could expand to include Kars (in April 1919) and the other territories of Russian Armenia. The *Paris Peace Conference* (winter–spring 1919) promised a united Armenia independent from Turkish rule, but under a Western mandate. The *Treaty of Versailles* (28 June 1919) between the Allied Powers and Germany did not deal with the Near Eastern and Armenian questions, leaving it to *Sèvres* (August 1920). The *Treaty of Alexandropol* (3 December 1920) between the representative of the newly resigned (two hours

for two that have entered Armenian national consciousness to such a degree that it is impossible to talk about modern Armenian identity—especially in the diaspora—without mentioning them. The first, the Treaty of Sèvres (10 August 1920) is an example of hope, of what could have been. The second, the Lausanne Treaty (23 August 1923) is considered by Armenians as the epitome of betrayal by the international community.[111] Sèvres recognised the independent Armenian republic and promised the creation of a much greater country based on the four (out of six) historic Armenian provinces in the Ottoman empire. The borders of the country were to be drawn by the US President, Woodrow Wilson. The final map was submitted in November 1920. It not only included the regions of Kars, Van, Bitlis and Erzerum (in addition to ex-Russian/independent Armenia), but also a wide stretch of coastline including Trebizond on the Black Sea. It was initially assumed by signatories that such a country would fall under the protective mandate of a Western power, most likely the United States (which was favoured by the Armenians as well).[112] The treaty, signed by the representative of

---

before!) Dashnak government and Kemalist forces accepted the reduced borders of the republic and forced the Armenians to renounce Sèvres. The *Moscow Treaty* (16 March 1921) between the Russian Bolsheviks and the Kemalists established friendly relations between the two; it set the border between the two countries where it is now, leaving Kars, Artahan and the south-west side of the Arax river, including Mount Ararat—all Russian Armenian territories since 1878—in Turkey; it also promised Soviet aid to Kemal in his struggle 'against imperialism'. This treaty had been initialled on 24 August 1920; days later Turkish forces attacked Armenia. The *Treaty of Kars* (13 October 1921) was almost identical to the Moscow Treaty, but it was signed between Kemalist Turkey and by each of the Sovietised South Caucasian republics. The last two treaties confirmed the borders accepted at *Brest-Litovsk* (3 March 1918) and renounced all territorial claims against Turkey. They also confirmed that Nakhijevan (a disputed territory between Armenia and Azerbaijan) was to be part of Soviet Azerbaijan.

[111] It is the reverse for the Turks: Sèvres is a symbol of ultimate defeat and betrayal, while Lausanne enabled the emergence of modern Turkey as a unified state.

[112] Much lobbying work was done by Armenians and their supporters in the West to convince the decision makers in Paris, London, Washington etc. to assist Armenia and to guarantee its security. In the United States the American Committee for the Independence of Armenia was set up in December 1918 and remained active until 1927 (for a brief study see G. Aftandilian, *Armenia*). In Britain, The British Armenia Committee was active. In one of its publications it is stated: 'In a region like this, where no race is in a majority over the rest and where the very rudiments of civilised life—security of person and property—have scarcely existed, only by the wise

the Sublime Porte, meant not only a complete defeat for the Ottoman empire, but its dismemberment and division among the victorious Western powers.

Sèvres was a stillborn treaty. It was superseded by the Lausanne Treaty in which the word Armenia was not even mentioned (although it was mentioned that Turkey was to respect the rights of non-Muslim minorities). This was a total victory for Turkey, now led by Mustafa Kemal. A defeated empire in the First World War, Turkey nevertheless expanded its eastern (Anatolian) frontier beyond the pre-war border at the expense of Armenia; Kemalist forces had successfully taken back territories the Ottoman empire had lost to Russia in 1878. Even Mount Ararat, the national symbol of Armenians, was now in Turkey. Lausanne bestowed international acceptance on this arrangement based on the earlier Turkish-Soviet agreements (the Moscow and Kars Treaties of 1921). In three years much had changed in international relations, which did not favour Armenians at all: Armenia was already Sovietised, nationalists had won the war in Turkey repudiating Sèvres, the West was no longer interested in a mandate over Armenia and the United States had entered its phase of isolationism—in fact the US Congress had not even ratified the Treaty of Sèvres. Lausanne was the ultimate letdown for the Armenians. With it the Armenian question was conveniently forgotten by the international community.

After the turmoil of the First World War and the subsequent Caucasian wars in 1920, the 1828 frontiers between the Ottoman, Russian and Persian empires emerged roughly as the final borders between Turkey, the USSR and Iran. The issue of the external borders was solved. By 1923 Soviet authorities had delineated the 'internal' borders between the three South Caucasian republics as well. This was not an easy task as Armenia and Azerbaijan had engaged in battles over disputed lands. There was even an armed skirmish between Armenia and Georgia. It is important to give some details

guidance of a powerful and impartial external authority can the peoples themselves hope to establish a stable political community.... Second only to the complete abolition of Turkish sovereignty is the need for a disinterested mandatory Power.... An American mandate for a united Armenia.... would be by far the best solution in every respect' (C. Leese, *Armenia*, pp. 14–15). And in France the position of the Armenian delegation was published in a book that contained supporting documentation, statistics and extracts from speeches of famous statesmen (*Délégation*).

of these disputes since the roots of the post-1988 conflict between Armenia and Azerbaijan, and the demands of the contemporary Armenian nationalist movement, lie in Moscow's 'solution' to opposing land claims.

There were five regions over which Armenians, Azerbaijanis and Georgians fought. The Armenian-Georgian dispute entailed two border regions: Lori and Akhalkalak, both with Armenian majorities. After a short armed conflict in December 1918 the two republics started negotiating over the two areas. The dispute was finally settled by the Soviets in 1921. Akhalkalak was made part of Soviet Georgia, while Lori was put under Soviet Armenian jurisdiction. Currently both republics accept the border finalised in 1921.

The Armenian-Azerbaijani conflict was much more protracted and violent. There were three disputed areas: Nakhijevan, Zangezur and Gharabagh. The first two had mixed populations, while (Mountainous) Gharabagh was overwhelmingly Armenian. The two republics constantly fought over these three regions—particularly Gharabagh—claiming them as their own territory. Eventually Nakhijevan was placed in Azerbaijan as an autonomous territory. The arrangement was formalised a year later when on 9 February 1924 it became an Autonomous Soviet Republic (ASSR) under the jurisdiction of Baku. Nakhijevan is an exclave bordered by Armenia, Iran and a ten kilometre frontier with Turkey. Zangezur, the territory that separates mainland Azerbaijan from Nakhijevan, was kept as part of Armenia. This was the last bit of the independent republic which fell to the Soviets in July 1921. Subsequently it became an integral part of Soviet Armenia.

The third dispute was the bitter and violent struggle over Gharabagh. Between 1918 and 1920 thousands of lives were lost in and around mountainous Gharabagh as Armenians and Azerbaijanis fought for control of the enclave.[113] Both peoples considered

[113] Ottoman troops were active in the area in September–October 1918. After the First World War ended, and until Azerbaijan's Sovietisation, the British played an important role in the region—mostly unfavourable to the Armenians—as they insisted in putting Gharabagh within Azerbaijan. As one French-Armenian historian put it, 'It is no exaggeration to say that the present (1991) problem of Karabagh is due largely to British diplomacy in the first half of the year 1919.' The British military representative at the time fully realised the effect of this on Armenia; Colonel J. C. Plowden 'declared at the end of August 1919: "The handing over of Karabagh

Gharabagh to be an integral part of their territory. The demographic and historical considerations favoured the Armenians, while the economic and strategic considerations (from Moscow's viewpoint) favoured the Azerbaijanis. On 5 July 1921, reversing earlier decisions, the plenary session of the Caucasian Bureau of Soviet Russia's Communist Party Central Committee decided to place Gharabagh in Azerbaijan. In July 1923 Gharabagh was officially made an Autonomous Region (*oblast*) within Azerbaijan. Armenians had to swallow another bitter pill of losing yet again a piece of territory they considered part of historic Armenia.[114] But the issue was never forgotten, as Soviet authorities discovered when the Gharabagh movement erupted in 1988 with the aim of reversing the decision taken 67 years earlier.

The two-year independent republic had a number of important effects on Armenian identity. It introduced a new set of symbols and dynamics, but it also reinforced certain traditional beliefs and attitudes.

First and foremost, the 1918 battles at Sardarapat, Bash-Aparan and Gharakilise, which ensured the survival of the independent

---

to Azerbaijan was I think the bitterest blow of all"' to the Armenians (Claude Mutafian's contribution in C. Walker, *Armenia and Karabagh*, p. 97; for a succinct overview of the struggle over Gharabagh between 1918 and 1923 see pp. 91–111). General Andranik (a veteran of the Bulgarian front against the Ottomans) played an important role in the military affairs of the region as well. He was instrumental in keeping Zangezur, the southern part of the republic, in Armenian hands, although owing to British pressure he could not reach Gharabagh to put it under Armenian control. Andranik died in Fresno in 1927 and was later buried in Père Lachaise cemetery in Paris—where a modest monument was erected on his grave. After years of debate and pressure, his remains were finally brought to Armenia in February 2000. On the occasion of his 'return' the Deputy Defence Minister of Armenia, A. Petrosian, said: 'The repatriation of this national hero is especially important now as Armenia crosses a difficult period while the issue of solving Nagorny Karabakh is raised…' (Agence France-Presse, as posted on *Groong Armenian News Network*, 18 Feb. 2000).

114 For details on these conflicts and related issues see, R. Hovannisian, *Republic*, Vol. I, pp. 79–125; R. Hovannisian, 'Armeno-Azerbaijani Conflict'; S. Blank, 'Bolshevik Organizational Development'; G. Libaridian, *Karabagh File*, pp. 34–7; L. Chorbajian *et al., Caucasian Knot*, pp. 133–9, 174–9; C. Walker, 'Armenian Presence', pp. 98–102; S. Alijarly, 'Republic of Azerbaijan', pp. 123–33; A. Altstadt, *Azerbaijani Turks*, pp. 100–5, 125–8; A. Altstadt, 'Nagorno-Karabagh', pp. 63–8. For a detailed account of the dynamics of the Gharabagh conflict between 1917 and 1920 written by a participant leader see the recently published diaries of Y. Ishkhanian, *Lernayin Gharabagh*.

republic, gave Armenians a real sense of victory. After the catastrophe of the Genocide these battles became the paradigm of the survival of the Armenian nation, akin to the battle of Avarayr in 451 (which had ensured the survival of Christianity in Armenia, although it was a military defeat). They are considered glorious moments in modern Armenian history. Until the late 1960s their celebration was confined to the Dashnaks and their followers, but Soviet Armenia also came to officially acknowledge their significance—especially that of Sardarapat—accepting the interpretation that 'due to the Sardarapat battle, eastern Armenia was saved from Turkish occupation.'[115] A massive memorial was built in 1968 at the battle site of Sardarapat (Soviet Armenia) and a museum of ethno-history was added in 1978. In this way the commemoration of the battle became a pan-Armenian event. Of the three battle sites Sardarapat is vested with the most symbolic value. Not only was it historically the major victory so close to Yerevan, it is also located at the current border with Turkey, at the foot of Mount Ararat.[116]

Second, and following from the above, the independent republic itself became the symbol of Armenian independence and statehood. This, however, was only publicly celebrated by the Dashnak side of the diaspora. The Soviets (and their allies abroad) branded the 1918 republic as 'bourgeois-nationalist' and 'reactionary'.[117] They officially denounced it and the ARF. Hence the republic as a symbol of independence divided the Armenians, particularly in the diaspora, for as long as Soviet rule existed. Celebrating 28 May 1918 essentially meant rejecting the legitimacy of Soviet Armenia. But as

115 *Haikakan Sovetakan hanragitaran*, vol. X, p. 228.

116 This symbolism is used to the maximum by the current leadership of Armenia. The closing reception (hosted by the Prime Minister) of the first ever Armenia-diaspora conference was held outdoors at Sardarapat on 24 September 1999. In the presence of close to 1,200 delegates from all over the world the late Prime Minister (formerly Defence Minister) Vazgen Sargsian said:

> Where we are sitting was one of the worst [i.e. most intense] locations of the 1918 battle for our existence. Every square metre of the land on which we are now sitting contains the blood of Armenian soldiers. With our supreme efforts we won an unequal war. Similar soldiers fought the war in Gharabagh and are now guarding our borders.... We are gathered at Sardarapat, because from Sardarapat our victories begin. And this must be our symbol, so that we will enter the 21st century once again from Sardarapat, together... (author's own recording).

117 *Hai zhoghovrdi patmutiun*, vol. VII, pp. 49–62.

became clear in 1988 the denunciation of the 'Dashnak republic' did not reflect the popular view of Soviet Armenians. At the end of communist rule between 1988 and 1991, the logic of 'Sardarapat saved us' publicly and easily extended to also mean 'If it was not for the first republic, the second (Soviet) republic would not have existed.' This position was always maintained by Dashnaks, but in the last decade it has become the dominant pan-Armenian view.[118] After all, the ARF did control the government of the independent republic, and it did play a central role in defending and running it for more than two years, despite very difficult conditions.[119]

Although the 1918 republic (its tricolor flag, heroes and symbols) was very much associated with—and to a large degree appropriated by—Dashnaks, independence entered the ARF programme only in the summer of 1919 at the party's Ninth General Congress in Yerevan. This *ex post facto* goal of independence superseded ear-

[118] Once again Vazgen Sargsian provides the best example of this line of thinking: 'If it was not for the first republic, there would not have been the second Armenian Socialist republic. This republic then became the basis of the future independent republic' (author's notes, 24 September 1999, at Sardarapat reception). Compare this with the following sentence from an ARF commemorative brochure published in May 1993 (celebrating the 1918 republic): 'Not even for one minute can we doubt the reality that the existence of today's Armenia is due to May [1918] independence' (*75-Amiak*, [p. 22]). For one typical example of the Dashnak press' celebration of 28 May before the latest (i.e. 1988) wave of nationalism see *Horizon Weekly* (Montreal), 23 May 1983.

[119] This seemingly neutral assessment, shared by many Western academics (R. Hovannisian, *Republic*, vol. IV, pp. 406–8; cf. R. Hovannisian, 'Role'; R. Suny, *Looking toward Ararat*, pp. 127–31), was hotly contested by Soviet Armenian historians and anti-Dashnaks in the diaspora. They argued that Dashnak rule in the independent republic was detrimental to the Armenians. In addition to the multitude of socio-economic problems they maintain that Kars and Artahan were lost to Turkey owing to the misguided diplomacy of the ARF (i.e. its post-1918 reliance on Western powers). In this view those two regions would have remained part of Armenia if Dashnaks had agreed to the republic's Sovietisation a few months earlier. For the 'standard' Soviet view see *Hai zhoghovrdi patmutiun*, vol. VII, pp. 95–105; for an example of a virulent Soviet attack on the ARF as 'treacherous' agents of 'American-Turkish imperialism' (written in the mid-1950s) see Kh. Badalian, *Dashnakneri kontrrevoliutsion*, particularly pp. 76–88; for one of the earlier (1925) Soviet publications denouncing Dashnak militancy and the overambitious refusal to 'let go' of the ideal of a 'united Armenia' see *Khorhdayin Hayastan*, pp. 2–3; for an anti-Dashnak diasporan view see A. Chelepian, *Zoravar Andranik*, pp. 609–13. Modern Armenian history—particularly at the popular level—was, and still is, highly ideologised and politicised. The role of the ARF is especially contentious.

lier demands for reform and autonomy within the Ottoman and Russian empires. Reality had outstripped the party programme.[120] Once again the fate of the Armenians was determined by external forces and much larger global dynamics. Armenians had obtained independence when there was a political and military vacuum in the South Caucasus. They skilfully and at times heroically maintained it for as long as possible. But in the end independence proved to be an unfeasible option given the geopolitical realities of the region.

The fact that Armenia became independent as a result of unforeseen circumstances does not prevent nationalists, particularly Dashnaks, from interpreting history in a way that sees the 1918 republic as a natural outcome of a long-lasting struggle—in which the ARF played a central role. In one of their typical commemorative pamphlets (in this case celebrating the 100th anniversary of the party) they write: 'The founding of United, Free and Independent Armenia on 28 May 1918 was the logical result of the Armenian liberation struggle.... After leading the battles that resulted in independence, the ARF was a protective presence in the life of the Armenian Republic, both at the levels of executive and legislative government.'[121] *After* 1918 independence became the cherished goal of Armenian nationalists. The Armenian delegation at the 1919 Paris peace conference demanded for the first time a 'sea to sea' independent Armenia (to be under an Allied mandate). And in a 1922 publication the delegation insisted on an Armenia that was '*absolument indépendant de la Turquie*'.[122] This became the declared goal of the ARF at its Tenth General Congress in Paris (November 1924 to January 1925) where the motto 'Free, Independent and United Armenia' was officially adopted as the party's supreme objective.[123]

120 The congress was held under two banners indicative of the two strains in the ARF ideology: 'United and Independent Armenia' and 'Toward the Socialist International' (R. Hovannisian, 'Ninth General Meeting', p. 7).

121 *H.H.D. 100*, p. 49. This theme is consistently maintained by Dashnaks. For another example see H. Marukhian, 'H.H.D Biuroyi nerkayatsutsich', p. 6. By contrast, the reality was that the actual declaration in 1918 contained 'No brave words about freedom or rights, no "cherished goal" rhetoric—not even the phrase "Republic of Armenia." Just a bare statement of the situation…' (C. Walker, *Armenia*, p. 257).

122 *Délégation*, p. 57.

123 H. Dasnabedian, *Histoire*, pp. 161–3. The actual commitment to a united and independent Armenia was made at an earlier smaller party conference held in Bucharest

Subsequently Dashnaks, with their uncompromising anti-Soviet attitude (at least until the 1970s) and maximalist public stance, kept the ideal of an independent Armenia alive in the diaspora. They did not monopolise it, but they were the most vocal and significant advocates of independence, always situating May 1918 and other events related to the republic at the core of their symbolic fund. The other two diasporan parties, the Ramkavars and the Hnchaks, had long accepted Soviet rule in Armenia as legitimate and even beneficial—although they too maintained an abstract and long term vision of a united Armenia. Nevertheless, they rejected the symbolism of 1918 and instead commemorated Armenia's Sovietisation. Needless to say the Communist Party in Armenia did not tolerate any public expression of sympathy towards the ARF and 'its' 1918–20 republic. The nationalist movement in Armenia in 1988 reappropriated the symbols of the 1918 republic: the flag, the emblem, the anthem, the heroes etc.

The third effect of the independent republic on Armenian identity was the familiar scenario of reliance on external forces. This was both indicative of, and further reinforced, the psychology of dependence. After the Bolshevik revolution Dashnak leaders decided to cast Armenia's fate with the Allied powers, as they realised that Armenia needed external support to survive. At the end of the First World War it seemed that their calculations would pay off and a Western power would assume a mandate over Armenia. Such reliance was built right into Armenia's foreign policy. The country's independence was to be dependent on the goodwill of European and American powers. With Russia preoccupied with its civil war, and the Allies promising so much, Dashnak leaders were 'never able to abandon their Western orientation, on which the hopes of a united Armenia rested.'[124] These were not naive men who believed

in April 1921 (p. 152). The Tenth General Congress formally declared this as the ARF's objective and introduced the idea in the party's Programme.

124 R. Hovannisian, 'Republic', p. 304. The following decisions—which effectively became the policy of the government—were taken at the Ninth General Congress of the ARF (1919): 'The present friendly attitude toward the Allied nations shall be continued.... In view of the prevailing political, economic and cultural conditions, the general meeting finds it desirable that, through a special mandate of the Allied nations, Armenia be placed under a temporary protectorate....' As to relations with Russia, given that the latter now had a Bolshevik regime, the Congress stated:

that the West would support the Armenians out of sympathy or Christian solidarity. They tried to present the importance of an independent Armenia as a politically beneficial entity to Europe (and to Russia). Nevertheless, they simply could not conceive an Armenian polity that would not at all rely on the benevolent attitude of some major foreign power. At the end the mentality that salvation needs to come from abroad persisted. Western humanitarian aid did come from abroad,[125] but the only tangible military forces that came were the Kemalist and Red armies intent on destroying the independent Armenian state, not saving it.

The fourth point was the territorialisation of national identity within a specific nation-state. The reality of independence transformed Armenian nationalism from its focus on communal rights and autonomy to independence and statehood. There was now a specific territory, with an Armenian majority, where Armenian identity could be rooted and supported by state institutions. The new republic established a state university, declared Armenian as the state language, printed its own currency, opened embassies abroad etc. Armenian armed units (be they regular or irregular) also drove out thousands of Muslims from mixed areas, particularly in Zangezur (which Azerbaijan claimed).[126] This cleansing—to use a current term—further enhanced the country's demographic balance in favour of the Armenians. Circumstances had dictated independence to the Armenians, but now that they had their own state they began to mobilise around it and redirected their nationalist aspiration towards it. The territorialisation of identity ushered in by the 1918 republic remained with the Armenians throughout the twentieth century. As the next chapter will show, it was emphasised by the Soviet authorities who consciously constructed and projected an

---

'While taking a thoroughly sympathetic attitude toward the Russian people and Russia's political restoration, our diplomacy must resist the attempts of the existing governments in Russia to spread Russian rule over former Russian Armenia, thereby precluding the realization of integral Armenia' (R. Hovannisian, 'Ninth General Meeting', p. 10).

[125] For details of the humanitarian assistance sent to Armenia in the face of mass starvation see, R. Hovannisian, *Republic*, vol. I, pp. 133–44, vol. II, pp. 397–402, and 'Republic', pp. 311–2.

[126] General Andranik and Garegin Nzhdeh were particularly active in this respect (see R. Hovannisian, *Republic*, vol. I, pp. 87, 194, vol. II, pp. 218–19, 226).

image of the Armenian SSR as the centre of national identity and as the natural locus of loyalty.

Having their own independent state did not transcend the east/west divide within the Armenian nation. The fifth point is the fact that this division was built into the domestic and international politics of the republic. Independent Armenia was in fact a manifestation of Russian Armenia, except with a different political arrangement—plus a few hundred thousand refugees from the Ottoman empire. The latter 'did not consider this their country. The Erevan republic, bearing the strong imprint of Russia, was alien to them.'[127] They simply wanted to go back to western (Ottoman) Armenia as soon as possible. There were accusations that the government was neglecting the needs of the refugees from the west, which led to political tensions between eastern and western Armenians. Furthermore, the east/west cleavage had some resonance in the internal politics of Armenia. Western Armenians tended to be more conservative, while easterners were more radical and internationalist. The conservative and bourgeois elements gathered around the People's Party in Armenia and around the Ramkavar party abroad. They supported the wealthy western Armenian leader Boghos Nubar Pasha who did not even live in Armenia, but wished to be prime minister (in order to negotiate with Allied leaders at the Paris Conference from a position of authority, so it was argued).

The most telling example of the east-west divide—and even antagonism—was the Populist and Ramkavar rejection of the government's May 1919 proclamation of the Act of United Armenia whereby, in a purely symbolic gesture, eastern and western Armenia were declared united as one country. Boghos Nubar was offended by this Act, seeing it as an attack on his 'representative' jurisdiction, while the Populists, reversing their initial support for the Act, argued that 'the proclamation had been an act of usurpation [because] Boghos Nubar and his Armenian National Delegation spoke for the Western Armenians [and] they had not been consulted regarding the act.'[128] Even while declaring the 'unity' of the nation and its ter-

[127] R. Hovannisian, 'Republic', p. 313.

[128] Ibid., p. 323, cf. 322–3, 325, and for further details, R. Hovannisian, *Republic*, vol. I, pp. 459–71; A. Hakobian, 'Mij-kusaktsakan paikare', pp. 5, 32–4.

ritory, Armenian politics split along the east-west divide intrinsic in collective identity.[129]

The division was also inherent in the external politics and diplomacy of the country, namely at the Paris peace conference in 1919. Armenians attended the conference not with one but two delegations: one was led by Boghos Nubar, claiming to represent western Armenians; the other was the official representation of the republic led by Avetis Aharonian. Sympathetic to the Ramkavar party, Nubar was the most prominent figure in western Armenian circles. Given that there was another delegation representing the Armenian state, he insisted that his presence was essential because Russian Armenians would not be able (or willing) to put forth and defend the interests of the Turkish Armenians (and the bourgeoisie). Avetis Aharonian was very much the contrasting image of Nubar: an eastern Armenian Dashnak intellectual-writer with left-leaning views. After a number of clashes (accentuated by personal dislike of one another)

[129] Many of these tensions and assumptions were evident in Boghos Nubar's own thinking even before Armenia's independence. In a handwritten report (probably for the British Foreign Office), Arnold Toynbee recounts his discussions with Boghos Nubar at a meeting in Paris on 6 November 1917. Toynbee first notes how Nubar's views are 'extremely moderate—so moderate that they are only to a limited degree representative of Armenian public opinion' (p. 2). Nubar, who would have been 'content with autonomy for the Armenian *vilayets* of the Ottoman Empire' before the war, now believed that the Armenian provinces, plus Cilicia, should enjoy independence from the Ottomans given 'Turkey's intervention in the war, and the Armenian Atrocities that followed' (p. 3). This independence should be under the protection of Western powers: 'The point on which Nubar insists is that if an independent Armenia is created, it cannot be left to itself. It must be warranted and assisted from outside, until it is strong enough to stand by itself' (pp. 4–5). However, what is remarkable is Nubar's more or less exclusive focus on western or Ottoman Armenia. Toynbee comments: 'Nubar has demanded the complete deliverance of the Armenian provinces from Turkish control—that is now the central point of his policy.... He never demanded the reunion with the Turkish provinces of the Armenian territories in the Russian Caucasus.... In this he is certainly out of touch with the main current of Armenian feeling at the present time' (p. 3). Toynbee adds: 'My impression is that Nubar does not follow Caucasian affairs closely.... Nubar's present programme is an independent Armenian state, *excluding of course the Armenian territories of Russia* [emphasis added]....' (untitled report in Toynbee Papers, Box 44, Bodleian Library, Department of Western Manuscripts, University of Oxford). Admittedly this discussion took place before it was clear that the Russians (Bolsheviks) were indeed totally abandoning the Armenian front, but it still showed Nubar's lack of interest in eastern Armenia—an attitude that did not change much two years later as it was recast in terms of a jurisdictional or representation issue.

the two men and their delegations managed to present a unified position at the peace conference in the form of the Delegation of Integral Armenia. But their united position could barely hide the cultural and political cleavages between eastern and western Armenians. The Dashnak-led government in the republic and the western Armenian representatives could not solve the issue of sharing power, nor the question of who had the right to represent the entire nation.[130]

The sixth and last point regarding the republic and identity was its confirmation of the spirit of rebellion. Two separate rebellions within Armenia provided two separate groups of people with a basis to claim legitimacy in their struggle against oppression. First, the Communists of Armenia staged a rebellion in May 1920 (centred in Alexandropol), which the Dashnak government put down. Second, the Dashnaks led a rebellion in February 1921 against the oppressive measures of the newly installed Soviet regime. The first incident, in typical Communist fashion, became part of history in Soviet Armenia as a glorious instance of workers' and peasants' struggle against the 'bourgeois-nationalist Dashnaks'. Although the uprising was not informed by nationalist demands and was a relatively minor set of events involving a few radical intellectuals and workers, it nevertheless provided the Soviet authorities with an opportunity to prove that the Armenians too were willing to rise up for communist principles.[131] The second incident, which actually did manage to topple the Soviet regime in Armenia between 18 February and 2 April, became part of the Dashnak and nationalist fund of episodes—on a par with Banque Ottomane—to be commemorated and celebrated as a heroic struggle against (Soviet) oppression.[132]

[130] For details see R. Hovannisian, *Republic*, vol. II, pp. 267–79.

[131] See, for example, *Haikakan sovetakan hanragitaran*, vol. VII, pp. 201–2; *Hai zhoghovrdi patmutiun*, vol. VII, pp. 83–94.

[132] For the Dashnak interpretation and celebration of the 'February rebellion' see H. Dasnabedian, *Histoire*, pp. 146–7. In addition, every February the Dashnak press devotes many articles to the subject. For the Soviet interpretation of February as 'counter-revolutionary agitation' see *Haikakan sovetakan hanragitaran*, vol. XII, p. 334; *Hai zhoghovrdi patmutiun*, vol. VII, pp. 136–54; Kh. Badalian, *Dashnakneri kontrrevoliutsion*, pp. 81–4. For a neutral account of the May 'uprising' and the February 'insurgency' or 'rebellion' see R. Hovannisian, *Republic*, vol. III, pp. 209–53 (on May), vol. IV, pp. 403–6 (on February). Interestingly, the 1921 February uprising and the 1988 Gharabagh movement are tied together in ARF ideology and popular culture

Despite fundamentally differing views on the two episodes by the Dashnaks and the Soviet Armenians, each side could claim a heritage of rebellion (dismissing the other as 'agitation' or 'disturbance') in relation to the independent republic.

Finally, it should be noted that the February rebellion was also important insofar as it enabled many Dashnak leaders and their followers to escape Soviet rule by retreating to the mountains of Zangezur. This region remained in Dashnak hands until early July 1921. Led by Garegin Nzhdeh, partisan units resisted Sovietisation until their defeat by the Red Army became inevitable. In fact they declared Zangezur as the independent Republic of Mountainous Armenia on 27 April 1921. Zangezur's resistance to Soviet rule had two significant effects. First, it provided an escape route for Dashnaks and other anti-Bolsheviks who retreated to Iran by crossing the Arax river. Henceforth these leaders and intellectuals became the organisers and leading figures of the Dashnak side of the diaspora. Second, by holding on to Zangezur for as long as possible, and insisting that it should remain Armenian, the partisans in all probability were a key factor in the decision of the Soviet central authorities to place the region in Soviet Armenia and not in Azerbaijan. Communist leaders in Yerevan explicitly promised Nzhdeh and the representatives of Mountainous Armenia that Zangezur would be incorporated into Soviet Armenia.[133]

Nationalism is not only an intellectual conceptualisation of collective identity, but a political movement. In fact it is the latter that makes nationalism such a potent force. Hence the importance of analysing the organisational dimension of Armenian nationalism and its consequences. In the fifty year period before the early 1920s Armenians experienced some of the most fundamental social and political transformations in their entire history. Their struggle began by demanding communal freedoms and security, but it was met with the catastrophe of the Genocide and the loss of their historic homeland; they witnessed the birth of an independent republic in

---

as part of a similar process of rebellion against injustice. For one example see the commemorative booklet *Petrvarian apstambutian*.

[133] Hovannisian, *Republic*, vol. IV, p. 406.

one corner of the homeland, fought for it, but in the end had to surrender independence to the forces of Sovietisation in order to survive.

By 1923 the Armenian Question was buried by the international community. Within the nation a fundamental shift had taken place between 1915 and 1923 in terms of identity construction. It was obvious that the western point of Armenian identity could no longer be centred in Istanbul and western Armenia, both of which were now an integral part of the newly formed Turkish and Turkifying republic. Hence the western point of Armenian identity was *completely* diasporised. It could only exist in a deeply wounded form in scattered survivor communities and some of the older intellectual centres. Meanwhile the eastern point was Sovietised, with its own administration, state structures and Communist elite. Although part of the USSR it was nevertheless the only surviving part of Armenia where identity could be maintained, albeit imbued with Soviet propaganda and thinking. Consequently, with the support of the Soviet state, the eastern point of Armenian identity was further entrenched, eventually acquiring the position of 'homeland' in Armenian thinking.

Ironically the most prominent eastern political party, the ARF, henceforth became in the diaspora a 'western' organisation—at least in some of its political thinking and vocabulary—but without at all giving up its eastern 'organic' and ethnic notion of nationalism. It saw itself as a party in exile. The ARF and the other political organisations outside Armenia emphasised the diasporan element of Armenian identity: a people condemned to live in exile without its historic homeland.

In short, despite some radical socio-political changes, the multilocal dimension of Armenian national identity continued into the twentieth century. The centres of identity were now Soviet Armenia (the inheritors of the eastern point) and the various (new) diasporan communities concentrated in the Middle East with some in Europe and North America (the inheritors of the surviving remnants of the western point). The wide gap between east and west remained and in fact was partly enhanced by the Iron Curtain. Nevertheless, the Soviets had the upper hand, with their state machinery, propaganda and resources. After all, Sovietisation, despite its problems and terror, did bring peace and tranquillity to Armenia.

The republic—the only remaining territory which had a real claim to be a homeland—experienced a 'national rebirth', especially during the 1920s and after Stalin's death in 1953. Of course this was a Soviet style rebirth and it only affected one segment of the nation. Soviet Armenia was not accepted by all Armenians—particularly not by the Dashnaks and their supporters in the diaspora—as an overarching and legitimate pan-national authority that could bring unity. Nevertheless, for the first time in centuries there was now a stable Armenian nation-state which could—and eventually did—become a national centre. These issues will be elaborated next.

6

DIFFERING IDENTITIES

SOVIET ARMENIANS, DIASPORA ARMENIANS (1921–87)

Despite the theoretical incompatibility between socialism and nationalism,[1] and the explicit anti-nationalist ideology of the USSR, Soviet rule either created or further consolidated and strengthened national identity in many of its constituent republics—especially in the South Caucasus and Central Asia. This process eventually led to the disintegration of the Soviet Union. The idea that the Soviets had a serious 'nationalities problem' that could lead to its demise was clearly articulated as early as the mid-1970s (mostly by anti-Soviet scholars). For example, Teresa Rakowska-Harmstone rejected the prevailing myth that the USSR had solved—or had at least firmly controlled—the 'nationalities question', and pointed out that in each major ethnic community in the USSR 'the sense of a distinct national identity is shared at the grassroots and among the modern elites and is used by the latter as the base for the maximization of national autonomy of their republics within limits allowed by the system.' Despite policies designed to neutralise ethnic self-assertion, she continued, 'It appears that, in the last two decades at least, the scale of development of ethnic nationalism has outstripped the rate of national Soviet integration' and is beginning to 'undermine the foundations of integration already achieved' since 1917. If this 'continues unchecked,' she concluded, it would, in the 'long run, con-

[1] For some theoretical works on the subject see W. Connor, *National Question*; R. Szporluk, *Communism and Nationalism*; cf. H. Davis, *Nationalism and Socialism*; R. Munck, *Difficult Dialogue*; S. Avineri, 'Toward a Socialist Theory'; Glenn, 'Nations and Nationalism'.

tribute to the disintegration of the *de facto* (if not *de jure*) unitary Soviet state.'[2]

The next generation of scholars, writing in the second half of the 1980s, and many from a more left perspective, further analysed the nationalities factor in the USSR. They advocated the thesis that the Soviet Union—more specifically, its federal structure—'created' or 'strengthened' nations. After December 1986, when the nationalities 'problem' erupted so unexpectedly in Central Asia, and then much more forcefully in Azerbaijan and Armenia over Mountainous Gharabagh (Nagorno-Karabakh)[3] in February 1988, this view gained ground and became the dominant mode of analysis; it is now the conventional wisdom in Soviet and post-Soviet studies. One scholar who, based on his earlier research, was instrumental in propagating the approach in English-speaking academia is Ronald Suny. In a seminal 1990 essay he wrote:

> ....the long and difficult years of Communist Party rule actually continued the 'making of nations' of the pre-revolutionary period. Not without its own contradictions and paradoxes, the Soviet experience resulted in stronger, more coherent and conscious nationalities than entered the federation at its inception. The Soviet Union, ironically, is the victim not only of its negative effects on the non-Russian peoples, but of its own 'progressive' contribution to the process of 'nation-building.'

[2] T. Rakowska-Harmstone, 'Integration', pp. 32–3; cf. T. Rakowska-Harmstone, 'Chickens Coming Home to Roost', and 'Study of Ethnic Politics'. At the same 1976 symposium where Rakowska-Harmstone first presented her article, Richard Pipes went as far as predicting that the 'Soviet empire, the last multinational empire, will fall apart roughly along the lines of today's republics.... [It will happen] if and when, for any reason, there is a weakening of authority within the central government and in the chain of command. [When it does happen,] it will proceed extremely rapidly, in weeks not in months' ('Reflections of a Nationality Expert', p. 10). Interestingly, 'Professor [Hugh] Seton-Watson called Pipes' ideas about the future a "wild scenario"' (Ibid., p. 11). Other scholars who belonged to the 'the-nationalities-issue-will-lead-to-the-destruction-of-the USSR' school of thought in the 1970s included H. Carrère d'Encausse, *Decline of an Empire*; Z. Brzezinski, 'Political Implications'; J. Azrael, 'Emergent Nationality Problems'; S. Bialer, *Stalin's Successors.*

[3] The spelling of 'Nagorno-Karabakh' comes from Russian transliteration. The Armenian name is Lernayin Gharabagh (i.e. Mountainous Gharabagh). Currently Armenians use 'Artsakh'—the ancient Armenian name—to refer to the region. Gharabagh is the more accepted term internationally and hence I use that, but with the Armenian transliteration. It comes from Persian and Turkic root words meaning 'black garden'.

In short, 'Rather than a "melting pot", the Soviet Union became the incubator of new nations'[4]—especially after Stalin. Consequently the union fell apart as it was unable to control the nationalist centrifugal forces of many of the republics.[5]

Numerous scholars have since examined the various aspects of the 'Soviet-style' nation-building process and its central role in the disintegration of the USSR. A plethora of publications in the early 1990s focused on the nationalities issue within the collapsing USSR. They highlighted, *ex post facto*, the inherent tensions and conflicts along national(ist) lines.[6] But to this date there are few detailed stud-

[4] R. Suny, 'Revenge of the Past', p. 22 for the first quote, p. 6 for the second. For an expanded version of the essay (covering the entire USSR and not just the Transcaucasian republics) see R. Suny, *Revenge of the Past*; cf. R. Suny, *Making of the Georgian Nation*, pp. 292ff. Other major scholars had come to similar conclusions in the second half of the 1980s onwards. For example, see G. Simon, *Nationalism and Policy*; H. Carrère d'Encausse, *End of the Soviet Empire*; R. Brubaker, *Nationalism Reframed*; G. Gleason, 'On the Bureaucratic Reinforcement', and *Federalism and Nationalism*; R. Karklins, *Ethnic Relations*; J. Dunlop, 'Language'.

[5] Soviet leaders themselves conceded that there were still 'many problems [regarding the relations between the nationalities] requiring the Party's tactful attention' (Brezhnev in 1981), and that 'successes in solving the nationalities question certainly do not mean that all the problems engendered... have disappeared' (Andropov in 1982; both cited in G. Lapidus, 'Ethnonationalism', p. 418). Andropov even acknowledged that 'national differences will continue considerably longer than class differences' (cited in H. Huttenbach, 'Conclusion', p. 290). However, the official Soviet version in 1986 remained: 'The path that has been traversed provides convincing proof that *the nationalities question inherited from the past has been successfully solved in the Soviet Union*. Characteristic of the national relations... are both the continued flowering of the nations and the nationalities and the fact that they are steadily and voluntarily drawing closer together on the basis of equality and fraternal cooperation' (*Programme of the Communist Party*, p. 47). It seems that Mikhail Gorbachev was the one First Secretary who actually believed in this statement (at least initially), even though he too acknowledged that the USSR faced certain nationalities-related problems (M. Gorbachev, *Perestroika*, pp. 104–7; M. Gorbachev, *Memoirs*, Chapter 15). Despite the above cited scholarly work, most Western sovietologists, with their Moscow-centred view of the USSR, failed in general to appreciate the absurdity of this statement; they either ignored, downplayed or underestimated the strength of the national factor. For a sensible article in this vein see, G. Lapidus, 'Ethnonationalism'; cf. A. Motyl, *Will the Non-Russians Rebel?* For a comprehensive discussion regarding the shortcomings of Sovietology see the special issue 'The Strange Death of Soviet Communism: An Autopsy', *The National Interest* no. 31, spring 1993, particularly the essays by P. Reddaway, 'Role of Popular Discontent', and R. Conquest, 'Academe and Soviet Myth'; cf. D. Lieven, 'Western Scholarship'; A. Motyl, *Sovietology*.

[6] For some of the general (mostly edited) volumes see I. Bremmer and R. Taras, *Nations and Politics*; R. Denber, *Soviet Nationality Reader*; L. Hajda and M. Beissinger, *National-*

ies that analyse the questions of how nations were built or strengthened under Soviet rule in a particular case or a specific republic, and what the key factors and mechanisms in this process were.[7]

Going beyond generalities in much of the literature on the subject, in this and the following chapters, I examine the 'how' and 'what' questions as I analyse the 'nation-building' process in Soviet Armenia and in the diaspora. The Soviet regime did not create Armenian nationhood, but it did strengthen it and consolidated it on a specific territory. In the words of Claire Mouradian, the Armenian SSR '*a pris l'allure d'un état-nation quasi parfait*'[8] by the 1970s. Consequently, in 1988 Armenians embarked on the transition from a nationalised republic to the politics of nationalism. The Armenian case also provides a unique opportunity to compare developments in a Soviet republic with similar dynamics in the diaspora. As before, my discussion will oscillate between Armenia and the diaspora. I will maintain that the east/west schism within the Armenian nation continued during the Soviet period. But it now manifested in terms of a clear-cut homeland/diaspora divide. Although the politics of the homeland-diaspora relationship did not rigidly reflect this divide (the Armenian SSR and *certain* diasporan organisations always maintained some links), and after the late 1950s there were controlled cultural exchanges between the republic and diasporan communities, the division between the two parts of the nation was entrenched further in social, political, and cultural terms.

The structure of this chapter is somewhat different from the previous chapters. First, I give an overview of the major developments in—and relating to—Soviet Armenia between 1921 and 1987, the emphasis being on the post-Stalin period. I then highlight

---

ities Factor; G. Lapidus *et al.*, *From Union to Commonwealth*; A. Motyl, *Post-Soviet Nations*; B. Nahaylo and V. Swoboda, *Soviet Disunion*; G. Smith, *Nationalities Question*; H. Huttenbach, *Soviet Nationality Policies*. For a similar volume, but focused on the South Caucasus, see R. Suny, *Transcaucasia* (Part 4). Many of these books contain articles or sections on or relating to the Armenians.

[7] For one excellent study (on Romania) see K. Verdery, *National Ideology*. Audrey Altstadt examines the relationship between Soviet power and identity in Azerbaijan, but she comes to the opposite conclusion. Using the 'colonialism' approach, she argues that the Soviets attacked and undermined the formation or strengthening of national identity (A. Altstadt, *Azerbaijani Turks*; cf. A. Altstadt, 'Decolonization').

[8] C. Mouradian, 'L'Arménie soviétique', p. 286.

some of the basic dynamics that affected diasporan Armenians and their process of identity construction. Subsequently, in the next chapter, I elaborate on the 'nation-building' argument through certain key factors or themes that emerged from my research in Armenia.

DYNAMICS IN SOVIET ARMENIA

Armenia was Sovietised in December 1920. It joined the USSR as a constituent part of the Transcaucasian Federal Soviet Socialist Republic at the Soviet Union's inception in December 1922. The December 1936 Constitution of the USSR granted Armenia the status of a separate Soviet Socialist Republic—the smallest of the then 11, later 15, Union republics.[9] Like other regions Armenia moved towards socialism at a 'leisurely pace'[10] until 1928. Subsequently it too was subject to the upheavals of collectivisation,[11] the Stalinist terror,[12] and the deprivations resulting from the Second World War (although Armenia was never occupied by German forces). After Stalin's death conditions eased somewhat, giving way to the rise of a 'new nationalism'. Armenia further developed economically in the 1960s, reaching a plateau by the early 1970s.[13] As in the rest of the USSR, stagnation set in, particularly in the realms of economics and politics. But the evolution of national consciousness did

[9] Numerous articles in Western journals and books cover various aspects of Soviet Armenia. There are two significant scholarly monographs devoted to the history of the Armenian SSR: the first covers the years up to 1953 (M. Matossian, *Impact of Soviet Policies*); the second analyses the period from Stalin to the Gharabagh movement (C. Mouradian, *De Staline à Gorbatchev*). See also R. Suny, *Armenia in the Twentieth Century*; C. Walker, *Armenia*, pp. 339–78, 391–407).

[10] C. Walker, *Armenia*, p. 341. For a poetic (and brief) description of Armenia in 1930 see Osip Mandelstam, *Journey to Armenia*.

[11] At the end of 1929 3.7 per cent of peasant households were collectivised. By February 1930 it was claimed that 63 per cent were collectivised. By the autumn of the same year, after the temporary easing of the process, the figure was back down to 8.9 per cent. By 1936 it had reached 80 per cent, and this time the trend was not to reverse. In 1926 four out of every five Armenians lived in the countryside (M. Matossian, *Impact of Soviet Policies*, pp. 59–60, 102–8).

[12] For details see M. Matossian, *Impact of Soviet Policies*, pp. 155–69; R. Suny, *Looking toward Ararat*, pp. 156–61.

[13] For an overview see C. Mouradian, *De Staline à Gorbatchev*, pp. 105–31.

not ebb. Soviet Armenia was on a 'march' towards nationalism rather than socialism.

The federal structure and centre-republic relations

Even though Soviet federalism was largely 'a fraud' given the centralised nature of the ruling Communist Party,[14] the federal structure of the USSR was not a complete sham—particularly in relation to some of the 'peripheral' republics. Moreover, the centralised Communist Party structures were themselves not so effective in controlling national(ist) sentiments in many regions. The Party too was subject to the policies of *khorenizatsiia* (the policy will be discussed below). Evidence suggests that both state and Party structures were used by the local elites and intellectuals to manipulate the system in their personal favour and, more importantly, in the favour of their 'own' republics. As Crawford Young affirms, in the post-Stalin period, 'ethnic machines emerged,... an informal ethnic patrimonialism' through which 'unacknowledged cultural bargaining could occur within the patron-client networks that linked the central organs of the Soviet state to its ethnic periphery.' These functioned 'alongside [and, I would add, within] the formal structures of coercive control and hierarchy.' Through such bargaining the Soviet federal cake was divided, with Russia holding the knife.[15] This was certainly the case in the Armenian SSR.

The federal structure gave Armenians a republic with clearly defined borders, albeit, importantly, with unsatisfactory territorial demarcations for most Armenians. On the basis of the Soviet Constitution,[16] and various policies and practices that will be examined

[14] D. Lieven, 'Gorbachev', pp. 2–3. The Party programme and statute were more '"fundamental" than the fundamental law' of the Constitution; they were also more difficult to revise than the Constitution (G. Gleason, *Federalism and Nationalism*, p. 45). And yet, as Eric Hobsbawm aptly puts it, 'The only form of constitutional arrangement which socialist states have taken seriously since 1917, are formulas for national federation and autonomy' (E. Hobsbawm, *Nations and Nationalism*, p. 172). Ronald Suny calls the USSR 'a pseudofederal state' which *both* 'eliminated political sovereignty for the nationalities and [yet] guaranteed them territorial identity, educational and cultural institutions in their own language' while promoting 'native cadres into positions of power' (R. Suny, *Revenge of the Past*, p. 101).

[15] C. Young, 'National and Colonial', p. 90.

[16] The first Soviet Constitution (of Russia) was adopted in July 1918; the second in Jan-

later, Armenians became the 'masters' in their own semi-autonomous—or more correctly somewhat-autonomous—state. Nevertheless there was finally an Armenian state that could be, and was, used to affect collective identity—even though it had emerged *after* the formation of national identity. What is more, through the Armenian SSR national identity came to be rooted in a specific territory, as one of the union republics with 'some paraphernalia of statehood'.[17] Rasma Karklins explains further: 'Territorially based group identity is at the core of self-perception of the major nations as well as the practice of Soviet nationality policy.... Soviet federalism has provided the fourteen non-Russian republic nations with some administrative and cultural prerogatives as well as the promise of group equality.'[18] The federal administrative-territorial system

---

uary 1924 (of the USSR); the third was the famous 'Stalin Constitution' of December 1936. The fourth Constitution was adopted in October 1977 and a new wave of amendments were incorporated in 1988. The 1936 Constitution formally enhanced the rights of republics; it gave them their own separate constitutions and the right to secede. Article 13 of Stalin's document stipulated that the USSR was a 'federal state formed on the basis of a voluntary association of equal Soviet Socialist republics' (G. Gleason, *Federalism and Nationalism*, p. 47). Of course this was a fraud and the whole idea of self-determination was not much more than a utilitarian device for the Soviet authorities, 'a versatile weapon in the Soviet diplomatic arsenal', as one expert puts it (V. Aspaturian, 'Union Republics', p. 462). The three criteria necessary to have republican status, according to Stalin (as outlined in his speech on 25 November 1936 at the Eighth All-Union Congress of Soviets), were: an external border, a population of at least one million, and a majority of the titular nationality. In February 1944 the republics were granted additional rights: to have their own military forces and the right to conduct foreign affairs (the latter had been outlawed in 1926). These changes were in the context of international relations and made the republics both subjects and pawns in Soviet diplomacy. In the end only Ukraine and Belorussia obtained some sort of international recognition with their own UN seats and limited foreign recognition (Stalin had initially asked for UN seats for all the republics). The 1977 Constitution eliminated the republics' right to have their own national armies, and the federal structure was centralised to a limited degree. However, the overall balance of powers between Moscow and the republics did not change. The final federal form of the USSR was settled in 1956, with fifteen constituent republics, sixteen ASSRs (all but one in the Russian Federation, plus Nakhijevan, the exclave of Azerbaijan) and eight Autonomous *Oblasts*, one of them being Mountainous Gharabagh. This basic set-up remained remarkably stable until the late 1980s, with very few structural changes.

[17] R. Szporluk, 'Nationalism after Communism', p. 312.

[18] R. Karklins, *Ethnic Relations*, p. 206; she points out that the territorial dimension is emphasised through the federal structure, the indigenisation campaigns and the rhet-

functioned as a 'licensing regime for ethnic sentiment' while at the same time acting as a control mechanism.[19]

Soviet federalism was justified by Lenin's nationality policy, although ideologically it was seen as a transitionary phase in the ultimate fusion of the various nations. The centralised party structure was the main mechanism through which the decentralised state system was kept in check. The tension between these two tendencies existed throughout the Soviet period, but by the 1960s and 1970s the balance began to favour the republics. One explanation for this is offered by Gregory Gleason as he highlights the power of the republican bureaucracies and the administrative elite in the 'bureaucratic reinforcement of nationalism':

> Given the limited capacity of the central government, the national republics wielded certain *de facto* powers by virtue of the fact that policy was implemented through the various branches of the administrative apparatus in the localities.... Despite administrative centralization, the authorities in Moscow were forced to rely upon the compliance of local officials.... [while] at the same time, satisfying local yearnings for local control.[20]

This was confirmed to me by the former First Secretary of Armenia, Karen Demirchian. With reference to the economic relationship between Moscow and Yerevan he explained:

> When we got the plan dictated from the centre, we tried to implement it, and to adapt it to our situation, to counter it, or to find ways around it, officially or unofficially. And the Centre knew this. Many times I was asked in Moscow why I did not do this or that in the plan, and I used to explain that in our context it did not make sense. And many times they accepted this and said OK. But it was dictated from above and we found ways around it, to make it fit.[21]

---

oric of Leninist nationality policy; this makes it difficult for the central authorities to counter national demands (pp. 96–7).

[19] A. Kagedan, 'Territorial Units', p. 164. I have discussed elsewhere some of the more general centre-periphery dynamics within the USSR using the concepts of ideology, hegemony, culture and civil society (R. Panossian, 'From Provincial Republics').

[20] G. Gleason, *Federalism and Nationalism*, pp. 52, 55. A number of other writers discuss the weakening control of Moscow over the republics: V. Aspaturian, *Union Republics*, p. 201; H. Carrère d'Encausse, *Decline of an Empire*, pp. 268–9; R. Suny, *Armenia in the Twentieth Century*, p. 73; P. Reddaway, 'Role of Popular Discontent', p. 58.

[21] Author's Interview with Karen Demirchian.

The federal structure gave such officials the legal basis to counter Moscow's directives based on local needs. It enabled them to develop an indigenous support base both in the Party apparatus and in the general population. Of course this begs the question, why did the local elite choose to do this? The answer lies in the elite's own nationalist and personal agenda. This will be discussed later.

Karlen Dallakian, a former Secretary of the Central Committee of the Armenian Communist Party (1976–85), explicitly discusses the tension between the federal system and the centralised Party structures as well, but on a more general level. He situates this dynamic at the heart of the collapse of the Soviet Union. The USSR could not solve the nationalities question because at its very core lay the decentralisation/nationalisation vs centralisation/Russification tension.[22] Comparing the situation with the West, he says that the issue of a 'national-state' was solved there 100–200 years ago; subsequently these societies moved onto the issue of human and individual rights. The Soviet leadership tried to skip the middle stage and go directly to the human rights 'stage', being under pressure from the West. But this could not succeed since it was against the 'laws' of historical evolution (Dallakian's analytical framework is after all based on dialectical-materialism). Hence when the system opened up in the late-1980s various nations rushed to solve problems emanating from the missing stage of 'national rights'—i.e. the need to create nation-states. The Union thus collapsed. The federal structure had enabled many of these nations to carry out the preparatory work needed to have a viable and modern nation-state. The Party itself, because of its own internal problems and inefficiencies, could not counter this powerful trend.[23]

Modernisation and national identity

The relationship between modernisation (including urbanisation, industrialisation, standardisation etc.) and national identity (including nationalism) is much analysed. There is no need to discuss the issue once again here since Soviet Armenia was not an exception to general trends.[24] Between 1928 and 1935 alone the 'proportional

[22] K. Dallakian, *Hushapatum*, pp. 335–7.

[23] Ibid., pp. 339–47.

[24] For an excellent study of the general trend see G. Simon, *Nationalism and Policy*, par-

value of industry in all economic production [in Armenia] increased from 21.7 per cent... to 62.1 per cent.'[25] Henceforth industrialisation continued steadily. The corresponding urbanisation rate was as follows: in 1926 82 per cent of the population lived in the countryside, in 1979 this figure was 34 per cent.[26] In the 1920s modernisation 'went hand in hand with nation-building,' states Ronald Suny; 'Economic development was seen as consistent with cultural and political renationalization.' This trend continued in the post-Stalin period. Modernisation did not lead to 'a reduction of ethnic cohesiveness and national consciousness.' Neither economic nor cultural progress accelerated the process of assimilation. Rather they led to the 'reconsolidation of the Armenian nation' and the 're-Armenization of the territory of Soviet Armenia.'[27]

The linkage between modernisation and national identity can be examined on many levels. Two examples would suffice to demonstrate the point. First, on the macro level economic and industrial achievements were seen as symbols and evidence of *Armenian national* success leading to collective ethnic pride, especially in the post-Stalin period.[28] This pride in Armenia's industrial might, as an advanced part of the Soviet economy, was constantly mentioned in

ticularly chapter 9, and more specifically pp. 278–9; cf. T. Rakowska-Harmstone, 'Study of Ethnic Politics', p. 26; H. Carrère d'Encausse, *Decline of an Empire*, p. 266; J. Azrael, 'Emergent', p. 378; G. Schroeder, 'Social and Economic', p. 309.

25 M. Matossian, *Impact of Soviet Policies*, p. 116. Some of the other economic figures are: the South Caucasus's share of total Soviet investment between 1950 and 1980 remained consistent at 3.5 per cent. Per capita investment rose two to five times—it was five times in the RSFSR, and over six to eight times in Latvia and Estonia. Between 1960 and 1980 the per capita average annual growth rate in Armenia was 5.5 per cent in national income and 6.4 per cent in industrial production. Its national income in 1980 was 86 per cent of the USSR level (G. Schroeder, 'Social and Economic', pp. 299–300). In terms of living standards, according to official data, Armenia was below the USSR level (p. 304). These figures do not take into account the significant shadow or non-official economy. In USSR's income distribution the principal gainers were the Central Asian republics, then came Georgia and Armenia (p. 308). For details of Armenian SSR's economic relations with other republics see S. Melkumian, *Sovetakan*, pp. 49–79 for an overview, pp. 80–122 for relations with the RSFSR.

26 M. Matossian, *Impact of Soviet Policies*, p. 59, cf. chapters 5,7,9 for further details and trends on Soviet Armenia's modernisation; C. Mouradian, *De Staline à Gorbatchev*, Chapter 3; R. Suny, *Armenia in the Twentieth Century*, pp. 45–52, 71–7.

27 R. Suny, *Armenia in the Twentieth Century*, pp. 45, 76.

28 V. Dadrian, 'Appraisal of the Communist Formula', part I, pp. 8–9.

many of my interviews. The well-developed scientific component and the related educational establishment were particularly emphasised. Communists highlighted them the most, but others too acknowledged past industrial and infrastructural accomplishments as major national achievements.[29] The sharpest quote comes from Sergei Badalian who had said in April 1993, 'The opinion was often stated that we [Armenia] were a colony of Russia. In reality it was probably the opposite.'[30] Second, at the micro level the Soviet regime modernised the family as well, but it did not alter some of its basic dynamics: patriarchal relations, the primary role of women as homemakers and its 'national character'. Mouradian and Ter Minassian point out that '*la famille arménienne constitue une unité de reproduction culturelle et nationale.*'[31] This was reinforced further because the traditional family was presented in the official discourse as 'progressive' and as the key to the individual's happiness and the 'bright future'.[32]

[29] See, for example, author's interviews with Sergei Badalian, Tital Davrishian, Artashes Shahpazian, Aram Sargsian and Rafael Ghazarian. Suren Harutiunian, a former First Secretary of Armenia (1988–91), made the same point in a 1994 published interview (S. Harutiunian, 'Verjin tarineri', pp. 4–5).

[30] As quoted in *Haik* (Yerevan), 3 October 1997, p. 2. This raises a theoretical point regarding the validity of the 'internal colonialism' theory used by certain scholars to explain nationalism (M. Hechter, *Internal Colonialism*; T. Nairn, *Break-up*). These theorists link uneven economic development and a cultural division of labour with the rise of nationalism in the periphery of a state. The internal colonialism argument might be applicable to some of the relationships between Moscow and certain republics or regions, but it was not the case with resource-poor Armenia and probably Georgia, and other 'southern' republics (although Audrey Altstadt uses a variant of it in the case of Azerbaijan; A. Altstadt, 'Decolonization'). Moscow did develop Armenia in diverse ways which gave the republic a sustainable and industrial economy, at least in the Soviet context. If the internal colonialism thesis is at all applicable to Armenia, it would be in the non-economic realms of political, social and cultural relations with Moscow. After all, as David Lane demonstrates, 'The Bolsheviks attempted to equalize standards between the regions', and with some success (D. Lane, *Soviet Society*, p. 196). For a good critique of internal colonialism models see A. Orridge, 'Uneven Development', particularly Part II.

[31] C. Mouradian and A. Ter Minassian, 'Permanence de la Famille', p. 70.

[32] Ibid., p. 72. The divorce rate in Yerevan was 0.2 per cent in 1979, up from 0.03 per cent in 1960!—the rate was less in the provinces (p. 78). The number of women in the Armenian Communist Party was in the 20–22 per cent range from the 1950s to 1980s; the Soviet average was 26.5 per cent (p. 76, Table 3). Currently there are practically no women involved in the Armenian political process.

Theoretical interlude: identity and modernisation

The Soviet experience highlights quite well the difference between the two approaches to the relationship between nationalism and modernity (and modernisation). The first school of thought, best represented by Ernest Gellner, would maintain that a crucial characteristic in modernisation and industrialisation is the homogenisation of culture, and that nationalism (more specifically, the education system) is a functional tool in this process. Gellner is correct, even in the Soviet context, to emphasise the importance of homogenisation as a precondition for industrial society.[33] The second school, best represented by Anthony Smith, does not dispute this linkage, but points out that someone like Gellner cannot satisfactorily explain why (and where) the nationalism of one group emerges and not of the other. Smith argues that it is not enough to examine the requirements of modernity and industrialisation in the emergence of nations and nationalism, but it is also necessary to analyse the 'genealogies of nations'.[34] Reformulating the question in the specific context of Soviet Armenia it can therefore be asked: why did the more powerful, official and state-sponsored form of homogenisation fail—i.e. the pan-Soviet and/or Russian identity so directly tied to modernisation—but the more specific, and initially weak, national (*qua* Armenian) form of identity succeed?[35]

The perspective represented by Smith assumes correctly that a nation does indeed have a genealogy (or at the very least can 'create' one with relative ease). What modernisation does is reinforce and homogenise the pre-existing sense of collective identity. But the

[33] E. Gellner, *Nations and Nationalism*, pp. 35–8, 48–9; cf. E. Gellner, *Nationalism*, particularly pp. 25–49.

[34] A. Smith, 'Memory and Modernity', pp. 377, 375–8; cf. R. Szporluk, 'Nationalism After Communism', pp. 304–5.

[35] I do not wish to imply that the Soviet system did not at all succeed in creating certain inter- and intra-national commonalities. Valery Tishkov emphasises this point: 'The overwhelming majority of Soviet citizens shared the same (or very similar) social, political and even cultural values. On the other hand, differences in cultural traditions, industrial development, demographic behaviour and political culture managed to survive all through the Soviet period' (V. Tishkov, *Ethnicity*, p. 42, cf. pp. 109–13). Tishkov does have a point, but he overemphasises the similarities. He does not see that pan-Soviet commonalities did not transcend national divisions. Non-national identity(ies) had the most impact on minorities living outside their titular republics—such as Armenians in Baku—but *in general* such identities did not *replace* a national sense of belonging.

imperative of modernisation is ineffective in rooting an externally induced and 'nation-less' (i.e. without a genealogy) ideology—in this case the Soviet belief system. Of course many levels of identity did co-exist (pan-Soviet, national, regional, local), but there were tensions and contradictions between these. It was fairly clear in the post-Stalin period that the 'national' end of the continuum was gaining strength. A number of factors were in its favour: the deepness of ethnic sentiments, a federal system and nationalities policies that could be manipulated to favour the particular rather than the universal, national elites, intellectuals and of course the institutions of modernisation (education, mass culture, large industries, urban centres and so forth).

Maintaining and strengthening (or even creating) national genealogies requires much work. The modernising institutions of the Soviet system provided the structural basis of this process. But owing to erroneous assumptions about the pan-Soviet universalising nature of modernisation, the Soviet leadership failed to realise that far from eradicating local nationalisms the Soviet path to modernity was in fact strengthening republic-based identity.

Soviet nationalities policies

Another set of policies that in the long run strengthened national and ethnic identities in the USSR can be grouped under the rubric 'Soviet nationalities policies'—yet again a much discussed topic. These policies oscillated between the nativisation (*korenizatsiia*) programme of the 1920s and the fusion (*sliianie*) ideal of the 1960s and early 1970s.[36] Soviet central authorities, despite the stated ideological goal of a post-national communist society, never pursued a *consistent* set of policies. Simultaneous encouragement for both assimilation and cultural diversity (1970s), or an abrupt switch from one policy to the other (early 1930s, late 1940s and early 1960s), meant that neither one could be implemented successfully.[37] In the end the

[36] For an overview see H. Carrère d'Encausse, 'Determinants'; R. Suny, *Revenge of the Past*, pp. 102ff. For an interesting critique of 'Great-Russian Chauvinism' from the late 1920s see P. Rysakov, 'Practice of Chauvinism'. For the Armenian context see R. Suny, *Armenia in the Twentieth Century*, pp. 48–9, 59, 65.

[37] Carrère d'Encausse puts it well. Since Stalin 'The national elites clearly understood that the Soviet system was oscillating between federal stability (which implied a fur-

process of instituting cultural diversity won out, but in a frustrated (and hence problematic) manner. Here four factors that had a significant impact—either in their success or their failure—in strengthening national identity must be pointed out.

First, the Soviet system institutionalised blood-based ethnic identity in its internal passport system. Introduced in 1932 it made nationality a 'fixed' category for all adult citizens based on parentage. This was a biological definition of identity rather than a linguistic or cultural categorisation. Hence in the legal and administrative codes there was no civic category of a *Soviet* nationality, despite the official rhetoric. In a mixed marriage one could change from one ethnicity to another; and children of such marriages would have to choose one of the ethnic identities of their parents. But none could transcend ethnic identity altogether and officially assume a Soviet sense of 'national' belonging. This led to situations in which there were ethnic Armenians, for example in Moscow or Baku, who did not know the language, were ignorant of Armenian culture, and did not necessarily feel Armenian, yet were defined as such (even though they saw themselves foremost as Soviets). In short, the internal passport system imposed an ethnic identity onto many individuals—especially outside their titular republics—who might have been much more comfortable with a civic definition of their identity rather than any particular ethno-national categorisation.[38]

Second, and in contrast to the above, there was a clear ideological emphasis on assimilating into the dominant nationality of the Soviet Union—i.e. the Russian nation. Soviet identity had come to mean, in its cultural essence, Russian identity. The clearest manifestation of this notion was Khrushchev's advancement of the idea of *sliianie* (fusion), 'implying a biological homogenization of the

ther diffusion of power) and the "construction of Communism" (which pointed to the eventual dissolution of the federal system). Stalin's successors were unable to choose between these paths, since they could neither dispense with a national consensus nor renounce their ultimate goal' (H. Carrère d'Encausse, 'Determinants', p. 53).

[38] On the other side of the spectrum, many Armenians in the republic had so internalised this ethnic categorisation in their documents that they resented not being classified as 'Armenian' in the newly issued post-Soviet passports. As one of my informants said, showing me his brand new Armenian passport, 'Look how anti-national these people are [i.e. the government of Armenia], they don't even say what nation you belong to in your passport…'

Soviet nationalities'.[39] It was taken for granted that this process of fusion would entail assimilation into Russian culture under the guise of Soviet culture. By 1976 the term *sliianie* had disappeared from official speeches. It was replaced by the notion of *edinstvo* (unity), but already many republics were pushing for further autonomy from Moscow.[40]

The assimilationist policies did not succeed for two reasons: (a) they were usually carried out in a half-hearted manner—even Stalin, the 'breaker of nations', did not abolish national categories and; (b) the earlier processes of nativisation and indigenisation (in the 1920s), and the unofficial process of nationalisation (in the 1960s), had taken root and could not be reversed.[41] The reality was that Soviet policies and practices had given many nationalities the tools to reinforce their separate sense of ethnic identity.[42] In short, one pillar of the policy was being used to negate the other pillar. The policies of the first decade of the Soviet Union were crucial in setting the precedence and the dynamics of future developments in favour of the nationalities and not in favour of the Russian centre.

Following on from the above, the third point was the most visible manifestation of the imposed Russophilia: the 'Elder Brother' approach towards the Russians. This tendency began to emerge in the 1930s in the form of 'national Bolshevism' which reflected the preoccupation of the Party hierarchy with state building and legitimacy. By the eve of the Second World War this state ideology assumed an 'undisguised Russian orientation'.[43] Already in 1938

[39] J. Dunlop, 'Language', p. 266.

[40] H. Carrère d'Encausse, 'Determinants', p. 57.

[41] Anthony Smith analyses this failure from the perspective of competing *mythomoteurs*: the USSR did not succeed in making Russia its 'ethnic core' into which other groups could assimilate. Just the opposite, it actually 'reawakened' the sentiments of the non-Russian *ethnie* (A. Smith, 'Ethnic Identity', pp. 62, 58).

[42] For example, Tishkov points out that Soviet authorities created written languages and textbooks for approximately fifty ethnic groups. And in the constitutive fifteen republics they created a stratum of professional cultural workers (music, theatre, literature, cinema), as well as 'other attributes of national statehood' such as academies of sciences, unions for writers, mass media and publishing, university education and so forth. These 'were developed, supported, and paraded to demonstrate the success of the system' (V. Tishkov, *Ethnicity*, p. 39).

[43] D. Brandenberger and A. Dubrovsky, 'People Need a Tsar', p. 883. The defining moment of this policy was Stalin's famous speech in 1945 at the Kremlin reception

learning Russian was made compulsory in all schools, and soon after the War 'Non-Russian nationalities [were] expected to acknowledge the leading role of the great Russian people and their indebtedness to the Russian "elder brother" for their economic and cultural progress.' This became a permanent feature of Soviet public rhetoric. For example, in May 1961 Armenia's First Secretary, Yakov Zarobian, declared: 'We acknowledge with pride that the cementing force of the inviolable friendship of our people was and remains great Russia. To the liberating struggle of the Russian proletariat and to advanced Russian culture have been drawn, as to the light, all the repressed peoples inhabiting the Russian empire.'[44] It seemed that this was the 'Soviet version' of the long tradition among eastern Armenians of relying on Russia. In subsequent years the cultural element was dropped and the security factor emphasised by Armenian leaders.

The fourth and last point is the resentment many non-Russians felt as a result of these policies. Armenians, Georgians and others particularly rejected the idea that their culture was in any sense inferior to that of the Russians. Just the opposite, they argued their indigenous cultures were much deeper and richer. Furthermore, many intellectuals viewed with alarm the stated goal of long term fusion, although it was more rhetoric than reality. Even Dallakian, who staunchly supports a pro-Russian orientation as the only security guarantee for Armenia, registers his resentment at the Soviet policies of fusion. As he puts it, 'The goal was clearly decided: the fusion [or assimilation—*dzulum*] of nations, [and] the creation of a state with a homogeneous population.'[45] According to him, non-Russians rejected this trend and asserted their own national identity. It was the ultimate failure of the Soviet nationalities policy.

Demographic issues and the homogenisation of Armenia

The Armenian SSR comprised 0.13 per cent of the territory of the USSR (it was the smallest republic). Its population ratio was some-

---

for Red Army commanders in which he effectively declared Russians to be the first among 'equal' nations (R. Conquest, *Soviet*, p. 90).

[44] Both quotes are from Conquest, *Soviet*, p. 91.

[45] K. Dallakian, *Hushapatum*, p. 337.

what higher. The following Table contains some of the more important population figures of the Armenians in the USSR.[46]

ARMENIANS IN THE SOVIET UNION

1989 Census	
Total in Armenia	3,283,000
Number of Armenians in Armenia	3,084,000 (93.9%)
Minorities in the republic	Azerbaijanis (2.6%), Russians (1.5%)
Total of Armenians in USSR	4,627,000 (1.6% of union total)
Percentage living in titular republic	66.6%
Numbers in other republics	
Russian Federation	532,000 (11.5% of all Armenians)
Georgia[47]	437,000 (9.4% of all Armenians)
Azerbaijan	390,000 (8.4% of all Armenians)
Ukraine	54,000
Uzbekistan	51,000
Turkmenistan	31,000
Kazakhstan	15,000
1979 Census	
Total in Armenia	3,037,000
Number of Armenians in Armenia	2,725,000 (89.7%)
Minorities in the republic	Azerbaijanis (5.3%), Russians (2.3%)

[46] I have given the 1926, 1959 and 1979 figures to demonstrate demographic trends. The 1939 and 1970 censuses are excluded simply because they do not provide any additional information regarding general trends (the 1939 census is also suspect owing to Stalin's manipulation of the figures). The last census taken was in 1989. I have included this to provide the latest numbers. However, its figures are not as reliable as the 1979 census because it was taken amidst the population transfers between Armenians and Azerbaijanis, and it was carried out almost immediately after the massive December 1988 earthquake in northern Armenia (killing at least 25,000 people). The figures are compiled from the following sources: *SSHM Bnakchutiune*; L. Mkrtchian, *Khorhrdayin; Natsional'nyi*; S. Afanasyan, 'Demographic Evolution', pp. 137–9; B. Anderson and B. Silver, 'Demographic Sources', pp. 612, 619, and 'Population Redistribution', pp. 488ff; R. Karklins, *Ethnic Relations*, pp. 230–2; M. Matossian, 'Communist Rule', pp. 185–6; C. Mouradian, *De Staline à Gorbatchev*, pp. 164–76.

[47] For a further breakdown of the Armenian population in Georgia in 1989 see, R. Gachechiladze, *New Georgia*, pp. 74, 89–90. In the Javakheti (Javakh) area, which includes the Akhalkalaki and Ninitsminda districts, Armenians made up 90 per cent of the population (approximately 100,000 people). This area is contiguous to Armenia and subject to irridentist claims by some nationalists. In the adjacent region of Akhaltsikhe Armenians comprised 50 per cent of the population and in Tbilisi 12 per cent (150,000). There were also some 76,000 Armenians in Abkhazia, comprising 14.6 per cent of that region's population.

Total of Armenians in USSR	4,151,000
Percentage living in titular republic	65.6%
Numbers in other republics	
Russian Federation	356,000 (8.8% of all Armenians)
Georgia	448,000 (10.8% of all Armenians)
Azerbaijan	475,000 (11.4% of all Armenians)

1959 Census

Total in Armenia	1,763,000
Number of Armenians in Armenia	1,551,600 (88%)
Minorities in the republic	Azerbaijanis (6.1%), Russians (3.2%)
Total of Armenians in USSR	2,787,000 (1.3% of union total)
Percentage living in titular republic	55.7%
Numbers in other republics	
Russian Federation	255,978 (9.2% of all Armenians)
Georgia	442,900 (15.9% of all Armenians)
Azerbaijan	442,100 (15.9% of all Armenians)

1926 Census

Total in Armenia	881,000
Number of Armenians in Armenia	744,000 (84.4%)
Minorities in the republic	Azerbaijanis (10.1%), Russians (2.6%)
Total of Armenians in USSR	1,568,000 (1.1% of union total)
Percentage living in titular republic	47.4%
Numbers in other republics	
Russian Federation	183,000 (11.7% of all Armenians)
Georgia	307,000 (19.5% of all Armenians)
Azerbaijan	282,000 (18.0% of all Armenians)

In the Mountainous Gharabagh Oblast (Azerbaijan) the figures were:[48]

1989

Total	189,000
Armenians	145,450 (76.9%)
Azerbaijanis	40,700

1979

Total	161,000
Armenians	123,000 (76.4%)
Azerbaijanis	37,000

1959

Total	118,000

[48] These numbers are included in the total number of Armenians in Azerbaijan as given above.

Armenians	110,000 (93%)
Azerbaijanis	8,000

In the Nakhijevan Autonomous Republic (Azerbaijan) the figures were:[49]

1989	
Total	294,000
Armenians	2,000 (0.7%)
Azerbaijanis	282,000
1979	
Total	247,000
Armenians	3,400 (1.4%)
Azerbaijanis	239,000
1959	
Total	142,000
Armenians	9,500 (6.7%)
Azerbaijanis	127,000

The entire Armenian population in the world was estimated at around 7 million in the early 1990s. In other words, only half of the total lived in the Armenian republic.

Three important points emerge from these figures and the general demographic trends with respect to the Armenians. The first is the obvious fact that the Armenian SSR was the most homogeneous Soviet republic. This homogenisation was reinforced throughout the Soviet decades through a dual process: on the one hand Armenians moved from other parts of the Soviet Union—especially from Azerbaijan and Georgia—to their 'own' republic, where they could get better jobs, a higher education in their native tongue, live more comfortably and without discrimination.[50] On the whole, between 1970 and 1982, for example, 352,000 people moved to Armenia, while 208,000 left the republic.[51] On the other hand, for similar rea-

[49] These numbers are included in the total number of Armenians in Azerbaijan as given above.

[50] See, for example, author's interview with Amalia Petrosian, who along with her family moved to Armenia from Tbilisi in 1962. 'In Tbilisi', she said, 'we never felt at home, but here I was like a queen.' For a discussion of the general trend of homogenisation in many parts of the USSR see G. Schroeder, 'Social and Economic', pp. 293ff.; cf. V. Tishkov, *Ethnicity*, p. 40.

[51] *Sovetakan Hayastan*, p. 24. According to Anderson and Silver, the titular nationality in Armenia and Azerbaijan contributed more than 100 per cent of the population

sons, the same process took place, but in reverse: many Azerbaijanis left Armenia for their own republic. These two trends—especially the latter—were seen as a positive development by almost all Armenians. The final push to get rid of the remaining Azerbaijanis in 1988–9 is seen by Armenians in the republic as one of the most important achievements of the national movement (by the end of 1989 the entire Azerbaijani community in Armenia, over 160,000 people, had been forced to leave).[52] A number of my interviewees mentioned this point. As one of them put it, 'One benefit of this war [over Gharabagh], despite its many hardships, is that Armenia was cleaned [or cleansed] of this weed [i.e. of Azerbaijanis].'[53] The end result was an extremely homogenised republic where Armenians now comprise some 98 per cent of the population.[54]

The second point is the popular perception emanating from these figures—especially the figures that showed the exodus of

increase between 1979 and 1989 due to the heavy out-migration of non-titulars. That is to say, for every one Armenian that moved to Armenia, more than one Azerbaijani left (B. Anderson and B. Silver, 'Demographic Sources', p. 630, cf. pp. 638–40). Earlier, from 1959 to 1970, 146,000 people migrated to Soviet Armenia from other parts of the USSR; 70 per cent of them were Armenian (C. Mouradian, 'L'immigration', p. 100).

52 Conversely, the entire Armenian population of Azerbaijan, outside of Mountainous Gharabagh, had to flee—some 300,000 people. A few thousand Armenians did remain in Baku; they were members of mixed marriage families.

53 Author's interview with Gurgen Geghamian. Note that Geghamian is not a nationalist politician but an economics professor at the Academy of Sciences. His argument was put in the context of Azerbaijanis slowly taking over the Armenian countryside by occupying deserted villages left vacant due to Armenia's urbanisation. The security issue was brought in as well: that many border areas were being settled by Azerbaijani farmers. There is also an economic side to this argument of exclusion: Azerbaijanis were settling on the most fertile lands in Armenia. Nationalists justified the transfer of population with the simple rationale of 'Armenia belongs to the Armenians'—full stop (author's interview with Mushegh Lalayan, and with Artashes Shahpazian). According to one informant, Armenians in a systematic and planned manner emptied Azerbaijani villages, especially from border regions in 1988. The inhabitants, along with some of their mobile belongings, were put on buses and taken to Azerbaijani border points where they were left. I did not meet a single Armenian in over eight months of research in Armenia who saw the Azerbaijani expulsion, or the extreme homogenisation of the republic, as a problem.

54 The largest minority are the Yezidi Kurds of approximately 60,000 people. Muslim Kurds fled along with the Azerbaijanis. Yezidis are not persecuted in Armenia, and are given some cultural rights.

Armenians from their historic lands. In this context the experience of Nakhijevan became the paradigm. Whereas the Armenian population in this region was slightly less than 50 per cent at the time of its Sovietisation, by the 1980s it was around 1–2 per cent. Armenians used the term 'Nakhijevanisation' to denote the depopulation of Armenians from historic Armenia. Mountainous Gharabagh was constantly cited as the 'next Nakhijevan' if the trend was not stopped. Armenians pointed out that in the regions under Azerbaijani jurisdiction the Armenian population declined steadily in favour of the Azerbaijanis. Of course they did not mention the similar process taking place in Armenia in favour of the Armenians. The 'Nakhijevanisation' argument, and the demographic trend it symbolised, was a powerful impetus in the 1988 Gharabagh movement.[55]

The last point is the fact that Russians never constituted a significant minority in Armenia. The few Molokan villages and the handful of professionals in Yerevan were not seen as a demographic threat to the Armenian republic. One other consequence of a small Russian minority was the fact that mixed marriages were very few in the Armenian SSR. Marriages with Azerbaijanis were almost nonexistent for cultural reasons. Marriages with Russians were more acceptable, but owing to the small size of that community, they were not frequent. In 1970 the mixed marriage rate was only 3.7 per cent in Armenia as opposed to the 14 per cent Union average and the 20–24 per cent rate in Central Asia.[56]

A national and nationalising political elite

Bagrat Ulubabian, one of the most famous and earliest Gharabagh activists, tells a story of how he was spared persecution by the Arme-

[55] For example, Artashes Shahpazian made this point very clearly (author's interview). Some nationalists also use the 'Nakhijevan paradigm' with reference to Javakh, the Armenian region in southern Georgia (where some 100,000 Armenians live). The issue was discussed in such terms at a public seminar hosted at the Constitutional Rights Union in Yerevan on 29 November 1997. It was given by Karine Manukian and entitled, '*Javakhahayutian nerkayis iravichake* [The Current Conditions of Javakh Armenians]' (author's research notes).

[56] C. Mouradian and A. Ter Minassian, 'Permanence de la Famille', p. 80; cf. R. Karklins, *Ethnic Relations*, pp. 156, 162–3, 178, 214. The mixed marriage rate (mostly with Russians) among the Armenians was much higher outside the republic.

nian Communist Party leadership in the late 1960s. He had written a 150-page manuscript in 1966 detailing the terrible conditions of the Gharabagh Armenians and recounting his visit to Moscow in 1965 to secure the enclave's unification with Armenia. This unpublished semi-legal manuscript circulated among the Armenian intelligentsia in Yerevan like a *samizdat*. In 1968 the Yerevan authorities received a Russian translation of the manuscript from the Central Committee in Moscow, with a strong condemnation and an order to investigate Ulubabian. Eventually the Central Committee of Armenia 'fixed' the matter by claiming that people intent on blackmailing Ulubabian had stolen his personal notes and using them had fabricated the manuscript. Ulubabian was left in peace. The most fascinating part of the affair was when the philosopher Aramayis Karapetian, one of Armenia's most notorious 'materialists' who was unhappy with the fact that Ulubabian was getting away with it, took a copy of the manuscript to the head of the Armenian KGB. The latter, an Armenian, looked at it carefully, then 'threw it back on [Karapetian's] face saying: "Take it away, and keep it with care, we have a few of them ourselves!"'[57]

This story illustrates how the Communist authorities of Armenia played the game of advancing their national interests while placating Moscow. After the 1960s the First Secretaries of the republic were instrumental in this nationalisation process. The three names mentioned the most in this respect are Yakov Zarobian (1960–6), Anton Kochinian (1966–74) and Karen Demirchian (1974–88).[58] All are remembered in Armenia as great 'nation builders', and their achievements quickly listed: national monuments, infrastructure, industry etc. A former high-ranking party official explained:

> The role of the individual was very important in the hierarchy. Zarobian succeeded in beginning to nationalise the republic. The leaders and the intellectuals turned to the diaspora and to the church to find 'the national.' The country opened up toward the diaspora. Moscow knew this, through the party and the KGB, but it did not do much, and allowed some freedoms. Demirchian, for example, was like a governor [a '*marzpan*'] with certain local freedoms; he balanced the pressure from above and below.[59]

[57] B. Ulubabian, *Artsakhian goyapaikare*, pp. 12–13.

[58] For short biographies of these men see C. Mouradian, *De Staline à Gorbatchev*, pp. 78, 88–9.

[59] Off the record Interview II with author. Similar ideas of the local leaders being like

Of course, Demirchian casts the Communist Party—and himself—in the role of a great nation builder. As he put it to me:

> The Communists first saved Armenia from guaranteed destruction in 1920. They took it out of the mouth of the lion or the crocodile and saved it.[60] Thereafter, they began to build it up. By the 1930s the Communist leadership of Armenia had already developed a sense of national identity and [the drive for] national development. Subsequent first secretaries and other leaders continued this and strengthened it. We prepared the country for independence, to be a strong republic. Hence, we did two things: (a) kept national identity unique [*iurahatkutiun*] and developed it further, and (b) built a strong economic base; we developed [*zargatsnel*] the country. This was very obvious by the 1960s. We had an army of 700,000 labourers with very high standards.... The population increased from 700,000 in 1920 to 3.5 million. This was unprecedented.... I am very proud that as First Secretary, 20 per cent of the history of Soviet Armenia belongs to me....[61]

Notwithstanding Demirchian's ostentation, it is a fact that from the very inception of Soviet Armenia the political elite of the republic were almost entirely Armenian, including the second secretaries until 1973.[62] Therefore, despite constraints from Moscow, the leadership of Armenia could claim to be 'from the people', and on most occasions it acted as a buffer between the centre and the republic rather than a simple conduit for implementing Moscow's commands. This was not unique to the Armenian SSR, but was part of a general trend. There were numerous cases of Party and state officials, including two republic first secretaries (Georgia and Ukraine), who had 'shown a certain laxity in combating the forces of "local nationalism" and [had] pursued the "parochial" interests of their

---

'princes' were also expressed by Levon Abrahamian and Levon Mkrtchian (author's interviews). The latter also said that such leaders were 'mediators' between the centre and the republic.

[60] Demirchian was very fond of using images from the animal kingdom to illustrate a point. He also used images from the family: the people are like a child, he said; they should be guided, looked after, and when needed spanked. It is up to the leaders to do this, to prepare the people for freedom.

[61] Author's interview with Karen Demirchian.

[62] In contrast, ten of the fourteen non-Russian republics had non-titular second secretaries in 1966 (R. Conquest, *Soviet*, p. 129; R. Suny, *Armenia in the Twentieth Century*, pp. 50, 62).

fellow nationals at the expense of their all-union responsibilities.'[63] Such officials were dismissed, but this did not help, because whoever was appointed next would inevitably follow the prevailing ethos of his nation first, the Union second. This was certainly the case with Demirchian, initially seen as 'an outsider' who was appointed in 1974 to 'do house cleaning'; soon he was drawn into, and perpetuated, the local conditions.[64]

The upshot of this was that Armenia was on the whole governed by Communists with a national agenda—especially in the post-Stalin period. Generally neither they, nor the people, contrasted nationalism with communism. They saw the two as compatible.[65] Dallakian puts it forcefully in the Preface of his autobiographical book: yes, he says, there were problems, and yes, we had ideological constraints, but Armenians built their fatherland through this system. He adds: 'I reject with anger any attempt to contrast the Armenian with the Communist. All the Communists, be they members or leaders, have been the most real and most authentic Armenians during the entire seventy-year period of Armenia's development [and] the construc-

[63] J. Azrael, 'Emergent', p. 377; this was written in 1978. A decade earlier Matossian had noted: 'At present the Party [in Armenia] is very tolerant of Armenian nationalism' (M. Matossian, 'Communist Rule', p. 193.)

[64] Ronald Suny characterises this as rule by 'national "mafias" that were centred within Communist parties and state apparatuses whose reach extended throughout society' (R. Suny, 'Revenge of the Past', p. 25). Tishkov explicitly links such elites in the 'weakly modernized republics... [which have] degenerated into feudal-clan relations or produced organized criminal-mafia structures' with 'local chauvinism' (V. Tishkov, 'Inventions and Manifestations', pp. 48–9).

[65] On a more sociological level, Mary Matossian divided the politically conscious adults of Soviet Armenia in the following four categories: (1) 'Communists of Armenian birth', a small group of hard core Communists to whom nationality did not matter; (2) the 'Soviet citizen of Armenian birth' who is neither a militant communist nor nationalist, and is unconcerned with the status of the Armenians—in general such a person is satisfied with conditions; many artists and scientists fell into this category; (3) the 'Armenian Communist' who had a stake in the progress of Soviet Armenia and believed that the progress of the republic is impossible without Soviet rule, and that over time the minor deficiencies of the system would be resolved; (4) the 'fellow-travelling Armenian nationalist' who attributed economic and cultural achievements to the talent and hard work of the Armenians, but believed that Armenians were better off in the Soviet Union and nowhere else could they be such first class citizens—such a person hated and feared the Turk, and with Russian/Soviet help wanted to claim back the lost lands (M. Matossian, 'Communist Rule', pp. 192–3). This perceptive analysis was made in the mid-1960s. Over time the third and fourth categories became the most numerous and significant forces in Armenia.

tion of its national character.'[66] Even the anti-Communist nationalist leader Vazgen Manukian agrees. In a speech on a 1995 US visit he said that communism was buried in Armenia long before the July 1995 parliamentary election (which ousted the last remnants of delegates elected under Soviet rule). He then explained that the leadership in Soviet Armenia knew how to 'Armenianise' communism successfully by applying it to the Armenian character.[67]

The gap between ideology and reality

As is obvious, there was a wide gap between the policies, ideology and rhetoric of the communist system in Armenia (and other republics) on the one hand, and the 'on the ground' realities and processes on the other. My focus is only on the national dimension of this gap. A number of scholars have highlighted this point on a general level. For example, according to Rasma Karklins,

[66] K. Dallakian, *Hushapatum*, pp. 6–7.

[67] As reported in *Armenian Reporter International* (New York), 11 Nov. 1995, p. 10. Similar ideas were expressed in the author's interview with Vazgen Manukian; of the post-war generation of Communist leaders he said: 'These were pragmatic people. They did not share communist ideology so deeply—they were not Khanchians or Miasnikians [i.e. the first generation of leaders]. They did not feel a contradiction between the national and the communist.' A number of my other interviewees expressed similar views: Sergei Badalian and Tital Davrishian (both of the Communist Party) naturally lionised the role of the Communists in nation-building but without giving too much credit to the actual leaders, especially Demirchian. Razmik Davoyan, a poet with strong ARF sympathies, said that despite the awful system, in the past 20–30 years 'leaders realised that Soviet ideology was a veil… underneath which national culture and values were being built.' Levon Mkrtchian, an ARF member, said that Zarobian, Kochinian, Demirchian and even Harutiun(ian/ov) under Stalin 'had a very clear idea to use Soviet or central resources to build up Armenia.' Aram Mayilian of the National Democratic Union stated that although the Armenian Communist Party had to implement all directives from Moscow, it nevertheless tried to do its own thing and protect its own republic; for example, when several very promising gold mines were discovered in Zod, the Armenian leaders did not tell Moscow about this so that the centre would not exploit the resource and the gold would remain in Armenia. In step with the elite there was an almost universal appraisal of Demirchian and before him Kochinian as 'nation builders' among the general populace. After his assassination on 27 October 1999, Demirchian was declared a national hero. In April 2000, on his birthday, the Yerevan metro system, which was opened during his tenure, was named after him, as was the 'Hamalir' Sports-Leisure complex, which he had constructed.

...it is clear that the official notion of the emergence of a new community of people—the Soviet nation—hardly applies, and that *sblizhenie* (drawing together) is extremely limited. In so far as the outward forms of the Soviet way of life and customs are accepted it is frequently in a superficial and formalistic manner. While contacts with other ethnic groups exist, they rarely extend into the familial and communal sphere.[68]

Peter Reddaway adds: 'Many Soviet citizens lived double lives in which they said orthodox things in public, but were much more critical of the existing order in private.'[69] Even Mikhail Gorbachev admitted that the one key factor he had not foreseen when he embarked on the reform process was the rise and power of ethnic nationalism.[70]

The one scholar who saw this gap in Soviet Armenia as far back as the early 1960s is Vahakn Dadrian. In a 1963 article, based on two field trips, he commented on the nationalising dynamics taking shape in Armenia. He observed: 'Nationalism in "Socialist" Armenia is a very live force in spite of and perhaps also because of the magnitude of purges and victims inflicted upon her by the communist regime.' There is 'a keen national consciousness transcending all the hollow Socialist confines insisted upon by the communists'; and '"Socialism" seems to be a factor not reducing but rather promoting nationalism.' Successes in the fields of the arts, sciences, industry, education etc. have become 'a powerful impetus to Armenian national sentiment.'[71] Moreover, he wrote, the 'nationalist mood [in the South Caucasus,] which by definition and logic is pregnant with ethnic conflicts [...] has indeed led to a climate of persistent rivalries before as well as after the advent of the Soviet regime.' The bitterness of past conflicts is still echoed, especially verbally. There is also an 'acute' rivalry in the top echelons of the Communist Party in the South Caucasus, and ambitions for personal power are 'often transposed... to the level of national conflicts thus amplifying existing discords and tensions.' Writing twenty-five years before the Gharabagh conflict (and Ronald Suny's analysis of Soviet-style nation-building), Dadrian pointed out that the Soviets did not solve ethnic

[68] R. Karklins, *Ethnic Relations*, p. 199, cf. pp. 40, 71–2.
[69] P. Reddaway, 'Role of Popular Discontent', p. 59.
[70] Ibid., p. 60.
[71] V. Dadrian, 'Appraisal of the Communist Formula', part I, p. 8.

conflicts in the region, but they inhibited them; this led to cumulative frustrations which eventually could prove 'more cataclysmic than the precipitation of actual armed collisions.... Viewed thusly, the Soviet formula of reliance on Socialist culture as an antidote to local nationalism is at best an act of incubation, protracting the forces of conflict, and at worst an act of self-deception disregarding needed solutions.'[72]

Dadrian identifies four episodes that demonstrate the strength of nationalism and the weakness of Soviet ideology:

(1) The first generation of Communist leaders and intellectuals in the republic, in the 1920s and early 1930s, who also had strong Armenian national beliefs (e.g. Yeghishe Charents, Aksel Bakunts *et al.*).

(2) The Armenian participation in the Second World War. This demonstrated that Armenians were a brave people willing to fight against the First World War friends (i.e. the Germans) of their arch-enemies (i.e. the Turks).[73] During victory celebrations after the War the bravery of the Armenian heroes 'symboliz[ed] the bravery and genius not of Soviet citizens or communists but of the Armenian people.'

(3) The rehabilitation mid-1950s onwards of purged intellectuals and leaders. Since many of them were condemned for bourgeois nationalism, their rehabilitation was interpreted by many to mean that their nationalism was now accepted. A year after Stalin's death, Anastas Mikoyan[74] gave a speech in Yerevan and urged the Armenians to republish the works of writers such as Raffi and Charents that were earlier banned. Within months, their works were in bookshops and the 25,000 print runs immediately sold out. Mikoyan's point was that 'national nihilism' is just as wrong as nationalism. This episode showed (a) how ready and enthusiastic the Armenians were, with their latent nationalism, to answer Mikoyan's call; (b) that Mikoyan,

[72] Ibid., part II, pp. 4–5.

[73] During the Second World War 500,000 Armenians, out of a population of 1.4 million, were mobilised. 175,000 of these men died in the war (C. Mouradian, 'L'Arménie soviétique', pp. 278–9).

[74] At that point he was the USSR's Vice-Premier and Minister of Trade. Up to 1966 he was a member of the Politburo. He was also President of the Supreme Soviet (1964–5).

a high-ranking Soviet leader, harboured such sentiments himself and expressed them as soon as an opportune moment rose and; (c) that the communist formula defining the relationship between the people, the nation and socialism could easily lend itself to nationalistic interpretations.

(4) The fourth episode was the massive official celebrations in 1962 of the 1,600th anniversary of the creation of the Armenian alphabet, during which 'once more Armenia gave vent to its emotions disregarding Socialist culture and admiring the marvels of her own'[75] (this celebration will be discussed below).

I cite Dadrian at length because of all the scholars writing on the subject he was the earliest to capture—and in a very perceptive manner—the processes propelling nationalism in Soviet Armenia. However, Vahakn Dadrian did not pursue research in this field and his articles on the topic remain obscure. His line of argument regarding Armenia was only picked up and advanced further in the Western scholarly community by Ronald Suny two decades later.

My own research confirms Dadrian's findings as many interviewees mentioned the duality of life in the Soviet Union. One former Communist leader stated, 'Our public life was Marxist, our private life was "*spekulatsia*". It was a game, using Marxism for national goals, especially in Armenia.'[76] Levon Ananian, the editor of the progressive magazine *Garun* (Spring) (which constantly pushed the limits on national issues during the Soviet period) explained further. He pointed out that despite its ideological shallowness, the system still exerted much pressure. Hence,

'There was such an absurd [*anhetet*] situation [in the 1970s]. All knew that it was absurd. The anecdotes showed this. Everyone saw the many stupid mistakes at the top. But all knew that this was such a deep swamp, that it is impossible to come out of it. In 1975 or 1985 no one could even think that Armenia can come out of the USSR.... Communist ideology was such that at 7 a.m., in [the rest area of] Tzaghkatsor they collected all the school kids and shouted at them "Live like Lenin!" and the kids responded,

[75] V. Dadrian, 'Appraisal of the Communist Formula', part I, pp. 9–12. In a subsequent and more theoretical article, Dadrian generalised his findings to show that nationalism and communism were becoming 'entwined' in the USSR. Using the term 'latent nationalism', he emphasised the role of culture, education etc. in 'tuning out' the official propaganda (V. Dadrian, 'Nationalism, Communism', pp. 201ff.).

[76] Off the record Interview II with author.

"Let us live like Lenin, let us learn like Lenin!" From a young age they were instilling these ideas in the minds of the kids—and all throughout their education, up to university.'
[Question: To what extent was this believed in?]
'People had seen 1937.... The effects of 1937 were deeply ingrained. But because the effects of 1937 were weakened because of Khrushchev, there was some psychological freedom. It was not like 1937 but in all places of work there were KGB agents.... Yes, there was this duality, of freedom in the home. But the mass of the people had very little [public] freedom. 1965 did a lot to loosen people, but again they clamped down. *On the one hand you did not believe, on the other you obeyed....*'[77]

Levon Abrahamian, a political anthropologist, characterised the condition as follows:

'The Brezhnevian period resembled more a medieval system [than anything else]. Communist ideology, or becoming a Communist, was more of an initiation [into adulthood]. People did not become Communists [i.e. party members] because of ideological belief. Rather, they needed to be a member to get a position.... In the villages they drank toasts to young men to become a party member; no one there was a Communist, no one believed in it. It was just so that the young man would become a valuable part of society. Communism never played a large role with us, as in Russia. That's why there is no Communist opposition here. It was just a system adopted by the Armenian people to preserve themselves.'[78]

Needless to say, current Communists strongly disagreed with this view. According to the late Armenian Communist Party leader, Sergei Badalian, 'The Soviet ideology had completely entered into the nature (*bnazt*) of the Armenian people; it was a natural part of its psychology.'[79] In a separate interview another leading figure in the Party, Tital Davrishian, put it in this way: 'In the Armenian people the ideas of communism are found in its blood.... Communist ide-

[77] Author's interview with Levon Ananian (emphasis added). Razmik Davoyan gave a similar analysis; he too emphasised the all-encompassing and 'heavy mechanism' which functioned mostly on inertia. The communist ideology was the veil of this system (author's interview with Razmik Davoyan).

[78] Author's interview with Levon Abrahamian. It is worth noting that as early as the late 1920s Party activists in some parts of the USSR realised that Communist ideology and policies were being fused with traditional elements within (rural) society such as local family clans. For one example, albeit far from Armenia, see K. Kulov, 'Clan Survivals'.

[79] Author's interview with Sergei Badalian. Contrast this to the assertion in a television news programme in Yerevan (broadcast 14 July 1996): 'The Armenian essence does not correspond with communism.'

als are also found in Christianity—brotherhood, justice, goodness.'[80] As mentioned, such Communists maintain that national and socialist ideals are completely compatible. But they are silent on the policies of 'fusion' and the anti-nationalist rhetoric of the Soviet regime.

A final quote, from Karen Demirchian, is indicative of the gap between official ideology and personal beliefs, even at the very top of the system. Demirchian was not speaking about national issues, but the general economic problems of the Soviet system:

> 'The socialist system tried to make everyone equal. This is unnatural and unrealistic.... People are not equal in their abilities, mentality and work. Is the cat the same as the tiger? No. And socialism, as interpreted here, was trying to do this. Instead, what it should do is give an equal chance and opportunity to all. Equality in real life for all is not realistic, and when an ideology moves away from reality, the outcome is disastrous.'[81]

Even though the quote is not about nationalism, it does demonstrate the contradictions between public pronouncements and personal views. Of course Demirchian's statement—based on the classic liberal idea—could be dismissed as an *ex post facto* (and insincere) explanation of the collapse of the system in which he did so well. However, my sense of him, based on the interview, and based on what others said of him, is that he was a pragmatic man who knew how to manipulate the system for his benefit and the benefit of Armenia. The rest—communist ideology, placating Moscow, praising the Russians, internationalism etc.—was a facade that he maintained. He certainly believed in the discipline and order of Soviet rule, but these were outside this 'commitment' to communist ideology. If the First Secretary of the republic (for fourteen years), the linchpin between Moscow and Armenia, embodied such a schism between the official ideology and reality, then one realises how wide the gap was in the rest of society.

CREATING A DIASPORAN NATIONAL IDENTITY

In parallel with the nationalisation of Soviet Armenia, the newly created post-Genocide diaspora went through a similar process. If

[80] Author's interview with Tital Davrishian. The irony of this quote is that Davrishian is not even an Armenian or a Christian, but a Yezidi Kurd.

[81] Author's interview with Karen Demirchian.

what was going on in the Armenian SSR was 'Soviet-style' nation-building, in the communities abroad it was 'diaspora-style' nation-building—particularly in the 1920s and 1930s. The process was typical of elite mobilisation efforts intent on moulding a conscious nation, except that it was done outside a homeland and without state institutions. If Stalin and Russification were the main threats in Soviet Armenia, parochialism and voluntary assimilation were the main threats in the diaspora. Nonetheless, under the leadership of competing organisations, a heterogeneous group of people with fundamental differences in terms of regional identity, religion (Apostolic, Catholic and Protestant), language (Armenian, Turkish, dialects), occupation and class, social status (refugees, assimilated elites, intellectuals), political loyalties and cultural influences from host-states were moulded into a relatively coherent community with a collective consciousness as a *diasporic nation.* In short, 'Armenianness' as *the* most important identity category was either created or reinforced in the diaspora, superseding the differences within and between the communities.

Different Armenian groups around the world engaged in differing processes of identity formation in the post-Genocide period. However, the best analytical commencing point is the Armenian diaspora in Lebanon where thousands of Armenian refugees had concentrated after the Genocide. There are two reasons for this: first, the Lebanese Armenians constituted the archetypical diasporan community in the 1920s and 1930s, subsequently Beirut becoming—until the civil war of the 1970s—the 'capital city' of the Armenian diaspora in terms of its political leadership and cultural production. Second, Lebanon, along with Syria and Egypt with their similar community dynamics, was the root of many other Armenian diasporan centres throughout the world. The diasporan 'nation-building' processes in Lebanon can, with certain circumscriptions, be generalised to the rest of the newly established post-Genocide Armenian communities, including, in varying degrees, those in Europe and America.

The most extensive research on the Armenian community of Lebanon is done by Nikola Schahgaldian. He argues that until the 1930s the Armenians of Lebanon were a politically undeveloped community because they lacked 'the ability to establish common, community-wide secular and political structures based on a common consciousness of ethnic belonging as opposed to loyalties to tribe, religious sect, or provincial localisms.... [The] bulk of Armenians in Lebanon had reached in the 1920s a level of political development equivalent to that of Eastern or Western Armenians in the last quarter of the nineteenth century.'[82] However, within one generation the secularising elite did manage to create a sense of national identity and a politically integrated community. The situation was similar in other major diasporan communities.[83]

The process of formulating a modern and secular national identity, which had taken root in the eastern and western points of Armenian nationalism some fifty years earlier, continued to shape Armenian identity, but in diasporan conditions, and after the catastrophe of the Genocide. However, the main cultural influence on this group came from the 'western' and 'central' points of the triangle mentioned in Chapter 4. The ideological influence came from both the eastern and western points—the first through the exiled Dashnak leaders, the second through the Ramkavar party (Hnchaks and other organisations also played some role in this, but were not as influential). Diasporan national identity was constructed on the model of the 'organic' eastern notion of nationhood. But this newly created diaspora itself came to be identified with the western point of Armenian identity. The Genocide survivors after all were all from western Armenia. Furthermore, the eastern point was under Soviet rule and the ARF's vehement opposition to that regime meant that a substantial element of the diaspora was going to create its sense of collective identity independently of the Armenian SSR. In sum, an Armenian diasporan national identity was created in the Middle East and elsewhere which was culturally western-Armenian (except in Iran), ideologically had an eastern

[82] N. Schahgaldian, 'Ethnicity and Political Development', p. 46, cf. pp. 50–1, 54.

[83] For some of the more noteworthy publications on specific Armenian diaspora communities which touch upon issues of identity formation and maintenance in the twentieth century see A. Bakalian, *Armenian–Americans*; R. Mirak, 'Armenians in America', and *Torn Between Two Lands*, pp. 150–79, 241–54; A. Mesrobian, '*Like One Family*'; S. Atamian, *Armenian Community*, pp. 353ff.; S. Pattie, *Faith in History*; A. Ter Minassian, 'Les Arméniens de France'. For more general studies see U. Björklund, 'Armenia Remembered'; R. Dekmejian, 'Armenians', and 'Armenian Diaspora'; C. Mouradian, *De Staline à Gorbatchev*, Chapter 7; A. Ter Minassian, *Histoires Croisées*, pp. 19–48; K. Tololyan, 'Exile Governments'; K. Dallakian, *Hai spiurki patmutiun*, pp. 141ff.

conception of nationhood, and politically was separate from the Soviet Armenian 'homeland'. The diasporan Armenian that emerged from this context was quite different from the Soviet Armenian being moulded in the USSR.

Diasporan mobilisation

The Armenian nationalist leadership that had fled the Sovietisation of the republic generally found itself among a broken refugee population with little or no political consciousness, with strong regional and religious identities, a weak pan-national sense of belonging and even limited or no Armenian language skills. It also faced strong opposition from the conservative clergy and compatriotic societies suspicious of political parties and their secular and national world-view. The modernising political and cultural elite had an uphill battle on its hands to transform such a disparate people into a cohesive nation.

The main agents of this change were the already existing Armenian political and revolutionary parties, especially the Armenian Revolutionary Federation. The ARF had restructured itself and at its Tenth General Congress held in Paris between November 1924 and January 1925 redirected its activities to diasporan conditions. The party declared 1925 as the beginning of '*une période d'action pour la restructuration des nouvelles colonies dispersées et la génération des orphelins devenus adultes*', particularly in the Middle East, Greece and France.[84] Yet in a 1925 party report it is lamented that in Lebanon the 'masses are confused and pessimistic.... Our party suffers from the fact that for the first time in recent history, the ARF has lost its influence among the masses.... The religious heads, exploiting the mentality of the refugees, continually try to disrupt and neutralize secular bodies and extend their rule over them.... [making them] radically opposed to our national understanding.'[85] Similarly the secular leadership was extremely wary of thirty or so compatriotic societies in Lebanon—calling them 'useless weeds'[86]—because of their fragmenting

[84] H. Dasnabedian, *Histoire*, pp. 162–3, 152. Even earlier, at a conference in Bucharest in April 1921, the ARF elected an Executive Organ responsible for diaspora affairs. The party leadership realised that its goal of an independent and unified Armenian was to be a long term objective, and in the meantime diasporan communities needed to be organised under the party's umbrella.

[85] Quoted in N. Schahgaldian, *Political Integration*, p. 155.

[86] N. Schahgaldian, 'Ethnicity and Political Development', p. 54, n. 18.

tendencies and specific loyalties based on regional identities. However, by the mid-1930s the ARF had asserted itself as the hegemonic party in many of the diasporan communities and had succeeded, along with its competing organisations, in instilling a strong and modern sense of pan-national identity among the newly-politicised masses. The influence of religious leaders and localising organisations in terms of identity had been generally overcome.[87]

Similar to what the Bolsheviks were doing in the Soviet Union, the ARF embarked on a programme of mass mobilisation, using the youth of the Armenian-speaking refugees as their core group of supporters.[88] An intensive propaganda campaign was launched to propagate the twin ideals espoused by the party: nationalism and socialism. Ultimately the campaign bore fruit and the new generation of Armenians grew up knowledgeable of Armenian culture, speaking the language, and identifying with the nation above all else. *Then* came commitment to social justice issues, broadly situated under the rubric of socialism. This was, Schahgaldian asserts, 'the emergence of an essentially modern sense of common ethnic consciousness and belonging among the broad sections of Lebanon's Armenian population.'[89] Generalising further, Karlen Dallakian labels the 1920s to the late 1950s period as the 'self-assertion phase'. He maintains that 'the endeavour of both Armenian identity maintenance [*hayapahpanutiun*], and Armenian identity construction [*hayakertutiun*], was organised [or institutionalised] with the [self-]organisation of [Armenian] diasporan communities.'[90] Though Dashnaks were at the forefront of this process, other Armenian organisations played a similar role for their constituents.[91] The 'bal-

[87] Interestingly, the theme of combating parochialism for the sake of a united national identity remained in the ARF programme into the 1980s. In the Declaration of the 22nd General Congress of the Party (1982) there was a call 'To struggle decisively against local, parochial mentalities and the effects of degenerative external factors, and to imbue the Armenian masses of the Diaspora with general Armenian concerns and goals' ('Public Message', p. 198).

[88] In the late 1930s of the 710 party members in Lebanon 88 per cent were Armenian-speaking, whereas about 60 per cent of Lebanese Armenians were non-Armenian-speaking refugees from Cilicia. Literacy rate among Lebanese Armenians was 30 per cent, but 95 per cent among ARF members (N. Schahgaldian, *Political Integration*, pp. 157–60).

[89] N. Schahgaldian, 'Ethnicity and Political Development', p. 57.

[90] K. Dallakian, *Hai spiurki patmutiun*, p. 146.

[91] Even Karen Demirchian, the former First Secretary of the Armenian SSR, acknow-

ance' between nationalism and political ideology (socialism, communism or liberalism) might have been different, but the end result, the reinforcement of Armenian national identity, was the same.

Such national consolidation within the Armenian diaspora was taking place in Europe and North America as well, but within a different set of conditions and difficulties. The socio-cultural and political boundaries around these communities were much more porous. The host society's emphasis on integration, and many Armenians' desire for assimilation into mainstream culture, restricted the en-masse success of the nationalising elites. For example, in the United States the integrative ideology and activities of the Americanization League (between the 1910s and 1930s) competed with the diasporan parties for the hearts and minds of community members. Certain Armenian organisations and publications, such as the Protestant *Gotchnag* (Church Bell), 'strove assiduously to assist the Americanization of Armenians through educating readers about American citizenship obligations, American history, and the virtues of republicanism.'[92]

Such civic education or the Americanization League were not necessarily against the nationalism espoused by Armenian party leaders and their followers, but they certainly made integration into mainstream society much easier, especially for the younger generation. In short, immigrants in Western societies had a much greater choice to 'opt out' of Armenian identity, and out of the nation-building or maintaining project of the Armenian elite. Consequently Armenians in Europe (specifically France) and North America (specifically the United States) were caught between the need to 'fit in', as required by the host society, and calls by the community leadership to be Armenian, to be committed to the nation, and to pass on Armenian identity to the next generation. On the whole the diasporan elite did succeed in creating a core of committed Armenians with a national (and nationalist) vision who formed the

---

ledged the central role of the ARF. To paraphrase him: Dashnaks in the diaspora were doing the same thing as the Communists were doing in Armenia—they were building the nation. But as an opposition, they had more freedom to talk about things we could not talk about here in Soviet Armenia (author's interview).

92 R. Mirak, *Torn Between Two Lands*, p. 250, cf. pp. 271–86; A. Mesrobian, '*Like One Family*', pp. 125–30. Both of these studies outline how Armenians built community life in the United States, instilling and maintaining a sense of national identity through various activities and institutions.

visible and active component of these communities. But many Armenians did assimilate, and some communities dwindled or disappeared altogether—especially where there was no 'new blood' coming from the Middle Eastern diaspora.

Throughout the diaspora national identity was intertwined with the traditional political parties and the community organisations they controlled—at least until the early 1970s. These parties (Dashnak, Ramkavar and Hnchak) and their affiliated institutions saw themselves as the guardians and interpreters of Armenian political and cultural identity. As such, according to the intellectual-diplomat Jivan Tabibian, the 'interdependence between political parties... and all aspects of community life, became the norm. It is still the norm whether in Syria or Lebanon or "exported" to the US and elsewhere.'[93] Only in the past two to three decades is this norm being questioned, a reflection of new emerging identities, as will be discussed below.

Education as the means

The most important element of this mobilisation and identity reformulation process was national education. It is again possible to generalise from the Lebanese paradigm: 'The main objective [with education] was the infusion of subjective and symbolic meaning into merely objective distinctions which separated most local Armenians from the native Arab population in Lebanon.'[94] The community had to be imbued with a national world-view through which it could interpret its difference from the host society. Education was crucial in this. A number of lay (i.e. party) controlled schools were set up in populous diasporan communities. The teachers of these schools were usually party workers or affiliates, and the curriculum was set—as well as the textbooks written—by nationalist and secular intellectuals.[95] A dozen or so schools were founded in the 1920s

[93] J. Tabibian, 'Risk of Democratization', pp. 29–30.

[94] N. Schahgaldian, 'Ethnicity and Political Development', p. 55.

[95] For example, the former Prime Minister of independent Armenia, Simon Vratsian, was the principal of the famed Jemaran (a lyceum) in Beirut, established in 1930. He succeeded Levon Shant, another politician-intellectual. The Lebanese confessional system of governance allowed quite a bit of internal community autonomy (much like the Ottoman *millet* system). Hence, more than the state, Lebanese Armenian organisations controlled the community schools. The few Catholic or Protestant

and 1930s in Lebanon alone. In 1926 Apostolic Armenians had four elementary schools with a few hundred students. By 1937 there were 16 elementary and secondary schools with an enrolment of 4,600 pupils. At this point close to 2,000 Armenians were in Catholic and Protestant schools. By 1949 the Armenian Apostolic community had 29 schools with 6,500 students. Most of these schools were under the jurisdiction of the lay controlled Educational Council, which in turn was usually controlled by the ARF. According to Schahgaldian, 'The only mission of such schools was the creation of a new breed of Armenians in the image of what the party considered "true Armenians", conscious of their history and culture, well-versed in their mother tongue and dedicated to the ideals of Armenian nationalism.'[96]

There were similar attempts to educate the young into an elite-defined Armenianness in diasporan communities outside the Middle East. But once again a different set of dynamics was at play. Unlike Lebanon, in Europe and North America Armenian community schools could not exist in lieu of state-run schools. They had to provide additional tuition, almost always in the form of Saturday or Sunday schools for children, or evening classes for adults. The first Armenian school in the United States was established in New York in the 1880s. By 1932, according to one calculation, there were sixty Armenian schools in the country with 5,000 pupils and 100 teachers, excluding California.[97] These schools were mostly run by volunteers with untrained and unprofessional teachers and dreaded by the young. However, some basic knowledge of Armenian history and the church, and minimal Armenian language skills, were passed on to those who attended (a minority of the community). The situation of Armenian schools began to improve only in the 1960s in some large diasporan communities in North America with the establishment of more professionally run private day schools. These schools taught the state's curriculum, to which were added Armenian subjects. Despite the problems associated with Armenian schooling in Western societies, such national education nevertheless

---

Armenian schools were not under the control of the ARF or secular educational councils, but their own respective organisations.

[96] N. Schahgaldian, *Political Integration*, p. 165, pp. 166–7.

[97] A. Mesrobian, '*Like One Family*', pp. 131–5; R. Mirak, *Torn Between Two Lands*, p. 275.

did play an important role in shaping the identity of diasporan Armenians. At least a core group of people who symbolised and manifested Armenian nationhood in the diaspora were somewhat knowledgeable about their history and culture—if not the language. They could place Armenian identity within a much wider context than family history and traditions.

Language as the marker

The nationalist leaders of the post-Genocide diaspora realised the importance of a key cultural marker around which modern Armenian identity could be cemented. Given their secular attitudes, religion and the Armenian church could not have been the means. Language was therefore used as the common denominator, as the unifying element—more specifically *western* Armenian, its literature and intellectual traditions. Henceforth the Istanbul variant of Armenian became the hegemonic language of the diaspora (with the major exception of Iran) outside the USSR. 'Old country' regional dialects were relegated to the private sphere, the use of Turkish was condemned, and Turkish speakers were shamed into learning Armenian. It was made very clear: to be Armenian one had to speak Armenian. In this way a polyglot community was reshaped into a monolingual community. Every other language, even the Arabic of the host society in the Middle East, was considered a second language.

In western diasporan communities—e.g. in France and the United States—the linguistic challenge was tougher. As mentioned earlier, acculturation into mainstream society was much more rapid owing to pressures from the host society, more fluid borders around the community and the lack of day schools. Hence even before the First World War maintaining the Armenian language became a problem: 'The language as a living instrument was not transmitted whole to the second generation.'[98] Consequently, Armenian communities in the West could not use language as an identity marker to the same degree as in the Middle East. This led to a serious division within the European and American diaspora regarding the relationship between language and identity: how crucial was knowing Armenian to being Armenian? One side downplayed the importance of lan-

[98] R. Mirak, *Torn Between Two Lands*, p. 276.

guage, the other side—often newcomers from the Middle East—maintained its central role.[99] In such communities the Apostolic Church—as controlled by the lay community and the Armenian political parties—replaced language as the key cultural marker of Armenianness.

'…And parents learnt from their children', writes Susan Pattie about the spread of Armenian among refugees in Cyprus. It 'became a powerful cohesive force. First the drive to teach and learn Armenian spread to all in the community. Before long, speaking Armenian became not just an ideal but a reality and a standard marker of being Armenian in Cyprus.'[100] The situation was the same in Lebanon,[101] and in many other similar communities. Even though the Armenian language was particularly prone to disappear from one generation to the next as an everyday medium of communication in the western diaspora, it nevertheless retained its symbolic centrality in Armenian national identity.

Ideology as the directive

Despite the ideological divisions over Soviet Armenia (to be discussed later), all diasporan Armenian organisations in the 1920s were in agreement as to what constituted Armenian identity:

(1) As already mentioned, language was the key (often idealised rather than used in the western diaspora). Then came
(2) knowledge of—and pride in—history;
(3) commitment to the 'Armenian Cause'—which included the liberation of the lost lands in Turkey, and in the case of the Dashnaks, liberation from the Soviet yoke;
(4) the central notion of the return to the homeland (i.e. to western Armenia);
(5) activism or participation in community organisations;
(6) membership of the Armenian Apostolic church, or at the very least of the Armenian Catholic or Protestant congregations;[102]

[99] For details see A. Bakalian, *Armenian–Americans*, Chapter 4.
[100] S. Pattie, *Faith in History*, p. 52 and p. 70 respectively.
[101] N. Schahgaldian, 'Ethnicity and Political Development', pp. 55ff.
[102] The Dashnaks (and the Hnchaks) eventually dropped their more extreme anti-religious and secularising tendencies in order win people over to their nationalising

(7) belief in socialism, loosely defined, in the case of the Dashnaks and the Hnchaks, and liberalism in the case of the Ramkavars;
(8) a strong element of anti-Turkishness.[103]

These ideas were propagated throughout diasporan communities in formal and informal manners until they were internalised as the norm or the ideal.[104]

This ideology was pan-diasporan in its scope, but it could not be—despite its claims—pan-national. Obviously it was in contrast to Soviet ideology. Some diasporans did support the Soviet regime (Hnchaks, Communists and ironically Ramkavars), but the ideological premises of the two parts of the nation contrasted with one another. The division was rather sharp between the ARF, the domi-

---

cause. Recalling the role of the Mkhitarist congregation centuries earlier, the Armenian Protestants and Catholics were instrumental in separating national identity from religious (Apostolic) identity, hence indirectly reinforcing the secular nationalism of Armenian political parties. This was most obvious in the 1920s and 1930s diaspora.

103 There is no one document which outlines the 'criteria' of Armenianness. This is based on the work of scholars cited above, on ARF and Hnchak party programmes and documents, period textbooks, novels and the general Armenian media. Since the mid-1920s different points on this list have been emphasised, but the actual logic of it has remained (and remains). After the mid-1960s recognition by Turkey of the 1915 Genocide has become a central component as well.

104 One example of the ARF mobilising young Armenians along these lines is the 1930s drive in North America to establish a youth organisation. A veteran party member, and a hero from the independent republic, Garegin Nzhdeh, went from community to community establishing 'Tseghakron' cells of active youth. The word *tseghakron* is derived from 'race' and 'religion'. Anti-Dashnaks called it 'race worshipping' (with clear connotations of fascism). Sympathisers translated it as 'devotees of the race', 'followers of the race' or 'believers of the race' (S. Atamian, *Armenian Community*, p. 392; cf. pp. 388–96). The basic idea behind Nzhdeh's activities was to link the North American youth to a clear notion of national identity. His main premise was that the race, or the nation, should be considered above all else. He and the ARF initially had some success mainly due to Nzhdeh's charismatic personality. But they could not maintain the momentum in the long run. Nzhdeh, who was an anti-Soviet and anti-Turkish Nazi sympathiser, eventually left for Europe where he sought allies to overthrow the Soviet regime in Armenia. He was eventually expelled from the ARF for his extreme and racist views. The youth organisation he had helped to set up was renamed Armenian Youth Federation. Nzhdeh himself was captured by Soviet forces in Sofia in early 1945; he died in a Soviet prison in 1954. In post-Soviet Armenia Nzhdeh is considered a national hero, his racism minimised and nationalism applauded. His Tseghakron ideology is adhered to by extreme nationalists (R. Panossian, 'Past as Nation', pp. 130–6).

nant party of the diaspora, and the Communist regime of Armenia.[105] The open nationalism of most of the diaspora was not at all compatible with the ideological atmosphere of the Soviet Union. Soviet propaganda did have some influence among certain diasporan groups, but not in its anti-national variant. Moreover, between the mid-1930s and 1945 there was not even any meaningful interaction between the diasporan communities and Soviet Armenia. Since all the old Communists in the republic were purged, the elites of the diaspora and the Armenian SSR did not even know one another. Whatever limited knowledge there was of the other side disappeared in Stalin's prisons.

Between the 1920s and the early 1960s, Armenia and the diaspora did not influence each other's nation-building processes in any significant manner—except indirectly as the 'Other' to be opposed. In this respect there was no interaction or dialogue, but polarity, competition and propaganda. Whatever contact there was, it was between the Soviet regime and its allies abroad. The latter were not ideologically anti-nationalists (with some minor exceptions), and they posed neither an alternative nor a threat to the overall nation-building process taking place.

The progressive nation-building ideology of the diasporan parties soon became a conservative force after they had successfully reformulated a modern national identity. For example, as Schahgaldian writes, the ARF, once a 'socialist and modernist national movement', became a 'socially conservative, Western oriented, and pro status quo political party by the early 1950s.'[106] All it wanted was to preserve the identity it had helped to create. A new set of ARF leaders emerged who equated patriotism with anti-Turkishness,[107] pub-

[105] An important editorial from the 1930s Dashnak press sees Soviet rule over Armenia—and its followers in the diaspora—as the enemy, criticising it much more than Turkey. The Armenian Cause is interpreted more as the liberation of Armenia from the Soviet yoke than Genocide recognition and the liberation of the lost lands in Turkey ('H.H.D.', pp. 1–7).

[106] N. Schahgaldian, 'Ethnicity and Political Development', p. 58. Socialism was downplayed as the ARF came to be controlled by pro-West conservative cadres (N. Schahgaldian, *Political Integration*, p. 171).

[107] One crucial element of this anti-Turkishness is the constant struggle against Turkish influences, which continues to this day. In the 1920s the slogan was 'Speak Armenian!' In a flyer distributed by the ARF youth organisation in Lebanon in the autumn of 1999 attention was drawn to the 'serious' influences of Turkish culture on the

lic service with clientelism, modernisation with mimicking European values and lifestyles. Such ossified thinking, coupled with political inertia and rhetoric, was meant to preserve intact what was created a generation before. But it backfired. It led to the weakening of national identity as many young people wanted to leave the stagnant community. Dashnaks had come full circle: 'They all nearly ceased to play any role in the process of ethnic consolidation, identity-formation, and national solidarity among the Lebanese-Armenians.'[108] The situation was similar for the other parties, and it was the same in other diasporan communities. Ideological and political stagnation was the main characteristic of traditional diasporan organisations after the 1950s (paralleling unrelated developments in the Soviet Union). This meant that they could no longer execute their previous task of reformulating national identity. They just wanted to preserve it in a static manner in order to combat assimilation—i.e. any form of 'dilution' from the ideal of the 1920s and 1930s.

The social milieu as the setting

The social settings of the Armenian communities were also very important in the shaping of identity. These were usually close-knit and compact communities, often geographically concentrated into certain neighbourhoods, much like a ghetto. With their shops, churches, social clubs, political parties, schools, sports teams and cultural centres they became 'little Armenias' in Beirut, Cairo, Marseilles, Watertown, Fresno, and later Los Angeles, to mention but a few of the centres. Social services were also provided—from neighbourhood policing in some Middle Eastern communities (particularly when there was a breakdown of the central state) to employment opportunities for the newly arrived in the United States. Many

---

Armenians. It is then declared:

> Struggle [*paikar*] against Turkish television channels!
> Struggle against Turkish-sounding songs!
> Struggle against Turkish-inspired appearances!
> Struggle against Turkish products!...
> Let us not forget our centuries-old culture.
> Let us not forget the memory of 1.5 million victims of the Genocide...
> Let us not forget that Turkey is our enemy.

108 Schahgaldian, 'Ethnicity and Political Development', p. 60.

communities also had old-age homes, hospitals and charity services. Khachig Tololyan refers to these activities using the concept 'governments-*of*-exile'. They have, he elaborates, 'done considerable work of political organization and cultural production, of the sort that preserves, invigorates and invents the concepts, narratives and symbols that empower exiles to live on as a collective, or at least to represent their situation as such to themselves and others.'[109]

As social boundaries between host societies and many Armenian communities loosened, paradoxically a strong diasporan national identity emerged. There was a dual process of acculturation on two levels. First, at the local level, within each diasporan Armenian community some people identified themselves wholly with Armenianness, while others chose to leave the community entirely; the majority of Armenians occupied the social space between these two extremes. For example, even when many families moved away from the 'ghettos' and into the suburbs of their respective cities (especially in the post-Second World War period), they kept some contact with Armenian institutions and they certainly continued to identify themselves as part of the Armenian nation. The extent of this process of acculturation into mainstream society and/or into Armenian identity varied immensely from one community to another (especially between the Middle Eastern and the western diasporas).

Second, at the general level of pan-diasporan dynamics, dual acculturation meant that a modern sense of Armenianness was being created, particularly in the Middle East, on the one hand, but on the other there was much assimilation *out of* Armenianness, particularly in North America and Europe. In the 1920s and 1930s the alarm had already been raised by nationalist leaders regarding the assimilation of the community in the West. A Dashnak journal published in Boston in 1931 put it this way: 'In the colonies [the word diaspora was not yet widely used at this point] Armenians are denationalising [*apazgainanum*] and are denationalising at a rapid rate, especially in those colonies where Armenians are "guests" of [and] culturally subject to nations on a much higher level (America, France etc.).... It is necessary to struggle on this "front" too... and not surrender to the "enemy".'[110] The attitude is clear: we must preserve what we have

[109] K. Tololyan, 'Exile Governments', p. 167; cf. S. Pattie, *Faith in History*, p. 87.
[110] 'Apazgainatsman vtange', p. 171.

by stopping the process of assimilation so that identity can be maintained until Armenians return to their homeland. For the ARF and other national leaders the 'diaspora could not be *inknanpatak*—that is, an end in itself. Rather it was to be thought of and lived as temporary and transitory.'[111]

This dual acculturation is indicative of the weakness of a nation-building process in the diaspora that would lead to one homogeneous entity. Different social settings led to different processes. North America never became a significant centre of identity formulation on the same terms as the Middle Eastern communities. The latter's definition of national identity did become the hegemonic vision of Armenianness for at least two generations (1920s to 1960s), and it still dominates within traditional circles. Armenian migration from the Middle East to the West ensured that this variant persisted in the United States, France, Canada, Latin America etc.[112] In short, the definition of what it meant to be a diasporan Armenian that developed in the Middle East, most notably in Lebanon in the 1920s, was on the whole the 'standard' by which identity was measured throughout the post-Genocide diaspora (outside the USSR). Armenians who wished to assimilate into mainstream society, who did not know the national language, and who were not involved in community activities were considered 'lost' according to this perspective. And indeed, many did leave the community, falling altogether outside Armenian national dynamics.

However, there is another dimension to this process which suggests an alternative vision of diasporan identity based on Western social realities. National identity, like all social identities (especially in a diasporan setting susceptible to many influences), is not static.

[111] K. Tölölyan, *Redefining Diasporas*, p. 9. The name Tololyan is spelt both with and without *umlaut*-like accents. For simplicity it is spelt without accents in the text here, but with accents in notes and the bibliography for certain works to achieve consistency.

[112] The predominant demographic dynamic within the diaspora since the 1950s has been one of east to west migration and relocation: the contraction of the Middle Eastern communities at the expense of the West, namely the United States (especially in the Los Angeles area). In the last twenty-five years the size of the US Armenian community alone has doubled from close to 400,000 to 800,000 people (based on figures cited by A. Bakalian, *Armenian–Americans*, p. 14)—which is usually rounded up to one million by the Armenian press. This is approximately one eighth of all Armenians, or about one-third to one-half of the entire diaspora, excluding the countries formerly republics of the USSR.

Whereas in the Middle East Armenian identity generally remained in the traditional mould of the 1920s, in the West it evolved in new directions that questioned the norms set decades earlier. By the last quarter of the twentieth century some of the more numerous North American and European Armenian communities had evolved into centres of identity formulation in their own right. I do not wish to use the term 'post-modern' or 'post-national' because of their confusing connotations, but this new identity was in its essence different from the notions of Armenian identity developed in the modern period. It was reformulated in ways that did not fit into the image of the earlier nationalists. In this identity the 'objective' factors of language, established community organisations and politics, the church and the notion of return are not central—but 'feeling' Armenian is. Anny Bakalian, based on the work of Herbert Gans, calls it an identity based on 'symbolic ethnicity'.[113] 'Affiliation is coming to replace filiation', adds Khachig Tololyan, 'subjectively chosen identity is challenging situationally ascribed collective identity wherever possible.'[114] This much looser notion of being Armenian emerged from the open social setting of the West.

A new diasporan identity and its politics

The stagnation of many diasporan communities, coupled with social changes, led to the emergence of a new type of diasporan identity, particularly in Western societies. The very meaning of 'Armenianness' was changed and remoulded into an identity far removed from its original meaning. Importantly, the notion of the homeland, and especially the idea of return to it was no longer central. The homeland had become a culturally foreign and emotionally remote concept for most diasporan Armenians in the West. The 'host' society, conversely, had become 'home' as the boundaries around the community eroded, making it increasingly susceptible to assimilation.[115]

But this did not mean that by the 1970s the diaspora was simply withering away (although some elements were); rather, it was—

[113] A. Bakalian, *Armenian–Americans*, pp. 6ff., 44ff., cf. chapter 5; H. Gans, 'Symbolic Ethnicity'.

[114] K. Tölölyan, *Redefining Diasporas*, pp. 55–6.

[115] Parts of this and following sections have appeared in R. Panossian, 'Between Ambivalence and Intrusion'.

and still is—developing into a unique entity based on a hybrid and hyphenated identity and dual loyalties. In short, the western diaspora has evolved, and is continuing to evolve, into a conscious body in its own right, based not so much on 'objective' delimiting features such as language and other traditional cultural markers, but simply on a subjective feeling of being Armenian—and American, French, British etc.—here and now. This is not the diaspora of a concrete or existing homeland but of an idealised homeland—a 'spiritual' diaspora of a 'spiritual' homeland. For this community, 'Armenia, Soviet or free, lies in the realm of the spirit. It is an emotional link', observes Anny Bakalian.[116] Whereas in the 1920s a diasporan nation was being created based on strong emotional ties to a clearly-defined lost homeland, a language, an everyday culture and a clear nationalist ideology, what has emerged in the West, despite the efforts of the traditional politically active minority, is a hybrid Armenian entity based on a *double* imagination: a diaspora which, to borrow Benedict Anderson's phrase, is imagining an 'imagined community' found somewhere between the hostland and the homeland—with these terms themselves becoming interchangeable. This diasporan identity is suspended between the 'homeland ideal' and the realities of the host society. It embodies the tension and the duality of 'post-modern' diasporan identity.[117]

What makes this community connected to Armenianness is its active commitment to the Armenian nation (however defined) as a distinct group, its political involvement in pursuit of the national cause, its mobilisation on behalf of other Armenian communities and on behalf of the homeland. All of this is underpinned by a subjective sense of belonging to a diasporan nation, but without the real desire for return.

Against this background of cultural and sociological changes in the western diaspora, certain elements of its politics began to change as well. Under the leadership of new elites and different types of activists, politics too was 'westernised'. Political activity left the confines of the community and began to act on the wider terrain of the

[116] A. Bakalian, *Armenian–Americans*, p. 161.

[117] For an analysis of the literary manifestation of this hybrid culture see, L. Shirinian, 'Transculturation and Armenian Diaspora Writing', pp. 39–46, *Armenian-North American Literature*, and his *Republic of Armenia and the Rethinking of North-American Diaspora in Literature.*

host state and regional bodies (such as the US Congress and the European Parliament). This meant that two different planes of diaspora politics had come into being. One was the traditional but still prevalent community oriented party politics. The other was the new professional politics of campaigning, lobbying and networking as an integrated group in the political system of the host country. These two planes competed and complemented each other in the diaspora, sometimes co-existing within the same political 'bloc' or in the same party (e.g. the relationship between the ARF and the lobby group Armenian National Congress of America based in Washington).

By the 1970s the first type of traditional politics was in a rut. Having established the organisational structure of the community, politics had settled into a stagnant pattern. Essentially conservative, this element tried to preserve and protect traditional Armenian identity from assimilation and social change. Shunning innovation and unable—or unwilling—to adapt to modern (Western) politics in its mentality and organisation, it withdrew further into its cocoon and concentrated its energy on community affairs. There is an element of despair in this approach. Its official ideology centres around the importance of language, the idea of return to the homeland, 'authentic' Armenian culture etc. But the reality is the permanence of a mostly non-Armenian speaking diaspora, cultural 'dilution' and no foreseeable chance of return to the lost lands in Turkey. For this group the diaspora condition cannot be accepted, much less endorsed or celebrated. According to this view the diaspora is an abnormality, an aberration to be rectified, and yet nothing could be done about it, except to preserve it and to wait.[118]

The second type of politics, specific to the diaspora in the West, rejects the existing political conditions, and questions the fragmentation of the community caused by the traditional parties and their blocs. It takes the route of professional activism, reflecting the more

[118] There are of course exceptions to this generalisation. Vahé Oshagan, a diaspora intellectual is one. For him the diaspora is a 'homeland' to be maintained and cherished (U. Björklund, 'Armenian Remembered', pp. 353–5; V. Oshagan, 'Poles Apart', pp. 12–15; V. Oshakan (Oshagan), 'Spiurke arterkir che', pp. 1–4). There is also a group of intellectuals around the Paris-based *Haratch* (Forward) Armenian daily with similar or related views; they include Krikor Beledian, Marc Nichanian, Khachig Tölölyan and Vartan Matiossian (see, for example, the series of articles on homeland-diaspora relations in the June to September 1995 issues). These writers do not fit into the traditional mould, nor are they the intellectuals of symbolic identity.

secure and hybrid identity of one part of the community. It is led by a self-confident alliance of educated and monied professionals 'at home' in the diaspora. They seek to be a dynamic new force ushering in politics of cooperation and unity which would transcend the established divisions. Many of them are first generation immigrants from the Middle East, but educated in the West. They believe Armenian interests could be served best through the institutions of host governments and societies, through established political norms and methods. This approach generally reflects the thinking of the non-partisan 'neutral' element of the diaspora which has become quite significant, if not the majority, in most western communities. The new politics ironically implies that the diaspora had to westernise—making it more susceptible to assimilation—in order to better serve Armenian interests. This is the politics of symbolic Armenianness.[119]

The evolution of symbolic identity is much more fluid and loose than the conscious reformulation of national identity of the 1920s. There are no schools teaching symbolic Armenianness, nor are there clear-cut cultural markers. This identity is emerging from the contact and friction of traditional Armenian culture and the culture of the host-society. It is a fractured identity insofar as it is evolving in various directions in various communities. In use of language (of the host state), cultural norms, political outlook, sense of belonging etc., Latin American, North American, French, Lebanese and other Armenians differ from one another.[120]

[119] One of the most notable 'alternative' organisations founded in the United States is the Armenian Assembly of America, established in 1972 in Washington. It is not a political party, but it does play an important political role. It seeks to represent the interests of the US Armenian community in Washington; it also lobbies on issues such as Genocide recognition, aid to Armenia, legislation in favour of the republic etc. (R. Vartian, 'Armenian Face on Universal Issues', pp. 35–8). In addition, there are more specialised or localised associations of professionals (lawyers, doctors etc.), as well as research centres and compatriotic societies based on place of ancestral origin (cf. A. Bakalian, *Armenian–Americans*, pp. 140–4). Most of these independent and new organisations are US or West European-based, with limited pan-diasporan linkages.

[120] My discussion of diasporan identity has excluded the large Armenian diaspora within the Soviet Union. Armenians referred to these communities as the 'internal' diaspora; until the post-Soviet period it was not perceived as a 'real' diaspora, even though it numbered approximately 1.5 million people. The dynamics at play in these communities were quite different, and varied from place to place. In some

In addition to these two prevalent political modes, there also emerged a radical element of terrorism which took centre stage for approximately a decade before the mid-1980s. Although Armenian diasporan terrorism is a spent force, it played an important part in nationalising and radicalising a generation of young Armenians. It emerged in the Middle East in the context of regional radicalism and in response to the stagnation of Armenian political parties—particularly the gap between the rhetoric and actions of the ARF (with its revolutionary ideology but conservative politics). This movement sought to shake Armenians out of their torpid state, and to put the Armenian cause (Genocide recognition and lost lands) back on the agenda of world politics. It was primarily driven by nationalist demands. The wave of terrorism in the diaspora (1975–85) did not have any substantial influence on the advancement of the Armenian cause internationally. Its primary audience remained, as was intended, the Armenians of the diaspora.[121] The main victims of the attacks were Turkish diplomats (some 33 were assassinated) and Turkish interests. The two organisations most active were the

---

cases there were no community structures at all (e.g. Central Asia), in other cases there were Armenian schools and cultural organisations (e.g. in Tiflis/Tbilisi and Baku). However, in terms of centres of Armenian identity, the internal diaspora did not play a significant role—even Tbilisi ceased to be a major centre in its own right, but dovetailed Yerevan, 'exporting' its brightest intellectuals to Armenia (author's interview with Ruben Torosian and Yuri Poghosian). The internal diaspora was culturally an appendix to the national hub of Yerevan, to where it had easy access. This diaspora, especially where there were no community structures, was quite susceptible to linguistic Russification and assimilation. However, it is important to note that the identity of many of these Armenians was reformulated in a denationalised direction under the pervasive influence of Soviet ideology. Armenians outside their titular republic, particularly in large cities like Baku and Moscow, assumed the identity of a Russophone Soviet citizen. There are no major published studies of the 'internal' diaspora; until the collapse of the USSR the topic was taboo in Soviet Armenia. In the post-Soviet period the number of Armenians living within the former Soviet republics, especially Russia, has increased substantially through economic migration out of Armenia. It no longer makes sense to speak of this diaspora as 'internal'. A more appropriate term would be the 'post-Soviet' diaspora. In the past decade or so it has become an important economic actor in its support for Armenia. It has also begun to organise politically. The post-Soviet Armenian diaspora is an understudied subject requiring much more research (cf. R. Panossian, 'Courting a Diaspora', pp. 142–4).

121 K. Tololyan, 'Terrorism', and 'Cultural Narrative'; cf. M. Gunter, *Pursuing the Just Cause of Their People*; F. Hyland, *Armenian Terrorism*.

Armenian Secret Army for the Liberation of Armenia (ASALA) and the Justice Commandos of the Armenian Genocide (JCAG). The latter acted against Turkish targets, while the former broadened its tactics and attacked Western interests in the 1980s. ASALA was responsible for at least two attacks in Turkey (at Ankara airport and in Istanbul), an assault on Orly airport in Paris and some other bombings of civilian targets including shopping centres in Paris; these caused the death and wounding of innocent civilians. Over a ten-year period the victims of Armenian terrorism numbered around 200. In addition to the 33 Turkish diplomats assassinated, some 30 civilians were killed (half in the Ankara and Istanbul attacks) and 100–200 people wounded.[122] Most diasporans found terrorist attacks against civilians repugnant, but a good number of Armenians showed some sympathy for acts committed against Turkish diplomats.

Interestingly, terrorism did have a profound resonance in Soviet Armenia, with widespread verbal support for it among the intellectuals and the masses. Famous poets such as Hovhannes Shiraz and Silva Kaputikian (who penned *The Lisbon Martyrs* and *Night Requiem* respectively) wrote and published poems in the Soviet Armenian press dedicated to the fallen activists who carried out the terrorist acts.

The Gharabagh movement that began in 1988 completely supplanted the diasporan terrorist movement as it became the main focus for nationalist demands. Many of the terrorists from this period—often viewed as freedom fighters by the more radical Armenians—entered nationalist 'folklore' on a par with turn of the twentieth century *fedayees*, and with the volunteers who fought in the Gharabagh war of 1991–4.

Theoretical interlude: the modern diaspora

As has been argued throughout the book, the Armenian diaspora played a crucial role in the creation and maintenance of national identity. However, the concept of 'diaspora' itself needs to be analysed at this point in order to clarify its meaning. There is a growing body of literature on the subject, and the term itself has recently

[122] Exact numbers are difficult to come by. Lists of the attacks are maintained by various Turkish sources: cf. www.ermenisorunu.gen.tr/english/diplomats and www.atmg.org/Armenian \Terrorism.html.

acquired wide usage often referring, in a confusing manner, to historic diasporas (Jews, Armenians etc.), as well as ethnic minorities, asylum seekers, refugees, economic migrants and similar groups outside their 'home' state. Therefore, it is imperative to provide a more precise definition.

The 'classical' definition of diaspora emphasises the forced dispersion of a clearly identified group of people from their homeland, with a distinct collective memory and a 'myth' of return. The group maintains its collective identity by establishing and controlling boundaries around it, while maintaining communication with other similar communities and the homeland.[123] This restrictive definition is countered on the other extreme by Walker Connor's simple assertion that a diaspora is 'that segment of a people living outside the homeland'.[124] The first limits the definition to the historic 'ideal type' cases of the Jews, Armenians, Greeks and Palestinians. The second extends the term to all people living outside their land of origin. The transnational conditions of late twentieth and early twenty-first centuries do indeed require a reworking of the term 'diaspora' from its restrictive parameters, but going as far as Connor entails the loss of the term's analytical usefulness. A middle ground position, which I would take as the basis of my definition, is offered by Gabriel Sheffer: 'Modern diasporas are ethnic minority groups of migrant origins residing and acting in host countries but maintaining strong sentimental and material links with their countries of origin—their homelands.'[125] However, there are some additional points to be made as highlighted by the Armenian case.

The first is that the reason for leaving the ancestral lands—or one diaspora location for another—is not limited to coercion. Certainly the post-Genocide diaspora was created because of the most extreme

[123] For further elaboration see Khachig Tölölyan's account of the 'paradigmatic' definition of diaspora and his critique of it (K. Tölölyan, 'Rethinking *Diaspora(s)*', pp. 12–15); cf. W. Safran, 'Diasporas in Modern Societies', pp. 83–99.

[124] W. Connor, 'Impact of Homelands upon Diasporas', p. 16. Robin Cohen's definition also falls in this wider conceptualisation of diasporas (R. Cohen, *Global Diasporas*, p. ix). Cohen provides a list of 'common features' of diaspora which are inclusive enough to incorporate 'victim diasporas' (e.g. Armenians) as well as 'imperial diasporas' (e.g. British colonisers) (pp. 26 and 180ff.).

[125] G. Sheffer, 'New Field of Study', p. 3. For a similar definition, but with an emphasis on the political dimension see Y. Shain, 'Ethnic Diasporas', p. 814.

form of violence. However, historically Armenians have left their homeland for various other reasons. People usually do get uprooted because of some traumatic experience, be it violence or extreme economic difficulty, but the *fact* of migration—leading to diasporacisation—is more important than the reason for leaving.

Second, an emotional and/or real link is maintained with the homeland, as well as with other communities of the same ethnic group throughout the world. Such connections could range from simple interest in the affairs of various parts of the dispersed community to family bonds and organisational ties. Such links lead to a sense of belonging to a much larger collective than the local community. A diaspora constitutes a web of socio-cultural connections—often intertwined with economic and political ties—that incorporates the local into the global community.

Third, a diasporic identity is not merely an extension of the homeland. It is rather (consciously or not) created as a diaspora, as I have demonstrated above with the Armenian case. 'A diaspora is never merely an accident of birth,' says Khachig Tölölyan.[126] Much like identity formation in a nation-state, the *diasporan* entity is constructed through the work of intellectuals and organisations.

Fourth, a certain amount of communal solidarity is preserved through the creation and maintenance of boundaries either by the diaspora community itself or by the host country, and often both, leading to hybrid identities and dual (political-cultural) loyalties.[127] These boundaries do shift and could differ from one diaspora location to another. But there is a conscious attempt not to assimilate, at least not completely, into the host society; complete assimilation is seen as an undesirable problem.

Fifth, diasporas have a 'cause' to pursue outside (but possibly connected to) the politics of the host country. This cause relates to 'their' nation, be it in the homeland or elsewhere. The community mobilises around 'The Cause' in varying degrees, more or less on a regular basis. Such political—or historical—concerns for 'national issues', and for related activities, differentiate a diaspora from ethnic

[126] K. Tölölyan, 'Rethinking *Diaspora(s)*', p. 30, cf. pp. 13, 15.

[127] G. Sheffer, 'New Field of Study', pp. 9–10; Y. Shain, 'Ethnic Diasporas', p. 815; K. Tölölyan, 'Rethinking *Diaspora(s)*,' p. 14; J. Armstrong, 'Mobilized and Proletarian Diasporas', pp. 394ff.

communities. Benedict Anderson has coined the phrase 'long-distance nationalism'[128] to denote such nationalist mobilisation in the host country on behalf of the homeland found elsewhere.

Finally, the last point is the *subjective* nature of diaspora identity and the sense of belonging it entails. This is a crucial factor, and similar to the subjective component of national identity discussed in the Introduction and throughout this book. It makes the diaspora community conscious of its existence *as a diaspora*, and not merely an ethnic minority group. Furthermore, it acts as the basis of the feeling of connectedness—be it real or imagined—between diverse parts of the diaspora and between the diaspora and the homeland, however defined. This provides a sense of unity as one nation and a sense of belonging to a collective identity, no matter how multi-located or diverse the various actual communities are. As such it transplants the sense of belonging from a specific home*land* and onto the terrain of a diasporic transnational entity which continues to maintain—and indeed insists on saving and nourishing—a sense of national identity, but *without necessarily* the idea of return. Hence the myth of return to the homeland loses its meaning in many cases (either quickly or gradually) and is no longer an operative concept with any deep emotional resonance, if any appeal at all, especially for the younger generations. It becomes an 'eschatological concept' much like the Second Coming.[129] But the subjective identity, importantly, entails a responsibility to survive as a conscious collective, as part of the nation, and a sense of responsibility towards members of the same national group, wherever located.

The above definition is centred on the internal dynamics of the diaspora, and not on the external boundaries imposed on it by the host society/state.[130] While the latter cannot be neglected, the drive to maintain some distinctiveness, some boundaries to avoid complete assimilation (i.e. 'fitting in' without 'disappearing' as a collective), comes from within. The host society might or might not be accommodating, but the impulse to keep a separate identity lies within the walls of the diaspora community.[131] But these walls are not rigid, nor

[128] B. Anderson, *Spectre of Comparisons*, pp. 72–4.

[129] W. Safran, 'Diasporas in Modern Societies', p. 94.

[130] For an approach which emphasises the external dimension, the host society's attitude toward minority groups, see W. Connor, 'Impact of Homelands upon Diasporas'.

[131] Diasporas are of course susceptible to wars, imperial divisions of territory, depor-

are the differences between a diaspora and an ethnic community so clear cut. Assimilation into the host society does take place, sometimes at an alarming rate (as far as diaspora leaders are concerned), particularly where the cultural differences between host and diaspora are not too stark. Diasporic and ethnic identities are fluid constructs in relation to one another, shifting and overlapping, that can differ both spatially and temporally between and within communities.

In sum, diasporan communities are conscious entities *qua* a diasporan identity; they are more specific entities than ethnic communities or minorities. Diasporas are connected and mobilised around their nation, their national cause and their homeland in a much more profound manner, insisting on the preservation of their identity (however defined). It is for this reason that victims of mass violence, economic migrants, political exiles, third and fourth generation immigrants, all in various parts of the world, mobilise around the idea of their nation-in-diaspora, despite many objective differences among them.

Between the early 1920s and the late 1980s *two* types of Armenian identity, broadly conceived, took shape and were reinforced, both particular to the settings in which they emerged. In Soviet Armenia and in the diaspora, Armenian identity was strengthened and the nation was built through various mechanisms. There was a conscious effort to do this. The federal structure of the USSR, modernisation, nationalities policies, demographic trends and a nationalising elite were all key factors in this process in the republic. A parallel process took place in the diaspora, but in more open and diverse conditions.

The history of the post-Genocide Armenian diaspora is one of simultaneous integration and disintegration, identity formation and reformulation. Some of the old centres of cultural production continued to operate (e.g. the Mkhitarists of Venice and Vienna), some declined (e.g. Istanbul) and others emerged (e.g. Beirut, Marseilles and later Los Angeles). They were all instrumental in the formation of an Armenian identity that was diasporan and national. In short,

tations, state policies and persecutions that might very well destroy the community. As with all minorities, weaker states and society at large, their fate is determined by the powers that be.

they succeeded in continuing the work of late nineteenth century intellectuals in creating a modern Armenian nation, even in conditions of exile, based on traditional cultural and political markers. In Soviet Armenia state institutions were used for the same purpose of identity building, but within the confines of communist ideology and politics.

National identity, like other forms of collective identity, is a changing phenomenon, subject to many—often divisive—influences. Two factors demonstrate this. First, fundamental differences of identity emerged between the homeland and the diaspora owing to the historical roots of the diaspora and variations of dialect (eastern and western Armenian) and language (speakers and non-speakers of Armenian), as well as differences in historical memories, cultural markers, tastes, work ethic and so forth. And second, the diaspora itself evolved in a heterogeneous manner. The influences of host cultures and states in each community are undeniable in terms of habits, food and music, perceptions of Armenianness and world outlook and, very importantly, in terms of belonging.

This leads to the possibility that members of one nation could have more than one 'homeland'—i.e. more than one root national identity and more than *one way* of belonging. For example, a diasporan Armenian's homeland can alternate between, or simultaneously be, the *host*-land, the home-*land*, or the diaspora condition itself as *home*-land. More specifically, by not having the idea of homeland fixed on one spot, a typical diasporan Armenian in the West might consider the homeland to mean the ancestral village in the Ottoman empire, the city of birth in the Middle East (or elsewhere), the country of residency or citizenship, present day Armenia, or the ideal of an Armenia to be—and probably a combination of all of these.

In Armenia itself there is a clearer conception of a homeland with visible boundaries and state institutions. Since its independence in 1991 the predominant discourse among Armenians has come to emphasise the republic as the homeland to which the diaspora is 'attached' by default. But only fifteen years earlier, during the Soviet period, the very idea of a homeland or fatherland in Armenia had a built-in crucial ambiguity: the overlap between the wider 'fatherland', i.e. the USSR, and the Armenian republic. The ambiguity does not end there. Many people in Armenia (and not just in the diaspora) trace their ancestry to historic western Armenian lands in Turkey, and view these territories as part of the more abstract homeland—even though, more generally, the 'lost lands' in Turkey are receding further and further into the background of collective memory. Moreover, irredentist views by certain nationalists regarding Armenian regions in Georgia (Javakheti), and the successful secessionist movement in Gharabagh (1988–94) and the enclave's declaration of independence, also demonstrate that even in Armenia, a clearly defined state, the notion of homeland is somewhat fluid.

Despite such ambiguities in Armenia and profound divisions in the diaspora, differences and competing identities, a sense of belonging to the same nation—of being, or feeling Armenian—still prevails. There is a thread that connects various diasporan communities together, as well as the diaspora as a whole to Armenia (and vice versa). In short, it makes it possible to speak of 'Armenianness' in the context of *one* nation. This thread is the subjectivity of national identity, the idea of belonging to one particular nation despite real differences in everyday culture and in the ways in which one can belong.

Perhaps the power of the thread comes from the fact that Armenians have very deep historical roots as a (persecuted) collective deprived of their homeland, of a state, and hence constantly feel either the insecurities of a diaspora existence or the precariousness of existence in an occupied or insecure homeland. Having an identity on the edge, that is, being on the threshold of disappearance, is a powerful incentive not to disappear—a dominant theme in twentieth century Armenian literature.

Despite the integrative forces of the past eighty years, the old multilocal pattern of identity formation remained among the Armenians.. The east/west cleavage not only survived, but was further reinforced through the Iron Curtain. It was expressed through the homeland/diaspora division, acquiring the additional level of a diasporan identity. The latter itself differed from community to community, the biggest difference being between the settlements in the Middle East and in the West. As will be discussed in the next chapter, when the thaw between Armenia and the diaspora came in the 1960s, it did not alter the basic tenets of identity in either half of the nation.

The Armenian case shows that in the formation, strengthening and maintaining of national identity, having a large and organised diaspora is as important as having (and perhaps even interchangeable with) state institutions. In the absence of 'objective' factors making up a nation on its own land, or in its own nation-state, the diaspora replaces them with a subjective sense of belonging. But if the diaspora has historically replaced the role of an independent nation-state in issues relating to national identity, it has done so for only one half of the nation in most of the twentieth century. The other half has had a state in one form or another. That state itself played a key role in maintaining and even augmenting feelings of subjective unity and belonging by viewing the diaspora as an extension of itself despite, once again, the realities of difference. Overall, then, Armenians are presently divided between various sets of institutions, polities, imaginations, cultures etc., each set itself fragmented along political lines. But they all maintain they are one nation, bound by a subjective sense of belonging.

The estimated population of Armenians in the diaspora was 3.5 to 4.5 million in the early 1990s. This is no more than a guesstimate in the absence of any reliable data. Of the seven to eight million Armenians worldwide, approximately 25 per cent live in the West (Europe, Americas and Australia—this figure was 1 per cent in 1914 and 11 per cent in 1925), 8 per cent in the Middle East, 20 per cent in former USSR countries, excluding Armenia. Less than half of all Armenians live in Armenia. In the mid-1920s close to 11 per cent (300,000) of all Armenians (2.5–2.8 million) lived in the Middle East and a similar number were in the Balkans.[132]

[132] For various estimates see A. Bakalian, *Armenian–Americans*, pp. 145–6; G. Bournoutian, *History of the Armenian People*, vol. II, pp. 177–89; C. Mouradian, *L'Arménie*, p. 111; C. Mouradian, *De Staline à Gorbatchev*, pp. 169–70; Amalia Petrosian, *Hayern Ashkharhum; Sovetakan Hayastan*, p. 27.

7

STRENGTHENING NATIONAL IDENTITY, SOVIET STYLE, 1921–87

Armenian identity was reinforced and reformulated, and the nation 'built', through a multitude of specific mechanisms in Soviet Armenia: the dissident movement, historiography, national art and literature, language, textbooks and education, monuments and rituals, the church, and more broadly national(ist) intellectuals. These were the key (but by no means the only) mechanisms through which national identity and even nationalism were manifested, undermining official Soviet ideology. Such factors were not in themselves unique. Most were generally applicable, in varying degrees, to the other republics in what was the Soviet Union (and can be used as bases of comparison). Of course the degree of importance of each factor was specific to the Armenians, as were some of the issues such as Gharabagh, Genocide recognition and diasporan repatriation.

On the diasporan side, new communities emerged while others declined, but nationalism on the whole continued to be articulated. Relations between the republic and the diaspora remained problematic throughout the Soviet period. Much of the conflict evolved around control over the church in the diaspora, and over the right to speak on behalf of the entire nation. A major 'repatriation' drive brought many diasporans to Armenia in the 1940s, but the schism between the two entities did not abate all that much, at least not until the 1970s. Profound divisions remained—and still remain—between the republic and important sectors of the diaspora. At the heart of these tensions and adversaries lay the crucial issue of the legitimacy of Soviet Armenia as the 'homeland' of all the Armenians.

The first part of this chapter analyses the various factors and mechanisms that played an important role in the strengthening of national identity in Soviet Armenia. The second part focuses on the Armenia-diaspora relationship. However, it is important to begin with a very specific Armenian event which set the stage for the subsequent nationalist revival: the 1965 protests in Yerevan.

1965: A TURNING POINT

April 1965 had profound repercussions for Armenian nationalism around the world, and it was a linchpin between fear and national assertion in the Soviet republic. On the 50th anniversary of the Genocide, Armenians 'woke up' and began to demand justice, recognition and their lost lands. The most dramatic development was in Yerevan. For the first time, and after intense behind-the-scenes lobbying by the republic's leadership, Moscow had allowed the Armenians to commemorate the Genocide. An official but relatively low-profile event was organised in the Opera building, attended only by the political leadership and prominent intellectuals. However, this one event was the catalyst that set loose the forces of nationalism in Soviet Armenia. While the official ceremony was taking place, 100,000 to 200,000 people spontaneously gathered outside, chanting 'Our Lands! Our Lands!' (i.e. western Armenia) and 'Justice! Justice!' (i.e. Genocide recognition). Some of the protesters turned violent, smashing the doors of the Opera building and rushing in. The official event was disrupted, the political leadership fled, and only Catholicos Vazgen I who was in the audience managed to calm the crowds. None of the officials, from Moscow to Yerevan, had realised that Armenians, constrained for so long, were going to unleash their emotions so suddenly and so powerfully.[1]

All scholars of Armenia refer to 1965 as an important moment. But many of my interviewees mentioned it as the turning point in the nationalisation process in Armenia. For example, Amalia Petrosian described how she (then a postgraduate student) and many aca-

[1] V. Dadrian, 'Nationalism in Soviet Armenia', pp. 246–7. There was also a Genocide commemoration, accompanied by minor disturbances, in Moscow on 24 April 1965. After a memorial service in the Armenian chapel students marched to the Turkish embassy and demanded that it lower its flag. The very first (and unofficial) commemoration of the Genocide in public in Soviet Armenia had taken place in 1961 when 22 individuals (intellectuals) had gathered around Komitas's tomb in the 'Pantheon' of Yerevan (Sargis Harutiunian, 'Ailakhohutian akunknerum', part II, p. 4).

demics had 'secretly' gathered in the small theatre of the Academy at 10 a.m. on 24 April 1965:

> 'It was quite something, for the first time people and academics were discussing the Genocide. All were awed, that the Genocide was being talked about openly. Then Paruir Sevak [the famous poet] leaped onto the stage and recited his poem written for the occasion: *We are a few, but we are Armenian*! There was dead silence. It was a miracle. From there, with great enthusiasm, we went to the Square and the Garden of Komitas [near the Opera].'[2]

This drive and enthusiasm stayed with Armenians and was expressed in many ways in subsequent years. Of course the outburst was denounced by the Soviet authorities and the First Secretary of Armenia, Yakov Zarobian, was dismissed a year later for failing to curb such a public and disorderly expression of national sentiments; there were also a number of arrests of the more 'extreme' elements.[3]

However, 1965 left a number of important legacies for the subsequent evolution of Armenian identity and nationalism. First, it propelled Soviet Armenia to the forefront of Armenian national and nationalistic issues, especially with respect to the preservation of identity and the commemoration of the past. The 'new nationalism'[4] in Armenia was directed through, and guided by, the Soviet Armenian state. The expression of Armenian identity was therefore in accordance with, *and* constrained by, the 'rules of the game' of the Soviet system—even though the rules themselves were getting looser over time. After 1965 nationalistic forces—mostly expressed through culture and history—could not be suppressed in Soviet Armenia; they could be controlled or manipulated, but they could not be stopped.

[2] Author's interview with Amalia Petrosian. Other interviewees who mentioned the importance of the April 1965 events include Levon Abrahamian, Levon Ananian, Galust Galoyan, Paruir Hairikian, Vazgen Manukian and Aram Sargsian. Sevak's poem (which was later set to music) ends with these words:

We are
We will be
And continue to multiply.

[3] R. Conquest, *Soviet Nationalities Policy*, p. 101. Paruir Hairikian says the authorities 'decapitated' the movement (author's interview with Paruir Hairikian).

[4] The term is borrowed from R. Suny, *Looking toward Ararat*, pp. 178ff; cf. R. Suny, *Armenia in the Twentieth Century*, p. 78.

Second, as a result of the above, Armenian nationalism never evolved in an anti-Soviet or anti-Russian direction. Hostility was directed against the Turks, and it was therefore not seen as a threat to the Soviet state. In fact Armenian anti-Turkishness often fitted the political goals of the USSR in its condemnation of the NATO ally Turkey.[5] With the exception of a few dissidents there never was a call for independence (until mid-1988) in Armenia. And in the diaspora, as will be discussed below, the ARF's criticisms of the Soviet Union decreased substantially after the mid-1960s.

Third, the 1965 demonstrations in Yerevan and subsequent official commemorations of 1915 in Armenia gave a new meaning to the Genocide. It was elevated from the personal and psychological level to the collective, official and political level. The diaspora had been commemorating the Genocide since the late 1910s. But after 1965 the commemorations were *reformulated*. Explicitly politicised in the diaspora, and implicitly in Armenia, the Genocide became the core of what it meant to be Armenian in the political domain (it was already central in the cultural, religious and psychological domains). Henceforth the personal experiences of a dying generation were passed onto the younger generations in a systematic and coordinated manner (annual commemorations, history texts, literature etc.). In addition to the traditional realm of 'grandmother stories', the Genocide was placed squarely in the realm of collective identity. Private grief was transformed into a key symbol of Armenianness on 24 April 1965. The power of the symbol was greater for diasporan Armenians because they were the descendants of survivors. The Genocide was at the core of their identity. In Soviet (formerly Russian) Armenia this was less so.[6]

[5] Certain analysts, mostly of the anti-Soviet persuasion, maintain that this anti-Turkish orientation was 'given' to Armenian nationalism in the 1960s through the conscious but subtle efforts of Moscow. In this way, the argument goes, the centre successfully directed the emerging Armenian nationalism away from independence and anti-Russian/Soviet sentiments, and towards Turkey and territorial demands; this eventually led to 'pro-empire' thinking in both Armenia and the diaspora (Sargis Harutiunian, 'Ailakhohutian akunknerum', parts I and II).

[6] Levon Abrahamian uses the last point to highlight differences between the identities of Armenia and the diaspora. He says that despite the symbolic power of the Genocide in Armenia, 24 April has not penetrated the identity of Armenians in the republic as much as the identity of diasporans. But Abrahamian adds an interesting observation.

The Yerevan protests did not occur in a vacuum. They were a product of the post-Stalin thaw and the slow emergence of national issues in the late 1950s and early 1960s. In the next twenty-five years this revival gathered momentum and was reinforced through the dialectical relationship between the Soviet state and Armenian nationalists. While the latter pressed on, the state tried to steer national sentiments in a 'safe' direction, putting a brake on more radical or anti-Soviet expressions.

THE KEY FACTORS AND MECHANISMS IN BUILDING NATIONAL IDENTITY

The dissident movement

Teresa Rakowska-Harmstone distinguishes between '"orthodox nationalism," i.e. ethnic nationalism which seeks recognition and maximum accommodation within the system[, i.e. it] is "orthodox" in the sense that it poses no threat to the basic principles of Marxism-Lenininism,' and '"unorthodox nationalism" [which] combines national self-assertion with rejection of the political system and is frequently coupled with the civil rights movement and separatism.' Since 1956, she adds, orthodox nationalism has been 'tolerated', but unorthodox nationalism 'invites immediate suppression'.[7] Soviet Armenia was no exception. Since 1963 there have been three waves of dissident movements, each taking national demands a step further—Armenian 'dissidentism' was always concerned with national issues.

The first wave, the 'affair of the Seven', started to organise in 1962–3. Seven men were soon arrested and condemned to prison sentences ranging from one-and-a-half to five years. According to

For some in the diaspora, Armenians became 'real' Armenians through the Genocide; hence Armenians of the republic are not 'real' Armenians (author's interview with Levon Abrahamian). I had not come across this observation before, but had sensed the reverse perspective among some people in Armenia: that the diasporans are not 'real' Armenians because they had not experienced Stalinism. It seems that for some Armenians some sort of suffering is essential to affirm national identity.... One of my informants in Yerevan constantly referred to 'Armenians bearing the cross' for being the first Christian nation.

[7] T. Rakowska-Harmstone, 'Study of Ethnic Politics', pp. 21–2.

one of them, their sentences would have been much more severe (10–15 years) if it was not for the behind-the-scenes intervention of First Secretary Zarobian.[8] They had not reached the stage of establishing a formal organisation or hammering out a programme. They were a group of intellectuals who wanted to 'scratch the surface of the national issue'. They primarily raised the question of uniting adjacent 'Armenian lands' in the Soviet Union to the Armenian SSR (Gharabagh and Nakhijevan from Azerbaijan, Javakh from Georgia); the lands in Turkey were to follow later. Other issues raised were Genocide recognition, the fear of Armenia's Russification and the move to reinforce 'national feelings' among the Armenians. Independence from the USSR was not raised and was treated 'with caution'. Although only seven people were arrested and found guilty, 189 people were questioned in connection with the group. After their release this group did not continue their dissident activities. Upon their return from prison, they had already observed how much more open and national Armenia had become.[9]

Unconnected to them, the second wave began on 24 April 1966 in the home of Sergei Khachatrian, its main leader being his brother, Haikaz.[10] It was more organised, and a secret 'party' was founded called *Azgayin Miatsial Kusaktsutiun* (National Unity Party [NUP]). It actually managed to publish a single issue of a paper called *Paros* (Lighthouse). It too was based on the land issue and a sense of betrayal that the Soviet regime was not, at the very least, transferring Nakhijevan, Gharabagh and Javakh to Armenia, not to

[8] Apparently, the families of the arrested people had good links with Zarobian's sister (author's interview with Khachik Safarian).

[9] Based on author's interview with Khachik Safarian. Parts of the trial of the Seven were published in the Armenian press after independence. Safarian also made available to me a seven-page letter he had written to First Secretary Demirchian in March 1975. This letter is a good example of the semi-official nationalism which was tolerated but not publicised. Its basic gist is that 24 April should be made even more of a significant day of remembrance—i.e. an official 'national day of commemoration', with the appropriate set of activities, educational work etc. It adds that the government's job should not be considered over with the construction of the Genocide monument. The letter also criticises the persecution of groups pursuing the 'Armenian Cause' in the republic since 1963. In essence, it uses 24 April and the Genocide commemoration (safe issues) as a platform through which wider national questions can be discussed (not so safe topics), but it does not make any overt nationalist demands (K. Safarian, 'Hayastani').

[10] Author's interview with Sergei Khachatrian.

mention claiming the Armenian lands back from Turkey. This, according to Khachatrian, made them turn against the Soviet regime. But the NUP went much further and advocated Armenia's independence from 'foreign domination', from the 'Russian domination of slavery [*rusastani strkatirakan gerishkhanutiunits*]'; they wanted a 'free, independent and politically neutral republic' that would maintain friendly relations with Russia and other neighbours.[11] Haikaz Khachatrian, along with co-founders Stephan Zatikian and Shahen Harutiunian, was arrested in 1968. Khachatrian was condemned to five years imprisonment. According to his brother, he came back a broken man. But his torch was picked up by Paruir Hairikian.[12]

Hairikian ushered in the third wave of the dissident movement, becoming the best-known Armenian dissident, both nationally and internationally. He joined the NUP in 1967 and a year later, at the age of nineteen, became its leader when the others were imprisoned. Arrested in 1969, he spent the next twenty years in and out of jail—but mostly in. He was even exiled from the USSR in 1988, and then pardoned two-and-a-half years later. Vehemently anti-Soviet, he consistently advocated Armenia's independence. His supreme goal was self-determination, particularly national self-determination, which he regarded as the most basic human right. From his viewpoint the root of all evil in relation to Armenia was the Soviet empire. He rejected arguments that the Soviet Union played a positive role in Armenia's development.[13]

[11] P. Hairikian, *Azkayin Miatsial Kusaktsutiun*, p. 5; D. Kowalewski, 'Armenian National Unity Party', pp. 364–6.

[12] In the mid-1960s a dissident movement also re-emerged in the Mountainous Gharabagh Oblast. Its main goal was unification with the Armenian SSR based on grievances of Azerbaijani discrimination (H. Tchilingirian, 'Nagorno Karabagh', pp. 442–4). Any such manifestations were severely denounced by the Communist Party leadership in the *Oblast* appointed by the Azerbaijani branch of the Party ('Nagorno-Karabakhia's Ideological Flaws', p. 3).

[13] Author's interview with Paruir Hairikian; cf. 'Secret Political Trials'. Hairikian was one of the very few people who rejected outright the thesis that the Soviets built-up Armenia. As he put it during the interview, 'To say that under Bolshevism we have had any kind of tendency of national statehood is completely false and a lie. There has been a state apparatus in Armenia, but not an Armenian state. That has been an administrative unit of Armenian speakers under Moscow's rule, without the minimum right of self-determination.'

Through Hairikian and some of his associates the dissident movement survived (but barely) until the late 1980s. In 1988 it was overtaken by the mass Gharabagh movement. But he and his small group of associates are the thread which connects elements of current Armenian politics with the NUP. From the ashes of the latter Hairikian founded in the spring of 1987 his National Self-Determination Union (NSDU), which began to operate relatively openly. The NSDU has obtained 3–8 per cent of the vote in subsequent elections in Armenia.[14] Others active in the dissident movement also became prominent politicians after independence. Ashot Navasardian (who had joined the NUP in 1968 and who had served seven years of a twelve-year sentence for such activities) established the nationalist Republican Party in 1990. He had also been active in the military defence of Gharabagh. On his death in 1997 another NUP veteran, Andranik Margarian, became the leader of the Republican Party. He was appointed Armenia's Prime Minister in May 2000.[15]

The dissident movement did not capture the imagination of the Armenians, neither in the republic nor in most of the diaspora.[16] Its

[14] Hairikian tried to make the most of his fame, and his association with the NUP, in Armenian politics. See, for example, *Paruir Hairikian*, a booklet on him obviously published by his supporters on the occasion of his first bid to be elected president of Armenia in 1991 (he received 8 per cent of the vote). It heavily draws on his dissident past. In the 1987–90 period the NSDU was one of the most active publishers of semi-legal papers, journals and leaflets in Yerevan—e.g. it published a newspaper called *Ankakhutiun* (Independence), a monthly magazine (May 1988 onwards) called *Hairenik* (Fatherland) and various other booklets and papers. 200–300 copies would be secretly printed on state-owned presses by printers who were paid plenty of money to do the job as 'after hours' work. At this point, being caught by the police did not lead to anything more than a reprimand. (Author's interview with Zohrap Aghapapian)

[15] Author's interview with Andranik Margarian; cf. D. Kowalewski, 'Armenian National Unity Party', pp. 364–5. In the mid-1970s the dissident movement split. The Hairikian 'wing' advocated peaceful means to achieve independence. Some of his followers or sympathisers worked through the Armenian branch of the Helsinki Group established in Yerevan in April 1977. The Zatikian 'wing' (it is assumed) advocated terrorism against the USSR. In January 1977 a bomb exploded in the Moscow metro, killing seven people. Stepan Zatikian, Hakob Stepanian and Zaven Baghdasarian were arrested, put on trial, and immediately shot. Their executions were announced two years later (R. Suny, *Armenia in the Twentieth Century*, pp. 79–80). The debate on their guilt or innocence continues to this day. For example, two long articles on the issue, translated from the Russian press, were published in the *Molorak* (Planet) newspaper (Yerevan), 2 and 3 December 1997. Armenians on the whole maintain that the three were innocent. However, outside some limited circles these men are not viewed as national heroes.

[16] One informant relayed a story to me which is indicative of the lack of popular sup-

call for independence and its anti-Soviet position never resonated among the population or the intellectuals. Most Armenians viewed the Soviet regime more as protection against Turkey than as an oppressive force to be resisted. Eventually the Gharabagh movement, with its own leadership, outpaced the dissidents. After some fame and popularity between 1987 and 1990, its *cause célèbre*, Paruir Hairikian, was dismissed as more of a buffoon than a serious politician. Arrogant and full of self-righteousness, he was viewed as a man of the past.[17] After 1991 his main cause—independence—was no longer relevant and all he could do was rest on his laurels and proclaim, 'I told you so, I was ahead of the times.' But Hairikian and his associates and followers did keep the flame of independence burning, however weakly, *in* Soviet Armenia. Without being part of the mainstream, or 'orthodox', nationalism, they nevertheless helped to push its limits further and further. Their unorthodoxy was suppressed, but it did help to loosen the constraints of Moscow on Armenia.[18]

Historiography

The Armenian Academy of Sciences was founded in 1943 (on the basis of the Armenian branch of the USSR Academy of Sciences

---

port dissidents had in the late 1960s: 250 leaflets were put in people's mailboxes; 225 of them ended up with the KGB because people voluntarily brought them in to 'avoid headaches'.

[17] For example, in the aforementioned booklet about him, *Paruir Hairikian*, he is called the 'Jefferson of his time' (p. 1). He was pretentious enough to suggest that Moscow began the Gharabagh movement to put a stop to him and his party, by redirecting national sentiments away from independence and on to the Gharabagh issue (author's interview with Paruir Hairikian).

[18] The activities, speeches, arrests and trials of the dissidents received some coverage in the diasporan press, particularly among the Dashnaks (for one example see A. Ter Minasian, 'Ailakhohutiune Khorhrdayin Hayastani mej'). The *Armenian Review*, in addition to articles on the subject, also published a regular section called 'Soviet Armenian Chronicle', which covered the dissidents (cf. vol. 27, no. 2, summer 1974, pp. 209–10; vol. 27, no. 4, April 1975, pp. 435–7; vol. 33, no. 2, summer 1980, pp. 179–80). But there is no evidence at all that diasporan groups had any links with the dissidents—at least not until the outburst of the Gharabagh movement in the late 1980s. ARF's nationalists ideology was considered by many dissidents as their 'guide' or as the basis of their moral legitimacy. They were often accused of being 'Dashnak nationalist-chauvinists' by the regime.

which was established in 1935). It soon began to publish a number of distinguished journals. The quarterly *Patma-banasirakan handes* (Historical-Philological Journal) was launched in Yerevan in 1958. It became a trend-setting journal for historians, linguists, philologists and for scholars in the humanities in general. This influential journal brought together all branches of Armenian studies, systematically consolidating research on culture, ancient law and philosophy, architecture, language and history.[19] From 1967 to 1984 the massive (8-volume) *History of the Armenian People* was published by the History Institute of the National Academy of Sciences under the directorship of Galust Galoyan and with the participation of some 130 experts.[20] Much earlier Yerevan State University was (re)opened in January 1921 with Armenian as the language of instruction. Beginning with 255 students, by the late 1970s it had 13,000 students.[21] Since 1927 (when it acquired a proper printing plant) it has been a major publisher of academic texts.

These were some of the institutions in Soviet Armenia through which national history was produced. For example, referring to the *History of the Armenian People*, Galoyan says: 'It was written with great national spirit', and is 'hugely beneficial to the nation', despite its shortcomings and enforced ideological flaws.[22] Although the volumes mostly dealt with the relatively 'safe topics' of ancient history, linguistics and art, they were nevertheless instrumental in instilling a sense of ancient grandeur and pride, and even a sense of frustrated history.[23] Moreover, academic institutions and research

[19] V. Barkhudarian and S. Harutiunian, 'Haygitakan Handese', p. 7; cf. J. Greppin, 'Armenian Studies', p. 399.

[20] Author's interview with Galust Galoyan.

[21] J. Greppin, 'Armenian Studies', p. 399.

[22] Author's interview with Galust Galoyan.

[23] Another source of much pride was the fact that *The Great Soviet Encyclopaedia*, and school and college history textbooks, identified the South Caucasus as the oldest ethnic region in the USSR. Armenia was specifically mentioned as the oldest civilisation on the territory of the Soviet Union, as the most ancient birthplace of art and culture, and specific mention was made to Ejmiatzin (V. Dadrian, 'Nationalism in Soviet Armenia', pp. 212–13, 216). Armenian experts systematically gathered information on all the ancient monuments in Armenia (mostly churches and monasteries). Some were renovated with state funds (e.g. the pre-Christian Garni temple), others through the private endeavours of citizens and ethnographic societies (for a multi-volume and multilingual detailed study of ancient Armenian monuments published by the Academy of Sciences see *Hayastani hnagitakan hushardzannere*.

circles were also centres in which intellectuals gathered and semi-privately discussed national issues. For example, an Armenian Cultural Club was set up in Yerevan State University in 1967; it became a forum for young nationalists. Many of the leaders of the 1988 movement had been through the 'curriculum' of this Club (Vazgen Manukian, for example, was a key member).[24]

Astute observers of the Soviet Union identified this post-1956 trend in the approach to the study of national history: 'Writing primarily in national languages, minority historians have begun to utilize archival materials to rewrite history from the national viewpoint. The new approach revives past national glory and achievements and frequently sheds dubious light on the past and, by extension, also on the present role of the Russians.' This 'battle of historiography' was particularly visible in the Ukraine, the Caucasus and Central Asia.[25] Valery Tishkov goes further (perhaps a bit too far) and highlights the explicitly one-sided nature of this endeavour: 'Most of the national histories, encyclopaedias, and cultural research churned out during recent decades [i.e. before the 1990s] reflect little of the people's actual history and ethnography. These texts and beliefs have been intended mainly to legitimize politically constructed ethnonations and their "own" states.'[26]

An important element of 'the battle of historiography' was the writing of the history of the titular nation—i.e. the minorities in the republic were 'forgotten'. Furthermore, it was the history of a *national people* irrespective of where they lived—i.e. it included the people of the titular nationality who happened to live in other

[24] Sargis Harutiunian, 'Ailakhohutian akunknerum', part III, p. 4; author's interview with Vazgen Manukian. In addition to the university or academy based intellectual centres, there was also a 'rapid increase in the membership of republic and local ethnographic societies' that aimed to preserve and renovate architectural and historical monuments (J. Azrael, 'Emergent Nationality Problems', p. 377; cf. J. Dunlop, 'Language, Culture, Religion', pp. 276–7). Such volunteer associations were the popular and the activist side of the emerging nationalist historiography.

[25] T. Rakowska-Harmstone, 'Study of Ethnic Politics', p. 28. In the case of the Armenians and the Azerbaijanis, the most vehement historiographical battle was over the origins and the descendants of the long disappeared (by the tenth century) Caucasian Albanians. They were the indigenous population of the Gharabagh region. Who Gharabagh 'belonged' to was based on who the Caucasian Albanians were (for details of the debate see S. Astourian, 'Search of their Forefathers').

[26] V. Tishkov, *Ethnicity*, p. 15.

republics. For example, Armenian historians did not write about Azerbaijanis living in Armenia, but they did write about Armenians living in Azerbaijan, Georgia etc.[27]

This approach was rooted in the Soviet perspective on ethnicity and national identity. The latter was 'heavily dominated by the primordial approach' whereby ethnicity was considered 'an objective "given", a sort of primordial characteristic of humanity.' There was even the view that 'a recognition of group affiliation is included in the genetic code and is the product of early human evolution.'[28] Accordingly, national histories were written that assumed that 'ethnoses [i.e. ethnic identity] are a *sine qua non* of all human evolution, of all existing political and cultural structures, of contemporary collective and individual strategies.'[29] If the 'ethnos theory' was the cultural side of the argument, the structural side was of course the Marxist-Leninist approach to historical evolution. National issues had to be situated within dialectical materialism, class analysis and, in the twentieth century, the economic benefits of socialism. The model in this respect was the official *History of the USSR*.[30]

The best way to demonstrate the post-Stalin emphasis on the national dimension in historiography is to examine its formulation in a specific text. In this respect one of the earliest works is a book by M. A. Melikian called *On the Question of the Formation of the Armenian Nation and its Socialist Transformation*, published in 1957.[31] The author still maintains Stalin's categories in the definition of a nation (i.e. historically constituted with a common language, territory, economy and psychological makeup), but argues that this long historical process was not confined to Russian Armenia. Hence the need to examine national evolution under different social conditions of the same people. It is then asserted that the *ethnos* can be old

[27] M. Saroyan, *Minorities*, pp. 141–4.

[28] V. Tishkov, *Ethnicity*, p. 1; cf. V. Tishkov, 'Inventions and Manifestations', pp. 42–3. He criticises the main Soviet proponents of this approach: Shirokogorov, Gumilev and Bromley (V. Tishkov, *Ethnicity*, pp. 2ff.). For a systematic treatment of Soviet ethnography and the work of Yulian Bromley see also E. Gellner, *State and Society in Soviet Thought*, particularly chapter 6.

[29] V. Tishkov, *Ethnicity*, p. 4.

[30] S. Velychenko, 'National History', pp. 26ff.

[31] M. Melikian, *Hai azgi kazmavorman*. All references to page numbers in this and the next paragraphs are to this book.

and pre-modern, but nation-formation is a modern phenomenon—i.e. from the seventeenth to the nineteenth century (p. 7). This formation is analysed through the Stalinist categories, but one of them is highlighted as the factor that can explain the persistence of a distinct identity in the face of external homogenisation and internal divisions: the unique psychological dimension of Armenian national identity (pp. 66–9). This gives the nation a deep sense of belonging, rooted in historical evolution (pp. 204–5). Clearly, then, 'psychological makeup is not class based, but a pan-national factor which is unique to all the classes of a nation' (p. 205). Although Melikian does not say it, the implication is clear: national identity, as understood through ethnos, is supra-class, it is unique, it unites a people, and it is applicable to co-nationals who live outside the borders of its state. To prove the point, he takes the example of the Armenian diaspora. Diasporan Armenians might not be on the same territory, they might be living under capitalist economies, nevertheless they remain part of the Armenian nation (p. 224).

The other side of Melikian's argument is to show how Soviet rule has reinforced the Armenian nation, using each of the Stalin criteria to prove his point. The Soviet system has strengthened the Armenian language (pp. 199–200); it has given Armenians a state territory which has become 'the fundamental central locale of Armenians scattered throughout the world' (pp. 201–2); it has given the nation economic growth and social development (pp. 202–4) and finally; it has further strengthened the unique psychological makeup—under Soviet rule 'the specific and unique characteristics of the Armenian culture were cultivated which distinguish the mentality of the representatives of the Armenian nation from the mentality and mode of operation of the representatives of other nations' (pp. 204–5). In all of this nationhood is being rooted and entrenched further. In Melikian's book there is one in-passing reference to the 'higher stage' of national fusion or merger (*miadzulum*, the Armenian word for *sliianie*).[32]

32 Another interesting example of the national 'creeping in', whenever there was a thaw, is a book published in 1945 on the twenty-fifth anniversary of Armenia's Sovietisation (Z. Grigorian, *Sovetakan Hayastane*). Amidst the standard glorification of Stalin and the Soviet system, the point of reference is the Armenian nation, its progress, survival and development through Soviet aid and guidance. One already sees the cracks

In the diaspora, two genres of historical literature were produced. Many works were published in Armenian, which were the memoirs or analyses of revolutionary and/or national leaders (e.g. Rouben, Armen Garo, Simon Vratsian [*Gianki Ughinerov*]), historical novels (e.g. Malkhas' *Zartonk*) and books written by 'amateur' historians (e.g. Mikayel Varandian, Gabriel Lazian and Arsen Kitur). The second genre consisted of the work in non-Armenian languages of professional academics usually based in universities (e.g. Nina Garsoïan, Mary Matossian, Vahakn Dadrian, Richard Hovannisian, Claire Mouradian). The first category was prevalent in the pre-Second World War period, the second in the postwar period. The second benefited from some of the original research done in Soviet Armenia. For the first, the reverse was the case—many of the books published in the diaspora, especially by Dashnak presses, were banned in Armenia. However, some were smuggled in and read as *samizdats*—particularly the memoirs of Dashnak leaders.[33] After the Second World War such texts were also read on the Armenian programme of Radio Liberty.

To conclude, national historiography in the Soviet Union was a curious mix of constructivism and primordialism. As Valery Tishkov puts it, 'During the Soviet period there were plenty of opportunities to design ethnicity, or to construct "ethnoses."'[34] The past was politicised, manipulated and at times created to fit with an ideology that was simultaneously structuralist and primordialist (when it came to nationhood). Nationalist historians used these mecha-

---

in the 'national in form, socialist in content' formula. For example, in the section on Soviet Armenian literature the first verse quoted is from Avetik Isahakian:

> *Your brilliant and powerful future*
> *Is like a lightening in front of me.*
> *You are forever Armenia*
> *Your name sweet and noble.* (p. 82)

Moreover, even the necessary quote from Stalin ending the preface is chosen to reflect this attitude. It is taken from *Pravda* of 4 Dec. 1920, two days after Armenia was Sovietised. Stalin had said: 'Only the idea of Soviet rule brought to Armenia peace and the possibility of *national* rebirth. Long live Soviet Armenia' (p. 21, emphasis added). From the 1960s onward such books openly talked about the successes of the Armenian nation.

33 Author's interview with Razmik Davoyan.

34 V. Tishkov, *Ethnicity*, p. 20.

nisms to reinforce their particular national identity. More often than not history was a weapon, or at the very least a tool, through which national rights were defended and advanced. Many of these 'weapons' were put to use to educate and to fuel the Gharabagh movement in 1988.[35]

Art and literature

Throughout the Soviet Union Marxism-Leninism had lost its appeal as an inspiring ideology after the Second World War. People were turning towards other belief systems that had a deeper resonance with their identity. According to John Dunlop, the 'increasingly irrelevant and "cold" ideology' of the state was being challenged 'by an appeal to nationalism or a combination of nationalism and religion'. Consequently, 'Nationalism and religion are increasingly, if cautiously, being utilized by Soviet writers, artists, and filmmakers to fill an obvious void.'[36] Armenian cultural workers were at the forefront of this trend.

As elsewhere in the Soviet Union there were no 'starving artists' in Armenia. The cultural elite generally lived well as long as they worked 'within' the system. Popular writers sold their works in print runs of 25,000 to 100,000 (sometimes overnight), while lesser known artists were at the very least guaranteed an income.[37] Of course many of these artists had to produce the required and standard glorifications of the Soviet system; Soviet literature is full of such examples. But there was also a very powerful nationalist trend in the arts in many republics.

I cannot adequately deal with the vast output of 'nationalist' works in Soviet Armenia. All branches of culture were affected:

[35] For example, Academy of Sciences historians mobilised in the spring of 1988 and within months produced a booklet, in Russian, on the history of Gharabagh and its Sovietisation. The authorisation to disseminate the publication was given very reluctantly by the Armenian Central Committee—it conceded only after mass protests. This was the first official publication on Gharabagh in decades (author's interview with Galust Galoyan). The book is called *Nagornyi Karabakh. Istoricheskaya Spravka* (Mountainous Gharabagh. Historical Report). Yerevan: Armenian SSR Academy of Sciences, 1988.

[36] J. Dunlop, 'Language, Culture, Religion', pp. 273 and 278.

[37] D. Kouymjian, 'Status of Artists', pp. 54–7. Cultural workers, just like every other work sector, were organised through unions. Kouymjian points out that the system was abused by union bosses, who treated the union as their own 'domain' and power base.

film,[38] theatre,[39] opera,[40] the fine arts,[41] music[42] and of course literature. It is the latter that I will examine by looking at some of the works of some of the more famous poets who had a huge impact on Armenians both in the republic and in the diaspora. The key themes that emerge from this literature are love of language, pride in Armenian history and culture, irredentism towards the lost lands in Turkey (especially the symbol of Mount Ararat), the need for unity, the beauty of Armenia and praise of Soviet Armenia as *the* national centre of *all* Armenians.

The paradigm of this genre of poetry and literature in the post-War period was set earlier by Yeghishe Charents (1897–1937), the most celebrated twentieth century Armenian writer. In 1920 he had penned the poem, *Yes im anush hayastani* (To My Sweet Armenia), which in the post-Stalin period became one of the most popular Armenian songs. In a 1933 poem entitled *Patkam* (Message), which sang the praises of socialist progress, he had cryptically written his real message: 'Oh, Armenian people, your only salvation is in your collective strength (*Ov hai zhoghovurd, ko miak prkutiune ko*

38 As D. Kouymjian ('Status of Artists', p. 54) puts it, 'The films [produced by HaiFilm Studio] are often national in content.' Cf. L. Micciché, 'Cinema', pp. 300–1; J. Dunlop, 'Language, Culture, Religion', pp. 276–7; author's interview with Artashes Shahpazian.

39 According to Sos Sargsian, a famous actor, stage director and the ARF's presidential candidate in 1991, 'After all, during these 70 years we were able to keep the essence of national theatre.' He then adds: 'The national is pan-human', it is not 'parochial' (Sos Sargsian, 'Piti ashkhatem', p. 5).

40 One example is Tigran Chukhajian's (1837–98) *Arshak II* opera which was constantly staged in Yerevan (D. Lang, *Armenia*, p. 256)—with a modified libretto. Another example is Armen Tigranian's (1879–1950) *Davit Bek* opera. Of the latter the *Soviet Armenian Encyclopaedia* writes, 'In the opera patriotism (*hairenasirutiun*), the heroic struggle for the liberation of the fatherland, bravery and love of freedom, as well as the friendship of the people (Armenian, Georgian, Russian) is praised' (vol. 11, p. 701).

41 For example, the work of Martiros Sarian (see V. Dadrian, 'Appraisal of the Communist Formula', part I, pp. 13–14).

42 For example, the acceptance into the canon of the pre-Genocide work of Komitas (1869–1935), the recording of the church liturgy and hymns, not to mention the setting to music of popular patriotic poems (e.g. Yeghishe Charents' *To my Sweet Armenia*, Paruir Sevak's *Sardarapat* and *Yerevan-Erebuni*, Hovhannes Shiraz's *Gharabagh*), and the composition of popular songs in praise of Armenia (for examples of the latter category see *Heghapokhakan yergaran*, pp. 195, 200–1, 220; K. Hannesian, *Heghapokhakan yergaran*, pp. 193–8; A. Ghaziyan, *Hai zhoghovrdakan*). The music of the most famous Armenian composer in the USSR, Aram Khachaturian, is a combination of the 'dialectical' and the 'national'.

havakakan uizhi mej e).' Charents lost his life in the purges, but his message and his patriotism, which he had dared to maintain even at the height of Stalinism, became a rallying cry for Armenians (even though his name could not be publicly uttered in Soviet Armenia until 1954).[43]

Hovhannes Shiraz (1914–84) published his *Knar Hayastani* (Lyre of Armenia) in 1958. There were of course the required poems to Lenin (p. 307), but there was also a whole section in the volume entitled *Hairenakan* (National). Shiraz, as with many other writers, was playing on the ambiguity of the term *hairenik*, meaning 'fatherland'. It could have meant the Soviet fatherland—i.e. the USSR—or (Soviet) Armenia (p. 308). But there are many poems which are unmistakably Armenian, with very strong nationalist overtones, especially with respect to Mount Ararat (in Turkey) and the irredentism it entailed. One of the most forceful poems is called *Ktak* (Bequest). Some of its lines are:

My son, what should I bequeath you? what should I bequeath, my boy?

...

I want to will you such a treasure as a father,
That no other father can will you in another country,

...

I will bequeath you our mountain, that you take it out of black clouds,
So you bring it home [based on] pure justice,

...

I am willing you Masis [i.e. Mount Ararat], that you keep it forever,
As the language of us Armenians, as the pillar of your father's home.[44]

Shiraz was also concerned with the Armenian language. Its importance is emphasised in a poem on people's names (pp. 440–6). He chastises people for giving their children foreign names instead of pure Armenian ones. This poem is an interesting mix of the glorifi-

[43] There is much literature on Charents. For a basic analysis see D. Gasparian and Zh. Kalantarian, *Hai grakanutiun*, pp. 23–69; G. Goshgarian, 'Eghishe Charents'; R. Peroomian, 'Expressions of Nationalism', p. 9. The poem *Message* is reprinted, among other places, in G. Lazian, pp. 428–9; one sees the 'message' by reading down the second letter of each line.

[44] H. Shiraz, *Knar Hayastani*, p. 46. There are many other poems with national themes, including one entitled 'To Ararat' (p. 353), and another which mentions the glory of Tigran the Great (p. 352).

cation of the Russians, for protecting Armenians against the Ottoman Sultans, *and* the glorification of the Armenian language:

If it had not taken us under its wings
Our protector, the light of our eyes,
The giant Russian pillar of our back,
Of peace
The victorious giant,
Who was exclaiming, O my son,
Even if you learn a multitude of languages,
Do not forget your mother tongue…

It concludes:

Because names in each nation
Are its costume, its language,
Its eternal holiness.
And it is the law of all humanity,
Whoever does not love that of his nation
Is the enemy of all nations.[45]

The theme of language and irredentism was also prevalent in the works of Paruir Sevak (1924–71) and Gevorg Emin (1919–99). Sevak, who never adhered to the official line with as much ease as the other prominent writers, died in a mysterious car accident. His collected works were published posthumously in six volumes. Sevak was lionised by the Soviet Armenian establishment as a great poet and patriot.[46] In a series of celebratory poems called 'Armenian Language', written in the early 1960s on the occasion of the

[45] H. Shiraz, *Knar Hayastani*, pp. 441–2 for the first verse, p. 446 for the last verse. Another noteworthy poem by Shiraz, from the early 1980s, is called *Hairenapakh Noyi agravnerin* (To Noah's Crows Escaping the Fatherland). It is a powerful and emotive attack on the Armenians emigrating from Armenia to the West. It combines irredentism, nationalism and the negative elements of exile or diaspora existence. The poem was reprinted in the diaspora press (see *Hairenik* [Fatherland] [Boston], 25 March 1982). When Shiraz died, he was given a huge state funeral (see *Haireniki Dzain* [Voice of the Fatherland] [Yerevan], 21 March 1984, for one example of a special issue devoted to him).

[46] For example, in the 28 March 1984 issue of the weekly *Haireniki Dzain* (Voice of the Fatherland) (Yerevan), there are a number of articles devoted to his 60th birthday. They emphasise the national character of Sevak. In the centre of the middle spread there is a quote by him which begins: 'There is no deeper feeling than love of the fatherland…' (p. 5). For a sympathetic biography of Paruir Sevak see L. Hakhverdian, *Paruire.*

1,600th anniversary of the creation of the Armenian alphabet, Sevak wrote:

> *He who calls you mother-tongue is blissful.*
> *Lucky is he who talks and judges through you,*
>
> ...
>
> *Not I, it is not I who masters you.*
> *You are, it is you who masters me—*
> *For ever and always!*
> *And now as well,*
> *Through you, you are glorified...*[47]

Emin, on the other hand, laments the division within the Armenian nation and its lands in a poem called *Menk* (We) dated from 1980:

> *What are we, after all,*
> *We and our land?*
> *Even if we try to mince the truth!*
> *We are tourists in our own land.*
> *Guests in our own homes.*
> *A river with only one bank,*
> *A mountain which we only view from afar,*
> *An unpeopled land,*
> *A landless people,*
> *And scattered beads which cannot be restrung.*[48]

Finally, Silva Kaputikian (born 1919), the grand lady of twentieth century Armenian poetry, is the perfect example of the Soviet Armenian intellectual who bridged the gap between nationalism and communism on the one hand, and culture and politics on the other. A longstanding Party member, she was also a prominent figure in the initial stages of the Gharabagh movement. Winner of the Stalin Prize for literature in 1952, and yet the people's 'representative' who was summoned by Gorbachev in 1988 to calm the

[47] As quoted in D. Gasparian and Zh. Kalantarian, *Hai grakanutiun*, p. 309.

[48] G. Emin, *We*, p. 50. The reference to 'A river with only one bank' is to the Arax and Akhourian rivers which mark the borders between Armenia and Turkey, separating (Soviet) Armenia from historic Armenian lands. The mountain viewed 'from afar' is of course Mount Ararat, clearly seen from Yerevan. Emin was one of the most successful writers who combined the Soviet with the national. His work was widely translated into English by Soviet publishers. For two examples see G. Emin, *Songs of Armenia* and *Seven Songs about Armenia*.

passions of the Armenian protesters. By the summer of 1988 she was already being booed by the crowds for being too conservative, pro-Russia and 'establishment-oriented'.[49] In post-independence Armenia she was mostly associated with the opposition, denouncing President Levon Ter Petrosian's government for destroying the country, reducing it to rubble, depopulating it, and being anti-national and unjust.[50] During the Soviet period she was one the few intellectuals who travelled extensively, visiting diasporan communities. She wrote mostly poetry and travel memoirs. She also published a candid autobiography/political anthology in 1997.

Kaputikian shot to fame in the 1940s. Her 1944 poem *Khosk im vordune* (Message to my Son) became a standard verse in asserting national identity. It was republished many times both in Armenia and in the diaspora. It ends with this verse:

Look, my son, wherever you are,
Wherever you go under this moon,
Even if you forget your mother,
Do not forget your Mother tongue.[51]

Republic first, diaspora second. Rather than focusing on the rest of her poetry, I will highlight one of the main themes which emerged from Silva Kaputikian's other writings. She was the key literary figure whose work entailed the diasporan dimension. But instead of viewing the diaspora as an entity on its own, she relegated it to a secondary position in relation to the republic. She made it very clear that the centre of the nation was Soviet Armenia. This was more than irredentism or exaltation of the language. It was the reinforcement of national identity which downplayed the importance of half of the nation. She was not alone in this approach and in fact her work was the literary reflection of Soviet policy toward the diaspora (to be discussed below). Her books are the clearest expression of this view.

[49] D. Kouymjian, 'Status of Artists', p. 62. For her own account of this period, her speeches etc. see S. Kaputikian, *Ejer pak gzrotsnerits*, pp. 221–426; for her meeting with Gorbachev see pp. 285–93.

[50] S. Kaputikian, 'Sere ser gberi' and 'Silva Kaputikianin khoske', p. 2. For a vehement attack on her by the post-Soviet authorities see *Hayastani Hanrapetutiun* (Republic of Armenia) (Yerevan), 1 Nov. 1997.

[51] S. Kaputikian, *Ejer pak gzrotsnerits*, p. 686.

Kaputikian made three extensive journeys to the diaspora (in the early years of the 1960s, 1970s and 1980s) and she wrote a book about each journey. She was instrumental in helping to bridge the gap between Armenia and the diaspora, although she mostly met the sympathisers of the Soviet regime abroad (i.e. the Hnchak and Ramkavar blocs). She wrote of the successes and achievements of the diaspora, but her theme remained the same: the diaspora condition is an unfortunate reality and Armenians should all live in their fatherland that had been built into a wonderful country under Soviet rule.[52] Occasionally Dashnaks were criticised for their lack of enthusiasm for Soviet Armenia and their belief that only they are true patriots (i.e. that Communists cannot be patriotic). She maintained that the fatherland is not built by singing revolutionary songs in the diaspora, but through the hard work being done in Armenia. 'It is in Armenia, on that small land, that the fate, the present and the future, of the dispersed Armenian people is being built.'[53] Throughout her entire writing career Kaputikian did not change her views on these fundamental Soviet Armenian 'truths'. Her last book on the subject (*Guiner nuin khchankarits* [Colours from the Same Mosaic]), written in 1988–9, ended with her speech in Lebanon in 1962, during her first trip. She was making it clear that she still held the same views on the diaspora.[54]

In the (autobiographical) book Kaputikian published in 1997 she discusses how in literature, and generally in Armenia, the national spirit grew from the mid-1940s onwards. She played a part in this as well. As she put it: 'So it emerged that instead of socialist ideas taking root, we became followers of national faith. In all of my poetry after the war, the national really became strong.'[55] Furthermore, on the basis of her knowledge of the diaspora she also tried to 'nationalise' the prevalent thinking in Armenia. For example, she tells the story of how she was invited to the KGB offices in 1963 to give her 'report' on her first journey abroad. She told them of all her impressions, her amazement at the successes of the diaspora etc. She then

[52] S. Kaputikian, *Karavannere der kailum en*, pp. 335–8, and *Guiner nuin khchankarits*, pp. 384–5.

[53] S. Kaputikian, *Khchankar*, p. 194, cf. pp. 183–94.

[54] The same ideas were expressed during the author's interview with her.

[55] Author's interview with Silva Kaputikian.

added, 'There was much "nationalism"—that is patriotism—in what I was telling them.... I told them that it is essential that we too commemorate 24 April, change our wrong policy toward the diaspora and be more accepting of [diasporan] opposition parties.'[56] But all of this was to increase the republic's image as a national centre vis-à-vis the diaspora.

Kaputikian's diasporan equivalent was Andranik Tzarukian (1913–89), a poet, novelist, publisher of the influential literary paper *Nairi*[57] and former Dashnak. He was raised in Aleppo, lived in Beirut, and died in Paris. He shot to fame with his long patriotic poem *Tught ar Yerevan* (Message to Yerevan) written in 1945. It exalted the ARF against the virulent accusations coming from Soviet Armenia. The poem did not denounce Armenia, rather it praised the *ideal* of a homeland while ridiculing the anti-Dashnak rhetoric.[58] In the late 1950s, no longer a member of the ARF, Tzarukian was one of the earliest diasporan intellectuals who visited Armenia (at the formal invitation of Catholicos Vazgen I). Upon his return he wrote a beautiful and perceptive book on his impressions and experiences. Tzarukian had been 'converted' to the Soviet Armenian perspective on the diaspora. Henceforth he too was instrumental in propagating the idea that there is a homeland being built in Armenia, that the communist system and Armenian national identity are compatible, and that Russian protection is securing Armenia's existence.

His trend-setting book in this respect was *Hin yerazner, nor chambaner* (Old Dreams, New Ways). The argument is obvious from the title: Soviet Armenia is the new road in the realisation of the Armenian dream of national survival, prosperity and development.[59] In one passage he says of Armenia: 'There is no independence here, but there is an unparalleled worship of the Armenian spirit and culture.... There is no Armenian military division here, but on the borders of Armenia there is such an army that can totally devastate

[56] S. Kaputikian, *Ejer pak gzrotsnerits*, p. 58. She also recounts how, in a closed speech to the Party in 1965, she argued that the diaspora must be more closely tied to the republic, adding that a positive image of Armenia abroad would translate into a positive image of the USSR (p. 64).

[57] On *Nairi* and its influence see H. Tashjian, 'Nairi'. The word 'Nairi' means Armenia, but is associated with ancient Armenia.

[58] A. Tzarukian, *Tught ar Yerevan*.

[59] A. Tzarukian, *Hin yerazner*, p. 172.

anyone who comes near it...' (p. 300). This fatherland, moreover, 'no longer needs us [the diaspora] all that much, but we need the fatherland more... to see the new roads taking us to our old dream' (p. 320).

Tzarukian continued to publish on these themes and eventually his essays were collected in a 1983 book entitled *Nor Hayastan, nor Hayer* (New Armenia, New Armenians). The new Armenian in Armenia is a communist, he observed, but his communism is not an either/or identity. Armenians are like Christians who do not follow every tenet of the Bible. Anti-Soviet Armenians in the diaspora do not see this about their communist brethren (this was originally written in 1962). Why should Soviet Armenians not believe in Lenin's miracle? he asked. Our national symbols became real in Lenin's Armenia; they became concrete and bronze: the monuments of Vardan Mamikonian, David of Sasun etc.[60] 'The new Armenian, with every thread of his spirit, is tied to the Russian people; but he does not suffer from slavery in front of the Russian. He lives with the Russian, with the latter's life, fate; he lives the past, builds the future with the strength of the Russian' (p. 45). Between the mid-1950s and the mid-1960s, he figuratively explains, the Soviet 'cage' became a 'nest' for the Armenians—but nevertheless, he adds, it remained a cage (p. 149). Eventually the cage became too small. Writing in the early 1980s, he already observes in the crowds who are visiting Tzitzernakabert on 24 April the 'repressed and constrained silence which has become dense like an explosive gas, immobile in the shell of prudence for now, and temperate in the straitjacket enforced on it by the times, it awaited....' (p. 288). Sure enough, in the last year of his life, Tzarukian saw this tension explode over Gharabagh.

Like Kaputikian, Tzarukian also argued that the diaspora is an unfortunate reality. In another book of collected writings (from the 1960s) he shared his impressions and thoughts about the diasporan communities he visited. He likens the diaspora to a broken branch from the main tree... still alive, but barely.[61] He then severely criticises those who further weaken this branch due to party divisions and internal politics.

[60] A. Tzarukian, *Nor Hayastan*, pp. 42–4.

[61] A. Tzarukian, *Amerikian koghmn ashkharhi*, p. 201.

The works of Kaputikian and Tzarukian are but two examples of Armenian literature in the post-War period that reformulated and strengthened Armenian identity. Many other writers, both in the republic[62] and in the diaspora,[63] wrote about similar themes or touched upon the issue of Armenian identity.[64] Of course Armenian literature had many other dimensions (love, existential angst, social ills etc.) that I do not examine, and the authors I discuss above were by no means unidimensional nationalist writers. What I am arguing is the clearly visible—and sometimes too stark and too obvious—nationalist tone in Armenian literature which led to the reinforcement of national identity and eventually to the politics of nationalism.

Language

As is obvious from the literature cited above, the Armenian language was revered to the point of being worshipped. As Catholicos Vazgen I put it in 1989, 'The Armenian language is our essence, our honour, our identity, the fountain of our culture, and the means of our psychological expectations. We cannot live without our mother tongue.'[65] But the Patriarch quickly added that the Armenian lang-

[62] For example, Gurgen Mahari, Hrant Matevosian, Vardkes Petrosian. For a brief overview of Soviet Armenian literature see R. Peroomian, 'Expressions of Nationalism'.

[63] For example, Hakob Oshakan (Hagop Oshagan), Simon Simonian, Shahan Shahnur, Vahan Tekeyan, Vazgen Shushanian, Mushegh Ishkhan. For a brief overview of diasporan literature see V. Oshagan, 'Modernization'. The Genocide was obviously a major theme in some of the diasporan literature. On this aspect see L. Shirinian, *Armenian-North American Literature* and *Survivor Memoirs.*

[64] In addition to the publication of books and anthologies of individual writers, there were literary journals both in Armenia and in the diaspora which provided the forums for the publication of such literature. The two most notable periodicals in Armenia were *Grakan Tert* (Literary Journal) of the Writers Union, and the earlier mentioned *Garun* (Spring). Both of these played important roles in the propagation of national identity (see Sargis Harutiunian, 'Ailakhohutian akunknerum', parts I and III). During my interview with Levon Ananian, editor of *Garun* in the 1990s, he explained how the magazine occasionally got into trouble for pushing the limits a bit too far: 'The leaders of Armenia, in the end, were also Armenian, also saw the problems. They looked at *Garun*, a bit more forgivingly, as just young people. The Bureau of the Central Committee, on occasion, called in the chief editor and gave him an official reprimand. Then added, you know, it wasn't possible not to do it [owing to pressure from above].'

[65] Vazgen I, 'T. T. Vazgen A. Hairapeti khoske', p. 49.

uage was not being adequately protected during the Soviet period. Much academic work and linguistic research was certainly being done since the 1920s, and Armenian was 'the official language for everyday business, government operation, and instruction.'[66] Armenian remained the official language of the republic even after the 1978 constitutional changes, largely thanks to Georgian protests in Tbilisi in favour of maintaining the official status of national languages.[67] However, many felt that Armenian was losing its prominence in the republic owing to the encroachment of Russian, particularly among the youth. There was no forced Russification, but many intellectuals pointed out that Russian was slowly becoming the lingua franca of research, administration and even everyday communication within the elite *in* the republic.[68] This was a major cause of discontent among nationally-minded Armenians and an important dimension of the 1988 nationalist movement.

According to official statistics, 45 per cent of all Armenians in Armenia claimed to know Russian (52 per cent of Armenians in Georgia and 69 per cent in Azerbaijan). The real numbers were probably higher.[69] This does not seem such a high figure, or a worrying development in terms of losing the mother tongue. But Armenians were concerned with the clear trend of an increasing number of Russian schools in the republic. Many of the children of the intellectual elite were being sent voluntarily to Russian schools. The latter were in general of better quality. In such schools they learned Armenian as a second language and not the other way

[66] M. Matossian, 'Communist Rule', p. 187 (writing in the 1960s). The two pioneering linguists in Armenia were Hrach Acharian and Manuk Abeghian; both joined Yerevan State University in 1923 (J. Greppin, 'Armenian Studies', pp. 399–400).

[67] Armenians did protest against the proposal to make Russian the only official language of all the republics, but their protests dovetailed the vehement Georgian opposition. Moscow backed down (see R. Karklins, *Ethnic Relations*, p. 62; J. Dunlop, 'Language, Culture, Religion', p. 268; author's interview with Levon Abrahamian, and author's group interview with members of the Institute for Philosophy and Law).

[68] Author's interview with Khachik Safarian; as he dramatically put it: 'In the diaspora preserving Armenianness was put on a much stronger basis than in the fatherland. There was step by step dilution (*lutsum*) here.' Gurgen Geghamian, in his interview with the author, also put it forcefully; he called the slow linguistic Russification a 'white massacre', a term usually reserved for diasporan assimilation. Others who mentioned the issue in interviews with the author include Rafael Ghazarian and Levon Mkrtchian. See also Rafael Ishkhanian, *Yerrord uzhi patsarman orenke*, pp. 24ff.

[69] V. Tishkov, *Ethnicity*, pp. 87–96.

around. Obviously mastering Russian was the key to (union-wide) social mobility. According to one education expert, 25 per cent of all students in Armenia went to Russian schools.[70] This loss of language, especially among the elite and their children, worried the nationalists—some of whom knew Russian better than Armenian! Russian schools were closed to Armenian students by the post-Soviet government in Armenia (the few that remain open serve the children of non-Armenian parents—e.g. Russian soldiers stationed in Armenia).

Of all the identity markers, language was the one emphasised the most by nationalist intellectuals. It was a 'safe' issue and *seemed* non-political—especially in the 1960s. But political connotations were never far from the surface. By glorifying such a unique and ancient characteristic as language, intellectuals and artists were emphasising not only the uniqueness of the Armenians, but also their cultural deepness and purported superiority. However, a sense of cultural superiority cannot be coupled with a sense of political inferiority (and historical injustice) for too long. On the one hand Armenians asserted the global importance of their culture and the uniqueness of their language, on the other they had to follow *Diktat*s imposed from 'above'. Such tensions could no longer be hidden by the 1980s; they were bubbling to the political surface. A good part of the discussion asserting national rights was couched in terms of the protection of the Armenian language.

One last point needs to be made on the language issue: the orthographic changes instituted by the Soviet regime in 1922 and then reinforced in 1940. There was never any serious attempt to replace the Armenian alphabet with Cyrillic. But orthographic rules were devised to make spelling and pronunciation simpler. Many Russian words—especially technical and political ones—were introduced into Armenian. The most important impact of the orthographic changes was to separate eastern Armenian further from the western variant. The divergence of the literary language of the nation's two spheres made the literature of each look and sound 'strange' in the eyes and ears of the other. The orthographic changes became an emotive issue for many diasporan intellectuals who

[70] Author's discussion with Vladimir Ossipov, 17 October 1996 (Yerevan); V. Tishkov, *Ethnicity*, p. 86.

called for the 'unification' of the language based on the pre-Soviet 'classic'—i.e. western—spelling.[71]

Textbooks and education

I love you,
Armenian language,
Like my mother
You are sweet.
I take pride in you,
As I read, write,
Speak [through you].

This is from the first year textbook (published in 1983) for children beginning school in Soviet Armenia. After learning the alphabet, they first read a story about St Mesrop Mashtots, the inventor of the Armenian alphabet, and then the above poem called *Armenian Language.* Of course this is shortly followed by a story about Lenin telling the students to learn well, to be respectful and disciplined. The rest of the stories in the textbook do not have ideological or historical content.[72]

This duality between the national and the communist existed throughout the Armenian educational system. However, what I would like to highlight here, by examining three Armenian history textbooks covering the same topics, but published decades apart, is the change towards national issues in textbooks over the years. The first was published in 1964 (for eighth graders).[73] In addition to the standard thesis that Soviet Armenia was advancing by leaps and bounds, its cultural progress is discussed—from the number of schools to the work of famous authors, theatre etc. (pp. 289–97, 325–9). The diaspora is covered and is clearly divided into two parts: the progressive element (i.e. those who supported Soviet Armenia) and

[71] The issue of orthographic unity was raised by Vahe Oshagan and some other diasporans at the Armenia-Diaspora Conference in Yerevan in September 1999. It was again discussed, at times with vehemence, at the insistence of diasporan intellectuals at the second Conference in May 2002. For one brief article on how the decision to change orthography was taken in 1921 see K. Gerogian, 'Inchpes partadrvetsav nor ughghagrutiune', p. 33.

[72] *Arevik aibenaran*; the poem is on p. 107.

[73] V. Parsamian *et al.*, *Hai zhoghovrdi patmutiun.*

the reactionary element (i.e. those who opposed it, *viz.* Dashnaks). No opportunity is missed to denounce the ARF. For example, in its coverage of the Second World War, it says that the struggle was at the same time 'against Dashnaks who had entered to serve in the German Fascist army, against the bitter enemies of the Armenian people,... the traitors who had sold out to fascism' (p. 318).[74] Interestingly, even in a school textbook the notion of 'fatherland' (*hairenik*) had acquired a dual meaning: on the one hand it clearly meant Soviet Armenia, on the other it was also used to refer to the USSR (cf. p. 320 in contrast to p. 333). This was not a contradiction, but an oscillation which favoured the Armenians because they could benefit from the ambiguity.

There are certain continuities and differences with history textbooks published in the mid-1980s (for grades nine and ten).[75] The theme of the USSR developing Armenia economically, socially and culturally is certainly there. But the anti-Dashnak rhetoric is considerably toned down, albeit not totally eliminated. For example, the same section on the Second World war and the support diasporan Armenians gave to the Soviet war effort mentions the contribution of the 'progressive' elements, but does not at all mention the ARF, let alone accuse them of being 'traitors' in the service of fascism (pp. 163–5). The discussion on the diaspora does not directly divide it into 'good' and 'bad'. There is reference to the 'progressive elements' but silence on the rest (pp. 222–8). The notion of 'fatherland' had crystallised to refer clearly to Armenia, although the 'national in form, socialist in content' formula was explicitly maintained (p. 221).

Comparing the above to an equivalent post-independence (1996) textbook is illustrative.[76] The tables are turned on the Communists, needless to say. Sovietisation is not seen as liberation, but inevitable to save Armenia from Turkish occupation; the book does not go as far as lionising the role of the ARF in the first (1918) republic

[74] It is true that certain elements within some of the Middle East branches of the ARF—but not the party as a whole—collaborated with the Nazis in the hope that German forces, if victorious, would liberate Armenia from the Soviet yoke. This dark episode of history almost never figures in Armenian public discourse. See C. Walker, *Armenia*, pp. 356–8.

[75] Tz. Aghayan *et al.*, *Hai zhoghovrdi patmutiun.*

[76] B. Barkhudarian, *Hayots patmutiun.*

(pp. 271–5). Communist repressions are mentioned (pp. 287, 316–20, 334–48, 369–72), and the 'new' issues of Gharabagh and the republic's borders are covered (pp. 288–96). The overall economic improvements under Soviet rule are not denied (pp. 297–306, 351–61), nor is the country's cultural, educational and scientific development. All reference to the beneficial role of the Russians is eliminated, but *not* replaced by any anti-Russian sentences. The 1960s is mentioned as the period of 'national renaissance' (pp. 377–9). The last chapters are devoted to the Gharabagh movement—a 'national liberation struggle'—and independence (pp. 388ff.). The diaspora is treated as a separate chapter at the very end (pp. 416–40). Over all the textbook is a fairly balanced treatment of Armenian history, with certain overtones of the nationalist discourse.

As in other societies, textbooks were key mechanisms through which collective identity was shaped in Soviet Armenia. The national and the communist were *simultaneously* reinforced, at least in the post-war period. But whereas the communist side remained consistent in its repetitive slogans and arguments, the national side increased more and more in its scope and frequency. The balance had clearly tipped in favour of the national by the 1980s; communist ideology had become a rather empty set of beliefs, even though it existed in the textbooks and was widely taught.[77]

Soviet Armenia was a highly educated society,[78] with an excellent educational system—particularly in the hard sciences. This instilled much pride in the Armenians. But it was also a double edged sword for the Soviet authorities. As Crawford Young puts it, 'The Schoolhouse was... at once weapon of integration and detonator of ethnicity.' A number of other experts have also pointed out that higher education serves a catalyst for the rise of ethnic consciousness and nationalism.[79]

[77] Armenian schools in the diaspora did not use the same textbooks as in Armenia. They had their own. Some of these were produced by diasporan educators, others were published in Yerevan specifically for the diaspora (in western Armenian)—namely in the subject areas of literature, language and geography.

[78] It ranked among the top five republics in terms of students in higher education (R. Karklins, *Ethnic Relations*, p. 238).

[79] C. Young, 'National and Colonial', p. 71. For an extensive argument linking education to the rise of national identity and nationalism see G. Simon, *Nationalism and Policy*, pp. 268ff. (particularly p. 279); cf. H. Carrère d'Encausse, *Decline of an Empire*, p. 272; R. Karklins, *Ethnic Relations*, p. 223.

The Soviet educational system was formally centralised. The subjects, curricula and textbooks were either provided or approved by Moscow. Textbooks of the hard sciences were written by Russian experts and translated into local languages. But national history texts were written in the republic and then approved by the centre. Over the years the system was decentralised in practice. By the 1980s Moscow no longer really intervened; it still gave the funds without paying too much attention to content. Hence many textbooks were approved locally by the Party leadership in the republic and contained strong national themes.[80] However, any *serious* ideological deviations would have been brought to Moscow's attention by devout 'materialists'.

Outside the formal educational system the central authorities tried to inculcate Soviet identity in the young through an expansive socialisation programme called 'patriotic and internationalist upbringing' or 'patriotic education'. The idea was to encourage a non-national sense of identity and inter-ethnic ties. With its rituals and stories this programme permeated every aspect of school life in order to encourage participation. However, participation in Armenia, Georgia and the Central Asian republics was generally lower than the all-Union average.[81] Like other attempts to foster 'internationalism' this programme backfired, at least in the South Caucasus. Karen Collias, who believes that it had some success in making the USSR a 'motherland', nevertheless admits that the patriotic programme was hijacked by the forces of nationalism: it 'succeeded in legitimizing ethnoterritorial pride, assuming this to be non-system-threatening[. Moreover, it] was not as successful in its planned next stage, which was the integration of these substate identities into an international union of Soviet citizens professing exclusive loyalty to the Soviet state.'[82]

Monuments and rituals

Monuments and rituals were the most visible element of Soviet life. In Armenia there were two types of monuments and celebrations:

[80] Based on discussion with Vladimir Ossipov, 17 October 1996 (Yerevan).

[81] K. Collias, 'Making Soviet Citizens', pp. 74–86.

[82] Ibid., p. 89.

national and Soviet. There is no need to elaborate on the latter; the all too present war memorials, statues of Soviet leaders (both all-Union and republican), Party celebrations etc.[83] The symbolic switch from Soviet monuments to national ones took place in 1962 when the huge statue of Stalin was removed from a hill overlooking Yerevan. In 1967 an equally large statue of Mother Armenia, sword in hand, was erected in its place, staring at Mount Ararat. This is a fascinating Soviet-style structure which is clearly 'national in content, socialist in form'. It is also indicative of the transition from the soviet to the national: the museum of the 'Great Patriotic War' is located at its base. There is also a carving of a church on its pedestal, with 'CCCP' written on top of it.

Other national monuments include the Tzitzernakabert Genocide Memorial, planned in 1965 and completed by 1967; the Sardarapat victory monument (1968), celebrating the pre-Soviet defeat of the Turks which paved the way for the establishment of the first Armenian republic in 1918; various statues of ancient heroes—among them Vardan Mamikonian (fifth century),[84] the legendary David of Sasun (*circa* tenth century), and the mythical founder of the Armenians Haik Nahapet. Statues of more modern and controversial non-Communist heroes were not built, especially if they had in any way been affiliated with the ARF (with the one exception of a modest monument to General Andranik). Finally, Yerevan itself became part of the 'national iconography' as its symbolic importance as the centre of Armenianness (of culture and industry) was emphasised.[85]

[83] For details see C. Binns, 'Changing Face of Power', parts I and II. He points out that the main features of the 'post-Stalin ceremonial innovations... are centrifugal rather th[a]n centripetal' (part II, p. 183).

[84] At the unveiling of this statue, of a sword-drawn Vardan riding on a horse, in December 1975, the mayor of Yerevan, in the presence of the First Secretary Demirchian and other official guests, called it a symbol of 'the centuries old epic struggle of the Armenian people against foreign invaders...' (as cited in V. Dadrian, 'Nationalism in Soviet Armenia', p. 227). On the Symbolism of the Tzitzernakabert monument see R. Khachatian, 'Inch e asum', p. 6.

[85] T. Ter Minassian, 'Yerevan'. The iconic treatment of Yerevan and its architecture was evident in a fierce public debate in the city in the summer of 1996 when the Armenian government began to dismantle the marble podium of Lenin's statue (which had been removed in the spring of 1991) in the centre of Yerevan. One side wanted to get rid of the last remnants of Lenin's symbol, the other side argued that the podium itself was part of national heritage, keeping an aesthetic 'balance' in the central square of

As to national rituals, in addition to the annual commemoration of certain events such as the Genocide and the 1965 protests, two other events had a powerful impact on Armenian national pride. The first was the May 1962 celebration of the invention of the Armenian alphabet, which Vahakn Dadrian describes: 'Armenians indulged in contagious exuberance and Yerevan became an arena of nationalist fervor and outburst.... Defying the atheistic contours of the regime, religion, and more specifically, the Armenian brand of Christianity, were singled out as the incubators of national genius.... Significantly, noted communists partook in this spectacle.'[86] There were wild exaltations at banquets, which were not described in the local press, although diasporan guests wrote about them on their return. 'Once more Armenia gave vent to its emotions disregarding Socialist culture and admiring the marvels of her own.' The political dimension was never far away; Hovhannes Shiraz composed a poem on the spot asking when Ani, Ararat, Kars and Artahan (all in Turkey) were to be returned to Armenia. The poem evoked 'stormy applause'. The excesses of these celebrations were subsequently condemned in the Soviet Armenian press, but a precedent was set as 'festivities went out of control, in an overwhelming rapture of nationalist exaltations dumbfounding the Communists.'[87] A similar celebration took place in 1968 on the 2,750th anniversary of the founding of Erebuni, the precursor of Yerevan. Again the occasion was used to emphasise the deep roots Armenians had in their land, the centrality of Yerevan in ancient civilisation, and the architectural and cultural genius of the Armenians.... Other such events, associated with various aspects of Armenian history and culture, took place (usually on a smaller scale) in the 1970s and 1980s.

Church and religion

Guests from abroad who visited Ejmiatzin during the Soviet period were sometimes given a private tour of the 'hidden' treasures at the monastery. In addition to some of the rare and old religious relics

---

the capital, and therefore it should not be destroyed. Communists were the most incensed. The podium was removed.

[86] V. Dadrian, 'Nationalism in Soviet Armenia', p. 215.

[87] V. Dadrian, 'Appraisal of the Communist Formula', part I, pp. 11–13.

held by the church, they were shown three items of impressive and modern wealth from the vaults of the Catholicosate. The first was a large cross. The second was the Armenian alphabet. The third was the emblem of the Armenian SSR, and below it a list of the ancient Armenian capital cities. All three items were crafted from pure gold and adorned with precious stones. Each was mounted on a separate marble slab, approximately one metre in height.[88] The symbolism of these *three* items shown was as impressive as their material value. Christianity, Armenian cultural identity and the Soviet Armenian state—with ancient Armenia at its base—were kept safely at the heart of Ejmiatzin, cherished and proudly displayed to diasporan visitors. The dynamics and overlap between these three elements (perhaps representing the Father, the Son and the Holy Spirit!) basically characterised the history of the Armenian church within the USSR since the early 1940s.

The role of the church in Soviet Armenia has been analysed considerably.[89] Hence the discussion can be kept quite brief. Like other religious institutions the Armenian church was severely attacked by the Communists in the 1920s and especially in the 1930s. By 1938 the church barely existed. However, in 1941 the church began to be active again. This was in the context of the Second World War and Stalin's drive to mobilise all sectors of society in support of the war effort. The Soviet authorities had realised that religious institutions could play a vital role in this respect. Restrictions were eased by 1945 and henceforth the Armenian church in Armenia operated within the limits set by the Soviet state. After the church had been

[88] I was on one such tour in the summer of 1987, as part of a group of diasporan university students from Montreal. The alphabet and the Soviet emblem were built with funds from diaspora Armenians in Marseilles (K. Dallakian, *Hushapatum*, p. 100).

[89] The most extensive history in the English language of the Armenian church in the post-war period is provided by Felix Corley's three-part article ('Armenian Church'). See also C. Mouradian's 'Armenian Apostolic Church', *De Staline à Gorbatchev*, chapter 8, and 'L'Arménie soviétique', pp. 271–3, 298–300; W. Kolarz, *Religion in the Soviet Union*, pp. 160–73; S. Torossian, 'Apostolic Church of Armenia'; E. Oganessyan, 'Armenian Church in the USSR'; S. Jones, 'Religion and Nationalism'; and V. Dadrian, 'Nationalism in Soviet Armenia', pp. 242–51. Karlen Dallakian, who was the head of the Armenian Council of Church Affairs between 1963 and 1970, provides a sympathetic but very interesting 'insider's' account of the thinking and activities of Catholicos Vazgen I (K. Dallakian, *Hushapatum*). For two works on the persecution of the church under Stalin see S. Stepaniants, *Hai Arakelakan*; and A. Manukian, *Hai Arakelakan*.

pushed to the brink of extinction as an institution in the mid- to late-1930s, by the early 1980s there were 33 active Armenian churches in the USSR, with 29 places of worship in Armenia (including one or two mosques).[90] This was still quite a low number compared to the hundreds before Armenia's Sovietisation.

Despite the visible presence of the church and the positive image the population had of Catholicos Vazgen I (he was on the throne of Ejmiatzin from 1955 to 1994), atheism had made considerable gains in Armenia. As one commentator observed in the 1960s, the Ejmiatzin church might be full and active, but 'there were no believers.'[91] Soviet Armenians in general did not take *religion* all that seriously.

However, this does not mean that the church as a *national* institution was dismissed. The Soviet state, the people and even the last two Catholicoi of Ejmiatzin perceived it as a national institution. According to Karlen Dallakian, Vazgen I used to say, 'The important thing is to serve the nation, the means is [based on] personal preferences or [is] a question of time.' On another occasion he had said: 'Serving the Church is not an end in itself. It is the way and means for me to serve my nation. I wish that every Armenian would find his way of serving the nation. You, for example, are a Communist, but I am convinced that is your chosen way to serve our nation.'[92] One might rightfully suspect Dallakian's rendition of a quote from Vazgen I, and keep the context of the conversation in mind (i.e. with a Communist Party official). But the same idea, with a different emphasis, was conveyed by Vazgen's successor, Karekin (Garegin) I.

[90] There were Armenian churches in Tbilisi and Baku, but not a single church was allowed to operate in Mountainous Gharabagh from the 1930s (H. Tchilingirian, 'Religious Discourse', p. 72). Interestingly, Catholicos Karekin I complained in private that when he first assumed the Ejmiatzin throne in 1995 he realised that 'there was a complete lack of organisational structures, no permanent parishes organisations, no church councils etc. Officially the church existed, in reality there was nothing. Plus, there was no knowledge of the basic Christian principles among the people. We need to build structures, we need to do lots of educational work' (author's interview with Karekin I).

[91] Andrei Bitov, as quoted in F. Corley, 'Armenian Church', part II, p. 300. Corley concludes his extensive study, 'As an institution, the Church in Armenia enjoys some residual respect, but is so far removed from the identity of most Armenian citizens that it is largely an irrelevance that impinges little on their daily lives' (F. Corley, 'Armenian Church', part III, p. 348; cf. E. Oganessyan, 'Armenian Church', p. 242).

[92] K. Dallakian, *Hushapatum*, p. 105 for the first quote, p. 97 for the second.

In my interview with him the Catholicos said:

'For me the national and the religious are united in their culture, in practices, and in consciousness. And therefore the division between religion and secularisation is not that great in the case of the Armenians. In the Armenian case the church and the nation are not divided.... Since the Armenian Church is a national church, and Armenians keep their cultural habits through religious symbols and activities (even in such things as food and dance), then the difference between secularism and believers is not that huge or deep... Religious culture and Armenian identity are intertwined [*hiusvats*].'[93]

This line of argument was a continuation from the Armenian religio-nationalist discourse a century earlier. Karekin I was not saying that the church is a means to serve the nation (and I doubt that Vazgen would have put it in quite the same terms that Dallakian says), but that church and nation are in unity.

The Soviet Armenian regime and the church were certainly not intertwined or united. But there was a clear *modus vivendi* between the two. Vazgen I supported the regime, made pro-Russia pronouncements, portrayed a very positive image of Soviet Armenia (including religious life in the republic), and when needed issued pro-Soviet statements on Cuba, Lebanon or Vietnam.[94] In return he enjoyed quite a bit of respect (both nationally and internationally), his churches stayed open, he could travel extensively, and he could obtain visas for just about anyone he wanted to visit Armenia. Dallakian suggests that Vazgen was semi-independent, with considerable indirect authority in Yerevan. Soviet rulers saw him as a 'wise man' and granted him *carte blanche.*[95] Dadrian refers to the relationship between the church and the Soviet Armenian state as a 'sym-

93 Author's interview with Karekin I.

94 During the turbulent months of 1988, Vazgen I denounced the strikes (called in favour of Gharabagh's unification with Armenia) and urged the protesters to respect law and order. He objected to any kind of extremism. He was criticised by nationalists for being pro-Soviet. In his 9 November 1989 address to the delegates of the (anti-regime) Armenian National Movement he outlined three points that the Movement should keep in mind: (1) Strengthening and safeguarding the political security of the republic, (2) safeguarding the economic rebuilding of the country, and (3) unity in further developing national culture (Vazgen I, 'T. T. Vazgen A. Hairapeti Khoske', pp. 45, 49).

95 K. Dallakian, *Hushapatum*, p. 113.

biotic relationship', although he quickly qualifies it as a form of 'antagonistic cooperation.'[96]

The church played a very significant role in the relationship between Soviet Armenia and the diaspora. It was, however, a negative (i.e. a divisive) role. Despite the respectful relations between the church and the Soviet state, the former was used by Soviet authorities—initially overtly and directly but later subtly and indirectly—as one of the main instruments in their attempts to control the diaspora.[97] Once the Communists managed to dominate Ejmiatzin (by 1929), they had a powerful tool in their hands.

Between 1930 and 1956 two major episodes of conflict engulfed the church—both taking place in the diaspora. The first led to the murder of an archbishop, the second to the *de facto* schism of the church between two political blocs. In 1931 Ghevond Turian (Leon Turian) was ordained as the Archbishop of New York by Ejmiatzin. However, he was opposed by the Dashnaks for being explicitly pro-Soviet. Although he was appointed by the Catholicos of All Armenians, his legitimacy and jurisdiction were not accepted by some churches and members of the congregation; consequently the diocesan assembly in New York split along the Dashnak/non-Dashnak division, the first wanting to get rid of him, the second supporting him. The dispute became so bitter that the Archbishop was stabbed to death on Christmas Eve in 1933 while celebrating mass in the Holy Cross Church in New York. Nine Dashnak members were found guilty of the murder, although the party officially denied any involvement. This event became the founding 'myth' of the North American diaspora, with its deep scars and profound division of the community, the consequences of which are still felt.[98]

[96] V. Dadrian, 'Nationalism in Soviet Armenia', pp. 242–3.

[97] For example, F. Corley ('Armenian Church', part II, p. 329) quotes Soviet documents from 1959: '[We need to] work out measures having as their aim the use of the Armenian Church of the USSR to strengthen Soviet influence among Armenians living in foreign countries.'

[98] For details see S. Atamian, *Armenian Community*, pp. 358ff.; U. Björklund, 'Armenia Remembered', pp. 342–3. In a 1934 booklet one vehemently anti-ARF author provides an 'indictment' of the 'terrorist' Dashnaks as 'an enemy of the nucleus of Armenian political life; as an organization that has degenerated so far, that it can be compared with the Italian Mafia, and the gangsters of this country' (K. S. Papazian, *Patriotism Perverted*, p. 67).

The division of the church was 'institutionalised' in 1956 with the election of the Catholicos of the See of Cilicia, in Beirut. Historically the head of the Cilician Prelacy is elected independently, although theologically there is no difference between Ejmiatzin and Cilicia. Armenian Catholicoi are elected not only by a college of bishops or other church officials, but also by a larger number of lay delegates; this makes the election of the Catholicos dependent on dynamics within the community and leaves the whole process open to political manipulation. Both heads of the church have the title 'Catholicos', and are institutionally independent of one another. But the rank of the Cilician office is lower insofar as it does not carry the title 'Catholicos of *all* Armenians'. The 1956 elections provided an opportunity for the Dashnaks to gain outright control of an important part of the Church in the diaspora, hence limiting Soviet domination of the institution through the latter's control of Ejmiatzin. To achieve this the ARF had to ensure the election of its 'own' candidate despite Ejmiatzin's objection and influence in the diaspora. Amidst accusations and counter-accusations of subverting the church, the ARF won this round of the battle and succeeded in having the Primate of Aleppo, Zareh Payaslian, elected as the Catholicos of the Great House of Cilicia. The Soviet authorities were outmanoeuvred even though the Catholicos of Ejmiatzin, Vazgen I (himself newly elected), had travelled to Lebanon to ensure the election of a candidate other than the 'pro-Dashnak' Zareh. The schism in the church became complete when Vazgen, under pressure from the Soviet authorities and some anti-Dashnak diaspora organisations, did not recognise the legitimacy of the elections. A battle of jurisdiction ensued as the Cilician church sought to extend its influence beyond the Middle East and into Europe and North America, or to wherever there was a large enough Dashnak community to sustain its own church. Henceforth the Cilician church came to be known—unofficially—as the 'Dashnak church', while diaspora Armenians, on the basis of their political persuasions, split their loyalty between one of the two Catholicoi. The schism prevented Soviet Armenia from using the church to exercise any control—or even to have any influence—over parts of the diaspora.

In sum, the Armenian church played a dual role. Insofar as church and ethnicity were intertwined it helped to reinforce national identity. It was a symbol of the nation, of national unity, at the abstract level. By attending church people affirmed their Armenianness both in the diaspora and in the republic (albeit less so in the latter), without necessarily having any religious beliefs.[99] Atheism was strangely compatible with the church because it was compatible with national identity (as mentioned above by Catholicos Karekin I). However, *simultaneously* the church played a divisive role. It further reinforced the Armenia-diaspora division. It became a political instrument in the hands of two opposing blocs, one led by the Dashnaks and based in the diaspora, the other by the Soviets and based in the republic. The latter also had diasporan allies in the form of the non-Dashnak bloc.

Theoretical interlude: the state-culture nexus

The final theoretical interlude has to briefly address the relationship between the state and national (or nationalising) culture. The marriage of culture and the state is a central argument in Ernest Gellner's *Nations and Nationalism* and the relationship is discussed by other major writers on nationalism. The basic argument is that the state plays an active role in the homogenisation of national culture. For example, Anthony Smith points out that the state has two effects on culture. First, 'It has instituted a single public or political culture, a kind of civil religion' which propagates 'an official version of the community's history'. Second, the state has sought to 'fuse cultural dimensions with other sources of power' because it cannot 'tolerate rival centres of cultural power'. Hence 'The modern state must destroy any hierarchy or institution that could challenge its efficacy and legitimacy in the cultural domain.'[100]

These points are particularly pertinent in the case of the Soviet Armenia for two reasons. The first relates to the very nature of the Soviet state. It was an extremely prevalent institution, involved in all aspects of life. The state was therefore intimately involved in the propagation of 'official' culture. It defined—directly or indirectly—the general parameters of this culture. Of course it was susceptible to many pressures, both from below and from above, but neverthe-

[99] V. Dadrian, 'Nationalism in Soviet Armenia', p. 222.
[100] A. Smith, 'Ethnie and Nation', pp. 130–1.

less the state was the main arbitrator of public culture. Hence the relationship between state and culture was much more direct in the Soviet context. However, this was not a singular relationship but a multilayered one.

The second point relates to the complexity of, and tensions within, this multilayered relationship. There were two levels of state and two levels of culture: the Soviet 'civic' culture largely propagated by the central state, and the 'ethnic' culture propagated by the republican state. Hence there were rival centres of cultural production, inexorably intertwined in many social, political and economic aspects, but competing with one another at the level of national culture. In the case of Armenia there was the added dimension of the diaspora as a rival centre of national culture. As will be pointed out in the next section, the Armenian SSR effectively neutralised the threat of the diaspora as a serious cultural rival. Importantly, it also successfully competed with the culture associated with the central state insofar as a homogenised national culture emerged in contradistinction to Soviet and Russian culture. The primary loyalty of the Soviet Armenian citizen was based on Armenian national identity, even though his or her national 'state' (i.e. the republic) was at best semi-independent from the central state. The republic was significantly more independent in cultural matters than in other realms.

The state in the Armenian SSR, and organisations in the diaspora, succeeded in making national identity 'banal', to borrow Michael Billig's argument. Nationhood was manifested and reinforced daily in banal and mundane ways in Armenia and in the diaspora. Nationalism, says Billig, 'far from being an intermittent mood in established nations [including in Western societies], is the endemic condition.'[101] In a chapter entitled 'Flagging the Homeland Daily,' he demonstrates how the nation is reproduced, as if naturally, as part of daily life by politicians, intellectuals, the media etc. Through the use of flags, monuments, words, images, rituals and so forth, *the* nation—i.e. 'our' nation—becomes the normal context of the world, an apparent given.[102] Armenia, along with many other Soviet republics, was

[101] M. Billig, *Banal Nationalism*, p. 6.

[102] Michael Billig and Partha Chatterjee, though writing about different contexts (the 'first world' and the 'third world'), address an interesting lacuna in the study of

no different, although the nation was 'flagged', ironically, in the anti-national ideological, aesthetic and political context of communism, and co-existed with the overt 'flagging' of communist symbols and practices. In the diaspora too Armenianness was being fortified, sometimes with difficulty, in the overall context of the host societies' prevalent cultures and nationalising policies—i.e. their own 'flagging' of their homelands.

REPATRIATION AND FORMAL ARMENIA-DIASPORA RELATIONS

Part of Soviet Armenia's self-reinforcement was the 'repatriation' of diaspora Armenians. Soviet authorities encouraged such immigration in ebbs and flows in order to augment the population of the republic and to demonstrate that the Soviet republic was the one and only fatherland of all Armenians. But repatriation was a double-edged sword. On the one hand it did augment a sense of united identity, at least on the ideological level, but on the other it introduced new cleavages in the republic and between Armenia and the diaspora. Between 1921 and 1936 42,000 Armenians immigrated to Armenia, almost all from neighbouring countries or the Balkans, a few from France and the Middle East. 4,000 arrived in the 1950s and 26,000 from 1962 to 1972. A few more thousands followed during the rest of the 1970s.[103] However, the largest and most significant 'repatriation' drive was launched by the Soviet authorities in 1945, ostensibly to populate the historic Armenian regions of Kars

---

nationalism: how people internalise the nation, and the power relations it entails, as a 'normal' part of life—as routine and common. The national ideal as such becomes the hegemonic view of the world because it affects the consciousness of nearly all citizens. The work of the anthropologists Jean and John Comaroff is particularly relevant. They talk of the 'colonisation of consciousness and the consciousness of colonisation' as they examine how power is internalised and obeyed in its 'silences' (J. Comaroff and J. Comaroff, *Of Revelation and Revolution*, chapter 1; cf. A. Ruud, 'Indian Hierarchy', pp. 718–19). The theoretical confluence of Antonio Gramsci (to whom Billig alludes twice) and nationalism literature could produce some very interesting insights on the durability and power of national identity.

103 C. Mouradian, 'L'immigration des Arméniens', pp. 99–100, and 'L'Arménie soviétique', p. 265.

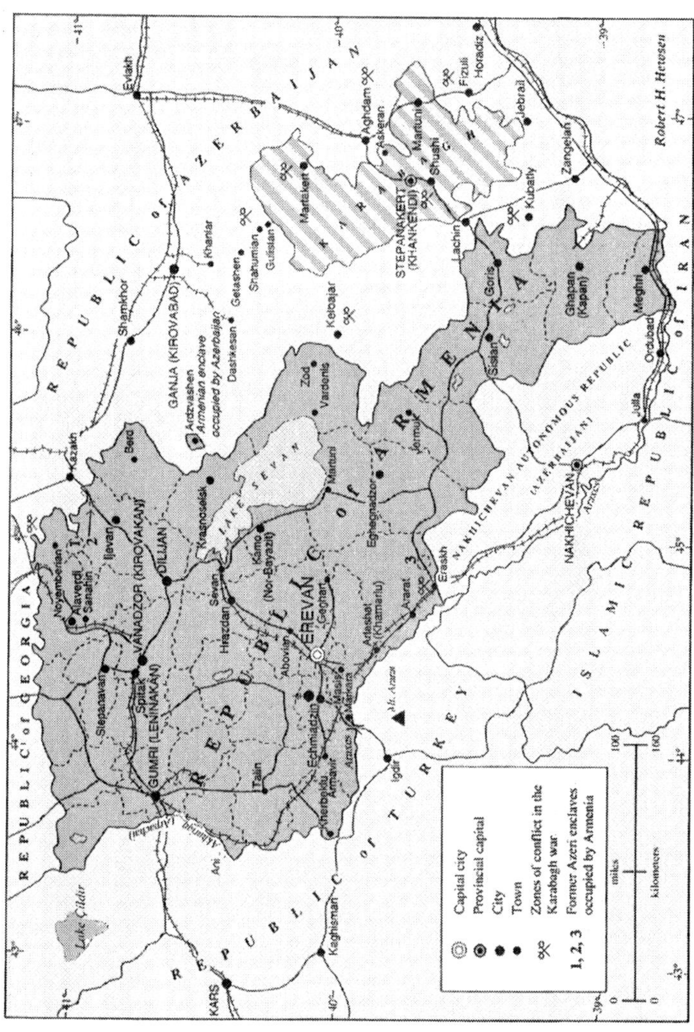

Soviet and Independent Armenia, 1920 to the present.

and Artahan to be acquired from Turkey.[104] The land claims, made in the context of post-war superpower geopolitical manoeuvring, came to naught, but between 1946 and 1948 100,000 Armenians immigrated to 'their' Soviet 'homeland'.[105] However, none of these immigrants were returnees in the strict sense, and the official term 'repatriation' is a misnomer. Approximately 90–95 per cent had originated in western Armenia; they were Genocide survivors and refugees who had not yet sunk deep roots in the countries where they were living. The reason they came was a combination of patriotism

[104] These were the same lands Stalin had claimed during his negotiation with the Nazis prior to the outbreak of the Second World War. A formal claim to Kars and Artahan was made secretly on 7 June 1945 by Molotov to the Turkish ambassador in Moscow. The Soviet claim was complicated by the fact that no Armenians lived on the lands being claimed. The repatriation drive could have been a solution to this problem. The land claims by (or on behalf of) the Armenians were part of larger Soviet demands (e.g. joint control of the Straits). Georgians too put forth land claims against Turkey, and Azerbaijan against Iran. The issue was practically dropped in 1949, with no border changes at all. Four months after Stalin's death Soviet claims against Turkey were formally renounced and diplomatic apologies issued. At the end of the Second World War, of all the territories which were part of the Russian empire in 1914, and with the exception of Poland and Finland, only Kars and Artahan were not retrieved by the Soviets (V. Aspaturian, 'Union Republics', pp. 470–2).

[105] 32 per cent came from Syria/Lebanon; 20 per cent from Iran; 18 per cent from Greece; 12 per cent from Egypt; 7 per cent from France; 8 per cent from Bulgaria and Romania; 3 per cent from Iraq and Palestine; 0.2 per cent from the United States. The official decree was issued on 21 November 1945 by the Soviet of People's Deputies of the USSR. It was published on 2 December. On 27 November Catholicos Kevork VI, urged by the Soviet foreign ministry, had already sent a note to the British Foreign Secretary and the foreign ministers of the United States and the Soviet Union asking them to restore the historic Armenian lands as per the Treaty of Sèvres (C. Mouradian, 'L'immigration des Arméniens', p. 80). A copy of the original decree can be found in the State Central Archives of History and Contemporary History (henceforth, SCAHCH), Fond 326, Folder 1, Item 74 (1945). The Soviet authorities prepared detailed reports on the Armenian communities abroad, based on which they decided who to admit and who to reject. For some of these reports see, 'Information about Armenian Colonies Abroad', SCAHCH 326/1/150 (1946) (a country by country overview of the Armenian diaspora); 'Report on Public Organisations among Armenians Abroad', SCAHCH 326/1/50(1945) (an overview of each of the organisations or parties); 'Report on the 1947 Repatriation', SCAHCH 326/1/196(1947) (a breakdown of the number of 'returnees' based on country of origin, resettlement area, occupation etc.). This is a sample of a wider collection of materials which are now open to researchers; almost all of the documents are in Russian. For further details on the repatriation drive see C. Mouradian, 'L'immigration des Arméniens' and 'L'Arménie soviétique'; R. Suny, *Looking toward Ararat*, pp. 163–9; and from the Soviet Armenian perspective, H. Meliksetian, *Hairenik-spiurk*.

and better economic opportunities (so they were promised). The demand to repatriate was higher than places being offered. This sudden influx of diasporan immigrants represented 9 per cent of the 1946 Soviet Armenian population of 1.2 million.

According to the official view, the immigrants were greeted with open arms and 'the best living conditions were created for the repatriates in Soviet Armenia. The state gave them many allowances. The issues concerning their work and maintenance was successfully organised.'[106] However, nothing can be further from the truth. The repatriates suffered much hardship, given the difficult conditions in Armenia, and many were sent, almost directly, to Siberia.

The repatriation had three important effects on Armenian identity, especially in the realm of diaspora relations. First, there was the tremendous sense of disappointment and betrayal. This had two dimensions to it. The first was the betrayal by the 'fatherland' of the diaspora. As news of the appalling conditions and the politically repressive regime started to leak out, diasporans felt cheated. One popular folk song in Beirut (one of the main departure points) from the period went as such:

> *You took out red papers, and deceived us,*
> *We sold our houses and are left homeless,*
> *Hey, yaman, yaman, sriga* [rogue, scoundrel or rascal] *Tevechian,*[107]
> *Syria and Lebanon curse you…*
> *We will not go to Armenia, but to Iran,*
> *We do not accept the Bolshevik regime…*
> *We were resurrected by passing the Arax river* [out of Armenia],
> *After that we began to worship the Tricolor* [flag]…[108]

[106] V. Parsamian *et al.*, *Hai zhoghovrdi patmutiun*, p. 320. This glowing view from a 1964 textbook was subsequently toned down a bit. But only after *glasnost* could Armenians in the republic openly talk about the real hardships they suffered (see M. Grigorian, 'Hairenadardzutian').

[107] Hrant Tevechian was the chairman of the repatriation organising committee in Lebanon. He was killed in Armenia in 1949.

[108] These verses are quoted in G. Shenian, 'Esker Misak', p. 3 (the article is not on the repatriation). Notes on some of the terms: the Turkish word *yaman* is used here to mean 'sly/cunning/shrewd'; it is used colloquially by Armenians in the Middle East. The Tricolour flag of the independent republic was at that point exclusively and emotively associated with the Dashnak side of the diaspora. For a fascinating personal account of the repatriation, of the hopes, the disappointment and the eventual emigration back to the West (to the United States in 1965) see H. Touryantz, *Search for a*

The other disappointment, both in Armenia and in the diaspora, was the fact that the Soviet authorities, after raising hopes over the land issue so much, completely dropped it. Once again Armenians felt cheated by a regime which, supposedly, was to defend their national interests. As mentioned earlier, this led some in Armenia to turn against Soviet rule as dissidents, while it fuelled the fire of irredentism in others. Once the Soviet regime had raised the issue of land claims on behalf of the Armenians it was impossible to eliminate the demands from the public domain—especially when Mount Ararat is so clearly visible from Yerevan.

The second effect was to introduce a new identity cleavage within Soviet Armenian society and polity. In addition to existing regional divides, the local/*aghpar* (meaning 'brother' but used as a derogatory term for Armenians from abroad) split was created. This cleavage continues, albeit in a milder form, to this day. It is not part of any official document or pronouncement, but it is clearly observable to anyone who spends time in Armenia. The following are some examples as they pertain to politics (from my own research notes). During the 1996 presidential elections the issue of Levon Ter Petrosian being an '*aghpar*' was raised by both the descendants of repatriates (as a reason to vote for him) and by the 'indigenous' Armenians (as a reason not to vote for him). The latter were particularly upset, according to the former, that *both* heads of the nation, the President and the Catholicos (Karekin I, who was widely perceived to be a supporter of the President) were Armenians from abroad. As one '*aghpar*' informant rather forcefully and in an exaggerated manner put it to me, 'We have nothing to do with the locals'. Another added, 'We should vote for Ter Petrosian, he is one of "us".'

On the other side of the fence, I witnessed the following fascinating tirade in *Communist* Party headquarters while waiting to interview an official. It was a few weeks before the presidential elections. The speaker seemed to be a high-ranking member.

'We, the Communists, built the country and now the present regime is destroying it under the name of 'mafioso-capitalism'... They are selling the country to foreigners, to Turks, to Iranians (who are really Azeris [i.e.

Homeland; the quote on the cover of this book is telling: 'No experience is ever a complete failure. It can always serve as an example not to repeat the same mistakes.'

from Iranian Azerbaijan]). They are letting these impurities pollute our country. How can it be that non-Armenians get citizenship to this republic? There are 1,500 Iranian kids born here and with Armenian citizenship—and Azeri Iranian! This is a disgrace. But what do you expect from the *foreign* leaders [of Armenia]? The leaders of a country have to be from that nation, from that blood and genes. They cannot be otherwise.... [Someone else continued, even more furiously] ...The present leaders are giving the land to the Turks, and blaming it on Lenin—having the nerve, in their smallness, to criticise the glory of Lenin.... And that Ter Petrosian, that son of Arab land, that traitor to the nation, insolent [*lkti*], hooligan.... They used to live under the Arabs, under the Turks, like slaves, and now they are 'leading' the country? Shame! You should have seen how pathetic the Armenians were under the Arabs, and afraid to raise their voice, while here, in the fatherland, we had so much pride, much higher standard of living, culture, education... The state has to be powerful for a small nation like Armenia, and we had such a powerful state, the Russian one, which was protecting us....'

Another lifelong member of the Communist Party offered to me the following 'genealogy' of the President at the height of an anti-Levon Ter Petrosian rally. She first asserted:

'Neither Talaat Pasha,... nor Sultan Hamid, nor Ataturk, nor King Shapuh [of Persia],... have damaged [Armenian] humanity as much as Levon.... Levon's father was an Arab whom Armenians had killed. His [maternal] grandfather was Armenian. Levon took the revenge of his father on the Armenians [by destroying this country]. His wife is Jewish, his mother is Assyrian, so is his maternal uncle.'[109]

These tirades, with their rich imagery and disturbing racism, can be analysed on many levels. In this context, I would just like to highlight their anti-*aghpar* nature. The second quote is particularly interesting, with its anything-but-Armenian 'logic'—never mind the obvious contradictions.

The third effect of the repatriation was to bring into Armenia a group of people who were much more knowledgeable about Armenian history, the nationalist revolutionary past, the Armenian heroes and their deeds (many were the successful products of the Armenian national schools in Lebanon and elsewhere). These peo-

109 Ter Petrosian's wife being of Russian-Jewish background was used against him by some nationalists—with all the usual conspiracy theories. I have analysed elsewhere the racist component of Armenian nationalism (R. Panossian, 'The Past as Nation', pp. 132–6).

ple could at least privately counter the state-propagated collective amnesia towards the national past in Armenia. They brought stories of heroic battles for the nation (rather than for the proletariat), of the *fedayees* and of nationalist revolutionary parties. Moreover, they brought with them very strong regional identities from historic and western Armenia.[110]

In my discussions with many *aghpars* and their descendants it became obvious how they had retained a remarkable sense of identity linked to their ancestral town or village, especially if it was one of the more 'famous' western Armenian centres of national resistance—e.g. Mush, Sasun, Van etc. The one group of people I observed closely were the descendants of repatriates from the Armenian village of Kessab (Kesap), currently in Syria. Even the Armenia-born generation felt very strongly about Kessab—without ever seeing it. There was much pride in the (mostly uneventful) history of the village. It was a strange type of longing for a *diasporan* community—albeit a very old one—as a 'homeland', while living in the 'real' fatherland. The dialect of Kessab (unintelligible to other Armenians) was proudly spoken and taught to children, and in some cases even to Russian brides.

The important dimension of this regional identity (for my argument) is how it is connected to nationalism. For example, the identity of a '*Kessabtsi*' (i.e. someone from the village) is fused with nationalist identity through past stories of heroes, *fedayees* and anti-Turkish battles. Moreover, knowledge of national history is tied to being an expatriate with certain suggestions that it was really the repatriates who brought national identity and knowledge of the past to Soviet Armenia. Therefore, it is implied, the returnees are 'better' Armenians. It was even explicitly stated a few times, and by a number of different ordinary people, that the 1988 movement began with the descendants of the repatriates (i.e. men who were the children of First World War refugees from Ottoman Armenia, and who went to school in the 1960s).[111] The returnees did have more knowledge

110 Ancestral regional roots are an important identity marker for Armenians. For example, both in the republic and in the diaspora, when one Armenian meets another for the first time he or she usually asks where the other person is 'really' from—i.e. which region of historic Armenia can the family roots be traced to.

111 Indeed, President Ter Petrosian, one of the key leaders of the 1988 nationalist movement, is a descendant from Musa Dagh (Musa Ler), the Armenian village that

of national history in the 1950s and 1960s, as compared with the Stalin-era educated Armenians. And, importantly, they passed down this (forbidden) knowledge from one generation to the next. The official history taught in schools, as national as it had become, could not compete in its nationalism with the experienced, uncensored and often exaggerated history of the '*fedayee* past' which was learnt from the stories of the elders. When the locals accused the repatriates of being uncultured, the latter retorted that the locals did not know Armenian history. The 'nationalising' role—however significant or not—the repatriates played in Soviet Armenia was certainly an unintended consequence that the Communist authorities had not foreseen. Again none of this can be discerned from official documents or publications, but it is clearly observable at the popular level.

A divided diaspora and Soviet Armenia's links with it

The repatriation drive further exacerbated the already tense Armenia-diaspora relations, and intra-community relations in most of the significant diasporan centres. By 1948 the ARF had reinforced its staunchly anti-Soviet stand. The Hnchaks and the Ramkavars had been supportive of the Soviet regime since the early 1920s.[112] The

---

defended itself against Turkish attack in 1915. As early as the 1930s the Musa Dagh battle had entered Armenian history as an episode of heroic national defence.

112 The ARF was initially divided on the issue of the repatriation. It supported the idea in the 1920s, but reversed its policy in the 1930s. A serious split emerged within the organisation between those who were staunchly against Soviet rule and those who were less opposing and in favour of repatriation. By 1947–8 the 'anti' side was firmly in control. The ARF thus came to associate its nationalism with anti-communism (N. Schahgaldian, *Political Integration*, pp. 93, 105–8, 202–4). Conversely, the Ramkavar Party, reorganised in Constantinople in October 1921, declared in its first congress (June 1922), and in its 1924 congress (in Paris), that it recognised the Soviet government of Armenia as legitimate and affirmed the Party's willingness to assist Soviet Armenia (C. Mouradian, 'L'Arménie soviétique', pp. 276–7). Relations between the Ramkavars and the Soviets were not always smooth. They deteriorated sharply in the 1930s to the point where the local representative of the pro-Ramkavar charity, the Armenian General Benevolent Union (AGBU), Haikaz Garakiozian, was shot in July 1938. The Armenian First Secretary of the time, Aghasi Khanjian, denounced the AGBU, Ramkavars, Hnchaks and Dashnaks—all diasporan organisations—as agents of Western imperialism who were preparing 'cannon fodder' for the imperialists to attack the USSR (E. Melkonian, *Haikakan Baregortzakan*, pp. 87–91, 181–2).

diaspora was divided fundamentally into two overall blocs: pro-Dashnak and non-Dashnak (including Ramkavar and Hnchak). By the 1950s, after the bitter conflict of the inter-war period, each segment had its own sphere of influence and its own institutional, psychological and sometimes even physical 'territory'.[113] There were two sets of umbrella organisations with global networks linking the various branches of each bloc, which were scattered over many countries. This meant that there existed two parallel Armenian Apostolic churches, two sets of cultural organisations, philanthropic societies, sports clubs, school systems, media outlets and so forth. Socialisation and intermarriage between the blocs were rare or non-existent as one was born and raised in his/her sub-community rather than voluntarily joining it or leaving it. The Cold War was also fought *within* Armenian diasporan communities and there was indeed an Iron Curtain separating one bloc from the other. Each bloc was under the hegemony of its respective political party. This entrenched system has been the operative dynamic within all major Armenian diaspora communities (excluding Istanbul) outside the USSR for the past half a century.[114] Only very recently—i.e. after the collapse of the USSR—there has been a limited thaw between the two blocs. It is mostly evident at the social level, especially among the young. But this limited rapprochement has not translated to political or institutional unity or even systematic cooperation.

The root cause of this political divide was each side's relationship with Soviet Armenia. The Ramkavar/Hnchak bloc supported the Soviet republic. Ironically the party that started as the organisation representing bourgeois-liberal interests was the main ally of Soviet

113 For example, by 1946 there was a 'complete division of Lebanon's Armenian community into two opposing and intensely hostile camps.... The two camps behaved as if they were entirely different sectarian groups.' There were even dozens of intra-community killings between 1947 and 1960; the vocabulary used for the opposing camps included words like 'traitors', 'lackeys' and 'agents' (N. Schahgaldian, *Political Integration*, pp. 221, 224). For the divide in the community in America see S. Atamian, *Armenian Community*, pp. 377ff. For party divisions in the Cyprus community see S. Pattie, *Faith in History*, pp. 93–6.

114 This is a generalisation of a complex dynamic. There are also 'neutral' (*chezok*) elements, especially large in North America by the 1980s. In addition, the diaspora is not just one homogeneous entity. As mentioned, there are marked differences in terms of habits and outlooks between communities in the West and the Middle East. Finally, within each bloc there are divisions, but not deep enough to undermine the bloc system.

Armenia; its logic was that the homeland must be supported whatever its regime.[115] The politically more significant Dashnak bloc was staunchly opposed to Armenia because of its Soviet regime. The Hnchak-Ramkavar-Armenian SSR alliance became a small hole in the global Iron Curtain, linking parts of the diaspora with the Soviet republic, but on the latter's terms.[116] This was the main link between Armenia and the diaspora—i.e. with one segment of the diaspora—until 1988.

Since the 1920s there has been either open conflict or low intensity opposition between the Dashnaks on the one side, and Soviet Armenia and its diasporan allies on the other. At the core of the bitter dispute were the questions: who was the legitimate representative of the diaspora, who were the 'true' leaders of the community *and the nation*? Whose version of Armenian identity was to be hegemonic? What were the basic tenets of this identity? The issue and the divisiveness it produced became the defining elements of Armenian politics throughout the entire life of Soviet Armenia. A two-pronged battle ensued: for the control of the diaspora, and for legitimacy.

The first instrument of the Soviet Armenian side in this battle was the government created *Hayastani Ognutian Komite* (HOK) (Aid Committee for Armenia), with the explicit purpose of generating material support for Soviet Armenia from diaspora communities.

115 As one of the Ramkavar leaders put it in a recent keynote speech (in Lebanon), the party supported Soviet Armenia without adhering to its political and party structure, because it wanted 'to see the fatherland secure, to resolutely support the fatherland, and to be nourished by the fatherland' (O. Potrumian, 'Orvan panakhos', p. 2). The thesis that Armenia could not have survived without Russian support and that the latter built the country is still prevalent in the Ramkavar press. One 1999 editorial concluded, 'It was Moscow which provided the day-to-day needs of Armenia,' not to mention the funds to build the nuclear power plant, the Yerevan metro etc. ('Hayastan yev Rusastan', p. 2).

116 One telling document about the close relationship between the Ramkavars and the Soviet authorities is a report from the Soviet Foreign Ministry to the Armenian 'Foreign Minister', B. G. Martirosian, dated 29 August 1959. It is based on the report of the USSR's ambassador in Lebanon of his meeting with Ramkavar leader Barunak Tovmasian. The ambassador recounts that Tovmasian explicitly asked for financial assistance from the government of the Armenian SSR for the 'Progressive Armenian Alliance' which included Ramkavars, Hnchaks, independents; and it was supported by the Armenian Communists of Lebanon (i.e. all the anti-Dashnak forces). They wanted the money to maintain party activities—from propaganda to paramilitary forces—as well as support for the anti-ARF electoral campaign (SCAHCH 326/1/271[1959]).

Founded on 13 September 1921, it was to collect funds for economic reconstruction and famine relief, aid refugees and engage in other humanitarian work: in short, to support the republic at a time of great difficulty. But it was also to be Armenia's means of influence and control of the diaspora. For fifteen years (it was dissolved in 1937) the HOK became the main political tool and propaganda conduit for Soviet authorities in dealing with Armenians abroad (it claimed to have 10,000 members worldwide).[117] In addition to soliciting aid, it was to 'tighten the links between the diaspora and the homeland'. Its declarations also called for support for Armenian workers' rights throughout the world and, more importantly, implored Armenians to wage battle against the Dashnaks who were accused of being 'the author of the immense crimes committed against our country.'[118] Despite the standard references to workers' rights, imperialism and communist revolution, the HOK's appeals for aid were essentially underpinned by Armenian patriotism. The main point was that only Soviet rule could provide the peace and security necessary for Armenia to rebuild and to prosper. Hence a truly concerned Armenian in the diaspora should support the Soviet government (and Union) because this would mean support for the fatherland.

The HOK set the stage for subsequent homeland-diaspora relations. But its methods needed to be refined. A new approach was developed after the 1957 decision of the Central Committee of the Armenian Communist Party which sought to augment the republic's influence over diaspora communities. This had become particularly pertinent after Soviet Armenia's 'defeat' in the elections of the Catholicos of Cilicia in 1956 (the ARF's candidate was elected). It was clear that a new, more sophisticated and long term approach was required. Instead of trying to directly control institutions and communities (as it had tried through the HOK in the 1920s), the

[117] There were also a small but active number of Armenian Communists in the diaspora, some of whom were quite involved in the setting up and operation of the Communist parties in the Middle East (T. Ter Minassian, *Colporteurs du Komintern*, pp. 154–62).

[118] C. Mouradian, 'L'Arménie soviétique', pp. 261–2, 265, cf. pp. 260–7. When the HOK was closed amidst the Stalinist terror, some of its local leaders were shot for being 'bourgeois nationalists' and 'rightist Trotskyites' (E. Melkonian, *Haikakan Baregortzakan*, pp. 160–9).

Soviet Armenian government implemented policies of rapprochement. Using—and strengthening—its close ties with one sector of the community, it tried to undermine the legitimacy of the other. The main instrument of the new policy was the *Spiurkahayutian Het Mshakutayin Kapi Komite* (SMKK) (Committee for Cultural Ties with Diaspora Armenians), established in 1964. It systematised, regulated and substantially increased the links with the diaspora. It promoted contacts and cultural exchanges, provided language and literature textbooks, invited sympathetic intellectuals to visit Armenia, sent dance troupes and music choirs abroad to perform in Armenian communities, and sponsored selected diasporan youth to study free of charge at universities in the republic.[119] It also oversaw the dissemination of specific journals and magazines aimed at Armenians abroad (e.g. the paper *Haireniki Dzain* [Voice of the Fatherland], which it began to publish in 1965, and the magazine *Sovetakan Hayastan* [Soviet Armenia]). It should be noted that these contacts were made explicitly on the terrain of culture and education with no overt political agenda or agitation.[120] It was a rather more subtle

[119] Armenian students from the diaspora were first admitted to institutions of higher learning in Armenia in 1957, when twenty arrived. After 1964 70 students came per year (SCAHCH 326/1/352[1969]). Between 1963 and 1985 1,244 students of the 1,590 admitted graduated from vocational schools and universities. Approximately 80 per cent came from Middle Eastern countries. In the 1985–6 academic year there were 108 diasporan students registered in Armenia (L. Gharibjanian, 'Krdakan-mshakutayin kianke', pp. 56–7). In 1975 there were a total of 531 foreign students from 28 countries studying in Soviet Armenia. Of these, 320 were Armenian. 82 Armenians had applied to study in Armenia (from 15 countries) in 1974–5, and 70 were accepted (SCAHCH 326/1/583[1975]; for an earlier report see SCAHCH 326/1/461[1969]). In some communities in the Middle East (e.g. in Syria), these graduates (doctors, teachers, engineers etc.) formed a significant part of the diasporan intellectual elite, affecting social relations and, of course, the diaspora's view of Soviet Armenia. The practice of having diasporan Armenians study in the republic continues to this day. In the 1998–9 academic year 70 university places were given to Armenians from abroad, including 13 from Mountainous Gharabagh. There were a total of 111 applications—As reported in *Zartonk* (Beirut), 11 Dec. 1998. For the year 1999–2000 60 places were reserved for diasporans and 30 for students from Gharabagh (*Zartonk*, 1 Sept. 1999).

[120] Author's interview with Karlen Dallakian. Note that Dallakian was the head of the SMKK between December 1985 to February 1991. For his (positive) assessment of the work and role of the Committee see K. Dallakian, *Hushapatum*, pp. 280–333. Obviously Dallakian had a very positive view of the SMKK and regretted that the post-Soviet government of Armenia closed it. This 'was the same as someone cutting

form of propaganda which portrayed the Armenian SSR as *the* homeland, the exclusive source of national identity where the nation was being conserved and advanced.[121] Economic development and social standards were also part of this message. Moreover, it was viewed as a concerned homeland providing cultural nourishment for the

---

the branch he was sitting on' (p. 332). Then he jokes that he was dismissed from his post as Armenia's ideology chief in 1985 for being too nationalist, and he was dismissed by the Armenian National Movement government from his post as the head of the SMKK for being too Communist (p. 332)! The ARF consistently criticised the SMKK as a propaganda tool (see H. Marukhian, 'Grakan Tert-i', p. 12; 'Hakadashnaktsakan arshavi', pp. 18–19.

[121] This 1974 document from the archives is indicative of the thinking behind Soviet relations with the diaspora. It is entitled 'Minister's [Foreign Minister?] Report Addressed to Armenian CP Central Committee and USSR Foreign Affairs Ministry Regarding the Implementation of Efforts to Neutralise the Anti-Soviet Propaganda of the Dashnaks in Armenian Colonies of the Diaspora' (SCAHCH 326/1/562[1974]). It includes the presentation of a detailed plan. These are some of the twenty-eight points listed:

— Soviet successes to be emphasised by Armenpress and the Ministry of Culture;
— Armenian films to be sent abroad, and film festivals organised (via Soviet central agencies);
— school textbooks, cultural workers and agitators to be sent abroad;
— exhibits of Armenian culture to be organised;
— Intourist to have people carrying out propaganda;
— book fairs to be organised;
— the USSR foreign ministry to send Armenian diplomats to countries where there are large Armenian communities (e.g. Beirut, Montreal, Argentina);
— counter assimilation through publications such as *Sovetakan Hayastan* and *Haireniki Dzain*;
— ask Soviet central authorities to allow Armenian teachers from the republic to teach in diasporan schools;
— invite progressive Armenian organisations to Armenia and help them solve their internal disputes and create a united pro-Armenia front;
— strengthen the sense of political responsibility in Armenian students from abroad studying in Armenia;
— central authorities to increase the number of students from the diaspora studying pedagogy to 50;
— invite diasporan children to come to Armenia for summer camp. Give financial aid to *Lraper* in the United States, and restart *Sevan* newspaper in Argentina (both being pro-Soviet Armenian publications);
— bring youth groups to Armenia on a subsidised basis through Intourist and the Ministry of Culture;
— organise symposia;
— apply to Ejmiatzin so that the Catholicos will further increase his activities relating to the diaspora.

diaspora so that it could preserve its 'weakening' Armenianness in foreign lands. Hence the diaspora came to be viewed as a mere annex with no purpose of its own. While the republic's security and prosperity were emphasised, there was no mention of liberty and independence, and no anti-Russian sentiment was expressed.[122]

Thanks to the efforts of the SMKK, a new mentality began to emerge which eventually took root in the diaspora, becoming the dominant paradigm of its relations with the Armenian SSR. In this view, the earlier roles of donor and recipient were reversed. The homeland became the 'aid' provider, while the diaspora needed assistance for its national 'survival'. This was not economic relief, but cultural support. The homeland was now perceived to be the bastion of Armenianness, coming to help its culturally 'poor' brothers in exile.[123] The diaspora came to be viewed as an appendix to the fatherland, its long-term survival as an Armenian entity depending on the nation-state existent on the territory of the Armenian SSR. It was pointed out that the diaspora was succumbing to the pressures of assimilation (particularly in the West), losing its language and identity, its culture was getting 'diluted' and it was susceptible to upheavals and persecutions in the host societies (e.g. Arab nationalism in Egypt and Syria in the late 1950s and 1960s). In short, the diaspora did not have the benefit of its own state and needed the Soviet Armenian one for its cultural fund and national-spiritual nourishment. So went the logic.

ARF-Soviet Armenia relations

It had become increasingly difficult for the Dashnaks and their supporters in the diaspora to oppose Soviet Armenia by the 1980s. On the one hand the republic was more amicable as a national centre owing to its clearly visible nationalisation; on the other the meaning of the 'Armenian Cause' shifted from the debate over Soviet rule to Genocide recognition and Turkish denial, to anti-Turkish propaganda and later terrorism. The impetus of this shift had come from

[122] For a similar argument see C. Mouradian, 'L'Arménie soviétique', pp. 287–90, 292; cf. U. Björklund, 'Armenia Remembered', p. 343.

[123] The literary manifestation of this was found in the works of Silva Kaputikian and Andranik Tzarukian, as discussed above.

the 1965 events in Armenia. The Soviet state was now accepted in all sectors of the community, but to varying degrees: from benign acknowledgement to active support. Even the Dashnaks, toning down their anti-Soviet rhetoric, accepted that the Armenian SSR was *a*—if not *the*—homeland, albeit imperfect and territorially incomplete. Independence was, therefore, put on the back burner of their agenda. Armenians throughout the world came to believe that being part of the Soviet Union—that is, being under Russian hegemony—was vital for the nation's physical survival. It was not free, but it was at least secure. However, the ARF had very little official or organisational contact with Armenia. It maintained control over its bloc in the diaspora while ceasing to question the legitimacy of Soviet rule in Armenia. A stable pattern of co-existence was the norm in the 1970s and 1980s, as there was now considerable conceptual overlap between Soviet Armenia and the 'homeland'. This is not to say that the Armenian SSR replaced the Dashnak ideal of the homeland which remained in the abstract and attached to the lost lands to be retrieved from Turkey.[124]

Evidence of the ARF's change of position come from its own publications, as well as from its opponents. The party had begun to change its confrontational attitude toward Soviet Armenia as early as 1963. Over the years this was reinforced at party congresses and clearly articulated in the publications of the organisation. For example, its 22nd General Congress in 1982 saluted

> the Armenians of Armenia, who have, during the last 60 years, overcome a world of difficulties and grim temptations, and have accepted superhuman sacrifices to protect and to reconstruct the fatherland; have grown in population; and have recorded honourable achievements in scientific, technological and cultural fields. With an ear to the echoes of Armenian History, they strive with all available means to reinforce the bases of our existence today and tomorrow, having a clear vision of the bright future for the whole Armenian nation.

Of course, the ideal of a united, free and independent homeland was not forgotten, nor the liberation of the 'occupied historic lands' in Turkey. But there was no attack on the Soviet regime. In fact,

[124] Some diasporan intellectuals also occasionally raised the issue of Mountainous Gharabagh, highlighting its subordination to Azerbaijan and the difficult conditions within the enclave (see, for example, G. Grigorian, 'Krkin Gharabagh').

echoing Soviet thinking, it advocated focusing 'on Armenia and to contribute to its security and progress directly and indirectly.'[125] The Party Programme of the 23rd Congress (1985) went further. It said that although the ARF does not accept communist totalitarianism, it nevertheless 'decides to limit its demands and criticisms in relation to Armenia, the Armenian nation and the Armenian Cause, and to refrain from taking one-sided positions in international issues against the Soviet Union.'[126] Nikola Schahgaldian points out that as early as

> ...1974 Dashnak intellectuals viewed Soviet Armenia as the 'national home' of the Armenian people and their 'only salvation and hope'. They now recognized Armenia as a place where Armenian culture and literature developed according to Armenian national traditions. Moreover, many Dashnaks came to accept the notion, already expounded for decades by the SDHP [Hnchak Party] and the DLP [Ramkavar Party], that without Soviet Armenia, the existence of the diaspora would become meaningless in the long run because sooner or later Armenian communities were bound to disappear as ethnic collectivities.[127]

Many of the ARF's critics attributed this change of policy to KGB infiltration of the party. When President Levon Ter Petrosian expelled the ARF leader, Hrair Marukhian, from Armenia in July 1992, among the various accusations he levelled against the Dashnak leader was the 'fact' that the latter had collaborated with the KGB in the past.[128] One 'objective proof' of this accusation from a

[125] 'Public Message', p. 197 (both citations).

[126] As published in the party organ, *Droshak* (Flag) (17:8–9, 6–20 Aug. 1986, p. 6; see also, 'Patmakan pataskhanatvutiun', p. 4). Another interesting revelation is made by Edik Hovhannisian, a high ranking Dashnak intellectual and leader. In his attempt to debunk criticisms from Soviet Armenia that the ARF is a tool in the hands of US imperialists, he cites a study of the ARF press in the first half of 1986 which found that, out of the 10,653 articles published, there was not a single pro-US article. Instead, there were 1,532 forceful anti-US articles, 943 forceful pro-Soviet articles, the rest being neutral or anti-Turkish. There were only 16–21 articles which were mildly critical of the USSR. He also goes on to say that since the early 1970s, there has not been any anti-Soviet activity such as demonstrations, flyers etc, organised by the ARF (E. Hovhannisian, 'Dashnaktsutiune', pp. 20–2).

[127] N. Schahgaldian, *Political Integration*, pp. 111–12.

[128] L. Ter Petrosian, 'Nerkaghakakan mtahogich taknap', pp. 40–1. The same accusation is made by S. Melik-Hakobian, 'Establishment of the Second Republic'; I. Muradian, 'Dashnaktsutiune', p. 4.

non-Armenian source came from Oleg Kalugin, a former Chief of Counter-Intelligence and Major General in the KGB. In his book he makes a passing reference to the ARF:

> ...the émigré organization we most thoroughly infiltrated was the Armenian exile group, Dashnak Tsutyun [sic]. Once, Dashnak Tsutyun had been a staunchly nationalist group that campaigned for an independent Armenian state. Over time, we placed so many agents there that several had risen to positions of leadership. We succeeded in effectively neutralizing the group, and by the 1980s Dashnak Tsutyun had stopped fighting against Soviet power in Armenia. The organization and some of its members had been co-opted by the KGB. Years later, in 1992,... I provided [President Ter Petrosian] and the Armenian press with information about KGB's deep penetration of that émigré group in the 1970s.[129]

This one paragraph in a 300-page book made Kalugin 'essential reading' for some Armenians. It seemed to confirm the suspicions of many both within and without the Party that certain ARF leaders were KGB 'operatives'.

Of course the ARF leaders vehemently denied any such infiltration by or cooperation with the KGB. Marukhian, at the centre of the accusation, admitted that since 1963 the ARF and Soviet Armenian representatives had met about once a year (or less) to discuss national issues such as the Armenian Cause, the rights of Soviet Armenian citizens, homeland-diaspora relations, attitudes towards Turkey, the reduction of media criticism of one another etc. The Soviet side was asked to be more national, to publish more balanced history texts and to lessen anti-ARF propaganda. The meetings were held in various cities including Yerevan, Moscow, Geneva and Beirut. These meetings did not constitute Dashnaks being agents of the KGB, Marukhian insisted, or being in the service of Soviet authorities. The ARF never met the KGB knowingly, but representatives of the republic—and if they were KGB members, the Dashnaks could not know. Concerning these representatives Marukhian maintained: 'Whatever was their *real* affiliation, the approach they were manifesting was *national*.'[130]

It was undeniable that by the late 1970s there was a rapprochement between the Communist authorities and the ARF, whatever

[129] O. Kalugin, *Spymaster*, p. 193.

[130] H. Marukhian, 'Hayastani Hanrapetutian', p. 19, cf. pp. 16–20.

the reasons. The first continued to issue the occasional anti-Dashnak pronouncement, but it was a matter of 'show'. According to Karlen Dallakian, they did this to demonstrate to Moscow that they had an external 'threat' and as such they could get more concessions on national issues from the centre. It was a strategic move and not necessarily a matter of belief.[131] In response the latter would occasionally criticise some of the policies of the republic, raise the Gharabagh issue or mention the dissident movement. In the long run, however, the ARF lost quite a bit of prestige both in Armenia and in the diaspora as a result of the rapprochement. This became obvious by 1989.

Since the early 1950s the republic had come a long way in its nationalisation. Armenian identity was reinforced, the culture was deeply rooted in the people and institutionalised through the state, and the language was relatively secure. Only national causes *outside* the republic remained to be solved, as did the question of the political control of the country. Armenia had become a fairly compact and secure nation-state. On the diasporan side its nationalist discourse remained and was getting increasingly closer to the Soviet republic in terms of cultural *cooperation*.

But none of this could lead to the 'unity' of the two parts of the nation. Cooperation is not the same as homogenisation or fusion into one overarching contemporary culture; rather it entails contact between two distinct entities. The Soviet republic had nationalised on its own terms, not on the terms of the diaspora. In the meantime diasporan identity had evolved in different directions. Diasporan Armenians might have felt an emotional affinity toward their 'homeland', might have shared some of the same ancient symbols and beliefs, but they were not speaking in eastern Armenian, their habits and outlook were quite different from those of their Soviet kin, their social life and education (with minor exceptions) were unconnected to Armenia, their political structures and community organisations were formally independent of the SSR, and they were not participating in the cultural production *of* the republic as such.

[131] Author's interview with Karlen Dallakian. Dallakian was aware that the ARF had come to the conclusion that Russian protection was essential for Armenia's security and survival (K. Dallakian, *Hushapatum*, pp. 302–3).

Hence, despite the close links between Soviet Armenia and the non-Dashnak bloc, and the fact that antagonisms between the Soviets and the ARF has eased considerably, there remained a deep divide between Armenia and the diaspora. Each side had a legitimate claim to being Armenian, but each was of a different sort.

Furthermore, there was a deep ignorance of each other. Closer cooperation did not mean that the two parts really understood one another. One faction of the diaspora more or less idealised the Soviet homeland, blind to its problems, the other side criticised it while dreaming of a greater Armenia. Both perceptions were based on superficial knowledge mostly obtained from one-sided information, propaganda and short visits (tourism was allowed from 1957 onwards). The view in Armenia regarding the diaspora was based on the perception that Armenians abroad were unfortunate because they lived outside their homeland, and that they were somehow incomplete in their national identity, especially those 'symbolic' Armenians of the West, and those who had lost the language. These Armenians were to be 'helped' (usually in a condescending manner) while they were simultaneously envied for their material wealth. The view in the diaspora regarding Armenia was mostly based on the positive image painted by the SMKK, the Catholicos and various intellectuals—it was of a modern country at the centre of Armenianness. On the whole, by 1988 the ancient east/west divide had not been overcome, although there was at least a small bridge between the two, the toll booth of which was operated by Soviet Armenia. Neither the homeland's nor the diaspora's vision of Armenianness had become hegemonic. Neither side could claim to be the legitimate 'representative' of all Armenians—although the balance was clearly in favour of the Armenian SSR. Onto this scene burst the Gharabagh movement, and homeland-diaspora relations entered a new stage of uncertainly.[132]

STAGNATION AND DISSATISFACTION

From the 1970s on a period of stagnation had set in, both in Armenia and in the diaspora. Social, economic and political stagnation

[132] For post-Soviet Armenia-diaspora relations see R. Panossian, 'Diaspora and the Karabagh Movement'; R. Panossian, 'Courting a Diaspora'.

might not appear to be directly connected to national identity, but many nationalist intellectuals in the 1988 movement in Armenia mobilised around social issues (corruption, environmental degradation, social justice), making them into *national* causes.[133] Moreover, the opponents of the Soviet regime interpreted the stagnation as an anti-national move. For example, Levon Mkrtchian, after pointing out that certain Soviet leaders did benefit the republic, added:

> Then came a generation which was not concerned with anything besides their own positions and benefits; they just wanted to live well and acquire wealth. This last generation of Communist Party workers is still harming us tremendously today because they are in third and fourth positions in the regime or state institutions. And they are still doing the same, benefiting only themselves.

Ashot Manucharian, overstating the point, said: 'Not a single secretary of the Communist Party [in Armenia in 1988] primarily cared for the national benefit. Their main goal was to keep their positions. Second was national interest.'[134] And in the sensitive area of art and culture, nepotism and corruption were common problems that stifled creativity, innovation and quality:

> In the mid-1980s a general malaise had set in all the arts. Theatre, ballet, opera, literature, music and the film industry had all displayed a stagnation and mediocrity uncharacteristic of Armenian cultural life, and everyone knew it. Unions were run like the mafia and indeed, the term *mafiosi* for union chiefs and their acolytes was very commonly used by the sensitive public of Yerevan.... The arts in Armenia should be thriving; they are not.[135]

There were of course those who argued that the Soviet system as a whole was destructive of the Armenian nation. Paruir Hairikian, as mentioned, was the most adamant in this argument. Razmik Davoyan spoke of the all encompassing 'machinery' which destroyed the human spirit. And Artashes Shahpazian argued that despite the fact

133 Author's interview with Ashot Manucharian. Manucharian was more on the 'social' wing of the movement than the 'national'.

134 The first quote is from the author's interview with Levon Mkrtchian; the second from the interview with Ashot Manucharian. The economic side of the stagnation meant irrational or 'stupid' activities and policies that damaged Armenia's economy (author's interview with Gurgen Geghamian).

135 D. Kouymjian, 'Status of Artists', p. 60.

of creating a 'powerful culture', economic benefits and a strong scientific basis, in the end, the Soviet system did 'more harm than benefit to us' because of its anti-national policies.[136] The stagnation of the 1970s and 1980s added fuel to such arguments.

After Gorbachev's reforms of *perestroika* and *glasnost* were announced, and First Secretary Demirchian was openly criticised by Gorbachev in June 1987, some in the Armenian leadership tried to institute reforms in the country. Haik Kotanjian, the First Secretary of the Hrazdan region, was one of these men. He gave his first speech in July 1987 on the issues of reform, corruption and deviation from the 'true path' of socialism. Despite his pro-Gorbachev and pro-reform stand, he was swiftly denounced by the local party leadership for being an anti-party 'deviant' and a 'careerist'.[137] Not much came out of his criticism, but it was already too late. Months later the Gharabagh movement had erupted, changing the political scene of Armenia. In short, until the very end the Party leadership in Armenia remained 'a tightly-woven network of friends and colleagues, even relatives, who manage through their loyalty to Moscow and their protection of one another within Armenia to maintain their positions of authority.'[138] Nationalist or not, these men tried to hold on to power for as long as they could. Eventually the top leadership gave up their positions in 1990 to a non-Communist and staunchly nationalist counter-elite. Soviet-style limited cultural nationalism—formally divorced from politics—was insufficient for the new politics of Armenia.

In the diaspora too there was a widespread sense of stagnation, especially among the traditional parties and community organisations. Petty internal disputes, corruption with respect to public funds, and moral bankruptcy clashed with the revolutionary rhetoric and the 'official' nationalism of the parties.[139] Many of the youth were alienated. Some in the Middle East turned to terrorism, while others in the West tried to establish new non-partisan and professional organisations. There was even dissidence within the tightly-controlled

[136] All from author's interviews with the respective individuals.

[137] Based on author's informal discussions with Haik Kotanjian (November 1996), and H. Kotanjian, *Haikakan 'yekrasharzhe'*, pp. 51ff., 73ff., 91ff. Kotanjian is currently Armenia's military attaché in Washington.

[138] R. Suny, *Armenia in the Twentieth Century*, p. 74.

[139] N. Schahgaldian, *Political Integration*, pp. 228–9, 254–5.

ARF. Many party members privately criticised their leadership for the stagnation of the organisation and its timid policies.[140] In many ways the diaspora as a whole was mirroring developments in Soviet Armenia, and the ARF was mirroring developments in the Communist Party—other diasporan parties did not fare any better.

Finally, as an indication of their dissatisfaction within Armenia, thousands voted with 'their feet' by leaving the republic. There was discontent over conditions, particularly among the post-Second World War immigrants who had had difficulties in assimilating into the mainstream of society. This was one more indication that even after a generation change, many diasporan repatriates could simply not fit into their 'homeland'. The last wave of people to leave Armenia for the diaspora before the 1990s was overwhelmingly made up of these 'repatriates' and their descendants. Almost all moved to the United States, a few to France, but almost none went back to their countries of 'origin' in the Middle East. Between the 1950s and the end of 1988 66,500 Armenians left the USSR.[141] This exodus from the republic was frowned upon by both homeland and diaspora nationalists, but for many ordinary people in Armenia emigrating to the West was a dream come true.

IDEOLOGY AS A GAME

With the exception of the 'security' argument (i.e. the importance of Russian protection against Turkey), communist ideology and

[140] The dissident 'movement' within the ARF finally became public in December 1994. Based in the United States, these members called themselves the ARF Revival Movement and began to publish *Yeraguin Droshak* (Tricolour Flag) in May 1995. Among other demands (e.g. better relations with President Ter Petrosian), they insisted that the party must be restructured into an open, decentralised and democratic organization. They accused its leadership (viz. Hrair Marukhian, who had been in top party positions for over thirty years) of corruption and of self-serving activities which had come to replace endeavours of genuine support for the homeland and the nation.

[141] 12,000 went to France between 1958 and 1960, and almost all of the rest to the United States (S. Heitman, 'Soviet Emigration', pp. 235, 242ff., 248). According to Anny Bakalian's estimates, from 1971 and 1989 some 60,000 entered the United States, 90–95 per cent of them settling in the Los Angeles area. Armenians from the Soviet republic did not comprise more than 5–10 per cent of the total diaspora population in the United States in the early 1990s (A. Bakalian, *Armenian–Americans*, pp. 12–13, 25, 80 n. 13). This number has probably doubled in the last five or six years.

belief in the Soviet system had all but disappeared by the 1980s in Armenia. It had been replaced by national identity and nationalism. In the previous chapter I discussed the gap between official policies and reality. But the whole situation had also become a 'game'. The metaphor of a game was constantly mentioned by many intellectuals. For example, it was clear to all that an 'appropriate' quote from the Marxist-Leninist canon or from the First Secretary of the Central Committee of the Communist Party of the Soviet Union had to be put somewhere in a publication. But, as Levon Abrahamian explained, certain experts would 'compete' with one another to see who could get away with putting the necessary quotation in the most inappropriate or weak place of a text. Others spoke of the 'negotiations' between intellectuals and the censors to try to get away with as much as possible.[142] Of course views on the levels of censorship differed and all saw it as a nuisance, but there was also a certain sense of camaraderie with the *glavlit* to 'get away' with as much as possible.[143] It was striking to see that even the former head of the Armenian censorship board saw the 'game' from this perspective.[144]

[142] Author's interviews with Levon Abrahamian, Levon Ananian, Razmik Davoyan, Gurgen Geghamian, and group interview with members of the Institute for Philosophy and Law.

[143] For example, Gurgen Geghamian told a story of how he was called in by the censors in 1968 to explain why he had written that the 'dekulakisation' of 10,000 peasants in Armenia was wrong because there were no kulaks in the republic. After he explained, the Armenian censor said of the people who would have objected to the book: 'F—their mothers! Send it for publication!' Geghamian was explaining how between the late 1950s and the 1970s censorship constantly eased 'because of the national renaissance' (author's interview with Gurgen Geghamian).

[144] Author's interview with Grigor Martirosian. Even Martirosian presented himself as a 'nationalist' and no doubt exaggerated certain elements of his story. But the fact that some of the intellectuals whom he censored referred to him in a relatively positive manner, and that he was employed to draw up laws on secrecy by the post-Soviet nationalist government, suggest that he too did his best to push the limits on national issues set by Moscow. According to him, when he was first appointed to the position in 1977, Karen Demirchian called him in and said: 'I don't want you to quit [due to various pressures from 'above']. Be nuanced and do such that the history of our people, our literature and art do not suffer, while people above don't talk about us.' The First Secretary had told him this after Martirosian had said that he would only stay in the job if he could 'increase the level reached in 1965, not decrease it'. According to Martirosian the real culprits were the KGB and its operatives in the censorship board 'who always made trouble' by reporting the board's activities and decisions to Moscow. He told of a number of cases where 'nationalist' literature was

Membership of the Communist Party itself was part of the 'game'. Certain educated people used to pay bribes in the range of 3,000 to 5,000 roubles just to join the Party. Being a Party member meant a lucrative job. Hence there was competition among many experts to become Party members not because of conviction, but because of position. On the mass level, Levon Chorbajian shows how people no longer believed in what they were shown on television. By the 1980s 'People would complain to one another about the same worn out ideas being aired repeatedly and expressed a desire for greater balance.'[145] Finally the whole idea of the 'brotherhood of nations' was dismissed by most people as yet another empty slogan. To paraphrase one cultural worker from Stepanakert (the capital of Gharabagh): In the Soviet period there was cultural cooperation, our dance troupes, theatre, musicians went to Baku, and Azerbaijanis came to perform in Gharabagh… But this was *forced cooperation dictated by the state.*[146] Chris Binns has also observed:

> …nowadays [late 1970s, early 1980s] any visitor to the Soviet Union knows how rare it is to come across anyone who sincerely and deeply believes in the principles, doctrines and practices of communism. The idealism and commitment have gone: cynicism, careerism and indifference prevail. Soviet communism can no longer be appropriately described as a secular faith.[147]

What is more, in whatever communist rituals people did participate, they generally ignored the ideological content. 'Marxist-Leninist ideals, [Soviet] patriotism etc… is completely absent [or…] it appears to be virtually ignored. Only those familiar with Soviet reality can appreciate the ability of Soviet citizens to "switch off" to the constant ideological barrage,' adds Binns.[148]

The Communist Party of the Soviet Union itself finally understood the situation, but it was too late to do much about it. At the

---

published, for which he got into trouble from Moscow. The local leadership supported him.

145 L. Chorbajian, 'For the Masses', p. 46. Although there was some further openness in the late 1980s owing to *glasnost*, television's mendacious coverage of the Gharabagh issue really incensed many Armenians turning them against the centre even more (pp. 48–50).

146 Despite the acknowledgement of the forced nature of the cooperation, it was clear that this particular individual was lamenting the current lack of inter-ethnic interaction.

147 C. Binns, 'Soviet Secular Ritual', p. 307.

148 C. Binns, 'Changing Face of Power', part II, p. 183.

CPSU's 19th All-Union Conference (June-July 1988) the resolution 'On Relations between Soviet Nationalities' stated, in the typically Soviet manner: 'Experience has shown that where the practice of Soviet patriotism and socialist internationalism is no more than perfunctory, national narrow-mindedness and chauvinistic arrogance come to the fore.'[149] What Moscow called 'chauvinistic arrogance' was the nationalism of many of the non-Russian republics, particularly that of the Armenians and the Azerbaijanis over Gharabagh.

The Soviet Union affected identity in various, often contradictory, ways. It did make some people more 'cosmopolitan'. It created a stratum of intellectuals who were at ease with being 'Soviet'—as long as it did not directly negate their national identity. Soviet propaganda and policies definitely created a strong pro-Russian mentality in Armenia where almost all of the intellectual elite were well versed in Russian culture. Not all Armenians were nationalists in 1987, and I do not wish to deny this fact. I have simply focused on the 'victorious' element of collective identity—the national dimension—and its politics of nationalism.

Neither capable of completely destroying the national, nor capable of replacing it with something else that would be just as meaningful and deep, the Soviet Union made do with basing its legitimacy on foundations incapable of supporting it. Economic integration, 'rational' arguments (on security or development) and the cultural contacts between the 'brotherhood of nations' proved to be rather shallow antidotes to the power of ethnic affiliation, cultural pride and secession and/or irredentism. Propped up by the threat of coercion, the communist regime languished in a hegemonic 'no-man's land'. Once the imperial centre loosened the controls, the system collapsed, torn apart by the nationalist centrifugal forces. The USSR had failed to achieve its stated goal. It could not create a *Homo Sovieticus* in Armenia (or elsewhere) since on the whole it did not transform the cultural 'essence' of the republic in a denationalising direction. Rather than creating a non-national sense of identity, many of its institutions and policies were used for national(ist) purposes. Seventy years of Soviet rule did, naturally, have some profound effects on identity, especially in the realms of social relations, relations with the state, work ethic and so forth. In addition to structural links, it did create a

[149] 19th All-Union Conference, p. 150.

multi-layered identity, the product of a national culture, Soviet ideology and practices, as well as Russian cultural trappings. The post-Soviet Armenian, for example, is a nationalist, but accepts—willy-nilly—the 'guidance' and some of the values and habits of the old imperial centre, as long as the latter is not too intrusive.

The Soviet Armenian identity was very different, even foreign, to the diasporan Armenian. Many in the diaspora would agree with the Russia-as-security argument, but not much more. The diasporan did not—and does not—see the world, human relations, rights and responsibilities, culture, social and political identity, and the nation from that all-too-obvious but difficult to define 'Soviet' perspective. Soviet Armenians did nationalise *their* republic, but they could not make *their* vision of identity—an Armenian-speaking, Armenia-residing, Russian oriented collective—the *pan*-Armenian ideal. In short, it was a *partial* victory of the homogenisation of identity. The multilocal process of identity formation continued. There were *parallel* processes in Armenia and in the diaspora, increasing contact between the two, but a definite sense of being separate. And yet, all legitimately claimed to be Armenian.

Finally, I began with 1965, and I would like to end with an observation about the significance of the 1965 protests in Yerevan since it is indicative of the political dimension of national identity. I have been describing the process of increased national awareness as national*ism*, rather than a renaissance or a cultural revival. In doing so I am emphasising the *political* dimension—even though much of what I have discussed can be termed as 'cultural nationalism'. The two are intertwined. Nearly every single person I interviewed, regardless of age, mentioned 1965 as a turning point. The other significant cultural events (celebrating the alphabet in 1962 or the 2,750th anniversary of Yerevan's founding in 1968 etc.)—building blocks of nationalism—were either mentioned in passing or not at all. One obvious reason for this is the fact that the occasion of 1965 was the Genocide. But 1965 was the cornerstone of contemporary Armenian identity for another reason. It was the only significant *event* with very clear *political* overtones. If the alphabet, the church, textbooks, literature etc., played an important role, after 1965 they were all filtered, in one way or another, through the political dimension of 1965. In many ways the 1988 national movement was an extension of 1965—but in a more focused and, eventually, organised manner.

8

CONCLUSION: A MULTILOCAL NATION CONTINUES

The Pandora's Box of the Soviet 'nationalities problem' was 'formally' opened in a remote corner of the USSR, in Stepanakert, the capital of the Mountainous Gharabagh Autonomous *Oblast*. Taking advantage of *glasnost*, the local soviet voted in February 1988 to secede from the Azerbaijani SSR and join the Armenian SSR. 76 per cent of Gharabagh's population of 161,000 were Armenian. Almost all the rest were Azerbaijani. Within two days, mass protests were spontaneously launched in Yerevan—with up to one million participants—in support of Gharabagh's decision. In response, counter protests and anti-Armenian pogroms began in Azerbaijan (mostly in Baku and Sumgait). As such, the Gharabagh movement was launched both in Armenia and in Azerbaijan. Henceforth Armenian—as well as Soviet—politics changed. By the summer of 1990 the Communist government had lost power in Yerevan. The new rulers of the country were the young men of the Gharabagh movement, the anti-Communist nationalist counter-elite which had emerged within four months of the beginning of the movement. In August 1990 Armenia had issued a declaration of its *intention* to secede from the USSR. In September 1991, after the failed August coup in Moscow, Armenia formally declared its independence. It was recognised as a sovereign country by the international community in December 1991, after the formal dissolution of the USSR.

The Gharabagh movement began as a 'simple' matter; the transfer of the enclave from Azerbaijan to Armenia. Within months, as it became clear that Moscow was not going to do this, the scope of the movement widened greatly. It started to incorporate issues such as corruption, environmental degradation[1] and other social ills; it then began to question the legitimacy of Soviet rule and started to vie for power. Finally, it incorporated the demand of independence in its programme—all within a period of two years.[2]

Organisationally a loose 'Gharabagh Committee' emerged to guide and coordinate the movement. Some of the early pro-Communist popular leaders and spokespersons (e.g. Igor Muradian, Zori Balayan and Silva Kaputikian) were pushed aside and a group of (mostly) non-Communist intellectuals took over (e.g. Vazgen Manukian, Rafael Ghazarian, Levon Ter Petrosian, Babgen Ararktsian and Vano Siradeghian). In the autumn of 1988 the Committee reorganised itself into the *Hayots Hamazgayin Sharjum* (Armenian Pan-National Movement [ANM]). Its leaders were arrested in December 1988–January 1989, in the aftermath of the massive earthquake in northern Armenia, but released six months later, returning to Yerevan even more popular. Between 1990 and 1998 the ANM was the ruling political force in Armenia; its candidate, Levon Ter Petrosian was the President of the republic. However, some of the founders of the ANM had left the organisation and had established alternative (i.e. opposition) parties—most notably, Vazgen Manukian and his National Democratic Union (NDU).

The Gharabagh movement in Armenia—as mobilised for and through the issue of the enclave's unification to the republic—is a prime example of a mass nationalist movement.[3] Armenians world-

[1] The ecological movement preceded the Gharabagh issue by about six months. In the autumn of 1987 there were mass rallies of thousands of people in Yerevan protesting against the pollution being produced by the Nairit chemical factory in the city. After February 1988 the environmental issue became one thread in the multi-dimensional Gharabagh movement.

[2] For some of the important articles, interviews, statements and documents which demonstrate the evolution in the thinking of the movement see G. Libaridian, *Armenia at the Crossroads*.

[3] For general overviews see S. Astourian, 'Nagorno-Karabakh Conflict'; M. Croissant, *Armenia-Azerbaijan Conflict*; N. Dudwick, 'Armenia'; R. Suny, *Looking toward Ararat*, chapter 12; K. Tölölyan, 'National Self-Determination'. For accounts sympathetic to the Azerbaijani position see S. Alijarly, 'Republic of Azerbaijan'; A. Altstadt, *Azerbaijani Turks*, pp. 195ff., and 'Nagorno-Karabagh'; A. Kyrou and M. Mardoukhaiev, 'Le Haut-Karabagh'. For accounts sympathetic to the Armenian side see L. Chorbajian, *Caucasian Knot*; C. Walker (ed.), *Armenia and Karabagh*, and 'Armenian Presence'. For the perspective within Gharabagh see H. Tchilingirian, 'Nagorno Karabagh'. For a fascinating eyewitness account of the movement in 1988 see M. Malkasian, 'Gha-ra-bagh!' For two PhD dissertations exploring the links between identity, memory and

wide mobilised in support of the 'cause', but the politics of nationalism which emerged out the movement, and the associated initial sense of unity, could not bridge the gap between the two parts of the nation: the diaspora and the homeland. In fact by 1995 relations had reached such a low level between the ANM government in Armenia and the ARF party based in the diaspora that one Dashnak member wrote in an Armenian language party newspaper in Montreal, 'At this stage [March 1995], it is possible to assert with a clear conscience that the situation would have been preferable [to the presidency of Levon Ter Petrosian] if Armenia was directly occupied by Turkey…'[4] This was a far cry from the euphoria of independence in 1991, when the diaspora and the homeland were metaphorically presented as two wings of the same bird. In four short years relations between the newly independent homeland and a significant element of the diaspora (but by no means the whole of it) had disintegrated to the level of declaring the rule of the Armenian President as worse than Turkish occupation. This was more than political opposition between two parties, it was a reflection of a deep divide and a distrust that emanated from historical roots.

After 1991 Armenians of the republic and of the diaspora clearly realised how different they were from one another. And the politics of the two entities reflected this difference. The interactions between these two parts of the nation demonstrated the vicissitudes and cleavages within the Armenian identity. The most interesting, and ironic, element of the relationship was the fact that when the pendulum in the republic swung in the direction of explicit and forceful nationalism between 1988 and 1991, the supposedly more nationalist diaspora remained ultra-cautious in its approach, rejecting early calls for independence and supporting Gorbachev until early 1991, well after he had lost all credibility in Armenia.

---

the movement (from an anthropological perspective) see N. Dudwick, *Memory*, and S. Platz, *Pasts and Futures*. For noteworthy sources in Armenian see Z. Balayan, *Dzhokhk yev drakht* (history of the 'national liberation war' as told by one of the main protagonists of the movement); V. Khojabekian, *Artsakhe* (historical overview); and B. Ulubabian, *Artsakhian goyapaikare* (the classic Armenian perspective), and *Artsakhian goyapaikari taregrutiun* (1988–94 diary of events).

[4] H. Shamlian, 'Levon Ter-Petrosiane', p. 16. The 23 Jan. 1995 issue of the same paper (*Horizon Weekly*) published a cartoon equating Ter Petrosian with Stalin and with Talaat Pasha, the architect of the Armenian Genocide and the embodiment of evil in the Armenian collective psyche. For further details see R. Panossian, 'Diaspora'.

'Being national is the condition of our times', Geoff Eley and Ronald Suny suggest.[5] And Armenians in the past ten years—and in the past 300 years!—have certainly demonstrated the correctness of this statement. This book has analysed the evolution of Armenian national identity and the processes through which an ancient collective identity became a modern national identity based on a subjective sense of belonging.

To recapitulate, briefly, Armenian identity began to take shape in the pre-Christian era. It reached its pre-modern peak in the fifth century AD as a clearly articulated ethno-religious identity based on a unique form of Christianity and a specifically invented alphabet. Religion/church and language/alphabet sustained collective identity for over a millennium, despite the lack of a state. From the seventeenth century onward, based on these cultural markers, Armenian identity was metamorphosed into a modern sense of national belonging. This evolution—usually referred to as the 'awakening'—was carried out mostly in diasporan communities by intellectuals who were supported by merchants. Hence, it was a multilocal process with various centres of identity construction. As a result the emergent sense of Armenian identity was subject to many divisions, the most profound of which was, and still is, the east/west divide. The divisions were most clear in the dialects of language, literature and political ideology. The organisational dimension of the renaissance was carried out by various community (including religious) institutions, political parties and revolutionary organisations. These played the same role as a 'national' state since Armenians did not have a state of their own. Armenians being at best a plurality in most of their historic homeland at the heart of Anatolia, Armenian nationalist demands were on the whole limited to autonomy and political rights as equal subjects of the empires in which they lived. However, Armenians wanted these rights to be guaranteed by European intervention in the Ottoman empire. The nationalist Young Turk leadership viewed Armenian demands as incompatible with Ottoman-*cum*-Turkish interests. Consequently, western Armenians were eliminated through the Genocide of 1915. This catastrophe ended Armenian presence in most of historic Armenia and reinforced the sense of victimhood and persecution within national identity.

[5] G. Eley and R. Suny, 'Introduction', p. 32.

In 1918 an independent Armenian state was established in eastern Armenia, but it was Sovietised in 1920. Henceforth eastern Armenians had a Soviet republic as their state and western Armenian existence was confined to the diaspora. Throughout the twentieth century Armenian identity continued to evolve in a multilocal manner. Yerevan emerged as the national centre, but the diaspora, containing the surviving western Armenian remnants, developed its own distinct identity. National identity was strengthened in Soviet Armenia through various factors such as the federal structure of the USSR, nationalist elites and intellectuals, Soviet policies, cultural practices and so forth. A parallel process of identity reinforcement took place in the diaspora. There was interaction between the two sides of the nation, mostly on the terms set by the Soviet republic, but the two entities, the 'homeland' and the diaspora, never developed a similar (i.e. homogenised) sense of national belonging. Armenian nationalism was alive and well in 1987 and burst onto the stage in early 1988 over the Gharabagh issue.

I will end this study by exploring the multiplicity of identities within contemporary Armenian realities. In other words, I would like to revisit my theoretical and historical arguments regarding intra-national differences made throughout the book, but in the contemporary settings of the Armenians.

The best way to demonstrate the different dimensions of this identity, which suggest potential trends in the evolution of Armenianness, is to present four vignettes. 'Being national' does not really explain *what exactly* one is being. I hope that these four examples shed some light on the variations possible in being Armenian at the beginning of the twenty-first century. Two of the cases are from the diaspora and two are from Armenia. They are—admittedly—extreme examples, but useful in demonstrating the range of possibilities in terms of both identity and nationalism.

The first is a series of questions a fourteen-year-old schoolboy (born and raised in Yerevan) asked his father in Armenia in 1997. Three of us were travelling on the highway parallel to the Turkish border and discussing the 'lost' historic Armenian lands on the other side of the river which divides the two countries. The boy asked: '*Where* is Mount Ararat, in Armenia or in Turkey?' '*What* is

Ani [the famous medieval Armenian city, now in ruins, on the Turkish side of the border and clearly visible from Armenia]?' 'What is a mosque? Do they worship fire there?' And 'What religion are the Turks?' The boy was a typical teenager and one should not expect too much historical knowledge from a fourteen-year-old in any country. But the nature of the questions he was asking demonstrated that ten years after 1988 Armenian nationalism had absolutely no relevance to his identity. He was not sure where the national symbol of the Armenians was. And he did not know the most basic difference that distinguished him from the 'Other'. This is one example of the 'weakness' of national identity in the homeland.

At the other extreme there is an intellectual association in Armenia called the 'Nationalist Club'. It is a grouping of a few of the more extreme nationalists. Its leading members used to form the intellectual core in the Republican Party of Armenia before the latter became a major political organisation in 1998 (the leader of the Republican Party, Andranik Margarian, was appointed Prime Minister in May 2000). These individuals pursue the '*tseghakron*' ideology (i.e. the idea of worshipping the Armenian race) and publish numerous books and articles on the subject. In one of their booklets they appeal to the youth of Armenia: 'Know your race!' They add: 'An essential element of race-religion is race-worship—worship of the race's qualities, values and sacredness.'[6] In another booklet, they state that national ideology is not 'created' but is born with the nation. It must be 'recognised and revealed'.[7] I asked one of the key figures in this club to explain to me what their ideology was based on, and how they envisioned the Armenian nation. He explained:

> 'Humanity is divided into nations; each nation is unique and has its own specific characteristics such as language, cultural traits, family values, territory etc. These must be kept and perpetuated in an unadulterated form without the influence of other values and races—i.e. the national blood must stay pure. Hence mixed marriages and cultural hybridity are not acceptable. The onslaught of the West must be rejected. For example, Western concepts such as human rights, feminism etc. are foreign to Armenian values and must be opposed. Armenians, furthermore, must occupy their own historic lands—to where true Armenians from the diaspora must

[6] *Tseghakronutiun*, pp. 5–6.
[7] *Azgayin gaghaparakhosutian ardiakanutiune*, p. 3.

return. *Tseghakron*s have nothing against other nations, as long as the other nations leave Armenians in peace and do not transgress on Armenian historic lands as Turks have done. Hence these territories must be returned to the Armenians without the current Turkish and Kurdish occupants, and the lands must be populated by Armenians.[8]

The teenager mentioned above, who did not even have the concept of 'lost lands' (and who wanted to be as 'Western' as possible), and the *tseghakron*s do not have all that much in common in their attitudes and worldviews. And yet they belong to the same nation. One wonders how, or even if, these two extremes will be able to reconcile their radically different attitudes with the same national identity in the future (even though history shows that ignorance and fear can bring such people together through political mobilisation).

Similarly, two examples from the diaspora demonstrate how differently Armenians can express their nationality. A heavy metal music band has been formed in Los Angeles by a group of young Armenians called System of a Down. It has acquired prominence as a rock band throughout the United States.[9] System of a Down is not an 'ethnic band'—and its members resent being pigeonholed as such—but some of its songs do mix Armenian political themes with American heavy metal music. One of the most striking examples is their song called *PLUCK*. This stands for 'Politically Lying, Unholy, Cowardly Killers' and it is about the Armenian Genocide. Band member Serj Tankian sings to *American* teenagers,

> *Die, why, walk down, walk down,*
> *A whole race Genocide,*
>
> ...
>
> *Revolution, the only solution,*
> *We've taken all your shit, now it's time for restitution.*
> *Recognition, Restoration, Reparation*
>
> ...
>
> *The plan was mastered and called Genocide.*[10]

[8] Paraphrased from an informal discussion with Mushegh Lalayan and Gevorg Hovsepian in November 1997; also, author's interview with Mushegh Lalayan. Andranik Margarian discussed the ideological basis of the Republican Party in terms of *tseghakron* ideology (author's interview with Andranik Margarian).

[9] Steve Morse, 'Rock Notes', *Boston Globe*, 21 Jan. 2000; Sarah Rodman, 'System of a Down is on its Way up', *Boston Globe*, 16 Feb. 2000 (*both posted on Groong Armenian News Network*, 31/1/00 and 16/2/00 respectively).

[10] Lyrics from the band's first album, *System of a Down* (1998). The group has also taken

I wonder what the *tseghakrons* would say to this heavy-metal style Armenian 'nationalism'!

Finally, the last vignette is an absurd newspaper advertisement for a public lecture and video presentation which was to be held in Los Angeles on 22 October 1999.[11] It was organised by the Educational Union of the Kessab compatriotic organisation (the actual Armenian village of Kessab still survives and is in Syria) in its newly-built centre in Los Angeles. The event was entitled 'Artsakh 2001'. Note that the diaspora (in Los Angeles) of a diasporan village (in Syria) was organising an event on Gharabagh.

The quarter page advertisement contains a number of symbols. In the centre there is a picture of the St John the Baptist church in Gharabagh (thirteenth century) with a caption (in Armenian) below it that reads: 'Who is in possession of the head of John the Baptist will rule the world'—this according to European knights in Jerusalem. It is then added that the head of John is actually buried in this church (according to Armenian legend). On the left of the church photo there is a sketch of Noah's Ark on Mount Ararat, and on the right one of Adam and Eve. There is also a drawing of St John the Baptist. The caption of the advert outlining the questions to be explored at the event is as follows (in its entirety):

> You have heard that Armenia's mountain range is considered the Biblical '*Place of Eden*,' and according to new research Artsakh is the *'Garden of Eden'*. Who were Adam and Eve? What scientific factors are there [proving] that the story of Noah's Ark is based on real geological changes? Why is Armenia considered the cradle of Aryan peoples from where international civilisations have spread? What irrefutable proofs are there that the Portuguese, the Spanish, the Bavarians of Germany, the Basques and the Kosovo Albanians have emigrated from Artsakh? What is the secret of Patriarch Haik's story [the mythical founder of the Armenians], and what links are there with the stars? Why are Armenians known as The Keepers of Christian Faith? And why have Armenians kept and protected the relics of the founders of Christianity? *Why is the third millennium called 'The Era of Armenian Aquarius?'*

---

part in charity concerts to raise funds for Genocide recognition activities in the United States.

[11] The advertisement appeared in the October 1999 issues of *Nor Gyank* (New Life) (Los Angeles), a mass-produced mainstream newspaper.

One could spend pages and pages deconstructing the rich ethno-symbolic imagery of this advertisement alone. It is quite a mixture of myths and symbols regarding the nation, race, territory, diaspora, religion and superstition. I do not know how many people attended this event, how 'convincing' the arguments were, how the speakers were received, or even how many people actually read the advertisement. Most Armenians would not believe in such nonsense, nor care much about it. But one does wonder about the 'logic' behind such thinking. The *tseghakron*s of Yerevan would have been proud of such an event, but certainly the people listening to System of a Down might find the whole idea rather absurd.

These four examples demonstrate the variations in the complex web of meanings and beliefs that tie Armenians together. The teenager with no national concerns, the ultra-nationalist who worships the race, the member of the heavy metal band singing about the Genocide and the organiser and speaker of the 'educational' event based on fantasy are all part of the same nation. There are not too many—if there are any—objective markers tying them together. This condition is not new: merchants, monks, peasants and revolutionaries living in the eighteenth and nineteenth centuries in various Armenian communities did not have much in common either. These examples are indicative of the fragmentation of Armenian identity. And yet they also show that there is a subjective sense of belonging which enables such diverse people to claim that they all belong to the same nation.

In the age of secularisation, particularly in the twentieth century under Soviet and diasporan conditions, a subjective sense of belonging has become what religion was in the past for the Armenians. Subjective belonging brings people together in a nation, even though subjectivity is much more fluid, dynamic and personalised than traditional religious practices and a rigid church organisation. Perhaps the most fitting image is that of a 'fragmented collective'. The term suggests *both* incoherence *and* unity. Two qualities that the Armenian nation has: diversity and connectedness.

Such fragmentation and unity are not unique to the Armenians. But drawing on the Armenian case it is possible to provide general conclusions about the nature of national identity. The four vignettes demonstrate the three main points of this book: the multilocal diversity in the 'imagined community' of the nation; the subjective 'will' which binds the various threads; and the modernity of national identity.

In three of the four cases mentioned there is a very clear political statement on behalf of the nation. It reflects the political nature of belonging necessary for national identity. From System of a Down in Los Angeles to the *tseghakrons* in Yerevan, Armenians see themselves, above all else, as members of a *modern political* community, in the widest sense of 'politics', *and* a *historically* constituted political community (which does not necessarily live in the totality of what it believes ought to be its state). Cultural markers change, language can be lost, habits may evolve differently, but this political sense of Armenianness—the notion of collective solidarity based on secular principles of national rights—remains. The notion is akin to 'citizenship', but this is a state-centric concept which must be used with caution in cases where the idea exists, but without necessarily a national state.

The fragmentation cited above is based on extreme examples, but it is useful to look at it as a point of reference for other nations and states. Such diversity is also found in many other cases—from Canada to Britain to Indonesia. Theories of nations and nationalism see such diversity as a 'problem' or as a 'failure' of the nationalist project to homogenise society. What is argued in this book is that diversity is not necessarily a problem as long as there is a strong sense of subjective belonging to the same political community defined as a nation.

BIBLIOGRAPHY

The transliteration of all Armenian sources is based on the *Armenian Review* key (modelled on the eastern pronunciation). Where there are transliteration variants in publication names or individuals, or there is a more widely used English-language variant, they are given in round brackets. The translations of Armenian titles are given in square brackets. The names of publishers listed for Armenian sources are given in translation if they are known institutions (e.g. Academy of Sciences), or as they appear in the text (i.e. without translation) if they are organisation/company names or abbreviations of such names (e.g. Hamazgayin, Haipethrat). Publisher names are given as they appear in the text, without being standardised for consistency. Dates in round parentheses are original publication or circulation dates; necessary additional notes on an item are also given in round parentheses at the end of the entry. Words such as Company (Co.) and Limited (Ltd) at the end of a publisher's name are excluded. In general the word 'Publisher', 'Publications' or 'Press' in a company name is also dropped. Armenian Revolutionary Federation is abbreviated to ARF.

ARMENIAN LANGUAGE SOURCES

75-Amiak [75th Anniversary], *1918–1993*, Toronto: ARF/Armenian Community Centre, 1993.

Abeghian, A., 'Haikakan mshakuite yev H. H. Dashnaktsutiune [Armenian Culture and the A(remenian) R(evolutionary) Federation]', *Hairenik Amsagir* [Fatherland Monthly] (Boston), 9:4/100, February 1931.

Abrahamian, A. G., *Hamarot urvagitz hay gaghtavaireri patmutian* [Concise Outline of the History of Armenian Colonies], vol. I, Yerevan: Haipethrat, 1964; vol. II, Yerevan: Hayastan, 1967.

Aghayan, Tz. P, *Hai zhoghovrdi azatagrakan paikari patmutiunits* [From the Liberation Struggle of the Armenian People], Yerevan: Armenian SSR Academy of Sciences, 1976.

——— *Rusastani dere hai zhoghovrdi patmakan chakatagrum* [The Role of Russia in the Historical Fate of the Armenian People], Yerevan: Hayastan, 1981.

——— Sh. R. Harutiunian and A. N. Mnatsakanian, *Hai zhoghovrdi patmutiun* [History of the Armenian People], Yerevan: Luis, 1987 (textbook for grade 9–10 students).

Aivazian, Armen, 'Ghazar Jahketsu gaghaparakhosutiune [The Ideology of Ghazar Jahketsi]', *Patma-banasirakan handes* [Historico-Philological Journal] (Yerevan), 1/159, 2002.

——— *Hayastani patmutian lusabanume amerikian patmagrutian mej* [The History of Armenia as Presented in American Historiography], Yerevan: Artagers, 1998.

Akçam [Agcham], Taner, 'Turk azgayin inknutiune yev haikakan hartse [Turkish National Identity and the Armenian Question]', *Haikazian hayagitakan handes/Haigazian Armenological Review* (Beirut), 15, 1995.

Ananian, Zh., 'Hai vacharakanutiune Rusastanum (17-rt d. verj—19-rt d. skizb [Armenian Trade in Russia (End of 17th century to Beginning of 19th c.)]' in V. B. Barkhudarian and Zaven Yekavian (eds), *Ejer hai gaghtavaireri patmutian* [Pages of Armenian Colonies], Yerevan: National Scientific Academy of Armenia, 1996.

'Anjatman dem ellalov handerdz, ankakhakan ke mnank! [Although Against Separation, We Remain for Independence!]', editorial, *Droshak* [Flag] (Athens), 21:3, 23 May 1990.

'Apazgainatsman vtange [The Danger of Denationalisation]', *Hairenik Amsagir* [Fatherland Monthly] (Boston), 9:6/102, April 1931.

Apinian, Abgar, 'Azgayin gaghaparakhosutiun, sahmanadrutiun hai hogu [National Ideology, Constitution of Armenian Spirit]', interview, *Zartonk* [Awakening] (Beirut), 18 Aug. 1998.

Arevelian Mamul [Eastern Press], 1871 (journal, published 1871–1909 in Smyrna [Izmir]).

Arevik Aibenaran [Little-Sun Alphabet-book], Yerevan: Luis, 1983/8 (textbook).

Armen, 'Kaghakakan arajnahertutiunneri hramayakane [The Imperative for Political Priorities]', *Droshak* [Flag] (Athens), 20:4, 7 June 1989.

Atikian, Hakob, *Hamarot patmutiun hai gaghtavaireru* [Concise History of Armenian Colonies], Antilias, Lebanon: Cilician Catholicosate, 1985.

Avetisian, Armen, 'Mi khpek azgainakanutiane [Do Not Knock Down Nationalism]', *Iravunk* [Rights] (Yerevan), 10–16 Oct. 1997.

Avetisian, Vardan, *Stepan Shahumian. Kensagrakan aknark* [Stepan Shahumian. Biographical Glance], Yerevan: Haipethrat, 1953.

Azgaser, char asatsial [A Discourse Called Love of Nation], San Lazzaro, Venice: Mkhitarian, 1815.

Azgayin gaghaparakhosutian ardiakanutiune [The Modern Relevance of National Ideology], Yerevan: *Hanrapetakan* newspaper publication, 1996.

'Azgayin sahmanadrutian aizhmeakanutiune [The Relevance of the National Constitution]', Special Supplement, *Horizon* (Montreal), November 1986.

Badalian, Kh. H., *Dashnakneri kontrrevoliutsion gortzuneutian mi kani pasteri masin (1918–1920 tt.)* [A Few Facts about the Counter-revolutionary Activities of the Dashnaks, 1918–1920], Yerevan: Haipethrat, 1955.

Balayan, Zori, *Dzhokhk yev drakht* [Hell and Paradise], Yerevan: *Azg* newspaper publication, 1995.

Barkhudarian, V[ladimir] (ed.), *Hayots patmutiun* [History of the Armenians], second edition, Yerevan: Luis, 1996 (textbook for grades 7–8 students).

Barkhudarian, Vladimir and Sargis Harutiunian, 'Hayagitakan Handese 40 tarekan e [Armenological Review is 40 Years Old]', *Hayastani Hanrapetutiun* [Republic of Armenia] (Yerevan), 21 Oct. 1997.

'Bazhake ke hordi [The Cup is Spilling]', editorial, *Droshak* [Flag] (Athens), 19:24, 15 March 1989.

Chamchiants, Mikayel, *Patmutiun hayots* [History of Armenians], Vol. 1 (of 3). Venice: Mkhitarian, 1784 (reprinted fascimile, Yerevan State University, 1985).

Chanashian, H. M., *Hai grakanutian nor shrjani hamarot patmutiun* (1701–1920) [Concise History of Armenian Literature in the New Period], San Lazzaro, Venice: Mkhitarian, 1973.

Chelepian, Andranik, *Zoravar Andranik yev Hai heghapokhakan sharjume* [General Andranik and the Armenian Revolutionary Movement], Los Angeles: n.p., 1984.

Cholakian, Hakob, *Kesap* [Kessab], Vol. 1 (of 2). Aleppo: Hamazgayin, 1995.

——— *Kesapi barbare* [The Dialect of Kessab], Aleppo: Dr Toros Toranian publisher, 1986.

Dallakian, Karlen, *Hai spiurki patmutiun* [History of the Armenian Diaspora], Hrachia Acharian University of Yerevan, 1998.

——— *Hushapatum* [Memoir], Yerevan: n.p., 1999.

Darbinian, Ruben, *Rusakan vtange* [The Danger of Russia], Yerevan: Azat Khosk, 1991 (1920).

Davtian, Vardges, *Araspeli yev irakani sahmanagtzin. Levon Ter-Petrosian, kaghakatsin yev kaghakagete* [On the Borderline of Myth and Reality: Levon Ter-Petrosian, the Citizen and the Politician], Yerevan: Nairi, 1996.

Devrikian, Vardan, 'Hayots patmutiune ibrev razmavarakan pashar [Armenian History as a Strategic Resource]', *Hai zinvor* [Armenian Soldier] (Yerevan), 20–7 Feb. 1999.

Eortekian, Hovik, *Hamarot patmutiun HRAK-i* [Concise History of A(rmenian) D(emocratic) L(iberal) P(arty)], Yerevan: Ankakhutiun, 1996.

Eplighatian, Melgon, *Gaghtakayanen khorhrdaran...* [From Refugee Camp to Parliament...], Aleppo: Cilicia, 1998.

Galemkiarian, Grigoris (Rev.), *Patmutiun hai lragrutian* [History of Armenian Journalism], vol. 1 (of 2). Vienna: Mkhitarian, 1893.

Galstian, J., 'Haikakan gaghtavaireri arajatsume Ukrainayum yev Lehastanum [The Development of Armenian Colonies in Ukraine and Poland]' in V. B. Barkhudarian and Zaven Yekavian (eds), *Ejer hai gaghtavaireri patmutian* [Pages of Armenian Colonies], Yerevan: National Scientific Academy of Armenia, 1996.

Gasparian, D. V. and Zh. A. Kalantarian, *Hai grakanutiun. Noraguin shrjan* [Armenian Literature. Latest Period], Yerevan: Luis, 1996 (textbook for upper grade students).

Gerogian, Karo, 'Inchpes partadrvetsav nor ughghagrutiune hayastani mej [How Was the New Orthography Enforced in Armenia]', *Nor Gyank* [New Life] (Los Angeles), 5 Nov. 1998.

Gevorgian, H. A., *Azg, azgayin petutiun, azgayin mshakuit* [Nation, National State, National Culture]. Simferopol, Russia: Amena, 1997.

Gharibjanian, Ludwig, 'Krdakan-mshakutayin kianke hayastani mech [Educational-Cultural Life in Armenia]', *Ararat* (Beirut), 1 Jan. 1986.

Ghazar-Chareg, *Hushamatian Pardzr Haiki, Karinapatum* [Commemorative book of Upper Armenia, Erzerum], Beirut: n.p., 1957.

Ghaziyan, A. S. (ed.), *Hai zhoghovrdakan razmi yev zinvori yerger* [Armenian Popular War and Soldier Songs], Yerevan: Armenian SSR Academy of Sciences, 1989.

Grigorian, Grigor, 'Krkin Gharabagh [Again Gharabagh]', *Horizon* (Montreal), 25 May 1981.

Grigorian, Marina, 'Hairenadardzutian hrchvankn u voghbergutiune [The Joy and Tragedy of the Repatriation]', *Aizhm* [Contemporary] (Yerevan), 27 Aug.–2 Sept. 1997.

Grigorian, Z., *Sovetakan Hayastane 25 tarum* [Soviet Armenia in 25 Years], Yerevan: Haipethrat, 1945.

Hai Heghapokhakan Dashnaktsutiun [Armenian Revolutionary Federation], *Tzragir* [Programme], n.c: ARF, 1998 (official Party programme as confirmed by the 27th ARF General Congress).

Hai zhoghovrdi patmutiun [History of the Armenian People], 8 volumes, Yerevan: Armenian SSR Academy of Sciences, 1967–84.

Haikakan sovetakan hanragitaran [Soviet Armenian Encyclopaedia], 12 volumes, Yerevan: Armenian SSR Academy of Sciences, 1974–86.

Hairikian, Paruir, *Azgayin Miatsial Kusaktsutiun. Tzragir-kanonadrutiun yev paragaik* [National Unity Party. Programme-constitution and Circumstances], Yerevan: National Unity Party, 1991.

'Hakadashnaktsakan arshavi "noreluk" voch me [A "New" Style in the Anti-Dashnak attack]', *Droshak* [Flag] (Athens), 17:6–7, 9–23 July 1986.

Hakhverdian, Levon, *Paruire* [Paruir (Hairikian)], Yerevan: Areg, 1997.

Hakobian, Ararat, 'Mij-kusaktsakan paikare 1919 T. [The Inter-party Struggle in 1919]', *Nor Gyank* [New Life] (Los Angeles), 28 May 1998 (originally published in *Droshak*, 7–20 May 1998).

Hakobian, Hakob, 'Hairenikn ibrev patmakan kategoria; taragrutiun yev hairenadardzutiun [The Fatherland as Historical Category: Expatriation and Repatriation]', *Patma-banasirakan handes* [Historio-Philological Journal] (Yerevan), 2/157, 2001.

Hambardzumian, Rafayel, 'Hayeris azgayin gaghaparakhosutiune 1700 tarekan e [The National Ideology of Armenians is 1,700 Years Old]', *Droshak* [Flag] (Athens), 28: 17, 28 Aug.–10 Sept. 1997.

Hannesian, Karapet (ed.), *Heghapokhakan yergaran* [Revolutionary Songbook]. Beirut: Social Democratic Hnchak Party/Shirak Publishers, 1984.

Harutiunian, Sargis, 'Ailakhohutian akunknerum [In the Springs of the Dissident Movement]', *Haik* [Armenians] (Yerevan), 8 Nov. 1997 (part I), 15 Nov. 1997 (part II), 29 Nov. 1997 (part III).

Harutiunian, Suren, 'Verjin tarineri dasere dazhan en, baits usaneli mer zhoghovrdi hamar [The Lessons of the Last Years are Hard but Educational for our People]', interview, *Azg* [Nation] (Yerevan), 7 April 1994.

'Hayastan yev Rusastan, Hayastan Sovetakan Miutian kazmin mej [Armenia and Russia, Armenia within the Soviet Union]', *Zartonk* [Awakening] (Beirut), 24 Aug. 1999.

Hayastani hnagitakan hushardzannere [Armenia's Ancient Monuments], vols 1–7, Yerevan: Armenian SSR Academy of Sciences, 1968–74.

Heghapokhakan yergaran [Revolutionary Songbook], Beirut: ARF Youth Union of Lebanon, 1988.

H.H.D. 100 [ARF 100]. Montreal: ARF Canadian Central Committee, 1990.

'H.H.D. karasnamiake (khmbagrakan Khoher) [ARF Fortieth Anniversary (Editorial Thoughts)]', *Hairenik Amsagir* [Fatherland Monthly] (Boston), 9:4/100, February 1931.

Hovhannisian, E(dik), *Azgayin kaghakakanutian pilisopayutiune* [The Philosophy of National Politics], Beirut: Hamazgayini Vahe Setian Tparan, 1979.

Hovhannisian, Edik, 'Dashnaktsutiune tkaratsnelu nor nakhadzernutiunner [New Undertakings to Weaken the ARF]', *Droshak* [Flag] (Athens), 17:6–7, 9–23 July 1986.

Hovhannisian, E(dik), 'Enkervarutiune, menk yev marksizme [Socialism, Us and Marxism]', *Horizon* (Montreal), 11 June 1984 (part I), 18 June 1984 (part II).

——— 'Inch kareli che yev petk che asel [What is not Possible to Say and Should not be Said]', *Droshak* [Flag] (Athens), 21:16–17, 5 Dec. 1990.

Hovhannisian, Edik, 'Mtermik pah me enk. Etik Hovhannisiani hed [An Intimate Moment of Discussion with Comrade Etik Hovhannisian]', interview, *Horizon* (Montreal), 3 July 1989.

Hovhannisian, P., 'Movses Khorenatsu "Patmutiun Hayotsi" angleren targmanutian masin [About the English Translation of Movses Khorenatsi's "History of the Armenians"]', *Banber Yerevani Hamalsarani* [Yerevan University Courier] (Yerevan), 3/45, 1981 (review of Robert Thomson's translation of Khorenatsi).

Hovhannisian, Raffi, 'Hayastanum haghtelu e aroghj banakanutiune [Healthy Reason Must Win in Armenia]', interview, *Hayatsk Yerevanits* [View from Yerevan] (Yerevan), 1:8–9, November–December 1998.

Hushamatian Hai Heghapokhakan Dashnaktsutian, Albom-atlas [Memorial book of the Armenian Revolutionary Federation: Album-Atlas], vols I–III, Los Angeles: ARF Western Central Committee, 1992.

Irazek, H. (Hakob Ter Hakobian), *Patmutiun hndkahai tpagrutian* [History of Indian–Armenian Printing], Antilias, Lebanon: Cilician Catholicosate, 1986 (1930s).

Ishkhanian, R. A., *Hai girke* [The Armenian Book], *1512–1920*, Yerevan: Armenian SSR Academy of Sciences, 1981.

Ishkhanian, Rafayel, *Yerrord uzhi patsarman orenke* [The Law of Excluding the Third Force], Yerevan: Azat Khosk, 1991.

Ishkhanian, Yeghishe, *Lernayin Gharabagh* [Mountainous Gharabagh], *1917–1920*, Yerevan: Hayastan, 1999 (1917–20).

Iuzbashian, Karen, 'Amerikian hayagitutiune A. Aivaziani datastani arjev [American Armeneology in the Judgement of A. Aivazian]', *Hayastani hanrapetutiun* [Republic of Armenia] (Yerevan), 16 Oct. 1999.

Jamalian, A., *H. H. Dashnaktsutiune yev enkervarutiune* [The A.R. Federation and Socialism], Beirut: Hamazgayin Vahe Setian Tparan, 1979 (1930–1).

Kaitzer [Sparks] (Beirut), 2:2–3, April–September 1985.

Kaputikian, Silva, *Ejer pak gzrotsnerits* [Pages from Closed Drawers], Yerevan: Apolon, 1997.

——— *Guiner nuin khchankarits* [Colours from the Same Mosaic], Yerevan: Khorhrdayin Grogh, 1989.

——— *Karavannere der kalum en* [The Caravans Are Still Walking], Yerevan: Sovetakan Grogh, 1984 (1965).

——— *Khchankar hogu yev kartezi guinerits* [Mosaic from the Colours of the Spirit and the Map], Yerevan: Sovetakan Grogh, 1976.

——— 'Sere ser gberi, atelutiune atelutiun [Love Brings Love, Hatred Brings Hatred]', interview, *Iravunk* [Rights] (Yerevan), 10–16 Oct. 1997.

——— 'Silva Kaputikianin khoske [Silva Kaputikian's Speech]', *Zartonk* [Awakening] (Beirut), 23 Jan. 1996.

Karapetian, Mher, *Hayots 1915–1916 tvakanneri tseghaspanutian hartsere hai patmagrutian mej* [Issues of the 1915–1916 Armenian Genocide in Armenian Historiography], Yerevan: Gitutiun Publications of the National Academy of Sciences of the Republic of Armenia, 1998.

'Kedronakan ishkhanutiants batsasakan ketsvatzkin tem [Against the Negative Stand of the Central Authorities]', *Droshak* [Flag] (Athens), 22:1, 24 April 1991.

Khachatian, Rusan, 'Inch e asum kareghen ait khorhrdanishe [What Does that Stone Symbol Say]?', *Azg* [Nation] (Yerevan), 23 April 1994 (on Tzitzernakabert monument).

Khachkonts, Davit, *Hayots patmutiun* [Armenian History], Constantinople: Siuniats, 1910 (textbook).

Khan-Azat, R. and G. Vardanian, *Hayastani patmutiun* [History of Armenia], second revised edition, Tiflis: N. Aghaniantsi, 1911 (textbook for grade 4 students).

Khazhak, 'Anjatman martavarutiune ke vnase Hayastani ankakhutian veranvachumin [The Struggle for Separation Damages Armenia's Regaining of Independence]', *Droshak* [Flag] (Athens), 22: 2–3, 22 May 1991.

Khojabekian, V. E., *Artsakhe pordzutian zhamin* [Gharabagh at the Hour of Adversity], Yerevan: Hayastan, 1991.

Khorenatsi, Movses, *Hayots patmutiun* [History of the Armenians], Yerevan State University, 1981 (1940 [5th/8th century]).

Khorhrdayin Hayastan, hing tari 1920–1925 [Soviet Armenia: Five Years, 1920–1925], Yerevan: Central Executive Committee of Soviet Armenia, 1926.

Khudinian, Gevorg, 'H. H. Dashnaktsutiune hayastanum; kasetsman u verabatsumi vorogaitnere [The A(rmenian) R(evolutionary) Federation: The Temptations of Banning and Reopening]', *Molorak* [Planet] (Yerevan), 3 Oct. 1997 (part I), 9 Oct. 1997 (part III).

Khurshudian, Lendrush, *Hayots azgayin gaghaparakhosutiun* [Armenians' National Ideology], Yerevan: Zangak-97, 1999.

Kirakosian, J., *Yeritturkere patmutian datastani araj (1915-its minchev mer orere)* [The Young Turks in front of the Judgement of History (from 1915 to our days)], vol. II, Yerevan: Hayastan, 1983.

Kitur, Arsen (ed.), *Patmutiun S. D. Hnchakian Kusaktsutian* [History of the S(ocial) D(emocratic) Hnchak Party] *(1887–1963)*, vols I–II. Beirut: Central Historiographical Committee of the Hnchak Party/Shirak Publishers, 1962–3.

Kotanjian, Haik, *Haikakan 'yekrasharzhe'* [The Armenian 'Earthquake'], Yerevan: Hayastan, 1992.

Lazian, Gabriel, *Hayastan yev hai date haiyevrus haraberutiunneru luisin tak* [Armenia and the Armenian Cause in Light of Armeno–Russian Relations], Iran (n.c.): Armen Publications, 1377 on the Iranian calendar (1986[?], original 1940s or 1950s).

Leo, *Yerkeri zhoghovatsu* [Collected Works], vols III(a), III(b), IV, V. Yerevan: Hayastan, 1969–86.

'Levon Ter Petrosiani mtahogich yeluite [The Worrying Speech of Levon Ter Petrosian]', *Droshak* [Flag] (Athens), 20:6, 5 July 1989.

Liparitian, Zhirair (Libaridian, Jirair), 'Hartsazruits [Interview], Zhirair Liparitian', interview, *Apaga (Abaka)* [Future] (Montreal), 13 Nov. 1995 (part I), 20 Nov. 1995 (part II).

——— 'Zhirair Liparitiani yeluite Los Anchelesi haikakan hiupatosaranin mej [Zhirair Liparitian's Speech in the Armenian Consulate of Los Angeles]', *Apaga (Abaka)* [Future] (Montreal), 10 July 1995.

Malkhas, *Zartonk* [Awakening], vol. I. Boston: Hairenik, 1933.

Manoyan, K. 'Hai Heghapokhakan Dashnaktsutiune "spiurkahai kusaktsutiun" che [The Armenian Revolutionary Federation is not a "Diasporan Party"]', *Droshak* [Flag] (Athens), 20:18–19, 3 Jan. 1990.

Manukian, Armenak, *Hai Arakelakan Yekeghetsu brnadatvatz hogevorakannere 1930–1938 (est PAK-i pastatghteri)* [The Clergy of the Armenian Apostolic Church Forcibly put on Trial 1930–1938 (According to KGB Documents)], Yerevan: Amrots, 1997.

Manukian, Vazgen, 'Gnatskits trchelu zhamanakn e [It is Time to Jump Off the Train]', *Harach* [Forward] (Paris), 7/8, 10, 11, 12, and 13 July 1990 (original in *Haik*, Yerevan).

Marukhian, Hrair, 'Grakan Tert-i hartsazruitse enk. Hrair Marukhiani hed [The Interview of *Literary Journal* with Comrade Hrair Marukhian]', Interview, *Horizon* (Montreal), Special Supplement, 26 March 1990 (original in *Grakan Terk*, Yerevan, 16 Feb. 1990).

——— 'Hai zhoghovurde ke pashtpane mer gaghaparnere [The Armenian People Defend Our Ideas]', interview, *Droshak* [Flag] (Athens), 19:19, 4 Jan. 1989.

——— 'Hayastani Hanrapetutian nakhagah Levon Ter-Petrosiani 1992-i hunis 29-i herustayeluiti aritov mer pataskhane [Our Answer to the 29 June 1992 Television Broadcast of the President of the Republic of Armenia, Levon Ter Petrosian]', *Horizon* (Montreal), Special Supplement, 26 Oct. 1992 (original in *Droshak*, 21 Oct. 1992).

——— 'H.H.D. Biuroyi nerkayatsutsich enk. Hrair Marukhiani khoske H.H.D. hariurmekamiaki tonakatarutian entatskin (Halep—Petruar 1992) [The Message of the ARF Bureau Representative Comrade Hrair Marukhian on the Occasion of ARF's Hundred-and-first Anniversary Celebration (Aleppo, February 1992)]', *Droshak* [Flag] (Athens), 22:25, 25 March 1992.

——— 'Petk e paipayel azat, ankakh yev miatsial hayastani teslakane [We Must Cherish the Vision of Free, Independent United Armenia]', *Droshak* [Flag] (Athens), 18:3, 27 May 1987 (also in *Droshak*'s English Supplement, 1:2, January 1988).

——— and Hrach Tasnapetian, 'Hartsazruits enkerner Hrair Marukhiani yev Hrach Tasnapetiani het [Interview with Comrades Hrair Marukhian and Hrach Tasnapetian]', interview, *Droshak* [Flag] (Athens), 21:9, 15 Aug. 1990.

Matevosian, A. S., 'Movses Khorenatsin yev Atanas Taronatsu zhamanakagrutiune [Movses Khorenatsi and the Chronology of Atanas Taronatsi]', *Patmabanasirakan handes* [Historio-Philological Journal] (Yerevan), 1/124, 1989.

Melikian, M. A., *Hai azgi kazmavorman yev nra sotsialistakan verapokhman hartsi shurje* [On the Question of the Formation of the Armenian Nation and its Socialist Transformation], Yerevan University, 1957.

Meliksetian, H. Yu, *Hairenik-spiurk arnchutiunnere yev hairenadardzutiune (1920–1980)* [Homeland-Diaspora Liaisons and the Repatriation (1920–1980)], Yerevan University, 1985.

Melkonian, Eduard, *Haikakan Baregortzakan Endhanur Miutiune Khorhrdayin Hayastanum, 1923–1937 tt* [The Armenian General Benevolent Union in Soviet Armenia, 1923–1937], Yerevan: History Institute of National Academy of Sciences of the Republic of Armenia, 1999.

Melkumian, S. A., *Sovetakan hayastani mijhanrapetakan tntesakan kapere* [The Inter-republican Economic Ties of Soviet Armenia], Yerevan: Luis, 1988.

Mikayelian, Kristapor, *Heghapokhakani mtkere* [Revolutionary's Thoughts], Yerevan University, 1990 (1900–3).

Mirumian, R. A., '"Azg-petutiun" haraberaktsutiune Stepanos Nazariani patmapilisopayutian mej [The "Nation-State" Relationship in the historio-philosophy of Stepanos Nazarian]', *Banber Yerevani Hamalsarani* [Yerevan University Courier] (Yerevan), 1/97, 1999.

Mkrtchian, Anahit, *Ugheghneri artahoski khndire hayastanum* [The Problem of the Brain Drain in Armenia], Yerevan: Armenian Center for National and International Studies, 1995.

Mkrtchian, L., *Khorhrdayin miutian hayere est 1970 tvi mardahamari* [The Armenians of the Soviet Union According to the 1970 Census], Beirut: Hamazgayini Vahe Setian Tparan, 1977.

Mnatsakanian, A. N., *Hai zhoghovrdi voghbergutiune rus yev hamashkharhayin hasarakakan mtki gnahatmamb* [The Tragedy of the Armenian People According to Russian and International Public Opinion], Yerevan: Hayastan, 1965.

Mshak [Cultivator] (newspaper published 1872–1921 in Tiflis [Tbilisi]).

Muradian, Igor, 'Dashnaktsutiune yev rusakan hatuk tzarayutiunnere [The (Armenian Revolutionary) Federation and the Russian Special Services]', *Iravunk* [Rights] (Yerevan), June 1996.

'Nichevo, kich men al k'espasenk [Nichevo, We Will Wait a bit Longer]', editorial, *Droshak* [Flag] (Athens), 21:5, 20 July 1990.

'Nshmarner [Glimpses]', *Yeraguin Droshak* [Tricolour Flag] (New Jersey), October 1996.

Ohanian, Murad, 'Hai zhoghovrdi patmutian tseghayin shrjanin masin [About the Tribal Period of the History of the Armenian People]', *Patma-banasirakan handes* [Historio-Philological Journal] (Yerevan), 1/159, 2002.

Oshakan (Oshagan), Vahe, 'Spiurke arterkir che, yerkir e! [The Disaspora in not Abroad but Homeland!]', interview, *Horizon* (Montreal), Literary Supplement, August 1992.

'Ov ke vakhna dashnaktsutenen [Who is Afraid of the ARF]?' *Droshak* [Flag] (Athens), 21:23, 27 Feb. 1991.

Parsamian, V. A., S. P. Poghosian and Sh. R. Harutiunian, *Hai zhoghovrdi patmutiun* [History of the Armenian People], Yerevan: Haipetusmankhrat, 1964 (textbook for grade 8 students).

Paruir Hairikian, n.c.: n.p., n.d. (Yerevan: National Self-Determination Union, 1991?).

'Patmakan pataskhanatvutiun [Historical Responsibility]', editorial, *Horizon* (Montreal), 11 Aug. 1980.

'Patmutian dzaine [The Voice of History]', editorial, *Droshak* [Flag] (Athens), 21:10, 29 Aug. 1990.

Perperian, N., 'Achalrjutian zhame [Time for Seriousness]', *Droshak* [Flag] (Athens), 19:20, 18 Jan. 1989.

——— 'Artsakhian sharzhume yev H. H. Dashnaktsutiune [The Gharabagh Movement and the A.R. Federation]', *Droshak* [Flag] (Athens), 19:22–3, 1 March 1989.

Peshiktashlian, Mkrtich, *Yerker* [Writings], Antilias, Lebanon: Cilician Catholicosate, 1995.

Petrosian, Amalia *et al.* (eds), *Haikakan harts hanragitaran* [Armenian Question Encyclopaedia], Yerevan: Armenian Encyclopaedia, 1996.

——— *Hayern ashkharhum* [Armenians in the World], Yerevan: Hayagitak/ Armenian Encyclopaedia, 1995.

Petrosian, Ashot, 'H.H.D. tsragri popokhutian masin [About Changes in the ARF Programme]', *Droshak* [Flag] (Athens), 11, 5–18 June 1997.

Petrvarian apstambutian yev Artsakian sharjman 10-rt taredardzi tonakatarutiun [Commemmorative celebration of the February Rebellion and the 10th Anniversary of the Gharabagh Movement], Canada (n.c.): n.p. (ARF), 1998.

Poghosian, Artashes, *Petakan ahabekchutiun AIM-K-i nkatmamb* [State Terror Towards N(ational) S(elf-determination) U(nion)—(C)hristianists], Yerevan: National Self-determination Union-Christianists, 1995.

Potrumian, Ohan, 'Orvan panakhos, enk. Ohan Potrumiani yeluite [Keynote Speaker, Comrade Ohan Potrumian's Address]', *Zartonk* [Awakening] (Beirut), 25 Nov. 1999.

Sadoyan, Arshak, 'Sotsialakan ardarutian sharzhume tzavalvum e glorvogh dznagndi pes [The Social Justice Movement is Developing like a Snowball]', Interview, *Iravunk* [Rights] (Yerevan), 10–16 Oct. 1997.

Safarian, Khachik, 'Hayastani Komunistakan Kusaktsutian Kentronakan Komitei arajin kartughar enk. K. Demirchianin [To Comrade K. Demirchian, the First Secretary of the Armenian Communist Party Central Committee]', unpublished letter, 10 March 1975 (author's private collection).

Sanjian, Ara, [Review of A. Aivazian's book, *Hayastani patmutian lusabanume* (see above)]. *Haikazian hayagitakan handes* [Haigazian Armenological Review] (Beirut), 20, 2000.

Sargsian, Armen, 'Patmutian chisht chanaparhe [The Correct Path of History]', *Hayastani Hanrapetutiun* [Republic of Armenia] (Yerevan), 27 Nov. 1999.

Sargsian, Sos, 'Piti ashkhatem, kani kam [I will Work as Long as I Exist]', Interview, *Hayastani Hanrapetutiun* [Republic of Armenia] (Yerevan), 14 Oct. 1997.

Shamlian, Haiduk, 'Levon Ter-Petrosiane mi meghadrek [Do Not Blame Levon Ter Petrosian]', *Horizon* (Montreal), 13 March 1995.

Shant, Levon, *Azgutiune himk martkayin enkerutian* [Nationality as Basis of Human Society], Yerevan: n.p., 1999 (1922–3).

Shenian, Grigor, 'Esker Misak—"grichin yerkatov chen pataskhaner" [Esker Misak: "One Does Not Answer the Pen with Steel"]', *Nor Gyank* [New Life] (Los Angeles), 5 March 1998.

Shiraz, Hovhannes, *Knar Hayastani* [Lyre of Armenia], Yerevan: Haipethrat, 1958.

Simonian, Hrachik, *Spiurkahayutiune sotsial-kaghakakan paikari ughinerum* [Diaspora Armenians in the Paths of Social-Political Struggles], Yerevan: Hayastan, 1968.

Sovetakan Hayastan [Soviet Armenia], Yerevan: Soviet Armenian Encyclopaedia, 1987.

SSHM bnakchutiune. Haikakan SSH bnakchutiune. Est 1979 tvakani hamamiutenakan mardahamari tvialneri [The USSR Population. The Armenian SSR Population. According to the results of the 1979 Union-wide Census], Yerevan: Hayastan, 1980.

Stepaniants, Stepan, *Hai Arakelakan Yekeghetsin Stalinian prnapetutian orok* [The Armenian Apostolic Church during the Time of Stalin's Dictatorship], Yerevan: Apolon, 1994.

Tasnapetian, Hrach, *Hai heghapokhakan sharjume minchev H. H. Dashnaktsutian Kazmutiune* [The Armenian Revolutionary Movement until the Formation of the A(rmenian) R(evolutionary) Federation], Athens: Revolutionary Library/Armenian Publications, 1990.

——— 'Purch Hamuti H. T. Melkonian Taterasrahin mej H.H.D. Biuroyi nerkayatsutsich enk. Hrach Tasnapetiani Artasanats Khoske [The Speech of the ARF Bureau Representative Comrade Hrach Tasnapetian at the H. T. Melkonian Hall in Purch Hamut (Lebanon)]', *Azdak* [Factor] (Beirut), 21 March 1995.

Tasnapetian, Hrach (ed.), *Niuter H.H.D. patmutian hamar* [Materials for the History of the ARF], vols I–IV. Beirut: ARF/Hamazgayin Vahe Setian Tparan, 1972–82.

——— *Rostom, mahvan vatsunamiakin artiv* [Rostom: On the Occasion of the Sixtieth Anniversary of his Death], Beirut: ARF/Hamazgayin Vahe Setian Tparan, 1979.

Teodik, *Tip u tar* [Edition and Font], Constantinople: Z. and H. Ter-Nersesian Publishers, 1912.

Teoleolian, Khachik (Tölölyan, Khachig), 'Hayastan-spiurk kaperu masin [About Armenia-Diaspora Links]', *Horizon* (Montreal), Special Supplement, 2 Oct. 1995.

Ter Minasian, Anahit, 'Ailakhohutiune Khorhrdayin Hayastani mej [The Dissident Movement in Soviet Armenia]', *Hairenik* [Fatherland] (Boston), 19, 20 and 21 Sept. 1984 (original in *Critique Socialiste*, autumn 1983).

Ter-Petrosian, L[evon], Review of R. Thomson's translation of Moses Khorenatsi, History of the Armenians (see below), *Patma-banasirakan handes* [Historio-Philological Journal] (Yerevan), 1/88, 1980.

Ter Petrosian, Levon, 'Dashnaktsutiune chi chanachi haikakan petutiune ainkan zhamanak, kani der chen haidnvel petutian glukhe [The (Armenian Revolutionary) Federation Will Not Recognise the Armenian State as Long as They Are Not at the Head of the State]', interview, *Apaga (Abaka)* [Future] (Montreal), 9 Dec. 1996.

——— 'Hajord serundneri gaghaparakhosutiune petk e lini mer petakanutian amrapndume [The Ideology of the Next Generations Should Be the Strengthening of our Statehood]', interview, *Hayastani Hanrapetutiun* [Republic of Armenia] (Yerevan), 27 Sept. 1997.

——— 'Nakhagah Levon Ter Petrosian, "Hai Gyank" in [President Levon Ter-Petrosian to *Hai Gyank*]', interview, *Hai Gyank* [New Life] (Los Angeles), 15 Nov. 1991.

——— 'Nerkaghakakan mtahogich taknap [Worrisome Internal Crisis]', *Nor Gyank* [New Life] (Los Angeles), 9 July 1992.

——— 'Paterazm te Khaghaghutiun? Lrjanalu Pahe [War or Peace? Time to Get Serious]', *Hayastani Hanrapetutiun* [Republic of Armenia] (Yerevan), 1 Nov. 1997.

——— 'Yeluit [Speech]', *Hayastani Hanrapetutiun* [Republic of Armenia] (Yerevan), 29 July 1993.

Tseghakronutiun [Race-Religion], Yerevan: Republican Party, 1994.

Tzarukian, A[ndranik], *Hin yerazner, nor chambaner* [Old Dreams, New Ways], Beirut: Meghag, 1960.

——— *Nor Hayastan, nor hayer* [New Armenia, New Armenians], Beirut: G. Tonikian and Sons, 1983.

——— *Tught ar Yerevan* [Message to Yerevan], Beirut: Etvan, 1957 (1945).

Tzarukian, Andranik, *Amerikian koghmn ashkharhi* [On the American Side of the World], Glendale: Tekeyan Cultural Association, 1999 (1960s).

'Tzerakir [Programme]', *Droshak* [Flag] (Athens), 17:8–9, 6–20 Aug. 1986.

'"Tzove-Tzov" anpataskhanatutiun ["Sea to Sea" Irresponsibility]', *Paikar Amsagir* [Struggle Monthly] (Watertown, MA), 1:9, December 1993.

Ulubabian, Bagrat, *Artsakhian goyapaikare* [The Struggle for Survival of Gharabagh], Yerevan: Gir Grots, 1994.

——— *Artsakhian goyapaikari taregrutiun* [Annals of the Struggle for Survival of Gharabagh], Yerevan: n.p., 1997.

Varandian, Mikayel, *H. H. Dashnaktsutian Patmutiun* [History of A(rmenian) R(evolutionary) Federation], Yerevan University, 1992 (1932).

Vasn hayutian, vasn hayrentiats [For the Sake of Armenians, for the Sake of Homeland], ASALA 1975–95, n.c: ASALA (Armenian Secret Army for the Liberation of Armenia), n.d.

Vazgen I, Catholicos, 'T. T. Vazgen A. Hairapeti khoske ughghvatz Hayots Hamazgayin Sharzhman patgamavornerin (Surb Ejmiatznum—9 Noyember 1989 in) [Message of His Holiness Patriarch Vazgen I to the Delegates of the Armenian National Movement, 9 November 1989 in Holy Ejmiatzin]', *Nor Gyank* [New Life] (Los Angeles), 8 Dec. 1989.

Vratsian, S(imon), *Gianki ughinerov. Depker, demker, aprumner* [In the Way of Life: Events, Individuals, Experiences], 6 vols, Beirut: Hamazgayin, 1967 (Cairo, 1955).

——— *Hayastane bolshevikian murchi yev trkakan sali mijev* [Armenia Between the Bolshevik Hammer and the Turkish Anvil], Beirut: Hamazgayin, 1953 (1940–1).

Yeapuchian, Avetis, 'Haikakan hartsin tzagume [The Origin of the Armenian Question]', *Zartonk* [Awakening] 1999 (Beirut), Special Issue, January 1999.

Zulalian, M. K. [Review of A. Aivazian's book, *Hayastani patmutian lusabanume* (see above)], *Patma-banasirakan handes* [Historio-Philological Journal] (Yerevan), 1/150, 1999.

NON-ARMENIAN LANGUAGE SOURCES

19th All-Union Conference of the CPSU, *Documents and Materials*. Washington, DC: USSR Embassy, n.d. [1988] (special supplement in *Soviet Life* Magazine).

Abrahamian, Levon, 'Armenia i diaspora: raskhozhdenie i vstrecha [Armenia and the Diaspora: Dispersal and Encounter]', *Diaspory* [Diasporas], 1:2, 2000.

Afanasyan, Serge, 'Demographic Evolution in Transcaucasia 1959–1989', *Armenian Review*, 44:1/173, spring 1991.

Aftandilian, Gregory, *Armenia, Vision of a Republic: The Independence Lobby in America, 1918–1927*, Boston: Charles River Books, 1981.

Ahmad, Feroz, 'Unionist Relations with the Greek, Armenian, and Jewish Communities of the Ottoman Empire, 1908–1914' in Benjamin Braude and Bernard Lewis (eds), *Christians and Jews in the Ottoman Empire*, vol. I: *The Central Lands*, New York: Holmes and Meier, 1982.

Aivazian, Armen, *The Armenian Rebellion of the 1720s and the Threat of Genocidal Reprisal*, Yerevan: Center for Policy Analysis, American University of Armenia, 1997.

Akçam, Taner, *Armenien und der Völkermord Die Istanbuler Prozesse und die Türkische Nationalbewegung*. Hamburg: Hamburger Edition, 1996.

Akiner, Shirin, 'Melting Pot, Salad Bowl—Cauldron? Manipulation and Mobilization of Ethnic and Religious Identities in Central Asia', *Ethnic and Racial Studies*, 20:2, April 1997.

Akkus, Oznur [Lucie], 'Les Arméniens restés en Anatolie orientale après le génocide à travers les témoignages oraux', Paris: Ecole des Hautes Etudes en Sciences Sociales, Master's dissertation, September 1999 (unpublished).

Alijarly, Sulejman, 'The Republic of Azerbaijan: Notes on the State Borders in the Past and Present' in John F. R. Wright *et al.* (eds), *Transcaucasian Boundaries*, London: UCL Press, 1996.

Alter, Peter, *Nationalism*, London: Edward Arnold, 1989 (1985).

Altstadt, Audrey, *The Azerbaijani Turks: Power and Identity Under Russian Rule*. Stanford, CA: Hoover Institution Press, 1992.

——— 'Decolonization in Azerbaijan and the Struggle to Democratize' in Donald V. Schwartz and Razmik Panossian (eds), *Nationalism and History: The Politics of Nation Building in Post-Soviet Armenia, Azerbaijan and Georgia*, University of Toronto Centre for Russian and East European Studies, 1994.

——— 'Nagorno-Karabagh—"Apple of Discord" in the Azerbaijan SSR', *Central Asian Survey*, 7:4, 1988.

Anderson, Barbara and Brian Silver, 'Demographic Sources of the Changing Ethnic Composition of the Soviet Union', *Population and Development Review*, 15:4, December 1989.

——— 'Population Redistribution and the Ethnic Balance in Transcaucasia' in Ronald Suny (ed.), *Transcaucasia, Nationalism, and Social Change*, revised edition, Ann Arbor: University of Michigan Press, 1996 (1983).

Anderson, Benedict, *Imagined Communities: Reflections on the Origin and Spread of Nationalism*, revised edition, London: Verso, 1991 (1983).

——— *The Spectre of Comparisons: Nationalism, Southeast Asia and the World*, London: Verso, 1998.

——— 'Western Nationalism and Eastern Nationalism: Is There a Difference?', *New Left Review*, 9, May–June 2001.

ARF, *Au Congrès International Socialiste de la Fédération Révolutionnaire Arménienne*. [Geneva?]: Droschak [central organ of the ARF], 25 July 1896.

Armstrong, John, 'Mobilized and Proletarian Diasporas', *American Political Science Review*, 70:2, June 1976.

——— *Nations Before Nationalism*. Chapel Hill: University of North Carolina, 1982.

——— 'The Autonomy of Ethnic Identity: Historic Cleavages and Nationality Relations in the USSR' in Alexander Motyl (ed.), *Thinking Theoretically about Soviet Nationalities. History and Comparison in the Study of the USSR*, New York: Columbia University Press, 1992.

Artinian, Vartan, *The Armenian Constitutional System in the Ottoman Empire, 1839–1863*, Istanbul: n.p., n.d. [1988?].

Aslanian, Sebouh, '"The Treason of the Intellectuals": Reflections on the Uses of Revisionism and Nationalism in Armenian Historiography', *Armenian Forum*, 2:4, 2003.

Aspaturian, Vernon, 'The Union Republics and Soviet Nationalities as Instruments of Soviet Territorial Expansion' in Vernon Aspaturian (ed.), *Process and Power in Soviet Foreign Policy*, Boston: Little, Brown, 1971.

——— *The Union Republics in Soviet Diplomacy: A Study of Soviet Federalism in the Service of Soviet Foreign Policy*. Geneva and Paris: Publications de l'Institut Universitaire des Hautes Etudes Internationales, 1960.

Astourian, Stephan, 'The Nagorno-Karabakh Conflict: Dimensions, Lessons, and Prospects', *Mediterranean Quarterly*, 5:4, fall 1994.

——— 'In Search of their Forefathers: National Identity and the Historiography and Politics of Armenian and Azerbaijani Ethnogeneses' in Donald V. Schwartz and Razmik Panossian (eds), *Nationalism and History: The Politics of Nation Building in Post-Soviet Armenia, Azerbaijan and Georgia*, University of Toronto Centre for Russian and East European Studies, 1994.

Atamian, Sarkis, *The Armenian Community. The Historical Development of a Social and Ideological Conflict*, New York: Philosophical Library, 1955.

Ataöv, Türkkaya, *The 'Armenian Question': Conflict, Trauma and Objectivity*, Ankara: Center for Strategic Research (Ministry of Foreign Affairs), 1999.

Avineri, Shlomo, 'Toward a Socialist Theory of Nationalism', *Dissent*, fall 1990.

Azrael, Jeremy, 'Emergent Nationality Problems in the USSR' in Jeremy Azrael (ed.), *Soviet Nationality Policies and Practices*. New York: Praeger, 1978.

Bakalian, Anny, *Armenian–Americans: From Being to Feeling Armenian*, New Brunswick, NJ: Transaction, 1993.

Balakrishnan, Gopal (ed.), *Mapping the Nation*. London: Verso, 1996.

Balekjian, Wahé, 'The University of Dorpat (Tartu) and the Armenian National Awakening in the 19th Century' in Aleksander Loit (ed.), *National Movements in the Baltic Countries during the 19th Century*, Uppsala: Centre for Baltic Studies, University of Stockholm, 1985.

Bardakjian, Kevork, *The Mekhitarist Contributions to Armenian Culture and Scholarship*. Cambridge, MA: Middle Eastern Department, Harvard College Library, n.d. [1976?] (pamphlet accompanying exhibit at Harvard University).

——— *A Reference Guide to Modern Armenian Literature, 1500–1920*, Detroit: Wayne State University Press, 2000.

——— 'The Rise of the Armenian Patriarchate of Constantinople' in Benjamin Braude and Bernard Lewis (eds), *Christians and Jews in the Ottoman Empire*, vol. I: *The Central Lands*, New York: Holmes and Meier, 1982.

Barraclough, Geoffrey and Geoffrey Parker (eds), *The Times Atlas of World History*, 4th edition. London: BCA/Times Books, 1994.

Barsamian, Meguerditch, *Histoire du village qui Meurt. Aboutcher, de Aghen*, Paris: V. Barsamian and A. Vycichl-Barsamian, 1990 (private publication).

Barsoumian, Hagop, 'The Dual Role of the Armenian *Amira* Class within the Ottoman Government and the Armenian *Millet* (1750–1850)' in Benjamin Braude and Bernard Lewis (eds), *Christians and Jews in the Ottoman Empire*, vol. I: *The Central Lands*, New York: Holmes and Meier, 1982.

——— 'The Eastern Question and the Tanzimat Era' in Richard Hovannisian (ed.), *The Armenian People from Ancient to Modern Times*, vol. II: *Foreign Domination to Statehood: The Fifteenth Century to the Twentieth Century*, New York: St. Martin's Press, 1997.

——— 'The Economic Role of the Armenian Amira Class in the Ottoman Empire', *Armenian Review*, 31:3/123, March 1979.

Barth, Fredrik, 'Introduction' in Fredrik Barth (ed.), *Ethnic Groups and Boundaries: The Social Organization of Culture Difference*. Bergen/Oslo/London: Universitets Forlaget/George Allen and Unwin, 1969.

Bedrosian, Robert, 'Armenia During the Seljuk and Mongol Periods' in Richard Hovannisian (ed.), *The Armenian People from Ancient to Modern Times*, vol. I: *The Dynastic Periods: From Antiquity to the Fourteenth Century*, New York: St. Martin's Press, 1997.

Beiner, Ronald (ed.), *Theorizing Nationalism*, Albany, NY: State University of New York Press, 1999.

Bhabha, Homi, 'DissemiNation: Time, Narrative, and the Margins of the Modern Nation' in Homi Bhabha (ed.), *Nation and Narration*, London: Routledge, 1990.

Bialer, Seweryn, *Stalin's Successors: Leadership, Stability, and Change in the Soviet Union*, Cambridge University Press, 1980.

Billig, Michael, *Banal Nationalism*, London: Sage, 1995.

Binns, Christopher, 'The Changing Face of Power: Revolution and Accommodation in the Development of the Soviet Ceremonial System', *Man*, part I: 14:4, December 1979; part II: 15:1, March 1980.

——— 'Soviet Secular Ritual: Atheist Propaganda or Spiritual Consumerism?', *Religion in Communist Lands* 10:3, December 1982.

Björklund, Ulf, 'Armenia Remembered and Remade: Evolving Issues in a Diaspora', *Ethnos*, 58:3–4, 1993.

Blank, Stephen, 'Bolshevik Organizational Development in Early Soviet Transcaucasia: Autonomy vs. Centralization, 1918–1924' in Ronald Suny (ed.), *Transcaucasia, Nationalism, and Social Change*, revised edition, Ann Arbor: University of Michigan Press, 1996 (1983).

Boghigian, Apo, 'A Challenge to Democracy', interview, *Armenian International Magazine*, November–December 1994.

Bournoutian, Ani Atamian, 'Cilician Armenia' in Richard Hovannisian (ed.), *The Armenian People from Ancient to Modern Times*, vol. I: *The Dynastic Periods: From Antiquity to the Fourteenth Century*, New York: St. Martin's Press, 1997.

Bournoutian, George, 'Eastern Armenia from the Seventeenth Century to the Russian Annexation' in Richard Hovannisian (ed.), *The Armenian People from Ancient to Modern Times*, vol. II: *Foreign Domination to Statehood: The Fifteenth Century to the Twentieth Century*, New York: St. Martin's Press, 1997.

——— 'The Ethnic Composition and Socio-Economic Condition of Eastern Armenia in the First Half of the Nineteenth Century' in Ronald Suny (ed.), *Transcaucasia: Nationalism and Social Change*, Ann Arbor: Michigan Slavic Publications, University of Michigan, 1983.

——— *A History of the Armenian People*, vol. I: *Pre-History to 1500 A.D.*; vol. II: *1500 A.D. to the Present*, Costa Mesa, CA: Mazda, 1993/4.

Bournoutian, George, trans., *Russia and the Armenians of Transcaucasia, 1797–1889: A Documentary Record*, Costa Mesa, CA: Mazda, 1998.

Brandenberger, D. L. and A. M. Dubrovsky, '"The People Need a Tsar": The Emergence of National Bolshevism as Stalinist Ideology, 1931–1941', *Europe-Asia Studies*, 50:5, July 1998.

Brass, Paul, 'Elite Groups, Symbol Manipulation and Ethnic Identity Among the Muslims of South Asia' in David Taylor and Malcolm Yapp (eds), *Political Identity in South Asia*, London: Curzon Press, 1979.

——— *Ethnicity and Nationalism: Theory and Comparison*, New Delhi: Sage, 1991.

Braude, Benjamin, 'Foundation Myths of the *Millet* System' in Benjamin Braude and Bernard Lewis (eds), *Christians and Jews in the Ottoman Empire*, vol. I: *The Central Lands*, New York: Holmes and Meier, 1982.

——— 'The Nexus of Diaspora, Enlightenment, and Nation: Thoughts on Comparative History' in Richard Hovannisian and David Myers (eds), *Enlightenment and Diaspora: The Armenian and Jewish Cases*, Atlanta, GA: Scholars Press, 1999.

——— and Bernard Lewis (eds), *Christians and Jews in the Ottoman Empire*, vol. I: *The Central Lands*, New York: Holmes and Meier, 1982.

Bremmer, Ian and Ray Taras (eds), *Nations and Politics in the Soviet Successor States*, Cambridge University Press, 1993.

Breuilly, John, 'Approaches to Nationalism' in Gopal Balakrishnan (ed.), *Mapping the Nation*, London: Verso, 1996.

——— *Nationalism and the State*, 2nd edn, Manchester University Press, 1993 (1982).

Brubaker, Rogers, *Nationalism Reframed: Nationhood and the National Question in the New Europe*, Cambridge University Press, 1996.

Brzezinski, Zbigniew, 'Political Implications of Soviet Nationality Problems' in Edward Allworth (ed.), *Soviet Nationality Problems*, New York: Columbia University Press, 1971.

Carrère d'Encausse, Hélène, *Decline of an Empire: The Soviet Socialist Republics in Revolt*, New York: Newsweek Books, 1979 (1978).

——— 'Determinants and Parameters of Soviet Nationality Policy' in Jeremy Azrael (ed.), *Soviet Nationality Policies and Practices*, New York: Praeger, 1978.

——— *The End of the Soviet Empire: The Triumph of the Nations*, New York: Basic Books, 1993 (1990).

——— *The Great Challenge: Nationalities and the Bolshevik State 1917–1930*, New York: Holmes and Meier, 1992 (1987).

Chaqueri, Cosroe (ed.), *The Armenians of Iran. The Paradoxical Role of a Minority in a Dominant Culture: Articles and Documents*, Cambridge, MA: Center for Middle Eastern Studies of Harvard University, 1998.

Chatterjee, Partha, *The Nation and its Fragments: Colonial and Postcolonial Histories*, Princeton University Press, 1993.

——— *Nationalist Thought and the Colonial World: A Derivative Discourse?* London: Zed Books, 1986.

Chorbajian, Levon, 'For the Masses: Television in the Armenian S.S.R.', *Armenian Review*, 42:3/167, autumn 1989.

Chorbajian, Levon *et al.*, *The Caucasian Knot: The History and Geo-politics of Nagorno-Karabagh*, London: Zed Books, 1994.

Chorbajian, Levon and George Shirinian (eds), *Studies in Comparative Genocide*, Basingstoke: Macmillan, 1999.

Cohen, Robin, *Global Diasporas: An Introduction*, London: UCL Press, 1997.

Collias, Karen, 'Making Soviet Citizens: Patriotic and Internationalist Education in the Formation of a Soviet State Identity' in Henry Huttenbach (ed.), *Soviet Nationality Policies: Ruling Ethnic Groups in the USSR*, London: Mansell, 1990.

Comaroff, Jean and John Comaroff, *Of Revelation and Revolution: Christianity, Colonialism, and Consciousness in South Africa*, vol. I, University of Chicago Press, 1991.

Connor, Walker, *Ethnonationalism: The Quest for Understanding*, Princeton University Press, 1994.

——— 'The Impact of Homelands upon Diasporas' in Gabriel Sheffer (ed.), *Modern Diasporas in International Politics*, London: Croom Helm, 1986.

——— *The National Question in Marxist-Leninist Theory and Strategy*, Princeton University Press, 1984.

——— 'When is a Nation?', *Ethnic and Racial Studies*, 13:1, January 1990.

Conquest, Robert, 'Academe and Soviet Myth', *The National Interest*, 31, spring 1993.

Conquest, Robert (ed.), *Soviet Nationalities Policy in Practice*, London: Bodley Head, 1967.

Corley, Felix, 'The Armenian Church Under the Soviet Regime, part 1: The Leadership of Kevork', *Religion, State and Society*, 24:1, 1996.

——— 'The Armenian Church Under the Soviet Regime, part 2: The Leadership of Vazgen', *Religion, State and Society*, 24:4, 1996.

——— 'The Armenian Church under the Soviet and Independent Regimes, part 3: The Leadership of Vazgen', *Religion, State and Society*, 26:3–4, 1998.

Cowe, Peter, 'Medieval Armenian Literary and Cultural Trends' in Richard Hovannisian (ed), *The Armenian People from Ancient to Modern Times*, vol. I: *The Dynastic Periods: From Antiquity to the Fourteenth Century*, New York: St. Martin's Press, 1997.

Croissant, Michael, *The Armenia-Azerbaijan Conflict: Causes and Implications*, Westport, CT: Praeger, 1998.

Cubitt, Geoffrey (ed.), *Imagining Nations*, Manchester University Press, 1998.

Curtin, Philip, *Cross-cultural Trade in World History*, Cambridge University Press, 1984.

Dadrian, Vahakn, 'An Appraisal of the Communist Formula "National in Form, Socialist in Content" with Particular Reference to Soviet Armenia', *Armenian Review*, part I, 16:3/63, autumn 1963; part II, 16:4/64, winter 1963.

——— 'The Armenian Genocide and the Pitfalls of a "Balanced" Analysis', *Armenian Forum*, 1:2, summer 1998.

——— 'The Determinants of the Armenian Genocide', *Journal of Genocide Research*, 1:1, March 1999.

——— 'Genocide as a Problem of National and International Law: The World War I Armenian Case and its Contemporary Legal Ramifications', *Yale Journal of International Law*, 14:2, summer 1989.

——— *The History of the Armenian Genocide: Ethnic Conflict from the Balkans to Anatolia to the Caucasus*, Providence, RI/Oxford: Berghahn Books, 1995.

——— *The Key Elements in the Turkish Denial of the Armenian Genocide: A Case Study of Distortion and Falsification*, Cambridge, MA/Toronto: Zoryan Institute, 1999.

——— 'Nationalism, Communism and Soviet Industrialization: A Theoretical Exposition', *Sociologia Internationalis*, 10:2, 1972.

——— 'Nationalism in Soviet Armenia—A Case Study of Ethnocentrism' in George Simmonds (ed.), *Nationalism in the USSR and Eastern Europe*, University of Detroit Press, 1977.

——— 'Ottoman Archives and Denial of the Armenian Genocide' in Richard Hovannisian (ed.), *The Armenian Genocide: History, Politics, Ethics*, New York: St. Martin's Press, 1992.

——— *Warrant for Genocide: Key Elements of Turko–Armenian Conflict*, New Brunswick, NJ: Transaction, 1999.

Dasnabedian, Hratch, 'The ARF Record: The Balance Sheet of Ninety Years', *Armenian Review*, 34:2/134, June 1981.

——— *Histoire de la Fédération Révolutionnaire Arménienne Dachnaktsoutioun (1890–1924)*, Milan: Oemme Edizioni, 1988.

——— 'The Hunchakian Party', *Armenian Review*, 41:4/164, winter 1988.

Davis, Horace, *Nationalism and Socialism: Marxist and Labor Theories of Nationalism to 1917*, New York: Monthly Review Press, 1967.

Davison, Roderic, 'The *Millets* as Agents of Change in the Nineteenth-Century Ottoman Empire' in Benjamin Braude and Bernard Lewis (eds), *Christians and Jews in the Ottoman Empire*, vol. I: *The Central Lands*. New York: Holmes and Meier, 1982.

Dekmejian, R. Hrair, 'The Armenian Diaspora' in Richard Hovannisian (ed.), *The Armenian People from Ancient to Modern Times*, vol. II: *Foreign Domination to Statehood: The Fifteenth Century to the Twentieth Century*, New York: St. Martin's Press, 1997.

——— 'The Armenians: History, Consciousness and the Middle Eastern Dispersion', *Middle East Review*, 9:1, fall 1976.

Délégation de la République Arménienne, *L'Arménie et la question arménienne*, Paris: H. Turabian, 1922.

Denber, Rachel (ed.), *The Soviet Nationality Reader: The Disintegration in Context*, Boulder, CO: Westview, 1992.

Derogy, Jacques, *Resistance and Revenge: The Armenian Assassination of the Turkish Leaders Responsible for the 1915 Massacres and Deportations*, New Brunswick, NJ: Transaction Publishers, 1990 (1986).

Deutsch, Karl, *Nationalism and Social Communication: An Inquiry Into the Foundations of Nationality*, 2nd edition, Cambridge, MA: MIT Press, 1966 (1953).

'The Dro Details', *Armenian International Magazine*, May–June 1996.

Dudwick, Nora, 'Armenia: The Nation Awakens' in Ian Bremmer and Ray Taras (eds), *Nations and Politics in the Soviet Successor States*, Cambridge University Press, 1993.

——— University of Pennsylvania: 'Memory, Identity and Politics in Armenia', PhD Dissertation, 1994.

Dunlop, John, 'Language, Culture, Religion, and National Awareness' in Robert Conquest (ed.), *The Last Empire: Nationality and the Soviet Future*, Stanford, CA: Hoover Institution Press, 1986.

Edwards, John, *Language, Society and Identity*, Oxford: Basil Blackwell, 1985.

Eley, Geoff and Ronald Suny, 'Introduction: From the Moment of Social History to the Work of Cultural Representation' in Geoff Eley and Ronald Suny (eds), *Becoming National*. New York: Oxford University Press, 1996.

Ełishe (Eghishe), *History of Vardan and the Armenian War* (5th/6th century), translation and commentary by Robert Thomson, Cambridge, MA: Harvard University Press, 1982.

Emin, Gevorg, *Seven Songs about Armenia*, Yerevan: Sovetakan Grogh, 1983.

——— *Songs of Armenia: Selected Poems*, Moscow: Progress Publishers, 1979.

——— 'We' in Gerald Papasian (ed.), *Sojourn at Ararat. Poems of Armenia*, Los Angeles: private publication, 1987 (originally published in Gevorg Emin, *Akh ais Masise* [Oh, this Ararat], Yerevan: Sovetakan Grogh, 1980).

Emin, Joseph, *The Life and Adventures of Joseph Émïn, an Armenian*, Second Edition. Calcutta: Baptist Mission Press, 1918 (London, 1792).

Eisenstadt, S. N., 'Center-Periphery Relations in the Soviet Empire: Some Interpretive Observations' in Alexander Motyl (ed.), *Thinking Theoretically about Soviet Nationalities. History and Comparison in the Study of the USSR*. New York: Columbia University Press, 1992.

Eriksen, Thomas Hylland, *Ethnicity and Nationalism: Anthropological Perspectives*. London: Pluto, 1993.

Fishman, Joshua, 'Social Theory and Ethnography: Neglected Perspectives on Language and Ethnicity in Eastern Europe' in Peter Sugar (ed.), *Ethnic Diversity and Conflict in Eastern Europe*, Santa Barbara, CA: ABC-Clio, 1980.

Forché, Carolyn (ed.), *Against Forgetting: Twentieth-Century Poetry of Witness*, New York: W. W. Norton, 1993.

Foss, Clive, 'Armenian History as Seen by Twentieth Century Turkish Historians', *Armenian Review*, 45:1–2/177–8, spring–summer 1992.

Gachechiladze, Revaz, *The New Georgia: Space, Society, Politics*, London: UCL Press, 1995.

Gans, Herbert, 'Symbolic Ethnicity: The Future of Ethnic Groups and Cultures in America', *Ethnic and Racial Studies*, 2:1, 1979.

Garo, Armen [Pasdermadjian, Garegin], *Bank Ottoman, Memoirs of Armen Garo*, ed. Simon Vratzian, trans. Haig Partizian, Detroit: Armen Topouzian, 1990 (originally published in Armenian in 1948).

Garsoïan, Nina, 'The Arab Invasions and the Rise of the Bagratuni' in Richard Hovannisian (ed.), *The Armenian People from Ancient to Modern Times*, vol. I: *The Dynastic Periods: From Antiquity to the Fourteenth Century*. New York: St. Martin's Press, 1997.

——— 'The Arsakuni Dynasty' in Richard Hovannisian (ed.), *The Armenian People from Ancient to Modern Times*, vol. I, op. cit. supra.

——— 'The Byzantine Annexation of the Armenian Kingdoms in the Eleventh Century' in Richard Hovannisian (ed.), *The Armenian People from Ancient to Modern Times*, vol. I, op. cit. supra.

——— 'The Emergence of Armenia' in Richard Hovannisian (ed.), *The Armenian People from Ancient to Modern Times*, vol. I, op. cit. supra.

——— 'The Independent Kingdoms of Medieval Armenia' in Richard Hovannisian (ed.), *The Armenian People from Ancient to Modern Times*, vol. I, op. cit. supra.

——— 'The *Marzpanate*' in Richard Hovannisian (ed.), *The Armenian People from Ancient to Modern Times*, vol. I, op. cit. supra.

Gellner, Ernest, 'The Coming of Nationalism and Its Interpretation: The Myths of Nation and Class' in Gopal Balakrishnan (ed.), *Mapping the Nation*, London: Verso, 1996.

——— 'Do Nations Have Navels?', *Nations and Nationalism*, 2:3, November 1996.

——— *Nationalism*, London: Weidenfeld and Nicolson, 1997.

——— *Nations and Nationalism*, Oxford: Basil Blackwell, 1983.

——— *State and Society in Soviet Thought*, Oxford: Basil Blackwell, 1988.

——— *Thought and Change*, London: Weidenfeld and Nicolson, 1964.

Ghazarian, Jacob, *The Armenian Kingdom in Cilicia during the Crusades*. London: Curzon, 2000.

Ghazarian, Salpi Haroutinian, 'The Great Divide', *Armenian International Magazine*, November–December 1994.

Ghougassian, Vazken, 'The Quest for Enlightenment and Liberation: The Case of the Armenian Community of India in the Late Eighteenth Century' in Richard Hovannisian and David Myers (eds), *Enlightenment and Diaspora: The Armenian and Jewish Cases*, Atlanta: Scholars Press, 1999.

Gleason, Gregory, *Federalism and Nationalism: The Struggle for Republican Rights in the USSR*. Boulder, CO: Westview, 1990.

——— 'On the Bureaucratic Reinforcement of Nationalism in the USSR', *Canadian Review of Studies in Nationalism*, 19:1–2, 1992.

Glenn, John, 'Nations and Nationalism: Marxist Approaches to the Subject', *Nationalism and Ethnic Politics*, 3:2, summer 1997.

Gökay, Bülent, 'The Battle for Baku, May–September 1918: A Peculiar Episode in the History of the Caucasus', *Middle Eastern Studies*, 34:1, January 1998.

Göl, Ayla, 'The Place of Foreign Policy in the Transition to Modernity: Turkish Policy Towards the South Caucasus, 1918–1921', London School of Economics and Political Science (University of London): PhD Dissertation, 2000.

Gorbachev, Mikhail, *Mikhail Gorbachev: Memoirs*. London: Doubleday, 1996.

——— *Perestroika: New Thinking for Our Country and the World*. New York: Harper and Row, 1988 (1987).

Goshgarian, Geoffrey, 'Eghishe Charents and the "Modernization" of Soviet Armenian Literature', *Armenian Review*, 36:1/141, spring 1983.

Gramsci, Antonio, *Selections from Prison Notebooks*, ed. and trans. Quintin Hoare and Geoffrey Nowell Smith. New York: International Publishers, 1971.

Greenfeld, Liah, *Nationalism: Five Roads to Modernity*. Cambridge, MA: Harvard University Press, 1992.

Gregorian, Vartan, 'The Impact of Russia on the Armenians and Armenia' in Wayne Vucinich (ed.), *Russia and Asia: Essays on the Influence of Russia on the Asian Peoples*. Stanford: Hoover Institution Press, 1972.

——— 'Minorities of Isfahan: The Armenian Community of Isfahan 1587–1722', *Iranian Studies*, 7:3–4, summer–autumn 1974.

Greppin, John, 'Armenian Studies and Language Reserch in Yerevan During the Soviet Period', *Armenian Review*, 32:4/128, winter 1979.

Grosby, Steven, 'Borders, Territory and Nationality in the Ancient Near East and Armenia', *Journal of the Economic and Social History of the Orient*, 40:1, February 1997.

——— 'Religion and Nationality in Antiquity: the Worship of Yahweh and Ancient Israel', *Archives Européennes de Sociologie*, 32:2, 1991.

——— 'Territoriality: The Transcendental Primordial Feature of Modern Societies', *Nations and Nationalism*, 1:2, July 1995.

Guaita, Giovanni, *Between Heaven and Earth. A Conversation with His Holiness Karekin I*, New York: St Vartan Press, 2000.

Guibernau, Montserrat, *Nationalisms: The Nation-State and Nationalism in the Twentieth Century*, Cambridge: Polity, 1996.

Gunter, Michael, *'Pursuing the Just Cause of Their People:' A Study of Contemporary Armenian Terrorism*, New York: Greenwood, 1986.

Gürün, Kamuran, *The Armenian File: The Myth of Innocence Exposed*, Nicosia, Northern Cyprus: K. Rustem and Brother, 1985 (1983).

Hajda, Lubomyr and Mark (eds), *The Nationalities Factor in Soviet Politics and Society*, Boulder, CO: Westview, 1990.

Hall, John (ed.), *The State of the Nation: Ernest Gellner and the Theory of Nationalism*, Cambridge University Press, 1998.

Hanioğlu, Şükrü, 'Turkish Nationalism and Young Turks, 1889–1908' in Fatma Müge Göçek (ed.), *Social Constructions of Nationalism in the Middle East*, Albany, NY: State University of New York Press, 2002.

Hartunian, Abtaham, *Neither to Laugh nor to Weep: A Memoir of the Armenian Genocide*, Boston: Beacon Press, 1968.

Hassassian, Manuel, *ARF as a Revolutionary Party, 1890–1921*, Jerusalem: Hai Tad Publications, 1983.

Hastings, Adrian, *The Construction of Nationhood: Ethnicity, Religion and Nationalism*, Cambridge University Press, 1997.

Hechter, Michael, *Internal Colonialism. The Celtic Fringe in British National Development, 1536–1966*, London: Routledge and Kegan Paul, 1975.

Heitman, Sidney, 'Soviet Emigration Policies toward Germans and Armenians' in Henry Huttenbach (ed.), *Soviet Nationality Policies: Ruling Ethnic Groups in the USSR*, London: Mansell, 1990.

Herzig, Edmund, 'The Armenian Merchants of New Julfa, Isfahan: A Study in Pre-modern Asian Trade', University of Oxford: DPhil dissertation, 1991.

——— 'The Deportation of the Armenians in 1604–1605 and Europe's Myth of Shah Abbas I', *Pembroke Papers*, 1, 1990.

——— 'The Rise of the Julfa Merchants in the Late Sixteenth Century', *Pembroke Papers*, 4, 1996.

Hewsen, Robert, 'Russian–Armenian Relations, 1700–1828', Cambridge, MA: Society for Armenian Studies Occasional Papers, no. 4, 1984.

Hobsbawm, E. J., *Nations and Nationalism Since 1780. Programme, Myth, Reality*, Cambridge University Press/Canto, 1991 (1990).

Hobsbawm, Eric, 'Introduction: Inventing Traditions' in Eric Hobsbawm and Terence Ranger (eds), *The Invention of Tradition*, Cambridge University Press/Canto, 1992 (1983).

——— 'Mass-Producing Traditions: Europe, 1870–1914' in Eric Hobsbawm and Terence Ranger (eds), *The Invention of Tradition*. Cambridge University Press/Canto, 1992 (1983).

——— 'The Opiate Ethnicity', *Alphabet City* (Toronto), 2, 1992.

Hopkins, J. Castell, *The Sword of Islam or Suffering Armenia: Annals of Turkish Power and the Eastern Question*, Brantford and Toronto, Canada: Bradley-Garretson, 1896.

Horowitz, Donald, *Ethnic Groups in Conflict*, Berkeley, CA: University of California, 1985.

Hosking, Geoffrey and George Schöpflin (eds), *Myths and Nationhood*, London: Hurst, 1997.

Hovannisian, Richard, *Armenia on the Road to Independence, 1918*, Berkeley and Los Angeles: University of California Press, 1967.

——— 'Armenia's Road to Independence' in Richard Hovannisian (ed.), *The Armenian People from Ancient to Modern Times*, vol. II: *Foreign Domination to Statehood: The Fifteenth Century to the Twentieth Century*, New York: St. Martin's Press, 1997.

——— 'The Armenian Question in the Ottoman Empire 1876 to 1914' in Richard Hovannisian (ed.), *The Armenian People from Ancient to Modern Times*, vol. II: *Foreign Domination to Statehood: The Fifteenth Century to the Twentieth Century*, New York: St. Martin's Press, 1997.

——— 'The Armeno-Azerbaijani Conflict Over Mountainous Karabagh, 1918–1919', *Armenian Review*, 24:2/94, summer 1971.

——— 'Denial of the Armenian Genocide in Comparison with Holocaust Denial' in Richard Hovannisian (ed.), *Remembrance and Denial: The Case of the Armenian Genocide*, Detroit: Wayne State University Press, 1998.

——— 'The Ninth General Meeting of the Armenian Revolutionary Federation, 1919', *Armenian Review*, 34:1/133, March 1981.

——— 'The Republic of Armenia' in Richard Hovannisian (ed.), *The Armenian People from Ancient to Modern Times*, vol. II: *Foreign Domination to Statehood: The Fifteenth Century to the Twentieth Century*, New York: St. Martin's Press, 1997.

——— 'The Republic of Armenia', vol. I: *The First Year, 1918–1919*; vol. II: *From Versailles to London, 1919–1920*; vol. III: *From London to Sèvres, February–August, 1920*; vol. IV: *Between Crescent and Sickle: Partition and Sovietization*, Berkeley: University of California Press, 1971, 1982, 1996, 1996 respectively.

——— 'The Role of the Armenian Revolutionary Federation in the Republic of Armenia', *Armenian Review*, 44:2/174, summer 1991.

Hovannisian, Richard (ed.), *The Armenian Genocide: History, Politics, Ethics*. New York: St. Martin's Press, 1992.

——— *The Armenian Genocide in Perspective*, New Brunswick, NJ: Transaction Books, 1986.

——— *The Armenian People from Ancient to Modern Times*, vol. I: *The Dynastic Periods: From Antiquity to the Fourteenth Century*; vol. II: *Foreign Domination to Statehood: The Fifteenth Century to the Twentieth Century*, New York: St. Martin's Press, 1997.

——— *Remembrance and Denial: The Case of the Armenian Genocide*, Detroit: Wayne State University Press, 1998.

Hovannisian, Richard and David Myers (eds), *Enlightenment and Diaspora: The Armenian and Jewish Cases*, Atlanta: Scholars Press, 1999.

Hroch, Miroslav, 'From National Movement to the Fully-formed Nation', *New Left Review*, 198, March/April 1993.

——— 'National Self-Determination from a Historical Perspective' in Sukumar Periwal (ed.), *Notions of Nationalism*, Budapest: Central European University Press, 1995.

——— 'Nationalism and National Movements: Comparing the Past and the Present of Central and Eastern Europe', *Nations and Nationalism*, 2:1, March 1996.

——— 'Real and Constructed: The Nature of the Nation' in John Hall (ed.), *The State of the Nation: Ernest Gellner and the Theory of Nationalism*. Cambridge University, 1998.

Hutchinson, John, *Modern Nationalism*, London: Fontana, 1994.

Huttenbach, Henry, 'Conclusion: Towards a Multiethnic Soviet State: Managing a Multinational Society since 1985' in Henry Huttenbach (ed.), *Soviet Nationality Policies: Ruling Ethnic Groups in the USSR*. London: Mansell, 1990.

Huttenbach, Henry (ed.), *Soviet Nationality Policies: Ruling Ethnic Groups in the USSR*, London: Mansell, 1990.

Hyland, Francis, *Armenian Terrorism: The Past, the Present, the Prospects*. Boulder, CO: Westview, 1991.

Jacobson, Matthew, *Special Sorrows: The Diasporic Imagination of Irish, Polish and Jewish Immigrants in the United States*, Cambridge, MA: Harvard University Press, 1995.

Jeni, Giulio, 'Architectural Typologies' in Adriano Alpago Novello *et al., The Armenians: 2000 Years of Art and Architecture*, Paris: Bookking International, 1995 (1986).

Jones, S(tephen) F., 'Religion and Nationalism in Soviet Georgia and Armenia' in Pedro Ramet (ed.), *Religion and Nationalism in Soviet and East European Politics*. Durham, NC: Duke University Press, 1989.

Kagedan, Allan, 'Territorial Units as Nationality Policy' in Henry Huttenbach (ed.), *Soviet Nationality Policies: Ruling Ethnic Groups in the USSR*, London: Mansell, 1990.

Kalugin, Oleg (with Fen Montaigne), *Spymaster: My 32 Years in Intelligence and Espionage against the West*. London: Smith Gryphon, 1994.

Karekin I (Catholicos), *In Search of Spiritual Life*, Ejmiatzin, Armenia: Catholicosate of Holy Etchmiadzin, 1995.

Karklins, Rasma, *Ethnic Relations in the USSR: The Perspective from Below*, London: Unwin Hyman, 1986.

Karpat, Kemal, '*Millets* and Nationality: The Roots of the Incongruity of Nation and State in the Post-Ottoman Era' in Benjamin Braude and Bernard Lewis (eds), *Christians and Jews in the Ottoman Empire*, vol. I: *The Central Lands*, New York: Holmes and Meier, 1982.

Kedourie, Elie, *Nationalism*. New York: Praeger, 1961 (1960).

Keshishian, Aram, *The Witness of the Armenian Church in a Diaspora Situation: Problems, Perspectives, Prospects*, New York: Prelacy of the Armenian Apostolic Church of America, 1978.

Kévorkian, Raymond, 'L'Extermination des déportés Arméniens Ottomans dans les camps de concentration de Syrie-Mésopotamie (1915–1916). La deuxième phase du génocide', *Revue d'histoire arménienne contemporaine*, vol. II, 1996–7–8.

——— and Paul Paboudjian, *Les Arméniens dans l'empire ottoman à la veille du génocide*, Paris: Les Editions d'Art et d'Histoire ARHIS, 1992.

Kévorkian, R.-H. and J.-P. Mahé, *Le livre arménien à travers les ages*. Marseilles/Venice: La Maison Arménienne de la Jeunesse et de la Culture/Mkhitarian Press, 1985.

Khorenatsi, Moses, *History of the Armenians* (5th/8th century), translation and commentary by Robert Thomson, Cambridge, MA: Harvard University Press, 1978.

Kolarz, Walter, *Religion in the Soviet Union*, London: Macmillan, 1961.

Kouymjian, Dickran, 'Armenia from the Fall of the Cilician Kingdom (1375) to the Forced Emigration under Shah Abbas (1604)' in Richard Hovannisian (ed.), *The Armenian People from Ancient to Modern Times*, vol. II: *Foreign Domination to Statehood: The Fifteenth Century to the Twentieth Century*, New York: St. Martin's Press, 1997.

——— 'The Status of Artists and Intellectuals in Soviet Armenia', *Armenian Review*, 42:3/167, autumn 1989.

Kowalewski, David, 'The Armenian National Unity Party: Context and Program', *Armenian Review*, 31:4/124, April 1979.

Krikorian, Mesrob, 'The Armenian Church in the Soviet Union, 1917–1967' in Richard Marshall Jr.(ed.), *Aspects of Religion in the Soviet Union, 1917–1967*, University of Chicago Press, 1971.

Kulov, K., 'Clan Survivals as a form of Class Struggle in North Ossetia' in Rudolf Schlesinger (ed.), *The Nationalities Problem and Soviet Administration*. London: Routledge and Kegan Paul, 1956 (article is from 1933).

Kyrou, Ariel and Maxime Mardoukhaïev, 'Le Haut-Karabagh, vu de côté Azerbaïdjan', *Hérodote*, 54–5, July–December 1989.

Lane, David, *Soviet Society Under Perestroika*, revised edition, London: Routledge, 1992.

Lang, David Marshall, *Armenia: Cradle of Civilization*, 2nd edition. London: George Allen and Unwin, 1978 (1970).

——— *The Armenians: A People in Exile*, 2nd edition. London: Unwin Hyman, 1988 (1981).

Lapidus, Gail, 'Ethnonationalism and Political Stability: The Soviet Case', *World Politics*, 36:4, July 1984.

——— *et al.* (eds), *From Union to Commonwealth: Nationalism and Separatism in the Soviet Republics*, Cambridge University Press, 1992.

Leese, C. Leonard, *Armenia and the Allies*, London: The British Armenia Committee, 1920.

Lewis, Bernard, *The Emergence of Modern Turkey*, 3rd edition, Oxford University Press, 2002 (1961).

Libaridian, Gerard, *The Challenge of Statehood: Armenian Political Thinking Since Independence*, Watertown, MA: Blue Crane Books, 1999.

——— 'The Changing Armenian Self-Image in the Ottoman Empire: Rayahs and Revolutionaries' in Richard Hovannisian (ed.), *The Armenian Image in History and Literature*, Malibu, CA: Undena Publications, 1981.

Libaridian, Gerald [*sic*], 'Democracy, Diaspora, and the National Agenda', *Nor Gyank*, 7 Feb. 1991 (part I), 14 Feb. 1991 (part II—text of his speech at the second congress of Armenian National Movement, 25 November 1990).

Libaridian, Gerard, 'The Ideology of Armenian Liberation: The Development of Armenian Political Thought Before the Revolutionary Movement (1639–1885)'. University of California, Los Angeles: PhD Dissertation, 1987.

Libaridian, Jirair (Gerard), 'Interview', 1 September 1992, as posted on *Groong Armenian News Network* (interviewed by Soren Theisen).

Libaridian, Gerard, 'Nation and Fatherland in Nineteenth Century Western Armenian Political Thought', *Armenian Review*, 36:3/143, Autumn 1983.

——— *The Karabagh File*. Cambridge, MA: The Zoryan Institute, 1988.

——— (ed.), *Armenia at the Crossroads: Democracy and Nationhood in the Post-Soviet Era*, Watertown, MA: Blue Crane Books, 1991.

Lieven, Anatol, 'Qu'est-ce qu'une nation? Scholarly Debate and the Realities of Eastern Europe', *The National Interest*, 49, Fall 1997.

Lieven, Dominic, *Empire: The Russian Empire and its Rivals*. London: John Murray, 2000.

——— 'Gorbachev and the Nationalities', London: Centre for Security and Conflict Studies, Institute for the Study of Conflict, 1988.

——— 'Western Scholarship on the Rise and Fall of the Soviet Régime: The View from 1993', *Journal of Contemporary History*, 29:2, April 1994.

Lima, Vincent, 'The Evolving Goals and Strategies of the Armenian Revolutionary Federation, 1890–1925', *Armenian Review*, 44:2/174, Summer 1991.

Lowry, Heath, *The Story Behind Ambassador Morgenthau's Story.* Istanbul: Isis Press, 1990.

Lynch, H. F. B., *Armenia: Travels and Studies*, vol. I: *The Russian Provinces*; vol. II: *The Turkish Provinces.* London: Longmans, Green and Co., 1901.

Maksoudian, Krikor, 'Armenian Communities in Eastern Europe' in Richard Hovannisian (ed.), *The Armenian People from Ancient to Modern Times*, vol. II: *Foreign Domination to Statehood: The Fifteenth Century to the Twentieth Century.* New York: St. Martin's Press, 1997.

Malkasian, Mark, *'Gha-ra-bagh!' The Emergence of the National Democratic Movement in Armenia*, Detroit: Wayne State University Press, 1996.

Mandelstam, Osip, *Journey to Armenia*, trans. Sidney Monas, San Francisco: George F. Ritchie, 1979 (1933).

Manoukian [Manukian], Vazgen, 'War Is Inevitable', interview (by Vartan Oskanian and Gayane Hambartzoumian), *Armenian International Magazine*, December 1991.

Marashlian, Levon, *Politics and Demography: Armenians, Turks, and Kurds in the Ottoman Empire.* Cambridge, MA: Zoryan Institute, 1991.

Mathossentz, Murad, *The Black Raven.* London: Policy Research Publications, 1988.

Matossian, Mary Kilbourne, 'Communist Rule and the Changing Armenian Cultural Pattern' in Erich Goldhagen (ed.), *Ethnic Minorities in the Soviet Union*, New York: Praeger, 1968.

——— *The Impact of Soviet Policies in Armenia.* Leiden: E. J. Brill, 1962.

McCabe, Ina Baghdiantz, *The Shah's Silk for Europe's Silver: The Eurasian Trade of the Julfa Armenians in Safavid Iran and India (1530–1750)*, Atlanta: Scholars Press, 1999.

McCarthy, Justin, 'The Anatolian Armenians, 1912–1922' in *Armenians in the Ottoman Empire and Modern Turkey, 1912–1922*, Istanbul: Boğaziçi University Institute for Atatürk's Principles and the History of Turkish Renovation, 1984.

——— *Death and Exile: The Ethnic Cleansing of Ottoman Muslims, 1821–1922*, Princeton: The Darwin Press, 1995.

——— *Muslims and Minorities: The Population of Ottoman Anatolia and the End of Empire*, New York University Press, 1983.

Melik-Hakobian, S., 'Establishment of the Second Republic of Armenia and the Dashnaktsutiun (ARF)', *Nor Gyank*, 28 Nov. 1996 (originally published in Armenian in *Hayastani Hanrapetutiun*, June–July 1995).

Melson, Robert, *Revolution and Genocide: On the Origins of the Armenian Genocide and the Holocaust*, University of Chicago Press, 1992.

Mesrobian, Arpena, *'Like one Family': The Armenians of Syracuse*, Ann Arbor, MI: Gomidas Institute, 2000.

Micciché, Lino, 'The Cinema of the Transcaucasian and Central Asian Soviet Republics' in Anna Lawton (ed.), *The Red Screen: Politics, Society, Art in Soviet Cinema*, London: Routledge, 1992.

Miller, Donald, 'The Role of Historical Memory in Interpreting Events in the Republic of Armenia' in Richard Hovannisian (ed.), *Remembrance and Denial: The Case of the Armenian Genocide*, Detroit: Wayne State University Press, 1998.

Minassian, Gaidz, 'Les relations entre le Comité Union et Progrès et la Fédération Révolutionnaire Arménienne à la veille de la Première Guerre Mondiale d'après les sources arméniennes', *Revue d'histoire arménienne contemporaine*, 1, 1995.

Mirak, Robert, 'The Armenians in America' in Richard Hovannisian (ed.), *The Armenian People from Ancient to Modern Times*, vol. II: *Foreign Domination to Statehood: The Fifteenth Century to the Twentieth Century*, New York: St. Martin's Press, 1997.

——— *Torn Between Two Lands: Armenians in America, 1890 to World War I*, Cambridge, MA: Harvard University Press, 1983.

Motyl, Alexander, *Sovietology, Rationality, Nationality: Coming to Grips with Nationalism in the USSR*, New York: Columbia University Press, 1990.

——— *Will the Non-Russians Rebel? State, Ethnicity, and Stability in the USSR*, Ithaca, NY: Cornell University Press, 1987.

Motyl, Alexander (ed.), *The Post-Soviet Nations: Perspectives on the Demise of the USSR*, New York: Columbia University Press, 1992.

——— *Thinking Theoretically about Soviet Nationalities. History and Comparison in the Study of the USSR*, New York: Columbia University Press, 1992.

Mouradian, Claire, 'The Armenian Apostolic Church' in Pedro Ramet (ed.), *Eastern Christianity and Politics in the Twentieth Century*, Durham, NC: Duke University, 1988.

——— *L'Arménie*, Paris: Presses Universitaires de France, 1995.

——— 'L'Arménie soviétique et la diaspora', *Les Temps Modernes*, 504/5/6, July–September 1988.

——— *De Staline à Gorbatchev. Histoire d'une république soviétique: l'Arménie*, Paris: Editions Ramsay, 1990.

——— 'L'immigration des Arméniens de la diaspora vers la RSS d'Arménie, 1946–1962', *Cahiers du Monde Russe et Soviétique*, 20:1, January–March 1979.

——— and Anahide Ter Minassian, 'Permanence de la Famille Arménienne', *Cultures et Sociétés de l'Est*, 9, 1988.

Munck, Ronaldo, *The Difficult Dialogue: Marxism and Nationalism*, London: Zed Books, 1986.

'Nagorno-Karabakhia's [*sic*] Ideological Flaws', *Current Digest of the Soviet Press*, 27:17, 21 May 1975.

Nahaylo, Bohdan and Victor Swoboda, *Soviet Disunion: A History of the Nationalities Problem in the USSR*, New York: Free Press, 1990.

Nairn, Tom, *The Break-Up of Britain: Crisis and Neo-Nationalism*, 2nd edition, London: Verso, 1981 (1977).

——— *Faces of Nationalism: Janus Revisited*, London: Verso, 1997.

Nalbandian, Louise, *The Armenian Revolutionary Movement: The Development of Armenian Political Parties through the Nineteenth Century*, Berkeley: University of California, 1963.

Nassibian, Akaby, *Britain and the Armenian Question, 1915–1923*, London: Croom Helm, 1984.

Natsional'nyi sostav naseleniya SSSR. Po dannym vsesoiuznoi perepisi naseleniya 1989 g [The National Content of the Population of the USSR. From the All Union Census of 1989], Moscow: Finance and Statistics, 1991.

Nichanian, Marc, 'Enlightenment and Historical Thought' in Richard Hovannisian and David Myers (eds), *Enlightenment and Diaspora: The Armenian and Jewish Cases*. Atlanta: Scholars Press, 1999.

——— 'The Style of Violence', *Armenian Review*, 38: 1/149, spring 1985.

——— 'The Truth of the Facts: About the New Revisionism' in Richard Hovannisian (ed.), *Remembrance and Denial: The Case of the Armenian Genocide*, Detroit: Wayne State University Press, 1998.

Nieguth, Tim, 'Beyond Dichotomy: Concepts of the Nation and the Distribution of Membership', *Nations and Nationalism*, 5:2, April 1999.

Nielsen, Kai, 'Cultural Nationalism, Neither Ethnic nor Civic' in Ronald Beiner (ed.), *Theorizing Nationalism*, Albany, NY: State University of New York, 1999.

Norbu, Dawa, *Culture and the Politics of Third World Nationalism*. London: Routledge, 1992.

Novello, Adriano A., 'Armenian Architecture from East to West' in Adriano Alpago Novello *et al.*, *The Armenians: 2000 Years of Art and Architecture*, Paris: Bookking International, 1995 (1986).

Oganessyan, Eduard, 'The Armenian Church in the USSR', *Religion in Communist Lands*, 7:4, winter 1979.

Öke, Mim Kemâl, *The Armenian Question, 1914–1923*, Nicosia, Northern Cyprus: K. Rustem and Brother, 1988.

O'Leary, Brendan, 'On the Nature of Nationalism: An Appraisal of Ernest Gellner's Writings on Nationalism', *British Journal of Political Science*, 27:2, April 1997.

Orel, Şinasi and Süreyya Yuca, *The Talât Pasha 'Telegrams': Historical Fact or Armenian Fiction?*, Nicosia, Northern Cyprus: K. Rustem and Brother, 1983.

Ormanian, Malachia (Archbishop), *The Church of Armenia*. New York: St. Vartan Press, 1988 (1910).

Orridge, A. W., 'Uneven Development and Nationalism' in *Political Studies*, part I: 29: 1, March 1981; part II: 29:2, June 1981.

Oshagan, Vahé, 'Cultural and Literary Awakening of Western Armenians, 1789–1915', *Armenian Review*, 36:3/143, autumn 1983.

——— 'Modern Armenian Literature and Intellectual History from 1700 to 1915' in Richard Hovannisian (ed.), *The Armenian People from Ancient to Modern Times*, vol. II: *Foreign Domination to Statehood: The Fifteenth Century to the Twentieth Century*. New York: St. Martin's Press, 1997.

Oshagan, Vah[é], 'Modernization in Western Armenian Literature', *Armenian Review*, 36:1/141, spring 1983.

Oshagan, Vahé, 'Poles Apart: Interview with Vahe Oshagan', *Armenian International Magazine*, July 1991 (by Ishkhan Jinbashian).

——— 'The Self-Image of Western Armenians in Modern Literature' in Richard Hovannisian (ed.), *The Armenian Image in History and Literature*, Malibu, CA: Undena Publications, 1981.

Özkırımlı, Umut, *Theories of Nationalism: A Critical Introduction*. London/New York: Macmillan, 2000.

Panossian, Razmik, 'Between Ambivalence and Intrusion: Politics and Identity in Armenia-Diaspora Relations', *Diaspora: A Journal of Transnational Studies*, 7:2, fall 1998.

——— 'Courting a Diaspora: Armenia-Diaspora Relations since 1998' in Eva Østergaard-Nielsen (ed.), *International Migration and Sending Countries: Perceptions, Policies and Transnational Relations*, Basingstoke: Palgrave Macmillan, 2003.

——— 'The Diaspora and the Karabagh Movement: Oppositional Politics between the Armenian Revolutionary Federation and the Armenian National Movement' in Levon Chorbajian (ed.), *The Making of Nagorno-Karabagh: From Secession to Republic*. Basingstoke: Palgrave, 2001.

——— 'The Evolution of Multilocal National Identity and the Contemporary Politics of Nationalism: Armenia and Its Diaspora', London School of Economics and Political Science (University of London): PhD dissertation, 2000.

——— 'From Provincial Republics to Independent Provinces: Centre-Periphery Tensions in the Transcaucasus', *Papers from the Second University of Manchester Workshop on Central Asia and the Caucasus, May 1995*, Research Group on Central Asia and the Caucasus, University of Manchester, 1996.

——— 'The Irony of Nagorno-Karabakh: Formal Institutions versus Informal Politics', *Regional and Federal Studies*, 11:3, autumn 2001.

——— 'The Past as Nation: Three Dimensions of Armenian Identity', *Geopolitics*, 7:2, autumn 2002.

Papasian, Gerald (compiler and ed.), *Sojourn at Ararat. Poems of Armenia*, Los Angeles: issued privately, 1987.

Papazian, Dennis, '"Misplaced Credulity": Contemporary Turkish Attempts to Refute the Armenian Genocide', *Armenian Review*, 45:1–2/177–8, spring–summer 1992.

Papazian, K. S., *Merchants from Ararat. A Brief Survey of Armenian Trade through the Ages*, New York: Ararat Press, 1979 (1930s).

——— *Patriotism Perverted: A Discussion of the Deeds and the Misdeeds of the Armenian Revolutionary Federation, the so-called Dashnagtzoutune*, Boston: Baikar Press, 1934.

Papazian, Pierre, 'Terrorism: The Constant Threat', *Armenian Review*, 45:3/179, autumn 1992.

Pattie, Susan, *Faith in History: Armenians Rebuilding Community*, Washington: Smithsonian Institution, 1997.

Peroomian, Rubina, 'Armenian Literary Responses to Genocide: The Artistic Struggle to Comprehend and Survive' in Richard Hovannisian (ed.), *The Armenian Genocide: History, Politics, Ethics*, New York: St. Martin's Press, 1992.

——— 'Expressions of Nationalism in Dissident and Post-Soviet Armenian Literature', paper presented at Middle East Studies Association 33rd annual meeting. Washington, DC, November 1999.

——— 'Problematic Aspects of Reading Genocide Literature: A Search for a Guideline or a Canon' in Richard Hovannisian (ed.), *Remembrance and Denial: The Case of the Armenian Genocide*, Detroit: Wayne State University Press, 1998.

Phillips, Jenny, *Symbol, Myth, and Rhetoric: The Politics of Culture in An Armenian–American Population*, New York: AMS Press, 1989.

Pipes, Richard, *The Formation of the Soviet Union: Communism and Nationalism, 1917–1923*, Cambridge, MA: Harvard University Press, 1954.

Plamenatz, John, 'Two Types of Nationalism' in Eugene Kamenka (ed.), *Nationalism. The Nature and Evolution of an Idea*, New York: St. Martin's Press, 1976.

Platz, Stephanie, 'Pasts and Futures: Space, History, and Armenian Identity, 1988–1994', University of Chicago: PhD dissertation, 1996.

The Programme of the Communist Party of the Soviet Union. A New Edition. Moscow: Novosti Press, 1986 (as approved by 27th Congress of CPSU in March 1986).

'Public Message of the XXII World Congress of the Armenian Revolutionary Federation', *Armenian Review*, 35:2/138, summer 1982.

Rakowska-Harmstone, Teresa, 'Chickens Coming Home to Roost: A Perspective on Soviet Ethnic Relations', *Journal of International Affairs*, 45:2, winter 1992.

——— 'The Dialectics of Nationalism in the USSR', *Problems of Communism*, 23:3, May–June 1974.

——— 'Integration and Ethnic Nationalism in the Soviet Union: Aspects, Trends, and Problems' in Carl Linden and Dimitri Simes (eds), *Nationalities and Nationalism in the USSR: A Soviet Dilemma*, Washington: Center for Strategic and International Studies, Georgetown University, 1977.

——— 'The Study of Ethnic Politics in the USSR' in George Simmonds (ed.), *Nationalism in the USSR and Eastern Europe*, University of Detroit Press, 1977.

Reddaway, Peter, 'The Role of Popular Discontent', *The National Interest*, 31, spring 1993.

Redgate, A. E., *The Armenians*. Oxford: Blackwell, 1998.

'Reflections of a Nationality Expert' (i.e. Richard Pipes) in Carl Linden and Dimitri Simes (eds), *Nationalities and Nationalism in the USSR: A Soviet Dilemma*. Washington: Center for Strategic and International Studies, Georgetown University, 1977.

Renan, Ernest, 'What is a Nation?' in Geoff Eley and Ronald Suny (eds), *Becoming National*, New York: Oxford University Press, 1996.

Riggs, Henry, *Days of Tragedy in Armenia: Personal Experiences in Harpoot, 1915–1917*, Ann Arbor, MI: Gomidas Institute, 1997.

Rouben [Ter-Minasian, Minas], *Mémoires d'un partisan arménien*, trans. Waïk Ter-Minassian, Marseilles: Editions de l'Aube, 1990 (abridged translation of multi-volume memoirs in Armenian).

Russell, James, 'The Formation of the Armenian Nation' in Richard Hovannisian (ed.), *The Armenian People from Ancient to Modern Times*, vol. I: *The Dynastic Periods: From Antiquity to the Fourteenth Century*, New York: St. Martin's Press, 1997.

Ruud, Arild, 'The Indian Hierarchy: Culture, Ideology, and Consciousness in Bengali Village Politics', *Modern Asian Studies*, 33:3, 1999.

Rykhlevski, K. S., 'Excerpts from: The Books of the Nationalities of the USSR During Fifteen Years' in Rudolf Schlesinger (ed.), *The Nationalities Problem and Soviet Administration*, London: Routledge and Kegan Paul, 1956 (article is from 1932).

Rysakov, P., 'The Practice of Chauvinism and Local Nationalism' in Rudolf Schlesinger (ed.), *The Nationalities Problem and Soviet Administration*, London: Routledge and Kegan Paul, 1956 (article is from 1930).

Safran, William, 'Diasporas in Modern Societies: Myths of Homeland and Return', *Diaspora: A Journal of Transnational Studies*, 1:1, spring 1991.

Salt, Jeremy, *Imperialism, Evangelism and the Ottoman Armenians, 1878–1896*, London: Frank Cass, 1993.

Sanjian, Ara, 'Taner Akçam's "Türk Ulusal Kimliği ve Ermeni Sorunu" and the Slow Emergence of a Revisionist trend in Turkish Historiography as Regards the Genocide of the Ottoman Armenians in 1915', *Haigazian Armenological Review* (Beirut), 15, 1995.

Sandjian, Avedis, *The Armenian Communities in Syria under Ottoman Dominion*, Cambridge, MA: Harvard University Press, 1965.

Sarafian, Ara (compiler), *United States Official Documents on the Armenian Genocide*, vol. I: *The Lower Euphrates*; vol. II: *The Peripheries*; vol. III: *The Central Lands*. Watertown, MA: Armenian Review, 1993, 1994, 1995.

Sarafian, Kevork, *History of Education in Armenia*, Pasadena, CA: PCC Press, 1978 (1930).

Sarkisyanz, Manuel, *A Modern History of Transcaucasian Armenia*, Ketsch, Germany: issued privately, 1975.

Saroyan, Mark, *Minorities, Mullahs, and Modernity: Reshaping Community in the Former Soviet Union*, Berkeley: University of California, 1997.

Schahgaldian, Nikola, 'Ethnicity and Political Development in the Lebanese–Armenian Community, 1925–1975', *Armenian Review*, 36:1/141, spring 1983.

——— '*The Political Integration of an Immigrant Community into a Composite Society: The Armenians in Lebanon, 1920–1974*'. Columbia University, New York: PhD dissertation, 1979.

Schroeder, Gertrude, 'Social and Economic Aspects of the Nationality Problem' in Robert Conquest (ed.), *The Last Empire: Nationality and the Soviet Future*, Stanford, CA: Hoover Institution Press, 1986.

'Secret Political Trials in Soviet Armenia: "An Unendorsed Communique"', *Armenian Review*, 31:3/123, March 1979.

Seers, Dudley, *The Political Economy of Nationalism*, Oxford University Press, 1983.

Seth, Mesrovb Jacob, *Armenians in India*, New Delhi: Oxford and IBH Publishing, 1983 (Calcutta, 1937).

Seton-Watson, Hugh, *Nations and States: An Enquiry Into the Origins of Nations and the Politics of Nationalism*, Boulder, CO: Westview, 1977.

Sevian, A., 'The Founding of the Armenian Revolutionary Federation', *Armenian Review*, 34:2/134, June 1981 (1936).

Shain, Yossi, 'Ethnic Diasporas and U.S. Foreign Policy', *Political Science Quarterly*, 109:5, 1994–5.

Shaw, Stanford and Ezel Kural Shaw, *History of the Ottoman Empire and Modern Turkey*, vol. II: *Reform, Revolution, and Republic: The Rise of Modern Turkey, 1808–1975*, Cambridge University Press, 1977.

Sheffer, Gabriel, 'A New Field of Study: Modern Diasporas in International Politics' in Gabriel Sheffer (ed.), *Modern Diasporas in International Politics*, London: Croom Helm, 1986.

Shirinian, Lorne, *Armenian–North American Literature: A Critical Introduction. Genocide, Diaspora, and Symbols*, Lewiston, NY: Edwin Mellen, 1990.

——— 'The Impact of the Armenian Genocide: Eighty-Three Years of Survival and Memory in the Armenian Diaspora', Lectures and Papers in Ethnicity, no. 27, University of Toronto, December 1998.

——— *The Republic of Armenia and the Rethinking of the North-American Diaspora in Literature*, Lewiston, NY: Edwin Mellen, 1992.

——— *Survivor Memoirs of the Armenian Genocide*. Reading, England: Taderon, 1999.

——— 'Transculturation and Armenian Diaspora Writing: Literature on the Edge', *Armenian Review*, 45:4, winter 1992.

Shmavonian, Sarkis, 'Mikayel Nalbandian and Non-Territorial Armenian Nationalism', *Armenian Review*, 36:3/143, autumn 1983.

Siegel, Evan, 'Armenophilia Among Azerbaijani Intellectuals', paper presented at Association for the Study of Nationalities 4th Annual Convention, New York, 15 April 1999.

Simon, Gerhard, *Nationalism and Policy toward the Nationalities in the Soviet Union: From Totalitarian Dictatorship to Post-Stalinist Society*, Boulder, CO: Westview, 1991 (1986).

Smith, Anthony, 'Chosen Peoples: Why Ethnic Groups Survive', *Ethnic and Racial Studies*, 15:3, July 1992.

——— 'Ethnic Identity and Territorial Nationalism in Comparative Perspective' in Alexander Motyl (ed.), *Thinking Theoretically about Soviet National-*

ities: History and Comparison in the Study of the USSR, New York: Columbia University Press, 1992.

——— 'Ethnie and Nation in the Modern World', *Millennium: Journal of International Studies*, 14:2, 1985.

——— *The Ethnic Origins of Nations*, Oxford: Basil Blackwell, 1986.

——— 'The Formation of National Identity' in Henry Harris (ed.), *Identity: Essays Based on Herbert Spencer Lectures Given in the University of Oxford*, Oxford: Clarendon Press, 1995.

——— 'The Golden Age and National Renewal' in Geoffrey Hosking and George Schöpflin (eds), *Myths and Nationhood*, London: Hurst, 1997.

——— 'Memory and Modernity: Reflections on Ernest Gellner's Theory of Nationalism', *Nations and Nationalism*, 2:3, November 1996.

——— *Myths and Memories of the Nation*, Oxford University Press, 1999.

——— 'National Identities: Modern and Medieval?' in Simon Forde *et al.* (eds), *Concepts of National Identity in the Middle Ages*, School of English, University of Leeds, 1995.

——— *National Identity*, London: Penguin, 1991.

——— 'Nationalism and the Historians' in Gopal Balakrishanan (ed.), *Mapping the Nation*, London: Verso, 1996.

——— *Nationalism and Modernism*. London/New York: Routledge, 1998.

——— *Nations and Nationalism in a Global Era*. Oxford/Cambridge: Polity, 1995.

——— *State and Nation in the Third World*. Brighton: Wheatsheaf Books, 1983.

——— *Theories of Nationalism*, 2nd edition. New York: Holmes and Meier Publishers, 1983.

Smith, Graham (ed.), *The Nationalities Question in the Post-Soviet States*, 2nd edition, London: Longman, 1996 (1990).

Smith, Roger W., Eric Markusen, and Robert Lifton, 'Professional Ethics and the Denial of the Armenian Genocide' in Richard Hovannisian (ed.), *Remembrance and Denial: The Case of the Armenian Genocide*, Detroit: Wayne State University Press, 1998.

Somakian, Manoug, *Empires in Conflict: Armenia and the Great Powers, 1895–1920*, London: I. B. Tauris, 1995.

Sonyel, Salahi Ramsdan, *The Ottoman Armenians: Victims of Great Power Diplomacy*, Nicosia, Northern Cyprus: K. Rustem and Brother, 1987.

Stalin, Joseph, 'The Nation' in John Hutchinson and Anthony Smith (eds), *Nationalism*, Oxford University Press, 1994.

Suny, Ronald, *Armenia in the Twentieth Century*, Chico, CA: Scholars Press, 1983.

——— *The Baku Commune, 1917–1918. Class and Nationality in the Russian Revolution*, Princeton University Press, 1972.

——— 'Eastern Armenians under Tsarist Rule' in Richard Hovannisian (ed.), *The Armenian People from Ancient to Modern Times*, vol. II: *Foreign Domination to Statehood: The Fifteenth Century to the Twentieth Century*. New York: St. Martin's Press, 1997.

——— 'Empire and Nation: Armenians, Turks, and the End of the Ottoman Empire', *Armenian Forum*, 1:2, summer 1998.

——— 'The Formation of the Armenian Patriotic Intelligentsia in Russia: The First Generations', *Armenian Review*, 36:3/143, autumn 1983.

——— 'Incomplete Revolution: National Movements and the Collapse of the Soviet Empire', *New Left Review*, 189, September/October 1991.

——— *Looking Toward Ararat. Armenia in Modern History*. Bloomington: Indiana University Press, 1993.

——— *The Making of the Georgian Nation*, 2nd edition. Bloomington: Indiana University, 1994 (1988).

——— 'Marxism, Nationalism, and the Armenian Labor Movement in Transcaucasia, 1890–1908', *Armenian Review*, 33:1/129, March 1980.

——— 'Populism, Nationalism, and Marxism: The Origins of Revolutionary Parties Among the Armenians of the Caucasus', *Armenian Review*, 32:2/126, June 1979.

——— 'Reply to my Critics', *Armenian Forum*, 1:2, summer 1998.

——— *The Revenge of the Past: Nationalism, Revolution, and the Collapse of the Soviet Union*, Stanford University Press, 1993.

——— 'The Revenge of the Past: Socialism and Ethnic Conflict in Transcaucasia', *New Left Review*, 184, November/December 1990.

——— 'Soviet Armenia' in Richard Hovannisian (ed.), *The Armenian People from Ancient to Modern Times*, vol. II: *Foreign Domination to Statehood: The Fifteenth Century to the Twentieth Century*, New York: St. Martin's Press, 1997.

——— *The Soviet Experiment: Russia, the USSR, and the Successor States*, Oxford University Press, 1998.

Suny, Ronald (ed.), *Transcaucasia, Nationalism, and Social Change*, revised edition, Ann Arbor: University of Michigan Press, 1996 (1983).

Süslü, Azmi *et al.*, *The Armenians in the History of Turks*, Kars/Ankara: Rectorate of the Kafkas University, 1995.

Szporluk, Roman, *Communism and Nationalism: Karl Marx versus Friedrich List*, New York: Oxford University Press, 1988.

——— 'Nationalism After Communism: Reflections on Russia, Ukraine, Belarus and Poland', *Nations and Nationalism*, 4:3, July 1998.

Tabibian, Jivan, 'The Risk of Democratization', *Armenian International Magazine*, August–September 1999.

Taras, Ray, 'Nations and Language-Building: Old Theories, Contemporary Cases', *Nationalism and Ethnic Politics*, 4:3, autumn 1998.

Tashjian, Hasmig, '"Nairi", A Beacon of Light in the Diaspora', Paper presented at Middle East Studies Association 31st Annual Meeting, San Francisco, November 1997.

Tchilingirian, Hratch, *A Brief Historical and Theological Introduction to the Armenian Apostolic Orthodox Church*, Montreal: Diocese of the Armenian Church of Canada, 1994.

——— 'Nagorno Karabagh: Transition and the Elite', *Central Asian Survey*, 18:4, winter 1999.

——— 'Religious Discourse and the Church in Mountainous Karabagh 1988–1995', *Revue du Monde Arménien Moderne et Contemporain*, 3, 1997.

Ter Minassian, Anahide, 'Les Arméniens de France', *Les Temps Modernes*, 504/5/6, July–September 1988.

——— *Histoires Croisées: Diaspora Arménie Transcaucasie 1880–1990*, Marseilles, Éditions Parenthèses, 1997.

Ter Minassian, Anaide [Anahide], *Nationalism and Socialism in the Armenian Revolutionary Movement (1887–1912)*, Cambridge, MA: Zoryan Institute, 1984 (1983).

Ter Minassian, Anahide, 'The Role of the Armenian Community in the Foundation and Development of the Socialist Movement in the Ottoman Empire and Turkey: 1876–1923' in Mete Tuncay and Erik Zurcher (eds), *Socialism and Nationalism in the Ottoman Empire, 1876–1923*, London: British Academic Press, 1994.

——— 'Sociétés de culture, écoles et presse arméniennes à l'époque d'Abdul-Hamid II', *Revue du Monde Arménien Moderne et Contemporain*, 3, 1997.

Ter Minassian, Taline, *Colporteurs du Komintern. L'Union soviétique et les minorités au Moyen-Orient*, Paris: Presses de Sciences Po, 1997.

——— 'Yerevan, a 20th Century Armenian National "Icon": The Role of a Capital-city in the Making of Territorial Identity'. Paper delivered at the Association for the Study of Nationalities Fifth Annual Convention, New York, April 2000.

Ter Petrosian, Levon, 'A Man and a State', interview, *Armenian International Magazine*, March 1994 (by Salpi Haroutinian Ghazarian).

Ternon, Yves, 'Freedom and Responsibility of the Historian: The "Lewis Affair"' in Richard Hovannisian (ed.), *Remembrance and Denial: The Case of the Armenian Genocide*, Detroit: Wayne State University Press, 1998.

Thomson, Robert, 'Armenian Literary Culture Through the Eleventh Century' in Richard Hovannisian (ed.), *The Armenian People from Ancient to Modern Times*, vol. I: *The Dynastic Periods: From Antiquity to the Fourteenth Century*, New York: St. Martin's Press, 1997.

Tiryakian, Edward and Neil Nevitte, 'Nationalism and Modernity' in Edward Tiryakian and Ronald Rogowski (eds), *New Nationalisms of the Developed West: Toward Explanation*, London: George Allen and Unwin, 1985.

Tishkov, Valery, *Ethnicity, Nationalism and Conflict in and after the Soviet Union: The Mind Aflame*, London: Sage Publications, 1997.

——— 'Inventions and Manifestations of Ethno-Nationalism in and after the Soviet Union' in Kumar Rupesinghe, Peter King and Olga Vorkunova (eds), *Ethnicity and Conflict in a Post-Communist World: The Soviet Union, Eastern Europe and China*, London/New York: Macmillan/St. Martin's Press, 1992.

Tololyan, Khachig, 'Cultural Narrative and the Motivation of the Terrorist', *Journal of Strategic Studies*, 10:4, December 1987.

——— 'Exile Governments in the Armenian Polity' in Yossi Shain (ed.), *Governments-in-Exile in Contemporary World Politics*, New York: Routledge, 1991.

Tolo[l]yan, K., 'Martyrdom as Legitimacy: Terrorism, Religion and Symbolic Appropriation in the Armenian Diaspora', Paul Wilkinson and Alasdair Stewart (eds), *Contemporary Research on Terrorism*, Aberdeen University Press, 1987.

Tololyan, Khachig, 'National Self-Determination and the Limits of Sovereignty: Armenia, Azerbaijan and the Secession of Nagorno-Karabagh', *Nationalism and Ethnic Politics*, 1:1, spring 1995.

Tölölyan, Khachig, *Redefining Diasporas: Old Approaches, New Identities. The Armenian Diaspora in an International Context*, London: Armenian Institute, 2002.

——— 'Rethinking *Diaspora*(s): Stateless Power in the Transnational Moment', *Diaspora: a Journal of Transnational Studies*, 5:1, spring, 1996.

Tololyan, Khachig, 'The Role of the Armenian Apostolic Church in the Diaspora', *Armenian Review*, 41:1/161, Spring 1988.

——— 'Terrorism in Modern Armenian Political Culture', *Terrorism and Political Violence* 4:2, summer 1992.

——— 'Textual Nation: Poetry and Nationalism in Armenian Political Culture' in Ronald Suny and Michael Kennedy (eds), *Intellectuals and the Articulation of the Nation*, Ann Arbor: University of Michigan, 1999.

Torossian, Sarkis, 'The Apostolic Church of Armenia' in Boris Iwanow (ed.), *Religion in the USSR*. Munich: Institute for the Study of the USSR, 1960.

Touryantz, Hagop, *Search for a Homeland*. New York: issued privately, 1987 (1982).

Türközü, Halil Kemâl, *Armenian Atrocity According to Ottoman and Russian Documents*, Ankara: Institute for the Study of Turkish Culture, 1986 (1918).

van den Berghe, Pierre, 'Does Race Matter?', *Nations and Nationalism*, 1:3, November 1995.

——— 'Race and Ethnicity: A Sociobiological Perspective' in *Ethnic and Racial Studies*, 1:4, winter 1978.

Vartian, Ross, 'An Armenian Face on Universal Issues', interview, *Armenian International Magazine*, February 2000 (by Salpi Haroutinian Ghazarian).

Velychenko, Stephen, 'National History and the "History of the USSR": The Persistence and Impact of Categories' in Donald V. Schwartz and Razmik Panossian (eds), *Nationalism and History: The Politics of Nation Building in Post-Soviet Armenia, Azerbaijan and Georgia*, University of Toronto Centre for Russian and East European Studies, 1994.

Verdery, Katherine, *National Ideology Under Socialism: Identity and Cultural Politics in Ceauşescu's Romania*. Berkeley: University of California Press, 1991.

Vorbach, Joseph, 'Monte Melkonian: Armenian Revolutionary Leader', *Terrorism and Political Violence*, 6:2, Summer 1994.

Voskeritchian, Taline, 'Armenians of Istanbul', *Armenian International Magazine*, 9:11, December 1998.

Vratzian, Simon, *Armenia and the Armenian Question*, Boston: Hairenik, 1943.

——— 'The Second World (Untanoor) Congress of the Armenian Revolutionary Federation', *Armenian Review*, 32:3/127, September 1979 (1938).

Walker, Christopher, *Armenia: The Survival of a Nation*, 2nd edition, New York: St. Martin's Press, 1990 (1980).

——— 'The Armenian Presence in Mountainous Karabakh' in John F. R. Wright *et al.* (eds), *Transcaucasian Boundaries*, London: UCL Press, 1996.

——— *Visions of Ararat: Writings on Armenia*, London: I. B. Tauris, 1997.

——— 'World War I and the Armenian Genocide' in Richard Hovannisian (ed.), *The Armenian People from Ancient to Modern Times*, vol. II: *Foreign Domination to Statehood: The Fifteenth Century to the Twentieth Century*, New York: St. Martin's Press, 1997.

Walker, Christopher (ed.), *Armenia and Karabagh: The Struggle for Unity*, London: Minority Rights Group, 1991.

Young, M. Crawford, 'The National and Colonial Question and Marxism: A View from the South' in Alexander Motyl (ed.), *Thinking Theoretically about Soviet Nationalities. History and Comparison in the Study of the USSR*, New York: Columbia University Press, 1992.

Young, Pamela, 'Knowledge, Nation, and the Curriculum: Ottoman Armenian Education (1853–1915)', University of Michigan, Ann Arbor: PhD dissertation, 2001.

——— 'Making a People into a Nation: Sanasarian Varzharan's Role in Educating the Armenian Communities of Erzerum'. Paper presented at International Conference on Historic Armenian Provinces and Cities: Erzerum, University of California, Los Angeles, 14–15 November 1998.

Zekiyan, Boghos Levon, 'The Armenian Way to Enlightenment: The Diaspora and its Role' in Richard Hovannisian and David Myers (eds), *Enlightenment and Diaspora: The Armenian and Jewish Cases*. Atlanta: Scholars Press, 1999.

——— *The Armenian Way to Modernity: Armenian Identity Between Tradition and Innovation, Specificity and Universality.* Venice: Supernova/Eurasiatica 49, 1997.

ARCHIVAL MATERIAL

Noraguin Patmutian Petakan Kedronakan Arkhiv yev Patmutian Petakan Kedronakan Arkhiv [State Central Archives of History and Contemporary History (SCAHCH)], Yerevan, Armenia.

ELECTRONIC SOURCES

Aragil Electronic News Bulletin, daily, Yerevan (www.aragil.am).

Groong Armenian News Network, daily, California (groong.usc.edu).

RFE/RL (Radio Free Europe/Radio Liberty), daily and weekly, Czech Republic (www.rferl.org).

FORMAL INTERVIEWS

Abrahamian, Levon. Prominent anthropologist, professor at Yerevan State University and leading member of the Ethnography Institute. *30 October 1996*, at his home, Yerevan. Recorded, 90 minutes.

Aghapapian, Zohrap. Dissident activist in the late 1980s, involved in the publication and dissemination of nationalist literature, affiliated with the National Self-Determination Union. *5 November 1997*, at his home, Yerevan. Recorded, 30 minutes.

Ananian, Levon. Editor of the progressive *Garun* literary magazine. Subsequently elected President of the Writers' Union of Armenia in May 2001. *5 September 1996*, at his office, Yerevan. Recorded, 85 minutes.

Aramian, Aram. Chief architect under Soviet rule. One of the directors of the Metro-building project in Yerevan, and involved with most other large architectural projects in Armenia. *27 November 1997*, at his home, Yerevan. Recorded, 120 minutes.

Badalian, Sergei. Leader of the Armenian Communist Party (opposition).[1] Died November 1999. *8 November 1996*, at Communist Party offices, Yerevan. Recorded, 50 minutes.

Bezirjian, Khachatur. Chairman of Central Election Commission. Member of Parliament (pro-government). *4 November 1996*, at his office, Yerevan. Recorded, 170 minutes.

Dallakian, Karlen. High-ranking Communist Party official and member of Central Committee of Armenia (until 1991). Former head of Armenian Council of Church Affairs, Ideology Secretary, and Director of Committee of Cultural Relations with Diaspora Armenians. Member of Academy of Sciences. *28 November 1997*, at his office, Yerevan. Recorded, 90 minutes.

Davoyan, Razmik. Poet, member of the Armenian Revolutionary Federation and former head of the Writers' Union of Armenia (1994–6). *6 November 1996*, at his office, Yerevan. Recorded, 60 minutes.

Demirchian, Karen. First Secretary of the Communist Party of Armenia, 1974–88. Subsequently retired from politics and appointed director of Hayelectromach industrial plant. Presidential candidate in 1998 (came second with 40 per cent of vote). Speaker of Parliament in 1999. Murdered in the 27 October 1999 Parliament shootings. *3 December 1997*, at his office, Yerevan. Unrecorded, 60 minutes.[2]

[1] The political position I give of the parties is at the time of the interview. Some opposition parties or individuals became close to the government/executive after the change of President in February 1998.

[2] This interview was initially 'off the record'. I made it 'on the record' after Karen Demirchian's death.

Eortekian, Hovik. Former diasporan student at Yerevan State University, active in student politics and in the establishment of the Ramkavar party in Armenia (1989–91). *5 November 1996*, at the author's residence, Yerevan. Recorded, 75 minutes.

Galoyan, Galust. Former President of the History Institute of the National Academy of Sciences (1970s). Former Vice-President of the Academy of Sciences and currently adviser to its President. Ideology Secretary, 1989–90. *27 November and 2 December 1997*, at his office, Yerevan. Recorded, 75 minutes.

Geghamian, Gurgen. Senior economist at Academy of Sciences. *28 November and 2 December 1997*, at his office, Yerevan. Recorded, 60 minutes.

Ghazarian, Rafael. Academician. Former member of Gharabagh Committee. Leader of Union of Scientific and Industrial Workers Party (opposition). *21 November 1997*, at the offices of the Socialist Forces Union, Yerevan. Recorded, 120 minutes.

Hairikian, Paruir. Dissident from the late 1960s to 1989. Leader of the National Self-Determination Union (until 1999). Presidential candidate 1991, 1996, 1998. Member of the National Assembly (until 1999). Later, human rights adviser to President Kocharian. *20 August 1996*, at his party headquarters, Yerevan. Recorded, 50 minutes.

Hovannisian, Raffi. Diasporan-born lawyer. First Foreign Minister of independent Armenia (1991–2). Director of the Armenian Center for National and International Studies (Yerevan). *19 November 1997*, at his office in Yerevan. Recorded, 45 minutes.

Institute for Philosophy and Law of the National Academy of Sciences. Group Interview/discussion with Hamlet Gevorgian, Vladimir Ossipov, Rafayel Seiranian, Natalia Tomassian, Armine Halajian; *11 October 1996*, at the Institute, Yerevan. Recorded, 120 minutes.

Kaputikian, Silva. Famous poet and writer. Winner of Stalin Prize for Literature in 1952. Communist Party member and part of the Soviet literary 'establishment'. Active in the initial stages of the Gharabagh movement. *6 November 1997*, at her home, Yerevan. Recorded, 60 minutes.

Karekin I, Catholicos of All Armenians. Formerly Catholicos of Cilician see in Beirut (1983–95), elected to the Ejmiatzin Catholicosate in April 1995. Died June 1999. *5 November 1996*, at his quarters in Ejmiatzin. Unrecorded, 120 minutes.[3]

Khachatrian, Sergei. Brother of dissident Haikaz Khachatrian, who founded the National Unity Party in 1966. Partly active in the dissident movement in Soviet Armenia. *12 November 1997*, at his home, Yerevan. Recorded, 85 minutes.

Khachatrian, Vardan. Current Member of Communist Party, member of the Party's Yerevan Political Committee (responsible for ideological issues).

[3] In this case also, I put this 'off the record' interview 'on the record' after the interviewee's death.

Lecturer in History and Religion at Yerevan State University. *2 September 1996*, at a café, Yerevan. Recorded, 60 minutes.

Kharatian, Hranush. Professor and Director of Ethnography Division at Yerevan State University. *11 November 1997*, at her office, Yerevan. Recorded, 75 minutes.

Lalayan, Mushegh. Editor of *Hanrapetakan* [Republican] newspaper, member of the ruling council of the Republican Party (pro-government). Activist in the Tseghakron (ultra-nationalist) movement. *12 November 1997*, at his office, Yerevan. Recorded, 35 minutes.

Manucharian, Ashot. Former head of Komsomol in Armenia, former member of the Gharabagh Committee, former Interior and Security Minister (1991–2). Leader of the Union of Scientific and Industrial Workers Party (opposition). 21 November 1997, at the offices of the Socialist Forces Union, Yerevan. Recorded, 60 minutes.

Manukian, Vazgen. Mathematician. Founding member of the Gharabagh Committee and the Armenian National Movement. Leader of the National Democratic Union (party). Presidential candidate (main challenger) in the 1996 elections. *2 November 1996*, at *Iravunk* newspaper headquarters, Yerevan. Recorded, 55 minutes.

Margarian, Andranik. Former dissident in Soviet Armenia. Leader of the Republican Party since 1997. Member of Parliament (pro-government). Appointed Prime Minister in May 2000. *12 November 1997*, at his office, Yerevan. Recorded, 45 minutes.

Martirosian, Grigor. Former head of the Censorship Bureau (Glavlit) of Armenia. *8 December 1997*, at his office, Yerevan. Recorded, 60 minutes.

Mayilian, Aram. Member of the executive council of the National Democratic Union Party (opposition). *29 October 1996*, at a cafe, Yerevan. Recorded, 70 minutes.

Melkonian, Edvard. Diaspora expert at Academy of Sciences. *28 November 1997*, at a café, Yerevan. Recorded, 60 minutes.

Mkrtchian, Levon. Director of the National Question and Genocide Studies Centre affiliated with the Academy of Sciences. Member of the Armenian Revolutionary Federation (opposition). Later, Minister of Education (1998). *7 November 1996*, at his office, Yerevan. Recorded, 60 minutes.

Movsisian, Jivan. Current Director of the Committee for Cultural Relations with Diaspora Armenians. *21 November 1997*, at his office, Yerevan. Recorded, 60 minutes.

Off the record interview I. High-ranking government official in Levon Ter-Petrosian's administration. *30 October 1996*, at his office, Yerevan. Unrecorded, 45 minutes.

Off the record interview II. Former high-ranking Communist Party leader, member of subsequent administration. *6 November 1996*, at his home, Yerevan. Unrecorded, 120 minutes.

Off the record interview III. Former cabinet minister in post-independence government. *19 November 1997*, at his office, Yerevan. Unrecorded, 60 minutes.

Off the record interview IV. Former member of the Gharabagh committee. *3 December 1997*, at his office, Yerevan. Unrecorded, 30 minutes.

Petrosian, Amalia. Senior editor at the *Armenian Encyclopaedia*. Member of Parliament (pro-government), a co-founder of the Shamiram women's party. *31 October 1996*, at her National Assembly office, Yerevan. Recorded, 120 minutes.

Poghikian, Apo. Member of the Armenian Revolutionary Federation (opposition) Bureau (i.e. top ruling body). He is based in Los Angeles. *31 October 1997*, at ARF offices, Yerevan. Recorded, 35 minutes.

Safarian, Khachik. Dissident from 1962–3. One of the defendants in the Trial of the Seven in 1963. Member of the National Assembly (pro-government). *5 and 8 December 1997*, at his office, Yerevan. Recorded, 110 minutes.

Sargsian, Aram. Former First Secretary of the Communist Party of Armenia (1990–1). Leader of Armenian Democratic Party (opposition). Subsequently adviser to President Kocharian. *2 December 1997*, at his office, Yerevan. Recorded, 75 minutes.

Shahpazian, Artashes. Member of Supreme Council of the Armenian Revolutionary Federation in Armenia (opposition), responsible for ideological/ public relations issues. Former employee of HaiFilm Studios. *21 August 1996*, at the ARF offices, Yerevan. Recorded, 50 minutes.

Tavrishian, Tital. Senior member of Communist Party of Armenia (opposition). *1 November 1996*, at Communist Party offices, Yerevan. Recorded, 50 minutes.

Torosian, Ruben and Yuri Poghosian. Editorial Board members of *Vrastan* [Georgia], Armenian language newspaper in Tbilisi. *24 November 1997*, at newspaper offices. Unrecorded, 60 minutes.

Zeynaltvantian, Nerses. Vice-President of National Self-Determination Union. Member of Parliament (opposition). *31 August 1996*, at party offices, Yerevan. Recorded, 60 minutes.

INDEX